Emerging Technologies in Virtual Learning Environments

Kim Becnel
Appalachian State University, USA

A volume in the Advances in Educational Technologies and Instructional Design (AETID) Book Series

IGI Global
DISSEMINATOR OF KNOWLEDGE

Published in the United States of America by
IGI Global
Information Science Reference (an imprint of IGI Global)
701 E. Chocolate Avenue
Hershey PA, USA 17033
Tel: 717-533-8845
Fax: 717-533-8661
E-mail: cust@igi-global.com
Web site: http://www.igi-global.com

Library of Congress Cataloging-in-Publication Data

Names: Becnel, Kim, editor.
Title: Emerging technologies in virtual learning environments / Kim Becnel, editor.
Description: Hershey PA : Information Science Reference, [2019] | Includes bibliographical references.
Identifiers: LCCN 2018041412| ISBN 9781522579878 (hardcover) | ISBN 9781522579885 (ebook)
Subjects: LCSH: Virtual reality in education. | Augmented reality. | Educational innovations.
Classification: LCC LB1044.87 .E544 2019 | DDC 371.33/468--dc23 LC record available at https://lccn.loc.gov/2018041412

This book is published in the IGI Global book series Advances in Educational Technologies and Instructional Design (AE-TID) (ISSN: 2326-8905; eISSN: 2326-8913)

British Cataloguing in Publication Data
A Cataloguing in Publication record for this book is available from the British Library.

For electronic access to this publication, please contact: eresources@igi-global.com.

Advances in Educational Technologies and Instructional Design (AETID) Book Series

Lawrence A. Tomei
Robert Morris University, USA

ISSN:2326-8905
EISSN:2326-8913

Mission

Education has undergone, and continues to undergo, immense changes in the way it is enacted and distributed to both child and adult learners. In modern education, the traditional classroom learning experience has evolved to include technological resources and to provide online classroom opportunities to students of all ages regardless of their geographical locations. From distance education, Massive-Open-Online-Courses (MOOCs), and electronic tablets in the classroom, technology is now an integral part of learning and is also affecting the way educators communicate information to students.

The **Advances in Educational Technologies & Instructional Design (AETID) Book Series** explores new research and theories for facilitating learning and improving educational performance utilizing technological processes and resources. The series examines technologies that can be integrated into K-12 classrooms to improve skills and learning abilities in all subjects including STEM education and language learning. Additionally, it studies the emergence of fully online classrooms for young and adult learners alike, and the communication and accountability challenges that can arise. Trending topics that are covered include adaptive learning, game-based learning, virtual school environments, and social media effects. School administrators, educators, academicians, researchers, and students will find this series to be an excellent resource for the effective design and implementation of learning technologies in their classes.

Coverage

- Bring-Your-Own-Device
- Educational Telecommunications
- Virtual School Environments
- Adaptive Learning
- Collaboration Tools
- Instructional Design Models
- Instructional Design
- Game-Based Learning
- Hybrid Learning
- Social Media Effects on Education

IGI Global is currently accepting manuscripts for publication within this series. To submit a proposal for a volume in this series, please contact our Acquisition Editors at Acquisitions@igi-global.com or visit: http://www.igi-global.com/publish/.

The Advances in Educational Technologies and Instructional Design (AETID) Book Series (ISSN 2326-8905) is published by IGI Global, 701 E. Chocolate Avenue, Hershey, PA 17033-1240, USA, www.igi-global.com. This series is composed of titles available for purchase individually; each title is edited to be contextually exclusive from any other title within the series. For pricing and ordering information please visit http://www.igi-global.com/book-series/advances-educational-technologies-instructional-design/73678. Postmaster: Send all address changes to above address.

Titles in this Series

For a list of additional titles in this series, please visit: www.igi-global.com/book-series

Care and Culturally Responsive Pedagogy in Online Settings
Lydia Kyei-Blankson (Illinois State University, USA) Joseph Blankson (Ohio Northern University, USA) and Esther Ntuli (Idaho State University, USA)
Information Science Reference • copyright 2019 • 423pp • H/C (ISBN: 9781522578024) • US $195.00 (our price)

Ensuring Quality and Integrity in Online Learning Programs
Esther Smidt (West Chester University of Pennsylvania, USA) and Rui Li (West Chester University of Pennsylvania, USA)
Information Science Reference • copyright 2019 • 325pp • H/C (ISBN: 9781522578444) • US $190.00 (our price)

Handbook of Research on Ecosystem-Based Theoretical Models of Learning and Communication
Elena A. Railean (Siberian Federal University, Russia & Moscow State Pedagogical University, Russia & Free International University of Moldova, Moldova)
Information Science Reference • copyright 2019 • 401pp • H/C (ISBN: 9781522578536) • US $245.00 (our price)

Comparative Perspectives on Inquiry-Based Science Education
Stuart Bevins (Sheffield Hallam University, UK) Louise Lehane (St. Angela's College, Ireland) and Josephine Booth (Sheffield Hallam University, UK)
Information Science Reference • copyright 2019 • 298pp • H/C (ISBN: 9781522554394) • US $185.00 (our price)

Opening Up Education for Inclusivity Across Digital Economies and Societies
Patricia Ordóñez de Pablos (The University of Oviedo, Spain) Miltiadis D. Lytras (Effat University, Saudi Arabia) Xi Zhang (Tianjin University, China) and Kwok Tai Chui (City University of Hong Kong, China)
Information Science Reference • copyright 2019 • 352pp • H/C (ISBN: 9781522574736) • US $185.00 (our price)

Mobile Technologies in Educational Organizations
Alona Forkosh Baruch (Levinsky College of Education, Israel & Tel Aviv University, Israel) and Hagit Meishar Tal (Holon Institute of Technology, Israel)
Information Science Reference • copyright 2019 • 383pp • H/C (ISBN: 9781522581062) • US $195.00 (our price)

An Invariant-Based Approach to Second Language Acquisition Emerging Research and Opportunities
Elena Orlova (Lobachevsky State University of Nizhny Novgorod, Russia)
Information Science Reference • copyright 2019 • 164pp • H/C (ISBN: 9781522582205) • US $145.00 (our price)

IGI Global
DISSEMINATOR OF KNOWLEDGE

701 East Chocolate Avenue, Hershey, PA 17033, USA
Tel: 717-533-8845 x100 • Fax: 717-533-8661
E-Mail: cust@igi-global.com • www.igi-global.com

Table of Contents

Detailed Table of Contents

This chapter highlights over a decade of literature and research findings related to new learning ecosystems such as personal learning environments including MOOCs. New structures and environments are now in place that provide opportunities for learning in open networks, but important challenges and issues persist. This chapter also highlights challenges and opportunities in the design and development of MOOC learning experience design, conditions that must exist for people to be involved and engaged in a connectivist learning environment, challenges related to personalization and support of individual learning needs, along with new ethical and privacy concerns related to the safeguarding of data in networked environments. In conclusion, further research in areas of machine-learning AI in data-driven learning systems is discussed with emphasis on human factors such as motivation, incentives, and support that encourage course participation and learning.

Students of higher education are complaining about their online courses or faculty perhaps because universities are pushing to have classroom lectures converted to virtual learning delivery methods but without hiring qualified professors and failing to train faculty to effectively teach online. Different skills are required to effectively teach online courses as compared to lecturing in the classroom. To examine this problem, the author discusses the results of a mixed-methods research design consisting of an experiment followed by constructive feedback analysis. The experiment measured student grades from a standard teaching approach as compared with applying constructivism theory in the same online course at a university. The student outcome effect size for the treatment group was substantial and the analysis of constructive feedback evidence from the students was moderately supportive of the teaching approach.

Section 4
Applications in Development: New Frontiers in Education and Training

Preface

Too often in pedagogical circles, the mention of online or tech-mediated learning evokes isolated, alienated, and confused students taught by instructors who simply upload content and grade student assignments without fully engaging the students behind the submitted work. The chapters in this volume fully dispel these notions. The authors describe tech-mediated instruction at its best, engaging and motivating students, forming communities and nurturing peer relationships, sparking problem solving and creativity, and providing opportunities for growth to a diverse array of learners across the globe. The instructors and scholars represented here are innovators, game-designers, world-creators, and boundary-pushers eager to leverage technology to provide the best educational opportunities possible for the students they serve.

SECTION 1: SELF-DIRECTED AND CONNECTED – PEDAGOGICAL GOALS AND ONLINE LEARNING

Although there are always emerging technologies to thrill us with their potential and new frontiers to be explored, the most profound conversations about technology and pedagogy often draw us back to core questions about the nature of education and learning. What is the role of the instructor in the learning process? How do we motivate students to critically and authentically engage with the concepts and content we present to them? How can we tell if students are learning? How do we provide meaningful feedback on their progress? How can we make our instruction work for every student? The chapters in Section 1: Self-Directed and Connected: Pedagogical Goals and Online Learning repeatedly revisit these fundamental questions as they explore the ways in which instructors can leverage technological capacity to enhance the student experience.

In the chapter titled "New Personal Learning Ecosystems: A Decade of Research in Review," Canadian researchers Helene Fournier, Rita Kop, and Heather Molyneaux describe the evolution of research on Personal Learning Environments (PLEs), environments designed to provide users with maximum control of their learning experience. Specifically, they look at MOOCs, Massive Open Online Courses, intended to be delivered freely to large numbers of people. Proponents of MOOCs reject the notion that knowledge is passed from teacher to student and embrace, instead, connectivism, the idea that learning happens by creating and shaping networks, and that it is within these networks that knowledge is constructed and shared. This chapter discusses the challenges inherent in creating a connectivist learning space such as a MOOC in which individual learning goals and styles are prioritized and privacy is protected, while learners are connected to peers in meaningful community and receive feedback on their progress in their desired area of study. The authors suggest that "research and development efforts in the new learning ecosystem include powerful data-driven visualizations aimed at providing valuable and meaningful feedback to learners based on trace data of their learning activities, machine-learning techniques to personalize the learning, learning analytics, recommender systems, big data and educational data mining applications"; however, these strategies will need to be developed along with protections for learners' privacy and the data they generate through their participation in MOOC-related activities. Further, developers of this technology will need to consider more nebulous but no less important factors such as support and motivation, which are fundamental to the success of any educational endeavor. This is a welcome reminder that for all of the advances in technological capability, developers and instructors need to be mindful of all of the various elements necessary to the enterprise of education. While some of them, in some cases, might be successfully automated, there are others which remain quintessentially human, and which require interaction among people who are invested in the subject at hand and in the students' success.

In his chapter titled "Teaching Virtual Online Courses in an Era of Negative Student Reviews: Mixed Methods Controlled Experiment and Feedback," Kenneth David Strang also acknowledges the difficulties inherent in delivering effective, meaningful instruction online. Strang is writing about fee-based university courses, which may have more in common with standard face-to face courses than MOOCs do, yet they still require instructors to radically reconceive what it means to teach a course. Nonetheless, Strang argues that many universities are encouraging professors to teach fully or partially online courses without providing the necessary training or support, leaving instructors to transform their face-to-face courses into uploadable content or to experiment with dramatically different teaching and learning approaches on their own. For his part, Strang hypothesizes that a constructivist learning approach would increase the effectiveness of an online business course, and he tested that hypothesis by comparing data from an online, constructivist-centered operations research course to data from a face-to-face section of the same course that did not employ constructivist instructional strategies. Like the connectivist learning described by Fournier, Kop, and Molyneaux, constructivist learning puts the learner in the proverbial driver's seat. It can be understood as a process in which leaners absorb and internalize new information by discovering the ways in which it is relevant to their own lives and related to prior knowledge and/or experience. In constructivist pedagogy, as Strang explains it, students build on their current knowledge, adding concepts and content in an active process through dialog with instructors and peers.

In the context of Strang's experiment, the traditional approach is defined as relying on textbooks and the analysis of case studies. Meanwhile, constructivism involves the professor exhibiting certain behaviors in online forums: using current examples in online discussions, replying to posted comments and questions publicly so that all students receive the benefit of exposure to the dialog, encouraging students to weave their own personal context into course conversations, and modeling the application of relevant theories to examples in his or her own research and in the cases introduced by students. The instructor also asked questions in both synchronous and asynchronous formats designed to encourage critical thinking about the knowledge management cycle at the heart of the course and assigned a final course activity which asked students to produce their own mental models representing what they learned. In this way, knowledge can be viewed as having been built dynamically by everyone participating in the course instead of being transferred in one direction from the professor to the student(s). In the comparative study, the group who participated in the online, constructivist course received higher grades in the course and produced more "positive pedagogy-related constructive feedback" when asked to rate the course. What is so compelling here is that, in his efforts to develop an instructional approach that would work in an online environment, Strang has not only discovered some new teaching techniques and strategies, he has experimented with a different conceptual framework, one that might work just as well in a face-to-face classroom as it does online. Good online teaching, after all, is just good teaching, and creative educators are adept at employing pedagogies that motivate, engage and empower students in spaces of all kinds, transforming, revising, and reinventing them as needed. It is exciting to think that experiments and discoveries in online learning will help educators improve their practice in face-to-face environments, thus benefitting students in all types of learning situations.

In their piece "#teachingbydesign: Complicating Accessibility in the Tech-Mediated Classroom," Cat Mahaffey and Ashlyn Walden, at the University of North Carolina Charlotte, describe their efforts to redesign aspects of their online and hybrid course offerings in sustained efforts to enhance accessibility. The authors teach writing-centered courses that meet face-to-face but incorporate web-based tools to deliver some instruction and communicate with students; they also require students to produce digital-mediated content as course products. Based on their experiences teaching writing intensive courses and their attention to student feedback, Walden and Mahaffey argue that while much has been written about accessibility regarding online and tech-mediated teaching for students with disabilities, the concept of accessibility should be dramatically broadened. "[A]ccess is about more than screen readers and transcripts," they write. "Content must also be designed for English language learners, those with limited technological literacy, and those for whom digital realms create barriers," for "students with colorblindness, dyslexia, or anxiety; and students disadvantaged by socioeconomics, gender, or race." The authors believe that "instructors should assume responsibility for and work toward offsetting the gaps in students' ability to engage with digital course materials rather than blaming students when they fail to do so". Despite the moniker "digital natives," in many ways, students lag behind their teacher-designers in higher education, having not been granted access to digital reading and writing through intentional instruction." This argument is a crucial one for those involved in online pedagogy; the assumption that many make that simply moving education online increases and improves access is one that must be interrogated. On a practical level, like Strang, Mahaffey and Walden argue that instructors should be offered more education and support to make the best use of technological tools. When this support is provided, technological tools are more likely to enhance students' experience in a course rather than serving as obstacles or barriers unintentionally set in place by unaware instructors. Further, Mahaffey and Walden make the compelling argument that instructors should make their process of accessible course design visible to their students, and that their course content should serve as models for students' own digital compositions.

In "Participating on More Equal Terms? Power, Gender, and Participation in a Virtual World Learning Scenario," Mats Deutschmann, Anders Steinvall, and Airong Wang report on a study conducted in Sweden that examined power relationships and linguistic acts in collaborative workshops conducted in Second Life. The authors are interested in the potential effects of the anonymity a virtual world offers on the process of language learning. They point to previous research suggesting that more powerful or expert individuals tend to monopolize situations, leaving some learners less able to participate in activities and practice their skills. In this study, the authors analyzed data from collaborative activities conducted in Second Life, where "a class of student language teachers was joined by professionals working with online language teaching and/or research in order to discuss two pedagogic case studies." Deutschmann, Steinvall, and Wang's study, focused on the dynamics at play between experts and students and between women and men, found that the students did not appear to be intimidated or silenced by the status or knowledge of the experts. Nor did the data bear out previous findings that male students would occupy more floor space than females while females would spend more time engaging in supportive speech than their male counterparts. In short, in this virtual interaction, participants did not exhibit the expected behaviors dictated by traditional hierarchies. The authors note that more research is necessary to establish to what extent the virtual environment is a factor in helping to disrupt established power structures in international language learning contexts such as those examined in this experiment. The possibility that virtual spaces provide a way to disrupt expected patterns certainly invites further study. Fascinating questions remain. "How [might] interaction through avatars alter conventional interactional patterns? Does an avatar teacher represent the same role as a face-to-face teacher? To what extent is the physical appearance of the avatar instrumental in establishing roles? What happens to traditional gender roles if participants act through avatars of the opposite sex?" This chapter, along with the others in this section, speak to the ways in which online and technology-mediated instruction can open up productive conversations and new avenues of research by disrupting the traditional structures that govern and organize instruction, our ideas of what successful instruction looks like—both online and in the classroom, our assumptions about the digital literacy of our students, and the traditional power dynamics that govern interactions in the classroom.

SECTION 2: 3D VIRTUAL ENVIRONMENTS – A CLOSER LOOK AT IMMERSION

Virtual Environments are spaces that foster the feeling of immersion in users, often by creating richly detailed worlds in which users can move, interact with objects and resources, and communicate with other participants. Virtual spaces can be used to create an environment relevant to the subject matter of a given lesson, to create virtual classrooms for students learning together at a distance, or to host short or long-term gaming activities. The use of immersive spaces for educational purposes is growing because the technology needed to access them is becoming more readily available; often, users need only a laptop or smart phone and an internet connection. No specialized equipment or gear is required. The chapters that comprise Section 2, 3D Virtual Environment: A Closer Look at Immersion, examine the ways in which virtual spaces can provide opportunities for meaningful learning, support the establishment and growth of a learning community, and enrich users' experience with opportunities for incidental learning as they complete the main tasks at hand.

In "Transitions in Student Motivation During a MUVE-Based Ecosystem Science Curriculum: An Evaluation of the Novelty Effect," Shari J. Metcalf, Jason A. Chen, Amy M. Kamarainen, Kim M. Frumin, Trisha L. Vickrey, Tina A. Grotzer, and Christopher J. Dede report on a study conducted using a two-week ecosystem science lesson conducted in EcoMUVE. MUVEs (multi-user virtual environments) are three-dimensional spaces in which users, represented by an avatar, can visit different places and times, exploring an intricately detailed environment while interacting with each other and with elements and objects planted in the space. The authors of this chapter were particularly interested in whether and how excitement with the technology would translate into excitement about the scientific content involved and scientific methods of discovery. As the students progressed through the curriculum, the researchers provided multiple surveys to ascertain how the students' perceived the experience and to gauge their levels of motivation and interest. They found that students' engagement with Eco-MUVE endured, but that their responses to it evolved from an initial pleasure at using the new technology to a conviction that the program, EcoMUVE, could help them to learn science. The authors investigated what it was about EcoMUVE that enabled this desired transition, discovering that the main factor is opportunity "for sustained, meaningful engagement, through self-directed learning, inquiry-based activities, and collaboration with a team." Significantly, the virtual world of EcoMUVE creates an experience that taps into "internally controlled motivators: autonomy (choice), competence, and connectedness." As students discover they can make choices, be successful in their navigation of the world and its tasks, and work as part of team, they become more interested in the virtual world and more open to learning both content and the process of scientific inquiry. This study addresses central questions that concern educators involved in technology-mediated and gamified learning. While motivating students to complete tasks or learn content through introducing new technologies, games, or competitive elements is a valuable goal, it is when extrinsic motivations translate to or ignite internal motivators that true success is achieved and excitement generated by well-designed instruction can grow and extend well past a single pedagogical unit.

Amelia Cheney, Terry McClannon, Les Bolt, and Robert Sanders, in their chapter "Perceptions of Presence and Community in Immersive Online Learning Environments" report on a study involving graduate students using immersive online learning environments for their coursework. Describing the evolution of online course delivery at their institution, the authors explain that when some faculty members at Appalachian State University in North Carolina, USA, began to teach online, they noted that the social constructivist framework to which the college subscribed and the community of practice they had relied on to support learning required opportunities for interaction among faculty and students that their online courses did not provide. Thus, they began to experiment with Virtual Worlds, specifically *ActiveWorlds*, which offered "persistent 3D immersive learning environments that provided multiple manifestations of presence (comprised of students, faculty, spaces, tools, and artifacts) that closely aligned with the real world in which these students were accustomed to working." Students and instructors, represented by avatars, could enter the virtual space at will, move around, view and share resources, and communicate with one another. Through shared anecdotes and their own observations, the authors believed that the immersive environment provided many opportunities for conversations and interactions and ultimately created the sense of community that had initially been missing from their online courses. The faculty embarked on a study to evaluate whether students who participated in courses conducted in the virtual world perceived themselves as part of a community. Their findings suggest that students felt both a sense of presence and a sense of community in this online environment, with students who worked and learned for longer periods of time in the virtual space developing an ever stronger sense of community with their peers. It would be interesting to find out how the online community established here compares with communities established in brick and mortar classrooms and whether connections developed in virtual spaces can persist past the conclusion of particular courses or degree programs to become operational professional networks.

In their chapter titled "Effects of Learning Traits and Information Display on Incidental Learning in 3D Virtual Environments," Wayne W. Thomas and Patricia M. Boechler explore whether and how incidental learning—learning facts or concepts not essential to the lesson or task at hand—occurs in virtual environments. More specifically, they investigated whether the following factors influence incidental learning in a virtual space: visual salience of texts and images, students' learning styles, and students' levels of digital literacy. In their study, the authors had one hundred and fifty-five education undergraduate students complete tasks in a virtual environment in which there were opportunities for incidental learning to occur. The results of the study indicate that incidental learning does occur in virtual environments and that visual salience—the extent to which text or images stand out against the background and call attention to themselves—does impact that learning. This finding reinforces the notion that virtual environments can be powerful educational tools, especially when designers and instructors pay attention to all parts of the environment and take advantage of considerable opportunities for learning outside of the main tasks students are asked to complete. In addition to this finding, the study concluded that the level of digital literacy students exhibit also impacts their incidental learning; students with higher levels of digital literacy were more likely to acquire more incidental learning than students with lower levels of digital literacy, probably because students who were more familiar with and comfortable with the technological tools were able to spend more time and energy paying attention to the environment than those who were working harder to navigate the platform. This finding sparks connections to Mahaffey and Walden's chapter about expanding the definition of accessibility; instructors who are aware of and who attend to students' digital literacy skills can help ensure that all learners are able to access and process as much of the course content as possible.

SECTION 3: GAMIFICATION – THE PURPOSE OF PLAY IN THE VIRTUAL CLASSROOM

Games and gamified activities in educational settings are becoming increasingly popular because of their motivational capacity. In addition to this motivational element, games can elicit interactivity among participants, encourage teamwork, and reward creativity and problem-solving. The games that produce the richest results meld the use of classic game design elements—including achievable and adaptable goals, a diverse array of rewards, and the capacity to take risks and experiment in a low-stakes environment—with complementary pedagogical approaches such as flow theory or constructivism. The chapters in Section 3, The Purpose of Play in the Virtual Classroom, discuss all types of games, from MMORPs to simulation-based gaming to role-playing activities, investigating which types of games are appropriate to achieve various instructional goals and exploring the mechanisms by which they work.

Research has demonstrated the capacity for role-play and simulation-based gaming designed to mimic real world and professional situations to teach students how to solve problems within these contexts. In "Games in Innovation Education: Simulated vs. Authentic Gamified Participation," Rikke Magnussen expands on this research, reporting on a study conducted with Danish public school students ages 13-15 which asked students to enact the roles of leaders of intelligent music design companies. They were introduced to innovative design strategies and skills in an effort to teach them innovation competencies. In the game-like scenario, each team had to produce a prototype for a new design and compete against the other teams to produce the best one. The study found that the game format, including rules of play, the narrative framework, and the element of competition, helped the students to achieve the desired innovation competencies, exhibited by their ability to create and nurture brand new ideas growing from user needs and desires. Magnussen notes that this type of gamification is an approach that might work in other academic areas as well, especially those in which creativity and problem solving are required. Exercises like the one Magnussen describes serve to simulate genuine scientific, research, and/or creative processes. While they produce open-ended and often unexpected results and products, these exercises are still, by their nature, simulations, pretend versions of the real world in which nothing is truly at stake. In contrast is the growing area of science discovery or citizen science games, in which games are designed to motivate large numbers of people to contribute to the data generation, collection, and analysis needed to solve some outsized scientific problems. Magnusson cites, for example, Foldit, an online game in which players discover new protein structures by manipulating the protein's chain and backbone to find the lowest-energy 3-D structure. In this case, and others like it, players are actually participating in the scientific process and contributing to society's overall understanding of the phenomena that make up our world. While both types of experiences have value, research into the difference between simulations and authentic game participation might help us to achieve a deeper understanding of the effects of various elements of gaming and how they might be utilized for different goals.

In a similar spirit, Jerremie V. Clyde and Glenn R. Wilkinson's chapter titled "Rhetorical Replay and the Challenge of Gamic History: Silencing the Siren Song of Digital Simulation" critiques the trend of using simulation-based games to teach history by discussing the limitations of this type of gaming for history education at the college level. The authors argue that simulations are simply a digital approach to historical reenactments, which are not adept at helping students to understand why events occurred, how they might be related, or how the historical record is created through a network of interrelated sources and stories. The authors propose, as an alternative to historical simulations, an approach to gaming that acknowledges history as a discipline with particular ways of thinking about and understanding the world and the past. Historians analyze and interpret evidence, reveal relationships among pieces of evidence, contextualize these relationships, and use them to construct an argument with a sound conclusion. It is this process, rather than the recitation of a record of facts, that is the goal of university level history instruction.

For this reason, Clyde and Wilkinson argue, students should be asked to "construct the past via procedural rhetoric, using games that mirror the structure of the historical argument." Ian Bogost describes procedural rhetoric as the way in which users involved in gaming develop their understanding of a concept or phenomena through the process of creating rules and building processes. The authors propose a gamic mode of history that asks users to employ procedural rhetoric to create "computer mediated gamic scholarly constructions of the past," which would encourage "students to explore and interact with the process of historical construction within a given argument." In this type of game, students would not be engaged in reenactments defined by the computer program they are using, but instead they would be asked to manipulate bits of evidence, such as texts, audio, and visual data, and use them to construct an argument in the way that historians do. If the computer's rule set provided feedback at various points in the process, the student could reflect on the work and reassess, rearrange, and reinterpret as necessary. Approaching gaming in this way may help students to develop the epistemic frame of a historian, which is the ultimate goal of advanced history courses. This chapter reinforces the importance of having clear goals for assignments and courses and serves as a model for in-depth exploration of whether and how various games and gaming types can support those goals.

In "Revisiting MMORPGs in Support of Learning: Changes in the Last Decade," Bodi Anderson examines a specific subset of educational gaming, Massive Multiplayer Online Role-playing Games, in which thousands of players, represented by avatars, engage in tasks and complete challenges in a 3D virtual space. Most MMORPGs use character archetypes to help define the characteristics of players, have as a main goal the progression or growth of the avatar through various levels of play, and employ competition between players as well as between players and the program as they complete various tasks. Anderson points out key differences between MMORPGs and classic video games: (1) the online environment persists and progresses whether or not a player is online (2) intense collaboration, rather than simple cooperation, is often required for successful play and (3) players are provided with many opportunities for a "large and varied amount of avatar creation and customization."

Participation in MMORPGs has been linked to cognitive, social, and psychological benefits, which points to their potential as educational tools. In terms of cognitive growth, MMORPGs foster critical thinking and problem-solving skills, and often require creativity to complete tasks as well. Concerning social and psychological growth, MMORPGs have been found to create and nurture community through their focus on teamwork and social interactions, elements which can be sorely lacking in some approaches to online pedagogy, and they can also foster rich and rewarding relationships among team players. Additionally, according to Anderson, educationally focused MMORPGs can help students maintain better concentration and enhance retention of concepts. Studies show that the MMORPG environment has successfully helped advanced students understand the research process as they pulled together game-based resources with resources obtained outside of the game to complete tasks. MMORPGs have also been shown to be useful in language acquisition because of the amount of interaction required and the feeling of community and trust the game promotes.

As Anderson points out, the effects of using avatars in virtual settings is an area of scholarly inquiry with a promising future. Initial research suggests that the anonymity of avatars can increase social interaction by helping reticent or anxious players to contribute more readily to conversations and activities. Also, the majority of players report creating and playing characters of the opposite gender and enjoyed the perspectives they gained in these explorations. The field of technology-mediated education, especially in the areas of gaming and virtual worlds, would benefit from additional investigations into the ways in which avatars allow users to engage new experiences and explore behaviors and perspectives not familiar to them. Finally, Anderson writes that "perhaps the greatest power avatars have to support learning lies in their potential use as pedagogical agents," which are defined as "personified computer-based teaching applications" designed to "help learners by stimulating social interaction and socially based cognition and motivation." MMORPGs make use of game-controlled agents with limited functionality to guide players in the right direction. These can be supplemented with instructor-controlled avatars who can act as more sophisticated pedagogical agents as they support players in their tasks. As do the other chapters in this section. Anderson's work points to the rich and varied ways in which the concept of play can serve educational goals when instructors and designers are clear about what those goals are and choose activities and games that are well-tailored to the course objectives.

SECTION 4: APPLICATIONS IN DEVELOPMENT – NEW FRONTIERS IN EDUCATION AND TRAINING

The chapters in Section 4, Applications in Development: New Frontiers in Education and Training, describe programs designed to improve education in the fields of construction, crime scene training, and language learning. The developers of each of these applications is pushing the boundaries of what is possible in an attempt to provide effective, efficient, and engaging learning experiences in these fields. The tools they are creating and exploring are immersive, interactive, and adaptable for varied purposes and multiple audiences. Similar development is occurring in other areas as well, as educators and designers take advantage of technical advances and increasingly available access to smart phones and internet connections to improve training and learning opportunities for students and employees.

In their chapter titled "Augmented Reality-Based Training Systems for Teaching Health and Safety Procedures in Construction," Inma García-Pereira, Cristina Portalés, Sergio Casas, María Vidal-González, and Jesús Gimeno argue that AR (augmented reality) and simulations can be particularly beneficial for instruction in areas such as construction in which real-life simulations are necessary. The authors describe AR as "a well-known emerging technology by which virtual data (images, sound, haptic stimuli, etc.) can be added to the user's perception of the real world. This is achieved by simultaneously combining real and virtual objects which are registered in a 3D space, making AR an interactive technology in real-time." The increasing use of smart mobile devices means that mobile AR applications can be more easily used in places where computers might be impractical, such as construction sites. One such program, a European project called ARFAT, (The Augmented Reality Formwork Assembly Training) is being used to teach elements of construction safety that are difficult to convey through traditional teaching methods, including lectures and hypothetical exercises. The program works in two modes; the first is an augmented reality mode, designed to be used on a construction site, in which virtual objects are superimposed on real world objects such that students can manipulate elements and visualize the consequences of certain actions they perform. This can give them a version of real-world experience without the dangers inherent in learning on the job. In a second mode, designed for classroom use, the program works through simulation, creating an entirely virtual scene for the user to manipulate. According to the chapter's authors, the fact that different modes of interaction are required to solve the exercises and that random elements are woven into several of the problems results in higher levels of motivation and engagement on the part of users. Another benefit is that the exercises and simulations can be repeated to test different variables or solutions or to reinforce the correct responses. The authors suggest that similar programs could be effective in teaching other construction skills as well as content and concepts in other, related areas.

In contrast to the construction field, in which traditional training occurs in a classroom or on an actual work site, crime scene investigation training typically occurs using strategically staged scenes that instructors painstakingly create. In the chapter by Ian Levstein and Lenora Jean Justice, titled "CSI4FS®: A Markerless Augmented Reality Game – A Novel Approach to Crime Scene Investigation Training," the authors describe the ongoing development of a "game-based markerless augmented reality smartphone application (CSI4FS®) that complements traditional crime scene investigation training." The authors highlight the limitations of current techniques for crime scene training, including the time and labor involved in setting and resetting the instructional scenes for training exercises. Using AR technology can make this process much easier and more flexible by allowing instructors to instantly recreate scenes, introduce new and different kinds of evidence for trainees to analyze, and adapt and modify the exercises to customize them for different audiences. The program the authors discuss here, employs markerless technology, which means that it makes use of GPS data to merge virtual and real-world content instead of relying on the creation of markers to link virtual and real world objects to create the AR experience. The use of markerless AR technology in combination with smart phones means that the application is fully mobile and may be used anywhere. The authors note that CSI4FS® is still in the development process and that "[g]ame elements such as fun, simplicity, multiple levels of play, story, and graphics will be developed and enhanced as the application evolves." Initial testing has been promising, and the developers anticipate that the application will ultimately feature "the ability to tag evidence (e.g. blood spatter, DNA, documents, shell casings, shoe prints, and tire treads), check for signs of arson or explosives, document bullet trajectory, and maintain a chain of custody." Ideally, the program will offer better, more detailed and adaptable instruction in a more efficient and engaging manner than traditional techniques.

In her piece, "A Constructivist Desktop Virtual Reality-Based Approach to Learning in a Higher Education Institution," Serpil Meri-Yilan describes an experiment with a new language learning application called ImmerseMe, which was established in 2015 and is still currently in development. ImmerseMe includes over 500 activities, many scenario-based, for language learners at various levels and in nine different languages. The program offers 360° YouTube-based videos in locations in which the target language is spoken and features simulations of common, real-world interactions, such as "ordering coffee in London, a baguette in Paris, tapas in Spain or an obento box in Tokyo." Google-based sound recognition software is able to recognize whether a learner supplies a correct response in a simulation, moving on the next activity upon a correct response and otherwise requiring the learner to try again. In her study, Meri-Yilan observes groups of students in Turkey interacting with the application on two occasions, once using an English program and once with a language of their choice. Interviewing the students after each experience, she discovered that the students believed that the program improved their speaking, listening, pronunciation, vocabulary, and critical thinking; further, students indicated that using the program increased both their motivation to learn and their cultural awareness. While students were largely positive about their experience with the application, they did express some frustration with the sound recognition software, which did not always recognize what they felt were correct responses and prevented them from moving to another activity. Studies such as Meri-Yilan's are invaluable to educators and also developers, who can use this research to evaluate and improve their applications so that they can provide experiences more closely tailored to user expectations and desires.

Taken together, the chapters in this volume provide a broad overview of approaches to incorporating emerging technologies in educational spaces. The discussions of augmented reality, virtual reality, gaming, simulations, and the use of immersive spaces have one important element in common—pedagogical goals and concerns drive the projects. Technological tools, no matter how advanced, cannot do the work of education. Educators must conceive, design, implement, and evaluate technology-mediated instruction, ensuring their most fundamental and significant objectives can be met through the methods they have devised. These chapters are both evidence of and models for the careful planning, continuous evaluation, and frequent revision required to implement technology in a way that is truly beneficial to learners of all types.

Section 1

Self-Directed and Connected:

Pedagogical Goals and Online Learning

Chapter 1
New Personal Learning Ecosystems:
A Decade of Research in Review

Helene Fournier
https://orcid.org/0000-0002-8470-3226
National Research Council, Canada

Rita Kop
Yorkville University, Canada

Heather Molyneaux
National Research Council, Canada

ABSTRACT

This chapter highlights over a decade of literature and research findings related to new learning ecosystems such as personal learning environments including MOOCs. New structures and environments are now in place that provide opportunities for learning in open networks, but important challenges and issues persist. This chapter also highlights challenges and opportunities in the design and development of MOOC learning experience design, conditions that must exist for people to be involved and engaged in a connectivist learning environment, challenges related to personalization and support of individual learning needs, along with new ethical and privacy concerns related to the safeguarding of data in networked environments. In conclusion, further research in areas of machine-learning AI in data-driven learning systems is discussed with emphasis on human factors such as motivation, incentives, and support that encourage course participation and learning.

DOI: 10.4018/978-1-5225-7987-8.ch001

INTRODUCTION

The proliferation of Information and Communications Technology (ICT) in recent years has changed the educational landscape. Social media and emerging informal learning ecosystems such as Personal Learning Environments, including Massive Open Online Courses, offer tremendous potential to enhance learning processes; but research and literature findings have underscored important challenges as well. This chapter presents highlights from over a decade of research on Personal Learning Environments and MOOCs with a glimpse into the new learning ecosystems. Some background will be provided which includes research on PLEs and MOOCs by the National Research Council Canada. As we enter into a new era of information abundance and learning opportunities, new ways of participating in educational experiences and learning are now available. We address possible new approaches and methods by examining next generation learning environments.

With new structures and environments in place, two areas of research are highlighted as foundational to examining learning in open networked environments: learner autonomy and a theory for learning in a digital age, that is, connectivism. Another section will look at self-directed learning, agency and autonomy as essential for learning in open networked environments with evidence from Connectivist MOOCs as a potentially disruptive pedagogy. This chapter will also look at how research on cMOOCs has informed MOOC learning experience design, specifically, what conditions must exist for people to be involved and engaged in a connectivist learning environment. The challenges related to personalization and support of individual learning needs will be highlighted along with new ethical and privacy concerns related to the safeguarding of data in networked environments. A glimpse into what the future holds in terms of next generation learning environments will also be revealed along with conclusions that will point to important area of research that are still lacking and recommendations for future areas of investigation.

Background

The National Research Council Canada has been conducting research on emerging technologies and learning innovation since 2008. One component of this research has focused on PLEs, including information gathering and user case studies exploring educational issues in massive open online courses (MOOCs). Research has been conducted in the context of four connectivist MOOCs (cMOOCs), namely Critical Literacies (#CritLit2010), Personal Learning Environments, Networks, and Knowledge (#PLENK2010), CLOM-REL-Open Educational Resources (#CLOM REL2014) and more recently E-Learning 3.0-Distributed Learning Technology (#el30 2018). Over a decade of research has identified important gaps, especially around the types of support mechanisms required by learners to be successful in these new open and accessible learning environments. #CritLit2010 was one in a series of cMOOCs facilitated by educational researchers at NRC and had over 600 participants who were interested in the particular new skills and competencies required to function well in the new media landscape as learner. It was followed by #PLENK2010 with around 1600 participants. The two had in common that they used the Moodle learning environment as a blended learning management system, but also made extensive use of a daily newsletter, The Daily, that was delivered to the inbox of all participants using RSS technology (gRSShopper) and the course hashtag to collect all Web distributed course related publications and creative productions, which then led to daily discussions. Both MOOCs also used weekly themes and guest speakers to create engagement, creative activity and thinking on the course network.

The format at #CLOM REL2014 was similar, although the Moodle environment was abandoned by this stage as the restriction of the discussion forum was felt to be unsuited for the networked environment because of the scale of the MOOCs and more suited to more traditional courses. A distributed learning environment was used instead which made for very different dynamics. The technical implementation of #CLOM REL2014 included: (1) gRSShopper platform to host content and aggregate the contributions of participants and their discussions, (2) the media chosen by the participants which also served as their portfolio, usually a blog, and (3) social media adopted to facilitate the creation and sharing of information via virtual communities and networks (i.e., Google community, Twitter, and a Facebook page). A total of 1,273 participants registered for #CLOM REL2014. Finally, #el30 held in 2018 was the most recent cMOOC with the number of unique visitors to the E-Learning 3.0 course website reaching 3000 participants. This cMOOC also used a distributed learning environment format, including gRSShopper and social media for creating virtual communities and networks for generating and sharing course related information.

Researchers at the NRC have contributed important findings which highlight some of the challenges in the research and analysis process, especially as significant amounts of both quantitative and qualitative data are involved. The NRC's contributions to the field span over a decade with the publication of early baseline data about user experiences with existing tools, applications, systems, and desirable features for creating new and improved personal learning environments, including learning in the context of MOOCs. The findings about the importance of human factors such as motivation, incentives, and support (organizational, social networks, either online or in the community) in creating high-quality learning experiences have been highlighted (Fournier & Kop, 2010). Findings from case studies of PLEs and MOOCs suggest that learning experiences are impacted by much more than tools and technologies. Some findings related to Big Data and Educational Data Mining (EDM), ethics and privacy issues in networked environments, and the use of personal learning data to feed into the research and development process remain fertile ground for further research (Fournier and Kop, 2015; Fournier, Kop & Durand, 2014; Kop & Fournier, 2010, 2015). One aspect of the development has been the use of data and data analytics to enhance learning and fertile research worldwide has enhanced the field.

New Learning Ecosystem Landscape

The proliferation of Information and Communications Technologies in recent years has changed the educational landscape, creating a plethora of new opportunities for learning. New learning technologies are emerging outside formal education, and academics and technologists are experimenting with these in formal and informal settings. PLEs, including MOOCs, are part of the new learning ecosystem landscape, offering a wide range of open and accessible learning opportunities to learners across the world. Novel technologies using datamining and analytics have been called for in a new era of information abundance, far beyond a point in time where information was scarce and inaccessible (Weller, 2011). Filtering and managing information have become a necessity rather than a luxury. This means that emerging technologies are no longer the simple tools Heidegger described in the 1970s (Walters & Kop, 2009). Recent developments have given us access to complicated assemblages of data and artefacts, and their availability to humans now involves multiple algorithms produced by computer scientists. This presents interesting opportunities to learn from data, with the potential to reveal many hidden insights and important challenges as well. However, this also complicates effective scrutiny of the technologies and the data they produce as well as an effective assessment of their value to enhance the human and technological way-of-being.

The emerging technologies that are currently shaping the Internet and the Web provide us with access to information and the ability to work and learn with others in a creative global collaboration outside the educational structures that have been the norm for centuries (Downes, 2010; Fournier & Kop, 2010). New structures and environments are in place where people can learn autonomously, but one might question if people will be able to do so effectively (Kop & Bouchard, 2011). Two areas of research are foundational to examining effective learning in open networked environments: learner autonomy and connectivism.

Self-Directed Learning, Agency, and Autonomy

Researchers in the field of self-directed learning see learner autonomy as an important component of self-directed learning (Ponton, 2005; Bouchard, 2009; Boucouvalas, 2009). The learning environment, the learning context, and the connections people make during their learning have also been highlighted as determining factors in the success of self-directed learning journeys (Bouchard, 2009; Boucouvalas, 2009). These elements are aligned with Bandura's (2002) ideas on "human agency" (p. 269). He emphasized three types of agency: personal agency exercised individually, proxy agency, in which people secure desired outcomes by influencing others to act on their behalf; and collective agency, in which people act in concert to shape their future in whatever cultural context they inhabit. Bandura underscored the importance of all three agencies and their interrelatedness in the complex world in which we now live.

Tough (1979) and Grow (1991) noted that learners move through different phases of self-direction while Bouchard (2009) identified particular factors that influence autonomous learning strategies including psychological factors, pedagogical factors, and environmental factors. While Bouchard's dimensions provide an important basis for exploration of learner autonomy, examining self-directed learning in an open networked learning environment also requires awareness of the challenges of connectivism.

Research on self-directed learning in MOOCs has revealed that self-evaluation, self-orientation, and self-regulation are important in relation to motivation in connectivist learning (Kop and Fournier, 2010). It is now possible for self-directed learners to participate informally in learning events on open online networks, such as cMOOCs. As such, cMOOCs have a very different educational philosophy from xMOOCs, in that cMOOCs place heavy emphasis on networking and in particular on strong content contributions from the participants themselves. In contrast, xMOOCs, which became popular in 2012 as spinouts of traditional universities, primarily use a teaching model focused on the transmission of information, with high quality content delivery, computer-marked assessment (mainly for student feedback purposes), and automation of all key transactions between participants and the learning platform. In an xMOOC, direct meaningful interaction between an individual participant and the instructor responsible for the course is very difficult because of the scale of the courses (Bates, 2014). Chen (2015) has described the differences between cMOOCs and xMOOCs on the basis of characteristics and platforms (Table 1).

In an xMOOC, there is almost no direct interaction between an individual participant and the instructor responsible for the course (Bates, 2014). cMOOCs have been described as including four key design principles according to Downes (2014): autonomy, openness, diversity and interactivity (Table 2).

Downes and Siemens (conveners of the first cMOOC in 2008, CCK08) have described four key MOOC activities as: aggregation (filtering, selecting, and gathering personally meaningful information); remixing (interpreting the aggregated information and bringing to it personal perspectives and insights); repurposing (refashioning the information to suit personal purposes); and feeding forward (sharing the

Table 1. A comparison of cMOOCs and xMOOCs

MOOCs	Characteristics	Major Platforms
cMOOCs	Focused on connection and building up community. Based on connectivist design principles which include aggregation, remixing, re-purposing, and feeding forward.	Rely on posted resources, learning management systems, and social networking sites.
xMOOCs	Focused on content, standardized assessment. Similar to traditional online courses.	Coursera, edX, Udacity, Udemy, P2PU, Openedup.

Table 2. Four key design principles for cMOOCs (Downes, 2014)

Autonomy	• Choice of contents • Personal learning • No curriculum
Openness	• Open access • Open content • Open activities • Open assessment
Diversity	• Multiple tools • Individual perspective • Varied content
Interactivity	• Encourage communication • Cooperative learning • Emergent knowledge

newly fashioned information with and learning from other participants) (Downes, 2013). These four key activities are what distinguish cMOOCs from xMOOCs (Chen, 2015).

Thus, for the proponents of cMOOCs, learning results not from the transmission of information from an expert to novices, as in xMOOCs, but from sharing of knowledge between participants (Bates, 2014). In order to develop empowering learning environments that foster active learning, designers and developers of such environments first need to understand the factors that influence people's attitudes, intentions and behaviours. They must also understand the prerequisites for people to thrive in such environments in order to create favourable components and conditions, to encourage agency and autonomy for learners to participate wholeheartedly.

Recognizing the challenges posed by innovations in Web-based learning, learning technologists have started developing structures to support autonomous learners in the negotiation of this new and ever-changing learning landscape. Kop and Carroll (2011) described a place where people feel comfortable, trusted, and valued as the crux to engaging learners in an online environment. The challenge involves moving to a space that aggregates content and imagine it as a community, a place where dialogue happens, where people feel comfortable, and interactions and content can be accessed and engaged with easily.

A place where the personal meets the social with the specific purpose of developing ideas and learning. In a learning environment characterized by change, the tools and application recommended to learners and the connections to others and resources are vitally important to create meaningful learning experiences. The flow of learning in a learning environment that supports learner self-direction on online networks, as is the case in cMOOCs, is illustrated in Figure 1.

Participants in PLENK2010 reported the following motivational factors:

Figure 1. Model of personal learning environment-based learning

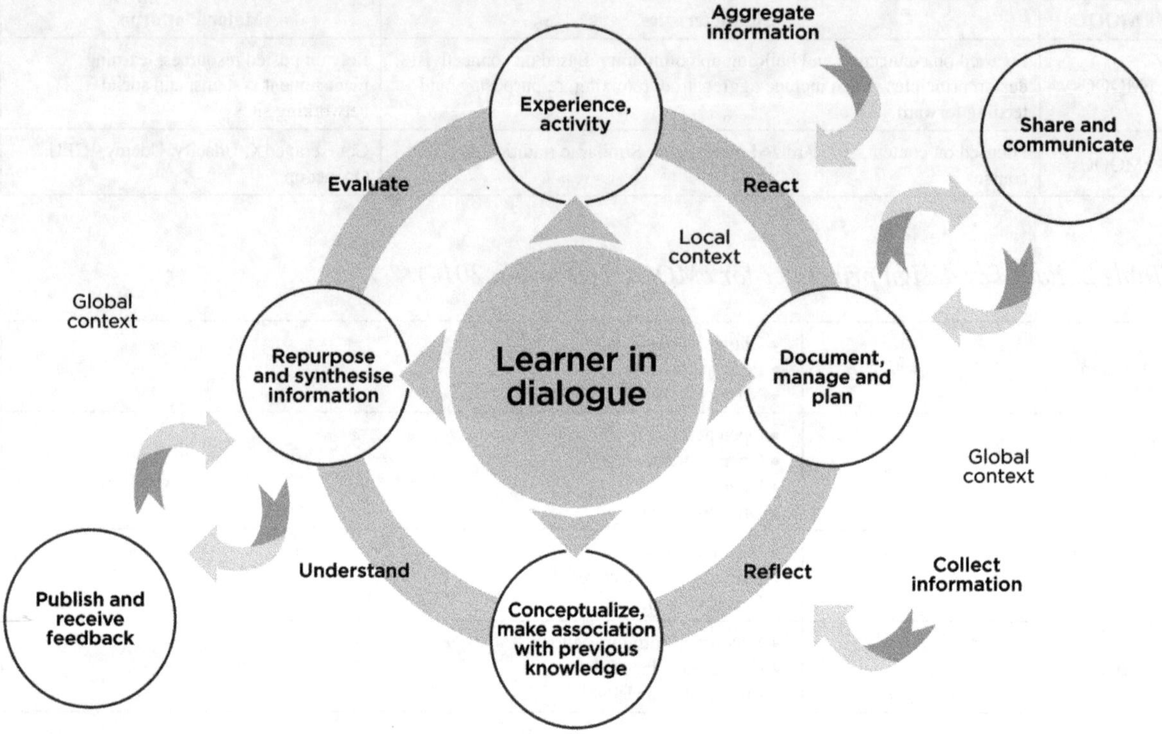

Kop, R. (2010) Model of learning in a Personal Learning Environment

- “Finding and sharing striking resources and information.”
- “Getting involved in an online community.”
- “The opportunity to learn something new.”
- “Learning alongside self-motivated peers as opposed to traditional training days where people were forced to be present.”
- “Learning how the new environment might improve my teaching and the learning of others” and
- “The topic of discussion” itself was a motivational factor.”

This suggests that active self-directed informal learning inspires learners. Downes (2009) has argued that new skills and competencies will develop while engaging in online communication with others, or via challenging feedback or recommendations through the PLE system itself. The system and technology itself, or the activity the learner is involved in, will have to be engaging and interesting enough for the learner to work his or her way through the problems that will undoubtedly come up during the learning journey. People have to be motivated to use the environment. Research and literature around connectivist learning in an online environment have underscored some key developments and challenges which will be presented in the next section.

Connectivist Learning in an Online Environment

A current example of self-directed learning promoted by Downes (2010) and Siemens (2008) is based on connectivism. They posit that being a member of an online network, communicating with others and filtering information and ideas that others provide will lead to knowledge creation and learning advancement. Connectivism advocates the active engagement of people with resources in communication with others, rather than the transfer of knowledge from educator to learner. Moreover, they promote a learning organization whereby there is not a body of knowledge to be transferred from educator to learner, and where learning does not take place in a single environment. Instead, knowledge is distributed across the Web and people's engagement with it constitutes learning. This model recognizes that the increasing influence of the eWeb and the global online connectedness of people will have implications for people's learning (Siemens, 2008; Fournier & Kop, 2010). The role of the educator is predicted to change (Downes, 2010) as learners have the option to move from a learning environment controlled by the educator and the institution to an environment where they find their own information and direct their own learning as they develop ideas and connect with (knowledgeable) others on networks away from the formal setting.

The current literature related to Web development highlights four challenges and pertinent developments to connectivist learning:

1. The nature of the network as a place to learn as opposed to a group in an educational institution and the levels of presence in each has been highlighted as an important factor in the willingness of participants to actively engage online (Dron & Anderson, 2007). Power relations in online networks and how these might influence the information and resources that self-directed learners will be able to access are other important issues. The structures of the Web are preventing it from developing into a network where equality is the norm, rather than the exception (Barabasi, 2003; Boyd and Crawford, 2012). In addition, the increasing influence of commerce on the Web might negatively influence the potential of the social Web for learning and education (Friesen, 2010; Mager, 2014).
2. Some literacies have been identified that are critical for learners to be able to effectively direct their own learning in an open online networked environment. Apart from reading and writing, these include information and media literacy and the ability to critically analyze resources and information in order to understand the new semantics of the Web. Creative abilities and a flexible mindset in an environment that is characterized by change and complexity have also been highlighted as important (Downes, 2009; Partnership 21st Century Skills, 2009; StriČević, 2018).
3. Cloud computing and the emergence of social media have altered the dynamics of the Web. Moving away from a linear process of printed text, they increasingly involve the production of digital artefacts and the storage of these away from local computing devices, as well as the use of a variety of communication, collaboration and sharing tools that people find and use on the Web. These tools have created a new demand on human agency in the form of creativity, innovation and self-expression (Fisher, Giaccardi, Eden, Sugimoto, & Ye, 2005; Nguyen, 2018).
4. The Semantic Web, Artificial Intelligence and learning analytics are the latest developments of the Web and can be used for the visualization of large amounts of data, creating a need for learners to be able to understand and critically analyze graphs, figures and recommendations. The analysis of this "Big Data" can also be used to improve learning in new ways, and some observers envisage the use of analytics in learning recommender systems to aid learners in their information aggrega-

tion strategies (Drachsler & Greller, 2016; Fournier, Kop, & Sitlia, 2011), but others suggest that caution is needed to maintain the human in learning and education (Ravipati, 2017).

Feedback from participants in connectivist-type MOOCs highlights the importance of having choices at the start of the learning activity and the need for a negotiation process regarding content, skills, and process to make courses meaningful and relevant to everyday life (Kop and Fournier, 2010). In PLENK2010, for instance, participants expressed the following: "It was motivational to be learning about connectivist learning in the company of the originators of the connectivism theory". Another participant drew inspiration from "learning in the company of self-motivated persons with a similar interest". There was "value in the opportunity to come in contact with, collaborate with, and meet people who would help to expand their personal network."

Different skills, abilities and competencies are required to learn in a complex learning environment such as a cMOOC. PLENK2010 participants shared these perceptions in an end of course survey: "A particular mindset is required", "Novices might need more time to feel comfortable with this change process, especially in relation to building self-confidence and a sense of community in such a large course", and "People need to develop . . . a host of new critical literacies in order to learn and to work effectively with intelligent data, with people, and within the network."

cMOOCs as a Disruptive Pedagogy

Connectivist MOOCs have been described as being pedagogically disruptive (Mackness, Waite, Roberts, & Lovegrove, 2013) and this can have a significant impact on participant learning experiences and their sense of personal identity. Connectivism is based on the idea that knowledge is essentially the set of connections in a network, and that learning therefore is the process of creating and shaping those networks. As part of a pedagogically disruptive learning experience, the course facilitator of E-Learning 3.0—a cMOOC on the topic of 'Distributed Learning Technology' expressed the following: "You might be thinking: this course looks too difficult, too technical, or too high level. This will be true for everyone, even me. But the course is structured so you can focus on what's interesting and accessible for you, and you can ignore the rest" (Downes, 2018).

Participants in the E-Learning 3.0 cMOOC expressed the following insights regarding their own journey in the course, the richness of shared experiences and some of challenges as well:

I'm a free range learner and like to take my own route through a course, often checking out related resources and ideas along the way. But I do appreciate the sense of a shared experience that synchronous components of a course creates [...] it's the surprising, sometimes disconcerting and shocking discoveries in a rich, deep, multilayered, unplanned environment that makes the experience memorable and, perhaps transformational.

A MOOC isn't like listening to a finished symphony, it's more like warming up in the pit with everyone else. It's improvised jazz. (#el30, duration—10 weeks, October-December 2018).

When asked to share their thoughts and experiences notions of community, openness and interaction were frequently mentioned for participants in the E-Learning 3.0 MOOC (Figure 2).

Figure 2. Wordle of text responses describing E-learning 3.0 MOOC experiences

In order to develop empowering learning environments that foster active learning, designers and developers of such environments first need to understand the factors that influence people's attitudes, intentions and behaviours. They must also understand the prerequisites for people to thrive in such environments in order to create favourable components and conditions. Despite the wealth of information now available on MOOCs through various scientific publications and social media including blogs, microblogs, wikis, and social networks, there is no shortage of challenges and issues to be addressed. The next section will highlight some of the obvious ones.

MOOC Learning Experience Design

Challenges Related to Learning and Experience

To date, research on cMOOCs has pointed to the conditions that clearly encourage the involvement and engagement of people in learning in a connectivist learning environment, including: (1) the social presence of the facilitators and of participants, (2) feeling competent and confident in using the different tools, (3) learning in an autonomous fashion without the provision of organized guidance by facilitators, and (4) the emergence of critical literacies such as collaboration, creativity, and a flexible mindset, which are prerequisite for active learning in a changing and complex learning environment (Kop, 2011).

Empirical research into the actual cMOOC experience is still sparse and areas of particular weakness include information on the types of support systems required by learners to be successful in MOOCs. There is also an overreliance on metrics commonly used in education to measure success in MOOCs, namely the number of enrollments, completion rates, and assessments. Clearly, it is easier to capture numbers than qualitative identifiers, such as motivation and engagement. Accreditation and the perception that courses need to be finished to be meaningful, stemming from traditional education, continue to pose a challenge in MOOCs as well, whether in dealing with the semantics of digital badges, automated grading, calibrated peer review, learning analytics for assessment and adaptive learning, distance proctoring, and engagement diagnosis and remediation (Alain, 2014). Moreover, individuals now need a wide range of competencies—social skills, communication, problem solving—in order to face the complex challenges of today's world; especially those related to an increasingly digital world and information systems (StriČević, 2018).

Challenges Related to Personalization and Supporting Individual Learning Needs

Efforts directed towards "mass customization" are currently aimed at restructuring MOOCs at the individual level and to personalize information, resources, and communication in order to best support each student, and not only the aggregate (Salvador, De Holan, & Piller, 2009). These efforts also tie into the persistent challenge of sustained and personal engagement across MOOCS (xMOOCs and cMOOCs). Participants in cMOOCs continue to express the need for greater presence of course facilitators, which makes cultivating a relationship with the course instructor or tutor a real challenge given the large number of students and the scale of the operation that can run in the thousands of participants. To this end, Coursera, an xMOOC developer has recommended an approach that borders in part on course automation, that is, a computer assigns classmates to give one another feedback. However, automated feedback does not provide students with a sense of being treated like an individual, nor does it create a sense of community that fosters learning, and, therefore, falls short in providing personalized learning. Additional inroads are also needed to begin to understand the specific types of resources that informal learners find valuable to their changing learning needs.

The factors or learning components which support participant retention in a MOOC are still not well understood nor are the online supports or scaffolds that can be embedded to increase weak completion numbers of most MOOCs to date (Catropa, cited in Bonk 2013). Comments received from cMOOC participant surveys underscore similarities between the barriers or challenges in MOOCs and many self-directed learning environments, which include less immediate feedback and guidance, lack of personalization, procrastination, and becoming overwhelmed by the resources made available (Graham, 2006). Furthermore, researchers should consider if learning on the network is different from the typical learning in groups that is prevalent in traditional educational institutions it seems that participants in informal networks do not find it necessary to finish the course. They seem to prefer to 'dip in and dip out' to get what they need from it. Further research in these behavioural and attitudinal issues is required. Increasingly, information about individual learners and their online behaviors are now made available and harvested from their participation in MOOCs, which makes it possible to do these types of analyses. However, researchers need to carefully consider the ethical implications related to how personal learning data is collected, analyzed, and reported.

De Laat (2006) highlighted the complexity of researching networked learning and emphasized as key problems the issues of human agency and the multitude of issues involved, such as the dynamics of the network, power-relations on the network, and the amount of content generated. It might also mean that qualitative analysis in addition to quantitative analyses are necessary to obtain meaningful answers to research questions. Effective analysis would require a multi-method approach and would need to address new ethics and privacy issues. The next section highlights some of these issues.

New Ethics and Privacy Issues in Networked Environments

Every researcher has to consider the ethical implications of the chosen methods of obtaining the data for a study and the use made of it. Sometimes obtaining data is a matter of accessing statistics or documents. When human subjects are involved in the research, careful consideration of the level of informed consent by participants is also required.

Miller and Bell (2002) argued that gaining informed consent is problematic if it is not clear what the participant is consenting to and where "participation begins and ends" (p. 53). Several ethical issues were raised in the literature, of which misuse of data and privacy issues were the most important. Van Wel and Royakkers (2004) and Boyd and Crawford (2012) caution that data could pose a threat to subjects when misused or used for different purposes than what it was supplied for. Researchers should at least anonymise data in order to respect privacy (Van Wel & Royakkers, 2004; Prinsloo & Slade, 2017; Boyd and Crawford, 2010).

It has also been suggested by network researchers that people should have the choice to opt in or opt out of the use of their data. If someone is not aware that the data is being collected or how it will be used, he/she has no real opportunity to consent or withhold consent for its collection and use. This invisible data gathering is common on the Web (Van Wel & Royakkers, 2004) and highlights new decisions and issues related to ethics that researchers will have to address. Ultimately, researchers have a responsibility to carefully consider the context of their research, and also the process that takes place between observing, collecting and analyzing "Big Data"; data that is left by traces of activities that might not at all be related to the visible participation of learners (Prinsloo & Slade, 2017).

In PLENK2010, boundaries of the research were identified on the consent form that participants were asked to read at the start of the course. Data collection involved quantitative as well as qualitative measures (demographic data, system data, surveys and focus groups), asking for informed consent, and using the course hashtag (#PLENK2010) to identify course-related data inside and outside the course environment as part of the research and specified in the consent request.

According to Koutropoulos et al. (2012), MOOCs need to evolve in areas such as data capture and learner and learning analytics. Their categories include: determining who is merely "window shopping" in the initial periods of a MOOC, who is a lurker, who is an active participant, and when and why participants drop out completely. These MOOC researchers also state that in order to better understand the learners and MOOC participation, rich and informative data needs to be available for analysis and systems that facilitate this collection need to be built. There is a need for powerful tools to allow analyses of the most important factors contributing to the quality of the learning experience "at a glance" to be useful to either the facilitator or those participants who are in need of targeted remediation at crucial points in the course – before their participation starts to decline or participants drop out altogether. Automated methods of educational data mining could readily add temporal information and clarity to the levels of learning activity of participants, with possible suggestions as to the nature of support, feedback, and tools they desire and require. Intelligent data analysis would overcome the limitations and challenges in using qualitative software analysis tools which are labor intensive and time consuming.

In an effort to facilitate research, analysis and smart explorative applications of massive datasets the LACE-Learning analytics community exchange project (EU funded project of the 7th Framework Programme) offered data sets as publicly available, machine-readable versions of research articles. The main goal of this initiative was to facilitate research, analysis, and smart explorative applications. Based on the insights gained from these data challenges, the idea was born to make more Learning Analytics data sets publicly available for researchers to get to a more open access data-driven research community within Learning Analytics. The intent was to collect more data and reward their creators through citing the datasets and connecting new research outcomes to them (Dietze, Siemens, Tabi, & Drachsler, 2016).

NEXT GENERATION LEARNING ENVIRONMENTS

The research over the years has led to some recommendations for future development of personalized learning ecosystems. The design and development of next generation learning environments, including PLE ecosystems needs to include a common set of standards to enable personalization from available tools and components, learning resources and interaction derived from learner profiles, and standard features designed specifically to meet individual needs and preferences. A review of literature highlights technology design considerations and strategic areas of focus related to the personalization of learning (Kondratova, Molyneaux, O'Donnell, & Al-Digeil, 2015). Table 3 provides a summary of findings related to personalization.

Several themes are discussed in the literature, including "the extensive use of multi-agent computing, artificial intelligence, recommendation algorithms, user profiling, learning analytics, and semantics/ontologies as the basis of personalization strategies. Natural language processing and interfaces are at the forefront of ongoing research, and the influence of mobile technologies is also apparent, as researchers design ways to reformat content and apply contextual (e.g., location-based) intelligence to learning platforms" (Schoefegger, Seitlinger, & Ley, 2010). However, the need for caution and transparency has been identified in the fields of educational datamining and learning analytics as a must, as examples have come to light of falsified and inaccurate data use so the need to set quality standards in learning analytics and educational datamining also need attention in these reasonably young research areas (Ropovic, 2015; Scheffel, Drachsler, Stoyanov, & Specht, 2014).

The use of contextual information (e.g., user's current mood or location) is widely used by recommendation systems for mobile devices to search for and present the best resources to the users (Hu, Du, Tong, & Liu, 2013). Social tags and resource metadata semantics (e.g., for deriving meaning from single words or text) are also used to enhance recommendation systems. Social networks like Facebook, Twitter, and LinkedIn are rich with detailed contextual information describing an individual's preferences and relationships. This contextual information can make recommendation more feasible and effective—extracting user social tags from external social networks while the collaborative tagging system is used as supplemental information (Hu, Du, Tong, & Liu, 2013).

Researchers have access to massive amounts of data that capture the entire digital experience in a constant stream of inputs and outputs, but the challenge is the effective analysis of such big data. It is easy for researchers to resort to the easiest way of capturing quantitative data, which would leave out the richness that more qualitative efforts could achieve. Some efforts are being made to develop data-driven learning environments that include features for visualizing traces of data that learners have left behind in their online learning activities (Duval, 2011; Downes, 2013). Machine-learning techniques to personalize the learning experience are also being pursued (Spice, 2014).

Table 3. Technology design considerations and industry focus

Technology Design Considerations: Areas Addressing Personalization	**Industry Focus: Strategic Areas Being Developed**
• Micro-credential and badges • Privacy considerations for a learning assistant • Using social media in the workplace • xAPI enabled systems facilitate immersive learning • User's e-portfolio data harvested by learning analytics	• Measuring improvement in learning outcomes • Improving learner engagement • Delivering personalized, competency based learning pathways • Having a mobile strategy • Supporting badges & micro-credentials

Among the major complaints from participants in CLOM-REL2014 (on Open Educational Resources) was the challenge of sifting through threaded discussions to find relevant contributions, an overabundance of discussions and content, and the difficulty of knowing who contributed what, especially in one's area of interest or learning. In response to these challenges, social learning analytic tools are being applied in MOOC environments to stimulate, monitor, and evaluate networked learning activities. Tools such as the Network Awareness Tool (NAT) plug-in increases the power of analytics such that participant can render their connected world more visible. Visualizing networked learning activities can help learners to decide which discussion topics they should join and which experts they should aim to connect with (Schreurs, de Laat, Teplovs, & Voogd, 2014).

Tools for visualizing networked learning activities could go a long way in helping to support learners in MOOCs. Still, with MOOC learning analytics there are the challenges of going beyond the logs, observing and making sense of interactions, annotations for assessment, dynamic adaptation of learning processes, and the need to provide avenues for deeper learning, while managing and protecting the identity and privacy of learners (Alain, 2014). Moreover, there are also difficult issues relating to identity fraud, plagiarism, peer learning, meaningful feedback, and assessment of learning outcomes which need to be addressed going forward.

At the NRC, the design and development of next generation learning includes data-driven visualizations of trace data learners have left behind in their online learning activities and machine-learning techniques to personalize the learning experience. Other development efforts have focused on personal and context-aware information about the learner to help to counter issues of human bias in collecting and analyzing data, and interpreting results. New recommendation systems now rely on artificial intelligence and techniques which take into account user learning styles, preferences, prior experience and knowledge to better predict and anticipate the needs of learners, and act more efficiently in response to learner behaviors (Verbert et. al., 2012). The application of various intelligent techniques from data mining and machine learning represents a more recent trend in attempting to study and model users' context-sensitive preferences. This is fertile ground for further research and development efforts.

CONCLUSION

This chapter has tried to cover over a decade of literature and research findings which have informed research and development efforts of new learning ecosystems such as Personal Learning Environments, including cMOOCs. These efforts have highlighted the potential of new learning environments and systems for enhancing learning processes but also highlight important challenges and issues as well; the need for further research in several areas has been emphasized.

Findings from case studies of PLEs and MOOCs suggest that learning experiences are impacted by much more than tools and technologies. Findings related to Big Data and Educational Data Mining (EDM), ethics and privacy issues in networked environments, setting quality standards and the use of personal learning data to feed into the research and development process remain fertile ground for further research (Scheffel, Drachsler, Stoyanov, & Specht, 2014). Initiatives have been created to explore applications to facilitate research, analysis of massive datasets which address ethics and data protection through publicly available, machine-readable versions of research articles (see LACE, Learning Analytics Community Exchange).

This chapter has also highlighted some challenges and opportunities in the design and development of Personal Learning Ecosystems. To support learners effectively in dealing with the abundance of information available through technological means (including algorithms and machine learning), a concerted collaboration of computer scientists, mathematicians and social scientists is taking place to ensure a quality ecosystem for the future. Technologies are now being developed to empower the learner to take control over the information stream him or herself and be proactive in collecting meaningful information that is filtered through interaction with other human beings.

Working across distributed platforms allows learners considerable autonomy, but also requires the associated technical, navigation, and critical thinking skills. For newcomers to MOOCs, case studies have revealed that the experience is most often difficult and disorienting. Fostering and encouraging learner autonomy is an essential part of the learning process and design but the constraints on autonomy must be recognized as part of the human factors involved in critical learning on an open network. Findings presented in this chapter point to the type of support structures needed to create a place or community where people feel comfortable, trusted, and valued, and can access and interact with resources and each other.

The notion of what it means to learn in a new learning ecosystem continues to expand, with opportunities for individuals to manage their own learning, improve on their competencies, add a new skill set for career advancement or pursue learning for personal enjoyment. Current research and development efforts in the new learning ecosystem include powerful data-driven visualizations aimed at providing valuable and meaningful feedback to learners based on trace data of their learning activities, machine-learning techniques to personalize the learning, learning analytics, recommender systems, big data and educational data mining applications, as well as the provision of safeguards for data protection and privacy in a complex networked environment. Further research in the area of AI and data-driven learning systems such as recommender systems will help learners filter information and online social interactions, but the challenge also lies in the human factors such as motivation, incentives and support that make people want to participate in a course and learn.

ACKNOWLEDGMENT

We would like to acknowledge Stephen Downes who has been at the heart of NRC research on MOOCs and technologies to develop personal learning ecosystems over the past ten years. His philosophy on open and accessible teaching and learning has made this research possible. This research received public funding through the National Research Council of Canada.

REFERENCES

Alain, M. (2014). *MOOCs: New research questions and method?* Retrieved from https://prezi.com/owhcvtpwsu5q/moocs-new-research-questions-and-method/

Bandura, A. (2002). Social cognitive theory in cultural context. *Applied Psychology*, *51*(2), 269–290. doi:10.1111/1464-0597.00092

Barabasi, A. (2003). *Linked: How everything is connected to everything else and what it means*. New York, NY: Penguin Books.

Bates, T. (2014). *Comparing xMOOCs and cMOOCs: Philosophy and practice*. Retrieved from https://www.tonybates.ca/2014/10/13/comparing-xmoocs-and-cmoocs-philosophy-and-practice/

Bonk, C. J., Lee, M. M., & Sheu, F.-R. (2014). *Research on self-directed informal learners in open educational environments and massively open online courses*. Presented at AECT, Anaheim, CA. Retrieved from http://trainingshare.worldisopen.com/pdfs/Self-Directed_Lrng_MOOCs_Open_Ed_AECT_Bonk_et_al_Friday_paper_session--Title-Change.pdf

Bouchard, P. (2009). Pedagogy without a teacher: What are the limits? *International Journal of Self-Directed Learning*, *6*(2), 13–22. Retrieved from http://www.sdlglobal.com

Boucouvalas, M. (2009). Revisiting the concept of Self in self-directed learning:Towards a more robust construct for research and practice in a global context. *International Journal of Self-Directed Learning*, *6*(1), 1–9. Retrieved from http://www.sdlglobal.com

Boyd, D., & Crawford, K. (2012). Critical questions for Big Data. *Information Communication and Society*, *15*(5), 662–679. doi:10.1080/1369118X.2012.678878

De Laat, M. (2006). *Networked learning* (Doctoral thesis). Retrieved from https://eprints.soton.ac.uk/20358/1/Maarten_De_Laat_Networked_Learning_2006.pdf

Dietze, S., Siemens, D., Tabi, D., & Drachsler, H. (2016). Edotorial: Datasets for learning analytics. *Journal of Learning Analytics*. Retrieved from https://learning-analytics.info/journals/index.php/JLA/article/view/5071

Downes, S. (2010, December 5). The role of the educator. *Huffington Post*. Retrieved from http://huff.to/g7Orh9

Downes, S. (2013). *The quality of massive open online courses*. Retrieved from http://mooc.efquel.org/week-2-the-quality-of-massive-open-online-courses-by-stephen-downes/

Downes, S. (2013, December 4). Learning and performance support systems. *Half an Hour Blogspot*. Retrieved from http://halfanhour.blogspot.com.es/2013/12/learning-and-performance-support-systems.html

Downes, S. (2014). *The MOOC of one*. Retrieved from https://www.slideshare.net/Downes/2014-03-10-valencia

Downes, S. (2018). *Approaching E-Learning 3.0*. Retrieved from https://halfanhour.blogspot.com/2018/09/approaching-e-learning-30.html

Drachsler, H., & Greller, W. (2016). Privacy and analytics: it's a DELICATE issue a checklist for trusted learning analytics. In *Proceedings of the Sixth International Conference on Learning Analytics & Knowledge (LAK '16)*. ACM. 10.1145/2883851.2883893

Dron, J., & Anderson, T. (2007). *Collectives, networks, and groups in social software for e learning*. Paper presented at World Conference on E-Learning in Corporate, Government, Healthcare, and Higher Education (ELEARN), Quebec City, Quebec, Canada.

Duval, E. (2011). Attention please! Learning analytics for visualization and recommendation. *Proceedings of 1st International Conference on Learning Analytics and Knowledge*. 10.1145/2090116.2090118

Fisher, G., & Eden, S. (2005). Beyond Binary Choices: Integrating Individual and Social Creativity. *International Journal of Human-Computer Studies*, *63*(4), 482–512. doi:10.1016/j.ijhcs.2005.04.014

Fournier, H., & Kop, R. (2010). *Researching the design and development of a Personal Learning Environment.* Paper presented at the PLE Conference, Barcelona, Spain. Retrieved from http://bit.ly/c5ehX4

Fournier, H., & Kop, R. (2015). MOOC learning experience design: Issues and challenges. MOOCs and Open Education. *International Journal on E-Learning, 14*(3), 289-304.

Fournier, H., Kop, R., & Durand, G. (2014). Challenges to Research in MOOCs. *Journal of Online Learning and Teaching / MERLOT, 10*(1). Retrieved from http://jolt.merlot.org/vol10no1/fournier_0314.pdf

Fournier, H., Kop, R., & Sitlia, H. (2011). The Value of Learning Analytics to Networked Learning on a Personal Learning Environment. *1st International Conference on Learning analytics and Knowledge*, Banff, Canada. 10.1145/2090116.2090131

Friesen, N. (2010). Education and the social Web: Connective learning and the commercial imperative. *First Monday*, *15*(12). doi:10.5210/fm.v15i12.3149

Graham, C. R. (2006). Blended learning systems: Definition, current trends, future directions. In C. J. Bonk & C. R. Graham (Eds.), The handbook of blended learning: Global perspectives, local designs (pp. 3-21). San Francisco, CA: Pfeiffer Publishing.

Grow, G. (1991). Teaching learners to be self-directed. *Adult Education Quarterly*, *41*(3), 125–149. doi:10.1177/0001848191041003001

Hu, L., Du, Z., Tong, Q., & Liu, Y. (2013). Context-aware recommendation of learning resources using rules engine. *IEEE 13th International Conference on Advanced Learning Technologies*. Retrieved from https://ieeexplore.ieee.org/stamp/stamp.jsp?tp=&arnumber=6601899

JISC. (2008). *Effective practice with e-Portfolios, supporting 21st century learning*. Bristol, UK: JISC Innovation Group.

Kondratova, I., Molyneaux, H., O'Donnell, S., & Al-Digeil, M. (2015). *Quick Dive Environmental Scan for the LPSS Visioning Exercise*. Internal report.

Kop, R. (2010). The design and development of a personal learning environment: Researching the learning experience. *Proceedings of the European Distance and E-learning Network Annual Conference 2010*. Retrieved from https://nrc-publications.canada.ca/eng/view/accepted/?id=0728bc9b-1907-49c1-90bd-0f7ea87a0cad

Kop, R. (2011). The challenges to connectivist learning on open online networks: Learning experiences during a massive open online course. *International Review of Research in Open and Distance Learning*, *12*(3), 19. doi:10.19173/irrodl.v12i3.882

Kop, R., & Bouchard, P. (2011). The role of adult educators in the age of social media. In M. Thomas (Ed.), *Digital education*. London: Palgrave MacMillan. doi:10.1057/9780230118003_4

Kop, R., & Carroll, F. (2011). Cloud computing and creativity: Learning on a massive open online course. *EURODL*, 1–11. Retrieved from http://www.eurodl.org/?p=special&sp=articles&article=457

Kop, R., & Fournier, H. (2010). New dimensions to self-directed learning in an open networked learning environment. *International Journal of Self-Directed Learning*, *7*(2).

Kop, R., & Fournier, H. (2013). *Developing a framework for research on personal learning environments.* ELearning Papers n.º 35. Retrieved from http://openeducationeuropa.eu/fr/node/131234

Koutropoulos, A., Gallagher, M. S., Abajian, S. C., de Waard, I., Hogue, R. J., Keskin, N. O., & Rodriguez, C. O. (2012). Emotive vocabulary in MOOCs: Context & participant retention. *European Journal of Open, Distance and E-Learning, 2012*(1). Retrieved from http://www.eurodl.org/materials/contrib/2012/Koutropoulos_et_al.pdf

LACE. (n.d.). Retrieved from http://www.laceproject.eu/lace/

Mackness, J., Waite, M., Roberts, G., & Lovegrove, E. (2013). Learning in a small, task-oriented, connectivist MOOC: Pedagogical issues and implications for higher education. *The International Review of Research in Open and Distributed Learning*, *14*(4). doi:10.19173/irrodl.v14i4.1548

Mager, A. (2014). Defining Algorithmic Ideology: Using Ideology Critique to Scrutinize Corporate Search Engines. *TripleC*, *12*(1), 28–39. doi:10.31269/triplec.v12i1.439

Miller, T., & Bell, L. (2002). Consenting to what? Issues of access, gate-keeping and 'informed' consent. In M. Mauthner, M. Birch, J. Jessop, & T. Miller (Eds.), Ethics in qualitative research (pp. 53-69). London, UK: Seven Oakes. doi:10.4135/9781849209090.n3

Nguyen, D. (2018). The university in a world of digital technologies: Tensions and challenges. *Australasian Marketing Journal, 26*(2), 79-82.

Ponton, M. (2005). The relationship between self-efficacy and autonomous learning: The development of new instrumentation. *International Journal of Self-Directed Learning*, *5*(2), 50–58. Retrieved from http://www.sdlglobal.com

Prinsloo, P., & Slade, S. (2017). Ethics and Learning Analytics: Charting the (Un)Charted, Handbook of Learning Analytics. Academic Press. doi:10.18608/hla17.004

Ravipati, S. (2017). *Outsmarting the Machine: Redesigning Education to Make Students, Teachers Relevant in the Algorithm Age, Transforming Education Through Technology*. Centre in discussion with Lee Rainie from PEW's Research Centre.

Ropovik, I. (2015). A cautionary note on testing latent variable models. *Frontiers in Psychology*, *6*, 1715. doi:10.3389/fpsyg.2015.01715 PMID:26594192

Salvador, F., De Holan, P. M., & Piller, F. (2009). Cracking the code of mass customization. *MIT Sloan Management Review*, *50*(3). Retrieved from http://www.ie.edu/microsites/comunicacion/Sem%2018%20mayo%202009/Salvador,%20De%20Holan%20&%20Piller.pdf

Scheffel, M., Drachsler, H., Stoyanov, S., & Specht, M. (2014). Quality indicators for learning analytics. *Journal of Educational Technology & Society*, *17*(4), 117–132.

Schoefegger, K., Seitlinger, P., & Ley, T. (2010). Towards a User Model for Personalized Recommendations in Work-Integrated Learning: A Report on an Experimental Study with a Collaborative Tagging System. *Procedia Computer Science, 1*(2), 2829–2838. doi:10.1016/j.procs.2010.08.008

Schreurs, B., de Laat, M., Teplovs, C., & Voogd, S. (2014). Social learning analytics applied in MOOC-environment. eLearning Papers. *OpenEducationEuropa, 36*, 45-48. Retrieved from http://openeducationeuropa.eu/en/download/file/fid/33697

Siemens, G. (2008). *Learning and knowing in networks: Changing roles for educators and designers*. Paper presented at the University of Georgia IT Forum, Athens, GA. Retrieved from http://bit.ly/170fVM

Spice, B. (2014). Press release. Google sponsors Carnegie Mellon Research to improve effectiveness of online education. Paying attention to how people learn promises to enhance MOOCs. *Carnegie Mellon News*. Retrieved from http://bit.ly/1l6NsON

Stričević, I. (2018). Literacies in the Digital Age New Teaching Paradigms and Solutions for Academic Libraries. In *Proceedings of the 5th International Symposium on Emerging Trends and Technologies in Libraries and Information Services (ETTLIS)*. Bettis University.

Tough, A. M. (1979). Choosing to learn. Toronto: The Ontario Institute for Studies in Education (OISE).

Van Wel, L., & Royakkers, L. (2004). Ethical issues in web data mining. *Ethics and Information Technology, 6*(2), 129–140. doi:10.1023/B:ETIN.0000047476.05912.3d

Verbert, K., Manouselis, N., Ochoa, X., Wolpers, M., Drachsler, H., Bosnic, I., & Duval, E. (2012). Context-aware recommender systems for learning: A survey and future challenges. *IEEE Transactions on Learning Technologies, 5*(4), 318-335. Retrieved from https://ieeexplore.ieee.org/stamp/stamp.jsp?tp=&arnumber=6189308

Walters, P., & Kop, R. (2009). Heidegger, digital technology and post-modern education: From Being-in-cyberspace to meeting on MySpace. *Bulletin of Science, Technology & Society, 29*(4), 278–286. doi:10.1177/0270467609336305

Weller, M. A. (2011). Pedagogy of abundance. *Revista Española de Pedagogía, 249*, 223–236.

KEY TERMS AND DEFINITIONS

Big Data: A field that addresses ways to analyze, extract, and manage data sets that are too large or complex to be dealt with by traditional data-processing application software.

Cloud Computing: Makes computer system resources, storage and computer power in particular, available on demand without direct active management by the user. The cloud makes data centers available to many users over the internet.

Educational Data Mining (EDM): A research field concerned with the application of data mining, machine learning, and statistics to information generated from educational settings.

Learning Analytics: The measurement, collection, and analysis and reporting of data about learners and their contexts, for the purpose of understanding and optimizing learning and the environments in which learning occurs.

Learning Ecosystem: An entity made up of components that work together to create a whole learning experience. The overall experience becomes more than the sum of its parts.

Moodle: A free and open-source learning management system used for blended learning and open education.

National Research Council Canada: The Government of Canada's largest research organization supporting industrial innovation, the advancement of knowledge and technology development, as well as fulfilling government mandates.

Personalized Learning Environments: Provide learning opportunities and instruction paced to the learners' needs, tailored to learning preferences and to the specific interests of different learners.

Semantic Web: An extension of the world wide web and a common framework that allows data to be shared and reused across application, enterprise, and community boundaries.

Chapter 2
Teaching Virtual Online Courses in an Era of Negative Student Reviews:
Mixed Methods Controlled Experiment and Feedback

Kenneth David Strang
https://orcid.org/0000-0002-4333-4399
W3Research, USA

ABSTRACT

Students of higher education are complaining about their online courses or faculty perhaps because universities are pushing to have classroom lectures converted to virtual learning delivery methods but without hiring qualified professors and failing to train faculty to effectively teach online. Different skills are required to effectively teach online courses as compared to lecturing in the classroom. To examine this problem, the author discusses the results of a mixed-methods research design consisting of an experiment followed by constructive feedback analysis. The experiment measured student grades from a standard teaching approach as compared with applying constructivism theory in the same online course at a university. The student outcome effect size for the treatment group was substantial and the analysis of constructive feedback evidence from the students was moderately supportive of the teaching approach.

INTRODUCTION

Online virtual learning is increasing in demand due to the changing needs of students who are working (Strang, 2017a), facing high debt and struggling to balance family with professional life (Strang & Shimer, 2017). The problem is according to student ratings and accreditation assessments, many universities offer very low quality online courses and/or they employ incompetent faculty to teach them (Arbaugh et al., 2009; Strang, 2016b).

DOI: 10.4018/978-1-5225-7987-8.ch002

There are many cases of poor online programs or unethical faculty conduct reported in the media for USA-based degree-mill institutions such as Corinthian College, University of Phoenix, and others (Levin, 2018; Costin & Hamilton, 2009; Popovich & Neel, 2005). There are numerous negative student reviews of online courses taught at USA-based public universities (Collegeconfidential, 2019; Niche, 2019; Ratemyprofessors, 2019; Studentsreview, 2019; Unigo, 2019).

Public universities have an additional challenge not faced by the private institutions: A lack of revenue (Collegeconfidential, 2019). Therefore, professors in public universities must be creative and strategically innovative in order to leverage learning theories to design and teach online courses in a way to appease emerging virtual learner demands. According to a virtual learning meta-analysis, many studies claim classroom pedagogy best-practices are effective when applied to online courses (Tallent-Runnels et al., 2006). In fact, a number of comparative empirical studies prove that online teaching can be just as effective as face-to-face instruction (Ginns & Ellis, 2007; Laurillard, 2007; Strang, 2015b; Strang, 2016a; Strang 2016b, Strang 2016c).

Contrary to the above, some researchers assert that simply imitating direct instruction in a virtual online course fails to motivate students to deeply learn knowledge as compared to direct in-person dynamic lectures (Joint, 2003; Strang & Vajjhala, 2017). More so, claims of effective online pedagogical strategies may be defective because they ignore confounding variables (Joy & Garcia, 2000). Furthermore, some courses may be more difficult to teach online than in the classroom due to their complex content (Arbaugh, 2005), especially in predominately quantitative fields like operations research or engineering (Affouf & Walsh, 2007; Cybinski & Selvanathan, 2005; Swan, 2003). Therefore, stakeholders need more information about what works when teaching online courses with applied content such as in the operations research field.

The objective of this chapter is to discuss the findings from a controlled experiment examining if constructivism learning theory can be more effective than not using it to teach a virtual online course in the operations research field. The purpose of the experiment was to measure the academic effectiveness of a constructivist instructional methodology applied to an online project management course, as compared to the traditional approach used to teach the same course online by another faculty. Independent student constructive feedback was collected from an online rating system and analyzed to explain what worked well and what did not. The aim of the chapter is to generalize the findings to faculty and management of universities in USA who offer online courses. Additionally, accreditation panel members, academic researchers and students may be interested in these findings.

Background

The phrase 'virtual online learning' is often used synonymously with online education, distributed learning, networked learning, web-based learning, and distance education (Weller, 2007). As applied to this study a virtual online learning environment is an educational delivery system and accompanied by a methodology or pedagogy for effectively teaching the material to students while leveraging technology to provide asynchronous and/or synchronous learning activities (Naidu, 2002; Strang, 2017b). A few researchers have experimented with Second Life and other gaming type technology as a way of delivering online courses to university students but this is not an effective pedagogy according to any scholarly literature (Helling, Dumire & Augustosky, 2009) and it is ineffective at contemporary universities for online instruction (Strang, 2014; Arbaugh, Godfrey, Johnson, Pollack, Niendorf & Wresch, 2009; Bernard, Abrami, Lou, Borokhovski, Wade & Wozney, 2004), and it is not considered further in this chapter.

Another issue is that unfortunately, instructional methodologies that strongly focus on student interaction and collaboration may function well in social sciences but emphasizing a constructivist learning strategy may be better for cross-disciplinary applied fields like operations research, project management, nursing, and so on. Applied disciplinary subjects are difficult to learn online because there is less dynamic personal interaction between the professor and student in virtual learning environments (Laurillard, 1993, 2007; Strang, 2016d). Notwithstanding this, it may be difficult to prove that constructivism is more effective than not using this theory, so a controlled experiment would provide better scientific evidence as compared to best practice case studies or similar research designs.

It is possible that cross-disciplinary operations research courses are more difficult to teach because they are cognitive and applied in nature. As a solution, constructivist learning theory can be applied for virtual online courses based on research, experimentation, critical thinking, and peer socialization but at the end of the process it is a student individual mental model which emerges as a learning outcome (Senge, Kleiner, Roberts, Ross, & Smith, 1999).

Therefore, a professor must spend time interacting online with each student using the course theory and materials applied to real life examples, and not just cut-paste text from books or notes (Strang,

(Strang, 2016c; Strang, 2016d). The online discussions initiated by the professor must be relevant to each student while interacting in a cognitive motivating approach in order to properly apply constructivism theory (Strang, 2014).

WHAT WE KNOW AND DO NOT KNOW ABOUT VIRTUAL ONLINE TEACHING

Unfortunately what we do not know a lot about is how to apply constructivism in a virtual learning approach for teaching applied business courses or whether it is effective (Arbaugh, 2005), especially in predominately quantitative fields like operations research or engineering (Affouf & Walsh, 2007; Cybinski & Selvanathan, 2005; Swan, 2003). Project management, a cross-disciplinary operations research profession, is typically a difficult subject to learn (Anderson & Jackson, 2000; Smith, Heindel, & Torres-Ayala, 2008) and students have raised concerns about teaching quantitative courses online (Niche, 2019; Ratemyprofessor, 2019; Unigo, 2019).

Smith and colleagues (2008) reported that the use of a virtual learning software tools was much lower in the pure disciplines (natural sciences, humanities, mathematics) and in cross-disciplinary operations research fields. Furthermore, studies in the literature suggest that online courses are not as well received by students as their classroom lecture counterparts (Anstine, 2005; Niche, 2019; Ratemyprofessor, 2019; Unigo, 2019).

There is certainly evidence in the literature that teaching online can be as effective as lecturing in the traditional classroom. According to Russell (2002), his meta-analysis of 355 research papers indicated distance education was just as effective as traditional classroom instruction. More recently higher education studies have come to the same conclusion of there being no significant student performance difference between online versus face-to-face modalities (Bernard et al., 2004; Sitzmann, Kraiger, Stewart, & Wisher, 2006). Strang found that online instruction can be more effective than classroom teaching as long as discussion questions were made relevant and motivating (Strang, 2015b).

On the other hand, evidence also suggests non-quantitative online courses may be better received than quantitative courses (Anstine, 2005). Furthermore, the no significant difference in "learning effectiveness between technology-based and conventional delivery media may be defective because it ignores confounding variables" (Joy & Garcia, 2000, p. 33).

Recent empirical e-learning studies focus more on testing student preferences, faculty satisfaction, and student motivation - few studies actually focus on VLE instruction and learning (Tallent-Runnels et al., 2006, p. 117). A number of researchers have called for new research to measure impact of online teaching on academic success and thinking skills (Arbaugh et al., 2009; Bernard et al., 2004; Tallent-Runnels et al., 2006, p. 117).

There are several sources of best-practices for teaching online material in any discipline (e.g., Jochems, Merriënboer, & Koper, 2004; Schunk, 2004). The constructivism design framework applied for the course in this study was based on the recommendations of Hutchings, which they state was derived from the work of Laurillard (2002) as well as Chickering and Ehrmann (1996). The course in their case study at Bournemouth University (UK) concerned "complexity, sustainable development as a multidisciplinary subject addressing economic growth, employment, and social progress" (Hutchings, Hadfield, Howarth, & Lewarne, 2007, p. 332) in the engineering industry. Although their subject matter was not entirely quantitative (as with this course), and their framework is not tested here, their research is laudable, and comparable to the instructional design/teaching theories applied in this study.

It should be noted that the design recommendations of Hutchings, Hadfield, Howarth and Lewarne (2007) consisted of seven guiding principles for online course design: variety, action, application, interaction, feedback, scaffolding and evaluation (Hutchings et al., 2007, pp. 334-335). Their concept applied a teaching-focused approach based on Laurillard's conversational framework, by specifying teaching strategies to engage the learner using dialogue, adaptation and interaction, feedback, and reflection (Laurillard, 2002). They also designed and taught using experiential learning cycle theory, by providing students with opportunities to experience, reflect, theorize and experiment (Kolb, 1984). For the last component of the course design (evaluation), they applied a rubric drawn from the work of Chickering and Ehrmann (1996). The seven principles of their online course evaluation are: encourages student-faculty contact, develops cooperation between students, applies active learning techniques, gives prompt feedback, adequate time allocated to studying topics, communicates high expectations, and respects diverse learning styles (adapted from: Hutchings et al., 2007, pp. 338-341).

An additional online course design approach was applied to this research, based on the work of Honebein (Honebein, 1996). According to Strang (2014; 2016b), he successfully adapted and applied a constructivist design concept to teach online human resources management, business strategy and project management courses in an MBA program. Strang's teaching methodology was premised on andragogical student-centered motivation and constructivist learning, calling for: knowledge construction, authentic learning, asynchronous plus synchronous discussions, vicarious social learning opportunities, covering multiple perspectives from case studies, goal setting, with peer and self-reflection (Strang, 2014; Strang, 2015b; Strang, 2016b). Other researchers have discussed similar online teaching approaches (Arbaugh, 2005; Maclellan, 2005; Moon, Birchall, Williams, & Vrasidas, 2005; Rovai, Wighting, Baker, & Grooms, 2009; Tsai, Hwang, Tseng, & Hwang, 2008).

Quantitative subjects can be very challenging for students to learn in an online context (Affouf & Walsh, 2007; McCabe, 2007; Mills, 2004). As noted earlier, an online design and delivery framework is still needed – it is just that additional facilitation procedures are recommended for complex math-oriented topics within any course. A few researchers have started the process of improving how they teach math-oriented subjects online, particularly in computer science and statistics courses – as evidenced by recent manuscripts published in the Statistics Education Research Journal (and other publications).

For example, Harvard University colleagues tested traditional and versus online/video-conferenced bio-statistics courses but "failed to identify a significant distance effect with regard to student grades" (Evans et al., 2007, p. 73). Joint and colleagues (2003) used simulation quiz software in a virtual online learning course to improve student learning in a computer science related course. The key to their success seems to be the process was learner-centered, individual, and it helped the student develop their own mental models of the theory. Much work has been done developing online course teaching ideas at the Open University (UK). For example Allan and Lawless (2003) studied 200 students in an 18-day course, which revealed there was a lack of trust and social presence.

By far the most interesting online course analysis relevant to this chapter utilized a combination of WebCT, Acrobat Connect Professional, e-mail, Google Docs, and Skype along with a collaborative-problem-solving instructional methodology. Their course subject was a unique educational technology project (not purely math-oriented) involving graduate students from a USA and a Denmark university. A noteworthy comment was "teams found audio/video conferencing essential for making important decisions because it allowed for immediate feedback" (Karpova, Correia, & Baran, 2009). Unfortunately they only provided qualitative feedback (without performance testing or experimental control).

Interestingly, Baker-Eveleth, Eveleth and Sarker (2005) found that providing a virtual online learning course helped social-relational development, collaboration, and cohesiveness in a computer science course. Borthick and Jones (2000) found that applying cognitive and social education theories in a synchronous VLE for a computer science course generated positive feedback and there was no significant difference in student performance when compared to a classroom based section of the same course. Vrasidas and colleagues used a constructivist approach in a virtual online learning course to help teach a project management course (Vrasidas & Zembylas, 2004, p. 333).

Many of the empirical examples discussed above applied a key learning theory: Constructivism. Constructivism (Bruner, 1990) is an educational psychology theory for instruction based on knowledge cognition requirements. Interestingly, constructivism was conceived from a 1960 conference focused on science and math learning (Bruner, 1990) so it was not necessarily designed for online or applied field courses.

Constructivist learning has been described as "the process whereby learners personalize and/or customize new information; it is the process whereby learners make the new information relevant and/or meaningful to themselves" (Mezirow, 2000, p. 49). Constructivist teaching uses an active process in which learners construct new ideas, concepts and/or mental models that build on their current and/or past knowledge. According to Bruner (1990), instructors should engage students in an active dialog. He recommends teaching using visual representations and logical knowledge structures, to help students build their own meaning and mental models. Therefore, constructivism can be used with online and applied field subject matter.

Knowledge management theory can also help explain constructivism. The socialization-externalization-combination-internalization (SECI) model (Nonaka, Toyama, & Konno, 2001) proposes that groups learn by sharing tacit and explicit knowledge through dialogues – thus interaction is needed and each participant uses constructivism to extend their individual mental models (Strang, 2016a). Constructivism and the knowledge management SECI model could be applied to a math-oriented topic in a virtual online learning course by the professor discussing applied examples to mandatory pre-assigned reading, then having students work in groups to externalize their understanding, synthesize (combine) their knowledge to solve and interpret/explain problem solutions, and finally having each student individually reflect on how this could be applied to a problem of their own (Strang, 2016c).

Motivation can be used at first to get the process started in constructivism then the excitement and peer-pressure of a competitive team challenge in a synchronous online course could maintain their interest and spurn students to try their best at understanding the problems (Strang, 2015b). Since students often have different learning styles, ability and experience, as a group they will often have the combined know how to learn to solve more complex problems that at first they may not fully comprehend. Later, once they have gone through this group experiential exercise in the online course, they can practice the concepts to internalize, in order to apply the theories to new problems. This is constructivism.

Furthermore, the disadvantages of computer mediated communications become advantages for online constructivist learning. In a virtual online learning course peers only see what you want them to (if video is used), what you type in the chat or whiteboard, and what you say – they do not see your facial expressions or physical aspects unless you as a professor are using video. Gestures, clothing, or other physical dimensions can be hidden if wished, or displayed (again if in video mode) if that is a preference. Theoretically this leverages what the younger digital-generation seems to prefer: The personal/impersonal in-your-face or camouflaged persona often exhibited on cell phones or on the Internet in Facebook. This teaching context can give students the self-efficacy they may not have in a physical class, while for others, there may be no difference (but not less) – thus, the aggregate learning outcome should increase (Strang, 2015b; Strang, 2016c).

When considering all teaching practices, this constructivist learning of operation research concepts in a virtual online learning course should make a positive difference for students. Therefore, based on the above literature review, the research goal is to identify if grade will increase when constructivism is applied by using a virtual online learning course in the manner described above. There are various ways to measure if and how constructivism is working. Measuring grade (academic outcome) is kind of a brute-force approach, but performance is quite important to all educational stakeholders, so it makes sense to do this. Also well-known researchers were cited earlier calling for more testing of instructional method impact on academic outcome.

There are four general approaches that could be used to test if it is the constructivist component of the teaching in the online environment which is actually impacting the grade (versus some other confounding factor, such as prior ability, instructor capability, etc.), or a combination, as enumerated below:

1. Test each student perception of all factors;
2. Test each student outcome based on learning (e.g., grade or assignment scores);
3. Test the professor perception of all the above factors;
4. An independent learning assessment such as a standardized exam or accreditation evaluation.

Regardless of the approach, if effectiveness of constructivism as a teaching method is the unit of analysis with grade as the dependent variable, the independent factors in the virtual learning environment including student characteristics must be accounted for in some way or the results will not be scientific or credible (Strang, 2015a).

This study can be classified as a sequential mixed research design because two of the above approaches (2 then 1) were carried out back-to-back in time. First, an experiment was executed using two different teaching methods for the same online course which was measured by grade. Then, constructive feedback was subsequently collected from students and analyzed to determine how factors in the online course or the treatment conditions impacted learning. The following simplified hypothesis was proposed based on the above literature review and research design. Additional technically-oriented hypotheses were tested but were not reported in this chapter so as to avoid detracting from communicating the research findings.

Hypothesis One: Student grade will be higher in the experimental test group (as compared to the control group), where the constructivist teaching approach is applied in the online course.

This study was categorized as a quasi-experiment because although the participants (students) were allocated to courses on a random basis, it was a self-selection basis, which could mean that professor reputation had a latent, mediating or moderating effect on assignment. However, students were not told about the experiment and the syllabus as well as tests was identical between the two courses. Descriptive statistics, correlation, T-tests, F-tests, ANOVA and regression techniques were used to test the hypothesis.

SOLUTIONS AND RECOMMENDATIONS

The final sample consisted of two in-tact cohorts (taught at the same university) using the same course taught online, with the same tests and syllabus, except taught by two different professors, the first using the traditional method and the second using the constructivism approach discussed in the literature review.

The course was a the same senior-level online 8-week project management course, common to the Master of Business Administration and other Management programs, at a USA-based public university. As noted, participant selection was quasi-random based on the students self-selected to a course with no prompting from administration but they were aware of who would be teaching each course.

The experimental test group (where constructivism was applied) contained 23 students, while the control group (with the traditional method) had 21. Prior ability, gender, and age were configured as experimental control factors. These were tested between groups to determine if there were any differences. Later these control factors were used in correlation and regression tests to determine if they impacted grade.

The mean grade of a prerequisite course (advanced finance) was not significantly different between the test and control groups as compared to their cohort population mean ($t=1.14$, [$M1=84.28$, $n1=23$, $M2=85.2$, $n2=21$], $p>.05$), and the variance was similar between test and control groups ($F=2.21$, [$DF=1,43$], $p<.05$).

Note this course was offered to two master level programs so another t-test as performed to determine if there were any differences in prior ability based on concentration, which there was not ($t=0.99$, [$n1=21$, $n2=23$], $p>.05$). This was a desired result proving there was no difference in cohorts. Furthermore, mean age was 34 in the test group and 33 in the control group. Additionally, the gender ratio was 62% male in the test group, 64% male in the control group. For experimental control purposes, it was now asserted that prior ability and demographics were the same between test and control groups. Note however prior ability was tested to illustrate there was also no difference in competence between groups (cohorts), but it will be later proven there is a correlation between prior ability and grade.

In this study Moodle was the Learning Management System (LMS). Moodle was developed in Perth Australia and is free from the Open Software Foundation (but requires technology expertise to configure it). For generalization purposes, the author and colleagues used other LMS products in similar experiments which worked equally well for online education (namely, Blackboard, as well as WebCT and

Angel which are now also owned by BlackBoard). The key LMS object utilized in this study was the discussion forum for the asynchronous group interactions. Both professors used this object for the lecture material as well as for delivering the material that students used to prepare for the learning assessments.

In this program, this project management course serves as an introduction to applied field of managing projects in operations research in two masters-level programs. It aims to provide students with the knowledge and skills necessary to apply the scientific method and to design projects in their chosen disciplinary topic and industry setting. The topics available for work in the course include quantitative and qualitative type projects. Additionally students were expected to integrate their work experience in to their projects and online assignments. The assignments take students through the process of producing four common project management plans, which could form the basis for commencing an operations research project in an actual setting.

There were three equally-weighted assessments: one was an exam, the second was interaction, and the other was an operations research project plan proposal. For the proposal, students had to select an appropriate methodology, and then describe how to apply it. Rubrics were used to assess all assignments (except the exam). The interaction assignment was where the experiment focused (this is discussed in more detail below in the procedures). The assignment marks were aggregated to produce a final grade, which was the dependent variable in the experiment (the interaction assignment mark was also tested as a dependent variable, to capture any treatment impact).

Both cohorts in the experiment (test and control groups) were treated identically in all respects except for the instructional method used after each lecture for the interaction assignment. In terms of workflow, generally there were two sessions each week, with the first being a brief theory-knowledge oriented lecture (sometimes involving statistical software examples), and the second a group-oriented learning activity. These sessions were conducted at a scheduled time, online, using the discussion forum with Zoom live synchronous participation, lasting approximately 1 hour (each week). Additionally, individual (un-graded) study materials were made available in the discussion forum (of the LMS) to help students self-prepare for the exam.

The weekly learning activity for the interaction assignment was where the constructivist instructional method treatment was applied. Both cohorts were assigned the same type of 'complex project management problems' (in total, two problems for the course, one with qualitative data, the other with quantitative data, each requiring different techniques). Students were expected to work together in their teams to solve the problem. They were expected to use the software systems provided to do their work. For example, students were required to use either the asynchronous discussion forum in the LMS and/or the synchronous Zoom rooms (after the lectures) to do their work. Although it was possible the students could have met face-to-face at a campus library (or elsewhere), from experience this rarely happened due to busy work schedules and traffic congestion, except that friends definitely would hang-out (if they happened to be randomly assigned to the same team – note this was not measured). Most importantly, all assignments were individual: each team member was required to take the group deliverable, add their own revisions to it (if necessary), then reflect on how they would apply that to another problem that needed to be selected and cited from their work or the literature. Optionally, individuals could submit a peer-evaluation of the group (this was a mechanism to indicate if there was social-loafing in the team, which could impact marks).

In terms of the constructivist instructional method treatment, each cohort had a different professor mentoring their work, but both were supervised by the author to ensure consistency of the experiment. In the control group, student teams were allocated private topic threads in the discussion forum. They were required to record their group activity there (this was assessed in the rubric). They were told that if they met elsewhere (physically, or virtually in Zoom), they needed to post a summary of their meeting minutes of the participants along with the outcomes/decisions. This was the interaction component. The professor attempted to apply constructivist instructional methods by occasionally asking the teams for clarifications (based on predetermined questions) as well as answering questions posed by teams (in their forum). Teams could not see one another's discussion forum (this was a security setting in the LMS).

For the experimental test group, break out rooms were setup in Zoom for each team after the lecture. The four teams in the test group simultaneously and synchronously worked on their problem in their breakout room each week. As noted in the rubric, points were given specifically for interaction (in the Zoom session). This could be checked by the professor during and after the session ended (as it was recorded for review). Although the breakout rooms were not recorded, the interaction statistics were still available and the processor downloaded both the whiteboard activity and the chat text message log in each break out room. During the Zoom sessions, the professor applied constructivist scaffolding by jumping between breakout rooms to check on progress, to answer occasional questions, and to specifically ask for clarifications (using the same pre-determined list of questions that were also posed to the control group in their discussion forums).

With respect to the treatment itself, the same constructivist scaffolding was also applied to both cohorts by reminding students to go through the Socialize-Externalize-Combine process (internalization was done at the end and during the individual reflection submission). Also, constructivism was applied during the individual reflection, as the student needed to apply the group solution (or their improved version) to another problem of their own. Thus, the treatment factor was the type of online course context as measured by the cohort: Experimental test group versus control group.

As required by the statistical procedures, normality tests were first conducted following the recommendations of Hair, Black, Babin, Anderson, and Tatham (2006) and Strang (2015a). The distribution shapes were adequate for a small sample and the dependent variable grade had a *skewness* estimate less than ±2.58 (Hair et al., 2006, p. 31). The Anderson-Darling normality test of the dependent variable grade was accepted ($p>.05$). In this test the null hypothesis is that the data approximates a normal distribution (no significant difference, with a relatively linear probability plot line), so the null hypothesis of normality is accepted when $p >$ alpha level (which was .05 level of significance in this study).

Table 1 lists key descriptive estimates (means with standard deviations in parenthesis), by experimental test group and the traditional control group. *T-tests* indicated there were no significant differences between the test and control groups with exception to grade (which supports the hypothesis).

First, it can be reiterated that earlier pretests of ability indicated the control and test groups were statistically similar with respect to scores on a prerequisite course in finance. As reported in Table 1, a *t-test* of the grade means (assuming unequal variance) between the two groups in this experiment indicated a significant difference with a $t(41)=2.93$, $p=.006$ (two-tailed), with the test group (using Zoom

Table 1. Descriptive statistics of sample by experimental group

Treatment factor	Age	Gender	Prior ability	Grade	N
1. Experimental group	33.9 (6.8)	61% female	84.3 (8.7)	82.1* (8.9)	31
2. Control group	32.6 (7.0)	57% female	85.2 (8.8)	74.7* (9.1)	32
Note: means shown except % counts for gender (standard deviations); difference t-test *p<.05					

for constructivist synchronous interaction) achieving higher academic performance (as compared to the control group using the asynchronous discussion forum for constructivist interaction). This supports the hypothesis.

Table 2 lists the Spearman correlation estimates at the sample level. The correlations of most interest here are those with grade. Prior ability had a very high positive correlation with grade *Rho*(+0.84), and a medium negative correlation with treatment *Rho*(-0.42). The latter indicates it is worthwhile to perform subsequent regression tests on the groups. It should also be noted that there was a medium positive correlation between age and treatment *Rho*(+0.64), but this may be due to chance since none of the control factors had significant correlation with grade. These results were tested more tested further with more rigorous statistical techniques discussed below.

The hypothesis testing strategy was to apply ANOVA to confirm the group grade variances were significantly different when all control and treatment factors were included, and then regression to determine if the treatment factor was the only significant predictor of grade in this experiment. The key assumptions of ANOVA were easily met: Cell sizes were larger than the number of dependent variables, the variances within the groups were equal and the dependent variables were normal.

First ANOVA was performed, using all control factors (gender, age, prior ability). The omnibus test failed and all coefficients were insignificant except the treatment factor (of interest in this experiment). A multiple regression on grade was run with treatment factor to distinguish between groups, with the results summarized in Table 3. These results clearly indicate that the model is statistically significant with an $F(1,42)=8.617$, $p=.005$ (one-sided), resulting in a small-to-medium effect size of 17% (adjusted $r^2 = 0.15$).

The regression indicated the treatment factor was a significant predictor of grade, with a $t(60)=-2.94$, $p=.005$ (one-sided), with a negative coefficient of -7.36232; which can be interpreted that the experimental test group using constructivism resulted in a higher grade since the coding was 1=test and 2=control. Furthermore, since the mean in Table 1 was higher for the experimental test group, the hypothesis can be accepted that constructivism as a teaching method resulted in a higher grade as compared with the traditional instructional approach for the same online project management course.

Constructive feedback was collected from independent online rating systems for both instructors of these courses. The most relevant comments were analyzed and related to teaching approach or pedagogy, so as to form a sequential link to the experiment where constructivism was found to be more effective. The results are summarized below in table 4, organized by key topic that emerged from the constructive

Table 2. Correlation statistics of sample

Control and treatment factors, dependent variable	Descriptive statistics		Pearson product moment correlation			
	Mean	SD	1. Age	2. Gender	3. Ability	4. Treatment
1. Age	33.2	6.95				
2. Gender	59%m 61%f		-0.631			
3. Prior ability	84.8	8.73	0.037	-0.097		
4. Treatment	n1=30 n2=31		0.641*	0.054	0.053	
5. Grade	78.2	9.02	0.052	-0.236	0.839*	-0.41261*
Note: SD=standard deviation or % counts for gender (m=male, f=female); *p<.05						

Table 3. ANOVA and regression model of constructivist treatment effect on grade

Regression	Estimates						
Model r^2	0.170244						
Adjusted r^2	0.150488						
Standard error	8.30952						
Sample size	44						
ANOVA	DF	SS	MS	*F*	*P-value*	η^2	Hypothesis result
Factors	1	595.0092	595.0092	8.617313*	0.00538	0.1702	H1 supported
Residual	42	2900.021	69.04812				
Total	43	3495.03					
Factors	Coefficient	SS	*T*	*P-value*			
Constant	89.40899	4.019218	22.24537*	7.34E-25			
Treatment	-7.36232	2.508007	-2.93553*	0.00538			H1 supported
*p<.05							

student feedback. From the student constructive feedback, it is clear that constructivism as a pedagogy works better since the professor uses current relevant examples in the online discussion, and also the professor engages each individual student to use their own problem context. Furthermore, the professor using constructivism makes individual constructive comments to the dominant students in the online course context to help all students even the passive learners to benefit from learning. The constructivist approach does not use textbooks but instead applies the theories cited by the textbooks using current research published by the professor and integrates examples using real life projects from either students or the professor according to the situation. By comparison, the traditional approach relies on textbook examples and materials such as case studies.

FUTURE RESEARCH DIRECTIONS

Given that the key factor in the model was constructivism online interaction, it is possible that other teaching methods and products could achieve this same effect on grade if students were given incentives – no incentives were provided in this study. Additionally, students get excited over games so it is possible that using Second Life avatar-based e-learning games could motivate students and make them respond positively to course opinion surveys and online student review systems. However, ultimately accredited universities must be responsible enough to evaluate actual student learning as measured by standardized exams and industry accepted best practice indicators, as applied in this course for the constructivism experimental treatment condition. More research must be done to measure actual student learning.

One limitation in this study is the relative small group sample sizes of 30, and 31, respectively, which can be remedied by replicating this experiment in more courses. Secondly, this was an applied operations research course, so results may not generalize other professional fields particularly social science disciplines. Secondly, students self-selected into these two courses, the traditional and experimental sections, so the reputation of the professor certainly would have impacted this and it was indeed clear

Table 4. Qualitative analysis of student feedback for constructivism versus traditional online teaching

Topic	Constructivism Experimental Test Group	Traditional Teaching Control Group
Project budgeting	• Discussing issues such as what financial amounts were actually known from the project sponsor • What percentage of the total budget can be controlled by the student project manager and why	• Reflecting on a textbook problem • Focusing on the expected cost of earned value using the formula from the textbook
Resources	• Discussing how team members are typically allocated to projects and who makes/made the decision in the selected project to assign members	• Discussing human resource management theories and the concept of resource leveling
Assignment	• In addition to face-to-face Zoom session, various discussions included letting several more talkative students discuss their projects with the professor adding subject matter expert feedback, listened to by all students and cited in the assignment	• Creating a project schedule using a popular software program and pasting the Gantt chart for the assignment
Examples	• Students work in groups but can use their own individualized work context as the project assignment with names removed to promote freedom of expression and honest discussion. • Professor presents examples from his own scholarly research and from actual industry projects with named corporations (asks students to not copy names or material outside of class).	• Students expected to reflect select a case project from textbook or from their workplace to use for project assignment but must disclose particulars. • Professor presents examples using more than five videos online and cites interesting examples with slides downloaded from the textbook (asks students to not plagiarize copyrighted material outside of class or for assignment).

that the latter was completely full very early. This could be remedied by replicating this experiment with a pure random selection. Other researchers are invited to perform these recommended studies.

CONCLUSION

Online virtual learning is becoming popular with the modern generation of employed students. Although operations research subjects (such as the project management course tested in this chapter) may be more difficult to teach – and learn – compared with social science courses, especially online, constructivist instructional methods can be used to assist students to learn more effectively. This was proven in this controlled experiment.

In this study, constructivism was applied in online course discussion forums which resulted in high student grades and more positive pedagogy-related constructive feedback from students through the independent rating systems not controlled by a specific university. Constructivism was applied by using probing questions during asynchronous discussions and synchronous sessions to encourage students to go through the SECI knowledge management cycle, resulting with internalization at the end where students would develop a mental model as part of their individual reflection. The hypothesis of this study was that applying a constructivist instructional approach in the online course would have a stronger positive predictive impact on grade (which it did).

The concept of applying constructivism learning theory in an online operations research course through the SECI cycle of knowledge management worked in this experiment, as judged by the results that the grade was higher as compare with the experimental test group as compared with an identical course taught online in the traditional approach during the same term at the same university. The study used an experimental design, with two groups (test and control), varying only the instruction method since the same syllabus and assessments were applied in both courses. Care was taken to verify there were no significant differences between the experimental groups, by using *t-tests* to compare prior ability (grade of a previous prerequisite course in finance), age, and gender. None of these control factors presented a significant difference between groups nor did they have any significant predictive effect on grade in this sample. Researchers claim that other factors confound studies such as this, mainly instructor or context differences (Arbaugh et al., 2009; Bernard et al., 2004; Joy & Garcia, 2000; Tallent-Runnels et al., 2006). This is true and it was impossible to control for the instructor in this experiment since it was a different professor. However, everything else was identical and controlled.

The end result of this experiment was: A constructivist instructional pedagogy applied in an online operations research project management course predicted 17% of grade variation (compared with the traditional approach). *T-tests* confirmed the mean grade was higher in the experimental test group using the constructivist teaching method.

The implications of this finding for other professors are that student academic performance in online operations research courses can be improved beyond what is achievable in a now-customary traditional method discussion forum, by using constructivist teaching methods with more customized problem based student-professor interaction. However, nothing can substitute for a traditional instructor who is incompetent, unqualified with no scholarly published research about the subject matter in question. Therefore, an additional applied finding is that universities must select online professors who are qualified for the job through education, experience and especially scholarly published research about the subject matter that can be utilized during discussions with students in the class.

Finally additional extant observation can be made from this study. The independent student rating systems were valuable for allowing students to enter objective opinions about the university, course, and instructor, without being monitored through email or any other covert system at the university. This is democracy. The future learning paradigm needs more independent democratic student rating systems, much as our current political environment now had. However, from a statistical control standpoint, independent online student rating systems must have mechanisms to prevent abuse, such as an authenticated logon process whereby a public monitored entity can ensure students are actually students and not the university marketing department, and that statistical independent non-replacement is maintained meaning that ratings are entered only once per student-course instance. For example, we have sophisticated online voting software that could be modified for use in student university course rating systems. This would be valuable for accreditation institutions and for governments to use in order to endorse and possibly fund universities. That would be true democracy and we need it in higher education to ensure students get the best online learning experience that they are paying for and deserve.

REFERENCES

Affouf, M., & Walsh, T. P. (2007). An assessment of web-based homework in the teaching of college algebra. *The International Journal for Technology in Mathematics Education, 14*(4), 163–167.

Anderson, M. & Jackson, D. (2000). Computer systems for distributed and distance learning. *Journal of Computer Assisted Learning, 16*(1), 213-228.

Anstine, J., & Skidmore, M. (2005). A small sample study of traditional and online courses with sample selection adjustment. *Journal of Economic Education, 36*(1), 107–127.

Arbaugh, J. B. (2005). How much does "subject matter" matter? A study of disciplinary effects in on-line mba courses. *Academy of Management Learning & Education*, *4*(1), 57–73. doi:10.5465/amle.2005.16132549

Arbaugh, J. B., Godfrey, M. R., Johnson, M., Pollack, B. L., Niendorf, B., & Wresch, W. (2009). Research in online and blended learning in the business disciplines: Key findings and possible future directions. *Internet and Higher Education*, *12*(1), 71–87. doi:10.1016/j.iheduc.2009.06.006

Bernard, R. M., Abrami, P. C., Lou, Y., Borokhovski, E., Wade, A., Wozney, L., ... Huang, B. (2004). How does distance education compare to classroom instruction? A meta-analysis of the empirical literature. *Review of Educational Research*, *74*(3), 379–439. doi:10.3102/00346543074003379

Bruner, J. (1990). *Acts of meaning*. Cambridge, MA: Harvard University Press.

Chickering, A. & Ehrmann, S.C. (1996, October). Implementing the seven principles: Technology as lever. *Association of Adult Higher Education Journal*, 3-6.

CollegeConfidential. (2019). *I found the following post about the college and wondering if it is true that they are bankrupt and have a super high crime rate?* Retrieved March 1, 2019, from: https://talk.collegeconfidential.com/suny-general/2107067-suny-plattsburgh-in-new-york.html

Costin, H., & Hamilton, D. (2009). Quality in business education as measured by accreditation and ranking systems. *International Journal of Management Education*, *3*(3/4), 249–269.

Cybinski, P., & Selvanathan, S. (2005). Learning experience and learning effectiveness in undergraduate statistics: Modeling performance in traditional and flexible learning environments. *Decision Sciences Journal of Innovative Education*, *3*(2), 251–271. doi:10.1111/j.1540-4609.2005.00069.x

Evans, S. R., Wang, R., Yeh, T.-M., Anderson, J., Haija, R., McBratbey-Owen, P. M., ... Zhang, J. (2007). Evaluation of distance learning in an introduction to biostatistics class: A case study. *Statistics Education Research Journal*, *6*(2), 59–77.

Ginns, P., & Ellis, R. (2007). Quality in blended learning: Exploring the relations between on-line and face-to-face teaching and learning. *The Internet and Higher Education*, *10*(1), 53–64. doi:10.1016/j.iheduc.2006.10.003

Grandzol, J.R. (2004). Teaching mba statistics online: A pedagogically sound process approach. *Journal of Education for Business, 79*(4), 237-246.

Helling, T. S., Dumire, R. D., & Augustosky, K. (2009). Incentives for scholarly activity at university and independent general surgery residencies: Current practices. *American Journal of Surgery*, *197*(3), 360–364. doi:10.1016/j.amjsurg.2008.11.004 PMID:19245915

Honebein, P. C. (1996). Seven goals for the design of constructivist learning environments. In B. Wilson (Ed.), *Constructivist learning environments: Case studies in instructional design*. Englewood Cliffs, NJ: Educational Technology Publications.

Hutchings, M., Hadfield, M., Howarth, G., & Lewarne, S. (2007). Meeting the challenges of active learning in web-based case studies for sustainable development. *Innovations in Education and Teaching International*, *4*(33), 331–343. doi:10.1080/14703290701486779

Jochems, W., Merriënboer, J. J. G. v., & Koper, R. (Eds.). (2004). *Integrated e-learning: Implications for pedagogy, technology & organization*. New York: RoutledgeFalmer. doi:10.4324/9780203416365

Joint, N. (2003). Information literacy evaluation: Moving towards virtual learning environments. The Electronic Library, 21(4), 322.

Joy, E. H., & Garcia, F. E. (2000). Measuring learning effectiveness: A new look at no-significant-difference findings. *Journal of Asynchronous Learning Networks*, *4*(1), 33–39.

Karpova, E., Correia, A.-P., & Baran, E. (2009). Learn to use and use to learn: Technology in virtual collaboration experience. *Internet and Higher Education*, *12*(1), 45–52. doi:10.1016/j.iheduc.2008.10.006

Kolb, D. A. (1984). *Experiential learning*. Englewood Cliffs, NJ: Prentice-Hall.

Laurillard, D. (1993). *Rethinking university teaching: A framework for the effective use of educational technolgy*. London: Routledge.

Laurillard, D. (2002). *Rethinking university teaching: A framework for the effective use of educational technolgy* (2nd ed.). London: Routledge. doi:10.4324/9780203160329

Laurillard, D. (2007). Modelling benefits-oriented costs for technology enhanced learning. *Higher Education*, *54*(1), 21–39. doi:10.100710734-006-9044-2

Levin, H. (2018). *Privatizing education: Can the school marketplace deliver freedom of choice, efficiency, equity, and social cohesion?* London, UK: Taylor & Francis. doi:10.4324/9780429498015

Maclellan, E. (2005). Conceptual learning: The priority for higher education. *British Journal of Educational Studies*, *53*(2), 129–147. doi:10.1111/j.1467-8527.2005.00287.x

McCabe, M. (2007). Assessment, blending and creativity: The abc of technology in mathematics teaching. *The International Journal for Technology in Mathematics Education*, *14*(1), 54–59.

McLaren, C. H. (2004). A comparison of student persistence and performance in online and classroom business statistics experiences. *Decision Sciences Journal of Innovative Education*, *2*(1), 1–10. doi:10.1111/j.0011-7315.2004.00015.x

Mezirow, J. (2000). *Learning as transformation: Critical perspectives on a theory in progress*. New York: Jossey-Bass.

Mills, J. D. (2004). Student's attitudes toward statistics: Implication for the future. *College Student Journal*, *38*(3), 349–360.

Moon, S., Birchall, D., Williams, S., & Vrasidas, C. (2005). Developing design principles for an e-learning programme for sme managers to support accelerated learning at the workplace. *Journal of Workplace Learning*, *17*(5/6), 370–384. doi:10.1108/13665620510606788

Naidu, S. (2002). Designing and evaluating instruction for e-learning. In P. L. Rogers (Ed.), *Designing instruction for technology-enhanced learning* (pp. 134–159). London: Idea Group. doi:10.4018/978-1-930708-28-0.ch008

Niche. (2019). *Terrible*. Retrieved January 19, 2019, from: https://www.niche.com/colleges/suny-plattsburgh/reviews/?rating=Terrible

Nonaka, I., Toyama, R., & Konno, N. (2001). Seci, ba, and leadership: A unified model of dynamic knowledge creation. In I. Nonaka & D. Teece (Eds.), *Managing industrial knowledge creation, transfer and utilization*. Thousand Oaks, CA: Sage. doi:10.4135/9781446217573.n2

Popovich, C. J., & Neel, R. E. (2005). Characteristics of distance education programs at accredited business schools. *American Journal of Distance Education*, *19*(1), 229–240. doi:10.120715389286ajde1904_4

Ratemyprofessors. (2019). *If possible don't attend*. Retrieved March 3, 2019, from: http://www.ratemyprofessors.com/campusRatings.jsp?sid=968

Rovai, A. P., Wighting, M. J., Baker, J. D., & Grooms, L. D. (2009). Development of an instrument to measure perceived cognitive, affective, and psychomotor learning in traditional and virtual classroom higher education settings. *Internet and Higher Education*, *12*(1), 7–13. doi:10.1016/j.iheduc.2008.10.002

Russell, T. L. (2002). *The no significant difference phenomenon as reported in 355 research reports, summaries and papers: A comparative research annotated bibliography on technology for distance education*. North Carolina State University: Office of Instructional Telecommunications. Retrieved from http://www.nosignificantdifference.org/

Schunk, D. H. (2004). *Learning theories: An educational perspective*. Upper Saddle River, NJ: Pearson Prentice Hall.

Senge, P. M., Kleiner, A., Roberts, C., Ross, R., & Smith, B. (1999). *The fifth discipline fieldbook: Strategies and tools for building a learning organization*. New York: Doubleday.

Sitzmann, T., Kraiger, K., Stewart, D., & Wisher, R. (2006). The comparative effectiveness of web-based and classroom instruction: A meta-analysis. *Personnel Psychology*, *59*(1), 623–664. doi:10.1111/j.1744-6570.2006.00049.x

Smith, G. G., Heindel, A. J., & Torres-Ayala, A. T. (2008). E-learning commodity or community: Disciplinary differences between online courses. *The Internet and Higher Education*, *11*(1), 152–159. doi:10.1016/j.iheduc.2008.06.008

Strang, K. D. (2014). Cognitive learning strategy as a partial effect on major field test in business results. *Journal of Education for Business*, *89*(3), 142–148. doi:10.1080/08832323.2013.781988

Strang, K. D. (2015a). *Handbook of Research Design in Business and Management*. New York: Palgrave Macmillan. doi:10.1057/9781137484956

Strang, K. D. (2015b). Effectiveness of instructor-led collaborative learning in the classroom. *Journal of Applied Research in Higher Education*, *7*(2), 1–16. doi:10.1108/JARHE-07-2012-0018

Strang, K. D. (2016a). Testing young business students for technology acceptance and learning performance. *International Journal of Learning Technology*, *11*(3), 238-265. doi:10.1504/IJLT.2016.079036

Strang, K. D. (2016b). How student behavior and reflective learning impact grade in online business courses. *Journal of Applied Research in Higher Education*, *8*(3), 390–410. doi:10.1108/JARHE-06-2015-0048

Strang, K. D. (2016c). Do the critical success factors from learning analytics predict student outcomes? *Journal of Educational Technology Systems*, *44*(3), 273-299. Retrieved from http://ets.sagepub.com/content/0047239515615844/0047239515615853/0047239515615273.abstract

Strang, K. D. (2016d). Can online student performance be forecasted by learning analytics? *International Journal of Technology Enhanced Learning*, *8*(1), 26–47. doi:10.1504/IJTEL.2016.075950

Strang, K. D. (2017a). Predicting student satisfaction and outcomes in online courses using learning activity indicators. *International Journal of Web-Based Learning and Teaching Technologies*, *12*(1), 32–50. doi:10.4018/IJWLTT.2017010103

Strang, K. D. (2017b). Beyond engagement analytics: Which online mixed-data factors predict student learning outcomes? *Journal of Education and Information Technologies*, *22*(3), 917–937. doi:10.100710639-016-9464-2

Strang, K. D., & Shimer, M. (2017). Compressed school week cultural bias against English Second Language student performance on standardized exams. *Global Journal of Human-Social Sciences-G:Linguistics & Education*, *17*(5), 37–48. doi:10.17406/GJHSS

Strang, K. D., & Vajjhala, N. R. (2017). Student resistance to a mandatory learning management system in online supply chain courses. *Journal of Organizational and End User Computing*, *29*(3), 49–67. doi:10.4018/JOEUC.2017070103

Studentsreview. (2019). *OMG!! worst school ever and only went beacause*. Retrieved January 18, 2019, from: https://www.studentsreview.com/NY/SUNYPL_comments.html?type=negative&page=2

Swan, K. (2003). Learning effectiveness: What the research tells us. In J. Bourne & J. C. Moore (Eds.), *Elements of quality online education: Practice and direction* (Vol. 3, pp. 13–45). Needham, MA: Sloan Consortium.

Tallent-Runnels, M. K., Thomas, J. A., Lan, W. Y., Cooper, S., Ahern, T. C., Shaw, S. M., & Liu, X. (2006). Teaching courses online: A review of the research. *Review of Educational Research*, *76*(1), 93–135. doi:10.3102/00346543076001093

Tsai, P.-J., Hwang, G.-J., Tseng, J. C. R., & Hwang, G.-H. (2008). Computer-assisted approach to conducting cooperative learning process. *International Journal of Distance Education Technologies*, *6*(1), 49–66. doi:10.4018/jdet.2008010104

Unigo. (2019). *What is your overall opinion of this school?* Retrieved March 2, 2019, from: https://www.unigo.com/colleges/suny-college-at-plattsburgh

Vrasidas, C., & Zembylas, M. (2004). Online professional development: Lessons from the field. *Education + Training*, *46*(6/7), 326–334. doi:10.1108/00400910410555231

Weller, M. (2007). *Virtual learning environments*. New York, NY: Routledge.

KEY TERMS AND DEFINITIONS

Project Budget: In the online course, total planned and actual expenditures of project. Manager must have ability to stay within initial expenditure estimates and secure additional funds if project scope expands.

Project Communications: In the online course, interpersonal communication with team members, project stakeholders, top management, user, and the like.

Project Human Resources: In the online course, effective and efficient use of project team members' time, talents, and skills.

Project Planning: In the online course, students need to understand the technical aspects of a project. A working knowledge of the specific technologies involved in a project such as tools, programs, hardware, software, and the like.

Project Scope: In the online course, refers to the definition stage in which specifications, objectives, and responsibilities are identified and described.

Chapter 3
#teachingbydesign: Complicating Accessibility in the Tech-Mediated Classroom

Cat Mahaffey
University of North Carolina at Charlotte, USA

Ashlyn C. Walden
University of North Carolina at Charlotte, USA

ABSTRACT

Much attention has been drawn toward issues of accessibility, but changes in course design have been slow at best. This chapter aims to expand notions of accessibility beyond students with visual or hearing impairments to include students with colorblindness, dyslexia, or anxiety; and students disadvantaged by socioeconomics, gender, or race. More specifically, this chapter serves as a call for instructors to incorporate accessibility practices in their course designs and to explicitly teach students what accessibility is and how to incorporate its principles into their writing/designing/creating processes.

INTRODUCTION

Online courses have been around since the 1980s when internet access spread to individual's homes. Since then, its expansion has been steady and now roughly 25% of higher education students are taking a course online (OLC, 2016). Furthermore, the digital revolution shifted course delivery to learning management systems like Blackboard and Canvas such that virtually all college courses are now technologically-mediated.

This chapter aims to expand notions of accessibility for both faculty and students, with emphasis on identifying gaps in accessible course design in the technology-mediated classroom. More specifically, this chapter serves as a call for instructors to incorporate accessibility practices into their course designs and to explicitly teach students what accessibility is and how to practice these strategies for themselves. But simply calling instructors to action is not enough. There are real concerns regarding workload; in short, it takes a great deal of time to design a truly accessible course that considers students' various

DOI: 10.4018/978-1-5225-7987-8.ch003

needs and learning preferences. And in the wake of such a call, rising to this challenge can be daunting, especially when instructors choose to tackle such a feat for the first time. This chapter shares the experiences of two writing instructors who sought to understand and practice accessibility as a part of two different course models. Their case studies provide a potential starting point for faculty that may yet be unsure of how to begin this process.

BACKGROUND

Much attention has been drawn toward accommodating students with visual and/or hearing impairments--position statements (CCCC, 2011; CCCC, 2012), collections (Hewett & DePew, 2015), and organizations focused solely on issues of accessibility (CEUD, 2014; GSOLE, 2016; Teach Access, 2019)--but scholars continue to point out that change in the classroom has been slow at best (Oswal, 2013; Oswal & Meloncon, 2014; Foley & Ferri, 2014; Boyle & Rivers, 2016; Hitt, 2018). Meanwhile, the bridge between secondary and postsecondary education grows increasingly flimsy, with all but the most prepared or technologically inclined students falling between the cracks. Consider the following from Maryanne Wolf's latest book *Dear Reader, Come Home*:

[Neuroscientists] are convinced that the next generation's deep-reading processes will be most endangered by the digital medium if we do not teach the proper uses of digital learning and screen reading from relatively early on, rather than leaving children to develop willy-nilly digital habits of mind that are counterproductive. (p. 176)

These "willy-nilly digital habits of mind" put students at a disadvantage that neither they nor their instructors fully comprehend, creating barriers to academic success that must first be revealed and then compensated for. For this reason, discussions of accessibility need to expand such that all learning paths, all those "willy-nilly digital habits of mind," become valued and accommodated. It is time to push beyond concerns regarding access for students with visual and hearing impairments and begin to also consider the varied learning preferences our students bring to the classroom. Furthermore, attention is needed to ensure success for students with unseen barriers like colorblindness, dyslexia, or anxiety. Most importantly, it is imperative to align course design and delivery to accommodate students disadvantaged by socioeconomics, gender, or race.

This chapter aims to put forth a new definition of accessibility informed by three major areas of scholarship related to digital literacy and digital design: Online Writing Instruction (OWI), Universal Design (UD), and User-Centered Design (UCD). The hope is that this new definition will be useful for instructor-designers who wish to enhance their course design and ensure that the diverse learners in their classes have equal opportunities to succeed.

Online Writing Instruction (OWI)

OWI is a branch of scholarship within Writing Studies. The Conference on College Composition and Communication (CCCC) established a committee in 2007 to "identify and examine best practices for online writing instruction in hybrid and distance-based composition classrooms" (Hewett & DePew, 2015, p. 5). The result of their years-long labor was "A Position Statement of Principles and Example

Effective Practices for OWI" (CCCC, 2013). Perhaps the most important discovery of the committee was that the best practices for teaching online overlap with best practices for teaching onsite. Specifically, the committee expanded the notion of "online teaching" to include "computer-based, Internet, or intranet instructional setting[s] [that use] online/digital media to provide instruction" (Hewett & DePew, 2015, p. 9). The first principle became an overarching one: "OWI Principle 1: Online writing instruction should be universally inclusive and accessible" (CCCC, 2013).

The committee's expanded definition of OWI aligns well with the findings of other scholars and reinforces a need for more research into best practices for digitally-mediated courses of all types, including face-to-face (see CCCC, 2012; Miller, 2015; Baron, 2017). Students remain perplexed about genre and audience in the various writing contexts they encounter in their highly digitized world. Today's college students have straddled print and digital in ways no other generation has or likely will. Their primary education was largely print, with worksheets, notebooks, and tomes of encyclopedias. This formative instruction via print shaped what Maryanne Wolf refers to as their "reading-brain circuit," which is influenced by what students read (content), how they read (print vs. screen), and what they are taught (instructional methods) (Wolf, 2018, p. 19). And even though many students were given mobile devices in middle grades, becoming adept at texting and writing and reading through social media, "their uses of technology [were] relatively unconnected to formal education [and] their experiences with digital technology make them different from the students instructors once knew and that may still inhabit the imagination" (Hewett, 2015, p. 11).

Budget constraints complicated this gap in digital literacy skills further as instructors were encouraged to rely more and more on the LMS to cut printing costs, and this move toward more digitally-mediated instruction expanded as composition pushed more toward multimodal composition, sparking many instructors to experiment with creating course materials that included images and videos. This went a long way toward modeling the kind of digital design needed for their success in the workplace, but it exacerbated issues of access because it pushed students toward digital reading and writing without proper instruction for how to navigate between digital and print materials (Wolf, 2018; Hewett, 2015).

In forming an expanded definition of accessibility, the authors of this chapter acknowledge the findings in OWI scholarship. An accessible course design considers the varied technological and digital literacy skills of students.

Universal Design (UD)

Universal Design is a concept coined by architect and scholar Ronald Mace in 1989 (CUD, 2008). His initial use of the term was to "describe the concept of designing all products and the built environment to be aesthetic and usable to the greatest extent possible by everyone, regardless of their age, ability, or status in life" (CUD, 2008). His initial set of principles has been taken up and expanded, creating spin-offs like the Centre for Excellence in Universal Design (CEUD), and becoming adopted and promoted by the National Disabilities Authority (NDA).

UD consists of a set of seven principles that call for accessible options in use and engagement with physical, virtual, and digital spaces:

- ***Principle 1: Equitable Use*** - *The design is useful and marketable to people with diverse abilities.*
- ***Principle 2: Flexibility in Use*** - *The design accommodates a wide range of individual preferences and abilities.*

- ***Principle 3: Simple and Intuitive Use*** *- Use of the design is easy to understand, regardless of the user's experience, knowledge, language skills, or current concentration level.*
- ***Principle 4: Perceptible Information*** *- The design communicates necessary information effectively to the user, regardless of ambient conditions or the user's sensory abilities.*
- ***Principle 5: Tolerance for Error*** *- The design minimizes hazards and the adverse consequences of accidental or unintended actions.*
- ***Principle 6: Low Physical Effort*** *- The design can be used efficiently and comfortably and with a minimum of fatigue.*
- ***Principle 7: Size and Space for Approach and Use*** *- Appropriate size and space is provided for approach, reach, manipulation, and use regardless of user's body size, posture, or mobility. (NDA 2016)*

The first four principles are most informative when considering a new definition of accessibility, specifically, the notions of designing for individual preferences and diverse abilities, regardless of the users' knowledge, skill, or visual or hearing impairment.

User-Centered Design (UCD)

The first inklings of user-centered design can be traced to Don Norman in 1986; he defines such design "as an approach that puts human needs, capabilities, and behavior first, then designs to accommodate those needs, capabilities, and ways of behaving" (Norman, 2013, p. 8). For Norman, the design thinking necessary for UCD lies in direct opposition with technology-centered design (TCD), which emphasizes what a technology can do rather than what users need, expect, or want the technology to do. At its core, UCD involves only two fundamental principles: "The first phase is to find the right problem, the second is to find the right solution," and this is accomplished through an iterative cycle of observation, ideation, prototyping, and testing (p. 220-222). Perhaps the most important concept around Norman's UCD approach is what he refers to as his "credo about errors":

Eliminate the term human error. Instead, talk about communication and interaction: what we call an error is usually bad communication or interaction ... Today, we insist that people perform abnormally, which includes always giving precise, accurate information. Humans are particularly bad at this, yet when they fail to meet the arbitrary, inhuman requirements of machines, we call it human error. No, it is design error ... It is easy to design devices that work well when everything goes as planned. The hard and necessary part of design is to make things work well even when things do not go as planned. (p. 67-68)

Inspired by the work of Norman, Still and Crane (2017) expanded Norman's two principles into a design methodology for UCD that "adapt[s] to the user's psychological, situational, emotional, and intellectual needs" (p. 12). In a nutshell, this methodology encourages designers to consider users' perspectives throughout the design process:

- How users might use a product
- How users think about a product
- How, where, when, and why users will interact with a product
- What users expect/need (p. 12)

The emphasis on users that Norman, Still, and Crane discuss goes beyond simply making things user-friendly. They also consider ethical obligations of designers. Specifically, they raise concerns about the cultural, political, and environmental impacts of design, recognizing that "design affects society [and] … takes on political significance" (Norman, 2013, p. 291). Likewise, for the purposes of this chapter, the authors recognize the impacts of the rapid advancements of the digital age such that "Our lives, our family size and living arrangements, and the role played by business and education in our lives are all governed by the technologies of the era" (Norman, 2013, p. 285).

Redefining Accessibility

The instructor-designers authoring this chapter see intersections in the three scholarship areas explored above, which means shifting at least part of the responsibility from students to instructors for errors and failures involving course navigation, assignments, and submissions. Thus, this chapter uses the following expanded definition of accessibility:

Accessibility refers to the ease of entry and use of a product, service, space, or text; and considers course design (navigation, layout, color scheme, font type, font emphasis), course tools (applications, discussion forums, quizzes) and course materials (instructional texts, resources, assignment descriptions, submission and evaluation guidelines).Thus, an accessible tech-mediated course is one that affords every learner the opportunity to succeed, regardless of technological skill, reading level, native language, learning preference, or physical impairment.

Yet, simply expanding the definition of accessibility may not be useful to all instructors, so it is necessary to articulate several concrete practices that any course designer may use in their tech-mediated classes no matter what the subject area:

- Ensure multiple points of access in navigation (also known as redundancy) so that students can move through the course in a way that makes the most sense to them.
- Provide alternate versions of course texts and materials (i.e. documents, screencasts, infographics, etc.) so that students can interact with them based on learning needs and preferences.
- Use preset styles (titles, subtitles, headings, etc.) so that digital course materials are navigable and accessible to screen readers
- Model for students the importance of best practices in digital compositions through course materials and design of the LMS.
- Practice user-centered design by providing opportunities for students to give feedback on the ease of navigation of the course and design of course resources.
- Discuss what accessibility means explicitly within the context of the course noting that accessibility is more than just accounting for disability, it considers all users' learning preferences and needs.
- Complicate student notions of accessibility by asking them to reflect on how their digital composing choices may include or exclude audiences.
- Be mindful of color schemes in course design (avoid neon or bright colors, colors that are too similar in terms of shade) allowing for adequate color contrast so items are easy to identify and accommodating to those with visual impairments and/or color-blindness.

What follows are two in-depth case studies of instructors and their course designs that explicate this new definition and exemplify ways of designing, modeling, and teaching the best practices spelled out above.

DESIGNING ACCESSIBLE COURSES: TWO CASE STUDIES

Situating the Instructors

Before sharing their journeys, a bit of background on these instructor-designers is necessary. Both are senior lecturers with extensive writing program administrative experience[1] in the independent writing program at the University of North Carolina Charlotte (UNCC), a large, urban public university with a population of about 29,000 students in the United States. At present, most faculty in their program primarily teach first-year writing with some also teaching in the writing minor as well as liberal studies courses grounded in the Writing Studies discipline. The program's core values revolve around inquiry-based research and digital composition, but faculty approaches to these concepts vary greatly. Furthermore, the program highly values innovation and encourages risk and creativity with attention to rhetorical awareness. Discussions of accessibility and the importance of intuitive design are still emerging in this program, with some faculty devoting their scholarship and professionalization to issues of diversity, equity, and best practices in digital design. But perhaps the most important feature of the program is the support of non-tenure track faculty pursuing a wide range of research interests within Writing Studies, and it is through this support that the authors are able to conduct focused inquiries into issues of accessibility, sharing experience and knowledge with various stakeholders in the program, across the institution, and beyond.

WALDEN'S FIRST-YEAR WRITING COURSE

At UNCC, most students are required to take a one-sequence first-year writing course which includes one extended inquiry project and the development of a digital writing portfolio. In fact, grades are primarily derived from portfolio work, meaning that digital composition practices and identifying target audiences are central to ongoing discussion in Walden's classes. Examples of this work include a recurring small group activity where students assess the expectations and purposes of various digital composing platforms including infographics, slides presentations, and screencast videos. Students first describe the features included in "successful" infographics, slides presentations, and screencasts. Next, they define several audiences and subjects for which these digital composing tools would be appropriate followed by the generation of an example that models the appropriate features of the selected composition. Finally, the work culminates in students comparing how an inquiry essay might change if one were to create an infographic snapshot of the subject, a slides presentation, or a screencast of the project. Walden's class strategically revisits this activity every three or four weeks in the course, each time exploring one of the digital composing mediums and considering how their research work as students may shift depending both on the type of composition and intended audience. Students range in terms of intended major, but as this course is a general education requirement, no student takes this class by choice. This often leads to some students struggling to understand the purpose and appropriate place for digital composing, as many are unaware of how their intended major or discipline uses digital composing--be it emails, modeling programs, coding, etc.

Accessibility: Instructor Preference vs. Best Practice

In Fall 2015, the school migrated from Moodle to Canvas, and most instructors were excitedly anticipating the change. For Walden, it invited opportunity for revision to the current course design and to potentially experiment with basic HTML coding commands. These were quite lofty expectations from someone who had yet to learn anything about how Canvas functioned; Walden is the type of learner-designer that benefits most from experimentation rather than taking a workshop on the basic functionality of an LMS or program. In short, what followed is that her initial experiments with designing online content did not yield positive results; instead of seeking out best practice in accessibility standards in her course, this instructor designed the course according to what was appealing and intuitive for her. Only when the instructor learned about accessibility and techniques such as Universal Design did her course design significantly improve.

Though Walden felt the move to a new LMS was an ideal time to reinvent the course design, what resulted, unfortunately, was a design very similar to her original Moodle page. It consisted of an incredibly long, list-formatted page that required quite a bit of scrolling. The new design still preserved three large units of content divided according to an overall theme, and relied heavily on a slides presentation to provide a daily agenda for class and homework. What changed in the Canvas site was asking students to provide some feedback on the unit content in the form of MEMEs and the addition of grading breakdown along with general expectations.

As demonstrated in both Figures 1 and 2, students had to scroll extensively to see all the content for the course. Under each unit, there were a series of subcategories including: daily agendas, unit materials (resources, assignments, modules, drafts, groupwork, and examples), course portfolio (checklists, examples, and guides), and an "I Need Help" discussion forum for students to post general questions to the whole class. Aside from the unit materials, the homepage included housekeeping resources such as the syllabus and attendance policy quicklinks, and general breakdown of the grading scale. The course design utilized bold, primary colors, incorporated images, included hyperlinks, varied font colors, bolded and italicized text, and highlights--all of which appeared, in the instructor's opinion, to be accessible and intuitively designed. At this point, Walden did not have a clear sense of accessibility; instead, she conflated the idea of intuitive design with the concept of accessible design.

There were many problems with the design in terms of accessibility and intuitive navigation for users, but perhaps the most glaring errors revolved around the volume of content, inattention to white space, and lack of alternative text for images. These concerns were confirmed in student evaluations throughout three iterations of this course (Fall 2015, Spring 2016, and Fall 2016); students routinely felt lost trying to locate material despite what were assumed to be clear labels and design. Rather than address these concerns repeatedly voiced in student evaluations, the instructor fell into a common trap for teacher-designers: assuming that the students were simply unwilling to spend the time and energy to seek out needed materials. The instructor herself was guilty of labelling students prematurely because of her own unwillingness to attend to accessibility and user-centered design.

By Spring 2016, the instructor was finally willing--albeit on a limited basis--to concede to student feedback that the design needed work. At the time, the loudest concern from students was the sheer volume of content; students were tired of dealing with a "scroll of death" on the homepage. There was too much

Figure 1. List model homepage

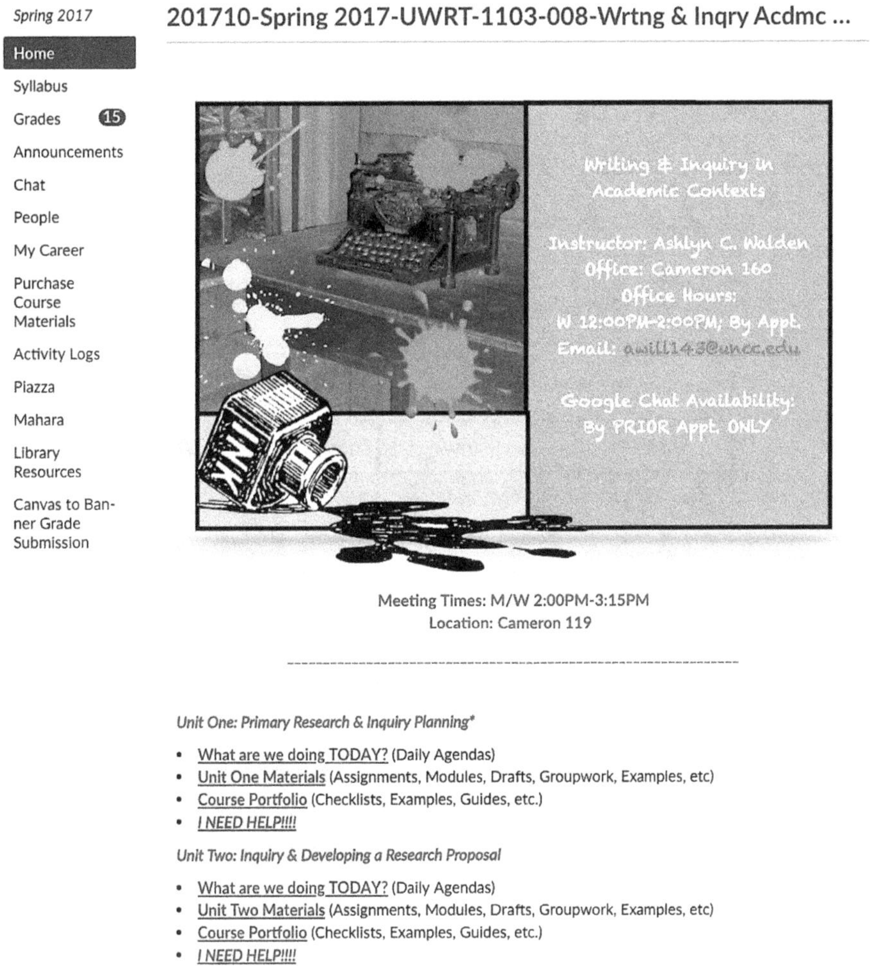

written content to sift through, and students had a difficult time identifying the salient information. The next goal was to address both the scrolling and overload of content by condensing the design to what is now shown in Figure 3. This time, the instructor-designer opted for a more muted color scheme, utilized buttons, and began experimenting with HTML codes by embedding newly designed slide agendas into the homepage. Items such as the syllabus, attendance policies, course portfolio, and the student learning outcomes were retained, but these were placed in a location of prominence under the course flag. The hope was to indicate these as items of importance by making them appear as menu items on a typical website. Images were used, but limited on this page (again without alternative text), various font type/styles were incorporated, and there was a more attentive focus on white space. The use of highlighting was eliminated, and instead, the instructor opted for a button feature that would circle the current unit, so students could easily identify where to go first. However, when a student navigated away from the homepage and began accessing the unit content, that problematic list format appeared yet again.

Looking at Figure 4, the image may be somewhat deceiving as it is zoomed out to make the contents entirely visible in one frame. Typically, this page on a computer screen is long enough to still require

Figure 2. List model homepage

Unit Three: Research, Inquiry, & Digital Composing

- What are we doing TODAY? (Daily Agendas)
- Unit Three Materials (Modules, Drafts, Groupwork, etc)
- Course Portfolio (Checklists, Examples, Guides, etc.)
- *I NEED HELP!!!!*

**The highlighted section is our current unit.*

"House Keeping" Resources

- Syllabus
- Attendance Quick Links (Accommodations, Dean of Students, etc.)

Grading

Your course grade will be based on percentages assigned to assignment drafts, the course portfolio, and various modules you will complete throughout course (i.e. Studio Responses, Class Participation, etc).

Assignment Groupings	Weight
Class Participation (In Class & Online)	15%
Studio, Group, & Homework Responses (Modules Online)	15%
Assignment Drafts (Peer Workshopping & 2nd Revised Drafts)	30%
Course Portfolio	40%
Course Total	**100%**

Grades are on a ten point scale (90-100 A, 80-89 B, 70-79 C, 60-69 D, and 59 and below, F).

All major assignments and a final portfolio must be completed in order to receive a passing grade in the course.

some scrolling. Hyperlinks were used throughout, as well as bolded and underlined text. The instructor's uninformed position at this point assumed that underlining demonstrated importance or a heading to a section or document; yet, according to accessibility research, underlined content in a digital space usually indicates a hyperlink, which was not the case for some of the items the instructor had chosen to highlight.

Perhaps the most troubling part of the design on this page was a lack of multiple points of access. In other words, this was the only way students could engage with the course content and turn in their course work. Canvas does provide options in the main left-hand menu for users to navigate to course content such as assignments, discussion forums, and modules (a sequenced list of course content), but none of these options were available to students because the instructor had chosen to hide them. At the time, the instructor did not yet understand the importance of providing multiple ways to navigate to content; instead, she was thinking of what was aesthetically pleasing to her preferences as a digital reader. Furthermore, consider the titles of the modules (e.g. modules 2.1, 2.2, 2.3, and so on). What do these titles tell students about the work they will be doing? Or maybe the better question: do these titles indicate that a student will be doing work at all? How would a student be able to return to an earlier piece of work? The simple answer: none of these questions can be answered with the titles such as they are.

Figure 3. Revised canvas course design

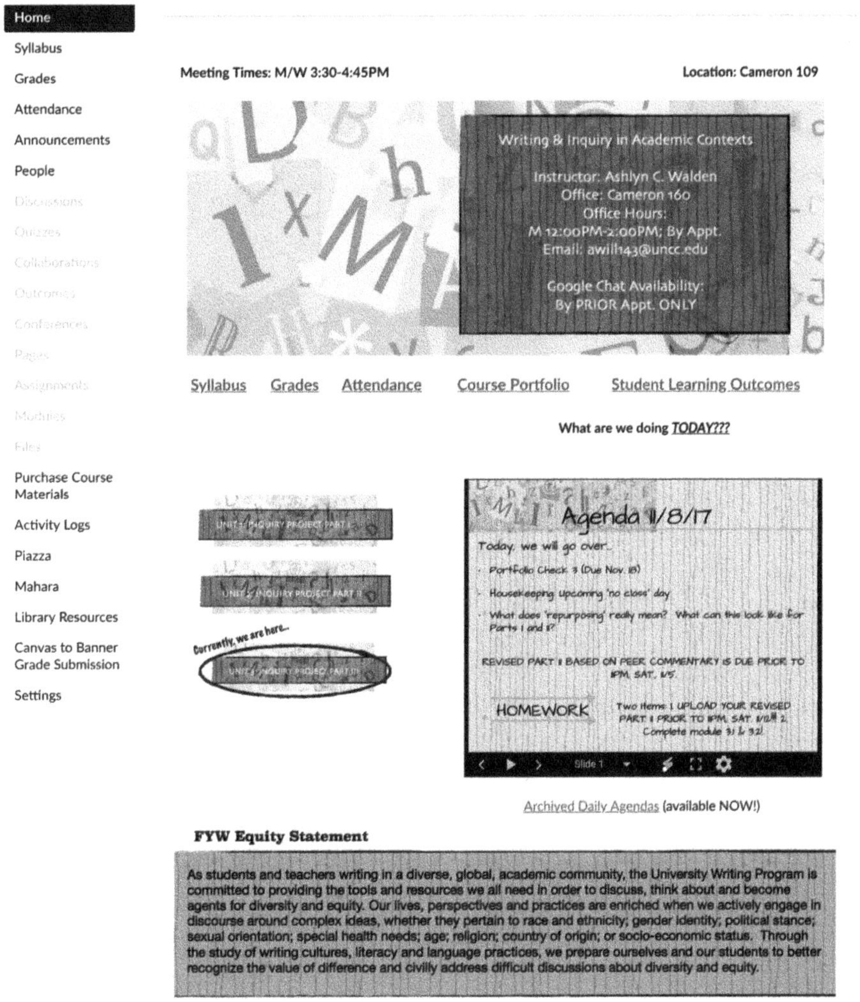

Users would have to click on the hyperlink and read the associated content before even having a vague inkling of what is expected. Students noticed this too, and they continued to struggle finding content.

Initially, Walden located the problem of finding material with the students and not in her course design. In fact, it wasn't until she undertook a new in-house training course[2] for best practices in Online Writing Instruction (OWI) that she was willing to concede that accessibility in design was truly an area in great need of improvement. Many things resulted from her participation in this course, including a more nuanced understanding of the importance of accessible course design, things like navigation and layout and the development of supplemental instructional texts to help students better navigate the course and its content; for the purposes of the discussion here, the author will focus on three areas where the most significant revisions occurred: (1) redesign of the course homepage, (2) development of "Start Here Module," and (3) allowing for multiple points of access to course material.

Figure 4. Module list page

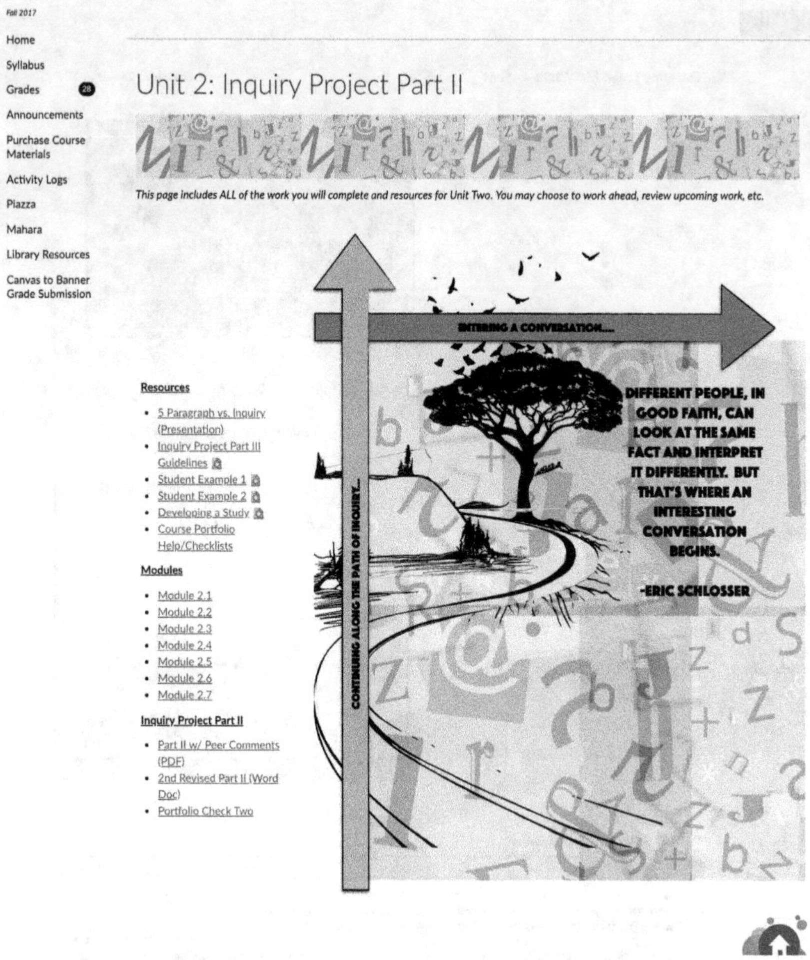

Redesigning the Homepage

The redesign of Walden's homepage was a really big step as she began to think more carefully about the accessibility concerns for her course. Figure 5 shows that the one-page frame was retained and that little to no scrolling was required. The color scheme still remained muted, and the underlined text was only for the "Course Calendar & Assignments" hyperlink. The course calendar was actually a pretty major shift; no longer was the slides format being used for daily course agendas. Though the slides tool was originally embedded from another source, it seemed best to make everything as internal to Canvas as possible. This led to the creation of a table format for each week of the course which included columns with the date, "Daily Agendas" and "What Do I Have To Turn In?" (See Figure 6). Here, the design retained the use of bolded text, limited the underlined text to only hyperlinks, and used highlighting to emphasize dates or important notes. Keeping in mind some of the concerns students had expressed previously with finding the most relevant information, the table was designed with alternating color contrast so students could easily identify what materials lined up with specific dates.

Figure 5. Current homepage

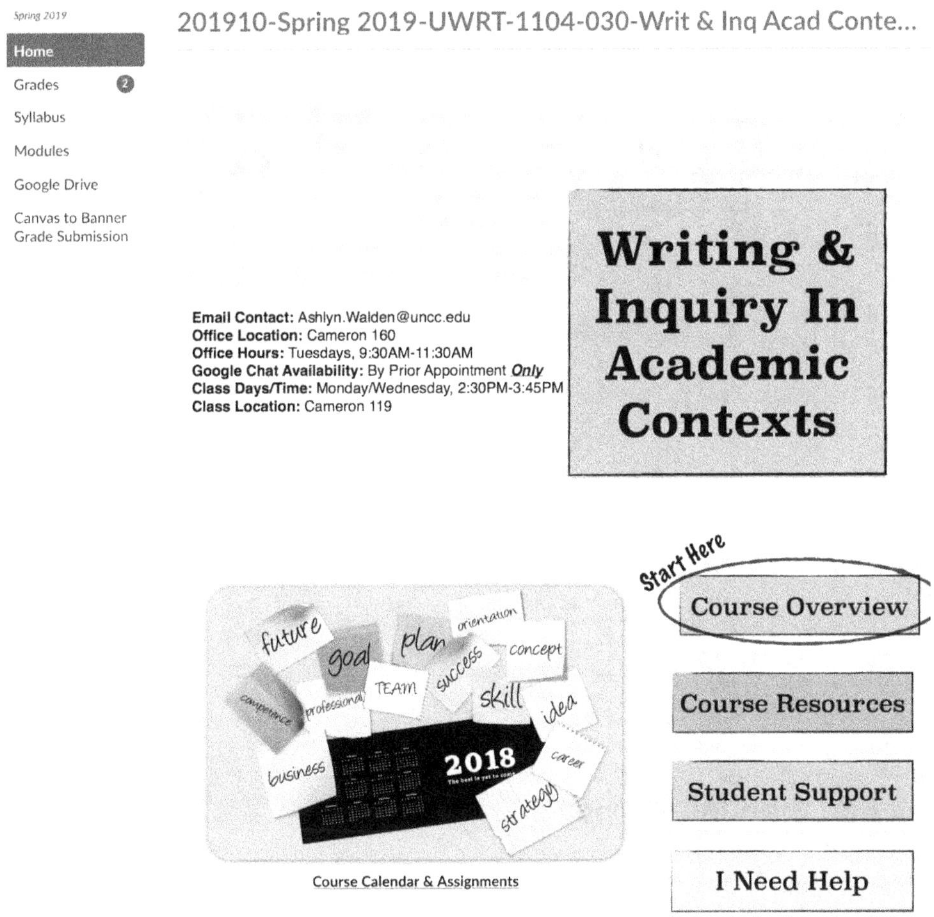

Another major revision was in the left-hand menu which can be seen in both Figures 5 and 6. Walden always tries to be keenly aware of overloading information in menus, thus she really attempts to limit the options available. The problem with this, as indicated earlier, is that this can sometimes restrict the opportunity for students to access the materials in the way that makes the most sense for them. Recognizing this problem, the instructor moved away from hiding the "Modules" from students and made sure this option was available to them in the left-hand menu. (See Figures 5 and 6). Other ways that students could access their materials and assignments also included: "Grades," the hyperlinks embedded in the "Course Calendar & Assignments," the "Course Resources" button located on the homepage, the Canvas "To Do List," and finally the Canvas calendar that collated all assignments students have across any Canvas course they are currently taking. In short, the course design went from three points of access ("To Do List," a list-formatted and poorly named unit page, and the Canvas course calendar) to five options. Looking at Figure 7, it can be seen that the issue of unclear naming was also addressed. Now students would know that "Discussion Post 1: Introduction to the Course" would cover content related to the beginning of the course, expectations, etc.

Figure 6. Canvas course calendar

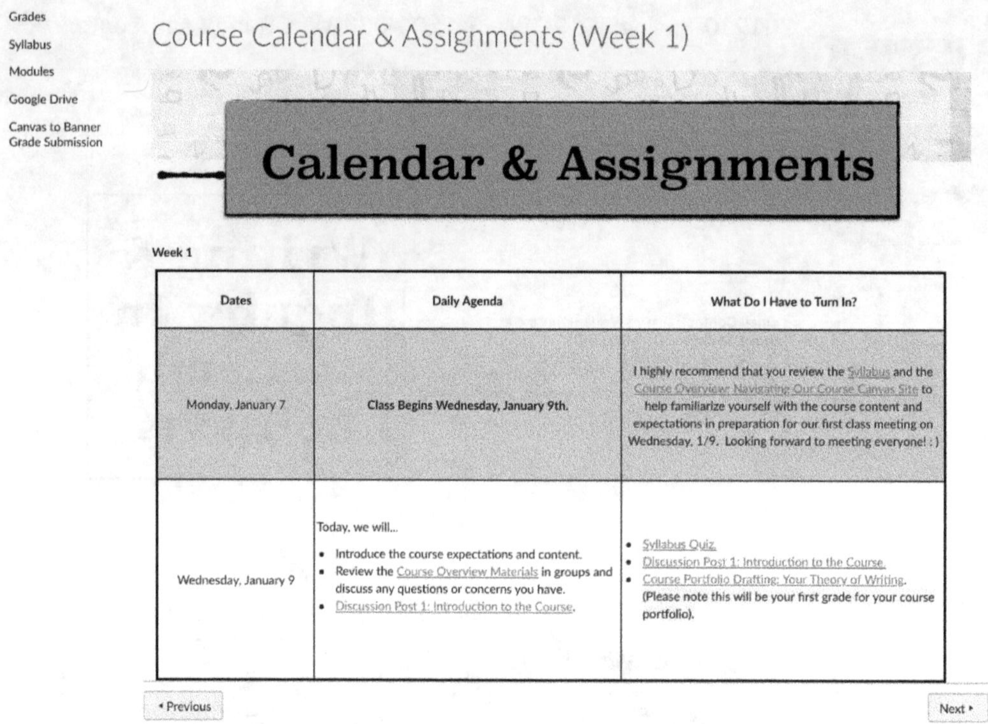

Developing the "Start Here" Module

As shown back in Figure 5, there is a "Course Overview" button with a large marker line noting "Start Here." This button immediately takes students into the first course module known as the "Start Here Module" that you can see partially outlined in Figure 7. Notice the top item on the list entitled "Course Overview: Navigating Our Course." This is a uniquely designed resource created through a combination of screencast and edited video demonstrating to students how to navigate through the course. Its overall purpose is to be an instructional text to show students how the teacher designed the course and to also note for them the many options for how to navigate to what they need and how to best determine when they need said content (see Figure 8). To build flexible access, aside from the video, a full PDF transcript is included for students to read if they wish. Notice also the language about accessibility options. Instead of referring to these as "accessibility options," this is framed in terms of having options for accessing the content in the way that makes the most sense for the student as a reader and a learner. The teacher-designer goes one step further, talking through her own preference for learning about a new concept or unfamiliar process. This is a key as instructors try to move beyond accounting for disability, and instead consider the way our students are engaging with content in both print and digital spaces.

Ensuring Multiple Points of Access

A cursory scan of Walden's course shows that she includes a lot of videos specialized for her courses. She enjoys the process, the design, and the challenge of creating content that is condensed and manage-

Figure 7. Revised modules screenshot

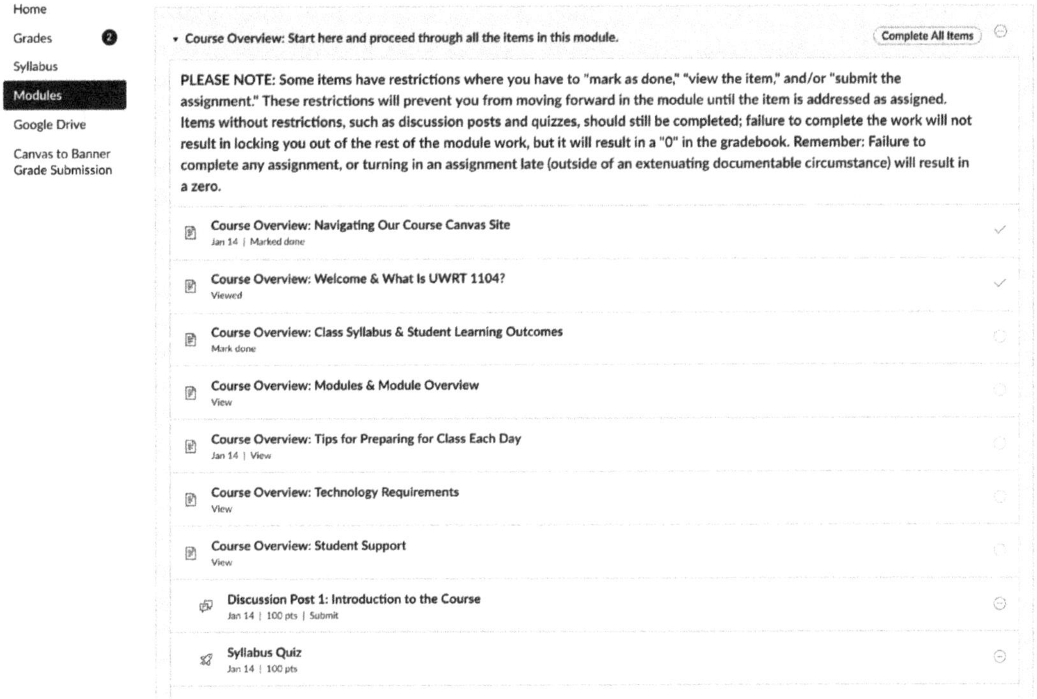

Figure 8. Course navigation video

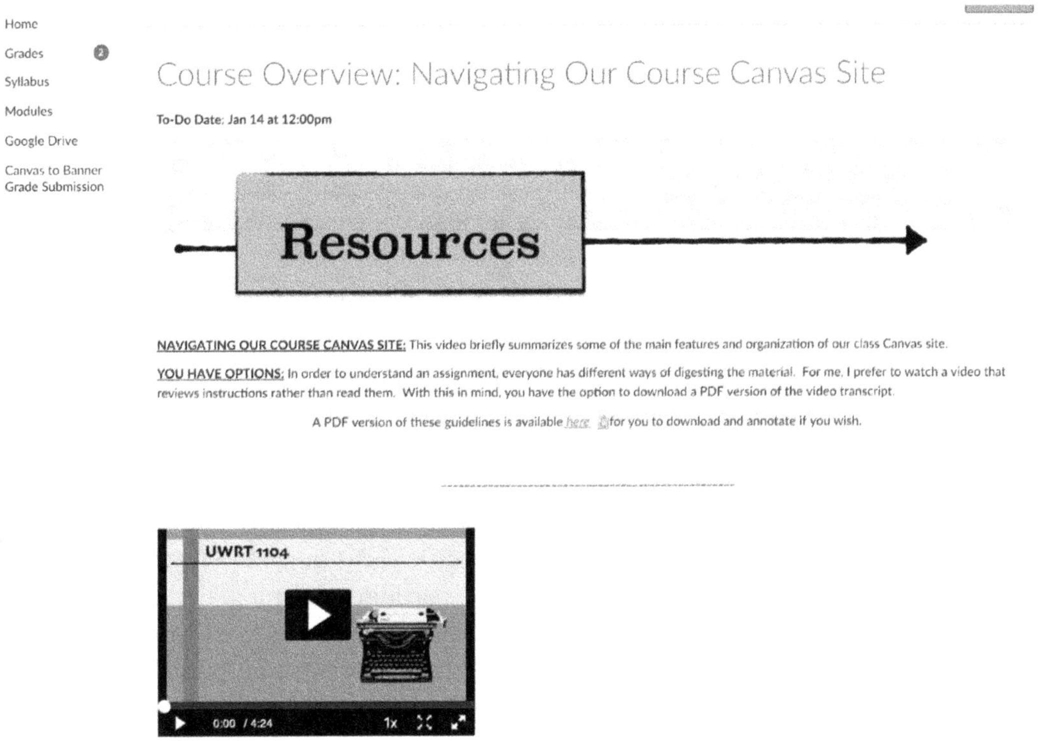

able while also maintaining relevancy. Yet, in the teacher's zeal for designing videos for the course, it became obvious that perhaps there were too many videos. Simply providing alternative text and transcripts is not enough for all students. Videos do not always work for everyone in terms of resources and support. Some students prefer verbal instructions or written instructions that allow for review at any point. One way to address this issue is by polling students to see the types of instruction that they find useful in video format and also inviting them to share other methods of resource presentation that may work for them as readers. Students have been gracious in providing ideas and feedback leading to the categorization of the types of resources that may work best as videos, infographics, slide presentations, etc. Interestingly enough, students respond best to video format when demonstrating a process such as how to navigate the Canvas site, how to develop a research question, consult source material, etc. Infographics tend to work best in breaking down a complicated concept into a series of steps such as how to identify a thesis-driven argument vs. an inquiry-driven argument, or how to develop a study proposal, etc. Slides presentations are often preferred when dealing with complicated abstract concepts that ground the practical work of the course such as understanding how the genre of a thesis-driven paper compares to an inquiry-driven research paper.

Moreover, as instructors continue the process of diversifying the type of resources in their courses, it is an opportunity for them to think more intentionally about how their course compositions can become models for students. Digital composition is in ever-increasing demand despite what the field of study may be--every job field requires some level of ability to communicate effectively in a digital space. As such, the authors wholeheartedly believe that teacher-designers need to be thinking purposefully about how course materials can become models for the quality and type of digital products that students are assigned to create across the disciplines. Being experts in a discipline requires thinking about what digital composition and design looks like for the field and to model this process for students. And as a part of this process, it is imperative to demonstrate the ways of providing multiple points of access for the content created for the online components of a course.

A Start: Students Practicing Universal Design

An emerging part of Walden's work with students on accessibility is making the step from practicing accessibility standards in the course design to having students demonstrate these principles in their own digital compositions. As indicated earlier, a major grade component of the first-year writing course is contingent upon the development of a digital writer's portfolio that charts and curates the student's work over the course of the term. Figures 9 and 10 show the currently in-process attempts to raise awareness of accessibility; this conversation begins with a brief video overview of Universal Design, which explains UD as a design approach that informs the creation of various environments, products, and/or communication. Again, as mentioned previously, this method of design can be used in any type of an environment (physical, digital, or virtual), to ensure that the content, objects, or physical space is accessible to any person. The studio[3] shown here in Figure 9 demonstrates more generally what UD practices look like in all three of these spaces, with specific focus given to what accessibility looks like in a digital composition in preparation for the course portfolio. Central to the video's message are parallels drawn between Walden's course design, course materials, and course tools and students portfolio design (navigation, layout, color scheme, font type, and font emphasis) embedded portfolio tools (quizzes to engage the reader, comment forums, and applications) and portfolio materials (assignment drafts, descriptions, and reflections).

Figure 9. UD studio video

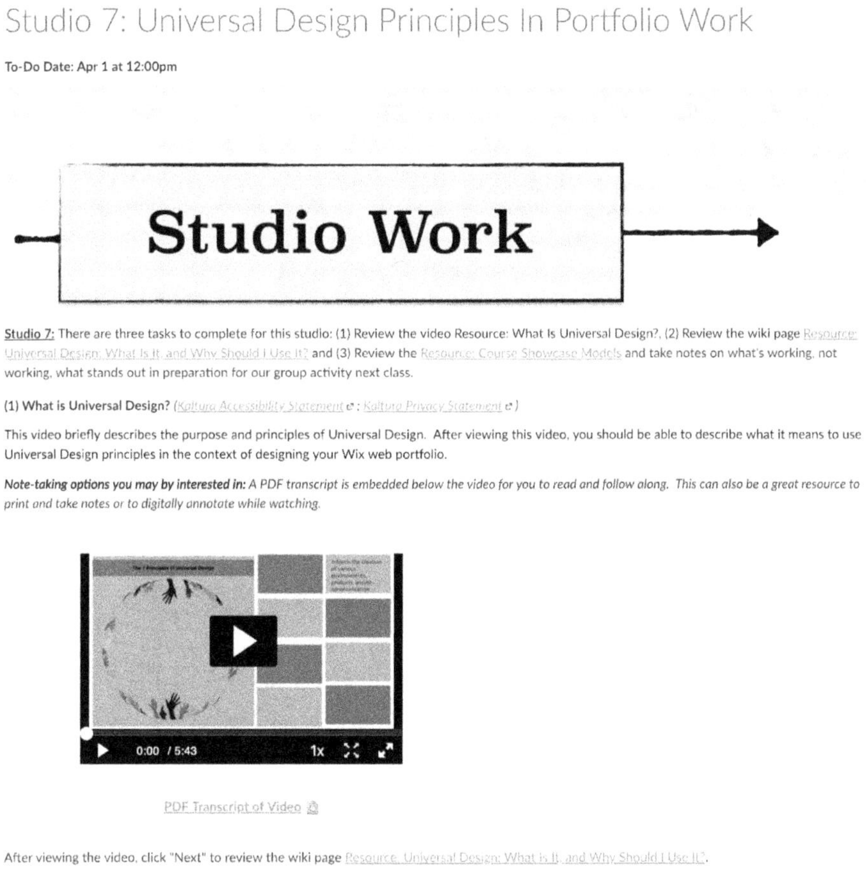

To review, students have been asked in this studio to first learn the principles of UD and try to locate examples of these practices within the Canvas course design. Next, students engage in an activity that asks them to identify Universal Design practices in previous student work noting what is working well and what needs further revision. Surprisingly, adding this step of identifying the practices in other student work has really helped a lot of students make the shift to understanding the importance of practicing accessibility in their own work.

MAHAFFEY'S DIGITAL DESIGN LIBERAL STUDIES COURSE

Early in her tenure as an administrator, an instructor came to Mahaffey in angst upon receiving a letter from disability services regarding one of her students. The student had visual impairments, so his accommodation request included video captions and course materials that could be read by screen readers. While university support afforded access for this student without much effort on the part of the instructor, this sparked a journey for Mahaffey, one that began with an exploration of and subsequent certification in Universal Design and has expanded into considerations of access way beyond this initial concern for students with disabilities.

Figure 10. UD infographic

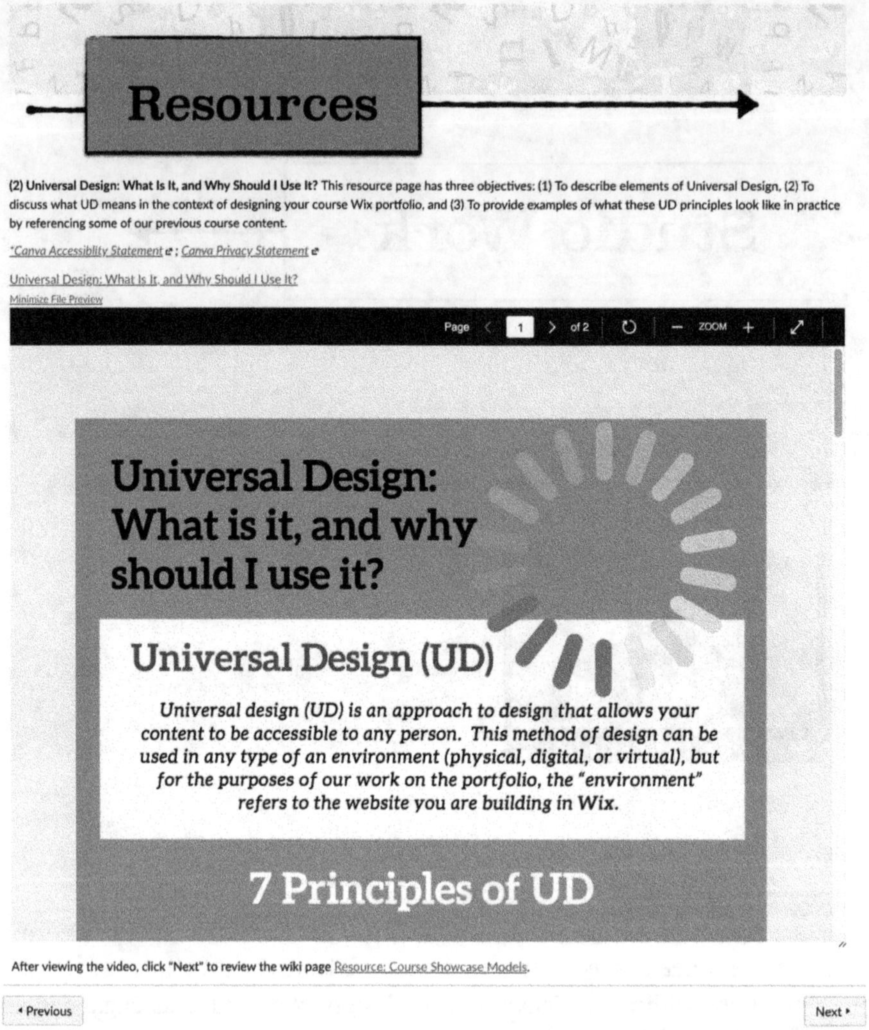

After becoming certificated in Universal Design and exploring OWI and UCD, it became apparent to Mahaffey that there was a need for an explicitly designed course around accessibility practices geared toward students and future employees. This desire, fortunately, was well-timed with an opportunity for her to move out the first year writing classroom and into an intentionally-designed sophomore-level liberal studies (LBST) course. As mentioned earlier, the program where Mahaffey teaches grants much freedom in course design according to instructors' strengths and interests. Thus, this new course afforded a space to explore the dynamics and challenges of practicing accessibility in digital design.

For context, this particular LBST course serves as a second-year general education writing requirement. Instructors from across the campus are invited to design courses related to their research interests so that students have a variety of themes/disciplinary foci to choose from. When Mahaffey began considering the idea of a course centered on accessibility, she was forced to keep in mind that her course theme and title needed to be something students could understand and would want to register for, so accessibility became a secondary theme, with digital design and rhetoric taking the lead. The course is called "The Rhetoric of Digital Design," with the following course description:

From academic essays to workplace memos, design and formatting can either grant or limit access to particular audiences. With special emphasis on digital texts, this course examines the rhetorical strategies employed to create documents and how those strategies impact the way various audiences interact with and interpret them. (University of North Carolina at Charlotte, 2019)

Most writing courses at this institution are capped between 22-25, and this LBST course is considered rather large for a writing course with a cap of 35 students. Therefore, the main project is a team-based inquiry assignment. Initially, this team setup addressed concerns regarding the ability to offer quality feedback to such a large class, but breaking the students into teams proved to be the single best approach for granting access to every student in the class. In essence, the instruction became more personalized. Rather than lecture, each class meeting consisted of team conferences, greatly enhancing student-instructor interaction and team community building.

What follows is a focus on three core aspects of the course: (1) revisiting the "Start Here Module," (2) explicitly teaching accessibility, and (3) weaving together accessibility and rhetoric.

Revisiting the "Start Here Module"

While this has been discussed earlier in this chapter, it is worthwhile to further consider ways to invite and grant access to courses. Setting up a clearly denoted "Start Here" module or section that students can review prior to the first day of class goes a long way toward this goal, especially for non-traditional students who may not be as acclimated to LMS's as continuing students. A start here module includes a lot of redundancy from the syllabus, and this is intentional. When thinking about access, instructors should consider the multiple points of entry through which different learners move in and out of a digital learning space. For some, a printable syllabus is necessary. For others, contact information for support services suffices. But for many, especially non-traditional students (i.e. returning adult students, international students, first generation students, etc.), repeated exposure to academic, disability, and technical support services invites them to take advantage of them.

The "Start Here" module does more than acclimate eager students who are motivated enough to browse early; it also serves as a valuable resource throughout the course. Figure 11 shows the pages students can quickly access if they come across an issue. For example, one of those pages is titled "Student Support & Accessibility" and includes information about how to get help for anything from tutoring to laptop repair. Another page is called "Grading and Feedback" so students can reference how and when their assignments will get responses. As previously stated, much of this is already included on the syllabus, but this redundancy makes the information more prominent for every type of learner.

One last point to make about "Start Here" modules and their importance: They allow access to students who register late or who need to visualize information by reading it on their own in order to process it. In a similar vein, Mahaffey and Walden advocate for all lecture notes and class agendas to be open and available to students during and after class so that students who learn best through written rather than verbal content have an equitable opportunity to absorb and understand new concepts. This continuous online access to course content also allows students to revisit concepts as they build their knowledge over the semester.

Figure 11. Start here module

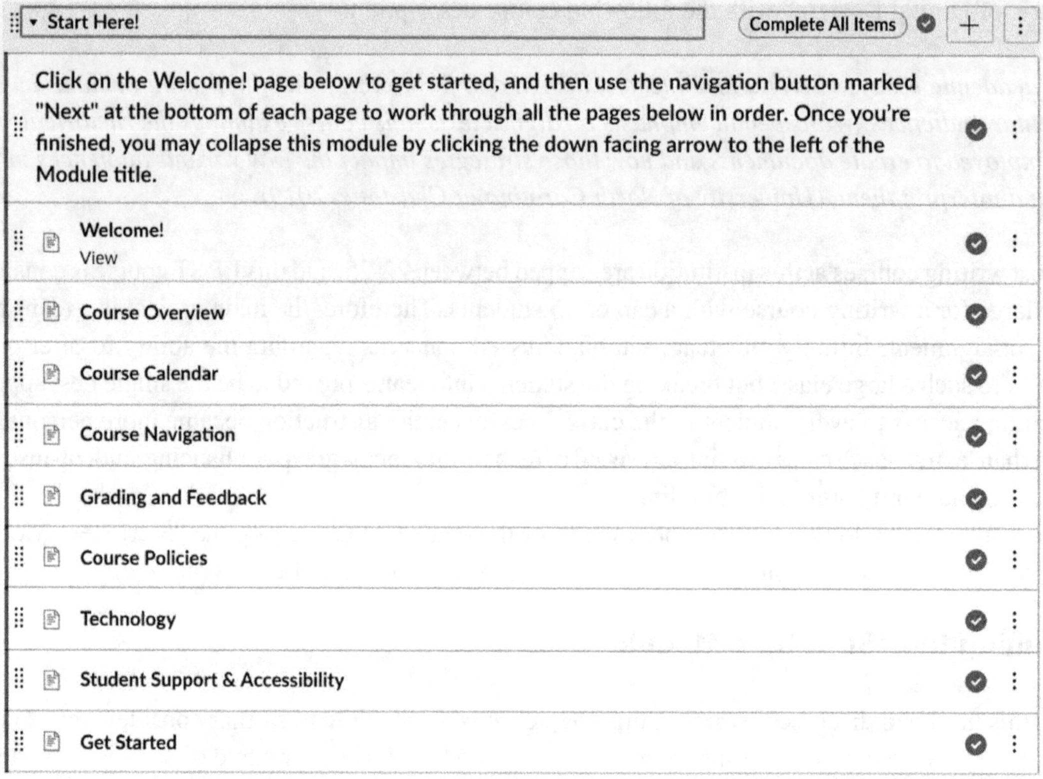

Explicitly Teaching Accessibility

This process of designing a liberal studies course on digital design granted new insight into ways to reinforce transfer of concepts. Several students had taken a prior course with Mahaffey or had been exposed through colleagues to the same emphasis on document design and accessibility, but, surprisingly, this did not grant them any advantage. Despite the modeling, direct instruction, and expectations, none of the continuing students performed basic skills like using headings and incorporating a hyperlinked table of contents until they were reminded to do so. Students had forgotten or perhaps missed the importance of what they had learned previously. This is not surprising and is emblematic of the larger issue with transfer of writing skills. Unless students encounter the vocabulary and are allowed to practice what they learned as they move through writing contexts, they revert back to what they learned in their formative years in K-12 (see Moore & Bass, 2017).

With transfer at the forefront, direct instruction of accessibility began with a brief introduction to the vocabulary. After a short overview of the class goals on the first day, students were asked to post to a discussion forum about what they thought the terms *access* and *accessibility* meant. These initial responses were referred to as "preliminary definitions" and served to frame the course's goal of expanding and refining those definitions. The intention was to empower them to look beyond the narrow emphasis on disability and begin to see themselves as granting or being granted access, to consider their own responsibilities and expectations as writer/designers.

The first group activity served as both an icebreaker on the first day and as a way to situate students with regard to their own accessibility needs and preferences (see Figure 12). They were tasked with generating a list of things that annoy or frustrate them as they go about their daily schedules. They had a lot of fun with this, coming up with a range of issues, from drivers not using turn signals to inaccessible campus maps. This activity concluded with students brainstorming why these things frustrate them and what could be done to make them less frustrating and, therefore, more accessible or user-friendly. For example, at least one group in every class mentioned being frustrated with playing against younger gamers in massively multiplayer online (MMO) video games like Fortnite. When asked to consider ways to improve this experience, the initial solution was to put age limits on the game interface, which of course would be intrusive and ineffective. Pressing them further resulted in rich discussions about designing for access, inviting or inhibiting target audiences. In this case, the students concluded that putting Fortnite on Facebook would disinvite younger gamers since Facebook is a space that young people avoid. This foundational conversation set the tone for helping them complicate their "preliminary definitions" of accessibility.

As the semester continued, students were invited to look for and share ways to make the Canvas course site more accessible. While this might be uncomfortable for some instructors, it encourages students to explore how they learn best. For this course, in particular, it was important for students to examine all sorts of digital texts around them, and the existing course design was as much fodder as any other. This openness creates balance between the instructor's expertise and the students' obligations to facilitate their own learning, reflecting on their own needs, becoming more aware of how to create access for themselves when barriers arise, and, more importantly, building empathy for how their own designs might impact users/readers. One request by students related to how they keep up with homework assign-

Figure 12. What frustrates you activity

Group Activity: What Frustrates You?

Step 1: Get into groups, introduce yourselves to each other, and use the nearest dry erase board to complete this activity.

Step 2: List each group member's first and last name (use preferred names)

Step 3: Generate a list of the following: **What things frustrate or annoy you about ...**

- Shopping (online or at the mall)
- Driving
- School
- Eating (dining out or eating in)
- Web Surfing
- Video games (tablet, console, computer, whatever)
- Board games
- Anything that involves doing something ...

I will come around and join your group at some point to meet you. Then we will wrap up the class by discussing how the activity relates to our course.

ments. Canvas has a built-in calendar populated automatically when instructors create assignments (see Figure 13). Since most of the assignments in this course were process-oriented and because they were submitted through Google Drive in team folders, most of the homework was initially communicated through modules rather than assignments. When students pointed out that they relied on the Canvas calendar and its notification center, it became clear that this initial setup limited their access and the overall usability of the course site. This was quickly remedied by shifting homework descriptions from pages to ungraded assignments. While some might say this accommodation was capitulating, in reality, this transaction benefitted both parties. The students gained understanding about what to ask for from future instructors, and the instructor came away with an enhanced course design that will increase accessibility for future students.

Weaving Together Accessibility and Rhetoric

As mentioned, designing this new course drew attention toward knowledge transfer in ways not previously considered. This desire for accessibility to become embedded into students' composing processes suggested the need to build explicit connections between rhetoric and access. The team inquiry project required each group to identify a "problem" text (one that had issues of access related to its design), analyze it, create prototype redesigns of it, and then revise the "problem" text to be more accessible/usable. Each stage included multiple opportunities for students to practice incorporating key concepts of the course. Rather than decide what those concepts were, each group contributed regularly to a Key Terms Glossary, building class vocabulary and defining the terms in their own words. At the end of the course, they were tasked with whittling the glossary down to ten concepts the students deemed most important to carry forward.

The first stage of the project, identifying a "problem" text (see Figure 14), was tricky, mostly because students had limited knowledge of what constitutes a "digital text." To them, a digital text was a website, something alphanumeric in nature, so most groups chose poorly-designed websites they found through simple Google searches. However, some teams focused on apps, restaurant menus, and flyers, creating a wide assortment of inquiries which benefited the class as a whole since it challenged and expanded their definitions of digital texts in general. Another area of concern that arose was difficulty in keeping teams focused on designing for access rather than aesthetics. This proved to be an opportunity to emphasize the class goals during team conferences such that the question "how does this 'problem' impact accessibility?" became somewhat of a mantra for the course. For example, when asked to identify opportunities for

Figure 13. Canvas calendar

Date	Details
Fri Jan 11, 2019	Preliminary Definitions (Access and Accessibility)
Mon Jan 14, 2019	Homework: Review the Start Here Module
Wed Jan 16, 2019	Homework: Preliminary Definitions (Usability)
Fri Jan 18, 2019	Homework: Syllabus Quiz
Wed Jan 23, 2019	Homework: Connections and Intersections

revising their "problem" texts, students discussed color but failed to connect color choices with access for readers with color-blindness or visual impairments.

Once they selected problem texts, groups analyzed them multiple times through different lenses. This is where rhetoric and accessibility were woven together, building and reinforcing connections through both the learning activities and the products students were creating. For example, each group was responsible for submitting regular progress reports as they moved through the project. These reports included things like meeting minutes and task schedules intended to hold each student accountable, but they also included audience, purpose, and genre analyses through the creation of user profiles, storyboards, paper prototypes, and report videos (see Figures 15, 16, and 17). In other words, students were practicing digital design through multiple modes, and because they were submitting work in groups rather than individually, virtually every concept was discussed at length during team conferences. Attention was drawn to revision opportunities for group documents, which were shared in folders through Google Drive. Notions of audience were expanded to include considerations of how to grant and/or limit access based on what they knew about those audiences. Barriers and frustrations to the overall purpose of their text were identified--things like distracting color schemes, confusing organization, and unclear navigation--and groups brainstormed appropriate ways to diminish or eliminate such barriers of purpose. And finally, students explored genre conventions in ways they had not before, which sparked rich discussions to connect those conventions to issues of access. For example, one team worked on a website that sells x-ray equipment. Their genre analysis pushed them past viewing the text as merely a website. Instead, they identified it as a digital storefront, leading them to consider the intersections between conventions of shopping and digital design. Overall, this emphasis on building explicit connections between the rhetorical situation and access encouraged students to expand their vocabulary, enriching both concepts.

The final project of the semester was an individual self-assessment report that can best be described as something between a reflective portfolio and an essay exam. Completed in three different stages across the semester, students considered what they learned or practiced and then curated samples and discussed their understanding of the ten key concepts the class had agreed were the most important. By this point, students were expected to demonstrate competence through both reflective writing and digital design, discussing and creating accessibility in what they produced.

Figure 14. Find a problem text assignment

Assignment

For this assignment, you will

1. Identify a digital text that commits at least six of the thirteen layout sins described in *White Space Is Not Your Enemy* chapter 4. You may choose any digital text. Feel free to have fun with this. A digital text is anything that conveys meaning through a screen, like a video, flyer, webpage, advertisement, menu, application, map ... anything!

Figure 15. Progress report 1 assignment

Create Progress Report 1: Audience Analysis

Purpose

The purpose of this assignment is to report on your team's work so far, and to demonstrate your understanding of the **audience** of your problem text.

Don't forget to update your Meeting Minutes!

What is a Progress Report?

From *Team Writing:*

> Usually an informal document that gives an instructor, supervisor, or client **information on the team's progress** on a project over a set period of time. This document is used primarily for projects that take at least three months to complete. (Wolfe, 2010, p. 24, emphasis added)

Consider that you have two audiences for this first Progress Report: the audience you are **writing to** and the audience you are **writing about.**

Format of a Progress Report

Your report should be **digital and multimodal**, should adhere to **best practices of digital design**, and should include the following:

- All team member's **names**
- A list of **tasks** the team has completed so far in the project, along with notes about which team member completed/contributed to each task
- A list of **issues** the team has worked through with details about how the team addressed each issue
- A **comprehensive audience analysis** of users of your problem text that should include the following:
  - **Research** into your audience -- a description of who they are and how you know this
  - User Profile of a hypothetical member of your audience
  - Discussion of **issues** the problem text poses for your audience
  - **Incorporate quotes** from the readings on audience and cite them properly using **APA format**

CONCLUSION

The extensive course redesigns described in the case studies above will likely be troublesome for some. There remains the lingering concern as to how much accommodation is necessary in light of faculty workloads. Furthermore, some faculty conflate student-centered design as capitulation or hand-holding, considering it to be a "watering down" of rigor. They believe that students must figure things out for themselves because struggle fosters learning, and the authors of this chapter agree with them to a certain extent. There is a fine line between providing accessible content that does not exclude students and expecting students to explore and learn for themselves. Perhaps one way to address this tension is to ask what students should figure out or struggle with? And is it fair to ask them to learn a new navigation system for every course they take or would their energies be better placed in grappling with course content?

In answering these questions about rigor and design, it is worth revisiting the definition of accessibility that frames this chapter and the ideas that inform it:

Accessibility refers to the ease of entry and use of a product, service, space, or text; and considers course design (navigation, layout, color scheme, font type, font emphasis), course tools (applications, discussion forums, quizzes) and course materials (instructional texts, resources, assignment descriptions, submission and evaluation guidelines).Thus, an accessible tech-mediated course is one that affords every learner

Figure 16. Progress report 2 assignment

Identifying a Purpose

When thinking about digital texts, the purpose is often layered. For example, if you're creating a **digital flyer for an event** that will be posted on a website and/or pushed out via email or social media, you have three different platforms to accommodate, and each platform will create a different interaction for users/readers.

The website version of the flyer might be a jpeg on a homepage with a hyperlink behind it that allows visitors access to a more accessible webpage with details about how to register for the event. **Its purpose is to serve as a gateway to registration.**

The emailed flyer might be an accessible pdf that includes hyperlinks within it so that users/readers can link to the website/wepbage and register for the event. **Its purpose is to entice readers to visit the website.**

The social media flyer might be a jpeg that includes a bitly or short url that can be pushed out to multiple platforms to raise the status of the event and make it more well-known. **Its purpose is to serve as a simple means of sharing/access/promotion for the event.**

So as you can see from this example, the flyer would likely have different versions that will be used differently by users on each platform.

The So What

To get at the purpose of your digital text and its redesign, you need to consider the multiple points of access and consider how different users might interact with it. The best way to do this is through **storyboards**.

Format of a Progress Report

Your report should be **digital and multimodal**, should adhere to **best practices of digital design**, and should include the following:

- All team member's names
- A list of tasks the team has completed so far in the project, along with details about which team members completed/contributed to each task
- A list of issues the team has worked through with details about how the team addressed each issue
- A **comprehensive purpose analysis** for users of your problem text that should include the following:
  - **Create two storyboards** that consider how different users might interact with the original version of your digital text. One user should be based on the user profile you created for Progress Report 1. The point is to help you clarify to stakeholders what problems users might encounter with the original version. Think of this as another tool to help you argue that the text needs to be revised. (See chapter 11 of WSINYE for guidance to creating Storyboards)
  - **Discussion** of the layered purpose of the problem text as you see it now
  - **Discussion** of how the problems with the text hinder its purpose

the opportunity to succeed, regardless of technological skill, reading level, native language, learning preference, or physical impairment.

Consider the issues displaced by this mindset to course design. First and foremost, it places responsibility for teaching digital reading and writing skills squarely onto instructors. It is not acceptable to continue to blame students for not reading dense assignments closely or for failing to transfer writing skills from high school. Instead, instructors should provide both explicit instruction and good modeling to offset gaps in students' digital literacy skills. Second, this new lens on accessible course design resituates students as *users* with varied learning preferences and technological skills. As such, when students cannot determine how to locate an assignment description or where to submit it, the error is not with them; the error is in the design. Finally, this new definition of accessibility clarifies the difference between capitulation and accommodation since it does not call for easier assignments. Instead, it insists on clarity, flexible access, and overall support for diverse learners.

The quickest way to undermine accessibility is to design a course without attention toward it or to assume that students have the same preferences as the instructor-designer. No matter the genre or platform,

Figure 17. Progress report 3 assignment

Create Progress Report 3: Genre Analysis

Purpose

The purpose of this assignment is to report on your team's work so far, and to demonstrate your understanding of the **genre** of your problem text.

Format of a Progress Report

Your report should be **digital and multimodal**, should adhere to **best practices of digital design**, and should include the following:

- All team member's names
- A list of tasks the team has completed since the last progress report, along with details about which team members completed/contributed to each task
- A list of issues the team has worked through with details about how the team addressed each issue
- A **comprehensive genre analysis** for your problem text that should include the following:
    - **An overview** of the conventions of the genre based on what you've read in WSINYE
        - NOTE: Conventions are rules and expectations for a given genre. For example, website users expect a homepage with links to other pages. Menu users expect prices next to entree options.
        - For this part of the analysis, identify which chapters, concepts, or elements in WSINYE are most important for the genre of your text.
    - **Discussion** of how the problem text fails to adhere to the conventions of the genre and the implications of those failures
    - **Incorporate quotes** from WSINYE and the readings on genre and cite them properly using **APA format**

all materials in a technology mediated course can model digital design that is accessible and effective. To reiterate access is about more than screen readers and transcripts. Content must also be designed for English language learners, those with limited technological literacy, and those for whom digital realms create barriers. It is important to think beyond personal preferences as digital readers. Instructors must think broadly about the various sponsors, histories, and experiences that have shaped the way students read. Furthermore, instructors should assume responsibility for and work toward offsetting the gaps in students' ability to engage with digital course materials rather than blaming students when they fail to do so. Despite the moniker "digital natives," in many ways, students lag behind their teacher-designers in higher education, having not been granted access to digital reading and writing through intentional instruction. In fact, it is worth taking time as teacher-scholars to reflect on the learning preferences that helped them shift from print to digital, share these preferences with students, and explain why these processes work with explicit examples. Then invite students to explore their own learning inclinations, connecting to examples of why these work for them. More often than not, these preferences and experiences are highly diverse, which ultimately means that instructors must move beyond defaulting to what works for them and personal preferences purely based on years of experience in the classroom.

This chapter has devoted much attention to the "so what?" of complicating accessibility in the tech-mediated classroom, but perhaps the more important question is "now what?" What suggestions can be offered for those who want to begin this sometimes-overwhelming work? The answer, unfortunately, cannot be packaged into a one-size-fits-all response. Because students and instructors have such varied skills, considering multiple points of access and options is key, and these points may look quite different depending on the values of the instructor, institution, and/or discipline. Furthermore, research in this area is just emerging and is ripe for more scholars to explore. To begin, instructors should seek out and join networks already in place, including professional organizations like the Global Society for Online Literacy Educators (glosole.org) and the Online Writing Instruction Community (owicommunity.org). These spaces are welcoming and invite colleagues, no matter where they are or how much knowledge they have, to brainstorm and collaborate in (re)designing courses that are more accessible and effective.

This call for modeling accessible design through course materials cannot be overstated. The only thing the authors can say with confidence is that students in their courses come away with more awareness of the terms access and accessibility, but there remains a disconnect between knowing the vocabulary and putting the concepts into practice. As writing and rhetoric instructors, the authors are keenly aware of how models shape developing writers, but limiting models to submission samples misses an opportunity. Modeling in course materials the kind of composing expected in student submissions makes assignments more accessible and also more fully immerses learners in practicing digital reading and writing.

Above all else, the work, modeling, and practice of accessibility is ongoing, and much like composing processes, this journey is rarely linear. Even as accessibility scholars, the authors are still grappling with finding a balance between theory and practical application in a way that makes the most sense given student need and faculty expectation. In closing, the authors invite all instructors alike to review their own courses and ask "now what?" in terms of the accessibility and practice they are imparting upon their students.

REFERENCES

Baron, N. S. (2017). Reading in a digital age. *Phi Delta Kappan*, *99*(2), 15–20. doi:10.1177/0031721717734184

Boyle, C., & Rivers, N. A. (2016). A version of access. *Technical Communication Quarterly*, *25*(1), 29–47. doi:10.1080/10572252.2016.1113702

Center for Universal Design (CUD). (2008). *North Carolina State University*. Retrieved from https://projects.ncsu.edu/design/cud/index.htm

Centre for Excellence in Universal Design (CEUD). (2014). *How to make accessible documents*. Retrieved from http://universaldesign.ie/Products-Services/Customer-Communications-Toolkit-for-the-Public-Service-A-Universal-Design-Approach/Digital-and-Web-Based-Communication-Systems-and-Services/How-to-make-accessible-documents/

Conference College Composition and Communication (CCCC). (2011). *A Policy on Disability in CCCC*. Retrieved from http://cccc.ncte.org/cccc/resources/positions/disabilitypolicy

Conference on College Composition and Communication (CCCC). (2013). *A position statement of principles and example effective practices for online writing instruction (OWI)*. Retrieved from http://cccc.ncte.org/cccc/resources/positions/owiprinciples

Foley, A., & Ferri, B. A. (2012). Technology for people, not disabilities: ensuring access and inclusion. *Journal of Research in Special Educational Needs, 12*(4), 192-200. Retrieved from https://onlinelibrary-wiley-com.librarylink.uncc.edu/doi/pdf/10.1111/j.1471-3802

Global Society of Online Literacy Educators (GSOLE). (2016). *Mission statement*. GSOLE.

Hewett, B. L. (2015). *Reading to learn and writing to teach: Literacy strategies for online writing instruction*. Bedford, MA: St. Martin's.

HewettB. L.DePewK. E. (Eds.). (2015). Foundational practices of online writing instruction. Retrieved from https://wac.colostate.edu/books/perspectives/owi/

Hitt, A. (2018). Foregrounding accessibility through (inclusive) universal design in professional communication curricula. *Business and Professional Communication Quarterly*, *81*(1), 52–65. doi:10.1177/2329490617739884

Miller, R. E. (2015). On digital reading. *Pedagogy*, *16*(1), 153–164. doi:10.1215/15314200-3158717

Moore, J. L., & Bass, R. (Eds.). (2017). *Understanding writing transfer: Implications for transformative student learning in higher education*. Sterling, VA: Stylus Publishing.

National Disability Authority (NDA). (2014). *The 7 principles*. Retrieved from http://universaldesign.ie/What-is-Universal-Design/The-7-Principles/

Norman, D. (2013). The design of everyday things (Revised & Expanded Ed.). New York: Basic Books.

Online Learning Consortium (OLC). (2016). *Report: One in four students enrolled in online courses*. Retrieved from https://onlinelearningconsortium.org/news_item/report-one-four-

Online Writing Instruction Community (OWI Community). (2015). *Our Mission*. Retrieved from http://www.owicommunity.org/

Organization Homepage. (n.d.). Retrieved from https://www.glosole.org/

Oswal, S. K. (2013). Exploring accessibility as a potential area of research for technical communication: A modest proposal. *Communication Design Quarterly Review*, *1*(4), 50–60. doi:10.1145/2524248.2524261

Oswal, S. K., & Meloncon, L. (2014). Paying attention to accessibility when designing online courses in technical and professional communication. *Journal of Business and Technical Communication*, *28*(3), 271–300. doi:10.1177/1050651914524780

Still, B., & Crane, K. (2017). *The fundamentals of user-centered design: A practical approach.* New York: Taylor & Francis Group. doi:10.4324/9781315200927

Teach Access. (2019). *About us.* Retrieved from http://teachaccess.org/about/

University of North Carolina at Charlotte. (2019, Spring). *LBST 2301: The rhetoric of digital design* [Course Syllabus]. Author.

Wolf, M. (2018). *Dear reader, come home: The reading brain in a digital world.* New York: HarperCollins.

KEY TERMS AND DEFINITIONS

Access: A way of entering or engaging with a physical location or space. For the purposes of the chapter, the primary definition is used as a way of engaging with course content and materials.

Accessibility: A way of designing physical/digital/virtual spaces, products, environments, and devices for stakeholders with various disabilities. This chapter complicates this notion by asking the readers to think beyond disability, and to also consider issues of socioeconomics, gender, race, and learning preference, all of which informs how users engage with content.

Course Design: This includes the overall technical structure of the course including syllabus, course expectations, grading, scheme, resources, and assignments that instructors use to develop the basic outline of a class.

Digital Design: The practice of developing digital compositions that may include text, hypertext, media, and various design elements to communicate meaning.

Online Writing Instruction (OWI): Acronym for online writing instruction, a branch of scholarship that seeks to raise awareness about teaching and learning in digital spaces, particularly through methods that are online or hybrid.

Rhetoric: The practice of generating and/or analyzing arguments that can be written, spoken, visually designed, or performed.

Universal Design (UD): A design approach that informs the creation of various environments, products, and/or communication. This method of design can be used in any type of an environment (physical, digital, or virtual), to ensure that the content, objects, or physical space is accessible to any person.

User-Centered Design (UCD): A design methodology that puts human needs, capabilities, and behavior first, then designs to accommodate those needs, capabilities, and ways of behaving.

ENDNOTES

1 Both instructor-designers have served as administrators of First-Year Writing and in the Writing Resources Center.

[2] This was an in-house training course developed by senior lecturers, Julie Cook and Cat Mahaffey, that focused on the delivery of online course content, quantifying instructional hours vs. outside student work, and ensuring accessibility of online course materials. Its purpose was to guarantee the quality of instruction was maintained as the courses moved from a primarily face to face to a 50/50 hybrid model.

[3] "Studio" is the term used at UNCC to refer to the one-hour online asynchronous lab that complements first-year writing courses.

Chapter 4
Participating on More Equal Terms?
Power, Gender, and Participation in a Virtual World Learning Scenario

Mats Deutschmann
Örebro University, Sweden

Anders Steinvall
https://orcid.org/0000-0001-6828-3009
Umeå University, Sweden

Airong Wang
Xi'an Jiaotong-Liverpool University, China

ABSTRACT

This chapter investigates the potential effects of unequal power relations on participation in a group of student teachers and invited professionals in two collaborative workshops in Second Life. The basic research enquiry addresses whether the relative anonymity afforded by virtual world environments has an effect on established power structures, thereby empowering relatively powerless language learners to more active participation than would be the case in more traditional learning set-ups. The data includes recordings, group reflections, and individual questionnaires. Participation was examined from the aspects of floor space, turn length, and utterance functions, and complemented with student reflections. The results show that the differences of floor space and turn length between the invited professionals and the students were small. The invited professionals did more conversational management than the students, while the students performed more supportive speech acts. No major gender differences in participation were found. There was, however, considerable individual variation.

DOI: 10.4018/978-1-5225-7987-8.ch004

INTRODUCTION

The pedagogical potential of virtual worlds for language learning was recognised early in the Computer Assisted Language Learning (CALL) community, and ever since the emergence of these environments in the mid-1990s, there has been a steady stream of studies investigating their potential as language learning environments (Wigham, Panichi, Nocchi & Sadler, 2018). Hew & Cheung's (2010) research review of studies up until 2008 points out that earlier studies were largely descriptive accounts of how environments had been used for learning, and also dealing with the affective domain: participants' likes and dislikes regarding platforms such as Active Worlds and Second Life, for example. Kim, Lee & Thomas' (2012) somewhat later review of 65 studies indicates that, while descriptive research still dominated, there was an increasing interest in experimental research, and also that the use of virtual worlds (VW) as communication spaces had increased drastically. According to Wigham et al. (2018), more recent VW CALL research has been empirical, focusing on the pursuit of finding pedagogic models for how the environments can be used successfully for language learning (see Blin, Nocchi & Fowley, 2013; Panichi & Deutschmann, 2012; Sadler, 2012; Wigham, 2012; Wigham & Chanier, 2013; Zheng & Newgarden, 2012; Panichi, 2014; Wang, 2017).

One feature highlighted as being of considerable significance in the pursuit of understanding and utilizing the full potential of VWs for language learning is that of interaction (Wigham et al., 2018). With reference to the current study, social interaction between the participants is of particular relevance. When studying interaction and participation in VWs, the complexity and the affordances of the environment, and how these in turn may affect participation, is of major interest (Boellstorff, 2015; Gregory, Lee, Dalgarno & Tynan, 2016). With this in mind, Lin, Wang, Grant, Chien & Lan (2014), call for further research into different teaching formats, and methods adapted specifically to VWs. Furthermore, according to Chen (2018, p. 964) a majority research into participation and interaction in VWs to date has been focused on text-based, rather than on voice-based task interaction, an area of research which therefore deserves more research attention according to Chen. The current study can thus be seen as an attempt to fill some of these gaps: we focus primarily on oral interaction between participants and try to evaluate how the learning environment (i.e. Second Life, hereafter SL) impacted the task design and our goals for the particular task at hand.

In spite of Chen's (2018) claims that most VWs studies looking at social interaction have focussed on text-based communication, there are some noteworthy exceptions. Aspects related to designing active and equal oral participation in Second Life language courses are the focus of two studies (Deutschmann, Panichi, & Molka-Danielsen 2009, and Deutschmann & Panichi, 2009b), which analyse variables such as floor space turn length and turn-taking patterns in oral tasks in order to identify how different oral task designs influence learners' participation. The teacher's role in encouraging active participation is also dealt with in Deutschmann & Panichi (2009). Here the authors are able to show how back-channeling and other ways of signaling active listening are important in this type of environment where facial expressions and body language are largely missing. Similar findings are confirmed in Wang (2017). With more specific focus on task design adapted to the affordances of Second Life, Jauregi & Canto (2012) show how a 'networking design' is used to bring native speakers and Dutch second language learners of Spanish together in meaningful interaction. Similarly, Chen (2018) is able to demonstrate how different networking task-designs trigger different types of language output in a mixed (ability and L1-background) group of English as a foreign language learners. Results indicated that more controlled so-called "jigsaw tasks" ("interactional tasks which require that each dyad member contributes equal pieces of information held by him/her in order to reach one single solution" (p. 964) prompted the most complex language output (negotiations and mixed strategy use), whereas freer opinion-exchange based tasks led to less complex interactions.

A key aspect of developing language skills is *usage*, and creating prerequisites for active conversations where learners develop their language skills is accordingly of special significance to task designers. VWs such as SL are open environments that have many tools that support social networking, aspects which make them perfect platforms for assembling participants in collaborative events. VWs thus answer to needs in communicative based language education, where intercultural experiences with more capable native or near native speakers are referred to as key factors of success (Guth & Helm, 2010). It is, however, not necessarily the case that pairing students with capable peers will give the desired result. Research shows that powerful individuals tend to take more space and control the conversation using discursive strategies such as controlling turn-taking, topic control and using elicitation strategies to maximize talking time (Abdullah & Hosseini, 2012). There is thus a risk that less capable students become intimidated by the situation. For example, Toyoda & Harrison (2002) report that native speakers could manipulate the chat communication in Active Worlds freely and elaborately, while the nonnative speakers' lower language proficiency often led to slow responses and confusions in communication.

In this study, we describe and analyse the outcomes of collaborative activities conducted in SL, where a class of student language teachers was joined by professionals working with online language teaching and/or research in order to discuss two pedagogic case studies. These professionals were recruited from all over Europe with the help of networks relating to SL and language learning. The basic research enquiry addresses the question of whether the relative anonymity afforded by virtual world environments has an effect on established power structures, and thereby empowers relatively powerless language learners to more active participation than would otherwise be the case in more traditional learning set-ups. The focus of our study is on quantitative and qualitative aspects of the participation in the activities, and how these can be related to the various power structures within the groups. As the goal of any activity of this sort is to give students an opportunity to learn as much as possible, participatory patterns, and how the environment may affect these, are of special interest.

BACKGROUND

Language Learning, Networking, and Social Software

The affordance of online communication in bringing intercultural learners together to create communities of practice and critical inquiry is particularly valuable in collaborative online language learning (Warschauer, 1997, p. 477). For this purpose, educators are increasingly integrating social software such as blogs, Skype, YouTube, Facebook, Twitter and SL in CALL. The open architectures of such social media support collective online activities, one of the main advantages being that the social networks of the students and the teachers can be integrated into the learning context thus adding to the authenticity of the scenario and increasing engagement (Bowers, Ragas, & Neely, 2009, p. 41; Otto & Pusack, 2009, p. 794). In the context of this study, our ambition was to integrate language teacher students in existing professional networks, a practice which will be discussed further below.

SL as a Learning Space

A recent development in online language learning involves the simulation of real world learning in three-dimensional virtual environments (3D VEs), where one of the most popular sites is SL (Warschauer & Liaw 2010, p. 13). Czepielewski (2012, p. 16) classifies SL as a *Serious Virtual World*, which though initially made for entertainment, cannot be seen as a game. It is rather an open virtual world, where each of the participants can realize his or her own objectives, which may be connected with social life, entertainment business or, indeed, language education. Designed as a place for socialisation, users can communicate in the target language synchronously using voice, chat and instant messaging, asynchronously using the group and private message function as well as note cards and even perform limited human gestures. SL also allows users to create objects and environments, which others can interact with. The 'self' is represented by a so-called avatar, which usually has a human shape (but does not have to). As an open environment with users from all over the world, it has been widely adopted as a learning environment by different educational institutions in the domain of language education, where it provides a contextually relevant language learning space for learners to interact with native speakers of a target language (Wang, Song, Xia, & Yan, 2009, p. 1). In all, SL affords group-based, project-based and student-centred teaching and learning where multiple avatars can engage in an activity simultaneously (Good, Howland, & Thackray, 2008, p. 164).

One of the main advantages of using SL in education, however, is the extensive community of educators that operates within its domains. Panichi (2012) lists a number of educational institutions and projects that operate within SL, and many of these educators are organised in more conventional asynchronous social network sites on the Internet (see also Wigham et al. 2018). In the domain of language learning, there are several forums and online networks such as the SLED List (SL Educators n.d.), the Avalon NING (2012), the Euroversity NING (2012), and the Eurocall/Calico Virtual World SIG NING (2012), where educators can exchange experiences and ideas and connect with others interested in this type of learning design. It is often in such forums that educators find partners for collaborative projects as the one described below, and indeed where we found volunteers in the form of experienced online educators to interact with our teacher trainee students.

However, SL is by no means an easy environment to master and strong technical skills and confidence with the platform are required for teachers and students to take full advantage of its learning potential (Longo, 2012). For this reason, many course designers point to the necessity of technical readiness in SL learning events. Proposed models include so-called technical initiations, where participants are required to attend pre-course session(s) in order to acquaint themselves with the program (Jarmon, Traphagan, Mayrath, & Trivedi, 2009; Mayrath, Traphagan, Heikes, & Trivedi, 2009; Wang, Song, Stone, & Yan, 2009; Blasing, 2010; Molka-Danielsen, Panichi, & Deutschmann, 2010).

The literature on virtual environments for educational purposes has explored some of the potentially important factors affecting participation. These include learner attitudes towards the environment, where some students may find the environment too game-like and inappropriate for serious learning events (Deutschmann & Panichi, 2009a, p. 33). Gender is another variable that has been contemplated as important, but little has been written about how gender may affect language learners' participation or other gender issues in SL (Inman, Wright, & Hartman, 2010, p. 54). Finally, many researchers have pointed to the advantages of computer mediated communication (CMC) in general, and VWs specifically, in reducing so-called Foreign language anxiety (FLA). Gamage, Tretiakov, & Crump (2011), for example, postulate that shy students participate more actively in VWs due to a sense of safety intermediated by the relative anonymity of the avatars. Similarly, Hammick and Lee claim that CMC provides a "sheltering effect" that reduces FLA (2014, p. 303). More systematic studies into FLA and VWs environments do indeed indicate that anxiety is reduced when learners can hide behind avatars (see Reinders & Wattana, 2015; Wehner, Gump & Downey, 2011; Melchor-Couto, 2017; 2018). However, as Melchor-Couto points out other aspects such as lack of facial expressions and lip movements, as well as lack of other non-verbal cues that come into play in VW interaction that may cancel out the presumed positive effects of anonymity (2018, p. 235).

Power in Conversations

The fact that the relational power of participants is an important aspect in conversations came to the fore through the study of gender and conversation. Early research applying a dominance framework (such as O'Barr & Atkins, 1980; West & Zimmerman, 1983) gave a fairly straightforward picture of how power relations and gender combine and affect conversations and the use of language pragmatic features related to conversational control. Later research, adopting a difference approach, identified the application of two conversational styles, collaborative and competitive, correlating with the genders female and male, respectively (see, for example Coates, 2004), as explanation to the imbalance in conversations. Women's collaborative style is supportive, whereas men's competitive style is more adversarial, leading to clashes in mixed-sex interactions and male domination.

Although these observations still hold to a certain degree, the appearance of new theoretical positions, for example a social constructivist perspective of gender as performance and construction, (e.g. Crawford, 1995; Holmes, 2006), and more detailed studies of specific contexts, e.g. workplace management (Ladegaard 2010; Holmes, 2006; Holmes and Schnurr, 2006), have indicated that the picture is quite complex. Holmes (2006, p. 6) points out that the stereotypical characterizations of the difference approach do not take the full complexity of sources of diversity and variation, such as context and power distributions, into account. Explanatory variables for a certain discursive behaviour (power, for example), thereby risk being blurred by gender factors simply because they happen to correlate. For example, Ladegaard (2010), was able to show that both male and female leaders tended to prefer "normatively feminine management styles" (indirect and mitigated directives, interrogatives and modal verbs, for instance). In another study, Hancock & Rubin (2015), were able to show that there were no overall gender differences in the use of such 'gendered' linguistic variables as fillers, hedges, interruptions, and tag-questions among their 40 test subjects.

Research has addressed whether gendered styles would be visible in and affect the climate in online discussions. Herring (2010) could find an effect of gendered styles in a study of floor patterns in asynchronous textual CMC (mailing lists). She concludes that professional recognition and male gender are key factors for gaining the floor in her corpus. Similarly, in a study of synchronous online group-discussion in chats among physics students, Sullivan, Kapur, Madden & Shipe (2015) found that the conversational styles in these chats followed the expected gendered lines. However, they could also identify male use of the stereotypically 'feminine' discourse style and female use of the stereotypically 'masculine' discourse style. More importantly, a careful analysis of contribution showed that, on average, females in male-dominated chats contributed slightly more amount of ideas than could be expected. In contrast, Lin, Dowell, Godfrey, Choi, & Brooks (2019) analysing online synchronous collaboration found no significant differences between men and women in terms of the degree of participation. Their results, however, indicate that women's communication is more likely to be effective and cohesive.

Conversations in some institutions tend to follow particular patterns. Have (1991) observed that certain asymmetries stem from institutional expectations. Although intimately linked to power, institutional conventions greatly dictate roles in most conventional learning contexts making them largely ready-made and expected. For example, Schleef (2008) found that instructors in academia, regardless of gender, tend to use the same speech style and only very seldom draw on wider identity resources. To what extent roles are re-negotiated in a different arena such as SL, and whether an informal role, such as 'expert peer' rather than teacher, affects the power situation has not been addressed previously.

Language proficiency is another variable that will affect the power relation in a conversation. This is especially true in a language learning context and Brislin (1981), for example, lists "language skills" as one of the key skills for opening for a learner's success in a cross-cultural conversation. As pointed out earlier (see Hammick & Lee, 2014, for example) more recent research, however, has shown that language learners tend to feel more comfortable in conversations and less concerned about language deficiencies when communicating online (see also Freiermuth, 2001). In this particular study, we deem language proficiency to be of lesser importance in creating potential power imbalances in the conversations since almost all participants, including the invited educators, could be classified as proficient non-native speakers of English.

Finally, we deem knowledge of the subject matter to be of relevance in deciding the power structures in the present context. This variable occurs in Brislin's (1981) aforementioned list of factors necessary for successful cross-cultural conversations and several studies have shown that non-native speakers communicating with native speakers will dominate conversational contexts where they are perceived as 'experts' in spite of their language difficulties (see Woken & Swales, 1989 and Zuengler, 1989, for example).

Aims

In the task design described below we introduced student teachers to outsiders, professional educators involved in online teaching and/or research, who were relatively more experienced and arguably more knowledgeable in the subject area being studied, namely participation in face-to-face and online educational contexts and pedagogic design to based on the ideas of collaboration and active participation. Given the potentially unequal power relations of the participants in this network design, the aim of this study is to investigate how the different power relations in the discussion groups may have affected participation both in terms of quality and quantity. Here the roles students vs. the invited online educators (so-called 'expert peers' in the context of the project) are of particular interest but we have also included a gender dimension. More specifically, we want to investigate participation in terms of floor space (i.e. the amount of time which different participants contribute to the conversation) and turn length, and examine what roles different individuals play in the conversations in terms of contributing to the task, managing the task at hand and being a supportive peer. In short, we want to find out who controls and 'owns the floor'. A final point of investigation is whether the VW environment had any effect on aspects related to power and participation.

METHOD

Participants and Course Context

The activities described in this article were part of a more extensive project carried out at Umeå University, Sweden, where SL was used in an attempt to explore gender and identity through experiments using gender and voice morphing and discussions with outside agents (for further information see Deutschmann, Steinvall, & Lagerström, 2011). In this chapter, we focus on a group of upper secondary student teachers attending a course on the theme of gender, sociolinguistics and second language education. During the course, two workshops were organised in SL under the project framework, where the purpose was to show how these tools could give access to international networks and contacts for second-language education. Another aim was to introduce the students to the use of Web 2.0 tools in language education and to let them experience the potential challenges and merits of this type of design first-hand.

Before describing the participants and specifics of the course, it is important to clarify the status of English in Swedish higher education, which more or less is that of a second official language. Much of the course literature in most university programs is in English and it is taken for granted that students are reasonably proficient in the language. In programs such as the one our students are partaking, the focus is thus mainly on theoretical content, but given the students' future roles as language teachers, an added ambition is to give students further opportunities to improve their English skills.

Given our course aims, we invited educators working with online language learning to join groups of three-four students as discussion partners in two problem-based case discussions on the subjects of classroom participation and online learning. In the course context, perhaps somewhat misleadingly, we chose to call these invited educators 'expert peers' in order to tone down their status. In the call for volunteers, it was made clear that an 'expert peer' merely had the role of a conversational partner rather than a teacher, coordinator, or facilitator and as such had no explicit responsibilities for the dynamics or outcomes of the discussions.

The 'expert peers' were recruited by sending calls for volunteers to various existing network sites in the domain of SL and language learning including the SLED List (SL Educators n.d.), the Avalon NING (2012), the Euroversity NING (2012), and the Eurocall/Calico Virtual World SIG NING (2012). All in all we recruited 11 volunteers of whom two were males and nine females. Their average age was 40, ranging between 28-54. All of the recruited volunteers were active language postgraduate students, researchers and/or language teachers from various educational institutions throughout Europe including France, Poland, Italy, Spain, Germany, England, Holland, Turkey, Sweden and Finland. Two of these were native English speakers and the rest were deemed to be highly proficient in English.

Participating on the course were 32 third-term students of English within the aforementioned program, English being their first university subject. Of the 32 students, 21 were females and 11 were males. The average age of the students was 24 years with almost all ranging between 20-27 years. There was only one older mature student (a female of 56 years). Their level of proficiency can be described as near fluent.

The invited professionals and the students participated two workshops. Workshop 1 was designed to let students reflect over individual and gender patterns of participation, and also the importance of the quality of attention a pupil gets. To this purpose, the students were given seven statements regarding gender and education from their course literature and were asked to discuss those in relation to participation data from 14 individual pupils in a fictitious second language classroom (very much inspired by Sunderland, 1998, 2000, 2004; the second of which the students later read). The invited professionals were asked to participate in the discussion, in their capacity of experienced teachers with insights from other environments.

The main task of Workshop 2 was to create a lesson or part of a lesson for a group of secondary school pupils in which the use of Computer Mediated Communication was to maximise the activity of the pupils. The participants were encouraged to design the lesson in order to address potential problems of inequality. Here we encouraged students to draw on their own previous experiences (from school, for example) and use the expertise of the invited professionals in order to optimise the design of their fictitious lesson. The invited professionals, on the other hand, had been informed about the tasks and were encouraged to help the students in drawing on their experience and using their expertise.

Collection of Data

The students were organised in groups of 3-4 individuals for the workshops and each group was joined by one so-called 'expert peer'. We had set up sound isolated collaborative spaces in SL where the avatars could sit and the groups could discuss the tasks at hand without disturbances from the other conversations going. The results and reflections on the discussions were later to be presented in a wiki site (*PBworks*) and in a final reflection paper. The two workshops were video recorded using the screen-recording software *Camtasia*. Both students and the invited participants were informed that the group discussions would be recorded and gave informed consent to this. The complete recorded material exceeded 20 hours, but given the practical limitations of a study of this kind, only a selection of this material was transcribed.

Also worth noting here is that participants were instructed to interact using voice primarily. We encouraged participants to limit their text chat conversations to technical issues, as we had two technical facilitators present who were instructed to deal with any technical problems using the chat mode (so as not to interrupt on-going conversations). There was, however, some conversation that went on using the text chat, and the overall distributions are summarised in the results below. Apart from solving technical issues, these contributions mainly consisted of greetings and goodbyes and we have thus not analysed this data qualitatively. Also note that since the students were relatively inexperienced using SL they did not use the 'gestures' tools and our main focus was thus limited to oral communication.

After each workshop, each group presented their group work and group reflections in the wiki. In addition, in order to get a fuller understanding of the students' perspectives, we asked them to fill in individual anonymous questionnaires at the end of the project in which they could react to what had happened in the workshops, and give their personal reflections without being influenced by the group or feel that they may be negatively judged by the teacher. The data from questionnaires plus the group pages from wiki were used as the qualitative part of the results in this study to complement the quantitative data with respect to factors that may have affected participation.

Analysis and Framework

For this analysis, we have limited ourselves to one discussion task only from each workshop. We decided to choose an entire task rather than a random span of time since the former would give a better insight into the group dynamics of how a group tackled the tasks from beginning to end. The discussions generated from the chosen tasks were transcribed, noting the identity and role of the interlocutor, the time of the turn (accurate to the second), utterance content, and utterance function in relation to how it functioned in the conversation.

For this last part, we identified three general pragmatic functions according to which most utterances could be classified: *support*, *management* and *content contribution*. Those that did not fall into these categories were classified in an "other" category. It is important to note that the turns were broken down into these functions, and that it is the time devoted to a particular function which is the main unit for the quantitative analysis. Such a procedure made it possible to relate functions to percentage of floor space and to avoid combined categories as longer turns could contain more than one function. The three categories that we focus on here are related to the macro-discourse marker categories (Starter, Elicitation, Accept, Attitudinal, Meta-statement and Conclusion) discussed by Bellés-Fortuño (2006), but we are considering the function of utterances, and not individual markers. Below a few instances of these categories are presented for illustration. Note here that the letter F represents female students, M, male students and E, 'expert peers'.

Example 1: Support

E4: Yes, yes, we can. (*support,* agreement)
M2: That is a really good question. (*support,* compliment)

As these two examples show, *support* is often given the form of agreements and compliments, thus typically containing an attitudinal discourse marker and markers of acceptance. Acknowledging what is being said through back-channelling is also included in this category.

Example 2: Management

F8: Should we move on to the third one? (*management,* elicitation)
E1: Let's move to statement three then. [To conclude] Women teachers are far more successful than men at giving girls fair share of their attention. (*management*, directions and conclusion)

Management often includes starting the task, suggesting topics for discussion, directing questions to others in order to elicit responses, closing topics, meta-statements, summaries and conclusions.

Example 3: Content Contribution

E1: if someone is raising their hands, and she directs the question to that person, [...] it is quite likely that the most active people, the people who raise their hands most, will get the most questions. (*Content contribution*)
F11: [speaking about a pupil in the case data from, Workshop 1] she almost didn't speak at all. But when she came online, she spoke the most. (*Content contribution*)

As the term *content contribution* suggests the function of such utterances is primarily to add factual substance to the conversation.

We have also included the students' reflections in the analysis, in order to shed more light on how they experienced the conversations, and their roles and we have tried to triangulate these reflections with the observed participation.

RESULTS

Floor Space and Participation

In this first section, we examine the overall tendencies related to floor space that we found in our material. The initial data is based on recordings of discussions of tasks from both workshops, 16 recordings in all. All in all the material constitutes 2 hours and 23 minutes of 'talk time' and the average 'talk time' of each recordings is about 9 minutes, but the lengths vary. Typically, the discussion groups were made up of four individuals: one expert peer (typically female), two female students and one male student, but there is some variation. All in all 43 individuals are represented in the data (32 students and 11 'expert peers').

The average floor space occupied by the different groupings was relatively equal (see Figure 1 below). The 'expert peers' occupied 2.25 minutes per session on average, closely followed by the female students (2.16 minutes) and the male students (2 minutes). It was encouraging to see that the students were not intimidated by the presence of the 'expert peers' and spoke almost as much as these on average. As we shall see in the next section, however, there was great individual variation.

We also examined the average turn length produced by the different groups. Longer turns are often associated with academic discourse of this nature where facts, figures and concepts are discussed, while more everyday conversation is typified by shorter turns (see *elaborated* and *restricted code* – Bernstein, 1971, for example). The turn length thus gives a rough indication of the type of input that was made. The average turn length produced by the 'expert peers' was slightly longer than that of the student groups. There was no difference between the turn length produced by male and female students (see Figure 2 below, turn length in seconds).

The text chat data for all the recorded material (20 hours) consisted of 2841 words in all, of which 1325 words (47%) were produced by the expert peers and 1516 words (53%) were produced by the students. The average number of words produced in text chat by each expert peer was 74 words and for the students the equivalent figure was 24 words. Note, however, that there was great individual variation here, with a few individuals who had technical problems or who were involved in solving these (mainly

Figure 1. Average floor space – all sessions, in minutes and seconds

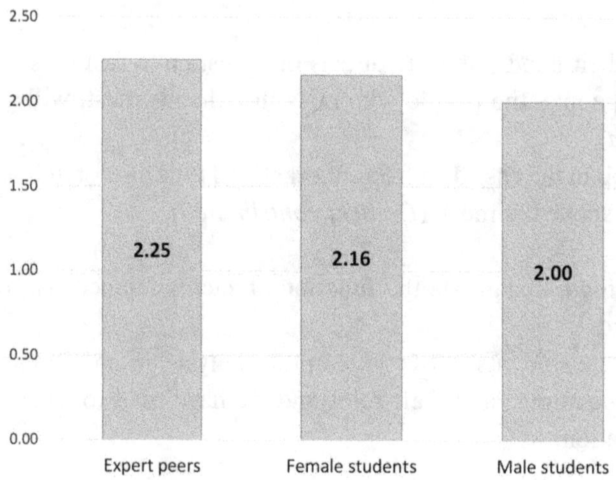

Figure 2. Average turn length – all sessions, in seconds

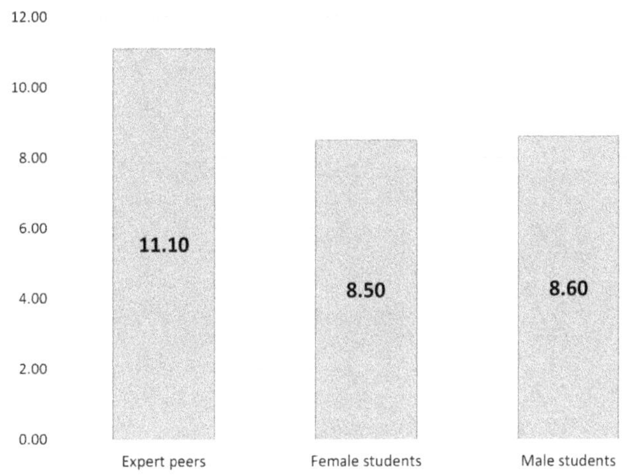

expert peers) producing the bulk of the text chat. Since the text chat was mainly used for solving technical issues, it will not be analysed further.

Examining Participation

In this section, we examine the conversational dynamics of the different discussion groups by analyzing the quantity and types of contributions different participants make. Since we want to compare individual performances in both workshops, we have only included recordings of groups that were of similar make-up in both sessions. This means that the data that forms the basis for this section is limited to 10 recordings.

Overall Findings

The analysed data represents spoken material from 22 individuals: six 'expert peers' (all females), and 16 students (11 females and 5 males). The total 'talk time' is 1 hour and 40 minutes and the average 'talk time' of each recording being approximately 10 minutes. The average floor spaces occupied by the different groups were: 'expert peers' 2.38 minutes, female students 2.33 minutes and male students 1.54 minutes. The average turn lengths for the 'expert peers' were 10.4 seconds, female students 6.9 seconds and male students 8.1 seconds. The data, thus, approximately mirrors the overall patterns found in the total recorded material.

The 'expert peers' occupied a slightly larger proportion of the floor space than the students, especially in Workshop 1. The male students were also the ones who were the least active, especially in Workshop 2 (see Figure 3 below).

We also looked at the functions of the utterances made in the conversations. The different speech functions of interest here are 'content contributions', 'conversation management' and 'supportive speech acts'. The category 'other' primarily constitutes utterances that could not be classified due to the quality of the recordings. The proportions of these speech functions for the groups 'female students', 'male students' and 'expert peers' in the two workshops are summarised in Figures 4 to 6 below.

Figure 3. Average proportion of floor space occupied by the different groups
**Note that the percentages above do not add up to 100 since there were generally two female students present in each group.*

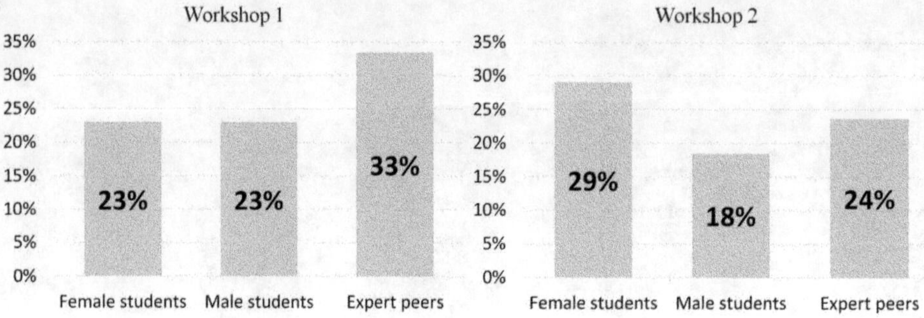

Figure 4. Proportion of speech functions, female students

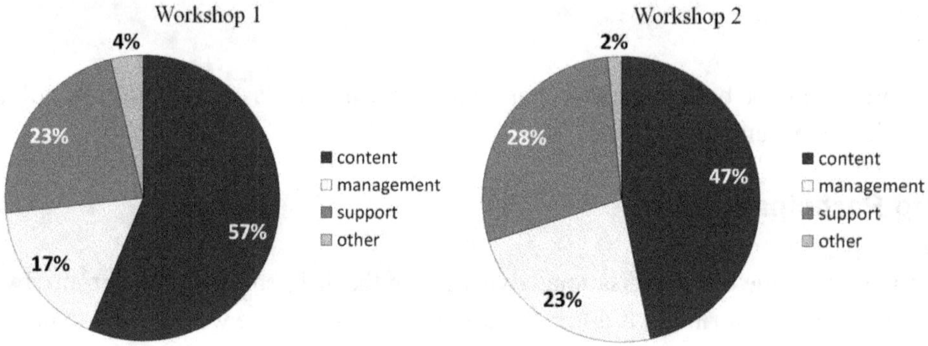

Figure 5. Proportion of speech functions, male students

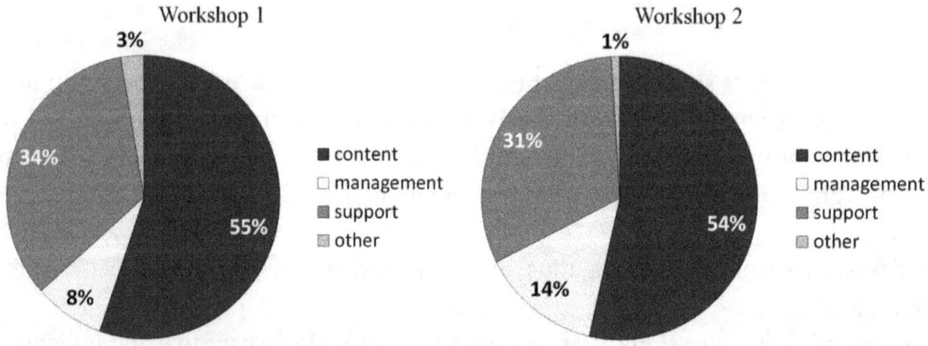

In the material, we find the following general tendencies: There was a slight tendency for students to contribute to the task content more than the 'expert peers'. There was a marked tendency for the 'expert peers' to do more conversational management than the students. On average, the female students also did more conversational management than the male students. Overall, the students performed more supportive speech acts, such as back-channelling and other conversational strategies that indicated active listening, than the 'expert peers'. Contrary to our expectations based on previous research in the field, which indicate that female speakers are more likely to signal active listening through supportive strate-

Figure 6. Proportion of speech functions, expert peers.

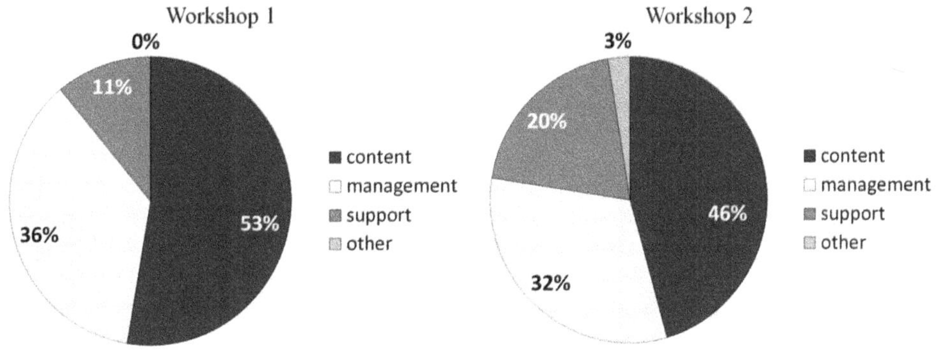

gies (see Coates, 2004, for example), we found that the male students were particularly active in this respect. Arguably, there were thus some indications (less floor time and more supportive speech acts) that the male students were in a relatively powerless position overall. This could be explained by the fact that they were typically in a 3:1 (female: male) minority in most groups. On the other hand, given the small size of the sample, it could just be individual variation.

Specific Findings From the Workshops

We now turn our attention to a more specific analysis of the individual recordings. The performances of each individual participant in the two workshops are summarised below in Figures 7–11. The data is represented as percentages of the total floor space in each recording so that the individual performances of different sessions can be compared. In each figure we have also included information of the total 'talk time' of each recording, each individual's average turn length, and the percentage of the total floor space taken up by each participant. Note that while the identities of the students are identical in the two workshops (with the exception of F3 who was absent in Workshop 2), some of the 'expert peers' differ.

The results in Figures 7–11 show that the general overall tendencies described above contain great individual variation. For example, there was great variation in the floor space occupied by different individuals. Although the 'expert peers' tended to be among the more active participants in most of the workshops, E4 and E6 were relatively passive in Workshop 2. In many cases, however, individuals tended to show similar behaviours in both workshops. Thus, on the basis of this data F6, F7, M1, M2 and E6 can be described as relatively inactive participants, while F1, F4, F5, F8, F10, M3, M5, E1, E2, E3 and E5 were more active. Others, such as F2, F9, F11, M4, and E4, display varied behaviour, being active in one workshop but less so in the other. One clear tendency that can be seen in almost all the individual data, however, was that active individuals tended to have longer turns on average.

There was also great individual variation as regards the use of speech functions, and from the data above it is clear that individuals had different roles in the conversations, roles that could vary between the two workshops. While most individuals contributed to the task content, some, such as M2 and E3 in Workshop 1, for example, hardly did so at all. While most males tended to do little conversational management, M5 was the most active participant in this respect in both workshops. He was, however, the least active student in displaying support. Some participants, such as F1, F4, contributed relatively little to the actual task content in Workshop 2, but instead spent more time managing the conversation

Figure 7. Group 1: Summary of individual participation in Workshops 1 and 2

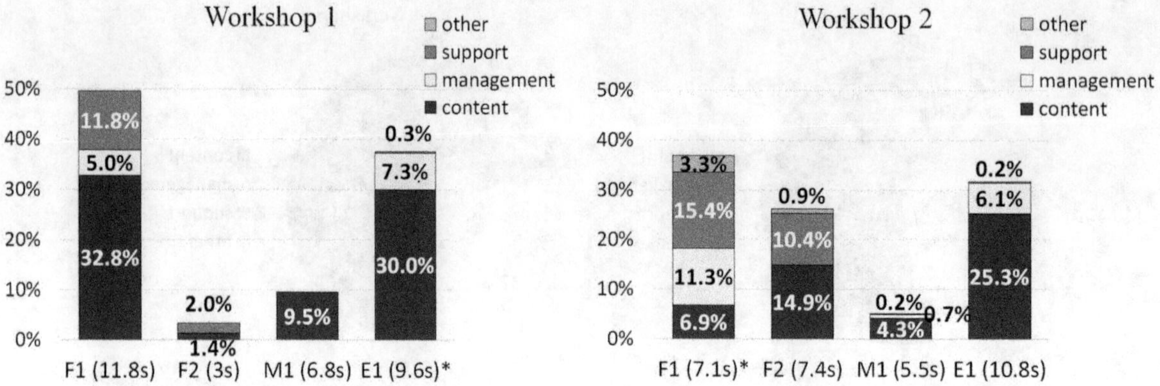

Total talk time = 5:57 min:
F1 (49.6%), F2 (3.4%), M1 (9.5%), E1 (37.5%)

Total talk time = 7:03 min:
F1 (36.9%), F2 (26.2%), M1 (5.2%), E1 (31.7%)

Figure 8. Group 2: Summary of individual participation in Workshops 1 and 2

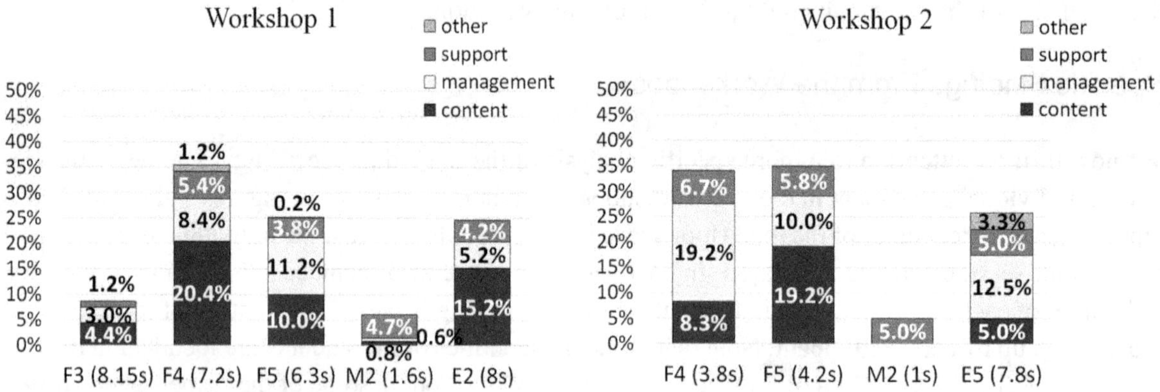

Total talk time = 22:06 min:
F3 (8.6%), F4 (35.4%), F5 (25.2%) M2 (6.1%), E2 (24.7%)

Total talk time = 2:00 min:
F4 (34.2%), F5 (35.0%) M2 (5.0%), E2 (25.8%)

and supporting the others, behaviours that had been less evident in Workshop 1. Other participants, such as F8 and E1, for example, were more focused on contributing to the task content, while M2's contributions almost entirely consisted of displaying support (agreeing with what was being said without coming with any opinions of his own).

Student Reflections

As pointed out in previous research, conversational behaviour cannot be explained by gender, power or relations alone (Kollock, Blumstein, & Schwartz, 1985, p. 44). In this section we employ qualitative data from group reflections and anonymous questionnaires in order to triangulate the quantitative results so as to shed more light on reasons for the observed behaviours.

Figure 9. Group 3: Summary of individual participation in Workshops 1 and 2

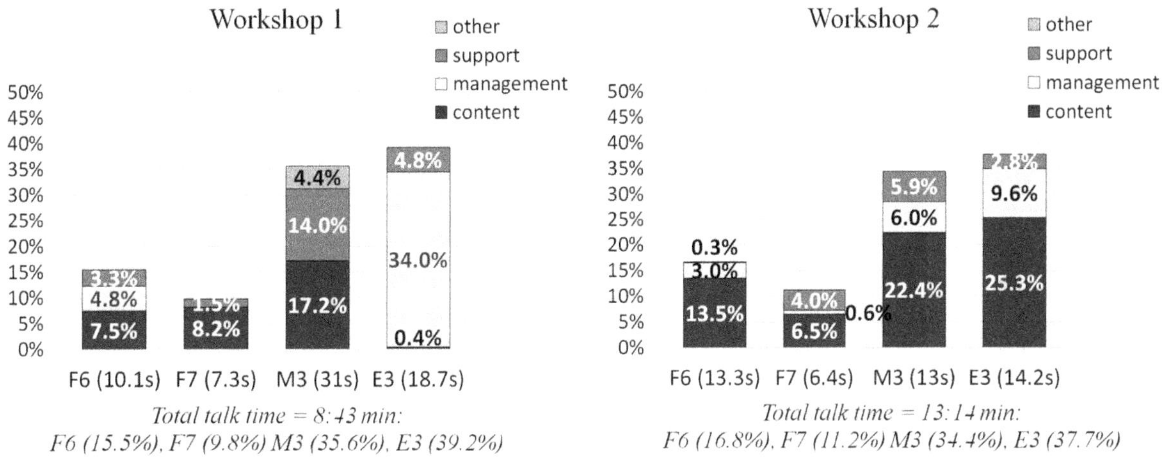

Figure 10. Group 4: Summary of individual participation in Workshops 1 and 2

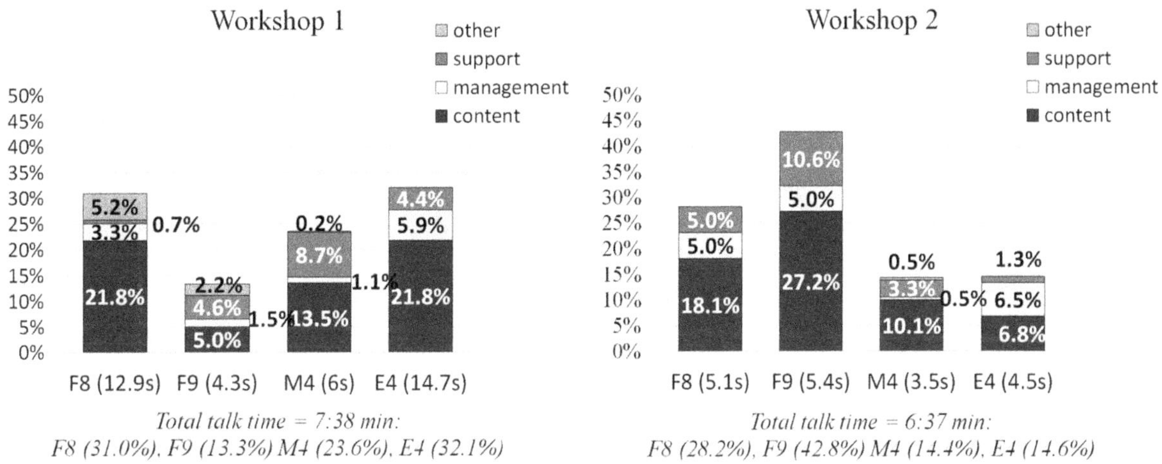

Overall Reflections

The data in this section was gathered from two sources: the group wikis and anonymous questionnaires. In the former, the students were asked to give general groups reflections on the tasks, and included in the directives students were specifically asked to reflect on the "role of the expert peer". Similarly, in the anonymous questionnaire the students were asked to give an open-ended personal reflection on the project, which could "include anything you think of. For example: [...] the expert peers etc."

The network design, i.e. using external invited professionals as conversational partners, was evaluated as useful and rewarding by nine groups out of ten who discussed this aspect in their group reflections. Similarly, 11 students (10 females and one male) of the 12 students who commented on this aspect in the anonymous personal reflections evaluated the design positively. Inferred from these evaluations, the invited professionals were appreciated since they facilitated group discussions and contributed with their

Figure 11. Group 5: Summary of individual participation in Workshops 1 and 2
**The numbers in brackets in the figures represent the average turn length for each individual.*

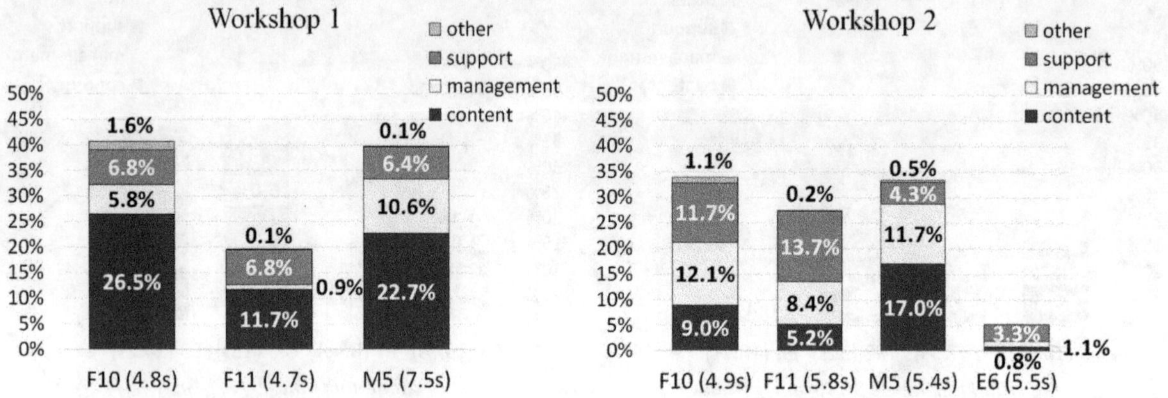

Total talk time = 15:55 min:
F10 (40.6%), F11 (19.6%), M5 (39.8%)

Total talk time = 10:34 min:
F10 (33.9%), F11 (27.4%), M5 (33.4%), E6 (5.2%)

superior knowledge and experiences, and helped with coordinating and supporting the discussions, as the following two quotes from the students' open reflections (answering the question "give your own reflections of the project") indicate:

1. We find that the presence of an expert peer is very useful, and can really help the discussion to move forward, and for the discussion to reach the desired goal. (group reflection)
2. He [the expert peer] was of great help and really facilitated the discussions, and came with good input. (individual reflection, male student)

This is consistent with the quantitative data result in Figure 6 that 'expert peers' spent much time to manage the conversations, but still paid much effort in contributing content and supporting discussions.

One positive finding was that the students contributed to the conversations almost as much as the invited professionals, which seems to suggest that they did not seem to be intimidated by the presence of the latter:

3. Our expert peer contributed with her experience and leadership qualities, and picked up the discussion whenever it was halted [...] and she did a good job not imposing her own opinions on us; on the contrary, she helped us voice our opinions and transfer them into ideas [...] (group reflection)
4. [...] we talked more at ease with our peer since we had no idea who she really was[...] (individual reflection, female student)

Interestingly, according to this female student teacher, the anonymity of the expert peer in their group was mentioned as a factor motivating participation. Other comments indicated that the presence of the invited professional was more problematic:

5. Using expert peers, while a good idea in theory, proved to be a rather unreliable method. (group reflection)

6. [...] our expert peer (though very nice and competent) hadn't really prepared for this. [...] But maybe there can be alternatives to expert peers. (individual reflection, female student)

Specific Reflections

In the results above, we looked at the individual conversational patterns in the different groups, and in this section, we attempt to triangulate the specific findings for groups 1, 2, 3, 4, 5 with the corresponding group reflections and individual comments in the questionnaire. Since the latter data was anonymous and most students did not mention the names of the 'expert peers', it is only when students did so that we can use the data here (limited to comments on E3 and E4).

Group 1

Group 1 only made one comment related to the presence of the expert peer:

7. Although we were technically anonymous to the expert peer, we did not feel like the pseudo-anonymity had much impact on our behavior. (group reflection, Group 1)

This, in contrast with the comment from the female student in (4), implies that the anonymity of invited professionals did not affect their participation (negatively or positively). The participatory patterns of this group were very uneven, with F2 and M1 being very inactive (especially in Workshop 1). From the group reflection we see that Group 1 was quite critical towards using SL as a collaborative tool because technological defects affected their participation negatively. For example, they criticised SL for its lack of visual cues:

8. In our opinion, using SL as a tool for collaborative work is problematic. First of all, there is the issue of not having any body language in the communication. This in turn leads to difficulties when it comes to turn-taking, resulting in interruptions and longer periods of silence where we felt that there was a great deal of uncertainty as to whether or not our messages had reached the other group members. (group reflection, Group 1)

In addition, they were frustrated by the voice quality at times. These negative attitudes towards the tools may explain the passive behaviour of two of its members.

Group 2

Group 2 had two different 'expert peers', E2 and E5, and although both were quite active, occupying approximately 25 per cent of the floor space, E2 did more content contributions while E5 did more conversational management. This data is mirrored in the group reflection:

9. [(E2)...] was very active in our discussions. [(E5)...] wanted us to come up with everything ourselves. [...] To work with expert peers was for us rewarding. They could give us helpful tips and ideas on how to work with virtual forums [sic. cf. online forums], something we know very little about. (group reflection, Group 2)

There are also some hints that the group thought that the presence of the expert peer helped to make the participation more equal:

10. The role of the expert peers as a moderator would be a suitable tool for making everybody talk and be listened to. (group reflection, Group 2)

It seems that for this group the expert peer(s) seems to have been important in coordinating and motivating participation. In spite of, this M2 was very inactive in both workshops.

Group 3

From the individual evaluations, there were indications that the anonymity of invited professionals had a motivating effect on participation, something which was supported by the reflections of this group:

11. However, we all agreed that the fact that we did not know our expert peer probably made us feel more comfortable talking about our personal feelings and experiences than if E3 would have been one of our teachers, or if we would have known her personally. (group reflection, Group 3)

One interesting finding from the data in 4.2 is that E3 spent much more time to manage the group discussion in Workshop 1 than in Workshop 2, where she mainly contributed to the discussion content. This may be explained by this group reflection:

12. […] when we entered the group discussions with our expert peer, it was hard at times to know who was going to speak, and when. (group reflection, Group 3)

It may be that the students were unfamiliar with SL initially and that E3 with her more advanced technology experience thus took a key role in coordinating the discussion. In addition, the first workshop was more complex in that it involved the discussion of statements in relation to data from classroom observations, which also could explain E3's greater emphasis on management in this session. On the whole, E3's efforts seem to have been appreciated as shown by a female students individual reflection stating that the expert peer "was great!" There were, however, some indications that the presence of the expert peer also may have had an inhibitory effect:

13. […] the expert peer might have caused us to be more cautious and over-polite. (group reflection, Group 3)

This may particularly have been the case for the female students in this group (F6 and F7) who were rather inactive in both sessions.

Group 4

The data in Figure 10 shows that the floor space of E4 was sharply reduced in Workshop 2. Some explanation for this variation is indicated from the questionnaires and Group 4's reflection:

14. Our expert peer (E4) was a good support in answering the questions in the cases. (individual reflection, female student)
15. Our expert peer was professional and did not take that much space in the discussions, which was her intended role. [...] our expert peer being quite inactive, however in a good way, since it made our discussions more fluent. [...] we felt that the second case worked out better, since that was more focused on our own experiences and discussions rather than looking at graphs. (group reflection, Group 4)

From these comments we may guess that in the more complex Workshop 1, E4 contributed more to the content. In Workshop 2, which was more based on the students' own experiences, E4 took less space and restricted her activities to coordinating the conversation. This illustrates a common dilemma in conversations of this nature, especially when in a position of power: the balance between contributing where necessary but at the same time not taking over the floor.

Group 5

Group 5 is interesting since it did not have an expert peer in the first session but did so in the second session. Two students in particular were active in both sessions: F10 and M5. Of particular interest here is F10, who is a mature student in her fifties and with over thirty years of teaching experience. Listening to the recordings, it is evident that she takes on a leader role in the group, which is also mirrored in the data. Similarly, M5 seems to be active and confident. The inactivity of E6 in Workshop 2 may thus be explained by the fact that the group already had established its roles. In this sense E6 is more of an outsider and in a less powerful position than the students. We may thus be seeing an example of "powerful participants controlling and constraining the contributions of non-powerful participants" (Fairclough, 2001, pp. 38-9). Alternatively, E6 may simply be satisfied with the way students are interacting and she may therefore be standing back intentionally.

In the group reflection, the students claim that the absence of the expert peer did not influence their participation. She was, however, appreciated in the second workshop for "bringing up useful technical suggestions". The results show that formal roles such as that of 'expert peer' do not necessarily mean that one is given a powerful position in a conversation. Other factors such as experience and charisma seem to play an important role too.

DISCUSSION

In our study, we tapped established networks active in SL language education in order to give our student teachers access to far more experienced 'peers' – active professionals in the domain of online language education, researchers and teachers, who could assist and stimulate them in their tasks.

In accordance with studies such as Jauregi & Canto, 2012 and Chen, 2018, this type of networking design turned out to be a good model for our particular purposes. On the one hand, it made it possible to meet the practical demands of the course (the time frame and content), while at the same time introducing an element of the "indeterminate" that so often leads to new meetings and insights. The volunteers also turned out to be engaging discussion partners who contributed with new insights without taking over the conversations. In contrast to Chen's (2018) findings, we found that freer topics (workshop two), where there was room for more personal accounts and opinions, and where students could draw on previous personal experiences, led to the most fruitful interactions. Interestingly, these conversations often became comparative in a cross-cultural sense, where the Swedish students would contrast the Swedish school system and their own school experiences with those of the expert peers', addressing issues such as gender, the role of the teacher, power in the classroom etc. in the different cultures. All in all, our impression was that there was a 'genuine' meeting going on in many groups and that this opened up new dimensions and contacts for our students. Important to note here, however, is that in contrast with Chen's (2018) study, all our participants were advanced learners of English.

One of our concerns was that real or perceived unequal power relations between the students and the invited professionals could have detrimental effects on conversation. There were several risk factors that could have affected the participation of the students negatively: we had an institutionalised situation of a university context where in spite of our efforts to tone down power differences it was likely that participants took on the traditional roles of students and teachers (cf. Have, 1991); we had students being put into a new collaborative arena, and linked to this, technological aspects that had to be overcome. Luckily, our fears were not realised.

Our results show that, on a general level, the division of floor space between participants was reasonably equal. 'Expert peers' occupied slightly more floor space and produced on average slightly longer turns. They also used the text chat more (although these contributions were mainly restricted to technical issues). However, the differences were very small, and the same was true of gender differences among the students. Thus the impact of the institutionalised setting appears to have had little or no negative influence. This may partly have been a result of the learning environment, and that the use of avatars in a VW setting may have blurred traditional power structures. Judging from the reflections, students did not feel inhibited by the formal status of the invited professionals. Here our findings support research claims that the SL technology could be liberating and reduce FLA, for instance by making shy students more active since the (pseudo-) anonymous environment reduced the force of face-threatening situations (c.f. Melchor-Couto, 2017; 2018; Gamage, Tretiakov, & Crump, 2011 above). On the other hand, we specifically instructed the invited professionals not to take on the teacher role, but rather the role of a well-informed conversational partner, so it is difficult, based on our results alone, to claim that it was the relative anonymity afforded by SL environment that alone contributed to the favourable participation patterns.

As far as gender is concerned, there was an unfounded fear that nature of the technology would affect the female students more negatively than the male. We based this erroneous assumption on research, which has shown that girls and women are less involved with virtual world online games (see Hartmann & Klimmt, 2006, for example). Neither the quantitative data nor the reflections suggest that this was the case. Furthermore, contrary to expectations (Coates, 2004; Herring, 2010), male students devoted more speech time to supportive utterances than did the female students. They also occupied slightly less floor space. We have no good explanation for this, but the findings do corroborate other studies that suggest that gender differences in conversational styles may not be as great as once thought (see Holmes, 2006; Ladegaard, 2010, above). More specifically, they support Lin et al.'s (2019) findings from online synchronous collaborations, where no significant gender differences in the degree of participation were found. One could also speculate that this may be the result of the demographics of the group constellations (and the class as a whole), where male students were in a 1:3 minority and may have perceived themselves in a slightly less powerful position. However, other studies have shown that such a configuration of genders does not affect the impact of male contribution (Coates, 2004, p. 116-7).

When looking at the dynamics of the individual groups we see a lot of variation, which can be related to individual traits and perhaps preparation for the tasks.

A general view expressed by the students in all the group reflections, however, was their positive experience of collaborating with the invited professionals. Some of the positives mentioned - that the task stimulated the use of the target language, and gave valuable input on how web tools could be used in language education (Workshop 2), and that students gained experience of how to conduct conversational management - were exactly those that we sought after when designing this project. Here it is important to note that it was the engagement of the SL community of language educators that made the design possible, and that the social network sites gave us access to this community. This active network is arguably the greatest asset of SL in language education.

Are there, then, no risks to recruiting peers in this way? After all, we had little control over whom exactly it was that we were inviting into our classrooms. Careful planning and initiation in combination with clear information on expected roles are probably prerequisites for a good result, as expectation on both students and invited participants have to be clear to all parties. Here others, such as Longo (2012), emphasise the importance of netiquette rules in order to reduce the risk of intercultural misunderstandings. However, this does not guarantee a positive result and in the end, it is up to the collaborating participants to maximise the benefits of their meeting. In our study, the results indicate that this was the case on the whole.

FUTURE RESEARCH DIRECTIONS

According to Wigham et al. (2018), VWs potential as learning environments need to be better understood, and in this pursuit the authors call for a "drastic change of approach" (p. 154), which takes the complexity of the environments into account. In addition, we would argue that more systematic empirical research is needed in order to understand the potential benefits and downsides that these environments represent in terms of language learning. In this respect, the research presented above is not without limitations, and we thus take this opportunity to propose a number of potential ways in which we, and others, can contribute to a better understanding of some of the central issues addressed in this study.

Firstly, we would suggest that much more systematic research is needed to address the question of how/whether VWs and other CMC environments can reduce FLA and alter established power structures in interactional language learning contexts. For this research to be robust, we maintain that more controlled research designs that include counter-balanced face-to-face control set-ups are needed. Melchor-Couto's studies (2017; 2018) go some way towards this, but fact remains that her face-to-face and VW learning groups did not interact in identical learning set-ups (only the VW-group interacted with native speakers, for example), and it is thus difficult to elucidate whether the positive outcomes for the VW group as regards FLA were truly the result of the anonymity afforded by SL. The same critique can obviously be made in relation to the current study.

As regards the question of 'power', roles and identity, and how these may affect interaction, we would also argue that more qualitative ethnographic research is needed to establish how interaction through avatars might alter conventional interactional patterns. Does an avatar teacher represent the same role as a face-to-face teacher? To what extent is the physical appearance of the avatar instrumental in establishing roles? What happens to traditional gender roles if participants act through avatars of the opposite sex (note here that voice to can be altered to simulate male or female voices)? These are just some of the issues that can be investigated, and here we would advocate a more qualitative approaches based on interviews, long term observations, careful discourse and conversation analysis.

In this study, we have really only looked at oral participation, but given the complexity of VWs there is obviously great scope to extend the object of investigation to include various modes of participation and interaction. This type of multi-modal research is at its infancy (see Panichi, 2015), and there is much to be done in this field. Here, as pointed out in Wigham et al. (2018), one of the great challenges is establishing research norms of how interaction can be captured, rendered, and interpreted methodologically, and in this field there is great potential for future research.

A final area of research which we think would contribute greatly to the field of language learning using VW environments is a systematic mapping and evaluation of tried learning designs, and how these can cater for different learning goals/learner profiles. As illustrated in this study, where we examined advanced learners of English, the freer task design in Workshop 2 rendered better outcomes in terms of participation than the more question-answer type design in Workshop 1. This result contradicts Chen's (2018) findings, but in the latter case the target learners were beginners and intermediate learners. As illustrated by this example, the suitability of different VW learning designs, depending on aspects such as learner profiles and desired outcomes, are thus an area that needs further mapping and investigation. Here we see great potential in methods involving systematic Action Research designs.

CONCLUSION

The present study provides one model for how online networks can be utilized in order to enrich university language courses and sets up an example of how VWs can be used to offer students opportunities to work with more capable peers from other countries. Our results also suggest that an arena such as SL may well reduce the anxiety associated with set-ups where collaboration is conducted among participants with unequal power relations. The study provides a first step towards further understanding the group dynamics of such meetings and the factors affecting participation – essential knowledge for language educators and practitioners designing more open online learning scenarios.

REFERENCES

Abdullah, F. S., & Hosseini, K. (2012). Discursive enactment of power in Iranian high school EFL classrooms. *GEMA Online Journal of Language Studies*, *12*(2), 375–392.

AVALON Learning NING. (2012). Retrieved June 6, 2012, from http://avalon-project.ning.com/

Bellés-Fortuño, B. (2006*). Discourse markers within the university lecture genre: A contrastive study between Spanish and North-American lectures* (Unpublished doctoral dissertation). Universitat Jaume I, Spain.

Bernstein, B. (1971). *Class, codes and control* (Vol. 1). London: Routledge and Kegan Paul. doi:10.4324/9780203014035

Blasing, M. T. (2010). Second language in Second Life: Exploring interaction, identity and pedagogical practice in a virtual world. *SEEJ*, *54*(1), 96–117.

Blin, F., Nocchi, S., & Fowley, C. (2013). Mondes virtuels et apprentissage des langues: Vers un cadre théorique émergent. *Recherches et Applications*, *54*, 94–107.

Boellstorff, T. (2015). Three real features for virtual worlds. *Journal of Virtual Worlds Research*, *8*(2), 1–5. doi:10.4101/jvwr.v8i2.7167

Bowers, K. W., Ragas, M. W., & Neely, J. C. (2009). Assessing the value of virtual worlds for post-secondary instructors: A survey of innovators, early adopters and the early majority in SL. *International Journal of Humanities and Social Science*, *3*(1), 40–50.

Brislin, R. (1981). *Cross-cultural encounters: Face-to-face interactions*. New York, NY: Pergamon Press.

Chen, J. C. (2018). The interplay of tasks, strategies and negotiations in Second Life. *Computer Assisted Language Learning*, *31*(8), 960–986. doi:10.1080/09588221.2018.1466810

Coates, J. (2004). *Women, men and language: A sociolinguistic account of gender difference in language* (3rd ed.). Harlow: Pearson Education Limited.

Crawford, M. (1995). *Talking difference: On gender and language*. London: Sage.

Czepielewski, S. (2012). The virtual world of Second Life in foreign language learning. In: S. Czepielewski (Ed.), *Learning a language in virtual worlds: A review of innovation and ICT in language teaching methodology, International conference*, *Warsaw*, *17th November 2011* (pp. 15-24). Warsaw: Warsaw Academy of Computer Science, Management and Administration.

Deutschmann, M., & Panichi, L. (2009a). Instructional design, teacher practice and learner autonomy. In J. Molka-Danielsen & M. Deutschmann (Eds.), Learning and teaching in the virtual world of SL (pp. 27-44). Trondheim: Tapir Academic Press.

Deutschmann, M., & Panichi, L. (2009b). Talking into empty space? Signalling involvement in a virtual language classroom in SL. *Language Awareness*, *18*(3-4), 310–328. doi:10.1080/09658410903197306

Deutschmann, M., Panichi, L., & Molka-Danielsen, J. (2009). Designing oral participation in SL – A comparative study of two language proficiency courses. *ReCALL*, *21*(2), 206–226. doi:10.1017/S0958344009000196

Deutschmann, M., Steinvall, A., & Lagerström, A. (2011). Gender-bending in virtual space: Using voice-morphing in Second Life to raise sociolinguistic gender awareness. In S. Czepielewski (Ed.), *Learning a language in virtual worlds: A review of innovation and ICT in language teaching methodology, International conference*, *Warsaw*, *17th November 2011* (pp. 54-61). Warsaw: Warsaw Academy of Computer Science, Management and Administration.

Eurocall/Calico Virtual World SIG NING. (2012). Retrieved June 6, 2012, from http://virtualworldssig.ning.com/

Eurocall/Calico Virtual World SIG NING. (2012). Retrieved June 13, 2012, from http://virtualworldssig.ning.com/

Euroversity, N. I. N. G. (2012). Retrieved June 13, 2012, from http://euroversity.ning.com

Fairclough, N. (2001). *Language and power* (2nd ed.). Harlow: Pearson Education Limited.

Fortuño, B. B. (2006). *Discourse markers within the university lecture center: A contrastive study between Spanish and North-American Lectures* (Doctoral Dissertation). Universitat Jaume I.

Freiermuth, M. (2001). Native speakers or non-native speakers: Who has the floor? Online and face-to-face interaction in culturally mixed small groups. *Computer Assisted Language Learning, 14*(2), 169–199. doi:10.1076/call.14.2.169.5780

Gamage, V., Tretiakov, A., & Crump, B. (2011). Teacher perceptions of learning affordances of multi-user virtual environments. *Computers & Education, 57*(4), 2406–2413. doi:10.1016/j.compedu.2011.06.015

Good, J., Howland, K., & Thackray, L. (2008). Problem-based learning spanning real and virtual words: A case study in SL. *Research in Learning Technology, 16*(3), 163–172. doi:10.3402/rlt.v16i3.10895

Gregory, S., Lee, M. J. W., Dalgarno, B., & Tynan, B. (Eds.). (2016). *Learning in virtual worlds: Research and applications (Issues in distance education).* Edmonton: AU Press. doi:10.15215/aupress/9781771991339.01

Guth, S., & Helm, F. (2010). *Telecollaboration 2.0.* Bern: Peter Lang. doi:10.3726/978-3-0351-0013-6

Hammick, J. K., & Lee, M. J. (2014). Do shy people feel less communication apprehension online? The effects of virtual reality on the relationship between personality characteristics and communication outcomes. *Computers in Human Behavior, 33*, 302–310. doi:10.1016/j.chb.2013.01.046

Hancock, A. B., & Rubin, B. A. (2015). Influence of communication partner's gender on language. *Journal of Language and Social Psychology, 34*(1), 46–64. doi:10.1177/0261927X14533197

Hartmann, T., & Klimmt, C. (2006). Gender and computer games: Exploring females' dislikes. *Journal of Computer-Mediated Communication, 11*(4), 2. doi:10.1111/j.1083-6101.2006.00301.x

Herring, S. C. (2010). Who's got the floor in computer-mediated conversation? Edelsky's gender patterns revisited. *Language@Internet, 7*, article 8. Retrieved April 9, 2013, from http://www.languageatinternet.org/articles/2010/2857

Hew, K. F., & Cheung, W. S. (2010). Use of three-dimensional (3-D) immersive virtual worlds in K-12 and higher education settings: A review of the research. *British Journal of Educational Technology, 41*(1), 33–55. doi:10.1111/j.1467-8535.2008.00900.x

Hirschman, L. (1994). Female-male differences in conversational interaction. *Language in Society, 23*(3), 427–442. doi:10.1017/S0047404500018054

Holmes, J. (2006). *Gendered talk at work: Constructing gender identity through workplace discourse.* Malden, MA: Blackwell. doi:10.1002/9780470754863

Holmes, J., & Schnurr, S. (2006). 'Doing femininity' at work: More than just relational practice. *Journal of Sociolinguistics, 10*(1), 31–51. doi:10.1111/j.1360-6441.2006.00316.x

Inman, C., Wright, V. H., & Hartman, J. A. (2010). Use of SL in K-12 and higher education: A review of research. *Journal of Interactive Online Learning, 9*(1), 44–63.

Jarmon, L., Traphagan, T., Mayrath, M., & Trivedi, A. (2009). Virtual world teaching, experiential learning, and assessment: An interdisciplinary communication course in SL. *Computer Education*, *53*(1), 169–182. doi:10.1016/j.compedu.2009.01.010

Jauregi, K., & Canto, S. (2012). Enhancing meaningful oral interaction in Second Life. *Procedia: Social and Behavioral Sciences*, *34*, 111–115. doi:10.1016/j.sbspro.2012.02.023

Kim, S. H., Lee, J., & Thomas, M. K. (2012). Between purpose and method: A review of educational research on 3D virtual worlds. *Journal of Virtual Worlds Research*, *5*(1), 1–18. doi:10.4101/jvwr.v5i1.2151

Kollock, P., Blumstein, P., & Schwartz, P. (1985). Sex and power in interaction: Conversational privileges and duties. *American Sociological Review*, *50*(1), 34–46. doi:10.2307/2095338

Ladegaard, H. (2011). 'Doing power' at work: Responding to male and female management styles in a global business corporation. *Journal of Pragmatics*, *43*(1), 4–19. doi:10.1016/j.pragma.2010.09.006

Lin, T.-J., Wang, S.-Y., Grant, S., Chein, C.-L., & Lan, Y.-J. (2014). Task-based teaching approach of Chinese as a foreign language in Second Life through teachers' perspectives. *Procedia Technology*, *13*, 16–22. doi:10.1016/j.protcy.2014.02.004

Lin, Y., Dowell, N., Godfrey, A., Choi, H., & Brooks, C. (2019). Modeling gender dynamics in intra and interpersonal interactions during online collaborative learning. *LAK19. Proceedings of the 9th International Conference on Learning Analytics & Knowledge*, 431-435. 10.1145/3303772.3303837

Longo, D. (2012). Learning a Second Language in a learning community "Second Life": Critical issues and possible developments. *Conference proceedings international conference ICT for language learning 5th conference edition*. Florence: Pixel.

Mayrath, M. C., Traphagan, T., Heikes, E. J., & Trivedi, A. (2009). Instructional design best practices for SL: A case study from a college-level English course. *Interactive Learning Environments*, *19*(2), 125–142. doi:10.1080/10494820802602568

Melchor-Couto, S. (2017). Foreign language anxiety levels in Second Life oral interaction. *ReCALL*, *29*(1), 99–119. doi:10.1017/S0958344016000185

Melchor-Couto, S. (2018). Virtual World Anonymity and Foreign Language Oral Interaction. *ReCALL*, *30*(02), 232–249. doi:10.1017/S0958344017000398

Molka-Danielsen, J., Panichi, L., & Deutschmann, M. (2010). Reward models for active language learning in 3D virtual worlds. In Y. Peng, G, Kou, F. I. S. Ko, Y. Zeng, & K. D. Kwack (Eds.), *Information sciences and interaction sciences: The 3rd international conference on information sciences and interaction sciences* (pp. 97-109). Chengdu.

O'Barr, W. M., & Atkins, B. K. (1980). "Women's Language" or "Powerless Language"? In S. McConell-Ginet, R. Borker, & N. Furman (Eds.), *Women and language in literature and society* (pp. 93–110). New York: Praeger.

Otto, S. K., & Pusack, J. P. (2009). Computer-assisted language learning authoring issues. *Modern Language Journal*, *93*(1), 784–801. doi:10.1111/j.1540-4781.2009.00973.x

Panichi, L. (2012). Virtual Worlds: An opportunity for thinking about learning. In: S. Czepielewski (Ed.), *Learning a language in virtual worlds: A review of innovation and ICT in language teaching methodology, International conference, Warsaw, 17th November 2011* (pp. 25-32). Warsaw: Warsaw Academy of Computer Science, Management and Administration.

Panichi, L., & Deutschmann, M. (2012). Language learning in virtual worlds: Research issues and methods. In M. Dooly & R. O'Dowd (Eds.), *Researching online foreign language interaction and exchange: Theories, methods and challenges* (pp. 207–234). Bern: Peter Lang.

Panichi, L. J. (2015). *Participation in language learning in virtual worlds: An exploratory case-study of a business English course* (Unpublished PhD thesis). University of Hull. Retrieved from https://hydra.hull.ac.uk/resources/hull:11583

Reinders, H., & Wattana, S. (2015). Affect and willingness to communicate in digital game-based learning. *ReCALL, 27*(1), 38–57. doi:10.1017/S0958344014000226

Sadler, R. (2012). *Virtual worlds for language learning: From theory to practice*. Bern: Peter Lang.

Scheelf, E. (2008). Gender and academic discourse: Global restrictions and local possibilities. *Language in Society, 38*(4), 515–538.

SLED list – SL Educators. (n.d.). Retrieved June 6, 2012, from https://lists.secondlife.com/cgi-bin/mailman/listinfo/educators

Sullivan, F. R., Kapur, M., Madden, S., & Shipe, S. (2015). Exploring the Role of 'Gendered' Discourse Styles in Online Science Discussions. *International Journal of Science Education, 37*(3), 484–504. doi:10.1080/09500693.2014.994113

Sunderland, J. (1998). Girls being quiet: A problem for foreign language classrooms? *Language Teaching Research, 2*(1), 48–62. doi:10.1177/136216889800200104

Sunderland, J. (2000). New understandings of gender and language classroom research: Texts, teacher talk and student talk. *Language Teaching Research, 4*(2), 149–173. doi:10.1177/136216880000400204

Sunderland, J. (2004). Classroom interaction, gender, and foreign language learning. In B. Norton & K. Toohey (Eds.), Critical pedagogies and language learning (pp. 222-241). Cambridge. doi:10.1017/CBO9781139524834.012

ten Have, P. (1991). Talk and institution: A reconsideration of the 'asymmetry' of doctor-patient interaction. In D. Boden & D. H. Zimmerman (Eds.), *Talk and social Structure: Studies in ethnomethodology and conversation analysis* (pp. 138–163). Cambridge, UK: Polity Press.

Toyoda, E., & Harrison, R. (2002). Categorization of text chat communication between learners and native speakers of Japanese. *Language Learning & Technology, 6*(1), 82–99.

Vygotsky, L. S. (1978). *Mind in society: The development of higher psychological process*. Cambridge, MA: Harvard University Press.

Wang, A. (2017). *Learning English in a Multi-User Virtual Environment : Exploring Factors Affecting Participation (PhD dissertation).* Sundsvall: Mid Sweden University. Retrieved from http://urn.kb.se/resolve?urn=urn:nbn:se:miun:diva-30795

Wang, A. (2017). Using Second Life in an English Course: How does the technology affect participation? *International Journal of Computer-Assisted Language Learning and Teaching*, *7*(1), 66–85. doi:10.4018/IJCALLT.2017010105

Wang, C. X., Song, H., Stone, D. E., & Yan, Q. (2009). Integrating SL into an EFL program in China: Research collaboration across the continents. *TechTrends*, *53*(6), 14–19. doi:10.100711528-009-0337-z

Wang, C. X., Song, H., Xia, F., & Yan, Q. (2009). Integrating SL into an EFL program: Students' perspectives. *Journal of Educational Technology Development and Exchange*, *2*(1), 1–16. doi:10.18785/jetde.0201.01

Warschauer, M. (1997). Computer-mediated collaborative learning: Theory and practice. *Modern Language Journal*, *81*(4), 470–481. doi:10.1111/j.1540-4781.1997.tb05514.x

Warschauer, M., & Liaw, M. L. (2010). *Emerging technologies in adult literacy and language education.* Washington, DC: National Institute for Literacy. doi:10.1037/e529982011-001

Wehner, A. K., Gump, A. W., & Downey, S. (2011). The effects of Second Life on the motivation of undergraduate students learning a foreign language. *Computer Assisted Language Learning*, *24*(3), 277–289. doi:10.1080/09588221.2010.551757

West, C., & Zimmerman, D. H. (1983). Small insults: A study of interruptions in conversations between unacquainted persons. In B. Thorne, & N. Henley (Eds.), Language, Gender, and Society (pp. 102-117). Rowley: Newbury House.

Wigham, C. R. (2012). *The interplay between non-verbal and verbal interaction in synthetic worlds which supports verbal participation and production in a foreign language* (Unpublished PhD thesis). Université Blaise Pascal - Clermont-Ferrand II. Retrieved from https://halshs.archives-ouvertes.fr/tel-01077857/document

Wigham, C. R., & Chanier, T. (2013). A study of verbal and nonverbal communication in Second Life – the ARCHI21 experience. *ReCALL*, *25*(1), 63–84. doi:10.1017/S0958344012000250

Wigham, C. R., Panichi, L., Nocchi, S., & Sadler, R. (2018). Interactions for language learning in and around virtual worlds. *ReCALL*, *30*(2), 153–160. doi:10.1017/S0958344018000022

Woken, M. D., & Swales, J. (1989). Expertise and authority in native-non-native conversations: The need for a variable account. In S. Gass, C. Madden, D. Preston, & L. Selinker (Eds.), *Variation in second language acquisition: Discourse and pragmatics* (pp. 211–227). Clevedon, UK: Multilingual Matters.

Zheng, D., & Newgarden, K. (2012). Rethinking language learning: Virtual worlds as a catalyst for change. *International Journal of Learning and Media*, *3*(2), 13–36. doi:10.1162/ijlm_a_00067

Zuengler, J. (1989). Performance variation in NS-NNS interactions: Ethnolinguistic difference or discourse domain? In S. Gass, C. Madden, D. Preston, & L. Selinker (Eds.), *Variation in second language acquisition: Discourse and pragmatics* (pp. 218–235). Clevedon, UK: Multilingual Matters.

KEY TERMS AND DEFINITIONS

Collaboration: The process of two or more people working together to complete a task or achieve a goal.

Floor Space: Or "floor apportionment" is the proportional amount of time each conversational partner gets in a conversation.

Network: A group with common interests that fosters the exchange of information and ideas. A task using "networking design" taps in on such networks for the purpose of collaborative learning.

Oral Interaction: The use of the target language in its spoken form in meaningful exchanges with conversational partners. It involves language production, but also active listening.

Power: A relative relationship where one person can be seen as having more, less or equal power compared another. Initially often based on formal roles, positions or conventions. A teacher, for example, possesses more power than a student in a conversation due to his/her formal role.

Second Life: A free, open, 3D virtual world where users act and move using avatars, and where they can create, connect, and chat with others using voice and text chat.

Turn Length: The measurable length of a "turn." Turn-taking characterizes the organization in a conversation whereby each participant speaks one at a time in alternating turns.

Utterance Functions: In this study, the functions of utterances in a conversation based on three categories: conversational management, support, and content contributions.

Section 2

3D Virtual Environments:
A Closer Look at Immersion

Chapter 5
Transitions in Student Motivation During a MUVE-Based Ecosystem Science Curriculum:
An Evaluation of the Novelty Effect

Shari J. Metcalf
Harvard University, USA

Kim M. Frumin
Harvard University, USA

Jason A. Chen
College of William and Mary, USA

Trisha L. Vickrey
University of Nebraska – Lincoln, USA

Amy M. Kamarainen
Harvard University, USA

Tina A. Grotzer
Harvard University, USA

Christopher J. Dede
Harvard University, USA

ABSTRACT

One issue involved in incorporating any new technology in science education is the concern that the value added is primarily due to the novelty effect. The authors address this concern by evaluating student motivation during a two-week, multi-user virtual environment (MUVE)-based curriculum for middle school ecosystems science. Analysis of multiple surveys at the beginning, middle, and end of the curriculum revealed that students continued to find the activity engaging from beginning to end, but differed in what specifically engaged them. Further, students' beliefs about EcoMUVE's utility in helping them learn science increased significantly. This transition is attributable to the curriculum's design, which supports internally controlled motivators: autonomy (choice), competence, and connectedness. Specifically, over time EcoMUVE provides opportunities for sustained, meaningful engagement, through self-directed learning, inquiry-based activities, and collaboration with a team.

DOI: 10.4018/978-1-5225-7987-8.ch005

INTRODUCTION AND THEORETICAL FRAMEWORK

Multi-User Virtual Environments in Education

Multi-user virtual environments (MUVEs) are 3-D graphical worlds used to create a simulated immersive experience. The user is represented by a virtual avatar, and interacts with the environment by controlling the moves and actions of this avatar through the 3-D environment. Participants in a MUVE may have a variety of tools with which to interact with virtual objects, and also opportunities to communicate and interact with other users and with computer-based agents in simulated environments.

MUVE's have become recognized as a powerful and effective educational platform (Fishman, Dede, & Means, 2015). MUVEs can simulate environments otherwise impossible in school settings, providing opportunities for classroom students to explore simulated worlds, travel in space and time, and explore events at different scales (e.g., Barab, Thomas, Dodge, Carteaux, & Tuzun, 2005; Kafai, 2010; Omale, Hung, Luetkehans, & Cooke-Plagwitz, 2009). In particular, there has been significant recent work on the use of MUVEs in science education, and MUVEs have been found to be effective in engaging middle and high school students in learning science, through shared participation in rich immersive experiences (Clarke, Dede, Ketelhut, & Nelson, 2006; Lim, Nonis, & Hedberg, 2006; Nelson & Ketelhut, 2007).

The Novelty Effect in Educational Technology

One issue involved in incorporating any new technology in science education, however, is the concern that the value added by technology is primarily due to the novelty effect, which Clark (1983) defined as, "the increased effort and attention research subjects tend to give to media that are novel to them" (p. 449). A recent meta-analysis of the effectiveness of virtual reality-based instruction on students' learning outcomes explored the novelty effect of desktop-based virtual reality learning environments. Their findings indicated that, particularly for game-based learning, if students spent more time playing games, the learning outcome gains started to diminish (Merchant et al., 2014).

Studies of MUVEs in education have found that, in the short term, students enjoy these virtual worlds primarily because the technology is new to them. In particular, students enjoyed: (1) the ability to move around freely in a 3D space; (2) interacting with virtual people; and (3) simulating new experiences (Hew & Cheung, 2010). Often, studies of virtual reality-based learning are based on only short-term implementations, and although they might show statistically significant learning outcomes, the novelty effect is an important caveat to the research because many of these studies do not account for the decay of outcomes over longer periods of time. One study of the learning effects of a virtual reality-based environment for learning about plant cells revealed an increase in learning over traditional learning modalities but noted that the "results may be partially because of the novelty of the VR equipment, so the improvements may not be sustained over longitudinal studies" (Allcoat & von Mühlenen, 2018).

Gamification and Novelty Effects

A related domain is that of *gamification* in education, a design approach in which game elements are implemented in learning environments. Studies of gamified learning environments often raise the issue of a novelty effect regarding the motivational impact of gamification, suggesting that its impact may not persist long-term, but is partially related to the novelty of the rewards (e.g. badges and points) (Hamari et al., 2014; Koivisto & Hamari, 2014; Hanus & Fox, 2015). As Koivisto and Hamari explain, "gamification could have some novelty value causing perceptions of usefulness and enjoyment to be higher in the beginning and to fade the longer the user continues using the service" (Koivisto & Hamari, 2014, p.183).

A potential negative effect of gamification relates to game elements that offer extrinsic motivation. Therefore, instead of using extrinsic rewards, many scholars have suggested that a better approach would be to identify ways to intrinsically motivate the learner to engage in the activity (Kim, 2015). In a recent paper, Nicholson (2015) advocated for the design of *meaningful gamification*, which encourages the learner to make a personal connection so as to make engagement more meaningful. This approach stands in contrast to reward-based gamification, which often reduces intrinsic motivation and makes learners feel as if they are being manipulated. Examples of meaningful gamification design include providing real-world contexts, and offering learners opportunities to explore multiple paths as they learn. How might meaningful engagement play out in a MUVE? We explore this next in a MUVE that we designed and implemented.

ECOMUVE: BACKGROUND AND RELATED RESEARCH

Overview of the EcoMUVE Curriculum

EcoMUVE is a 10-day middle school science curriculum that supports learning about causal patterns in ecosystems. It consists of two ecosystem modules, Pond and Forest, each centered on an immersive virtual environment that represents a complex causal scenario. The software is designed using an inquiry, role-based jigsaw pedagogy. Students work individually on computers, using a virtual avatar to explore the 3D ecosystem. They work together in teams of four in which each student has a distinct "role" (water chemist, microscopic specialist, naturalist, and private investigator). Students collect data specific to their roles, and then work with their team to analyze the combined data and understand the ecosystem interrelationships and investigate an ecological "mystery." The module culminates in each team creating an evidence-based concept map representing their understanding of the causal relationships in the ecosystem and presenting it to the class.

In the EcoMUVE Pond module, used for the study presented in this paper, students explore a pond and its surroundings (Figure 1). They can travel in time over eight virtual days during a simulated summer. They discover that on one day late in the summer, all of the large fish in the pond have died. To figure out the causal relationships that led to this event, they explore, observe, and collect data – they find and photograph organisms, shrink to microscopic size, travel in time, collect water, weather, and population measurements, track atoms, and use tables and graphs to view and analyze data over time (Figure 2). Each team creates a final concept map and presentation of their hypotheses, which may include factors including fertilizer runoff from a nearby housing development or golf course, measurements of phosphates, nitrates, turbidity, temperature and dissolved oxygen, weather factors of wind, temperature, and cloud cover, and populations of fish, herons, algae and bacteria.

Prior Research With EcoMUVE

In a number of prior studies using EcoMUVE, we have demonstrated student gains in ecosystem science knowledge and causal understanding (Kamarainen, Metcalf, Grotzer & Dede, 2015; Metcalf, Tutwiler,

Figure 1. Pond module

Figure 2. Water measurements

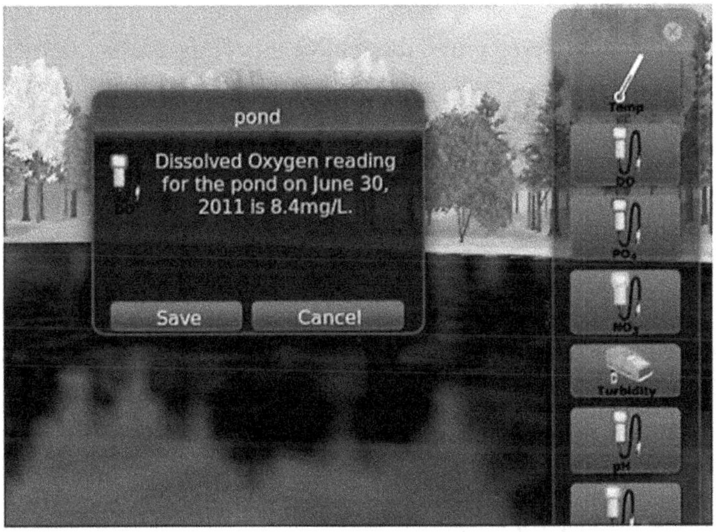

Kamarainen, Grotzer & Dede, 2013; Grotzer, Kamarainen, Tutwiler, Metcalf & Dede, 2013). A study on teacher perceptions of EcoMUVE in the classroom surveyed 16 teachers who had used the curriculum with their students, about the value, effectiveness, and feasibility of EcoMUVE based on their experiences, and some teachers additionally participated in a comparison study of EcoMUVE with a non-MUVE curriculum (Metcalf, Kamarainen, Tutwiler, Grotzer, & Dede, 2013). Teachers felt EcoMUVE was effective, aligned well with standards, and compared favorably with a non-MUVE alternative. Particular technological and curriculum features that were identified by teachers as valuable included both technological aspects such as immersion in the virtual environment and easy-to-use data collection and analysis tools, and also pedagogical features, particularly the opportunity for self-directed learning by students, and the inquiry, role-based pedagogy.

In another study we explored changes in student motivation as a result of using EcoMUVE (Chen, Metcalf, and Tutwiler, 2014). Self-report survey data indicated that, on average, students' interest in *science* did not change from pre-intervention to post-intervention. However, a closer analysis revealed that students who identified more strongly with science did become more interested in science, whereas those who did not identify with science evinced no change in interest for science. This finding showed that particular students benefited from the virtual world (i.e., students who identified with science), whereas others showed little to no motivational benefit. But we were interested in whether other changes were happening, which the surveys could not capture. Interview data and classroom observations suggested that, although students' interests for science may have stayed quantitatively equivalent, there were substantive *qualitative* changes that were occurring, which suggested that students' interests were indeed changing.

Finally, EcoMUVE researchers (Chen, Tutwiler, Metcalf, Kamarainen, Grotzer & Dede, 2016), explored whether there were different ways that students evince a novelty effect while participating in EcoMUVE, and whether these different ways were related to differential outcomes. For example, did some students show sharp gains in interest for the technology only to sharply decline again by the end of the curriculum? And did this type of novelty effect result in outcomes that were different from students who perhaps evinced sharp gains in interest for the technology but a very gradual decline in interest by the end? In the Chen et al. study we used Hidi & Renninger's (2006) four-phase model of interest development to characterize the novelty effect as a phenomenon in which people's situational interests are sparked, but not sufficiently maintained to develop into more robust and long-lasting individual interests. Using latent growth modeling, we found that some students in EcoMUVE evinced a sharp increase in interest for *the technology*, but then a relatively quick drop-off in that interest by the end of the curriculum. For these students, whose situational interest in the technology was *not* maintained, their self-efficacy and their interest *for the field of science* did not grow over time. However, for students whose situational interest in the technology was both sparked and maintained (i.e., there was a very gradual decrease in interest for the technology), their self-efficacy and interest *for the field of science* grew. What aspects of EcoMUVE allowed students to transfer their interest *for the technology* into a more robust interest *for science*? This is a main question we sought to address in the present study, which we describe next.

METHODS

Participants and Study Procedures

Participants were the 6th grade students (11-12 years old) of two science teachers at a relatively affluent and 70% White suburban school in the Northeastern United States The classes used the EcoMUVE curriculum for two weeks in 2012. Each teacher taught five classes, for a total of 250 students. Of that population, we analyzed data only from the students who completed all three checkpoint surveys, for a total N=198.

The students were not surveyed for computer literacy or prior experience with MUVEs, but computer gaming is almost universal among this demographic – a 2010 survey found that in the United States 11- to 14-year-olds spend an average of an hour and a half a day playing video games (Rideout, Foehr, & Roberts, 2010), and another survey reported that 97% of American youth aged 12 to 17 play computer, console, portable or cell phone games (Lenhart, Kahne, Middaugh, Macgill, Evans, & Vitak,, 2008). However, MUVE-based classroom curricula are rare; this was almost certainly the students' first experience with MUVEs in a classroom environment. Some of the students' survey comments indicated their initial excitement at that novelty, e.g., "This is kind of like playing a game in school!"

Students used the EcoMUVE Pond curriculum module over 10 consecutive classes. Students were polled with identical "checkpoint" surveys at the beginning, middle, and end of their use of EcoMUVE: after day 1, day 5, and day 10. The survey included a total of 8 Likert-scale questions on their value beliefs, and four open-ended questions.

Instruments

The Likert-scale variables assessed were as follows: Interest (four questions such as, "I like using EcoMUVE"), utility (two questions such as, "I think the skills that I'm using with EcoMUVE will be useful"), and cost value (one question: "It was a waste of time doing EcoMUVE."). One additional Likert-scale question assessed whether students thought they learned anything by using EcoMUVE. We did not include this in the quantitative analysis, however, because this question did not necessarily fit into a specific theoretical framework of motivation. Instead, we looked at students' thoughts about what they had learned using EcoMUVE during the open-ended response section (see below).

Students used a 6-point scale to select how true or false each statement was for them: 1=Definitely false, 2=Mostly false, 3=A little bit false, 4=A little bit true, 5=Mostly true, 6=Definitely true. Mean scores were then calculated for each variable, with the exception of cost value, which only had one item.

The four open-ended questions were designed to probe for qualitative responses about interest and utility, as follows:

- What do you like about EcoMUVE so far?
- Is there anything you don't like about EcoMUVE?
- In what ways do you think EcoMUVE is helping you learn science?
- How is learning science with EcoMUVE different from typical activities you've done in science class?

The open-ended questions were analyzed using an initial coding that focused on our research questions about the impact of the technology and the impact of the curriculum. Since students often wrote answers that included more than one element, a long answer might receive more than one code. Emergent codes were added during the coding process to classify responses that did not match previous codes. A second phase of analysis identified similarities and grouped the codes into larger themes. Using the final set of codes, the responses were scored by two independent scorers with inter-rater reliability assessed at 89% overall, ranging from 73% to 100% for the categories.

FINDINGS

Quantitative Changes in Interest, Utility, and Cost Value

Two one-way, repeated measures ANOVAs were conducted to evaluate the change in students' beliefs about interest, utility, and cost value across the three time points. Sphericity tests showed that the sphericity assumption was not violated in any of the cases. Therefore, degrees of freedom did not need to be corrected. Results from these analyses showed that interest in EcoMUVE decreased significantly from Checkpoint 1 to Checkpoint 2 [$F(1, 194) = 10.14$, $p=.0017$] and from Checkpoint 2 to Checkpoint 3 [$F(1, 194) = 6.70$, $p=.0104$]. Despite this, students' interest in EcoMUVE overall remained very high throughout the duration of the two-week activity (i.e., ratings remained between 5 and 6, which correspond to responses of "mostly true" and "definitely true").

Regarding students' beliefs about the utility of EcoMUVE, results showed that students' evinced a significant improvement in their beliefs about how useful EcoMUVE was from Checkpoint 1 to Checkpoint 2 [$F(1, 195) = 20.73$, $p<.001$], but no significant change from Checkpoint 2 to Checkpoint 3 [$F(1, 195) = 1.03$, $p=.3110$]. Finally, regarding students' beliefs about whether EcoMUVE was worth the time and effort, students reported a significant decrease in EcoMUVE being a "waste of time" from Checkpoint 1 to Checkpoint 2 [$F(1, 194) = 47.69$, $p<.001$], and a small but significant increase in that belief from Checkpoint 2 to Checkpoint 3 [$F(1, 194) = 5.20$, $p=.0237$]. Mean Likert-scale responses for each of the three measures, over the three checkpoints, are presented in Figure 3.

To look for potential population-level differences in student engagement with EcoMUVE, we also examined Pearson product-moment correlations between a proxy measure of student learning potential, a question asking teachers to rate how well they expect their students to be able to learn science content, and three of the affective outcomes: interest, utility, interest, and cost value. We found that teacher expectation was not linearly related to utility and interest, though there was a moderate negative statistically-significant correlation ($r=-0.243$, $p<.05$) between teacher expectation and cost value.

Figure 3. Mean Likert-scale responses for interest, utility value, and cost value, over the 3 checkpoints

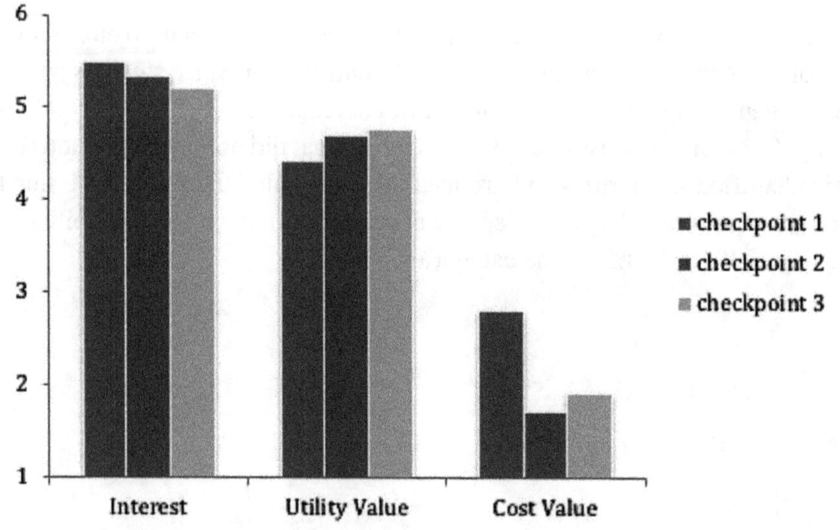

Qualitative Changes in Interest and Utility

Open-Ended Response 1: "What Do You Like About EcoMUVE so Far?"

Students gave a wide variety of answers to this question, from a simple "It was fun" to long answers describing details of the software and/or the activities. Many of the answers were given multiple codes. In our analysis, we focused on two categories of responses – elements of the technology and elements of the curriculum.

Responses that were coded for *technology* include those that mentioned computers, virtual worlds, games, or being online. For example:

- *That you got to use a computer.*
- *I like that there is a virtual pond.*
- *It is like a video game, also it has lots of animals and stuff.*

Responses coded for *interactive features* include those that mentioned features like realistic graphics, specific EcoMUVE tools, or interactive activities like searching, finding, and exploring. For example:

- *in EcoMUVE, I really like how you can go underwater with a submarine and take pictures of living things. Two of the reasons I like EcoMUVE is because I can travel through time and gather different measurements.*
- *I liked the animals and taking pictures and finding populations.*
- *I liked how you had a field guide to know more about living things.*

Some responses were coded for both technology and for interactive features. For example:

- *What i like about ecomuve so far is that it is a virtual world kind of like simms the game. It is fun to search for objects.*
- *I like how it is easier to do things, and I can take measurements quicker. It is fun going online and doing science.*

The percentage of responses that specifically mentioned the *technology* itself remained about the same through the three checkpoints, around 20%. References to *interactive features* were found in 70% of responses in checkpoint 1, decreasing but still frequent at 42% at checkpoint 2 and 46% at checkpoint 3 (Figure 4).

The second category of coding referred curricular elements – aspects of the pedagogical design. Here, the specific codes we identified referred to *self-directed*, *collaborative*, and *inquiry-based* activities.

Responses that were coded for *self-directed* include those that mentioned freedom, being on your own, getting to control elements of the interface, work independently, or take on a role. For example:

- *I like how I can learn to do new things by myself.*
- *I like that it's created so that I'm in control. I like that I can change the date whenever I want to.*
- *There was a lot of freedom.*

Figure 4. Percentage of responses to the question "What do you like about EcoMUVE so far" that were coded for "technology" and for "interactive features of the software." The same response might include more than one code. (All percentages reported based on (N=198) responses.)

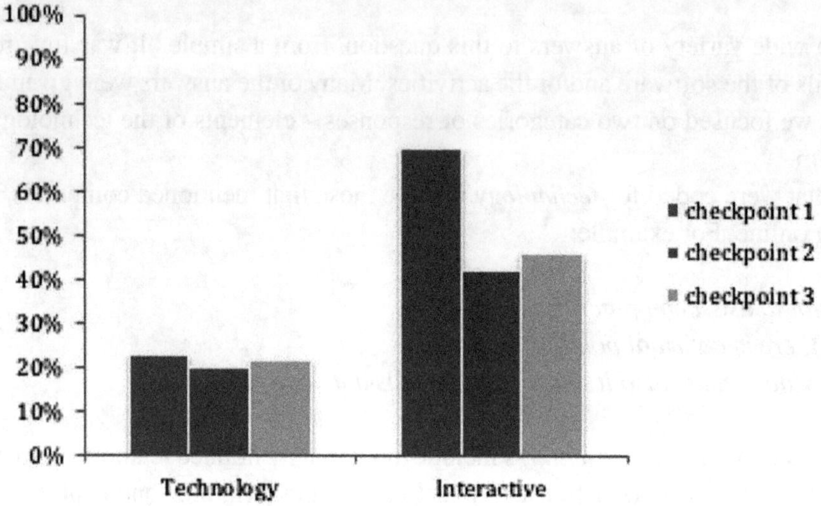

Responses that were coded for *collaborative* mentioned working with others or on a team. For example:

- *I liked how we were able to interact and work together with people in our groups.*
- *I love it! I think it is an amazing idea to get students working together.*

Responses that were coded for *inquiry-based* mentioned solving a mystery, figuring out what killed the fish, or being like a scientist. For example:

- *I liked how you could go into nature to find out what was wrong. Not just talking about it.*
- *I like how you learn facts, and face problems like a scientist.*
- *The fact that we are using what we find in the pond to solve the mystery of the fish dying.*

Some responses included more than one of these elements, as follows:

- *I like that you can see and chat with your friends in your group. Also I like how we can try to solve a mystery.* (collaborative and inquiry-based)
- *I like to use EcoMUVE because I love to play different roles with my friends to find a solution to a problem.* (self-directed, collaborative, and inquiry-based)
- *It helps us in science because we do this with a group to help us. Instead of having the answer told to us, we did the EcoMUVE to find it out ourselves.* (self-directed, collaborative, and inquiry-based)

The percentage of responses started low and increased in each of these three pedagogical categories increased over time, up to 26% who mentioned inquiry-based learning in checkpoint 3 (Figure 5).

Figure 5. Percentage of responses to the question "What do you like about EcoMUVE so far" that were coded for "self-directed", "collaborative," or "inquiry-based learning". The same response might include more than one code.

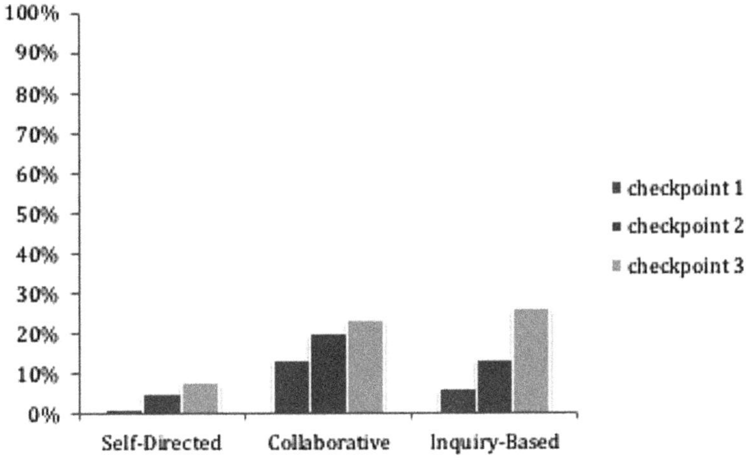

Open-Ended Response 2: "Is There Anything You Don't Like About EcoMUVE?"

The second question on each checkpoint survey asked if there was anything the student *didn't* like about EcoMUVE. Gratifyingly, we found that by far the most common response to this question was that there was nothing the student didn't like about EcoMUVE:

- *No. I like everything.*
- *No, I love it.*

Consistently over the three checkpoints, about half the student answers were that they did not dislike anything about EcoMUVE, decreasing slightly from 54% to 49% (Figure 6).

The other most commonly mentioned category referred to the *technology*. In this code we included both the technology itself and also features of the interface.

For example:

- *I don't like that I keep seeing the same animals.*
- *I think that it would be better with better graphics.*
- *I thought some of the fish swam too fast and they were hard to track.*

Responses in this category decreased over the three checkpoints from 39% to 31%. (Figure 6).

A third coding emerged as students criticizing about aspects of *active and inquiry-based learning*. Interestingly, these responses primarily focused on wanting even *more* of it. For example:

- *I don't like that you can't explore the world very far or else it will stop you short, like it is a dead end.*
- *I think there should have been more character selections and more things to do.*

Figure 6. Percentage of responses to the question "Is there anything you don't like about EcoMUVE?" The same response might include more than one code.

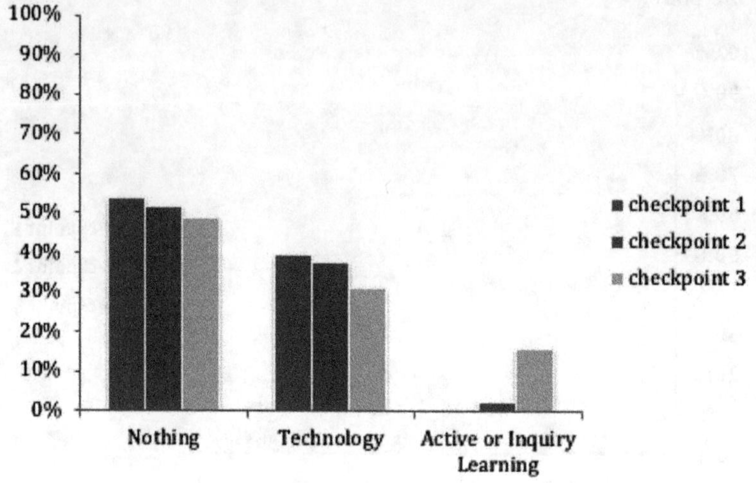

- *The world needed to be bigger, to have more places to go and have a bigger problem.*

Responses in this category increased over the three checkpoints from 1% to 16%. (Figure 6).

Finally, we note that by checkpoint 3, there also seemed to be a slight uptick in complaints (up to about 5% of responses) about other aspects of the activity, the most common being boredom, not enough time to complete activities, too many worksheets, and in reference to this research, too many surveys.

Open-Ended Response 3: "In What Ways Do You Think EcoMUVE Is Helping You Learn Science?"

For this question about science learning with EcoMUVE, we coded for responses that mentioned technology, active and inquiry learning, content learning, and process learning.

Responses that mentioned *technology* features were highest in checkpoint 1 and decreased in checkpoints 2 and 3 (Figure 7).

For example:

- *I think EcoMUVE is helping me learn in science because it is a fun kind of way to discover new things in a model of a real world.*
- *it shows me how the organisms look like if they were under a microscope.*

Between checkpoints 1 and 2, there was a large increase in responses about *active and inquiry-based learning*, which included all references to hands-on activities and figuring things out. In checkpoint 3, these responses decreased slightly but remained high (Figure 7). Examples:

- *I am learning ways to document discoveries, explore, work with a team, and use my data to draw conclusions and solve problems. All these skills help prepare me to be a better scientist.*

Figure 7. Percentage of responses to the question "In what ways do you think EcoMUVE is helping you learn science?" The same response might include more than one code.

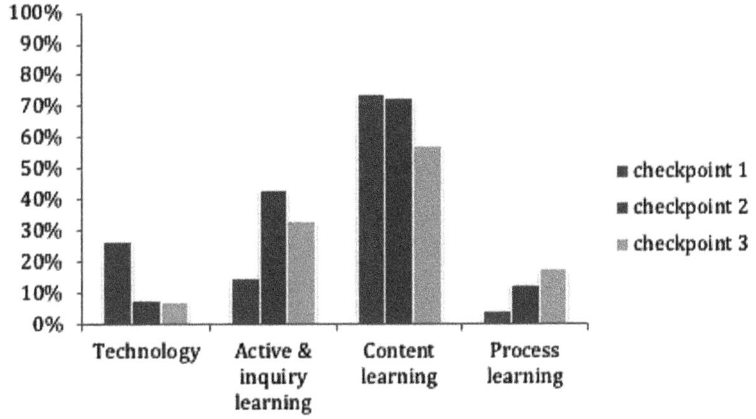

- *By exploring the world and taking pictures, you learn about different species in the real world.*
- *I think EcoMUVE helps me figure out how to solve problems.*
- *It helped me learn science by letting me do it by myself, not by a day to day manual.*

The coding for this question also added two categories about what students felt they were learning – coding for both science *content* learning – organisms, measurements, atoms and molecules – and science *process* learning - relationships, cause, effect, and how things happen. Content learning was the referenced most often, 74% in checkpoint 1, decreasing to 57% in checkpoint 3. Process learning increased from 4% in checkpoint 1 to 18% percent in checkpoint 3, as students described learning to make connections about relationships in ecosystems. Examples:

- *It helps me see what organisms live in a local pond.* (content)
- *It helped me learn more information about atoms.* (content)
- *It helped me to connect my knowledge and figure out how things are related.* (process)
- *It helped me learn to link behavior to past events, and that to the ecosystem.* (process)

Open-Ended Response 4: How Is Learning Science With EcoMUVE Different From Typical Activities You've Done in Science Class?

Responses to the question about differences between what they usually do in science class and EcoMUVE are presented in Figure 8. By far the most frequent response included *technology*. This response remained largely unchanged throughout the checkpoints (checkpoint 1: 79%, checkpoint 2: 77%, and checkpoint 3: 77%).

The second largest coding of responses referred to the activity being more *fun* than other activities. This response also didn't change much for the first two checkpoints, but decreased some for the third checkpoint (checkpoint 1: 32%, checkpoint 2: 34%, checkpoint 3: 26%).

Finally, responses that referred to pedagogical aspects of the activity were coded for *active* learning (e.g., interactive, hands-on, doing things) and *inquiry* learning. Responses coded as *active* learning

Figure 8. Percentage of responses to the question "How is learning science with EcoMUVE different from typical activities you've done in science class?" The same response might include more than one code.

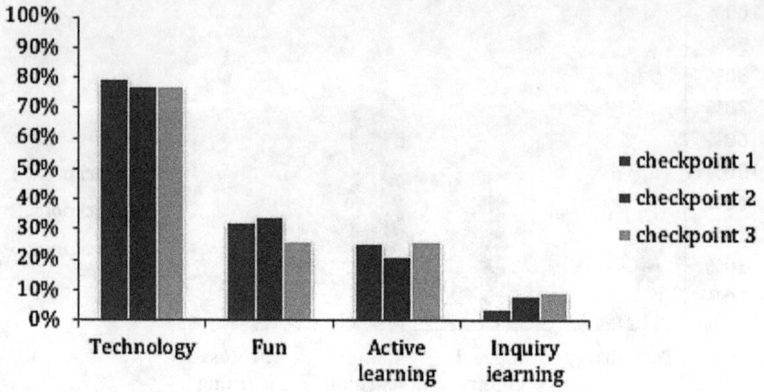

remained largely unchanged throughout the checkpoints (checkpoint 1: 18%, checkpoint 2: 14%, and checkpoint 3: 18%). Responses coded as *inquiry* increased from 4% to 10%.

Sample responses are as follows:

- *Its different because you are online.* (technology)
- *It's like playing a video game in school. And I realize that I'm learning at the same time as I'm having fun.* (technology, fun)
- *A lot more hands-on activities.* (active learning)
- *It is a different way to learn, instead of listening to a teacher you get to interact with a real world.* (active learning)
- *Usually, science class activities are reading and doing labs. EcoMUVE however, is more like being in the real world and solving real life problems.* (inquiry learning)

Progressions of Answers Over Checkpoints

In the analysis presented above, student answers were analyzed and compared between the three checkpoints, but without regard to progressions of answers by the same students through the checkpoints. Informally, however, we note some characteristics of student answers over time.

Some student answers stayed about the same through the checkpoints. For example, for question 1, one student wrote these very similar responses for checkpoints 1, 2, and 3.

1. I like that EcoMUVE is on the computer. I also like that it is like a game.
2. I like the virtual world part of EcoMUVE and how its on the computer.
3. The fact that it was on the computer.

The more interesting results are for the students whose answers progressed following the trends identified in our analysis. For example, another wrote these three responses, referencing technology and interface features for checkpoint 1, expanding to include collaborative aspects for checkpoint 2, and inquiry for checkpoint 3.

1. I like the virtual pond and the way you could explore underwater and on land.
2. I like the interesting features on EcoMUVE like people, the chatting feature, the submarine feature, and the ability to time travel to discover new things.
3. I liked the multiple features that could be used and the different people you could meet. I also liked how you could piece clues together that led to the answer of why the fish died.

Another factor to note is that the average length of student responses decreased from checkpoint 1 (100 characters) to checkpoint 3 (84 characters). Some students who wrote thoughtful responses in earlier checkpoints answered very briefly in checkpoint 3. Eg.

1. I like the interactivity. It is fun to do something where you get to control what you do.
2. I like how you can interact with virtual "people", animals, and each other.
3. There was a lot of freedom.

We postulate that this result may stem from reluctance or boredom in answering the same question for a third time, or more general survey fatigue.

DISCUSSION

Interest in EcoMUVE Becomes Interest for Science

Recall that one main goal of the present study was to explore features of EcoMUVE that sparked students' interests in the technology and then helped them translate that interest for the *technology* into interest for *science*. As Chen et al. (2016) noted, "technology-rich activities that spark an interest in an activity, but then sustain students' interests in the actual tasks of scientific inquiry may encourage students to turn their attention from the technology-rich activity to the field of science" (p. 21). In our present study, we found that students generally found working on a computer using an interactive simulation to be novel and therefore interesting. Roughly 70% of students mentioned enjoying something about the technology at the first checkpoint. That number decreased by roughly half by the second and third checkpoints, which indicates to us that the qualitative data also provide empirical evidence for a novelty effect. However, we also found that, although fewer people mentioned liking the technology as the curriculum progressed, more people mentioned being interested in curricular aspects. Specifically, students' enjoyment of the self-directed, collaborative, and inquiry-based nature of the curriculum increased. One question that follows from this finding concerns possible *mechanisms* for how EcoMUVE facilitated this transition from interest in the technology to interest for science. We discuss this next.

Choice, Connectedness, and Competence Beliefs Facilitate Interest Development

Self-determination theory (see Ryan & Deci, 2000) helps us understand how technology activities can facilitate the transition from interest in the technology to interest in the field of science. Ryan and Deci hypothesized that, three factors drive the move from more externally-controlled motivators (e.g., rewards, badges) to more internally-controlled ones (e.g., personal values): autonomy (choice), competence, and connectedness. When individuals have opportunities to make their own choices about what actions they take, their motivation for doing the activities is more likely to become internally driven rather than externally driven. Also, as individuals feel like they are becoming more competent in a class of activities, their motivation for engaging in those activities is more likely to be internally driven. Finally, the more that individuals feel a sense of connection or relatedness to others in the social context where they are engaging in tasks, the more likely their motivation is to be driven internally.

In the context of EcoMUVE, it is not surprising that student answers, particularly after the first day, focused on the technology and features of the virtual world interface. The opportunity to use computers in science class is rare and exciting, and that excitement is conveyed by students' focus on how "cool" the virtual world is, and how much more "fun" it is than traditional science activities. This is a common type of finding regarding educational technologies.

What this study demonstrates, however, is that over time enthusiasm about the technology begins to fade, and students become more aware and appreciative of the kinds of activities that EcoMUVE supports – the opportunities it affords for *self-directed learning* (choice), for *inquiry-based activities* (competence), and for *collaboration with a team* (connectedness). Even the question about what students *didn't* like, followed this pattern – over time there was an increase in requests for *more* active and inquiry-based learning, wanting more exploration, more things to find, more mysteries to solve. Phrases from students such as, "I like that it's created so that I'm in control. I like that I can change the date whenever I want to" show that once the novelty of the technology wears off, providing students with the *choice* to decide what to do facilitates interest development. Ryan and Deci (2000) rightly noted that "support for autonomy allows individuals to actively transform values into their own" (p. 74). We hypothesize that the more that students feel like their actions in scientifically inquiring through a complex problem are of their own choice, the more they begin to transform these values of scientific inquiry into their own values.

Furthermore, we point to student responses such as: "I like the fact that we are using what we find in the pond to solve the mystery of the fish dying" and also "I liked how you could go into nature to find out what was wrong. Not just talking about it." These responses describe students developing a greater facility with thinking scientifically through a problem. Although the present study does not have empirical evidence that students actually improved in their science inquiry skills, prior work has demonstrated that students do improve over time in their science inquiry (see Kamarainen, Metcalf, Grotzer, & Dede, 2015). Thus, it stands to reason that students, over time, begin to see themselves as more *competent* in doing the authentic tasks that scientists do—a key factor in developing students' intrinsic motivation for a set of tasks.

Finally, EcoMUVE is social—it fosters a sense of *connectedness*. For example, one student noted that, "I liked how we were able to interact and work together with people in our groups." In a similar fashion, another student said that, "I love it! I think it is an amazing idea to get students working together." Developing a sense of connection with other people who are all working on the same context helps to facilitate the development of interest, as Ryan and Deci (2000) hypothesized: "relatedness, the need to feel belongingness and connectedness with others, is centrally important for internalization" (p. 73). Thus, as students in EcoMUVE develop a stronger sense of connection with their peers, all of whom are working together to solve a complex problem, students are more able to internalize the value of scientific inquiry.

In light of the next generation science standards and their focus on the practices of science (NGSS Lead States, 2013; National Research Council, 2012), it was interesting to see that an increasing number of students referred to process and inquiry-based aspects of the learning experience. Further, the NGSS emphasize the need to address content learning in conjunction with development of process-based skills. Our work suggests (Figure 7) that students have opportunities for both types of learning within this richly contextualized virtual world. Education reform efforts over the past two decades have focused on inquiry-based approaches to learning and aim to support teachers in implementing rich inquiry curricula.

Inquiry-based teaching can be difficult to implement (Anderson 2002) and even in cases where a "hands-on" activity is used to engage students in scientific inquiry, those activities may not be "minds-on." Here we present a study in which the curriculum is not "hands on" in a traditional sense, yet seems to support students in their application of scientific thinking. Recent work suggests that carefully designed technology-supported curricula can support the creative synergy of thinking and doing that we hope students will engage in when conducting scientific inquiry (Campbell and Jane 2012), and our work aligns with these ideas in that significant numbers of students cited the utility of EcoMUVE for both active/inquiry learning and content learning. New and emerging technological approaches to teaching science bring to light interesting research questions around blending hands-on inquiry lessons with technology tools that support students in implementing "minds-on" approaches that are engaging on a deeper level than the 3-D graphical interface.

CONCLUSION

In summary, over the two-week EcoMUVE curriculum experience, student interest in EcoMUVE decreased somewhat but remained high; students' beliefs about EcoMUVE's utility increased; and students saw EcoMUVE as less of a "waste of time". Student responses to questions of what they liked about EcoMUVE changed from being primarily about the opportunity to interact in a virtual computer environment, to an increasing appreciation of the pedagogical aspects of the self-directed, collaborative, inquiry-based activities. These findings demonstrate that, although there is a novelty effect for EcoMUVE, student engagement didn't ultimately depend on novelty. The novelty of the technology, an attractor that fades over time, was supplanted by an intrinsic motivation to engage with the curriculum, a demonstration of Nicholson's goal for *meaningful* engagement (2015), and demonstrating the powerful motivational drives identified by Ryan and Deci (2000), through supporting Choice, Competence, and Connectedness.

This research is an important contribution to the teaching and learning of science because it demonstrates and reinforces the importance of sound pedagogical methods. As technology becomes more prevalent in science classrooms, this study serves as a reminder that, regardless of the medium, it is fundamental to design the technology to allow for active, collaborative student involvement in inquiring about scientific phenomena. As technology becomes more ubiquitous in everyday life, and as computer access improves across all schools, we can expect that there will be more development of technology-rich science curricula. With increased accessibility, research on the effectiveness of immersive environments to support student learning is becoming increasingly important. Affordances of technology merged with best practices in teaching can contribute to bolstering students' interest in doing science, and facilitating the belief that learning science is a useful and worthwhile pursuit.

ACKNOWLEDGMENT

This work is supported by the Institute of Education Sciences, U.S. Department of Education, Grant No. R305A080514 to Chris Dede and Tina Grotzer. All opinions, findings, conclusions or recommendations expressed here are those of the authors and do not necessarily reflect the views of the Institute for Education Sciences.

REFERENCES

Allcoat, D., & von Mühlenen, A. (2018). Learning in virtual reality: Effects on performance, emotion and engagement. *Research in Learning Technology*, 26.

Anderson, R. D. (2002). Reforming science teaching: What research says about inquiry. *Journal of Science Teacher Education*, *13*(1), 1–12. doi:10.1023/A:1015171124982

Barab, S., Thomas, M., Dodge, T., Carteaux, R., & Tuzun, H. (2005). Making learning fun: Quest Atlantis, a game without guns. *Educational Technology Research and Development*, *53*(1), 86–107. doi:10.1007/BF02504859

Campbell, C., & Jane, B. (2012). Motivating children to learn: The role of technology education. *International Journal of Technology and Design Education*, *22*(1), 1–11. doi:10.100710798-010-9134-4

Chapman, J., & Rich, P. (2017, January). Identifying motivational styles in educational gamification. *Proceedings of the 50th Hawaii International Conference on System Sciences*. 10.24251/HICSS.2017.157

Chen, J. A., Metcalf, S. J., & Tutwiler, M. S. (2014). Motivation and beliefs about the nature of scientific knowledge within an immersive virtual ecosystems environment. *Contemporary Educational Psychology*, *39*(2), 112–123. doi:10.1016/j.cedpsych.2014.02.004

Chen, J. A., Tutwiler, M. S., Metcalf, S. J., Kamarainen, A., Grotzer, T., & Dede, C. (2016). A multi-user virtual environment to support students' self-efficacy and interest in science: A latent growth model analysis. *Learning and Instruction*, *41*, 11–22. doi:10.1016/j.learninstruc.2015.09.007

Clark, R. E. (1983). Reconsidering research on learning from media. *Review of Educational Research*, *53*(4), 445–459. doi:10.3102/00346543053004445

Clarke, J., Dede, C., Ketelhut, D. J., & Nelson, B. (2006). A Design-based Research Strategy to Promote Scalability for Educational Innovations. *Educational Technology, 46*(3), 27-36.

Dalgarno, B., & Lee, M. J. W. (2010). What are the learning affordances of 3-D virtual environments? *British Journal of Educational Technology*, *41*(1), 10–32. doi:10.1111/j.1467-8535.2009.01038.x

Fishman, B., Dede, C., & Means, B. (2015). Teaching and technology: New tools for new times. In D. Gitomer & C. Bell (Eds.), *Handbook of Research on Teaching* (5th ed.). Washington, DC: American Educational Research Association.

Grotzer, T. A., Kamarainen, A., Tutwiler, M. S., Metcalf, S., & Dede, C. (2013). Learning to reason about ecosystems dynamics over time: The challenges of an event-based causal focus. *Bioscience*, *63*(4), 288–296. doi:10.1525/bio.2013.63.4.9

Hamari, J., Koivisto, J., & Sarsa, H. (2014). Does Gamification Work? – A Literature Review of Empirical Studies on Gamification. *Proceedings of the 47th Hawaii International Conference on System Sciences*. 10.1109/HICSS.2014.377

Hanus, M. D., & Fox, J. (2015). Assessing the effects of gamification in the classroom: A longitudinal study on intrinsic motivation, social comparison, satisfaction, effort, and academic performance. *Computers & Education*, *80*, 152–161. doi:10.1016/j.compedu.2014.08.019

Hew, K. F., & Cheung, W. S. (2010). Use of three-dimensional (3-D) immersive virtual worlds in K-12 and higher education settings: A review of the research. *British Journal of Educational Technology*, *41*(1), 33–55. doi:10.1111/j.1467-8535.2008.00900.x

Hidi, S., & Renninger, K. A. (2006). The four-phase model of interest development. *Educational Psychologist*, *41*(2), 111–127. doi:10.120715326985ep4102_4

Kafai, Y. B. (2010). The World of Whyville: Living, Playing, and Learning in a Tween Virtual World. *Games and Culture*, *5*(1), 3–22. doi:10.1177/1555412009351264

Kamarainen, A., Metcalf, S., Grotzer, T., & Dede, C. J. (2015). Exploring ecosystems from the inside: How immersion in a multi-user virtual environment supports epistemologically grounded practices in ecosystem science instruction. *Journal of Science Education and Technology*, *24*(2), 148–167. doi:10.100710956-014-9531-7

Ke, F. (2016). Designing and integrating purposeful learning in game play: A systematic review. *Educational Technology Research and Development*, *64*(2), 219–244. doi:10.100711423-015-9418-1

Kim, B. (2015). Designing Gamification in the Right Way. *Library Technology Reports*, *51*, 29–35.

Koivisto, J., & Hamari, J. (2014). Demographic differences in perceived benefits from gamification. *Computers in Human Behavior*, *35*, 179–188. doi:10.1016/j.chb.2014.03.007

Lenhart, A., Kahne, J., Middaugh, E., Macgill, A. R., Evans, C., & Vitak, J. (2008). *Teens, Video Games, and Civics: Teens' Gaming Experiences Are Diverse and Include Significant Social Interaction and Civic Engagement*. Pew Internet & American Life Project.

Lim, C. P., Nonis, D., & Hedberg, J. (2006). Gaming in a 3D multiuser virtual environment: Engaging students in science lessons. *British Journal of Educational Technology*, *37*(2), 211–231. doi:10.1111/j.1467-8535.2006.00531.x

Merchant, Z., Goetz, E. T., Cifuentes, L., Keeney-Kennicutt, W., & Davis, T. J. (2014). Effectiveness of virtual reality-based instruction on students' learning outcomes in K-12 and higher education: A meta-analysis. *Computers & Education*, *70*, 29–40. doi:10.1016/j.compedu.2013.07.033

Metcalf, S. J., Kamarainen, A., Tutwiler, M. S., Grotzer, T. A., & Dede, C. J. (2013). Teacher perceptions of the practicality and effectiveness of immersive ecological simulations as classroom curricula. *International Journal of Virtual and Personal Learning Environments*, *4*(3), 66–77. doi:10.4018/jvple.2013070105

Metcalf, S. J., Kamarainen, A. M., Torres, E., Grotzer, T. A., & Dede, C. (2018). EcoMUVE: A Case Study on the Affordances of MUVEs in Ecosystem Science Education. In Y. Qian (Ed.), *Integrating Multi-User Virtual Environments in Modern Classrooms* (pp. 1–25). Hershey, PA: IGI Global. doi:10.4018/978-1-5225-3719-9.ch001

Metcalf, S. J., Tutwiler, M. S., Kamarainen, A. M., Grotzer, T. A., & Dede, C. J. (2013). Multi-user virtual environments to promote middle school ecosystem science learning and attitudes about science. American Educational Research Association (AERA) Conference, San Francisco, CA.

National Research Council. (2012). *A framework for K-12 science education: Practices, cross-cutting concepts, and core ideas*. Washington, DC: The National Academies Press.

Nelson, B. C., & Ketelhut, D. J. (2007). Scientific inquiry in educational multi-user virtual environments. *Educational Psychology Review*, *19*(3), 265–283. doi:10.100710648-007-9048-1

NGSS Lead States. (2013). *Next Generation Science Standards: For States, By States*. Achieve, Inc.

Nicholson, S. (2015). A recipe for meaningful gamification. In *Gamification in education and business* (pp. 1–20). Cham: Springer.

Omale, N., Hung, W. C., Luetkehans, L., & Cooke-Plagwitz, J. (2009). Learning in 3-D multiuser virtual environments: Exploring the use of unique 3-D attributes for online problem-based learning. *British Journal of Educational Technology*, *40*(3), 480–495. doi:10.1111/j.1467-8535.2009.00941.x

Rideout, V. J., Foehr, U. G., & Roberts, D. F. (2010). *Generation M^2: Media in the Lives of 8-to 18-Year-Olds*. Henry J. Kaiser Family Foundation.

Ryan, R. M., & Deci, E. L. (2000). Self-determination theory and the facilitation of intrinsic motivation, social development, and well-being. *The American Psychologist*, *55*(1), 68–78. doi:10.1037/0003-066X.55.1.68 PMID:11392867

KEY TERMS AND DEFINITIONS

Autonomy: A situation in which the learner is able to make his/her own choices within a learning activity.

Cost Value: A perception of how the time and effort required for a task relates to its utility.

Ecosystem: A community that includes all the living and nonliving things found in a certain area.

Extrinsic Motivation: Choosing to do an activity for external rewards or to avoid negative consequences.

Gamification: A design approach in which game elements are implemented in learning environments.

Immersive: Feeling as if one is really taking part in the experience; feeling as if one is really in a virtual environment.

Inquiry-Based Learning: Active learning that is based on posing questions, problems or scenarios to investigate.

Intrinsic Motivation: Choosing to do an activity because of internal factors such as personal satisfaction or accomplishment.

Novelty Effect: An improvement in learning when a new technology is introduced, attributable to increased interest in the new technology, that tends to diminish as students become more familiar with it.

Utility: A perception of how a task relates to future goals, rewards, or outcomes.

Chapter 6
Perceptions of Presence and Community in Immersive Online Learning Environments

Amelia Cheney
Appalachian State University, USA

Terry McClannon
Appalachian State University, USA

Les Bolt
Appalachian State University, USA

Robert Sanders
Appalachian State University, USA

ABSTRACT

This chapter is based on survey research conducted between 2010 and 2017, involving 1053 graduate students using immersive online learning environments for their coursework. Investigators used course structural factors and student engagement factors to predict students' perceptions of community and presence in the online immersive space. Utilizing the Sense of Community II index (SCI-2) and the Community of Inquiry survey (COI) median scores as cut scores for predicted outcomes, researchers demonstrated that purely online environments which encouraged student engagement in the online immersive space can enhance sense of presence and sense of community. In addition, students in graduate programs that used online immersive delivery methods longer developed a stronger sense of community. Both dependent measures proved to have stable subscale structures for this inquiry based on a cursory confirmatory factor analysis.

DOI: 10.4018/978-1-5225-7987-8.ch006

INTRODUCTION

More than a decade ago, faculty members in the Instructional Technology program at Appalachian State University realized that something was missing from their online courses. These faculty members subscribed to the tenets of their college's social constructivist conceptual framework but noticed that despite their best efforts, many of these tenets were not being fully addressed in the online components of their courses; in particular, learning was not occurring through students' participation in a Community of Practice, nor was knowledge being socially constructed within such a community. At that time, the university had adopted and was promoting the use of a commonly used learning management system (LMS) to support the delivery of hybrid courses (combination of online and face-to-face), primarily as a supplement for students taking coursework at remote extension sites throughout western North Carolina. While the faculty using these tools believed that there was potential value in teaching and learning in an online environment, it was apparent to these educators that their students were not as engaged in the online component of the courses as they were when classes met face-to-face. The online learning components were passive, isolating, and utilitarian, albeit unintentionally, and lacked opportunities for social connections to be made with other students or faculty. Students had little, if any, sense that others were present when logged into the LMS. There was no sense that others were online to help, collaborate, or interact. The only opportunities for students to feel part of a learning community were during the limited time spent in class, face-to-face with their peers and instructors. The online component to the class did little to further the development of this community. Therefore, a new set of tools that afforded a new approach better aligned with a social constructivist philosophy was needed.

Following extensive research and exploration, these faculty members discovered an emerging technology that provided the type of online forum they desired; one that supported both scholarly activity and social interactions between and among students and faculty. Virtual Worlds, specifically *ActiveWorlds*, offered persistent 3D immersive learning environments that provided multiple manifestations of presence (comprised of students, faculty, spaces, tools, and artifacts) that closely aligned with the real world in which these students were accustomed to working. They believed that this virtual world might have potential for creating an online learning environment that was as engaging as the face-to-face classes they offered, if not more so. In fact, these faculty noticed that over time, the interactions they had with their students, the interactions between students, and the students' interactions with the tools and resources in this new virtual environment began to resemble the learning communities of practice promoted by the aforementioned conceptual framework of their college.

More than ten years later, the use of similar 3D immersive learning environments has spread worldwide and expanded at Appalachian State University to be the environment of choice for nearly two dozen faculty members in the Department of Leadership and Educational Studies in the Reich College of Education. During this last decade, numerous studies have been conducted and many changes have occurred to improve on quality of the teaching and learning experiences offered. However, the fundamental questions about the role of presence and the resulting formation of community have remained and continue to guide the work done by these educators.

FORMATION OF ONLINE COMMUNITIES

Learners' sense of "community" is a common theme found in the literature related to online learning, particularly that experienced in virtual worlds or 3D immersive learning environments. These communities are referred to in the literature as "learning communities," "virtual communities," and "communities of practice" but all refer to the same general description of learner groups. Regardless of the term used, each refers to what Sadera, Robertson, Song, and Midon (2009) describe as "a group of participants in a distance-based environment with a shared purpose and the relationship among them including their sense of belonging, trust, and interaction" (p. 278). These online communities develop around a shared understanding and exist as "real" communities in that they are simultaneously situated in the real world (Sanders & Melton, 2010, p. 65). Jonassen (1997) argues that online learning communities should be "active, constructive, collaborative, intentional, complex, contextual, conversational and reflective". Wilson and Ryder (1996) add the term "dynamic" to this list of characteristics of a learning community to emphasize a group characterized by the "distribution of control, commitment to generation and sharing of new knowledge, flexible and negotiated learning activities, autonomous community members, high levels of interaction, and shared goals and project". Preece further supports these definitions of an online learning community by stating that these particular communities include: (a) people establishing meaningful relationships; (b) a common purpose, interest, need, or task; (c) shared policies in the form of rituals, protocols, rules and laws to guide interactions; and (d) a sense of togetherness, once the virtual space becomes more and more inhabited (as cited in Ligorio & Van der Meijden, 2008, p. 12).

The formation of community is an essential ingredient to the success of online learners. Wilson and Ryder (1996) point out that "learning cannot be separated from action" and that "community sharing [has] a consensual goal to support each other in learning". Learning is inextricably tied to the learners' participation in a community (Oliver & Carr, 2009) and according to Perry and Edwards, the formation of an online learning community "serves as the foundation for a successful learning environment" (As cited in Scherer Bassani, 2011, p. 932). A study by Liu et al. (2007) showed significant relationships between sense of community and perceived learning engagement, perceived learning, and student satisfaction with online learning experiences. Lear, Ansorge & Steckleberg (2010) report that a sense of community is necessary for students to be active, engaged learners online. Furthermore, Edirisingha et al. state that "studies of online socialization within distance learning have found positive correlations between opportunities for socialization and students' perception of learning (as cited by Barkand & Kush, 2009, p. 223). In the COI model discussed below, "the abilities of both student and teacher to project themselves into the learning space [and into the learning community] are key elements to successful learning transactions" (Warburton, 2009, p. 419).

PRESENCE

Central to the idea of creation of community is that its members be present with one another. The concepts of presence and co-presence are often found in discussion of pedagogy in virtual environments, though definitions of the terms vary. One useful definition of presence can be found in Rodgers and Raider-Roth: "To be present is to come into relation, into connection, with students, their learning, subject matter and oneself" (2006). Gardner and Elliott (2014) describe an immersive online learning environment as one that gives:

Participants a sense of 'being there' even when attending a class or training session in person isn't possible, practical, or desirable, which in turn provides educators and students with the ability to connect and communicate in a way that greatly enhances the learning experience. (p. 2)

This notion of presence as one of relationships and connections is of great importance in online learning experiences. In a 2005 study, students' perception of presence of other students and instructors in online classes significantly related to their positive attitudes about courses and levels of satisfaction with their own learning (Russo and Benson). Selverian and Hwang (2003) noted that the sense of spatial and social presence in virtual learning environments plays a positive role in supporting learning. These findings were reiterated by Joksimovic et al (2015), in a study which reiterated the relationship of social and teaching presence to academic achievement in online courses.

Not only does a sense of presence have an impact of students' impressions of learning and satisfaction, but it may well have an effect on their levels of participation within online communities. A 2008 study by Shen and Khalifa found that affective social presence has significant effects on both extrinsic and intrinsic motivation of members of virtual communities; that within the context of online communities:

...the sense of psychological attachment is an important aspect of social presence and related to both external and internal goals in participating in online communities. When the individual member has a strong sense of psychological connection with the online communities, he or she is more likely to believe the online community will fulfill his or her needs for information, social support, or simply enjoyment. (p. 739)

They continue their analysis by noting that social presence has a significant independent effect on participation – that it is a driver distinct from motivational variables.

Bronack et al (2008), in their discussion of Presence Pedagogy (P2), note that manifestations of presence enabled by the combination of content, context, and activity in a well-designed virtual world are the critical attributes for engagement among students in a social constructivist learning environment. In this pedagogical model designed to capitalize upon the sense of presence in immersive environments, some similarities may be found to interactions in face-to-face environments; however, there are fundamental differences: "Unlike F2F presence, P2 can provide continuous access to instructors, colleagues and other students...students and faculty may be present in a virtual space at most times of the day, week and semester" (Cheney et al, 2009, p. 91). As all members of the learning community participate in ongoing interactions, both planned and unplanned, this feeling of presence can contribute to the formations of communities of shared learning in ways unique to virtual spaces.

COMMUNITIES OF INQUIRY

The community of inquiry theoretical framework is one that "represents a process of creating a deep and meaningful (collaborative-constructivist) learning experience through the development of three interdependent elements - social, cognitive and teaching presence" (Garrison, Anderson, Archer & Rourke, 2011). The three elements of cognitive presence, social presence, and teaching presence, all contain indicators within each of the areas that, serve as a guide to educators for the development of optimal online learning communities. The initial studies related to the community of inquiry model aimed to use the

COI framework within text-based CMC settings, primarily threaded discussions, in order to determine the effectiveness of such instructional settings (Garrison, Anderson, & Archer, 1999), and was utilized as an evaluation and assessment tool aimed at identifying categories and indicators of cognitive, social and teaching presence within these settings.

Within the model, cognitive presence is discussed as being the element that addresses the ability of community participants to construct meaning through sustained communication, and it is described as being the element that is most basic to successful learning. Social presence is defined as the ability of participants to represent themselves as 'real people' within the community, and it addresses many affective components of learning. The element of teaching presence consists of indicators that address both the design of the instruction and the actual facilitation (Garrison, Anderson, & Archer, 1999).

Since the initial application of the model to text-based CMC environments, the framework has been applied to a variety of online settings (Garrison, 2007), and has included hybrid settings as well (Arbaugh, Bangert, & Cleveland-Innes, 2010; Vaughan, 2010; Shea & Bidjerano, 2010). Although studies that address the COI framework within immersive learning environments have begun to emerge, there are still many avenues to be investigated within growing MUVE educational settings. McKerlich & Anderson (2007), laid the groundwork for being able to assessing the applicability of the COI model within Multi User Virtual Environments (MUVE) by utilizing an exploratory, observational methodology as they observed several educational events that occurred within the popular Second Life environment. Their findings indicated that the core construct of the community of inquiry framework does indeed transfer to immersive learning environments and that the indicators within the original model were indeed observable within this environment.

This finding was further validated by Burgess, Slate, Rojas-LeBouef, & LaPrairie, (2010) who evaluated class sessions conducted within Second Life and found that their study "supports the efficacy of assessing social, teaching and cognitive presences within a MUVE from the points of view of both participant perceptions and objective observations (p. 87). The validity of the COI framework within virtual environments was also noted by McKerlich, et al. (2011).

There is much more to be learned about the impact of presence has on students' sense of community and how an improved understanding of this impact can guide the ongoing design and development of effective and engaging online learning environments. Two tools that have the potential of providing some additional insight are the Community of Inquiry (COI) survey and the Sense of Community Index 2 (SCI-2).

Much of the research conducted to this point using the COI scale to analyze students' sense of community in an online environment have focused on the use of commonly used learning management systems like those first used by the instructional technology faculty mentioned above. Likewise, the use of the SCI-2 scale has been used primarily to examine students' sense of presence in a learning environment in both face-to-face environments and online environments created using similar learning management tools. While studies examining presence and community formation in virtual worlds are now beginning to emerge, more research is necessary to understand the unique impact of 3D immersive learning environments have on both students' sense of community and presence in these unique spaces.

PURPOSE OF THIS STUDY

The purpose of this exploratory study was to examine factors that may predict graduate students' development of a collaborative community of inquiry (as measured by the COI scale) and their development of a sense of presence in an online virtual environment (as measured by the SCI-2 scale).

In particular, four questions were examined:

- Does the time in the graduate program impact learners' sense of community as measured by the COI and/or SCI-2 scale scores?
- Does the level of online immersion impact learners' sense of community?
- Does the time per week actually spent in the online environment impact the learners' sense of community?
- What is the nature of the relationship between the COI and SCI-2 scale scores?

METHODS

Data Sources

Presence and Sense of Community appear to be two distinct yet related concepts. Therefore, two different instruments were chosen to assess the development of community within the MUVE: the Sense of Community Index 2 (SCI-2) and the Community of Inquiry (COI) survey.

The SCI-2 is a survey that is used as a measure of sense of community, and it has been used as such in a variety of educational settings and a number of different cultures (Chavis, Lee, & Acosta, 2008). The instrument includes subscores for reinforcement, membership, influence, and shared emotion with several distinct item sets for each subscore. The SCI-2 is an instrument that has been revised from an earlier version due to issues with reliability and concerns of cross-cultural measures. The new version, however, has been shown to be a reliable measure (coefficient alpha= .94), with subscales that are deemed reliable with coefficient alpha scores of .79 to .86 (Chavis, Lee & Acosta, 2008). For this study, the overall alpha was .95 with sub scores alphas ranging from .80 for membership to .92 for reinforcement.

The COI instrument is a 34-item likert-type scale that assesses all three areas of teaching, cognitive and social presence with a distinct item set for each sub score. The instrument has been widely utilized, and it has been deemed a valid and reliable instrument for measuring the dimensions of the model within a variety of educational settings (Arbaugh et al., 2008; Swan et al., 2008). For this study the overall alpha was .98 with alpha for the three sub scales ranging from .95 to .97.

Respondents

The respondents for this study included 1053 unique students enrolled in various graduate programs within the Department of Leadership and Educational studies during the spring and summer of 2010 thru 2017. Classes that included a virtual component and were either fully online or a hybrid of online and face-to-face meetings were included in the sample.

FINDINGS

In answering the first three research questions, categorical independent variables were recoded to dichotomous variables based on an inspection of frequencies and an Independent t-test was run for each question. Stepwise discriminant analysis techniques were then used to identify the most significant subscale predictors and the most significant question or question set predictors for the significant relationships identified in the t-tests.

In order to answer the fourth question, Pearson correlations were run for relationships between the overall scale scores and then between subscale scores. This analysis was used to identify the level and direction of shared variation between the two instruments.

Does the Time in the Graduate Program Impact the COI and/or SCI-2 Scale Scores?

Time in the graduate program had no significant impact on the overall SCI-2 ($p < .990$) score nor on the overall COI scores ($p < .073$) (Table 1). Although the t does not rise to the level of two-tailed significance for the overall COI score, it is a significant outcome ($p < .073/2 = .037$) for a directional one-tailed question. However, that was not the nature of this inquiry.

Does the Level of Online Immersion Impact the COI and/or SCI-2 Scale Scores?

See Table 2.

COI

Level of immersion in the virtual environment had a significant impact ($t = -7.55$, $p < .000$, $N = 902$) on the overall COI score (Table 2). In a previous 2013 analysis with a smaller N (193) this significance

Table 1. Time in program / SCI-2 & COI

		t-Test for Equality of Means		
		t	df	Sig. (2-Tailed)
COI_Overall	Equal variances assumed	-1.795	901	.073
SCI-2_Overall	Equal variances assumed	-0.012	901	.990

Table 2. Hybrid vs. total online/ SCI-2 & COI

		t-Test for Equality of Means		
		t	df	Sig. (2-Tailed)
COI_Overall	Equal variances assumed	-7.55	901	.000
SCI-2_Overall	Equal variances assumed	-8.835	901	.000

was not present ($p < .073$). Subject in fully online settings had higher overall COI scores (4.33) than those in hybrid environments (3.98).

Discriminant analysis (Table 3) revealed that the Social Presence sub score of the COI was the single significant sub score predictor of the discrimination between fully online cohorts and hybrid cohorts (Wilks' Lamba = .965, $p < .000$, N = 902).

Additional discriminant analysis of the question sets that composed the Social Presence sub score revealed that only the Affective Presence question set accounted for the discrimination attributed to the sub score (Wilks' Lamba = .907, $p < .000$, N = 902).

SCI-2

The level of immersion in the virtual environment had a significant impact on the SCI-2 overall scale (Table 2) score ($t = -8.835$, $p < .000$, N = 902). Subjects in fully online cohorts had a significantly higher overall score (2.86) than subjects in hybrid or hybrid formats (2.49).

Discriminant analysis (Table 4) revealed that the Reinforcement and Shared Emotional sub scores of the SCI-2 were significant predictors of the discrimination between fully online cohorts and hybrid cohorts (Wilks' Lamba = .890, $p < .000$, N = 977).

Additional discriminant analysis across those specific item sets in the Reinforcement subscore identified items related to Members Success Needs Met and Similar Values predicted the significant discrimination between subjects in fully online cohorts and those in hybrid cohorts (Wilks' Lamba = .882, $p < .000$, N = 965) .

Additional discriminant analysis across those specific item sets in the Shared Emotional subscore identified items related to Important Part of Community, Shared Important Events in Community, and Hope About Future predicted the significant discrimination between subjects in fully online cohorts and those in hybrid cohorts (Wilks' Lamba = .923, $p < .000$, N = 965) .

Table 3. Hybrid vs. total online discriminant analysis by COI sub scores

Step	Entered	Wilks' Lambda							
		Stat	df1	df2	df3	Exact F			
						Stat	df1	df2	Sig.
1	Social Presence	.965	1	1	901.00	32.835	1	901.00	.000

At each step, the variable that minimizes the overall Wilks' Lambda is entered.

Table 4. Hybrid vs. total online discriminant analysis by SCI-2 sub scores

Step	Entered	Wilks' Lambda							
		Stat	df1	df2	df3	Exact F			
						Stat	df1	df2	Sig.
1	Reinforce	.896	1	1	966.00	111.716	1	966.00	.000
2	Shared Emotional	.890	2	1	966.00	59.743	2	965.00	.000

At each step, the variable that minimizes the overall Wilks' Lambda is entered.

Does the Time Per Week Actually Spent in the Online Environment Impact the COI and/or SCI-2 Scale Scores?

See Table 5.

COI

Time spent in the virtual environment had a significant impact (Table 5) on the overall COI scores (t = -4.982, p < .000, N = 902). In particular, subjects that spent two hours or less in the environment per week had a significant lower score (4.05) than subjects that spent more time (4.28).

Discriminant function analysis (Table 6) revealed that the Social Presence subscore of the COI was the sole significant predictor of the difference between subjects that spent less than one hour per week and those that spent more time (Wilks' Lamba = .965, p < .00, N = 902).

Additional discriminant analysis across those specific item sets in the Social Presence subscore identified the item set related to Affective Presence predicted the significant discrimination between subjects in engaged more than two hours per week and those engaged less. (Wilks' Lamba = .958, p < .000, N = 902).

SCI-2

Time spent in the virtual environment (Table 5) had a significant impact on the overall SCI-2 scores (t = -9.348, p < .000, N = 972). In particular, subjects that spent less than two hour in the immersive environment per week had a significant lower score (2.47) than subjects that spent more time (2.87).

Discriminant analysis (Table 7) revealed that the Reinforcement sub score of the SCI-2 was the sole significant predictor of the discrimination between subjects that spent less than two hours per week and those that spent more time (Wilks' Lamba = .905, p < .000, N = 966).

Table 5. Time spent per week/ SCI-2 & COI

		t-Test for Equality of Means		
		t	df	Sig. (2-Tailed)
COI_Overall	Equal variances assumed	-4.982	901	.000
SCI-2_Overall	Equal variances assumed	-9.348	971	.000

Table 6. Time spent per week discriminant analysis by COI sub scores

Step	Entered	Wilks' Lambda							
		Stat	df1	df2	df3	Exact F			
						Stat	df1	df2	Sig.
1	Social Presence	.965	1	1	901.000	7.027	1	901.000	.000

At each step, the variable that minimizes the overall Wilks' Lambda is entered.

Table 7. Time spent per week discriminant analysis by SCI-2 sub scores

Step	Entered	Wilks' Lambda							
		Stat	df1	df2	df3	Exact F			
						Stat	df1	df2	Sig.
1	Reinforce	.905	1	1	966.000	101.152	1	966.000	.000

At each step, the variable that minimizes the overall Wilks' Lambda is entered.

Within the SCI-2 Reinforcement sub scale, two items (Success in Meeting Member Needs and Similar Community Needs) predicted the discrimination between subjects that spent less than two hours in the immersive environment per week versus those that spent more time (Wilks' Lamba = .900, p< .000, N= 898).

What Is the Nature of the Relationship Between the COI and SCI-2 Scale Scores?

Responses to the two instruments were highly positively correlated to each other in the overall score ($r = .602$, $p < .01$, $N = 903$). The r^2 of .362 between the two overall scores would indicate that the two instruments share about 36% of the variation between them and thus are relatively strong congruent predictors of a sense of community. In addition the subscores in the two instruments (Table 8) were also positively correlated (r's between .416 and .604, $p < .000$, $N = 903$) with subscores on the other. This would seem to indicate that the two instruments share some of the same dimensions, just described in different conceptual models.

DISCUSSION

The purpose of this study was to examine the impact of 3D immersive learning environments on students' sense of community and presence. Researchers utilized two previously validated instruments, the Community of Inquiry (COI) and the Sense of Community Index-2 (SCI-2), to assess students' perceived

Table 8. Correlations between SCI-2 and COI sub scores

		SCI2_Reinforce	SCI2_ Membership	SCI2_Influence	SCI2_ SharedEmotional
COI Teaching_Pres	r	.504**	.416**	.473**	.447**
	N	903	903	902	902
COI Social_Pres	r	.604**	.512**	.523**	.538**
	N	903	903	902	902
COI Cognitive_Pres	r	.569**	.468**	.516**	.507**
	N	903	903	902	902

sense of community and presence while taking graduate coursework. Significant findings were found for both instruments to address the study's four research questions.

Does the Time in Graduate Programs Impact the COI and/or SCI-2?

Researchers examined the overall SCI-2 scores to find that there was no significance in regard to the length of time that students were in graduate programs. While the researchers expected that it could potentially become significant, bi-annual surveys of students did not bear this out in either instrument.

Does the Level of Online Immersion Impact the COI and/or SCI-2 Scores?

There are varying degrees of immersion when one discusses teaching and learning online. The graduate programs involved in this study have two primary forms of formal meetings: hybrid (face-to-face classes and online meetings in virtual environment) and online (fully online meetings in virtual environment). For the purpose of this study, we will define the level of immersion by the standard meeting types used in the virtual environment. Low indicates that students met in a hybrid type or both face-to-face and online meetings. High indicates that students met completely online for meetings and interactions.

The impact of the level of immersion of students in the virtual environment on students' sense of community and presence was of interest to the researchers. Student levels of immersion in LMS type systems and virtual environments are often quite different from one another. Students' experiences in LMS environments tend to be focused more on the interaction and management of content of the course, whereas students immersed in a virtual environment tend to be much more interactive and collaborative with both content and the community of fellow students and faculty. With the virtual environment, the coursework and course interactions are interdependent and seamless. Therefore, students are part of a much more meaningful and engaging community of learners whereby learning is supported through socially and intellectual interactions.

The researchers found that Level of Immersion in Online environments had a significant impact on the COI score and the SCI-2 scores. The fully online cohorts had a significantly higher overall score than the hybrid cohorts. Therefore, the results indicated students in fully online cohorts had a greater perceived sense of presence than those in the hybrid cohorts. For the sub-score analysis of COI, the Social Presence Score was the only significant predictor of Cohort type, with the Affective Presence item set predicting cohort type.The SCI-2 sub scores for both Reinforcement of Needs and Shared Emotional Connection werealso found to be significant predictors between the groups. For SCI-2 and the Reinforcement sub-score, items 3 and 2 predicted the strongest significant discrimination between subjects in fully online cohorts and those in hybrid cohorts (3. *The community has been successful in getting the needs of its members met.*; 2. *Community members and I value the same things.*). Furthermore, for SCI-2 and the Shared Emotional Connection sub-score, items 19, 22, and 23 predicted cohort type. (19. *It is very important to me to be a part of this community.*; 22. *Members of this community have shared important events together, such as holidays, celebrations, and disasters.*; 23. *I feel hopeful about the future of this community.*)

These findings indicate the willingness of fully online groups to work together to accomplish mutually beneficial tasks and goals. The virtual environment provides students opportunities to interact with other members on a much more intimate ways than traditional LMS asynchronous systems and even face-to-face environments. Interactions often take place in small groups that include text chats, audio-conferencing and video-conferencing, while collaboratively sharing resources within the virtual environment. Students utilize the variety of synchronous and asynchronous tools of the virtual environment that work best for their group dynamics. As a result of the high levels of close interactions, groups develop close personal and professional bonds that help to develop close communities of practice where individual and group needs are met.

Does the Time Per Week Actually Spent in the Online Environment Impact the COI and/or SCI-2 Scale Scores?

The amount of time spent in the virtual environment was found to have a significant impact on the overall SCI-2 Scores. Subjects that spent one hour or less in the environment per week had a significantly lower score that subjects that spent more time. This finding should not be a revelation to anyone. Just as with any environment, the more time spent in that environment will have an impact on one's sense of community and presence. Virtual learning environments should be no different. Therefore, subjects spending more than one hour in the virtual environment had a greater sense of presence that those who spent less.

Analysis of the data revealed specific indicators of Reinforcement that proved to be predictors for this finding. For SCI-2 and the Reinforcement sub-score, items 3 and 2 significantly predicted cohort type (3. *The community has been successful in getting the needs of its members met.*; 2. *Community members and I value the same things.*). Members that felt that they had their needs met, membership feels good, and similar community needs responded more positively that those subjects who spent one hour or less in the virtual environment. Students in completely online cohorts who spent two or more hours in the virtual environment had a great sense of having their needs reinforced.

Time spent in the virtual environment also had a significant impact on the overall COI Scores. Subjects who spent one hour or less in the environment per week also had a significantly lower score than those who spent more time. For the COI scale, Social Presence was the sole significant predictor between groups. For COI and the Social Presence sub-score, Affective Presence item set predicted cohort type. Members of the community who spent more time online were more successful in projecting their "real selves" to other members of the cohort and conveying affect through their interactions with others.

What Is the Nature of the Relationship Between the COI and SCI-2 Scale Scores?

Researcher analysis found that the two instruments were highly positively correlated to each other in the overall score. The two instruments were found to share approximately 27% of the variance between them and were relatively strong congruent predictors of a sense of community. These results indicate that the two instruments share some of the same dimensions, just described in different conceptual models.

Limitations

The researchers acknowledge that the transition from one virtual environment to another may have impacted students' perceptions of community and presence in this study. Some of the initial students in the study worked within an ActiveWorlds virtual environment as well as a Teleplace environment during their courses, while others may have only worked within Teleplace. There are distinct differences between these platforms in the way that students and faculty can communicate, collaborate, and share resources. Student populations were surveyed at points before and after the department transitioned to a new virtual learning platform. The Teleplace environment provides a much more rich and integrated setting. The addition of new collaborative tools could have led to new pedagogical practices that may have had an impact on students' sense of community and presence.

Lastly, the researchers did not attempt to assess the pedagogical approaches used by faculty from the various programs. Variations in styles, interactions, and resources could potentially impact student perceptions.

Implications for Future Research

The researchers plan to continue research within the AET Zone virtual learning environment. Data collection will continue at periodic times throughout the academic year to accurately assess student perceptions of community and presence. As the data set grows the researchers will be able to continue provide more accurate analysis of community and presence within the virtual environment.

Continued research is needed to ensure that the study results are consistent within a single AET Zone platform (Teleplace). Given that some students received instruction and interacted with peers and faculty in one or both virtual learning environments, it is imperative that researchers compare activities that were perceived to produce students' sense of community and presence in a setting where the tools and interactions are consistent. At this time, Teleplace is the sole virtual platform used by departmental faculty for instruction. Therefore, all future student responses to surveys will be based on one instructional platform and set of collaborative tools.

An area of interest that emerged from this study is the potential correlation of sense of community and presence. Study results indicated that that these two factors were highly positively correlated and have a potential impact on each other. While these factors appear to be independent they appear to be indicators of the other. Future research would attempt to isolate the factors that contribute to their correlation and indications.

Much of the literature related to the Communities of Inquiry framework, and other work on presence in online environments, deals with the impact of social presence in instruction. The significant findings in the area of social presence and Reinforcement indicate that future focus is needed in these areas, particularly related to the relationship between these two areas and subsequently, the respective roles of the instructor and the other students in immersive learning environments.

CONCLUSION

Previous research has indicated that community is fundamental to learning (Oliver & Carr, 2009). The uses of 3D immersive environments for educational purposes are no different than traditional face-to-face experiences in this regard. Proponents of the use of immersive environments in education have often espoused the notion that important concepts such as community and presence can be replicated, if not improved, in these settings. The findings of this study support these ideas: that community and presence in online learning are related concepts, that students participating in these virtual spaces can have a strong sense of both, and that well-utilized immersive spaces give students a strong sense of connection to instructors.

REFERENCES

Anderson, T., Rourke, L., Garrison, R., & Archer, W. (2001). Assessing teacher presence in a computer conferencing context. *Journal of Asynchronous Learning Networks*, *5*(2), 17.

Arbaugh, J., Cleveland-Innes, M., Diaz, S., Garrison, D., Ice, P, & Richardson, J. (2008). Developing a community of inquiry instrument: Testing a measure of the Community of Inquiry framework using a multi-institutional sample. *The Internet and Higher Education, 11*(3-4), 133-136. doi:10.1016/j.iheduc.2008.06.003

Arbaugh, J.B., Bangert, A., & Cleveland-Innes, M. (2010). Subject matter effects and the Community of Inquiry (CoI) framework: An exploratory study. *The Internet and Higher Education, 13*(1-2), 37-44. doi:10.1016/j.iheduc.2009.10.006

Barkand, J & Kush, J. (2009). GEARS: A 3D virtual learning environment and virtual social and educational world used in online secondary schools. *Electronic Journal of e-Learning, 7*(3), 215 – 224.

Bronack, S., Sanders, R., Cheney, A., Riedl, R., Tashner, J., & Matzen, N. (2008). Presence pedagogy: Teaching and learning in a 3D immersive world. *International Journal on Teaching and Learning in Higher Education*, *20*(1), 59–69.

Burgess, M. L., Slate, J. R., Rojas-LeBouef, A., & LaPrairie, K. (2010). Teaching and learning in Second Life: Using the Community of Inquiry (CoI) model to support online instruction with graduate students in instructional technology. *The Internet and Higher Education, 13*(1-2), 84-88. doi:10.1016/j.iheduc.2009.12.003

Chavis, D. M., Lee, K. S., & Acosta, J. D. (2008). *The Sense of Community (SCI) Revised: The Reliability and Validity of the SCI-2*. Paper presented at the 2nd International Community Psychology Conference, Lisboa, Portugal.

Cheney, A., Sanders, R., Matzen, N., & Tashner, J. (2009). Instructional design and pedagogical issues with Web 2.0 tools. In T. Kidd & I. Chen (Eds.), *Wired for Learning: An Educator's Guide to Web 2.0.* Charlotte, NC: Information Age Publishing.

Gardner, M. R., & Elliott, J. B. (2014). The Immersive Education Laboratory: Understanding affordances, structuring experiences, and creating constructivist, collaborative processes, in mixed-reality smart environments. *EAI Endorsed Transactions on Future Intelligent Educational Environments*, *1*(1), e6. doi:10.4108/fiee.1.1.e6

Garrison, D., Anderson, T., & Archer, W. (1999). Critical inquiry in a text-based environment: Computer conferencing in higher education. *The Internet and Higher Education*, *2*(2-3), 87–105. doi:10.1016/S1096-7516(00)00016-6

Joksimovic, S., Gaševic, D., Kovanovic, V., Riecke, B. E., & Hatala, M. (2015). Social presence in online discussions as a process predictor of academic performance. *Journal of Computer Assisted Learning*, *31*(6), 638–654. doi:10.1111/jcal.12107

Jonassen, D. H. (1997). *INSYS 527: Designing constructivist learning environments.* Retrieved July 20, 2011, from http://www.coe.missouri.edu/~jonassen/INSYS527.html

Lear, J., Ansorge, C., & Steckleberg, A. (2010). Interactivity/community process model for the online education environment. *Journal of Online Teaching and Learning*, *6*(1).

Ligorio, M. B., & Van der Meijden, H. (2008). Teacher guidelines for cross-national virtual communities in primary education. *Journal of Computer Assisted Learning*, *24*(1), 11–25. doi:10.1111/j.1365-2729.2007.00240.x

Liu, X., Magjuka, R. J., Bonk, C. J., & Lee, S. (2007). Does sense of community matter? An examination of participants' perceptions of building learning communities in online courses. *The Quarterly Review of Distance Education*, *8*(1), 9–24.

McKerlich, R., & Anderson, T. (2007). Community of inquiry and learning in immersive environments. *Journal of Asynchronous Learning Networks*, *11*(4), 35–53.

McKerlich, R., Riis, M., Anderson, T., & Eastman, B. (2011). Student perceptions of teaching presence, social presence, and cognitive presence in a virtual world. *Journal of Online Teaching and Learning*, *7*(3).

Oliver, M., & Carr, D. (2009). Learning in virtual worlds: Using communities of practice to explain how people learn from play. *British Journal of Educational Technology*, *40*(3), 414–426. doi:10.1111/j.1467-8535.2009.00948.x

Rodgers, C. R., & Raider-Roth, M. B. (2006). Presence in teaching. *Teachers and Teaching*, *12*(3), 265–287. doi:10.1080/13450600500467548

Russo, T., & Benson, S. (2005). Learning with invisible others: Perceptions of online presence and their relationship to cognitive and affective learning. *Journal of Educational Technology & Society*, *8*(1), 54–62.

Sadera, W. A., Robertson, J., Song, L., & Midon, M. N. (2009). The role of community in online learning success. *MERLOT Journal of Online Teaching and Learning, 5*(2), 277-284. Retrieved September 15, 2011 from http://jolt.merlot.org/vol5no2/sadera_0609.pdf

Sanders, R.L. & Melton, S. (2010). The AETZone experience: A qualitative analysis of the use of presence pedagogy in a 3D immersive learning environment. *MERLOT Journal of Online Learning and Teaching, 6*(1).

Scherer Bassani, P. B. (2011). Interpersonal exchanges in discussion forums: A study of learning communities in distance learning settings. *Computers & Education*, *56*(4), 931–938. doi:10.1016/j.compedu.2010.11.009

Selverian, M., & Hwang, H. (2003). In search of presence: A systematic evaluation of evolving VLEs. *Presence (Cambridge, Mass.)*, *12*(5), 512–522. doi:10.1162/105474603322761306

Shea, P., & Bidjerano, T. (2010). Learning presence: Towards a theory of self-efficacy, self-regulation, and the development of a communities of inquiry in online and hybrid learning environments. *Computers & Education, 55*(4), 1721-1731. Elsevier Ltd. doi: . doi:10.1016/j.compedu.2010.07.017

Shen, K., & Khalifa, M. (2008). Exploring multidimensional conceptualization of social presence in the context of online communities. *International Journal of Human-Computer Interaction*, *24*(7), 722–748. doi:10.1080/10447310802335789

Swan, K. P., Richardson, J. C., Ice, P., Garrison, D R., Cleveland-innes, M., & Arbaugh, J. B. (2008). Validating a measurement tool of presence in online communities of inquiry. *E-Mentor, 2*(24), 1-12. Retrieved from http://www.e-mentor.edu.pl/e_index.php?numer=24&all=1

Vaughan, N. D. (2010). A hybrid community of inquiry approach: Linking student engagement and course redesign. *The Internet and Higher Education, 13*(1-2), 60-65. Elsevier Inc. doi: . doi:10.1016/j.iheduc.2009.10.007

Warburton, S. (2009). Second Life in higher education: Assessing the potential for and the barriers to deploying virtual worlds in learning and teaching. *British Journal of Educational Technology, 40*(3), 414–426. doi:10.1111/j.1467-8535.2009.00952.x

Wilson, B., & Ryder, M. (1996). Dynamic learning communities: An alternative to designed instructional systems. *Proceeding of Selected Research and Development Presentations at the 1996 National Convention of the Association for Educational Communications and Technology.*

KEY TERMS AND DEFINITIONS

Cognitive Presence: An element of the communities of inquiry model, referring to communication and meaning-making among participants in an online learning system.

Community: A group of people associated with one another through common proximity, interests, and/or goals.

Community of Inquiry: A framework for assessing the development of communities in technology-mediated environments.

Immersive Learning Environment: A technology-based learning system in which participants can interact in real-time with others, as well as resources and tools situated within the environment – one in which they feel truly immersed.

Presence: A sense of "being there" with others, even though not physically in the same space.

Social Presence: An element of the communities of inquiry model, referring to the ability for participants' ability to view themselves and others as "real people."

Teaching Presence: An element of the communities of inquiry model, referring to instructional design and facilitation.

Virtual World: A technology-based environment in which participants typically interact as avatars, and can have synchronous interactions with other participants and resources in the environment.

Chapter 7
Effects of Learning Traits and Information Display on Incidental Learning in 3D Virtual Environments

Wayne W. Thomas
University of Alberta, Canada

Patricia M. Boechler
University of Alberta, Canada

ABSTRACT

In this chapter, the authors sought to determine if learning style or digital literacy predict incidental learning, that is, learning that occurs without learners being instructed to attend to or learn presented information. One hundred and fifty-five education undergraduate students completed a series of tasks in a virtual environment where additional information unrelated to the tasks was present. The results indicate that in addition to incidental learning taking place in virtual environments, learning style and digital literacy seem to predict incidental learning in some instances. An additional analysis explored learning styles by "strong" and "moderate" indicators and found that there was no significant difference in their incidental learning score by learning style strength. The results also suggest that information display, in this case visual salience, plays a role in incidental learning as the participants performed better on recalling information that was made more salient.

INTRODUCTION

Virtual Learning environments (VLEs) are increasing in popularity in educational contexts (see Eschenbrenner, Nah, & Siau, 2008; Ghanbarzadeh & Ghapanchi, 2018). According to New Media Consortium and EDUCASE Learning Initiative (2007), virtual environments are "richly immersive and highly scalable 3D environments" (p. 18). Users explore virtual environments using an avatar, which is a virtual representation of the user within the world. Dickey (2003; 2011) proposes that VLEs are "networked,

DOI: 10.4018/978-1-5225-7987-8.ch007

desktop virtual reality in which users move and interact in simulated 3D spaces" (p. 105). Warburton (2009) suggests, "a virtual environment provides an experience set within a technological environment that gives the user a strong sense of being there" (p. 415). In their research on learning in virtual environments, Voinescu and David (2019) qualify virtual environments as desktop environments that are three dimensional. Although sharing similarities with video games, a key difference between games and virtual environments is that a game is more limited to a particular contextual setting and goal, while a virtual environment can be created and modified for any situation, allowing for greater flexibility. Virtual environments can be created for almost any discipline because they are not as contextually based as games (New Media Consortium and EDUCASE Learning Initiative, 2007).

Virtual learning environments are visually complex spaces that include multiple forms of information as well as opportunities for interaction with others. Although immersive to some degree, it cannot be assumed that learning processes and interactions are comparable to those observed in real-world learning spaces where learners are physically within the environment. In this study, the authors tested several elements of learning spaces that can impact learning to determine if these effects may exist in VLEs as well. First, the authors were interested in the impact of the traits that individual learners bring to the VLE (e.g., learning styles and digital literacy) on learning. Second, given VLEs can be information rich environments, the authors were interested in what information learners may retain beyond their intention to learn or engage in instructed activities. The unconscious retention of information that has not been purposefully studied is referred to as unintentional or incidental learning. It has been posited that this kind of unconscious learning is relatively robust over time because it is resistant to interference from explicit memory processing (Frensch & Miner, 1994). Stadler (1997) suggested that information acquired incidentally may later be retrieved for explicit reporting or manipulation. Hence, it is possible that incidental learning might enhance overall learning without placing additional demands on cognitive resources. Finally, the authors were interested in the form and degree of the visual salience of information that is required to capture attention and result in increased incidental retention (images vs. text, plain vs. bolded text). In addition to these, the authors examined learning styles by strength on the dimension scales in order to determine whether the strength of a given learning style made a difference in incidental learning scores.

BACKGROUND

The background covers the definitions of four key elements of this study: 1) incidental learning, 2) learning styles, 3) digital literacy, and 4) information display: visual salience.

Incidental Learning

Incidental learning is a term that is both similar to, and a subset of, other terms in the learning literature. For example, Schugurensky (2000) considers incidental learning to be "learning experiences that occur when the learner did not have any previous intention of learning something out of that experience, but after the experience she or he becomes aware that some learning has taken place. Thus it is unintentional, but conscious" (p. 4). Paek, Hoffman and Saravanos (2017) in their exploration of incidental learning also consider it to be learning that occurs unintentionally. Incidental learning can be considered both a subcategory and a form of, informal learning. Marsick and Volpe (1999) define informal learning as the unstructured learning that takes place as people go about their daily lives; it typically occurs outside of formal institutions. As a simple explanation, Gass (1999) presents incidental learning as a "byproduct of other cognitive exercises…" (p. 319). Kelly (2012) suggests that incidental learning is learning that does not happen by plan or purpose but "it develops while engaging in a task or activity and may also arise as a byproduct of planned learning." (p. 1517). Simply put, incidental learning happens unintentionally while the learner is doing something else. This can have implications for education and student learning because, while learners are receiving explicit instruction, they could also be acquiring other information that exists within the learning context.

Learning Styles

The concept of learning styles has a lengthy history, and an even longer list of interpretations. The term "learning style" has multiple definitions in the literature. Pashler, McDaniel, Rohrer, and Bjork (2008) refer to the idea of learning styles as "…the concept that individuals differ in regard to what mode of instruction or study is most effective to them" (p. 105). A study by Moser and Zumbach (2018) considers learning styles to be the different types of instruction or representations of information that a learner finds most preferable. Essentially, it refers to the idea that there are different ways of learning for different individuals. Dunn (1990) defines learning style as "the way each learner begins to concentrate, process, and retain new and difficult information" (p. 224). Hartley (1998) defines learning style as a characteristic approach to learning demonstrated by students. When attempting to learn new information, learners have the option to employ many learning styles, or simply utilize a single learning style. In another view, Sternberg, Grigorenko, and Zhang (2008) simply use the term "style" and define it as a difference in approach used by a learner to help them complete various tasks.

There has been so much disagreement on a definition for the term "learning styles" that a group of leading researchers in the field ran a survey which asked other researchers how they would define learning style. Peterson, Rayner, and Armstrong (2009), recruited 94 researchers from around the world to complete a questionnaire. After two rounds of voting the majority agreed upon the following definition of learning styles. "Learning styles are an individual's preferred ways of responding (cognitively and behaviorally) to learning tasks which change depending on the environment or context. Therefore, a person's learning style is malleable" (p. 12). This definition contains similarities to Moser and Zumbach's (2018) version. Given all of the debate around learning styles, many researchers still question and critique their existence as a concept (see An & Carr, 2017; Kirschner, 2017)

Learning styles were included as a possible predictor in this study because, despite disagreement surrounding definition and measurement, their measures are frequently used in various educational contexts (e.g., Kolb, 1984, 2015; Coffield, Moseley, Hall, and Ecclestone, 2004; Adkins & Guerreiro, 2017). In addition, our virtual environment represents a novel educational environment for which the authors cannot assume comparable results to physical world educational contexts.

To assess Learning Style the authors used the Index of Learning Styles (ILS), which was created by Felder and Solomon (1994). The instrument consists of eight categories along four spectrums. The spectrums consist of active-reflective, sensing-intuitive, visual-verbal, and sequential-global. The scales measure scores in terms of 'balanced' (a score of 1 to 3), 'moderate' (a score of 5-7), and 'very strong' (a score of 9-11). The scores have different implications for learners. If a learner is balanced, they will have an easier learning experience in an environment where that learning style is prioritized. If the learner has a very strong preference, the ILS suggests that they will experience more difficulty attempting to learn when that learning style is not prioritized in the surrounding teaching environment. Felder and Solomon (1993) state that everyone is in one of the two categories on each spectrum at any given time, which fits into the general definition of learning styles that suggests that a style is more flexible and adaptable as the situation or environment requires. Learners categorized as 'active' learn information most ideally when working with it. This could include teaching the information to others or having open discussions about it, resulting in the preference of working with others in pairs or groups. Learners categorized as 'reflective' learn information best by taking time on their own to think and process the information obtained. Learners categorized as 'sensing' prefer learning factual information and set problem solving methods, while 'intuitive' learners like open-ended information that is non-repetitive, with relationships that can be explored. Learners categorized as visual have a better memory for what they see, while verbal learners have a better memory for words they see or hear. Authors suggest that ultimately a combination of visual and verbal information is best for all learners. Those categorized as sequential tend to use a linear and logical process of learning information whereas global learners tend to make leaps in their learning by obtaining bits of information and suddenly are able to put it together and see the bigger picture.

Digital Literacy

The term digital literacy has also been a difficult one to define, again, because there are multiple interpretations. The term was originally introduced by Gilster (1997) who asserts that digital literacy has more to do with thought processes and conceptualizations than about mastering mere keystrokes (Gilster, 1997) and includes "…the ability to access networked computer resources and use them…" (p. 1). Other terms (sometimes incorrectly used as synonyms) are: (1a) information literacy, (1b) computer literacy (used synonymously with: IT/information literacy, and technology/electronic/electronic information literacy), (2) e-literacy, (3) network literacy (used synonymously with: Internet literacy and hyper literacy), (4) informacy, (5) media literacy and (6) mediacy, (7) digital skills, and (8) web literacy (Bawden, 2001, 2008). Hobbs and Coiro (2019) refer to digital literacy as a conceptualization of literacy that addresses the changes seen in various technologies used every day.

The term that best aligns with the purposes of this research seems to be that of operational internet skills because the authors were interested in finding out how a learner's ability to interact on-line influences their ability to learn incidentally in virtual environments, which aligns with van Dijk and van Deursen's (2014) consideration. In a recent study, van Deursen and van Dijk (2016) considered "Internet skills to be a multidimensional concept, accounting for both medium-related Internet skills, or skills related to the more basic and technical aspects of Internet use, and content-related Internet skills, or skills required to use Internet content" (p. 14). The definition of operational skills is based upon a collection of definitions from other authors within the digital literacies field (e.g., Carvin, 2000; Steyaert, 2002; Mossberger, Tolbert, and Stansbury, 2003; van Deursen & van Dijk, 2016). Instrumental skills are defined by Steyaert (2002) as "the ability to use technology to handle the basic functionality of the hardware or software involved" (p. 205). Technical competence is defined by Mossberger et al. (2003) as "the skills needed to operate hardware, such as typing, using a mouse, and giving instructions to the computer to sort records in a certain way" (p. 38). Technological literacy is defined by Carvin (2000) as "the ability to utilize common IT tools, including hardware, software, and Internet tools like search engines" (p. 42). Finally, the idea of technical proficiency is included in the concept of operational skills. Technical proficiency is defined by Søby (2003) as "the basic component of digital literacy, including a foundational knowledge of hardware, software, applications, networks, and elements of digital technology" (p. 13). van Dijk (2005) used these definitions to compose the concept of operational skills, which is ultimately defined as "the skills used to operate computer and network hardware and software" (p. 73). After investigating multiple definitions and frameworks of digital literacy, Alexander, Becker, Cummins, and Giesinger (2017) suggest that around the world digital literacy institutions view the concept as being multifaceted. It is a literacy that involves technical, psychological, and interpersonal aspects.

Information Display: Visual Salience

An important variable to consider in this study is that of salience or the properties of objects that draw learners' attention within the virtual environment. The concept of salience appears in two main areas throughout the literature. The first area that concerns itself with the notion of salience is that of reading and language acquisition. Reynolds (1992), a prominent researcher in the field, accepts the Webster's Dictionary definition of salience, which is "the property of standing out" (p. 349). This definition suggests that the manipulation of text can lead to various elements of the text standing out. While investigating visual salience, Keil, Edler, Dickmann, and Kuchinke (2019) relied on definitions that combined the likeliness of visual attention being attracted and a comparison of how an item's objective attributes differ from the surrounding.

The field of reading and language acquisition goes on to look at ideas such as the selective attention strategy (SAS) and how it factors into salience and learning. The SAS suggests that readers rank information they read in order of importance and then process information in order of its importance. SAS is summarized into three points by Anderson (1982). The summary states:

1. Text elements are initially processed to some minimal degree and graded for importance.
2. Extra attention is devoted to elements in proportion to their importance.
3. Because of the extra attention, or a process supported by the extra attention, important text elements are learned better than other elements (as cited in Reynolds, Shepard, Lapan, Kreek, & Goetz, 1990, p. 749).

This suggests that importance in attention leads to learning in students. Therefore, text that the reader determines to be most important is better attended to and subsequently better learned.

In the second area concerned with salience, cognitive psychology and neuroscience, there exists a slightly different perspective on salience. Itti (2007) looks at the concept of visual salience, and defines it as "...the distinct subjective perceptual quality which makes some items in the world stand out from their neighbours and immediately grab our attention." In this view, "the core of visual salience is a bottom-up stimulus-driven signal that announces 'this location is sufficiently different from its surroundings to be worthy of your attention'" (para. 4). Zhu, Luo, Dai, Shao, Zhou, Itti and Lu (2018) further support this idea by stating that something salient will always be distinguishable from the rest of its immediate environment. Goldstein (2008) refers to stimulus salience as areas that are "...conspicuous, and therefore attract attention based on their stimulus properties" (p. 120). Yeo and Alibali (2018) refer to visual salience as how much a person's attention is engaged by a visual stimulus. From this review of the salience literature it is evident that although the definitions are not exactly the same across the disciplines, they are similar in their main idea that salience is a quality possessed when an item, object, text, or scene is overt, or stands out in comparison to other things in its surroundings.

RESEARCH QUESTIONS

Focusing on the above-mentioned elements, the following research questions were addressed in this study:

Research Question 1: Does incidental learning occur in virtual environments?
Research Question 2: Does making text visually salient make a difference in incidental learning within virtual environments?
Research Question 3: Does learning style as measured by Felder and Solomon's (1994) Index of Learning Styles predict incidental learning within virtual environments?
Research Question 4: Does digital literacy as measured by Hargittai's (2005) Measure of Web-Oriented Digital Literacy inventory predict incidental learning within virtual environments?

METHODS

Participants

The participant sample consisted of 155 undergraduate students enrolled in the Education program at the University of Alberta. The participants were represented through a convenience sample recruited by the Faculty of Education's research participant pool, which draws its participants from two Educational Psychology courses for pre-service elementary and secondary education teachers.

Pretest Measures

Index of Learning Styles

The Index of Learning Styles or ILS (Felder & Solomon, 1994), was used to gauge student's learning styles and preferences. It consists of 44 forced choice questions forming four dimensions or subscales: Active/Referencing, Sensing/Intuitive, Visual/Verbal, and Sequential/Global. Each dimension has 11 corresponding questions within the inventory (Felder & Spurlin, 2005).

Internal consistency reliability of the ILS was estimated by Cronbach's alpha (Cronbach, 1957) for four samples. The active/reflective, sensing/intuitive, visual/verbal, and sequential global scores were found to be 0.595 (n= 540), 0.697 (n= 539), 0.633 (n= 544), and 0.530 (n= 532) respectively. Tuckman (1999) suggests that an alpha value of 0.50 or above for attitude tests is acceptable. A Pearson correlation was used for test-retest reliability analysis for each of the four dimensions with a time lapse of 8 months was used between testing. For the Active/Reflective, Sensing/Intuitive, Visual/Verbal, and Sequential/Global scores, a Pearson's correlation (n= 124) of 0.683, 0.678, 0.511, and 0.507 were found respectively (Zywno, 2003). This demonstrates a moderate to strong correlation between the scores of the first and second administration of the ILS. The inter-item correlation for internal consistency reliability calculations within each dimension also showed a very little if any correlation between the items with results ranging from 0.09 to 0.17 suggesting that the ILS assesses different qualities between the dimensions as it claims (Zywno, 2003). In investigating the internal consistency, temporal stability, and factor structure of the ILS, Hosford and Siders (2010) found it to be an appropriate tool for measuring learning style.

Survey Measures of Web-Oriented Literacies

The survey measures of Web Oriented Literacies (Hargittai, 2005), was used as a web literacy measure determining the extent to which students were familiar with internet use. It consists of 27 Likert-type items. Responses are scored from 5 (full) to 1 (none); the higher the average overall score, the higher degree of web literacy skills.

Prior studies by Hargittai and Hsieh (2012) using the Web-Oriented Literacies measure determined an internal consistency reliability well above the standard minimum consistency coefficient of 0.80 (Cronbach, 1951). The web-use skill measures that comprise the web-oriented literacies survey has maintained a Cronbach's alpha value of above .90 in each of Hargittai and Hsieh's (2012) studies using first-year university students.

PROCEDURES

Students completed the study in a computer lab with anywhere from 4 to 20 students per session. Each session took approximately one hour to complete. Participants were instructed to begin by completing the ILS and the Web-Oriented Literacies survey. Participants were then tasked with walking their avatar around the virtual space using the arrow keys on the keyboard and were told to follow the directional arrows on the sidewalk. Figure 1 contains a 'path view' of the virtual world. Participants were also instructed to complete the tasks on the colored boards along the pathway called distractor tasks (see Figure 2). A second set of boards was designed to look like billboards containing factual information about the University of Alberta (see Figure 3). Participants were only directed to complete the tasks on the colored boards. In accordance with previous research on the conditions of testing required to detect incidental learning, the information billboards were not mentioned or acknowledged and participants were not advised of the fact that they would be questioned later about the information presented to them during the experiment (See Baddeley, 1997; Hulstijn, 1989).

Figure 1. Path view from virtual world. Participant's avatars entered at the surface level

Once logged into the OpenSim virtual environment, participants were briefly reminded of how to navigate within the virtual space and to notify the researcher when finished (their avatar had returned to start). Upon completion of the path in the virtual space, participants were given two post-tests to test their incidental learning. The first post-test was a 20-item forced-choice image recognition test, which asked participants to identify images they recognized from the virtual campus. The items contained pictures taken from the bulletin boards lining the pathway in the virtual campus. The second post-test consisted of one 10-item sentence completion questionnaire where participants had to fill in the blank to complete the sentence with information that was presented on the bulletin boards lining the pathway of the virtual campus.

RESULTS

The research questions were addressed with a series of regressions and t-tests. For correlations and simple regressions, the assumption of linearity was verified using a scatterplot and a linear relationship was observed (Field, 2009, 2018). The assumption of homoscedasticity was verified using predicted vs. residual plots. Equal distribution of data points was observed, which confirmed the assumption according to Field (2009, 2018). Also according to Field (2009, 2018), having a sample size larger than 30 tends to result in a normal distribution. For the ANOVA test, the assumption of homogeneity of variance was verified by Levene's test to examine equal variances. The test results were not significant, which indicates that the variances were in fact similar and the assumption was met.

MAIN ANALYSIS

In the analysis of the Index of Learning Styles (ILS), the totals were treated as continuous data. Previous researchers have taken a similar approach using different values (see Hosford & Siders 2010; van Zwannenberg, Wilkinson, & Anderson, 2000; Zwyno, 2003). The descriptive statistics for both the independent and the dependent variables are listed in Tables 1 and 2.

Figure 2. An avatar walks through the virtual campus answering a distractor task question

Figure 3. An avatar walks through the virtual campus passing a billboard

Table 1. Descriptive statistics for learning style dimensions and digital literacy

Learning Style Dimension	*n*	*M (SD)*	95% CI
Active-Reflective	155	5.32 (2.29)	[4.95, 5.68]
Sensing – Intuitive	155	4.74 (2.58)	[4.33, 5.15]
Visual – Verbal	155	3.68 (2.61)	[3.27, 4.10]
Sequential - Global	155	4.92 (2.02)	[4.60, 5.24]
Digital Literacy Score	155	2.99(0.68)	[2.89, 3.10]

Table 2. Descriptive statistics for incidental learning of text

Incidental Learning	*n*	*M (SD)*	95% CI
Salient Text Score	155	2.44 (1.45)	[2.21, 2.67]
Non-Salient Text Score	155	2.05 (1.43)	[1.82, 2.28]
Total Text Score	155	4.49 (2.66)	[4.07, 4.91]
Image Score [a]	155	12.46 (3.04)	[1.98, 2.95]

Note. CI = Confidence Interval; [a]Test Value set to 10

Research Question 1

Does incidental learning occur in virtual environments?

In order to answer this question, two separate analyses (one for text, one for images) were performed and the results are listed in Table 3. To help clarify, the question can be rephrased into two parts. First, does incidental learning of text occur in virtual environments? And second, does incidental learning of images occur in virtual environments? To answer the first question, a one-sample t-test was performed to determine whether there was a difference between the total text score mean and mean of zero. There was a significant difference from a mean of zero found (see Table 3). These results suggest that students do learn textual information incidentally in virtual environments. To answer the second part of this research question, another t-test was applied. For this particular analysis, the test value for the expected difference was adjusted from 0 to 10 to account for the possibility of participant guessing. Because the basic probability for true/false multiple choice questions, the probability of getting one question right by random guessing is 0.5, and the expected score for a student who random guesses every question out of 20 questions is 10 (20*0.5). Because the test value is based on an 'expected value' as per Field (2009, 2018), this test value was adjusted to the expectation of a participant guessing. The t-test found a significant difference from a mean of 10 (see Table 3). The resulting effect size for the total text score was 0.86 (large effect) and for the image score was 0.63 (medium effect). The large and medium designations were determined according to Cohen's (1988) effect sizes. These results suggest that students do learn pictorial (image) information incidentally in virtual environments.

Research Question 2

Does making text visually salient make a difference in incidental learning within virtual environments?

In order to answer this question, a dependent samples T-test was conducted to compare the salient text scores to the non-salient text scores. Table 4 shows that there was a significant difference in the scores for salient text, and non-salient text conditions. These results suggest that visual salience, in this instance bolded text, really does have an effect on the incidental learning of text. The data also shows a strong and significant correlation between the salient and the non-salient text scores (r=0.71), which is to be expected, as they are subsets of the same incidental learning text variable. This correlation also suggests that if a student performs well on the salient portion of the incidental learning test, they also performed well on the non-salient portion of the incidental learning test. The test also resulted in an effect size of 0.50 (medium effect).

Research Question 3

Does learning style as measured by Felder and Solomon's (1994) Index of Learning Styles predict incidental learning within virtual environments?

This question was answered for each of the four learning styles and for each of the forms of incidental learning.

A series of simple regressions were performed (see Table 5). Table 6 shows that the SEQGLO variable was correlated with the incidental learning of salient text (n=155, r=0.17, p-value=0.04), and text overall (n=155, r=0.17, p-value=0.04). Although the correlations are weak, they are positive, linear, and statistically significant. A small effect size of 0.02 was found for both the salient and overall text. This suggests that the more global a learner was, the better they tended to score on the incidental learning

Table 3. One-sample t test for incidental learning

Incidental Learning Type	*N*	*t*	*df*	Sig.	Mean Diff	95% CI
Total Text Score	155	21.03	154	0.00*	4.49	[4.07, 4.91]
Image Score [a]	155	10.11	154	0.00*	2.46	[1.98, 2.95]

Note. *P-value is significant at the 0.05 level (2-tailed); [a]Test value set to 10

Table 4. Dependent sample t test for textual incidental learning

	Salient		Non-Salient		*n*	95% CI	*r*	*t*	*df*
	M	*SD*	*M*	*SD*					
Textual Incidental Learning	2.44	1.45	2.05	1.42	155	[0.22, 0.57]	0.71	4.47*	154

Note. *P-value is significant at the 0.05 level (2-tailed)

test for text overall, but more so for salient text. From the analysis of the data, there did not appear to be any learning style that correlated significantly with the incidental learning of non-salient text. Each of the four learning style dimensions resulted in statistically non-significant and weak correlations between learning style and incidental learning of non-salient text.

It appears that one particular learning style predicted the incidental learning of images within virtual environments. A significant correlation was found for the Sensing/Intuitive (SNSINT) learning style dimensions and the image (pictorial) incidental learning score and a small effect size of 0.03 resulted (Table 7). Although the correlation was somewhat weak, it suggested a positive linear relationship between learning style and pictorial incidental learning, suggesting that as a learner moved from sensing to intuitive along the SNSINT spectrum, their incidental learning score of images increased. Those who performed better on the incidental learning measure tended to be intuitive learners.

Table 5. Correlation matrix of learning styles and incidental learning

Measure	ACT/ REF	SNS/ INT	VIS/ VRB	SEQ/ GLO	Image Score	Total Text Score	Salient Text Score	Non-Salient Text Score
ACTREF	1.00	0.09	0.27**	0.025	0.03	0.05	0.08	0.02
Sig. (2-tailed)		0.28	0.00	0.758	0.72	0.50	0.34	0.78
SNSINT		1.00	0.03	0.473**	0.18*	0.09	0.10	0.07
Sig. (2-tailed)			0.69	0.000	0.028	0.27	0.22	0.36
VISVRB			1.00	-0.114	-0.06	0.09	0.10	0.07
Sig. (2-tailed)				0.158	0.47	0.26	0.21	0.41
SEQGLO				1.00	0.13	0.17*	0.17*	0.14
Sig. (2-tailed)					0.11	0.04	0.04	0.09
Image Score					1.00	0.53**	0.49**	0.49**
Sig. (2-tailed)						0.00	0.00	0.00
Total Text Score						1.00	0.93**	0.92**
Sig. (2-tailed)							0.00	0.00
Salient Text Score							1.00	0.71**
Sig. (2-tailed)								0.00
Non-Salient Text Score								1.00

**Correlation is significant at the 0.01 level (2-tailed).*. Correlation is significant at the 0.05 level (2-tailed).

Table 6. Simple regression for the sequential/global learning styles as predictors of the incidental learning of text and images in virtual environments

	B	*SE B*	*β*	*t*	*r*	Adjusted R^2	Sig
Incidental Learning (total)	0.22	0.11	0.17	2.07	0.17	0.02	0.04*
Incidental Learning (salient)	0.12	0.06	0.17	2.09	0.17	0.02	0.04*

Note: *Correlation is significant at the 0.05 level (2-tailed); N=155

Research Question 4

Does digital literacy as measured by Hargittai's (2005) Measure of Web-Oriented Digital Literacy inventory predict incidental learning within virtual environments?

A simple regression was performed and the results are displayed in Table 8. The results indicate that digital literacy did predict incidental learning of overall text within virtual environments (small effect size 0.04). The simple regression resulted in a weak, but statistically significant linear correlation. This correlation suggests that the higher a learner's digital literacy score, the better they performed or the higher their overall score on the incidental learning test for text. The same trend occurred for the incidental learning of salient text (small effect size 0.04). In that regression, a weak but statistically significant positive linear correlation was found. This result suggests that the higher a learner's digital literacy score, the better they performed on the salient component of the incidental learning test for text. A similar trend was found for digital literacy as a predictor of the incidental learning of non-salient text (small effect size 0.03). This correlation was weaker than the previous two, but still statistically significant. This correlation suggests that the higher a learner's digital literacy score, the higher their score on the incidental learning test for non-salient text. In terms of the fourth question of digital literacy predicting the incidental learning of images, the results are similar to the first two text results. A weak, but statistically significant positive linear relationship was found (small effect size 0.07). This result suggests that the higher a learner's digital literacy score, the better they performed on the incidental learning test for images.

Table 9 presents the Pearson correlation coefficients and the significance value for each variable. The analysis has revealed that there are two cases of correlation between two sets of independent variables. The first is between the Visual/Verbal (VISVRB) and the Active/Referencing (ACTREF) learning style dimensions. This correlation appears to be statistically significant, but has a weak positive linear correlation. The second case is the Sequential/Global (SEQGLO) and the Sensing/Intuitive (SNSINT) learning style dimensions. The analysis resulted in a moderate and statistically significant positive linear correlation. This result was expected as the authors Felder and Spurlin (2005), in the validation literature for the ILS indicate an overlap between the sequential/global dimensions and the sensing/intuitive dimensions.

Table 7. Simple regression for the sensing/intuitive learning styles as predictors of the incidental learning of images in virtual environments

	B	*SE B*	*β*	*t*	*r*	Adjusted R^2	Sig
Incidental Learning (image)	0.21	0.09	0.18	2.24	0.18	0.03	0.03*

Note: *Correlation is significant at the 0.05 level (2-tailed); N=155

Table 8. Simple regressions for digital literacy as a predictor of the incidental learning of text and images in virtual environments

Dependent Variable	*B*	*SE B*	*β*	*t*	*r*	Adjusted R^2	Sig
Incidental Learning (total)	0.85	0.31	0.22	2.74	0.22	0.04	0.01**
Incidental Learning (salient)	0.45	0.17	0.21	2.67	0.21	0.04	0.01**
Incidental Learning (non-salient)	0.40	0.17	0.19	2.37	0.19	0.03	0.02*
Incidental Learning (image)	1.26	0.35	0.28	3.62	0.28	0.07	0.00**

Note: *Correlation is significant at the 0.05 level (2-tailed); **Correlation is significant at the 0.01 level (2-tailed); N=155

Other researchers (see Hosford & Siders 2010; van Zwanenberg et al., 2000; Zywno, 2003) have also pointed out this overlap in dimensions. Felder and Spurlin (2005) suggest that while this poses a psychometric issue (colineraity or multicolinearity), it does not interfere with the original purpose of the ILS, which is to inform instructors as to how they can improve their lessons and teaching styles for students.

Additional Analysis

In order to more fully explore the data on learning styles, an additional analysis targeted how participants who ranked as 'strong' or 'moderate' as opposed to 'balanced' on the dimension scales performed. The analysis sought to begin answering the question of whether or not the strength of learning style preference was relevant. This additional question was asked because Felder and Spurlin (2005) suggested it as an area for future researchers to consider. In order to complete this investigation the effect of learning styles, the data of the participants who scored a "balanced" value in the ILS, was removed. The analysis was re-run using only the data of those participants who scored a "moderate" or "strong" on the various dimensions (see Figure 4).

Prior to running this analysis, the data was recoded to represent the 'moderate' and 'strong' ends of the eight categories on the four dimensions of learning styles, and a series of independent sample t-Tests were run. To verify the assumption of normality after having dropped the 'balanced' cases from the data set, a Levene's Test for Equality of Variances was run as recommended by Field (2009, 2018). No significance was found for the assumption of equal variances for any of the recoded variables, therefore each of the variances can be considered equal.

The t-test results in Table 10 show that there was no significant difference between the means when the dimensions were separated into their strong and moderate components. This means that regardless of whether or not a student was strong/moderate on the active side or strong/moderate on the referencing side of the ACTREF dimension, there was not a significant difference in their incidental learning score.

The t-test results in Table 11 show that there were no significant differences between the means when the dimensions were separated into their strong and moderate components, although the incidental learning of images was near the point of significance. This means that regardless of whether or not a student was strong/moderate on the sensing side or strong/moderate on the intuitive side of the SNSINT dimension, there was not a significant difference in their incidental learning score.

The t-test results in Table 12 show that there were no significant differences between the means when the dimensions were separated into their strong and moderate components. This means that regardless

Table 9. Complete correlation matrix for all variables

Measure	ACT/ REF	SNS/ INT	VIS/ VRB	SEQ/ GLO	Digital Lit	Image Score	Total Text Score	Salient Text Score	Non-Salient Text Score
ACTREF	1.00	0.09	0.27**	0.025	0.05	0.03	0.05	0.08	0.02
Sig. (2-tailed)		0.28	0.00	0.758	0.56	0.72	0.50	0.34	0.78
SNSINT		1.00	0.03	0.473**	0.30**	0.18*	0.09	0.10	0.07
Sig. (2-tailed)			0.69	0.000	0.00	0.028	0.27	0.22	0.36
VISVRB			1.00	-0.114	-0.06	-0.06	0.09	0.10	0.07
Sig. (2-tailed)				0.158	0.45	0.47	0.26	0.21	0.41
SEQGLO				1.00	0.28**	0.13	0.17*	0.17*	0.14
Sig. (2-tailed)					0.00	0.11	0.04	0.04	0.09
Digital Lit					1.00	0.28**	0.22**	0.21**	0.19*
Sig. (2-tailed)						0.00	0.01	0.01	0.02
Image Score						1.00	0.53**	0.49**	0.49**
Sig. (2-tailed)							0.00	0.00	0.00
Total Text Score							1.00	0.93**	0.92**
Sig. (2-tailed)								0.00	0.00
Salient Text Score								1.00	0.71**
Sig. (2-tailed)									0.00
Non-Salient Text Score									1.00

**. Correlation is significant at the 0.01 level (2-tailed).

*. Correlation is significant at the 0.05 level (2-tailed).

Figure 4. Combination regions of scoring data. New scoring scale used to account for moderate/strong scores

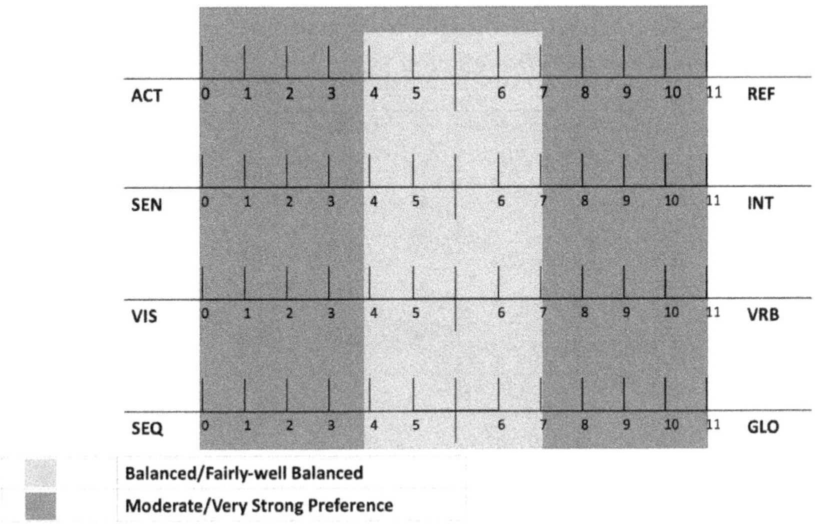

Table 10. Independent samples t-test for recoded 'strong' and 'moderate' combined learning styles for the active and referencing categories of the actref dimension

Incidental Learning Type	Learning Style Category	*N*	Mean *(SD)*	*t*	*df*	Sig.	Mean Diff	95% CI
Incidental Learning (total)	Active	35	4.14 (2.63)	-0.95	58	0.35	-0.66	[-2.04, 0.73]
	Referencing	25	4.80 (2.66)					
Incidental Learning (salient)	Active	35	2.17 (1.42)	-1.15	58	0.25	-0.43	[-1.17, 0.32]
	Referencing	25	2.60 (1.41)					
Incidental Learning (non-salient)	Active	35	1.97 (1.50)	-0.60	58	0.55	-0.23	[-0.99, 0.53]
	Referencing	25	2.20 (1.38)					
Incidental Learning (image)	Active	35	12.20 (2.87)	-1.043	58	0.30	-0.84	[-2.45, 0.77]
	Referencing	25	13.04 (3.35)					

Table 11. Independent samples t-test for recoded 'strong' and 'moderate' combined learning styles for the sensing and intuitive categories of the SNSINT dimension

Incidental Learning Type	Learning Style Category	*N*	Mean *(SD)*	*t*	*df*	Sig.	Mean Diff	95% CI
Incidental Learning (total)	Sensing	55	4.36 (2.50)	-1.65	75	0.10	-1.05	[-2.31, 0.22]
	Intuitive	22	5.41 (2.58)					
Incidental Learning (salient)	Sensing	55	2.44 (1.37)	-1.76	75	0.08	-0.61	[-1.30, 0.08]
	Intuitive	22	3.05 (1.36)					
Incidental Learning (non-salient)	Sensing	55	1.93 (1.33)	-1.26	75	0.21	-0.44	[-1.12, 0.25]
	Intuitive	22	2.36 (1.47)					
Incidental Learning (image)	Sensing	55	12.20 (3.08)	-1.97	75	0.05	-1.57	[-3.16, 0.02]
	Intuitive	22	13.77 (3.37)					

Table 12. Independent samples t-test for recoded 'strong' and 'moderate' combined learning styles for the visual and verbal categories of the VISVRB dimension

Incidental Learning Type	Learning Style Category	*N*	Mean *(SD)*	*t*	*df*	Sig.	Mean Diff	95% CI
Incidental Learning (total)	Visual	81	4.30 (2.79)	-0.31	96	0.76	-0.23	[-1.71, 1.25]
	Verbal	17	4.53 (2.81)					
Incidental Learning (salient)	Visual	81	2.30 (1.50)	-0.28	96	0.78	-0.12	[-0.93, 0.70]
	Verbal	17	2.41 (1.66)					
Incidental Learning (non-salient)	Visual	81	2.00 (1.47)	-0.30	96	0.76	-0.12	[-0.89, 0.65]
	Verbal	17	2.12 (1.32)					
Incidental Learning (image)	Visual	81	12.60 (3.17)	0.09	96	0.93	0.08	[-1.57, 1.72]
	Verbal	17	12.53 (2.70)					

of whether or not a student was strong/moderate on the visual side or strong/moderate on the verbal side of the VISVRB dimension, there was not a significant difference in their incidental learning score.

The t-test results in Table 13 show that there were no significant differences between the means when the dimensions were separated into their strong and moderate components. This means that regardless of whether or not a student was strong/moderate on the sequential side or strong/moderate on the global side of the SEQGLO dimension, there was not a significant difference in their incidental learning score.

To summarize, after looking at the combined data of those in the strong and moderate category for each dimension, it turned out that while the learning style preference did correlate with incidental learning, the strength of learning style preference did not make a significant difference. In the ACTREF dimension, the results showed that regardless of whether or not a student was strong/moderate on the active side or strong/moderate on the referencing side of the ACTREF dimension, there was not a significant difference in their incidental learning score. In the SNSINT dimension, the results showed that regardless of whether or not a student was strong/moderate on the sensing side or strong/moderate on the intuitive side of the SNSINT dimension, there was not a significant difference in their incidental learning score. When it came to the VISVRB dimension, the results demonstrated that regardless of whether or not a student was strong/moderate on the visual side or strong/moderate on the verbal side of the VISVRB dimension, there was not a significant difference in their incidental learning score. And lastly, with regard to the SEQGLO dimension, the results indicated that regardless of whether or not a student was strong/moderate on the sequential side or strong/moderate on the global side of the SEQGLO dimension, there was not a significant difference in their incidental learning score.

DISCUSSION

The purpose of this study was to investigate whether or not learning style or digital literacy served as predictors of incidental learning in a virtual environment. It also looked at whether visual salience, in this instance operationalized as bolded text, increased the occurrence of incidental learning and whether the strength of a learning style impacted incidental learning.

Table 13. Independent samples t-test for recoded 'strong' and 'moderate' combined learning styles for the sequential and global categories of the SEQGLO dimension

Incidental Learning Type	Learning Style Category	*N*	Mean *(SD)*	*t*	*df*	Sig.	Mean Diff	95% CI
Incidental Learning (total)	Sequential	40	4.35 (2.50)	-1.70	57	0.10	-1.23	[-2.68, 0.22]
	Global	19	5.58 (2.81)					
Incidental Learning (salient)	Sequential	40	2.40 (1.39)	-1.67	57	0.10	-0.65	[-1.44, 0.13]
	Global	19	3.05 (1.43)					
Incidental Learning (non-salient)	Sequential	40	1.95 (1.38)	-1.45	57	0.15	-0.58	[-1.37, 0.22]
	Global	19	2.53 (1.54)					
Incidental Learning (image)	Sequential	40	11.75 (3.16)	-1.35	57	0.18	-1.20	[-2.97, 0.58]
	Global	19	12.95 (3.24)					

The findings suggest that students do learn textual and pictorial information incidentally in virtual environments, which concurs with the results of an earlier pilot the authors had conducted with a smaller sample (Thomas, Boechler, deJong, Stroulia, & Delaney, 2012). When given a test of incidentally learned textual information, participants were able to recall a statistically significant amount of the information presented to them. This aligns with the interpretation of incidental learning by other researchers (see Marsick & Watkins, 1990; Schugurensky, 2000; Kelly, 2012; Paek et al., 2017) as an unintentional occurrence; something that takes place during engagement in some other task. While engaged with the distractor tasks, the learners were also interacting with and learning other information along the way.

The results also indicate that visual salience does have an effect on incidental learning within virtual environments, in that learners performed significantly better on the learning of visually salient text than on non-salient text. This finding aligns with the claims of Reynolds (1992) that salience assists learners in focusing attention and, therefore helps them to, better recall information. It also aligns with Yeo and Alibali's (2018) reference to visual salience as how much an individual's attention is engaged by a visual stimulus. It may be surprising that such a small change in visual salience impacts incidental learning but this result highlights the need for further exploration of what visual elements elicit attention within virtual environments.

As for Learning Styles, the results indicate the sequential/global (SEQGLO) dimension as a significant predictor of overall text learning and also visually salient text learning within virtual environments. Although the correlation was weak, it still suggested that the more global a learner was, the better they tended to score on the incidental learning test of text which is consistent with the research of Felder and Solomon (1994). In contrast, there was no relationship between the acting/referencing (ACTREF), sensing/intuitive (SNSINT), or visual/verbal (VISVRB) dimensions and the incidental learning of text. On the other hand, as a learner moves from the sensing end to the intuitive end of the SNSINT dimension, their incidental learning score for images increased. Those who performed better on the image incidental learning measure tended to be intuitive learners. This finding aligns with Felder and Solomon's (1994) description of intuitive learners. They suggest that intuitive learners may be more comfortable with new concepts and like discovering possibilities.

Digital literacy does predict incidental learning as well. The higher a learner's digital literacy score was, the better they performed on the incidental learning of text. This was true for visually salient text as well. In addition, the higher a learner's digital literacy score, the better they performed on the incidental learning test for images.

One might speculate here that higher digital literacy scores equal less demand on the cognitive resources required to simply operate the technology and navigate the virtual environment and, thus, allows learners to attend to and process non-target information.

Concerning learning style strengths, one possible reason that the results did not detect a significant difference with any of these learning style dimensions is that, upon combining the categories, the data of all of the balanced participants had to be discarded. This in turn significantly dropped the number of participant data left to work with and it is possible that the number of remaining data was simply too small to detect a difference. A remedy to this problem for future research would of course be to obtain a much larger sample size so that discarded data does not have such a dramatic impact. Another possibility is that the test used simply was not rigorous enough for the question being asked. It is very possible that the methods Felder and Solomon (1994) used to differentiate learners works well for the purposes of instructors modifying their lessons, but not for the purpose of predicting incidental learning. This is important to note because it also raises the question of whether or not other types of learning can be, or are best measured with this instrument. Lastly, it is also possible that learning styles is not the best variable to use as a predictor of incidental learning in students. Perhaps variables such as gender or age may better serve this purpose and this is where future research can help further the field. The implications that this has for education lie in the fact that it did not seem to matter what learning style was preferred. In the classroom that could indicate that teachers and instructors need not consider what a learner's preference is before embarking upon the process of incorporating virtual worlds into their teaching. This is an interesting implication because there is much debate in the literature as to whether or not learning styles are a valid concept (see An & Carr, 2017; Kirschner, 2017), let alone a valid concept in education (e.g., Roher & Pashler, 2012). If the literature is suggesting that learning styles are invalid, and the research seems to be presenting inconclusive results, then perhaps it is time to take a more in-depth look at what the concept of learning style really means.

FUTURE RESEARCH DIRECTIONS

There are a few limitations to note about this study. First, due to time constraints, the number of questions presented to the participants was limited, so future research should consider including more questions on assessments such as sentence completion tests. It should also be noted that this study only tested factual knowledge and not conceptual or other types of knowledge. Another limitation was the instrument used for measuring learning styles. As mentioned in the results section, the two learning style predictors SEQGLO and SNSINT were correlated. Future research could attempt the study again using a different instrument for measuring learning styles. One last limit to this study was the fact that it did not test participants for their reading ability. If there happened to be participants who were poor readers, this may have affected their ability to perform within the virtual environment and on the post-tests for incidental learning. Future research could test for reading ability in participants as one of the pre-test measures and incorporate that data into the study.

CONCLUSION

This study sought to provide some insight into the relationship between individual differences (learning style and digital literacy) and the occurrence of incidental learning within virtual environments. Using Felder and Solomon's (1994) Index of Learning Styles and Hargittai's (2005) Survey of Web-Oriented Digital Literacies measures, the authors were able to discern that particular digital literacies and particular learning style preferences served as predictors of incidental learning in virtual environments. Overall, learners performed better when information was made visually salient. The authors also concluded that the strength of a given learning style does not significantly impact an individual's incidental learning.

These findings have implications for educators who may want to integrate virtual environments into their teaching practices. It is not enough to simply present all information in a virtual environment in the same manner. Careful analysis of the learning task, presentation of information and an understanding of their students' strengths/preferences may be necessary to optimize these learning environments.

Further research is required to determine how best to display target information within virtual environments to elicit learning. This may also have ramifications for information presented via other visual and audio mediums as most virtual environments allow for a variety of media input. Future research should also consider the impact of virtual environment characteristics on other types of learning, such as conceptual vs. factual learning, while using different versions of visual salience. It is hoped that the results of this research will assist educators in their planning as educational institutions continue to use more technology-rich learning environments.

REFERENCES

Adkins, D., & Guerreiro, M. (2018). Learning styles: Considerations for technology enhanced item design. *British Journal of Educational Technology*, *49*(3), 574–583. doi:10.1111/bjet.12556

Alexander, B., Becker, S. A., Cummins, M., & Giesinger, C. H. (2017). Digital literacy in higher education, part II: An NMC horizon project strategic brief.: Vol. 3. Austin, TX: The New Media Consortium.

An, D., & Carr, M. (2017). Learning styles theory fails to explain learning and achievement: Recommendations for alternative approaches. *Personality and Individual Differences*, *116*, 410–416. doi:10.1016/j.paid.2017.04.050

Anderson, R. C. (1982). Allocation of attention during reading. In A. Flammer & W. Kintsch (Eds.), *Discourse processing* (pp. 292–305). New York: North Holland Publishing Company. doi:10.1016/S0166-4115(08)62699-0

Baddeley, A. D. (1997). *Human memory: Theory and practice* (Rev ed.). Hove, UK: Psychology Press.

Bawden, D. (2001). Information and digital literacies: A review of concepts. *The Journal of Documentation*, *57*(2), 218–259. doi:10.1108/EUM0000000007083

Bawden, D. (2008). Origins and concepts of digital literacy. In C. Lankshear & M. Knobel (Eds.), *Digital literacies: Concepts, policies & practices* (pp. 17–32). New York: Peter Lang Publishing.

Carvin, A. (2000). More than just access: Fitting literacy and content into the digital divide equation. *EDUCAUSE Review*, *35*(6), 38–47. Retrieved from http://www.educause.edu/ero

Coffield, F., Moseley, D., Hall, E., & Ecclestone, K. (2004). *Learning styles and pedagogy in post-16 learning: A systematic and critical review.* Retrieved from Learning and Skills Research Centre: www.LSRC.ac.uk

Cohen, J. (1988). *Statistical power analysis for the behavioral sciences* (2nd ed.). Lawrence Erlbaum.

Cronbach, L. J. (1957). The two disciplines of scientific psychology. *The American Psychologist*, *12*(11), 671–684. doi:10.1037/h0043943

Dickey, M. D. (2003). Teaching in 3D: Pedagogical affordances and constraints of 3D virtual environments for synchronous distance learning. *Distance Education*, *24*(1), 105–121. doi:10.1080/01587910303047

Dickey, M. D. (2011). The pragmatics of virtual worlds for K-12 educators: Investigating the affordances and constraints of ActiveWorlds and SecondLife with K-12 in-service teachers. *Educational Technology Research and Development*, *59*(1), 1–20. doi:10.100711423-010-9163-4

Dunn, R. (1990). Understanding the Dunn and Dunn learning styles model and the need for individual diagnosis and prescription. *Journal of Reading, Writing, and Learning Disabilities International*, *6*(3), 223–247. doi:10.1080/0748763900060303

Eschenbrenner, B., Nah, F., & Siau, K. (2008). 3-D virtual environments in education: Applications, benefits, issues, and opportunities. *Journal of Database Management*, *19*(4), 91–110. doi:10.4018/jdm.2008100106

Felder, R., & Soloman, B. (1994). *Index of learning styles* [Questionnaire]. Unpublished instrument. Retrieved from: http://www4.ncsu.edu/unity/lockers/users/f/felder/public/ILSpage.html

Felder, R., & Spurlin, J. (2005). Applications, Reliability, and Validity of the Index of Learning Styles. *International Journal of Engineering Education*, *21*(1), 103–112. Retrieved from http://www.ijee.ie/

Field, A. (2009). *Discovering statistics using SPSS* (3rd ed.). Thousand Oaks, CA: SAGE.

Field, A. (2018). *Discovering statistics using SPSS* (5th ed.). Thousand Oaks, CA: SAGE.

Frensch, P. A., & Miner, C. S. (1994). Effects of presentation rate and of individual differences in short-term memory capacity on an indirect measure of serial learning. *Memory & Cognition*, *22*(1), 95–110. doi:10.3758/BF03202765 PMID:8035689

Gass, S. (1999). Discussion: Incidental vocabulary learning. *Studies in Second Language Acquisition*, *21*(2), 319–333. doi:10.1017/S0272263199002090

Ghanbarzadeh, R., & Ghapanchi, A. H. (2018). Investigating various application areas of three-dimensional virtual worlds for higher education. *British Journal of Educational Technology*, *49*(3), 370–384. doi:10.1111/bjet.12538

Gilster, P. (1997). *Digital literacy*. New York: Wiley Computer Pub.

Goldstein, E. B. (2008). *Cognitive Psychology: Connecting mind, research, and everyday experience*. Thompson-Wadsworth.

Hargittai, E. (2005). Survey Measures of Web-Oriented Digital Literacy. *Social Science Computer Review*, *23*(3), 371–379. doi:10.1177/0894439305275911

Hargittai, E., & Hsieh, Y. P. (2012). Succinct Measures of Web-Use Skills. *Social Science Computer Review*, *30*(1), 95–107. doi:10.1177/0894439310397146

Hartley, J. (1998). *Learning and Studying. A research perspective*. London: Routledge. doi:10.4324/9780203270189

Hobbs, R., & Coiro, J. (2019). Design features of a professional development program in digital literacy. *Journal of Adolescent & Adult Literacy*, *62*(4), 401–409. doi:10.1002/jaal.907

Hosford, C. C., & Siders, W. A. (2010). Felder-Soloman's index of learning styles: Internal consistency, temporal stability, and factor structure. *Teaching and Learning in Medicine*, *22*(4), 298–303. doi:10.1080/10401334.2010.512832 PMID:20936578

Hulstijn, J. (1989). Implicit and incidental second language learning: Experiments in the processing of natural and partly artificial input. In H. W. Dechert (Ed.), Interlingual processes (pp. 47-73). Tubigen: Narr.

Itti, L. (2007). *Visual Salience*. Scholarpedia. doi:10.4249cholarpedia.3327

Keil, J., Edler, D., Dickmann, F., & Kuchinke, L. (2019). Meaningfulness of landmark pictograms reduces visual salience and recognition performance. *Applied Ergonomics*, *75*, 214–220. doi:10.1016/j.apergo.2018.10.008 PMID:30509529

Kelly, S. W. (2012). Incidental learning. In N. M. Seel (Ed.), *Encyclopedia of the sciences of learning* (pp. 1517–1518). Boston, MA: Springer US. doi:10.1007/978-1-4419-1428-6_366

Kirschner, P. A. (2017). Stop propagating the learning styles myth. *Computers & Education*, *106*, 166–171. doi:10.1016/j.compedu.2016.12.006

Kolb, D. (1984). *Experiential learning: Experience as the source of learning and development*. Englewood Cliffs, NJ: Prentice Hall.

Kolb, D. (2015). *Experiential learning: Experience as the source of learning and development* (2nd ed.). Upper Saddle River, NJ: Pearson Education.

Marsick, V. J., & Volpe, M. (1999). The nature and need for informal learning. *Advances in Developing Human Resources*, *1*(3), 1–9. doi:10.1177/152342239900100302

Marsick, V. J., & Watkins, K. E. (1990). *Informal and incidental learning in the workplace*. London: Routledge.

Moser, S., & Zumbach, J. (2018). Exploring the development and impact of learning styles: An empirical investigation based on explicit and implicit measures. *Computers & Education*, *125*, 146–157. doi:10.1016/j.compedu.2018.05.003

Mossberger, K., Tolbert, C. J., & Stansbury, M. (2003). *Virtual inequality: Beyond the digital divide*. Washington, DC: Georgetown University Press.

New Media Consortium and EDUCAUSE Learning Initiative. (2007). *The horizon report: 2007 edition*. Retrieved from http://www.nmc.org/publications/2007-horizon-report

Paek, S., Hoffman, D. L., & Saravanos, A. (2017). Spatial contiguity and incidental learning in multimedia environments. *British Journal of Educational Technology*, *48*(6), 1390–1401. doi:10.1111/bjet.12488

Pashler, H., McDaniel, M., Rohrer, D., & Bjork, R. (2008). Learning styles: Concepts and evidence. *Psychological Science in the Public Interest*, *9*(3), 105–119. doi:10.1111/j.1539-6053.2009.01038.x PMID:26162104

Peterson, E. R., Rayner, S. G., & Armstrong, S. J. (2009). Researching the psychology of cognitive style and learning style: Is there really a future? *Learning and Individual Differences*, *19*(4), 518–523. doi:10.1016/j.lindif.2009.06.003

Reynolds, R., Sheperd, C., Kreek, C., Lapan, R., & Goetz, E. (1990). Differences in the use of selective attention by more successful and less successful tenth-grade readers. *Journal of Educational Psychology, 82*(4), 749–759. doi:10.1037/0022-0663.82.4.749

Reynolds, R. E. (1992). Selective attention and prose learning: Theoretical and empirical research. *Educational Psychology Review, 4*(4), 345–391. doi:10.1007/BF01332144

Rohrer, D., & Pashler, H. (2012). Learning styles: Where's the evidence? *Medical Education, 46*(7), 634–635. doi:10.1111/j.1365-2923.2012.04273.x PMID:22691144

Schugurensky, D. (2000). *The forms of informal learning: Towards a conceptualization of the field* (Working paper 19-2000). Retrieved from: http://www.oise.utoronto.ca/depts/sese/csew/nall/res/19formsofinformal.htm

Søby, M. (2003). *Digital competence: From ICT skills to digital "bildung" (ITU Report June 10, 2003).* Oslo: University of Oslo.

Stadler, M. A. (1997). Distinguishing implicit and explicit learning. *Psychonomic Bulletin & Review, 4*(1), 56–62. doi:10.3758/BF03210774

Sternberg, R. J., Grigorenko, E. L., & Zhang, L. (2008). Styles of learning and thinking matter in instruction and assessment. *Perspectives on Psychological Science, 486*(6), 486–506. doi:10.1111/j.1745-6924.2008.00095.x PMID:26158974

Steyaert, J. (2002). Inequality and the digital divide: Myths and realities. In S. Hick & J. McNutt (Eds.), *Advocacy, activism, and the Internet* (pp. 199–211). Chicago, IL: Lyceum.

Thomas, W., Boechler, P., deJong, E., Stroulia, E., & Delaney, M. (2012). Incidental Learning and Salience in Virtual Worlds. In T. Bastiaens, & G. Marks (Eds.), *Proceedings of World Conference on E-Learning in Corporate, Government, Healthcare, and Higher Education 2012* (pp. 1686-1690). Chesapeake, VA: AACE.

Tuckman, B. W. (1999). *Conducting Educational Research* (2nd ed.). Belmont, CA: Wadsworth Group.

van Deursen, A. J. A. M., & van Dijk, J. A. G. M. (2009). Using the internet: Skill related problems in users' online behavior. *Interacting with Computers, 21*(5–6), 393–402. doi:10.1016/j.intcom.2009.06.005

van Deursen, A. J. A. M., & van Dijk, J. A. G. M. (2010). Measuring internet skills. *International Journal of Human-Computer Interaction, 26*(10), 891–916. doi:10.1080/10447318.2010.496338

van Deursen, A. J. A. M., & van Dijk, J. A. G. M. (2016). Modeling traditional literacy, internet skills and internet usage: An empirical study. *Interacting with Computers, 28*(1), 13–26. doi:10.1093/iwc/iwu027

van Dijk, J. A. G. M. (2005). *The deepening divide: Inequality in the information society.* Thousand Oaks, CA: Sage Pub.

van Dijk, J. A. G. M., & van Deursen, A. J. A. M. (2014). *Digital skills: Unlocking the information society.* New York, NY: Palgrave Macmillan; doi:10.1057/9781137437037

Van Zwanenberg, N., Wilkinson, L. J., & Anderson, A. (2000). Felder and Silverman's Index of Learning Styles and Honey and Mumford's Learning Styles Questionnaire: How do they compare and do they predict academic performance? *Educational Psychology, 20*(3), 365–380. doi:10.1080/713663743

Voinescu, A., & David, D. (2019). The effect of learning in a virtual environment on explicit and implicit memory by applying a process dissociation procedure. *International Journal of Human-Computer Interaction, 35*(1), 27–37. doi:10.1080/10447318.2018.1424102

Warburton, S. (2009). Second life in higher education: Assessing the potential for and the barriers to deploying virtual environments in learning and teaching. *British Journal of Educational Technology, 40*(3), 414–426. doi:10.1111/j.1467-8535.2009.00952.x

Yeo, A., & Alibali, M. W. (2018). Does visual salience of action affect gesture production? *Journal of Experimental Psychology. Learning, Memory, and Cognition, 44*(5), 826–832. doi:10.1037/xlm0000458 PMID:29648868

Zhu, D., Luo, Y., Dai, L., Shao, X., Zhou, Q., Itti, L., & Lu, J. (2018). Salient object detection via a local and global method based on deep residual network. *Journal of Visual Communication and Image Representation, 54*, 1–9. doi:10.1016/j.jvcir.2018.03.017

Zywno, M. S. (2003). *A contribution to the validation of score meaning for Felder-Soloman's Index of Learning Styles.* Paper presented at 2003 Annual Conference, Nashville, TN. Retrieved from http://asee.org

ADDITIONAL READING

Hulstijn, J. (2003). Incidental and intentional learning. In C. Doughty & M. Long (Eds.), *The handbook of second language acquisition* (pp. 349–381). Oxford, United Kingdom: Blackwell Publishing. doi:10.1002/9780470756492.ch12

Manolis, C., Burns, D. J., Assudani, R., & Chinta, R. (2013). Assessing experiential learning styles: A methodological reconstruction and validation of the kolb learning style inventory. *Learning and Individual Differences, 23*, 44–52. doi:10.1016/j.lindif.2012.10.009

Marsick, V. J., & Watkins, K. E. (2001). Informal and incidental learning. *New Directions for Adult and Continuing Education, 2001*(89), 25–34. doi:10.1002/ace.5

Reynolds, R. E., Wade, S. E., Trathen, W., & Lapan, R. (1989). The selective attention strategy and prose learning. In C. McCormack, G. Miller, & M. Pressley (Eds.), *Cognitive Strategy Research: From Basic Research to Educational Applications* (pp. 159–190). Springer-Verlag. doi:10.1007/978-1-4613-8838-8_7

Treisman, A., & Gelade, G. (1980). A feature integration theory of attention. *Cognitive Psychology, 12*(1), 97–136. doi:10.1016/0010-0285(80)90005-5 PMID:7351125

van Deursen, A. J. A. M., van Dijk, J. A. G. M., & Peters, O. (2012). Proposing a survey instrument for measuring operational, formal, information, and strategic internet skills. *International Journal of Human-Computer Interaction, 28*(12), 827–837. doi:10.1080/10447318.2012.670086

Vygotsky, L., & Cole, M. (1978). *Mind in society: The development of higher psychological processes.* Cambridge: Harvard University Press.

Warburton, S. (2009). Second life in higher education: Assessing the potential for and the barriers to deploying virtual worlds in learning and teaching. *British Journal of Educational Technology*, *40*(3), 414–426. doi:10.1111/j.1467-8535.2009.00952.x

KEY TERMS AND DEFINITIONS

Digital Literacy: The ability to successfully utilize a computer and navigate the internet.

Incidental Learning: Learning that occurs unintentionally. The learner may not be aware of what they have learned.

Index of Learning Styles: An instrument created by Richard Felder and Barbra Solomon to measure learning preferences on a four-dimensional scale. The questionnaire is based on a model created by Richard Felder and Linda Solomon with the dimensions of Active/Reflective, Sensing/Intuitive, Visual/Verbal, and Sequential/Global.

Learning Style: A learner's preferred method or format of having information presented.

Salience: The extent to which an object stands out from its environment.

Survey Measures of Web-Oriented Literacies: An instrument created by Ezster Hargittai to measure an individual's digital literacy in an internet-based context.

Virtual Environments: A three-dimensional space in which users can move about as an avatar and interact with other objects or avatars within the space.

Section 3

Gamification:

The Purpose of Play in the Virtual Classroom

Chapter 8
Games in Innovation Education:
Simulated vs. Authentic Gamified Participation

Rikke Magnussen
Aalborg University Copenhagen, Denmark

ABSTRACT

This chapter examines the methodological challenges and perspectives of designing game-like scenarios for the implementation of innovation processes in school science education. It presents a design-based research study of a game-like innovation scenario designed for technology education for Danish public school students aged 13-15. Students play the role of company heads who develop intelligent music technology. This game-like learning environment was designed to develop innovation competencies through the simulation of a practical learning situation. The focus of the design was to include practices and tools from innovative professions and use game principles and elements to create a meaningful frame around the creative and innovative practices. This chapter describes the results of this design and discusses the perspective of games in innovation education in relation to the more recent trends in research of games designed for citizen science.

INTRODUCTION

One key-adage of our time is that Western countries will only survive based on their populations' abilities to be innovative, flexible and creative in a world of global warming and foreign industries that exploit cheap labour (Drucker, 1993). To meet these challenges, the primary task of educators has been defined as preparing learners to participate creatively in the knowledge economies that most Western countries have become (OECD, 2000). In spite of this being one of the main educational challenges of the 21st century, schools still teach students that knowledge is static, and as a result, students are being taught to become experts at consuming knowledge rather than producing new knowledge (Sawyer, 2006). Past science and technology studies of actors in the field have led to a discussion of what is meant by "authentic science" in school education (McGinn & Roth, 1999). Rather than the traditional picture of the scientist as the isolated genius endowed with superior mental abilities, scientific knowledge in the field

DOI: 10.4018/978-1-5225-7987-8.ch008

of science and technology studies is seen as emerging from disciplined ways of organising and making sense of the natural world, as well as being a construction of visual representations (Latour, 1999; Lynch & Woolgar, 1990; Latour & Woolgar, 1986). Visual representations such as graphs, x-ray images, maps, models, diagrams and hybrids of these are central in creating and communicating science, and it has been argued that this view of scientific practice should have implications for how science is taught (diSessa, 2000; McGinn & Roth, 1999). Games that simulate scientific practice have been mentioned as an approach for implementing innovation in school education (Shaffer, 2007). The game media is well suited for simulating complex rule systems and real-life settings. Game scenarios offer a medium equipped for complex simulations integrating many different aspects of real-life learning environments and framing them in a simulation a player can identify with and relate to. Access to a wide range of professional tools and representations supports authenticity and allows for players to tackle complex problems from professional contexts (Magnussen, 2008). Though the potentials of game media in technology innovation education are clear, how innovative practices in game-based environments occur has yet to be fully understood. In this paper, the design of a game-like technology innovation scenario is presented. The scenario was developed as part of a design-based research study of how to implement innovative learning environments into cross-disciplinary science education in schools. The design, results and methodological discussions that arose from the first application of the design are discussed in relation to the more recent focus in the serious games field on development of citizen science games.

BACKGROUND: GAMES AS FRAMEWORK FOR INNOVATION

The empirical data in this paper is gathered from a technology innovation scenario, which was part of a new generation of theory-based educational games that simulate professional environments. One characteristic that these games share is that they simulate elements of the objectives and environments in a specific profession by using and making available the technology, tools and/or methods of that profession to students playing the game. Examples of simulations include environmental engineers trying to locate a polluted site (Squire & Klopfer, 2007), urban planners redesigning a central pedestrian street of a town (Shaffer, 2006), or criminal investigators investigating a murder using forensic techniques (Magnussen, 2007, 2008). The objective for creating these types of games is to use the game media to design complex settings based on the learning environments of real-life professionals, thus allowing students to engage in complex, creative, and innovative problem solving and learning processes of the professions. The motivation for developing these types of games stems from a critique of the teaching of standardized skills to children in today's school system. The skills acquired in this system do not prepare them for a future that involves a constantly changing, complex work life (Shaffer & Gee, 2005). Critics believe that, under the current system, students do not learn to deal with problems that do not have readymade answers and do not solve problems using creative, innovative thinking or collaboration. As a result, the aim of this type of game is to use the game media to create environments with simulations of complex real-life situations where students have to think like professionals and solve problems in innovative ways as professionals do (Gee 2003; Shaffer, 2007). Simulating professions is not new. Commercial games such as Counter-Strike or the game version of CSI simulate the professional practices of counter-terrorists and forensic detectives. The primary difference between commercial games and the new generation of educational games is that the latter's designs are based on learning theories and/or detailed studies of the learning processes and the tools of real life professionals. Some of these games are also designed to meet the goals of the formal school science curriculum (Magnussen, 2008), while others, known as epistemic games, "create the epistemic frame of a socially valued community by re-creating the process by which individuals develop the skills, knowledge, identities, values and epistemology of that community" (Shaffer, 2007, p. 164). Even though innovation is mentioned as an integrated part of the epistemic frame of professionals, the ways in which professional innovative processes may be implemented in game-like scenarios have not been studied in depth.

In the following, I present the design and play-analysis of a technology-supported scenario in which students play the role of company heads that develop intelligent music technology. This game-like learning environment was designed to develop innovation competencies through the simulation of a practical learning situation. The term "game-like" is used here to denote that the scenario should not be considered as an educational game, such as the educational computer games used in many school educations today. This design-research approach is based on an understanding of "game-like" as environments which are not constructed as games as such but are focused on creating scenarios based on game-like learning or activities. The term "game-like thus refers to scenarios or situations where game elements - such as missions or scores - are applied non-game contexts (Gee, 2005). This has later been defined as "gamification" by Deterding et al. (2011).

The focus of the educational design presented in the current paper was thus to include practices and tools from innovative design professions (IDEO, 2009) and then use game principles and elements such as roles and scores to create a game-like framework around the creative and innovative practices.

METHODOLOGY: DESIGNING GAME-LIKE INNOVATION EDUCATION

The study presented in this paper is part of a four-year research project entitled, "Serious Games on a Global Marketplace" (2007-2011), which explores the design and use of educational games within various school contexts. The project was set up as a collaborative endeavor in which academics work with companies to redesign, implement, and explore the use of games in order to generate knowledge about serious game challenges and educational design, with the aim to develop new formats of serious games for school education. The empirical case presented in this paper is a design-based research project, which involves the design of a technology innovation scenario for cross-disciplinary science teaching for students aged 13-15, in Danish public schools. The educational goal in the game-like scenario is to teach students how to take part in innovative thinking and the creative construction of new technologies that characterize professional designers and innovative companies. The scenario was designed to simulate professional innovators' innovation processes. Technological innovation was chosen to make the construction processes cross-disciplinary, since technology construction involves an understanding of social (e.g., user behavior), technical and scientific processes. The technology innovation education project is a design-based research project. Design-based research combines empirical educational research with the theory-driven design of learning environments (Brown, 1992; Design-Based Research Collective, 2003). Design experiments are therefore described both as a method to "engineer" learning environments and to develop domain-specific theories (Cobb et al., 2003). The design of learning environments and the development of theories of learning are closely intertwined and characteristic of the method, because they occur through continuous cycles of problem definition, design, enactment, analysis and redesign (Collins, 1992). In this chapter, I present the first cycle of problem definition, design and intervention, and the different methodological reflections and hypotheses the design-research process was based on.

Being a design-based research project, there were two praxes design foci: to understand how game elements can be used in designs of technology innovation education; and the research focus—understanding how students construct and mobilize representations of knowledge in these scenarios. The design of the technology innovation scenario was to simulate professional innovation methods, but also to provide students with the tools of professionals. When entering the meeting places and workspaces of professionals in the natural sciences or creative and innovative businesses, we find a variety of visual representations and visualisation tools such as white-boards, tablets, mind maps, Lego process tools, etc. These tools are an integrated part of the generation and development of new ideas. Professionals such as scientists develop knowledge through sketching and presenting models (McGinn & Roth, 1999; Latour, 1999). When entering a classroom and observing students' work processes, we see few of these tools used for visualizing new ideas and thinking processes. Most student work is conducted with pen and paper, text processing tools, or by listening to a teacher who is standing at the front of the class, using a blackboard. One hypothesis behind the project was that technology and visualization tools are actors in professional innovative thinking processes, and if we want to integrate innovative processes in schools, we have to integrate the tools of professional technology innovators. The main hypothesis behind the technology innovation design was that students' practices in using visual representations in game-like simulations of professional environments are formed by whatever artefacts are made available in their schools' workspaces, as well as by human actors and references to the profession that the game presents. Earlier studies have shown that the way students create and mobilise visual "inquiry representations" depended on relations to the simulated profession, complexity in the game, teachers' encouragement, other students' design formats as well as artefacts such as boards, posters, whiteboards or interactive boards available in school workspaces (Magnussen, 2008). Providing students with these tools to create visual representations of their ideas therefore became central in the design of the technology innovation space.

The second hypothesis behind the design centred on the creation of a meaningful frame for the technology innovation tools and practices. Introducing innovation tools in classrooms does not necessarily spark innovative thinking processes. To ensure that these tools become an integrated part of the school practice, we have to create contexts where they can become possible actors in innovative thinking processes. To do this, we may draw on inspiration from the educational game field and its ability to frame complex professional practices and create meaningful game and learning experiences (Magnussen, 2009). The challenge is to design contexts that, through narrative elements or elements such as rules and consequences, frame highly complex creative contexts, but which are still open enough for flexible working processes that allow students to develop and approach a topic with their own process tools and creative ideas. We have to create a space where children are given inspirational demands. These demands should, however, not constitute rigid restrictions that limit innovative processes. Innovation processes need frames to develop but may be obstructed by rigid rules. This is a difficult balance to strike, and part of the project is to develop design methods for the development and study of these flexible spaces.

FINDINGS: THE SCENARIO DESIGN

The theme of the first game-like innovation workshop in this study was "Development of future music technology." Students were given three days to develop and build prototypes of a future intelligent music technology. The design-based research study of technology innovation was part of the research conducted at the Playware Centre at the Technical University of Denmark, which was one of the partners of the

Serious Games on a Global Marketplace research project. Playware Centre is involved in advanced digital products that create play and experiences among users of all age groups. The centre works with technology and physical user interaction, including play media developed on the basis of robot technology, modern artificial intelligence and mobile technology. The three-day innovation camp was planned so that students would undergo three phases: user survey, brainstorm, and prototype building. The three phases had rules designed to stimulate innovative thinking and work processes at the different stages, such as "understanding needs of the user" and thinking "out of the box." The three-day camp was designed in collaboration with a professional innovation process consultant in Denmark, using, among other things, the Innovation Toolkit developed by the design consultancy company, IDEO (2009). The innovation camp was set up at the Science Talent Centre in Sorø, Denmark. The aim of this centre is to develop young science talents. The centre has recently opened and the facilities are very good; new laboratories with the latest technology, such as interactive whiteboards and flat screen PCs, are set up in most rooms. The group in the first observations of the game-like technology innovation scenario comprised of 25 students aged 13 - 15. Students were selected from seven different classes at a school in Northern Sealand in Denmark. Together with their two teachers, who also participated in the innovation camp, students designed a climate board game, which won a local competition in designing education materials. The teachers invited 25 of the students who had participated most actively in the design of the winning project to participate in a four-day camp at the science centre as a reward. The three-day technology innovation scenario was part of the four-day camp. The 25 participating students were described by their teachers as active students and 'above average' in science. Most of these students had a specific interest in technical and scientific subjects as well, and a few of them had creative interests outside school and played in bands or composed their own music. The overall structure of the game was designed by the author of this paper, who also, assisted by two additional researchers, conducted video observations of student participation throughout the three days. The camp was run by the director of the Science Talent Centre who played the role of local manager of the teams. She was assisted by the class' two teachers, who supervised the groups according to processes and rules in the different phases of the technology innovation. At the end of the camp, students presented their prototypes to a panel of four judges; two were from the Science Talent Centre, and two were from the Playware Centre (Lund et al., 2005).

Phase 1: Inspiration, Introduction, and User Survey

The technology innovation camp was planned for three days with participating groups of students camped at the Science Talent Centre participating full-time in the technology innovation camp. In the first day's evening, before the official introduction to the technology innovation camp, students were introduced to, and had a chance to play with, intelligent music technology developed by Playware as well as other types of robot technology. The idea was to introduce the concept of artificial intelligence to students and inspire them to think beyond existing formats, such as those offered by iPod or YouTube. They were introduced to the Playware-developed "Beat Blocks" (Nielsen et al., 2009). These consist of coloured building blocks, where each block is an instrument, and different rotations of each block produces different expressions of an instrument. A user can play with the blocks to combine different instruments and tracks and compose alternative versions of songs by famous artists. The idea was to inspire students to think "out of the box" and in intelligent formats that would help them produce and use music in new ways. Overall, students were enthusiastic in their play with the intelligent technology and used extensive periods of time to experiment with creating alternative versions of songs by their favourite artists. On the following morning, students were formally introduced to the camp through a narrative frame. Students were instructed that they would be innovative teams, who were to develop the future of innovative intelligent music technology in the course of the next two days. The target group was said to be young people, aged as participating students were, and the client was presented as the Playware Centre, which did not have the same intimate knowledge about the target audience as the students. To make these excellent new innovations, students would have to use the same techniques and tools as professionals. Students were shown an episode of the ABC Nightline show from 1999, where IDEO designers were given the task of developing a futuristic shopping cart. In the TV clip, the systematic user survey processes designers go through was shown, as well as brainstorming activities and prototype building. The idea was both to give the students a visual understanding of the different phases of design, but also to introduce the visual representations and process tools IDEO designers use. This last point was verbally repeated following the TV clip demonstration. Students were encouraged to use whatever papers, coloured pens, pins and whiteboards they would find in their workspaces.

Following this, the local manager, the director of the Science Talent Centre, introduced the first process: teams were to choose two members of their six-member groups and interview them about times of the day they listened to music and what problems there might be in the playing of or listening to music at different times of the day. They were also asked to produce a time-line that illustrated music listening/playing timelines. The user survey was designed with the assistance of a professional innovation consultant who advised students to start with the user survey, because brainstorms without a basic understanding of the needs of users often produce poor results. After the introduction, teams went to their workspaces to start working. Overall, groups were highly motivated and began making visual representations as part of their discussions and working processes; poster-size paper was put on walls, which students wrote on with coloured pens. The groups were supposed to start with the user survey, but almost all groups went straight into the brainstorm phase and started developing ideas instead of investigating the needs of the users. Teachers had to intervene and get them to start with the user survey. It seemed difficult for students to focus on mapping the users' daily use of music, without letting this lead directly into designing technologies to meet user needs. These difficulties led teachers to comment on how open innovation processes were fundamentally different from the processes students were used to work with in school. They said that most students are used to working with what they called "recipes." Both in science subjects as well as in other subjects, students are used to being told every step of a task, rather than working with open innovation processes. All teams eventually managed to produce timelines that mapped user needs as well as several ideas for technologies that could respond to these needs.

Phase 2: Brainstorm

The brainstorm phase was introduced to students in the afternoon of the second day, after teams had completed and presented their user surveys in the morning. The local manager (the director of the Science Talent Centre) encouraged students to start anew and put previous ideas in the background. Also, she introduced students to the set of rules they were to follow in the brainstorm process: 1. They must write as many wild ideas (the wilder, the better) as possible within 15 minutes, without talking to one another; 2. They must present ideas to the team—wild ideas should be encouraged, and team members must try to build on each other's ideas. Rejecting ideas was not allowed; 3. They must put ideas into different categories and vote – all members were given three points they could give to the different ideas they liked. All groups initially started out with the 15-minute idea development period, where they were writing down ideas on post-it notes. Following this, students began presenting their ideas to their team members by hanging post-it notes on the available boards and walls. Studying this process, it became clear that it was difficult for students to follow the given rules of coming up with many creative ideas. To help, groups were encouraged by their teachers to go to the "inspiration table," where, for inspiration, they could play with toys, music instruments, and the Playware music technologies they had been introduced to earlier. In most groups, there was also a dominant tendency to reject wild ideas, and the focus in team discussions within groups centred on what was technically possible, instead of the development of ideas. Later in the afternoon, the manager and teachers went around to the teams for a short briefing. The groups had been told that they should present their preliminary ideas and that they would have a chance to discuss problems with the manager and the supervising teachers. All teams went around to the different workstations to participate in this briefing and get inspired by the other groups' work processes. At the briefing, it became clear that most of the developed ideas resembled existing formats, such as those offered by iPod or internet music services. The manager again encouraged students to think of wild ideas and to more actively integrate elements of AI. In spite of difficulties (and in one group, frustrations) experienced within the different stages of the brainstorm processes, teams worked intensely for the balance of day two—with some groups continuing until late in the evening—on developing new ideas related to intelligent music technology. This impression from the observations was supported by the teachers who stressed that students were highly motivated and eager to develop their designs further for the coming day.

Phase 3: Prototype Building and Presentations Before Judges

The third and final day of the innovation camp was initiated with an introduction to the prototype building phase. Students had been given the task of selecting the one idea they wanted to make a prototype of and presenting it to the manager and her team. The overall impression of the finished ideas was that they had greatly developed into being more wild and futuristic concepts, which included intelligent technology. One group had developed an idea for a hand-held wireless music player with a claylike tangible interface for stress relief and in-built intelligent technology with sensors for response to the mood of the user. Another group had developed a music system shaped as blocks. The system was design as three blocks; One block was a music player and a watch- The watch and the music player was represented on each their side so users could use any of the functions by turning either the clock- or music player-side upwards. A second block was design to be used for making music by users shaking or twisting it for different sounds and instruments. The third block was designed as a speaker that could be turned and placed in a room depending on where the user was situated. The blocks could be used separately or combined for collective functions such as playing music made on the blocks. A third group presented the idea of a robot called a "Kaj" that would follow people around their homes and use voice recognition to respond to orders or go quietly to a corner if nobody talked to him. Kaj's brain could be removed and used as a wireless music player, outside the home. The fourth group of students created an idea for a wireless micro player with no sound that was to be placed behind one's ear, where it would align with the brain through emission of electronic waves in a way that users would think that they are hearing music, without actually hearing any—essentially eliminating the risk of damaging ear drums. Teachers encouraged this last team to conduct research on whether this technology was actually possible and how.

In general, it was at this stage that students started doing more specific research to specify the details of their idea. Students were highly engaged and almost ecstatic at this stage. In an interview with one of the groups, team members described the phase of having selected one idea for prototyping as "being in control again." This was compared to the more open brainstorm process where they had been discussing and debating pros and cons of many different ideas. Students were asked to make models of their idea in paper, cardboard, dough and similar materials, to present the different aspects of functionality of the technology and how it would meet the user needs to a panel of judges from the science talent centre and Centre for Playware. By the end of the day, teams presented their prototypes and visual presentations of functionalities to the four external judges. Based on the criteria 1) ability to think new, 2) inclusion of intelligent technology and 3) usefulness to a potential user group, the team with the modular block technology was announced as the winner.

DISCUSSION: RECENT TRENDS IN INNOVATION GAMING

In this chapter, the first cycle of a design-research study of a game-like technology innovation education has been presented. It became clear, from the above-described study, that participating in the various phases of technology innovation was both highly motivating and highly challenging for the involved group of children. In the observations of the different phases of innovation, it was clear that certain processes of user survey and brainstorming were particularly challenging to the groups. Students found it difficult to distinguish between the processes of user survey and brainstorming, and most went straight into the idea generating phase without understanding the process of identifying the needs of the user group. It also proved to be a massive challenge for most students to think outside existing formats and to develop ideas for intelligent technology. The members of the teams had a tendency to be too realistic with their own ideas, while rejecting other team members' wild ideas. We saw, however, that over the course of three days students became able to think beyond existing formats and develop futuristic ideas for intelligent technology which would meet the identified needs of the user group. This capacity for creative and innovative thinking within the given frame was a central result of the camp. Overall, the 25 students participated creatively and were motivated in the activities of the different phases of innovation. Also, they actively challenged themselves to think of new and intelligent technologies that they had identified user needs for. These stages in innovative processes, thinking "out of the box" and not rejecting wild ideas, are challenging, even to professional innovators (IDEO, 2009). Future studies should thus be focused on designing innovation learning environments where development of competences in idea generation is central. One idea could be to appoint facilitators who are given the task of facilitating the different processes for each group. This is, however, a highly difficult job, and including this element in the design would require reflections on the choice and role of facilitators. Another idea for future developments could be to build upon IT or technology-supported elements that would structure processes such as feedback from game characters or fictional clients. In designing for innovation, the balance between creating space for creative processes and instructing to make an activity meaningful is difficult to strike.

The study, however, showed that game-like scenarios, including narrative and competitive elements, and rules of play, create an interesting, meaningful, and engaging frame for integrating technology innovation in school education that can be developed more broadly for other types of school contexts. One trend in development and studies of science game formats in the past decade is exploring the ways in which game media can facilitate new approaches to authentic science education. Where the major trends have been to *simulate* authentic technical or scientific processes in game environments for the purpose of students learning *about* authentic science, *scientific discovery* games or *citizen science* games now focus on gamifying professional research or technical processes, allowing and motivating players to take part in generating results for authentic application in scientific research (Cooper, 2015; Magnussen et al., 2014). Interesting issues arise, however, in relation to discussing the various types of games that need to be addressed when discussing the integration of creation of new knowledge and authentic science practice in science education. Even though games simulating professional practice integrate professional values and tools, they remain simulations of professional practices. This aspect of the games brings up the matter of whether students learn to work as a scientific expert or whether they learn how to be a scientific expert. The difference between the above two learning approaches can be described comparing the various design elements in the two types of gamified science learning environments. First, the clients and experts students collaborate with in the games are fictional characters with fictional problems that need to be solved to play the game in school but that do not have relevance in the world outside school. Second, the fictional problems to be solved in these games often follow a linear path and have a clear starting and end point. This is clearly different from real-life professional problem solving, where the processes are more multidimensional. Finally, even though these types of science simulation games have been shown to support student creation of new process tools (Magnussen, 2007), the solutions are often pre-defined and already known by the teachers. This stands in contrast to the real-life open-ended tasks professionals face and that can be carried out in various ways, the chance of success or failure always an issue to be considered.

The development of scientific discovery games within the past couple of years introduces new elements into the issue of game-based participation in a science classroom setting. The main goal of this category of games is to create a platform that enables and motivates players to contribute in solving scientific problems (Cooper et al., 2010). Scientific discovery games also address issues that exist outside a formal learning setting (Magnussen, 2017). The main goal of this type of game is to create a platform that motivates players to contribute to solving scientific problems. Involving citizens or laypeople in production of science outside the walls of formal research institutions is traditionally defined as citizen science. Opportunities to involve citizens have increased with web 2.0 technologies and other types of digital platforms. New digital platforms are changing how laypeople are involved in technical and scientific processes and production that affect their lives (Delfanti, 2010). Overall, there has been an increasing focus on how lay people and other communities outside of traditional research institutions can be involved in all levels of research activities, including data collection and categorization. The development of the so-called citizen science games or scientific discovery games within the past few years has brought new elements into the issue of game-based participation in a knowledge domain. The main goal of this class of games is to create a platform that enables and motivates players to contribute to solving real scientific problems (Cooper et al., 2010). The most well recognized example of this class of games is Foldit, which is an online puzzle game where players participate in folding amino acid chains to form new protein structures. Presented with a primary protein sequence or partially folded structure, players need to find the – often-unknown – lowest-energy three-dimensional structure. Players manipulate the protein structure by pulling, twisting and tugging the protein backbone and side chains into various configurations (Good & Su, 2011). However, there are educational challenges in designing this type of games. Scientific discovery games have the potential to introduce authentic environments, grounded in real-world experience, generating new scientific knowledge in science education. Therefore, it is crucial to understand if and how the game environment contributes to students' experience of participating in research. Understanding the potentials and implications of this type of citizen-driven game environment and the effects of the game and subsequent learning experience on different types of students and in different contexts is therefore crucial.

CONCLUSION

Studies and research-based development of game-like education has matured over the past 10 – 15 years from focusing on developing learning games to developing gamified learning environments based on authentic collaboration with scientists. The current chapter has presented studies of gamified innovation education and discussed recent developments of scientific discovery games as a frame for collaboration between researchers and citizens. These type of games and gamified learning environments have opened new questions in regard to what learning practices researchers and citizens participate in, what motivate participants, and what expertise they contribute. Understanding these elements will be subject for future studies.

ACKNOWLEDGMENT

This research was supported by the Aalborg University Cross-disciplinary strategic fund.

REFERENCES

Brown, A. (1992). Design experiments: Theoretical and methodological challenges in creating complex interventions in classroom settings. *Journal of the Learning Sciences*, *2*(2), 141–178. doi:10.120715327809jls0202_2

Cobb, P., Confre, J., diSessa, A., Lehrer, R., & Schauble, L. (2003). Design experiments in education research. *Educational Researcher*, *32*(1), 9–13. doi:10.3102/0013189X032001009

Collins, A. (1992). Toward a design science of education. In E. Scanlon & T. O'Shea (Eds.), *New directions in educational technology* (pp. 15–22). New York, NY: Springer. doi:10.1007/978-3-642-77750-9_2

Cooper, Treuille, Barbero, Leaver-Fay, Tuite, Khatib, … Players. (2010). The challenge of designing scientific discovery games. Proceedings of Foundations of Digital Games.

Cooper, S. (2015). Massively Multiplayer Research: Gamifying and (Citizen) Science. In S. P. Walz & S. Deterding (Eds.), The Gameful World: Approaches, Issues, Applications (pp. 487–500). Academic Press.

Delfanti, A. (2010). Users and peers: From citizen science to P2P science. *Journal of Clinical Outcomes Management, 9*(1).

Design-Based Research Collective (DBRC). (2003). Design-based research: An emerging paradigm for educational inquiry. *Educational Researcher, 32*(1), 5–8. doi:10.3102/0013189X032001005

Deterding, D., Dixon, D., Khaled, R., & Nacke, L. (2011). From game design elements to gamefulness: defining "gamification". *MindTrek '11 Proceedings of the 15th International Academic MindTrek Conference: Envisioning Future Media Environments*, 9-15. 10.1145/2181037.2181040

diSessa, A. A. (2000). *Changing minds: Computer, learning, and literacy*. Cambridge, MA: MIT Press. doi:10.7551/mitpress/1786.001.0001

Drucker, P. F. (1993). *Post-capitalist society*. New York, NY: HarperBusiness.

Gee, J. P. (2003). *What video games have to teach us about learning and literacy*. New York, NY: Palgrave Macmillan. doi:10.1145/950566.950595

Gee, J. P. (2005). Good video games and good learning. *Phi Kappa Phi Forum, 85*(2), 33–37.

Good, B. M., & Su, A. I. (2011). Games with a scientific purpose. *Genome Biology, 12*(12), 135. doi:10.1186/gb-2011-12-12-135 PMID:22204700

IDEO. (2009). *Human centered design toolkit* (2nd ed.). Retrieved from http://www.ideo.com/work/item/human-centered-design-toolkit/

Latour, B. (1999). *Pandora's hope: Essays on the reality of science studies*. Cambridge, MA: Harvard University Press.

Latour, B., & Woolgar, S. (1986). *Laboratory life: The construction of scientific facts* (2nd ed.). Princeton, NJ: Princeton University Press.

Lund, H. H., Klitbo, T., & Jessen, C. (2005). Playware technology for physically activating play. *Artificial Life and Robotics Journal, 9*(4), 165–174. doi:10.100710015-005-0350-z

Lynch, M., & Woolgar, S. (1990). Introduction: Sociological orientations to representational practice in science. In M. Lynch & S. Woolgar (Eds.), *Representation in scientific practice*. Cambridge, MA: MIT Press.

Magnussen, R. (2007). Games as a platform for situated science practice. In Worlds in play: International perspectives on digital games research (pp. 301–311). New York, NY: Peter Lang.

Magnussen, R. (2008). *Representational inquiry in science learning games* (Unpublished doctoral dissertation). Aarhus University, Copenhagen, Denmark.

Magnussen, R. (2009). Representational inquiry competences in science games. In S. G. A. Rodrigues (Ed.), *Multiple literacy and science education: ICTs in formal and informal learning environments* (pp. 360–370). Hershey, PA: IGI Global. doi:10.4018/978-1-61520-690-2.ch017

Magnussen, R., & Elming, A. L. (2017) Student re-design of deprived neighborhoods in Minecraft: Game-assisted community-driven urban development. In *12th International Conference on Computer Supported Collaborative Learning, CSCL 2017.* Drexel University and The University of Pennsylvania.

Magnussen, R., Hansen, S. D., Planke, T., & Sherson, J. F. (2014). Games as a Platform for Student Participation in Authentic Scientific Research. *The Electronic Journal of E-learning*, *12*(3), 258–269.

McGinn, M. K., & Roth, W. M. (1999). Preparing students for competent scientific practice: Implications of recent research in science and technology studies. *Educational Researcher*, *28*(3), 14–24. doi:10.3102/0013189X028003014

Nielsen, J., Bærendsen, N. K., & Jessen, C. (2009). Music-making and musical comprehension with robotic building blocks. *Proceedings of the 4th International Conference on E-Learning and Games: Learning by Playing. Game-based Education System Design and Development*, 399-409.

OECD. (2000). *Knowledge management in the learning society*. Paris, France: OECD Publications.

Sawyer, R. K. (2006). Educating for innovation. *Thinking Skills and Creativity*, *1*(1), 41–48. doi:10.1016/j.tsc.2005.08.001

Shaffer, D. W. (2006). Epistemic frames for epistemic games. *Computers & Education*, *46*(3), 223–234. doi:10.1016/j.compedu.2005.11.003

Shaffer, D. W. (2007). *How computer games help children learn*. New York, NY: Palgrave Macmillan.

Shaffer, D. W., & Gee, J. P. (2005). *Before every child is left behind: How epistemic games can solve the coming crisis in education* (Tech. Rep. No. 2005-7). Madison, WI: University of Wisconsin-Madison, Center for Education Research.

Squire, K., & Klopfer, E. (2007). Augmented reality simulations on handheld computers. *Journal of the Learning Sciences, 16*(3), 371–413. doi:10.1080/10508400701413435

KEY TERMS AND DEFINITIONS

Citizen Science Games: Games designed to facilitate collaboration between researchers and citizens in solving authentic scientific challenges such as protein folding.

Gamification: The application of game elements such as missions and scores to a non-game context.

Innovation: A new idea or development in form of a device or a method that creates value.

Innovation Education: Education designed for learners to develop competences in developing new ideas and concepts.

Profession Simulation Games: Games that simulates the practices of a specific profession including values and perspectives of the members of the community.

Scenario: A description or plan of possible actions or events in the future involving specific actors.

Scientific Discovery Games: Games designed to involve gamers in scientific discoveries as part of playing the game.

Chapter 9
Rhetorical Replay and the Challenge of Gamic History:
Silencing the Siren Song of Digital Simulation

Jerremie V. Clyde
University of Calgary, Canada

Glenn R. Wilkinson
University of Calgary, Canada

ABSTRACT

This chapter explores the limits of simulations for university-level historical education. The authors develop an alternative gamic mode more fit for purpose by focusing on epistemology and procedural rhetoric. This chapter will start by examining how history functions as a form of disciplinary knowledge and how this disciplinary way of knowing things is taught at the post-secondary level. The manner in which history is taught will be contrasted with its evaluation in order to better define what students are actually expected to learn. The simulation will be then examined in the light of learning goals and evaluation. This will demonstrate that simulations are in fact a poor fit for most post-secondary history courses. The more appropriate and effective choice is to construct the past via procedural rhetoric, using games that mirror the structure of the historical argument.

INTRODUCTION

This chapter seeks to do two things. It outlines some of the limitations and responds to the use of digital simulations, such as *Sid Meir's Civilization*, in historical instruction. The simulations that will discussed here are computer video games, either commercial or designed expressly for teaching, that attempt to recreate the past by being as factually accurate as possible. They then let the player engage with that reconstructed past. In general, they do not actually construct the past as history in the same way that a history textbook, academic article, or lecture do. Secondly, his chapter puts forward an alternate gamic

DOI: 10.4018/978-1-5225-7987-8.ch009

approach to historical instruction, one that utilizes Ian Bogost's ideas of procedural rhetoric; the unique way in which games create reasonably justified truths. The authors look at how history is taught, and more importantly evaluated, to determine the actual goals of historical instruction. They then explore what a game needs to do in order to better match those goals. The main focus is on university and college level historical education, although the general idea of matching game play to learning objective could be applied in any field for any learner. The authors suggest a different approach to game-based learning for history and challenge the more common and popular use of digital simulations. The chapter builds upon the authors' previous work on a digital mode of history, where a case was made for history being non-mode or media specific, demonstrated by the use of a game-based procedural rhetoric to author scholarly history in a gamic form.

This chapter examines how that gamic form can be applied directly to historical education and student learning. Due to the authors' reliance on Bogost's conclusions regarding how games engage the player to make arguments and construct truths, this chapter is based largely, although not exclusively, on the North American work addressing game-based learning over the past few decades. It will start by examining how history functions as a form of disciplinary knowledge and how this disciplinary way of knowing things is taught in post-secondary history courses. The manner in which history is taught will be contrasted with how student learning is evaluated to better define what students are actually expected to learn. The simulation, a very popular tool for digital game-based attempts to teach history, will then be examined in the light of those learning goals. This will demonstrate that simulations are in fact a poor fit for most post-secondary history courses. The authors assume that the intent or goal of most history instruction, teaching how one constructs the past as history, is a worthwhile goal. In consideration of that particular goal the more appropriate and effective choice is to construct the historical arguments themselves as game, as opposed to trying to recreate a factually accurate past in a simulation. Historical instruction acts as a case study that can be applied to any discipline. This chapter is primarily focused on how a game is more suitable than a simulation for historical instruction, it does not necessarily argue that a game is always the best choice for historical instruction, just that it is a better choice than a simulation.

BACKGROUND

An ideal interactive gamic digital mode for history results from the application of procedural rhetoric to scholarly history with the aim of producing a valid argument that optimizes the use of computers for university and college level historical studies. This gamic digital mode of history was first presented as a way of communicating scholarly research at the *Seventy Years On: New Perspectives on the Second World War* in the Fall of 2009. The paper discussed how history as a disciplinary form of knowledge is not mode dependent, where mode is the technological medium through which the scholarly argument is constructed and conveyed. For example, historical arguments can be conveyed through the printed scholarly article and monograph, the oral classroom lecture, documentary film or computer video game. History is not mode dependent because it is defined by its epistemologies which are dependent upon a series of creative processes such as empathetic re-enactment, limited counterfactual, and narrative reconstruction. The point of a gamic digital mode is not to replace the textual mode found in print, but to offer a multi-modal approach to presenting valid scholarly interpretations of the past, whether they are constructionist, de-constructionist, or re-constructionist histories. In the realm of education, it does what Karras (1994) has stated is essential in an approach to teaching historical argumentation, in that it can be explicitly taught, performed, and evaluated. A gamic or digital mode of history allows new questions to be asked, old questions to be addressed in new ways, and constructions of the past to be communicated more effectively. The digital mode also offers exactly what students want; challenging content, exciting methodologies, and engagement with the material (Russell & Pellegrino, 2008).

This chapter considers the application of this digital or gamic mode to historical education and describes how arguments are created in this mode using Ian Bogost's ideas of procedural rhetoric. Procedural rhetoric becomes a significant tool to understand how this gamic mode constructs an argument in a way that is relevant in the context of historical education.

CONSTRUCTING THE PAST AS HISTORY

In order to express knowledge in a different format, whether that format be a digital simulation or a gamic representation of a scholarly argument, it is important to know how that knowledge exists. It is crucial to make the decision to use a different format or media intentionally, demonstrating the epistemic awareness that one also wants to see in students as critical thinkers. Epistemic cognition is particularly important for history students as valid representations of the past are constructed radically differently depending on the epistemic choices made. Epistemic cognition is the process that enables individuals to develop the criteria for limits and certainty of knowing (Maggioni, VanSledright, & Alexander, 2009), which enables a constructive approach to ambiguity as opposed to the common student misapprehension that historical certainty exists.

While there have been many attempts to address the epistemological question, "what is history?", Alun Munslow provides a functional answer that is useful for analyzing digital expression of the past. In his works *Narrative and History* (2007) and *The New History* (2003), he defines three broad epistemological approaches for historical scholarship: construction, deconstruction, and reconstruction. This chapter will borrow these categories to understand the nature of history and place it as a form of disciplinary knowledge in the post-secondary history classroom. Munslow's three epistemological approaches make it clear how some expressions of the past, such as history-themed commercial digital games and simulations, are fundamentally different from the scholarly history that is often taught.

Munslow suggests that the majority of historians working today are constructionists who construct the past as history through reasoned argument. Constructionist history relies on empirical methods and analyses as well as narrative to create adequately justified truth claims and theories about the past. Such claims and theories function as the basis of both historical knowledge and the traditional epistemology of history. As a form of history, constructionism recognizes that "history" is not the past. Constructionism builds up knowledge of the past and expresses the past as history by both analyzing how and what individual pieces of evidence can do, and what conclusions about the actions of historical agents (be they individuals or corporate entities) can be established through the relationships between fact, evidence, and interpretation.

In this case, evidence itself is separate from a notion of historical fact, despite these terms often being used interchangeably, as the fact only becomes evidence based upon its relationship to the question at hand. This differs from popular approaches to history where one often hears claims of factual accuracy as basis for veracity. The claim to factual accuracy as a source of veracity, as a trait of quality and applicability to education is common. Muzzy Lane produced a series of detailed military and diplomatic simulations of World War II that were promoted for educational use. They claimed that their *Making*

History series allowed one to understand history by accurately simulating all aspects of the conflict and letting the player manipulate them. This approach to history, proving what must have been through the use of counterfactuals is not how we generally understand, communicate, or teach history. Counterfactuals are sometimes employed as very limited thought experiments but not as basis for understanding, one cannot observe what might have been, only what was and then try to interpret it. The constructionist approach to history, while allowing almost any question to be asked, provides constraints around how the question can be answered.

Deconstructionist approaches to history tend to be more self-aware and will apply analysis and interpretation to both the historical source and the scholar's contemporary thinking. It is, at least in part, an attempt to deal with the scholar's bias, the bias inherent in the mode of communication, and the bias in the original information. It does not necessarily follow the standard constructionist procession of fact to interpretation to evidence to conclusion for building reasonably justified truths about the past. The deconstructionist approach to history is more open to how questions are answered and at first glance seems a more flexible approach for a digital mode or gamic version of history. The rules of each individual historical argument become wholly dependent and defined by that argument. The deconstructionist approaches implies an unknowable past, or past that can be known in a multitude of ways, which suggests that a gamic mode of history could be almost anything as long as it could be shown to create unambiguous arguments and shared understandings about a given topic. Taking a deconstructionist approach then might be simpler, or at least offer more freedom to scholars working in a gamic mode who wants to create entertaining history games for their students, than a more common constructionist approach to history. However, this approach offers two challenges. First just as in a constructionist approach the simulation would have to make unambiguously clear all aspects of the argument it is making, but it would not simply need to make clear how a given argument transforms fact in to evidence via interpretation leading to a conclusion, it would also have to make clear how the "text" the game itself creates meaning. Second it would also be contradictory to most historians' aspirations for themselves and their students, which is to achieve something approaching objective truth in mainstream historical scholarship (which is predominantly constructionist in approach). This aspiration exists because for a history (as an expression of the past) to have meaning and achieve adequately-justified truth claims and theories about its subject matter, these claims and theories must be recognizable as history and be part of the scholarly discourse at all levels.

Reconstructionist history is a third choice for the gamic mode of history, and like deconstructionist history does seem to present some benefits to educators working in the digital mode of history. The reconstructionist historian attempts to recreate the past as it actually was through the use of sources, which by their nature as facts are considered objective. The potential to use computers to collect, compile, arrange and present a vast array of historical data seems to hold the promise an accurate recreation of past. Of course, the utilization and arrangement of facts or data, is an interpretive activity and even the use of a computer to compile and present them is tainted by subjectivity. Research has shown that procedural and AI generated content and systems replicate social bias, and often reinforce them (Philips, Smith, Cook, & Short, 2016). Like deconstructionist history, this also taxes the historian's ideal of objective scholarship and then becomes a significant problem for education. The reconstructionist mode is now commonly that of the popular historian, the entertainment-documentary and many digital video games, where an attempt is made to tell the "real" story. It is clear that they are reconstructionist forms of history as the main claim to authenticity is based on the volume of data used. Reconstructionist history claims that history is the past, as opposed to a constructionist view where the argument is the past as history. History and the past are not the same thing, no more than the Tower of London and a description or photograph of the Tower of London are the same thing. Reconstructionist history fails to recognize the difference between the thing and the description of the thing. It is often believed that one can become the other, the description can become the Tower of London if that description is full enough. The vast majority of scholarly history recognizes explicitly or implicitly that that history is not the past, it is the exercise in constructing reasonably justifiable truth claims about the past.

Irrespective of the epistemological choices outlined above, there are no hard and fast rules in history as to what constitutes evidence, the limits of evidence, or the relationships between fact, evidence and interpretation. Even simply reading existing historical arguments students find it extremely difficult to understand this process and "it is likely that many students will be stopped at the beginning of the learning process" (Pace, 2004, p.13). Rules are established by the student or scholar in the creation of the argument itself, its use of facts as evidence, and the relationship between evidence interpretation and conclusion. That argument is generated by the scholar or student even if the decision is made to convey the argument through a computer-mediated gamic format. Even though constructions of the past as history can be computer mediated, it is not the case that the process of constructing the past as history can be automated. It is only within a given historical argument that one can find the rules that govern that particular construction of the past. It is that argument and the process of its formation (including historical imagination and empathetic re-enactment) where one finds the rules used to construct the argument. Those rules are then used to create the gamic version. They constrain what counts as a fact, examine how interpretation converts that fact in to evidence, and determine how that builds to a conclusion. If one looks at games, whether a computer game like Tetris or a soccer match, certain rules govern one's behaviors and it is the manipulation of those rules to a desired end that give the exercise its meaning. When one constructs the past as history one is creating a set of rules that apply within that argument, that give that particular exercise of history meaning.. The rules of the given argument or construction of the past are dependent upon the question being asked, the known facts and methods applied. In order to be considered "good history" these three factors must be interdependent. Once the relationships are set the logic of the argument can be used to generate a set of rules and procedures that are then mediated by a computer. That set of computer mediated rules and relationships is the digital version of the historical argument.

HISTORICAL TEACHING AND EVALUATION

The instructional goal of the post-secondary history course is both a particular understanding of the past and the creation of the historical argument, which is the process of establishing the relationships between facts, evidence, interpretations, and conclusions. The essay is traditionally used to evaluate student ability to create a historical argument using these processes. In fact, the American Historical Association in its "Statement of Excellence in Classroom Teaching of History" states that the final evaluation of student learning should include written or other work that provides evidence of analysis and interpretation of the factual information that students collected to address a significant historical question (AHA, 2010) It is interesting to note that evidence of analysis and interpretation is more important than format; even a game that provides adequate evidence of these would suffice.

However, instead of interpretation and analysis, what most students seem to focus on is the content of the course—dates, people, places, things, and the mechanical attributes of the essay—rather than process of constructing arguments about the past as history. When course lectures or readings try to contextualize those facts in different constructions of the past, students see those only as alternate opinions, and secondary to the facts themselves with the main issue at hand being whether something happened or not (Voelker, 2008). Often the way courses are organized re-enforces this separation of content and process with a minimal amount of class time given over to the construction of historical arguments and essay writing. Even essay writing is often treated as the mechanics of presentation rather than a heuristic process that is used to form the historical argument. It is usually relegated to being dealt with outside of class, by teaching assistants, sessionals, librarians, writing centre tutors, or through online tutorials, special lectures or drop in seminars, and written guides. The mechanics of presenting the argument in essay form and the lecture as a model of the process of constructing an argument are rarely brought together for the student.

Faculty want students to learn facts as both the building blocks of history and the basis of cultural literacy (Maxwell, 2010), but they also want the students to learn the process of constructing narrative interpretations of the past based on those building blocks. The research of Russell and Pellegrino (2008) suggests that the lecture and reading combination is an efficient way to transmit a great deal of factual information but fails to promote notions of how historical meaning is constructed. While professors imply the process of constructing the past as history through the structure of their lectures, students focus primarily on that which is being explicitly taught: people, places, and things in the past. It is only those students who are aware of this implicit modeling of process through lecture and course readings that will be successful. It could be argued that most history teachers are not even aware of this failure by students to connect process and content, but they are aware of many of their students being unable to produce a reasoned historical argument for their term papers.

PEDAGOGICAL TOOLS

In essence, there is a disconnection between the main evaluative tool of the history course, the essay, and what students are being taught in the classroom. What students most often come equipped to do from Secondary School is to summarize the factual content with many of them "eager to learn but relatively unable to initiate or carry out projects on their own" (McClymer & Moynihan, 1977, p. 360). It is important to recognize and address this disconnection because merely changing the mode or introducing digital learning objects, such as simulations or history games, will not result in effective student learning of the process of history. The essay as an evaluative tool does not just measure historical knowledge, but also the construction of the past as history. Indeed, it is the quality of the argument that receives the most scrutiny, as factual accuracy will not necessarily gain marks and inaccuracy will *cost* them. What the essay evaluates in student learning is the process of constructing the past as history despite this only being implied by the instructor (Beaufort, 2004).

This process is generally only taught indirectly through modeling via the students' readings and through lecture, rather than constituting a major part of the courses content. Student demonstration of that implied knowledge often takes place through the practical application during their assignments, not before, which is a high stakes process of trial and error from the students' point of view. There is no opportunity to explicitly demonstrate and evaluate those skills, particularly in a low stakes environment where learning could take place. So while the students are evaluated on their understanding of the processes of reasoned argument, and evidential attributes and relationships, they are not directly taught it. They are rarely able to play with the process to gain a better understanding of how it functions.

There are other techniques in history courses, such as annotated bibliographies, document analyses, seminars, and class presentations, that are used to better equip students to construct the past as history. The document analysis assignment is designed to encourage students to think critically about primary sources. They are given a primary source, which is a document produced in the time period under study, and asked to interpret its value as a historical source with respect to such concepts as authorship, intentionality, context, reception, and significance. Document analyses exercises have been used to help develop students' historical imagination and can also be merged with the final paper, asking students to comment on the context of their primary sources within their essays (Tobin, 2001, p.499). The outline and annotated bibliography assignments are given to students in advance of their term paper as a way to check the students progress on their research, the logic of their thinking, and to encourage them to get an early start.

While both these assignments do encourage students to think about the nature of historical evidence and the structure of their argument, they are rarely integrated into their term papers, being seen instead by many students as discrete exercises. In addition, there is some evidence to suggest that without significant support, students are not even adequately prepared to deal with these initial scaffolding exercises (Britt & Aglinskas, 2002). Unless class time is given over to teaching the process of building historical arguments, these assignments are no better than the term paper for expecting students to engage in trial and error learning (although fewer grades are attached, and so have lower risk) based on implied concepts from their lectures and readings. These assignments are intended to help build skills so that students are better equipped to deal with a term paper, but they do not necessarily teach the process of constructing the past as history. Instead, they focus on discrete parts of the process, and it is no wonder that students see them as individual and unrelated assignments. These issues can be ameliorated by class discussions, tutorials and seminars, but the use of these tools is often impractical in the face of shrinking budgets, large classes, and too few teaching assistants.

Online learning objects have been developed in response to student inability to write an essay and barriers to the instructor's ability to teach these skills in the classroom. They provide a way to reach the hundreds of students enrolled in history courses in any one semester. For instance, Workshop for the Information Search Process for Research (WISPR), developed at the University of Calgary, was based on Dr. Alex Hayden's phenemological research into how students handle the research and paper writing process (2003; Hayden, Rutherford, & Pival, 2006). WISPR, and tools like it, teach a student to write a paper and conduct research effectively, yet the tools fail to introduce students to thinking historically and considering the process of constructing reasonably justified truth claims in a discipline specific way.

The increasingly popular digital response to the problem of student inability to write a historical essay, engage with history, or think historically utilises everything from online discussion groups around a course to online learning objects like *Heaven & Hell on Earth: The Massacre of The "Black" Donnellys* (Pettit & Street), *Salem Witchcraft Trials* (Hurter, 2003), *The Estate Inventories of Early* Virginians (Phillips, 2002). In most cases they do one of two things: in attempting to teach the process of historical construction they become exercises in the mechanics of paper writing and/or research; or they end up teaching content and not process. They tend to either explicitly or implicitly use the metaphor of historian as detective searching for existing clues and solving a mystery by finding out the truth behind it. This is the popular metaphor of documentary media, such as the History Channel's series *Battlefield Detective,* or fiction such as Josphine Tey's *The Daugher of Time*. The idea of historian as detective only works as a metaphor for re-constructionist history, where the historian is uncovering a truth that is already there, as opposed to constructing a valid interpretation of the past. The current process of historical education concerns teaching this process via modeling it through lecture and readings. It does work for a limited number of students, but instead of trying to find a way to make that modeling more effective, instructors are turning to very different approaches. For example, the computer-based *Salem Witchcraft Trials* (Hurter, 2003) continues to emphasize content over process and models an obsolete way of reconstructing the past. This misplaced emphasis and modeling are particularly evident in the case of digital historical simulations for education, whether they are scratch built or modified commercial-off-the-shelf (COTS) digital games.

DIGITAL SIMULATIONS OF PAST

In the end, the history that is taught in most courses and that most students are evaluated for creating is one that constructs the past out of an argument, instead of attempting to recreate or simulate the past. Attempts to simulate the past through digital video games are exercises in re-enactment that are outside scholarly history's epistemology for assigning truth attributes. Prensky argues convincingly that "... *whenever* one plays a game - video, computer or otherwise - and *whatever* game one plays, learning happens constantly, whether the players want it to, and are aware of it, or not." The question then becomes, what is it exactly that students are learning? What one should actually be creating in a digital game-based mode is in fact the digital version of the valid empirical reasoned argument that is taught to students, and is more commonly communicated by the mechanical means of print or through the oral presentation of the lecture rather than in the digital simulation.

Kurt Squire has suggested that "...the important question is not *can* games be used to support learning, but *how*" (Changing the Game, 2004, p.1). Within the context of game-based historical education, the most important question is actually *what* is being taught, as *how* will be predicated on that. While there has been an explosion of interest in the field of history education regarding the use of games and simulations, a thorough consideration of what is actually being taught in the post-secondary history course does not seem to have taken place. There have been a number of articles focusing on the classroom use of non-digital simulations, where the students take on the role of historical actors during a particular time "to get into the shoes of historical people and to move around in them" (Monahan, 2002, P.74). Monahan claims that "a simulation comes closer than any other tool to helping students understand the past from the perspective of those who lived it" (Monahan, 2002, P.74). Despite this and claims of student enjoyment, he does not explain how a simulation creates student understanding, how that understanding is a valid form of history, and what learning is actually evaluated. This raises the question as to whether or not what they are learning is history or another form of knowing. The valid history course focus on the process of constructing the past as history in student assignments suggests that most historical simulations, digital or otherwise, are a poor fit for academic historical education. Monahan's (2002) implementation of simulations also involves a great deal of instructor mediation to ensure that learning takes place. Simulations fail to do what Royle and Clarke suggest games should be doing in education to be effective, namely to put the individual at the centre of the learning experience, to focus on the students interacting with the content to create knowledge, and to match what is actually being taught (Royle & Clarke, 2003). At best for simulations to be effective in post-secondary historical education, they require instructor mediation, through discussion, seminars, reflective writing, and the like. This suggests that the learning is not taking place in or through the simulation but as a result of the follow up exercises. This in turn means they are failing as game-based learning because the learning is not taking place during the play experience. It would be better if the game mechanisms were developed "where players literally perform the kinds of understandings, we want them to have" (Squire, Giovanetto, Devane, & Durga 2005), which should be the function of the digital, or even table top, gamic modes of history.

By focusing wholeheartedly on simulation-based learning objects and exercises, instructors are likely to take secondary and post-secondary historical education down the wrong path. There are several examples of the use of simulations for teaching history at different levels, including Squire and Barab's (2004) use of *Civilization III,* Aaron Whelchel (2008) using *Civilization III* and *Age of Empires,* and Julian DelGaudio (2002) scratch building role play simulations such as *Eunice: A Captivity Simulation* and *In Search of Freedom: Navigating A Slaves' [sic] Journey.* More recently in Canada, the Social Sciences and Humanities Research Council of Canada has funded *The Simulating History Project: Best Practices for History Simulations* (Kee, Graham, Dunae, Lutz, Large, Blondeau & Clare, 2009) which focuses on historical simulation through games to be used in teaching.

Even if the *Simulating History Project* and others like it were able to develop good history simulations, this pedagogy brings to mind Prensky's (2003) exhortation regarding digital games and education: "just because one learns *how* to do something, it doesn't mean one has learned *when* or *whether one should* do it." When one considers what is actually being taught, or more to the point, evaluated in most academic history courses, and what a student would need to learn to function as a history scholar, these simulations are of limited to no use. They are exercises in historical re-enactment, which is not even a new way to teach, as it has been used in role play in the classroom or visiting historical sites, particularly those with costumed interpreters. As paradigms of constructing the past, re-enactments are flawed because their accuracy is based on their ability to replicate historical events (Monahan, 2002). This is problematic because there is nothing in how one observes or interprets the past that enables one to declare events unfolded as they had to; one can only say they unfolded as they did. Kurt Squire, in his 2005 perspective paper, points out that "it is increasingly clear that simply replicating existing paradigms of instruction is unwise in the information age" (p.18).

Digital historical simulations may seem to do historical re-enactments and counterfactuals differently than their live action counterparts. They allow replications, recording and reviewing, and inclusion of more role-players or larger environments than would otherwise be possible. However, making the reconstructions bigger, better, faster, is not changing how they express the past; they still fail as expressions of scholarly history. The students need to know how to construct the past as reasoned historical argument. It might very well be the case that there are ways to use these computer mediated re-enactments as sources to greater conclusions, but students still need to know how to come to those conclusions, how to move that experience from event to evidence, to relate it to other pieces of evidence, move from evidence to interpretation and finally to conclusion. In looking at what it means to know something in the simulation *EnerCities,* Barzilai (2017) explores an inherent epistemic challenge. Players may have varying epistemic aims in the game world, they may want to know how to facilitate successful play and have a separate set of aims about the game itself based on its real-world importance. Those differing and conflicting aims are not necessarily in line with the instructional aims within a course, although inherent to a student's use of the tool. The result is that transfer of knowledge from game play to real world experience is not guaranteed. It may be incomplete or misdirected as the game or simulation is only concerned with encouraging and enabling the first epistemic aim, the facilitating of successful play, while the second aim and associated transfer of knowledge is entirely up to the player.

Epistemic challenges aside, computer games, even commercial quality games like *Civilization III*, are not immediately motivating for students because it is not always clear to them how a computer game can teach history (Squire, 2004). There is another problem with simulations. Many of them, like *Civilization III,* utilize the computer itself to generate game content for the player to experience. This is known as procedurally generated content and can play a major role in a simulations initial game design or as part of the users experience of the simulation. This is a problem because while studies show that race, class, and gender bias are present in procedurally generated content, game play itself can obscure embedded meanings from the player and students are unlikely to assign bias to what appears to be objective computer-generated content (Philips et al, 2016). The students then, in addition to learning how to succeed at the simulation, are having contemporary biases reinforced. The game should allow for the performance of disciplinary ways of thinking that provide a more active interpretative role to students (Anderson & Hounsell, 2007). This means it must focus on the process of constructing the past as history, where student interaction with the game creates knowledge of this process, rather than requiring supplemental learning activities. Their success in exploring the gamic procedural rendering of the reasoned historical argument should be the arbiter of their understanding of how to construct the past as history.

GAMES AND PROCEDURAL RHETORIC

Since simulations are not a legitimate constructionist expression of the past as history and are out of synch with what is being taught in the history class, one could begin to wonder whether or not computers should even be used. Using computers requires one to consider how the past as history is constructed as a reasoned argument and how arguments and truth claims are constructed in procedural environments. Ian Bogost argues convincingly that procedural environments persuade and make arguments in a sufficiently different way than classic text-based forms of rhetoric. Bogost calls this new form of persuasion "procedural rhetoric". Applying Ian Bogost's ideas of procedural rhetoric (2007) to how history is constructed suggests a possible method for the creation of a digital gamic scholarly expression of the past as history. Historians construct the past as a series of evidential relationships, which are procedural within a given argument. Those procedures could be expressed as rules that govern how the parts of an argument move towards a verifiable conclusion with a reasonably established truth attribute. Procedural rhetoric could be used to build a gamic mode of history that creates computer mediated gamic scholarly constructions of the past, the gamic nature of which allows students to explore and interact with the process of historical construction within a given argument.

The historical narrative offers explanations of events by constructing relationships and placing them in an order and context. Narrative explanation is dependent upon the idea that order and relationships are explanatory, and it is in the ordering and constructing of relationships of the historical narrative that one finds the processes. In order to identify the process of a given argument, one has to consider how facts are evidence, the relationships between individual pieces of evidence, the way in which evidence builds towards inference, and lastly how inferences lead to a conclusion and the formation of a justified belief. This is exactly what professors expect and assess in student essays. David Pace (2004) argues that students tend to be unable to read the historical narrative and understand the process of how it constructs the past, seeing it instead as a series of historical facts. His responses to this challenge include six steps such as using hyperlinks and audio files to make his own thought process knowable to his students while doing the assigned readings or reformatting them to emphasize those parts of a reading that are most important.

In a gamic mode of history Pace's six steps can be addressed as the evidence and resulting arguments are explored as a multi-modal rule set. One is not constrained by trying to recreate the past, but instead one is allowing the student to play with a historical argument. The elements of that play can include hyperlinks and audio files to make the historians thoughts known, reformatting and emphasizing parts of text. There can be secondary elements of play, often called mini-games, for the students to engage in that make clear the historians though processes, how they interpreted evidence, and came to their conclusions. In addition, by having a computer mediate those rules for the player, it allows a deeper exploration of the historian's thinking through trial and error (as opposed to allowing for trial and error only at the point of evaluation). In this way, students can gain a much deeper and more critical understanding of how the past is constructed as history. They can explore parts of the historical process that normally take place within the historian's mind, such as the use of evidence, the limits of empathetic re-enactment and the explanatory narrative, before anything is set down on paper. Since the historical process is taught through modeling, allowing students to explore the process itself, as opposed to just the historical facts or mechanics of writing, the emphasis is placed on the construction of the past as a reasoned argument. Students have an interest in the past and learning about history but how it is taught causes them to lose this interest. What is required is a way for students to be engaged with the material, such as readings, in an insightful and meaningful way (Russell and Pellegrino, 2008, p. 13-14). In the digital mode of the argument itself, they are explicitly engaged in the process of historical construction. This interaction enables them to understand how the past is constructed as history and as a result, they are better able to meet the requirements on which they are evaluated.

Allowing students to read and, better still, author their own work in this way will result in less focus on flowery prose and hollow rhetoric and more focus on the logic and structure of the well-reasoned empirical argument about the past. Tsui (1999) found that it was not a particular discipline that encouraged the development of critical thinking in students but writing assignments and instructor feedback. While authoring in a gamic mode may seem intimidating, the work of James Paul Gee (2010) suggests that most students can handle the technical aspects of authoring in this way. From the instructor perspective "the inclusion of computer games within formal learning is a necessity" and is now "an issue of curriculum and teaching methodology rather than a technological issue." (Royle, 2009) One does *not* require an entire games studio, professional programmers, artists and game designers in order to produce a high quality serious game (Blackman, 2005).

Authoring in a digital gamic mode can be done in a number of ways, including creating original code, modifying a COTS game with its bundled editors, using a COTS focused on user generated content like Minecraft,or using a commercial game engine licensed at a nominal cost for educational use such as *Source SDK* or *The Hero Engine* (Valve 2008, Whatley & Harris, 2010; Clyde &Thomas, 2008). Table top games, card games, role playing games, could also all be created, in this case with minimal technical expertise (Kim, Gupta, & Clyde, 2016). Modifying a commercial game, using purchased playing pieces or accessing a 3D printer makes analog game development reasonably accessible, so time can be spent authoring the rules and gameplay, that when combined construct the experiences argument.

Benjamin Hoy modified a COTS board game to produce "Policing the Sound," a game that modeled disciplinary approaches in history and the limits of the archival record. The resultant game play experience was useful to enable historical empathy, which is a crucial and difficult to develop component of crime and social history (Hoy, Benjamin, 2018). There is the potential for a great deal of flexibility in design as direct detailed factual authenticity is not necessary to create reasonable gamic expressions of history. Game mechanics, graphics, music, text, voice, mode of engagement are all rhetorical resources and it is their creative and intentional interplay that constructs the argument (Rughini & Matei, 2015). Johannes Koski (2017) in his analysis of the COTS game *Valkyria Chronicles,* demonstrates how a game uses selective authenticity, which is establishing a historical narrative by prioritizing some elements to the foreground while relegating others to the background. He shows how the combination of recognizable WWII tropes with Japanese Role Playing Game (JRPG) fantasy operate in both representational and ludic elements. This allows players of *Valkyria Chronicles* to engage in a narrative that is unique in WWII-themed games, as it acts as a commentary on how WWII history is created and explores difficult issues such as anti-Semitism and genocide (Koski, 2017). Students working creatively in a gamic mode, expressing their arguments via procedural rhetoric, can make all the evidential and interpretive relationships of their historical narratives clear through translating them into an interdependent set of rules. Working in a gamic mode creates the learning environment that Dickey (2005) states is the ideal for using digital video games for teaching where the "learner plays an active role in the construction of knowledge, while the role of the teacher is to provide materials and environment that support learner's engagement in the learning tasks." Where reading essays and listening to lectures may passively teach students something of the method for creating history, the iterative process used to develop games allows students to actively mirror historical scholarship; providing another advantage to working in this mode (Spring, 2015). Students authoring in this way are forced to think deeply and intentionally how they define and construct an argument. By reviewing the evidence, rule set, design, and finished product the educator is better able to evaluate student understanding of history.

If at least some of the course "readings" are in the form of a digital game and students can construct their own assignments in the same way, they will be introduced not only to historical skills, but also to procedural literacy. Procedural literacy is "not limited to the abstract ability to understand procedural representations of cultural values, it also uses that understanding to interrogate, critique and uses specific representations of specific real or imagined process" (Dickey, 2005, p246). It is an important skill in a world where media are increasingly dominated by all types of digital video games. It is also a critical literacy for academic work in other disciplines regardless of mode because it is an abstract approach applicable to all reasoned arguments. It provides students with a means to determine what counts as evidence such as empirical observation or predicative models and how reasonably justifiable truth is being created. As the thinking skills that are encompassed by procedural literacy are really the attributes of critical thinking, it provides students with a way to develop critical thinking skills in a media context they are familiar with. While defining critical thinking can be problematic for some, most definitions include the ability to recognize important relationships, make correct inferences, evaluate evidence or authority and deduce conclusions. Critical thinking has been touted by institutions of higher learning as the main benefit they offer society, as they claim it ensures a thinking citizenry and competent work force in an increasingly complex world (Tsui, 1999).

CONCLUSION

A gamic mode of history, digital or otherwise, is a way to avoid the siren song of simulations which, while fun, only seem to offer student engagement. They fail to address the important issue of how the past is constructed as history. A gamic mode provides an engaging way to introduce the process of scholarly history to all students, particularly those new to the university environment. This is more effective than digital simulations and even current classroom practice at universities where historical methods and process are often taught only at a senior level in courses primarily aimed at history majors. While a gamic mode of history, like course readings, would benefit from additional in-class discussion or seminars, it does not require them, unlike digital simulations. This means that a gamic mode of history is particularly practical for engaging large first-year classes in the process of constructing history because it does not require seminars, class discussion, or tutorials to be effective.

There are other benefits of a gamic mode for teaching the process of constructing the past such as peer learning through digital palimpsests and graffiti. Digital palimpsests are seen in games like *Demon's Souls* (Miyazaki, Takeuchi, & Nakajima, 2009) where the server automatically records one player's actions and makes them available for others to see. In *Demon's Souls* they have an instructive role as they show a player the last moments leading up to another player's demise. In this context graffiti refers to the ability to leave behind notes and comments, often context specific for other players by writing them in the game environment, acting as a form of virtual class participation. The potential for peer learning and more effective evaluation of student participation and learning offered by the gamic mode of history is the topic for further study. All epistemic approaches to history allow one to create reasonably justifiable truths regardless of mode. Procedural rhetoric is a useful tool in creating those truths about the past and communicating them via a gamic mode without changing epistemologies. This chapter has demonstrated how one might use procedural rhetoric to construct a gamic mode of history to support student learning in post-secondary history classrooms. This is different than history in the high school classroom or the type of memorialization found in historic sites. Creating "factual" digital simulations to recreate the past, while popular, is unlikely to enhance historical education unless the creators are aware of exactly how they are creating the past as history; epistemic awareness is the key to good gamic histories.

REFERENCES

American Historical Association. (n.d.). *Statement of Excellence in Classroom Teaching of History.* Retrieved May 26, 2010 from http://www.historians.org/teaching/policy/ExcellentTeaching.htm

Anderson, C., & Hounsell, D. (2007). Knowledge practices: 'doing the subject' in undergraduate courses. *Curriculum Journal, 18*(4), 463–478. doi:10.1080/09585170701687910

Barzilai, S. (2017). "Half-reliable": A qualitative analysis of epistemic thinking in and about a digital game. *Contemporary Educational Psychology, 51*, 51–66. doi:10.1016/j.cedpsych.2017.06.004

Beaufort, A. (2004). Developmental Gains of a History Major: A Case for Building a Theory of Disciplinary Writing Expertise. *Research in the Teaching of English, 39*(2), 136–185.

Blackman, S. (2005). Serious Games...and Less! *Computer Graphics, 39*(1), 12–16. doi:10.1145/1057792.1057802

Bogost, I. (2007). *Persuasive games: the expressive power of videogames*. Cambridge, MA: MIT Press.

Britt, M. A., & Aglinskas, C. (2002). Improving Students' Ability to Identify and Use Source Information. *Cognition and Instruction, 20*(4), 485–522. doi:10.1207/S1532690XCI2004_2

Clyde, J., & Thomas, C. (2008). Building and Information Literacy First Person Shooter. *RSR. Reference Services Review*, *36*(4), 366–380. doi:10.1108/00907320810920342

Clyde, J., & Wilkinson, G. (2009, Fall). *The Digital Mode of History*. Paper presented at Seventy Years On: New Perspectives on the Second World War, Lake Louise, AB. Retrieved from http://www.ucalgary.ca/newperspectives/

DelGaudio, J. J. (2002). Creating Simulations for Use in Teaching Lower Division U.S. History. *History Computer Review*, *18*(1), 37–52.

Dickey, M. D. (2005). Engaging by Design: How Engagement Strategies in Popular Computer and Video Games Can Inform Instructional Design. *ETR&D*, *53*(2), 67–83. doi:10.1007/BF02504866

Gee, J. P. (2010). *New Digital Media and Learning as an Emerging Area and "Worked Examples" as One Way Forward*. Cambridge, MA: The MIT Press.

Hayden, K. A. (2003). *Lived experience of students searching for information* (Unpublished doctoral dissertation). University of Calgary, Alberta, Canada.

Hayden, K. A., Rutherford, S., & Pival, P. (2006). WISPR (Workshop on the Information Search Process for Research) in the Library. *Journal of Library Administration*, *45*(3), 427–443.

Hayden, K. A., Rutherford, S., & Pival, P. (2006). *WISPR (Workshop on the Information Search Process for Research)*. Alberta: University of Calgary Libraries and Cultural Resources. Accessed on May 26, 2010 at http://webapps3.tlc.ucalgary.ca:9080/wispr/app

Hoy, B. (2018). Teaching History with Custom-Built Board Games. *Simulation & Gaming*, *49*(2), 115–133. doi:10.1177/1046878118763624

Hurter, S. R. (2003). Elusive or Illuminating: Using the Web to Explore the Salem Witchcraft Trials. *OAH Magazine of History*, *17*(4), 60–61. doi:10.1093/maghis/17.4.60

Karras, R. W. (1994). Writing Essays That Make Historical Arguments. *OAH Magazine of History*, *8*(4), 54–57. doi:10.1093/maghis/8.4.54

Kee, K., Graham, S., Dunae, P., Lutz, J., Large, A., Blondeau, M., & Clare, M. (2009). Towards a Theory of Good History Through Gaming. *The Canadian Historical Review*, *90*(2), 303–326. doi:10.3138/chr.90.2.303

Kim, B., Gupta, D., & Clyde, J. (2016). Gamefulness in designing digital game-based learning through a role playing game. In M. A. Tekeuchi, P. Preciado, & J. V. Koc (Eds.), *Ideas 2016: Designing for Innovation Selected Proceedings* (pp. 41–55). Calgary, Canada: University of Calgary.

Koski, J. (2017). Reflections of history: Representations of the Second World War in *Valkyria Chronicles*. *Rethinking History*, *21*(3), 396–414. doi:10.1080/13642529.2016.1256625

Maggioni, L., VanSledright, B., & Alexander, P. A. (2009). Walking on the Borders: A Measure of Epistemic Cognition in History. *Journal of Experimental Education*, *77*(3), 187–213. doi:10.3200/JEXE.77.3.187-214

Matei, S. (2015). Games as a Genre of Historical Discourse. The Past on Fast Forward. *Proceedings of DiGRA 2015: Diversity of play: Games – Culture – Identity.*

Maxwell, A. (2010). Assessment Strategies for a History Exam, or, Why Short-Answer Questions are Better than In-Class Essays. *The History Teacher*, *43*(2), 233–245.

McClymer, J. F., & Moynihan, K. J. (1977). The Essay Assignment: A Teaching Device. *The History Teacher*, *10*(3), 359–371. doi:10.2307/491847

Miyazaki, H., Takeuchi, M., & Nakajima, E. (2009). *Demon's Souls* [video game]. Atlus & Sony Computer Entertainment.

Mojang. (2009). *Minecraft* [video game]. Sweden.

Monahan, G. W. (2002). Acting Out Nazi Germany: A Role-Play Simulation for the History Classroom. *Teaching History*, *27*(2), 74–85.

Munslow, A. (2003). *The New History*. Toronto: Pearson Longman.

Munslow, A. (2007). *Narrative and History*. New York: Palgrave MacMillan.

Muzzy Lane. (2010). *Making History: The Calm and the Storm & Making History II: The War of the World.* Making History Series. Accessed on May 26, 2010 http://making-history.com

Pace, D. (2004). Decoding the Reading of History: An Example of the Process. *New Directions for Teaching and Learning*, *2004*(98), 13–21. doi:10.1002/tl.143

Pettit, J., & Street, K. (2007). *Heaven & Hell on Earth: The Massacre of The "Black" Donnellys.* Great Unsolved Mysteries in Canadian History. Accessed on May 26, 2010. http://www.canadianmysteries.ca/sites/donnellys/home/indexen.html

Phillips, A., Smith, G., Cook, M., & Short, T. (2016). Feminism and procedural content generation: Toward a collaborative politics of computational creativity. *Digital Creativity*, *27*(1), 82–97. doi:10.1080/14626268.2016.1147469

Phillips, J. (2002). The Dinosaurs Didn't See It Coming, But Historians Had Better: Computer-Aided Activities in the History Classroom. *History Computer Review*, *18*(1), 27–36.

Prensky, M. (2003). Computer Games and Learning – digital game-based learning. In Handbook of Computer Game Studies (pp. 97-122). Cambridge, MA: MIT Press.

Royle, K. (2009). Computer games and realising their learning potential: Crossing Borders, Blurring Boundaries and Taking Actition. *Game Based Learning Video Games, Social Media & Learning*. Retrieved May 26, 2010 http://www.gamebasedlearning.org.uk/content/view/67/

Royle, K., & Clarke. (2003). *Making the case for computer games as a learning environment*. University of Wolverhampton. Retrieved May 26, 2010 http://citeseerx.ist.psu.edu/viewdoc/download?doi=10.1.1.110.2561&rep=rep1&type=pdf

Rughinis, R., & Matei, S. (2015). Play to Remember: The Rhetoric of Time in Memorial Video Games. In Human-Computer Interaction, Part II (pp. 628-639). Springer International Publishing.

Russell, W. B. III, & Pellegrino, A. (2008). Constructing Meaning from Historical Content: A Research Study. *Journal of Social Studies Research*, *32*(2), 3–15.

Spring, D. (2015). Gaming history: Computer and video games as historical scholarship. *Rethinking History*, *19*(20), 207–221. doi:10.1080/13642529.2014.973714

Squire, K. (2005). *Game-Based Learning An X-Learn Perspective Paper*. MASIE Centre: ELearning Consortium.

Squire, K., & Barab, S. (2004). Replaying history: engaging urban underserved students in learning world history through computer simulations games. *International Conference on Learning Science. Proceedings of the 6th international conference on Learning sciences*, 505-512.

Squire, K., Giovanetto, L., Devane, B., & Durga, S. (2005). From Users to Designers: Building a Self-Organizing Game-Based Learning Environment. *TechTrends*, *49*(5), 34–74. doi:10.1007/BF02763688

Squire, K. D. (2004). Changing the Game: What Happens When Video Games Enter the Classroom? *Innovate*. Retrieved May 26, 2010 http://www.innovateonline.info/index.php?view=article&id=82

Tey, J., (1968). *The Daughter of Time*. Scarborough, Canada: Bellhaven House ltd.

Tobin, K. (2001). To Think On Paper: Using Writing Assignments in the World of History Survey. *The History Teacher*, *34*(4), 497–508. doi:10.2307/3054202

Tsui, L. (1999). Courses and Instruction Affecting Critical Thinking. *Research in Higher Education*, *40*(2), 185–200. doi:10.1023/A:1018734630124

Valve Corporation. (2007). *Source SDK*. Bellevue, WA: Valve Corporation.

Voelker, D. J. (2008). Assessing Student Understanding in Introductory Courses: A Sample Strategy. *The History Teacher*, *41*(4), 506–518.

Whately, D., & Harris, N. (2010). *Hero Engine*. Simutronics Corporation. Author spoke Harris at Game Developers Conference, San Francisco, CA. Website accessed May 26, 2010 http://www.heroengine.com/home

Whelchel, A. (2007). Using Civilization Simulation Video Games in the World History Classroom. *World History Connected*, *4*(2), 1–14.

KEY TERMS AND DEFINITIONS

Digital Simulation: These are computer-based attempts to recreate the past. They may be produced for entertainment or education and generally tie their claims of validity and value to their factual accuracy. They allow the player to explore their argument through infinite what-if scenarios.

Empathetic Reenactment: An essential tool in historical understanding. It is how one makes judgements about the motivations of historical agents (whether individual or corporate). It is the ability to imagine and empathize with a historical actor's situation and then make rational judgements about why he or she took particular actions.

Epistemic Awareness: This describes an individual's ability to understand how reasonably justified truth claims are being made by themselves and others. It is their awareness of the choices they make about what counts as facts, reasonable interpretation, and how they choose to construct truth. This could apply to how they know the world about them, or more narrowly to how a particular argument, regardless of media format, is constructing truths.

Epistemology: The theory or study of how we form reasonably justified truths about our world. It explores the limits of knowledge and how we transform facts into evidence and how evidence and interpretation are used to come to conclusions.

Explanatory Narrative: This is the mechanism used by historical studies to create reasonably justified truths about the past. It describes the idea that a narrative has an inherent ability to carry an explanation of why things happened or why historical agents acted in a particular way. The explanatory narrative relies upon empathetic reenactment to create meaning.

Game-Based Learning (GBL): The field of game based learning is broad and it can describe a wide range of learning objectives, learning environments, and teaching techniques. Essential to game-based learning is the idea that the learning takes place within a game where learners have the opportunity to make meaningful choices and have some self-determination of valorized outcomes.

Gamic Mode of History: This is the translation of historical arguments into procedural rhetoric while maintaining its original epistemologies. The rules of evidence and interpretation, explanatory narrative, and empathetic reenactment are translated in to game rules for a particular historical argument. The reader then becomes a player who explores those relationships and the reasonably justified truths they create (or fail to create) through meaningful choice within the context of a game.

Procedural Rhetoric: This is a theory put forward by Ian Bogost who argues that computer games create arguments in a way that is unique from other forms of rhetoric. It is the persuasive nature of procedural, designed, interactions that one finds in digital games. The players meaningful interaction with the game, the games narrative, and its rules are the substance of the argument.

Chapter 10
Revisiting MMORPGs in Support of Learning:
Changes in the Last Decade

Bodi Anderson
Indian River State College, USA

ABSTRACT

This enhanced chapter revisits a previous literature analysis of research on the potential educational benefits of the use of massive multiplayer online role playing games (MMORPG) by considering both changes in the medium itself and recent trends in research. Initially, a working operational definition of MMORPGs in education is considered in light of research to date with a focus on how MMORPGs differ from most video games in terms of types of player-game interaction, levels of player-player interaction, and environments in which interaction occurs. Next considering previous and current theoretical and empirical studies on MMORPGs from a variety of disciplines, including education, psychology, and linguistics, a conceptual framework for the use of MMORPGs in support of learning is created. Finally, an overview of current research trends in MMORPGs is provided, concluding with suggestions concerning future research of the use of MMORPGs in support of learning.

INTRODUCTION

Video games continue to increase in popularity worldwide and are the dominate earners of the entertainment market, making more than movies and music combined (Foote, 2018) with top games almost doubling the earnings of Hollywood's biggest blockbusters (Griffith, 2018). By now the concept of Massive Multiplayer Online Role Playing Games (or MMORPGs) is known to many in the general populace, thanks much in part to the success of *World of Warcraft*, the highest grossing game of all time, earning over $9.23 billion in revenue since its inception in 2004 (Fredrick, 2017). Now in its fifteenth year of release *World of Warcraft* has also spawned the highest grossing video game movie of all time and still enjoys a multi-million subscriber base (Gadgets 360, 2018).

DOI: 10.4018/978-1-5225-7987-8.ch010

Given the popularity of MMORPGs, and the continued use of video games in support of various learning contexts, educators began using MMORPGs in instructional settings in the mid 2000s. Instructors from various academic disciplines ranging from childhood education, communication technology, psychology and computer assisted language learning began to experimentally investigate the use of MMORPGs in instructional settings. For instance, the virtual world of *Second Life* is home to a multitude of K-12 classes and over one hundred virtual university projects and campuses including Harvard, Stanford and New York University, all of whom have ongoing virtual classes taking place within the MMORPG (Second Life, 2018). Furthermore, an educational institution within the game also controlled by Linden Labs (the creators of *Second Life*) is maintained to offer potential educators advice and pedagogical rationale for the creation of lesson plans and virtual campuses within Second Life (Waters, 2009).

Since 2010, research into the use of MMORPGs as an instructional medium has fluctuated, and while it has ultimately increased, it remains a focused subfield of game based learning and serious game research.

Naturally, each specific academic discipline is driven by different purposes, pedagogy, and field specific theoretical issues. Likewise, each discipline has particular needs for both instructors and students. For instance, a study by the Instructional Technology Council (2008) determined that disciplines such as foreign languages, hard sciences, and nursing faced many great adaptive challenges in distance education when compared with other subjects. This understood, in the conceptualization of a general definition of distance education, and thus in part MMORPG research, Deshler and Hagen (1989) suggest the pressing need for an interdisciplinary and multidimensional approach noting that anything short of this would be short-sighted and end up being either discipline restricted or capable of producing misrepresentative results in terms of any research done. However, MMORPGs, while being a distinct medium of distance education, also fall equally under the umbrella of game based learning and serious game research, another field that has a large body of research across many different academic disciplines. Thus, in order to understand their full implications for the use in support of learning, MMORPGs must be viewed in light of both current distance education and serious game research standards.

Considering these implications, this chapter will highlight important previous research done on MMORPGS and focus on more recent trends both in the changing status of the genre itself and more recent findings. First, an operational definition of MMORPGs will be established, particularly with regards to current research of serious game theory and concepts. Once established, this operational definition will be used in conjunction with current research on MMORPGS in order to propose a conceptual framework for MMORPGs in support of learning. Here, a focus will be placed on combining interdisciplinary research in order to create a general theoretical model that may hopefully serve as a foundation for further research into the MMORPG medium. Next, an overview will be provided of current research trends in MMORPGs across disciplines, and finally suggestions concerning future research in the medium will be proposed. It is hoped that by developing a foundational conceptual framework and providing an overview of MMORPG research to date that better planned and consolidated efforts for future research into the medium will be made.

BACKGROUND

Drawing game mechanics from Dungeons and Dragons style pen and paper (PnP) RPGs as well as their later computer based counterparts the term *massively multiplayer online RPG* was first coined by *Ultima* creator Richard Garriott for the release of *Ultima Online* in 1996 and is viewed by many as the first

MMORPG to reach a high level of popularity and success (Hill, 2005). Following the success of *Ultima Online*, launched a rival game, *Everquest* . Released in 1999, *Everquest* was the first 3-D MMORPG. By 2003, *Everquest* had nearly 500,000 player subscriptions (MMOG Chart.com) and was considered the most popular game released at the time. This success was then followed by Blizzard Entertainment's well-known *World of Warcraft*, released in 2004 and popularized the MMORPG genre to a whole new level. In essence, the MMORPG combines the social interaction found in online multi-user dungeons (MUDs) with the complex rule systems and graphics of computer role playing games (CRPGs) and thus can be viewed as a natural progression of the two mediums. A typical MMORPG functions much like a normal Internet chat room or MUD; however, there is an added element, in that all interaction takes place in large polygonated three-dimensional virtual world(s) wherein players are represented by virtual personifications, again called avatars or characters. Players create and assume control over their avatars and use them as a vehicle to interact with the virtual world and to communicate with other players' avatars. This interaction occurs in a manner similar to that of many other video games and particularly CRPGs, where the player takes control of a character and uses it to interact with challenges and puzzles within the game. In the simplest of forms, MMORPGs can be seen as chat rooms with interactive tasks (Yee, 2006). However, given the progress of current technology, MMORPGs go beyond both MUDs and PnP RPGs by allowing tens of thousands of players to simultaneously inhabit and interact in the same virtual world.

Many of the virtual worlds in which MMORPGs take place are immense in size, each with multiple virtual cities and towns and large wildernesses. Depending on the game, each virtual world can also house tens of thousands of avatars (as a result of technological restrictions that are being lifted as server technology advances, particularly scalable server hardware/software technologies), allowing for an avatar and player to interact with many others over the course of a play session. Additionally, most MMORPGs allow players to create multiple avatars (although in most cases, only one can exist in the virtual world at a time). This allows players to take on different personas and different paths for each of their avatars if they so wish.

WHAT ARE MMORPGs?

To develop a definition, it is best that one first understand the basic frameworks used to create and guide MMORPGs. Current MMORPGs generally follow a few basic design frameworks that have evolved out of the most successful titles in the genre. Here, some of the most prominent frameworks will be detailed; this is, however, by no means an exhaustive list.

Levels and Skills

One common rule here is that almost all MMORPGs center on the advancement and progression of the avatar. Psychology studies on player motivations have found that player attachment to their avatars (along with socializing) is one of the key reasons for continued game play, something also found in MUDs (Turkle, 1995; Yee, 2006) This is often done through accomplishing specific in-game goals (such as defeating a powerful enemy or creating in-game items with one's avatar) or through a natural progression of the game's rule system (many games use the "level" system, popular to PnP RPGs to rank a character's progress and relative power, e.g., a level 10 avatar will most likely be much weaker when compared to a similar level 30 avatar). It should be noted though that not all MMORPGs use level systems as a measurement of avatar progression.

Character Classes

Another major defining feature found more often in level-based games is that they often make use of character classes (from PnP RPGs) or avatar archetypes, which guide and limit how an avatar will progress. For instance, upon avatar creation, one might choose a wizard over a priest. The wizard will be able to destroy things more quickly and may have the ability of teleportation, while the priest, on the other hand, can help to heal wounded avatars and even resuscitate dead avatars. Even upon reaching the level cap in a game, avatars can still "progress" via the acquisition of rare items, which can make them more proportionately powerful, or special titles, which follow an avatar's in-game name and serve as a badge of success or pride in game.

Goal-Based vs. Sandbox

Another major framework difference lies in the difference between "goal-based" (also sometimes called quest-based) and "sandbox" MMORPGs. Much as with rule-based systems, goal-based MMORPGs occupy a large majority of the current market. These games follow a pattern similar to CRPGs in which there are game-generated tasks, quests, and storylines for players to complete. Such goals help serve to increase player immersion and provide a larger story to a game. Most of the quests and tasks offer sizeable in-game rewards as an incentive to get players to undertake them (e.g., if you accept a quest to kill a dragon, upon completion, the NPC who assigned the quest will reward the avatar with a magic sword). Sandbox games, on the other hand, simply provide players with a virtual world (supplemented with lore and history) and rules, but beyond that, expect players to create their own adventures and experiences. Players in a sandbox-based MMORPG may choose to group together and slay a dragon, but there is no in-game-based road pointing them there.

Player vs. Environment and Player vs. Player

Finally, a major distinction among rule-based systems lies in player vs. environment (PvE) and player vs. player PvP content. The former is modeled on CRPG gameplay, in which computer-controlled and computer-generated avatars (called NPCs, as in PnP RPGs), creatures/enemies (often referred to as "mobs," from the military slang for mobile object) and environments are the main focus of player interaction with the game. Players will group together in numbers ranging from one to hundreds of avatars to challenge pre-generated content (such as slaying a dragon). PvP play, on the other hand, focuses on competing with other players. This competition is most often realized through combat. Players can defeat or even kill other players; although most MMORPGs fall short of permanent avatar death, most all have some sort of in-game penalty for letting one's avatar die, such as reviving a dead player's avatar in a weakened state for a short amount of time. However, PvP can also take less violent forms such as controlling certain virtual economic markets or routes of supply, as in the complex sandbox MMORPG *EVE Online.*

An Operational Definition

Now that basic frameworks for the different types of MMORPGs have been established, a few additional observations about how MMORPGs are and are not related to other video game genres is warranted. MMORPGs primarily differ from other video games in that (1) they take place in a persistent, naturalistic online environment which continues to exist and progress/change whether or not players are logged on, (2) interaction between players goes beyond simple cooperative and tactical play, and encourages rich and collaborative social interactions, and (3) MMORPGs offer players an increasingly large and varied amount of avatar creation and customization. (Childress & Braswell, 2006; Riegle & Matejka, 2006 Yee, 2006;). Unlike other video games, MMORPGs need to account for the different play styles and times of their players; thus, the virtual world in which the games take place is a persistent world which exists whether or not a particular player is logged on and, furthermore, is modified in the form of frequent content updates by the developers of the games. MMORPGs have a dynamic model compared with standard video games, as time continues and events progress in the "persistent" world, regardless of who is (or is not) playing (Schrader & McCreery, 2007). Other players, computer-controlled avatars, and even virtual weather and day and night patterns will progress regardless of an individual player's presence. This persistent world creates many opportunities for players for different types of interaction with the world and other players.

Social interaction in MMORPGs also exceeds that of standard video games in that at any given time a player has the chance to interact with one or many thousands of other players in the same virtual world. Much research has shown that levels of social interaction between players in MMORPGs equals or exceeds that of traditional CMC settings (Anderson 2014; Bryant, 2008; Yee, 2006). MMORPGs also have a greater variety of possible social interaction than found in most video games. Furthermore, based on the need in many MMORPGs for players to often work together to achieve in-game goals organized social networking is often inherent to players' success and progression in the virtual word of an MMORPG (Chen, Sun, & Hsieh, 2008; Ducheneaut, Yee, Nickell, & Moore, 2006).

The creation and use of avatars in MMORPGs also goes beyond most video game models. Many players report great enjoyment derived from designing and customizing their avatars (Yee, 2005). Most MMORPGs allow highly detailed avatar customization during the creation process and throughout the game. Players can select the gender, race, hair color, and hairstyle of their avatars in most MMORPGs, with some being even more detailed, allowing players to make many subtle variations in facial structure and build. Furthermore, as avatars progress throughout the virtual world, they can often modify their roles or appearances by either specializing in certain skills and/or changing their clothes. Some games go so far as to have in-game barbershops and plastic surgeons allowing players to reformulate the entire look of their avatar down to the gender. In this sense MMORPGs allow gamers to explore a large range of identities by playing a character created and customized by the player (Eatough et al., 2006; Hussain & Griffiths, 2008).

We have seen how MMORPGs draw on various concepts from videos games, including typical adventure and combat styles, tap into creativity and construction skills, provide deep and varied levels of social interaction, and offer a wide range of avatar customization. This large range and variety of interaction and task type also has been found to be conducive of MMORPGs functioning as naturally occurring learning environments, and particularly so in relation to the constructivist idea of socially constructed knowledge (Steinkuehler, 2004, 2005). Thus, MMORPGs operate on a complex level, incorporating features from both standard video games and CMC, making them unique in the study of serious gaming, yet informed by research on games and CMC.

A Current Examination of the State of MMORPGs

Despite a large increase in the number of MMORPGs, many industry experts have reported an overall decline in the genre. Richard Bartle (2013), known for his admittedly flawed gamer personality type test, and considered by many to be one of the founding fathers of MMORPGs, first identified this trend in an open publication. Citing a fracturing of the player base as companies and designers rushed in on the then MMORPG market boom creating inferior or unoriginal products, increasing lack of game immersion with a focus on revenue models over meaningful content, and a lack of understanding by designers of the fundamentals of a good game. Economists also noted the pitfalls of real money trading and in-game micro transactions being seen as a key factor (Royce, 2017). Indeed, while the number of MMORPGs has grown greatly, many recognizable franchises with multi-million dollar development have failed. Due to the failings of big name titles such as 2010's *Star Wars* and other major titles which have shut down their servers, the genre has not seen a major franchise tie in or major new game in a few years.

In addition to the internal factors mentioned above, many industry experts have noted external challenges such as the fact that most video games, even if they are primarily single player, also currently offer an online mode, something which takes away from some of the uniqueness of MMORPGs (Appleton, 2016). Similarly, new genres of online games have become immensely popular, particularly Massively online battle arena (or MOBA) games such as *League of Legends*, a game in which teams of players compete in online battles which use many of the same mechanics of Action Role Playing Games and MMORPGs. As of 2018, *League of Legends* boasted 67 million monthly players, 27 million daily players and 7.5 million peak concurrent players (Heimer, 2018). Finally, the increased popularity of mobile online games is also seen by experts as detracting from traditional MMORPG player base numbers (Appleton, 2016). These combined internal and external factors would seem to indicate troubled waters for MMORPGs, and they have indeed seen a loss of players and revenue in the last five years.

In looking to the future of MMORPGs, some in the field still feel the genre is continuing to evolve, noting that with the increase of technologies and mobile gaming that MMORPGs can now be played most anytime or anywhere, even for a short time during a lunch or study break (Stargame, 2018). Bill Murphy, longtime chief editor of MMORPG.com, the longstanding de facto home for MMORPG trends and insights, sees the diversifying of the genre as strengthening. Now that the player base is not as congested around one of a few behemoth titles such as *World of Warcraft,* developers are backing away from trying to create the next big thing by copying *Warcraft's* success model and instead going back to the fundamentals of creative and immersive game design (Murphy, 2017). Murphy also argues that the current waning of MMORPGs is part of a typical market boom, bust, and repeat cycle seen across the gaming industry in which genres redefine and perfect themselves. From the standpoint of the player this offers a wider choice of options and experiences as new and original titles continue to be released which are now appealing more to niche markets, and while the industry may be in a recession now, the new diversified MMORPG market has much more to offer potential educators looking for games to meet the needs of more specific learners or situations.

In reexamining an operational definition of MMORPGs and looking to more current research, the three basic characteristics unique to the genre identified above hold true: A persistent world which remains active even when players are offline (Kim, 2018; Sourmelis, Ioannou & Zaphris, 2017); complex and collaborative social interactions occur frequently (Anderson 2014; Gallup et al., 2017; Manocha, 2017); and, finally, a complex system for avatar creation and growth is presented (Paik, 2017; Sibilla & Mancini, 2018; You, Kim & Lee, 2017). In addition to the traits previously identified, current research has proposed additional key features that define MMORPGs. Chen et al., (2018), Di Filippo (2017) and Kim (2018) have identified a strong narrative design including a continuing storyline. Chen et al. (2018) note that a strong continuing storyline allows learners to focus on collaboration with each other and computer controlled avatars to progress the plot. Indeed, looking to MMORPG behemoth *World of Warcraft,* the homepage references a well-developed, in-depth lore in the form of videos, books, short stories and comics (World of Warcraft, 2018). *Warcraft's* lore was also the primary inspiration for the movie based on the game (Gadgets 360, 2018). Alone, driving narrative elements are not unique to MMORPGs as they are central to CRPGs and even pen and paper role playing games, however, the persistent world and large and complex social interactions found in MMORPGs make unique narratives possible. One of the greatest complex narratives in *World of Warcraft* was called *The Gates of Ahn'Qiraj* in which hundreds or thousands of players of two different warring factions on each server worked collaboratively to complete a multifaceted epic quest resulting in the opening of interdimensional gates followed by a live 10 hour showdown with invaders from the other side. The quest took individual servers weeks and often months to complete and is noted as the greatest complex collaborative narrative event in the MMORPG world (Zeibart, 2018). Even when not engaged in server wide extended narratives, individual players still are able to interact with stories in a unique and sophisticated manner: as traditional viewers and readers, as avatars interacting with computer elements, avatars interacting with other human controlled avatars, and finally outside of the game discussing it with fellow players. Di Filippo (2017) notes that it is the culmination of these different perspectives and interaction that help to formulate narratives exclusive to the MMORPG genre.

Another key area to examine when considering an updated operational definition of MMORPGs is the evolution of the technology away from being nearly computer exclusive; currently, popular titles such as *Final Fantasy XIV* and *Elder Scrolls Online* have found also found a large player base on home consoles such as the PlayStation and Xbox. Similarly, mobile MMORPGs continue to gain popularity on phones and tablets across the world. Players can now engage in MMORPGs on multiple platforms and access them from nearly anywhere (Stargame, 2018). How this will influence the genre is yet to be seen as current published research still focuses mainly on traditional computer based MMORPGs. Mobile MMORPGs in particular, while gaining in popularity, do not have the quick synchronous language based CMC capabilities their computer counterparts have, which could limit player to player interactions. This would naturally have the potential to negatively influence the benefits of using MMORPGs as learning mediums as complex social interaction is key. As the genre and release platforms of MMORPGs continue to progress, research is needed on the effectiveness of the use of different platforms.

Another more recent development to consider is the use of Massively Multi-user Virtual Environments games (MMUVEs) in addition to MMORPGs. Game based MMUVEs such as the immensely popular *Minecraft* differ from typical virtual worlds such as *Second Life* in that they also have strong underlying game based mechanics driving players. In recent years *Minecraft* has gained immense popularity as an educational platform, compelling its publisher to release *Minecraft: Education Edition.* In Nebel et al.'s (2016) metasynthesis of research on *Minecraft*, the authors found many advantages of the platform as a learning environment. MMUVEs such as *Minecraft* emulate many of the key characteristics of MMORPGs in that they are conducive to advanced social interaction and allow players to interact with player controlled avatars to complete complex tasks. Virtual worlds in *Minecraft* remain persistent across multiple player servers, allowing for asynchronous interaction with other users via the virtual world. And while avatar creation and customization in *Minecraft* is present, it is greatly simplified and more generic than that found in MMORPGs and does not allow for comparative customization and progression. Narrative elements in *Minecraft* are also minimal as the game adopts a sandbox model depending on players to create their own stories and worlds. Nebel et al. (2016) also found across studies reviewed that this lack of central progression or story was distracting to learners at times. Finally, while complex social interaction was possible, intrinsic collaborative motivation was minimal as the game can reward bad behaviors such as resource hoarding or destroying the creations of others. One advantage to educators the platform does offer, however, is its smaller, more malleable scale. It is easy to set up and maintain servers in *Minecraft* allowing for further customization and specialization of learning environments. Regardless, comparative research further investigating potential overlapping benefits of both MMORPGs and MMUVEs is needed.

A CONCEPTUAL FRAMEWORK: HOW MMORPGs SUPPORT LEARNING

MMORPGs combine elements of video game play with the high levels of social interaction found in synchronous CMC as well as the use of avatars, or virtual representations of the self, as a means for interacting with the virtual world. This comes from blending the play styles and mechanics from both CRPGs and MUDs. In order to develop a conceptual framework for MMORPGs and pedagogy, three basic factors will be considered: (1) The use of video games in education and their effects on learning, cognition, and (to a lesser extent) motivation; (2) the role online social interaction plays in aiding learning; and (3) the sociopsychological research on self-projection through the use of avatars and the benefits it offers to learning and motivation. Thus, this conceptual model consists of analyzing the benefits of MMORPGs in terms of learning (cognition), social, and psychological factors.

The Cognitive Benefits of MMORPGs in Support of Learning

As described by O'Neil, Wainess, and Baker (2005), games can be seen as being potentially supportive of learning in four distinct ways: (1) the presence of complex and diverse approaches to learning processes and outcomes, (2) high levels of various types of interactivity, (3) the ability to address cognitive as well as affective learning issues, and (4) the ability to tap into motivation for learning. One outstanding feature of MMORPGs is that they expose players to a large variety of interaction and goal types when compared to most video games (Childress & Braswell, 2006; Yee, 2006). In that players can encounter a wider range of interaction when compared with traditional games, MMORPGs are theoretically suited to meet all four of the effective characteristics of games in learning.

In the *World of Warcraft* and *Everquest 2,* players are offered many different choices regarding how they choose to interact with the game. They can, for instance, choose to test their strategic and teamwork-based skills in tackling PvE content against challenges in the game. Many of the more difficult PvE encounters require large groups of players, (also called raids, varying in size from ten to 40 or more players), and require precise timing and teamwork to overcome a particular raid challenge, in addition to the development-specific strategies that differ from raid to raid. Players often are required to research game forums and discuss with other players effective strategies needed to successfully overcome raid encounters (Steinkuehler & Duncan, 2008). Furthermore, players are then required to put that research into action not only as part of an individual effort but also in coordination with other players.

Additional forms of interaction can be found in in-game crafting skills, which require players to assemble components and possibly barter with other players in order to craft complex in-game items. Such interaction builds both cognitive planning skills as well as social interaction skills (Smiyh, 2007). Most MMORPGs have in-game auction houses where players can "play the market" in hopes of trading their way to virtual wealth. *Eve Online* adds in elements of territorial control, thus limiting access to raw materials. The economic structure of *Eve Online* is so complex that the developers have hired professional economists to help monitor the game.

Smyth (2007) states that MMORPGs help to promote problem-solving skills and critical thinking and further creativity at levels significantly higher than standard video games as can be seen in the complex strategies, interaction, and often-needed teamwork described above. Similarly, Steinkuehler and Duncan (2008) note that players in MMORPGs often must collaborate to solve complex problems within the virtual world, such as determining what combination of skills, proficiencies, equipment, and strategy are needed to overcome a particular challenge, which in turn promotes naturalistic learning and helps to develop cognitive skills. Furthermore, the wide range of interaction and task types found in most MMORPGs can appeal to a broad range of learning types in promoting the development of cognitive skills (Steinkuehler, 2005). In the above examples, we can see this as players in a given game can choose to tackle PvE content alone or with friends, attempt to craft in-game items or property, or even choose to risk their avatar's virtual goods and cash on the economic market. Finally, all MMORPGs to an extent employ a nonlinear model, allowing players to either follow guided missions and quests, or simply explore their virtual world as they wish, even simply sitting around talking to friends (Wei, 2007). This flexibility permits players much more freedom of choice in their interaction and time spent in the game world, thus allowing players to choose which types of interaction they wish to engage in and when.

With specific reference to motivations for learning delineated in O'Neil et al.'s model (2005), current research notes that much of the advantage of the use of video games in support of learning comes from the fact that they can provide students with high levels of intrinsic motivation and a sense of accomplishment from conquering various aspects of the game, whether it be solving puzzles, defeating antagonists, or constructing items in a simulation (Ebner & Holzinger, 2007; Pan & Sullivan, 2008). The constantly changing nature of MMORPGs can far outlast interest in a standard video game (Yang et al., 2007).

Additionally, unlike most traditional games, there is no way to beat an MMORPG; rather, they provide multiple paths and constantly changing goals to be achieved. MMORPGs have higher levels of the ability to both tap and sustain player motivation and interest. This is perhaps most evident as noted by Yee (2005), who argues that MMORPGs are so successful in tapping into player motivation that a very small number of individuals can become addicted to them. While this is a negative factor from an educational standpoint, and it suggests some active monitoring of player/learner habits is necessary, it is also evidence of the power of MMORPGs to tap and keep player interest. Finally, the highly interactive nature of MMORPGs would suggest that more in-depth levels of instructor interaction are possible and needed when compared with the use of standard video games in instructional settings, in that instructors need to take an active role in guiding their students (Childress & Braswell, 2006).

As can be seen from the studies referenced above, MMORPGs combine elements of many different types of video games and give players potential exposure to many of the different cognitive benefits video games offer in a single medium. A common misconception in the use of video games in support of learning, however, is that teachers can let their students go unmonitored and the game will take care of the learning process. Though we have seen evidence of MMORPGs promoting naturalistic learning (Steinkuehler & Duncan, 2008), it should be stressed that whenever any video game is used in support of learning, the instructor needs to take an active role in the process.[1]

The Social Benefits of MMORPGs in Support of Learning

As the interaction which occurs in MMORPGs takes place primarily though IRC (Internet relay chat, or more commonly known as simply "chat") much of the research on IRC used in educational technology in general, and distance learning in particular, is relevant to MMORPGs. While overall research points to CMC-based education as being able to provide more support for collaborative projects and encourage students to be more outspoken and in-depth in their discussions (Gunawardena & McIsaac, 2003; Rovai, 2007), one hindrance of CMC-based instruction that distance education researchers have noted is that sometimes some users feel disconnected socially, lacking solidarity. Thus, distance education classes tend to have higher dropout rates when compared to traditional classes (Instructional Technology Council, 2008). Studies on MMORPGs, however, have found both psychological (Smyth, 2007; Yee 2005, 2006) and linguistic evidence (Anderson 2014; Weininger & Shield, 2003) pointing towards high levels of solidarity and interaction in MMORPGs. It has been suggested that explicit socialization processes are embedded into many MMORPGs and that trust and responsibility are both fostered by them.

Jakobsson and Taylor (2003), in their study of *Everquest* found that by design many of the challenges in the game required social interaction. Additionally, groups of formal player organizations frequently called "guilds" in which avatars belong to a recognizable, hierarchically structured group permit advanced levels of organization often needed to complete many of the cooperative challenges faced in an MMORPG. Chen et al. (2008) note guilds as being the most social organization in online game societies, in many ways mirroring a combination of both business and family online. A high percentage of MMORPG players report that joining guilds is either highly preferable or perceived as almost necessary for game progression; sometimes the importance of guilds approaches that of the game itself (Chen et al., 2008; Ducheneaut et al., 2006). Guilds also allow for stronger and deeper social relationships to develop between players, as players in guilds will regularly interact with their guild mates more so than with other avatars, specifically with regard to completion of collaborative goals. Furthermore, guilds will often form alliances or rivalries with other guilds, allowing players more varied social interaction. Finally, while anecdotal evidence suggests video games on the whole may be more of a male-oriented interest, Yee (2006) found that roughly 43% of the MMORPG population he examined was female, and that most female players listed the deep social relationships formed in MMORPGs as one of their top motivations for continued play. Hussain and Griffiths (2008) added that female players, in particular, often logged on simply for the sake of socialization suggesting that, compared with standard video games, MMORPGs may be more likely to be positively received by female players.

Yee (2005) also found that high levels of player solidarity are due to the fact that many of the in-game goals in MMORPGs are designed around cooperative and collaborative quests, in which players need to interact with each other and develop teamwork mechanics in order to be successful. This is confirmed in corpus-based register comparison studies by Anderson (2014, 2008), who found four of six linguistic features of interaction to be more frequent in MMORPG communication when compared with traditional IRC. Features representative of collaborative and cooperative interaction were found at particularly high levels, suggesting that MMORPGs not only have greater levels of interaction but features which are important in distance education settings.

MMORPG also have out-of-game asynchronous discussion forums that are used by players and developers to discuss issues in the game and to socialize with each other. Steinkuehler and Duncan (2008) conducted an analysis of MMORPG discussion forums and found that players who used these forums presented complex models in their discussion of game mechanics and strategies to apply to games. When presenting comments tied to a critique of game rules or changes, and of effective in-game performance, players were often expected to supply empirical and often quantitative data in combination with complex logical arguments much in the same way academic research papers are constructed. To support these discussions, a number of second-party database and data management home pages and programs are available. For example, one such Web site that is often used in conjunction with the game *The World of Warcraft* is *WoW Web Stats* (often referred to as WWS by players). This program advertises itself as "a unique tool to enhance your experience in *The World of Warcraft*. With WWS, you generate and share reports of your raids, which include a tremendous amount of information and statistics" (WoW Web Stats, 2009). Players use information and statistics from program sources such as WWS in order to provide logical, data-backed critiques of the game and each other and to analyze their own performance within the game.

The Psychological Benefits of MMORPGs in Support of Learning

MMORPGs are seen as being cognitively and psychologically productive in terms of both collaboration and interaction (Wagner, 2008; Yee, 2005). Furthermore, the social relationships players have in MMORPGs can be just as fulfilling and deep as in traditional relationships (Yee, 2006). Over half of the players surveyed by Yee also reported that their MMORPG friendships were comparable to or better than their material world friendships. Moreover, almost all players also felt a degree of attachment to their in-game personas, or avatars. Yee (2005, 2006) found that players noted that they enjoyed the creative aspects of modifying their avatar's initial appearance and subsequent customizations, with some players even going as far as inventing fictitious background stories for their avatars. Players also reported being invested emotionally and psychologically in what happened to their avatars. Thus, successes and failures as realized through the avatar can have a psychological impact on players and, because most MMORPGs are designed to reward players regularly, this could have potential effects on long-term motivation and esteem.

To date, a growing body of psychological literature has examined the use of avatars in virtual settings. Avatars offer the potential for therapeutic benefits as well as a means for heightened social interaction. Hussain and Griffiths (2008) explored gender-swapping in MMORPGs and found that 56% of players surveyed, both male and female, engaged in creation and play of avatars of the opposite gender. Players surveyed stated that they enjoyed virtual gender-swapping, as it gave them insight into how the other gender perceives, and more so, is perceived, in the world. Hussain and Griffiths (2008) suggest that the possible explanations include greater anonymity online, less importance on physical appearance, and the greater control gamers have over the time and pace of their interaction. This idea of avatars as a means of increased social interaction is supported by Svensson (2003), who anecdotally reported that the use of avatars served to encourage shy students to interact more, as they felt safe behind the anonymity of their avatars. Bryant (2008) also observed the high levels of linguistic interaction and negotiation in MMORPGs to be conducive of second language acquisition. He notes that social motivations for communication as well as the desire to progress within the game itself helped promote a feeling of accomplishment among students and a social and goal-oriented environment for the classroom.

Still, perhaps the greatest power avatars have to support learning lies in their potential use as pedagogical agents. Baylor (2002, 2003) and Baylor and Kim (2006) have done extensive research supporting the uses and advantages of pedagogical agents in computer-based learning, as have others (Lester et al., 1997; Moreno, Meyer, Spires, & Lester, 2001; Shaw, Johnson, & Ganeshan, 1999). Agents are described as personified computer-based teaching applications (such as the famously annoying paperclip character that often popped up in older versions of Microsoft Windows offering help). Thus, one can see a definite connection between avatars and agents. Overall, the research here suggests that pedagogical agents help learners by stimulating social interaction and socially based cognition and motivation and allow for more naturalistic learning, making them an invaluable tool in computer-based educational technology. Baylor (2003) also found that multiple pedagogical agents focusing on distinctly different roles (e.g., expert, motivator) facilitated greater learning. Furthermore, Baylor and Kim (2006) note that one great advantage of pedagogical agents is that they can be tailored to the needs of specific learners and learning environments. MMORPGs already have a number of computer-controlled NPC agents which are used to focus players on in-game tasks and act as in-game guides to game mechanics (thus one will tend to find a large number of NPCs in the starting or tutorial zone of an MMORPG). Additionally, player-controlled avatars theoretically possess abilities far beyond those of any preprogrammed pedagogical agent, because as human instructors, they are able to quickly adapt to the needs of learners individually as well as provide deeper elements of social interaction. Thus, MMORPGs are able to facilitate computer-based learning with the presence of a wide range of potential pedagogical agents, including instructor-controlled avatars.

The motivation and engagement of MMORPGs does not come without potential drawbacks. Smyth (2007) purports that some players, deemed predisposed to addiction, reported that MMORPGs interfered with their homework and social life schedules to an extent. While this might be said of any game genre or entertainment source, this may be particularly true of MMORPGs, given their persistence and lack of a predetermined end-goal state. When compared to control and standard video game groups, MMORPG players displayed no loss of academic performance, and Smyth (2007) also observed that the use of avatars allowed shy or socially inhibited students to improve their social skills significantly. While the potential for addiction is an important factor to consider with any educational application, in the popular press, there have been many warnings about addiction to computer games. Additionally, limited data suggest that, when users begin playing MMORPGs in excess, social anxiety in real-world relationships can increase; however, light to moderate use is implicative of only positive gains (Lo, Wang, & Fang, 2005). As was discussed in the section on cognition, there is a need here for instructors to be closely involved with students when using any sort of computer game, both for guiding instruction and to make sure students are using applications properly.

Benefits of MMORPGs in Support of Learning Found in the Last Decade

Sourmelis, Ioannou and Zaphris' (2017) study provided a literature review of (n=49) articles written from 2011-2016. Examining further cognitive benefits of MMORPGs, Sourmelis, Ioannou and Zaphris (2017) found a commonality amongst studies (n=11 studies) that learning in MMORPGs is a progressively complex process that involves the use of in-game and external resources, and that referencing external resources such as game discussion forums and wikis helped players to focus on retainable knowledge. Similarly, they reported that learners playing MMORPGs modified for education purposes maintained better concentration. Smith (2017) found that learning in MMORPGs resulted greater degrees of comprehension of course materials as well as mental retention of lectures and primary sources. Snelson et al. (2017) also reported that the MMORPG format helped doctorate level students better understand the complex challenges of the research process as they discussed research methods and engaged in activities together to practice research within the game, drawing on external sources. This new body of research suggests that outside of previously discussed benefits that MMORPGs can potentially help learners better integrate external resources alongside game play including but not limited to focused academic content.

Recent research on potential cognitive benefits associated with MMORPGs also suggests that the skills learned within the medium transfer well into real life situations. Barr (2017) found that the fluid, unpredictable nature of in-game challenges played an important role in essential academic survival skill development, such as adaptability and resourcefulness in graduate level learners. Similarly, both Yasar (2018) and Zhang et al. (2017) found MMORPG enhanced instruction provided second language learners with benefitted reading, writing and listening skills which transferred to classroom and beyond. Di Filippo (2017) also argues that the MMORPG platform, allowing the user to both focus as actor and spectator, has the potential to positively influence the skills and understanding of media studies learners. Finally Malliarakis et al. (2017) used a pre and post test model MMOPRG to successfully teach computer programming skills to learners, with the experimental MMORPG group performing better on a post-test compared to the control group while also reporting more motivation to learn.

Research also looked at the potential of MMORPG to hone leadership skills and interactions. Thumlert et al. (2018) studied the potential of MMORPGs as training grounds for leadership competencies focusing on complex actions such as raiding in MMORPGs, where a group of 10-40 players will gather to achieve a collective goal of confronting an enemy in battles which require large amounts of pre, during and post coordination. Some raids in *Warcraft* are only attemptable once a week and require preparations such gathering in-game materials and crafting items. The composition of the jobs and classes of the players must also be carefully preplanned. During a raiding experience, complex coordination is required to successfully complete it. Following the raid, winnings and treasures must be allocated to participants in a fair manner with some not getting a desired item without participating multiple times. For these reasons, Thumlert et al. (2018) argue guild and raid leadership in game to be an excellent simulated environment for developing leadership skills and that MMORPGS were ahead of their time in anticipating leadership models that are increasingly heterarchical, distributed, driven by teams instead of individuals, self-organizing and networked, with a likelihood of transient membership. Yee (2014) also found multiple parallels between guild leadership and real world managerial skills with successful guild leaders performing well in the real world. Manocha (2017) observed that *Warcraft* players had higher levels of civic engagement in both the video game and in real world with community leaders displaying a higher chance of civic engagement than any of the other ranks. Finally, Sourmelis, Ioannou and Zaphris' (2017) observed (n=5) articles between 2010-2016 which reported MMORPGs as potential areas for leadership ability gains adding that leadership ability increase and practice was uninfluenced by gender.

Sourmelis, Ioannou and Zaphris (2017) found more research (n=6) supporting that MMORPGs can be used to increase user motivation to learn. These findings were echoed by Akcaoglu (2013), Adris and Yamat (2015), Malliarakis et al. (2017), Yasar (2018), and Zhang et al. (2017) with many studies showing the collaborative nature of MMORPG tasks added to motivation levels. Furthermore, Gallup et al. (2017) found that MMORPGs helped learners with an autism spectrum disorder support a recognition and reciprocation of emotions, friendship development, and role identification. And while additional study has been done on the potential of MMORPG addiction, Snodgrass et al. (2017) add that only a small portion, less than five percent, of users play problematically. However, a new potential limitation is present in the form of in-game micro-transactions. As noted earlier, with a larger, more competitive market many MMORPGs have resorted to a free to play model with micro-transactions instead of a traditional subscription model. In a growing number of online games these appear as what is commonly referred to as "loot boxes" in which users purchase a onetime use consumable item which in turn rewards them with a randomized item or benefit (Pu, 2018). These often times have the potential to be either a power in-game item or a rare cosmetic alteration to one's avatar with a focus on rare randomized items brining more prestige and uniqueness. A number of psychological studies have found a correlation between these "loot box" mechanics and symptoms of gambling addiction (Griffiths & King, 2015; Griffiths et al. 2015; Kardefelt-Winther 2015). For this reason when adapting an MMORPG for educational purposes a careful study of the economic system funding must be done. Loot box mechanics are far from rare and a $30 billion a year industry in video games on the whole (Pu, 2018), luckily this practice is usually frowned upon by most players who see the downsides of such systems and does not appear at all in some of the most popular titles including *World of Warcraft* and *Final Fantasy XIV*.

More recent research has also studied the potential therapeutic advantages of MMORPGs to counter social and interaction anxiety. Zhang and Kaufman (2017) looked at the socio-emotional well being found that older adults were able to develop meaningful friendships in-game, something which was furthered by the quality of guild play. However, they noted that it would be difficult for these adults to integrate their friends into their real life personal lives. Ramirez (2018) further explored friendships in-game and found three levels of friendship present: in-game associate, social friend and true friend. She found that while many players were able to find social game-based friendships in MMORPGs that few players were able to develop true friendships which took years to form, and would transcend the limits of games. Martončik and Lokša (2017) added that many online friendships generated in MMORPGs helped to alleviate feelings of loneliness and social anxiety in players, again strengthened by finding a quality community or guild to be a part of. They note that the game environment served as an excellent platform for forming relationships as everyone players meet has a default shared interest (the game) and that this creates a gateway of conversation for players allowing for personal relationships to form. Finally studies on second language learners the MMORPG environment was found to reduce interaction anxiety and increase confidence amongst learners (Adris & Yamat, 2015; Bytheway, 2015; Yang & Quadir, 2018).

INITIAL TRENDS IN MMORPG RESEARCH

It should first be noted that one overall problem currently is the lack of published research on MMORPGs as instructional mediums. This lack of research is further compounded by the small number of empirically based studies. A majority of the published research on MMORPGs falls into either loose theoretical work or anecdotal accounts of classroom use. While such reports can be useful for direct classroom implementation, there is a definite need for a higher level of scholarly examination. This current chapter has attempted to place emphasis on empirical work; however, it is somewhat limited by the current lack of quality empirical research directly on MMORPGs. Thus it has taken studies and theoretical concepts from multimedia learning, CMC, social relationships in virtual environments, online social behaviors, and traditional serious game research into consideration. Reasons for an overall lack of research on MMORPGs are conjectured as resulting from the relative newness of the medium as well as a perceived social stigma in academia on the study of video games (Bonk & Dennon, 2005; de Freitas & Griffiths, 2007; Riegle & Matejka, 2006).

MMORPG Research in Education

Focus here has been placed primarily on techniques and methods for the integration and use of MMORPGs in classroom settings (Bonk & Dennen, 2005; de Freitas & Griffiths, 2007;). Studies have reported that students responded well to MMORPG-based lesson models (Bonk & Dennen, 2005). Cognitive skill gains, exposure to various levels of interaction, and appeal to multiple learning styles have also been noted (Childress & Braswell, 2006; O'Neil et al., 2005; Riegle & Matejka, 2008; Steinkuehler & Duncan, 2008). There is, however, a lack of *longitudinal* studies present in this body of research with most studies employing a one-shot design and examining the use of MMORPGs over a few lessons at most. Additionally, there is a large amount of qualitative research when compared with quantitative studies. More empirically based studies in education might be beneficial in that they could better contribute to data sets for potential meta-analyses. Finally, Castronova et al. (2009) offer an interesting model for using virtual worlds as evaluative instruments to replicate social science experiments. They stress that although full understandings of the surroundings and mediums for interaction in virtual worlds is necessary for researchers to make generalizable results, virtual worlds allow researchers to more accurately manipulate and observe variables as well as offer (in the form of motivation) the potential for greater participant retention in longitudinal studies. The guidelines proposed by Castronova et al. (2009) make an excellent case and foundation for researchers interested in using MMORPGs as a method for data collection.

MMORPGs Research in Psychology

In psychology, studies have examined the ability of MMORPGs to motivate and tap the interests of players as well as develop social and emotional skills (Smyth, 2007; Schroeder, 2002; Wagner, 2008; Yee, 2005, 2006). Results point to MMORPGs as being valuable educational tools, specifically for traditionally shy or introverted students (Smyth, 2007; Svensson, 2003). Initial research into the psychological effects of MMORPGS focused on the fact that some players might run the risk of becoming overly immersed in the virtual worlds of MMORPGs and could face the possibility of becoming addicted. Conversely MMORPGs can provide positive influences such as support for depression or socially disadvantaged players (Lo et al., 2005; Morgan & Cotten, 2003: Peris et al., 2002). Other studies examined more subtle psychological factors present in MMORPGs with particular attention to the use of avatars, representations of the virtual self, life in virtual space, and potential therapeutic uses of games (Eatough et al., 2006; Hussain & Griffiths, 2008). Most all studies in the realm of psychology on MMORPGs have stuck to traditional quantitative empirically based models. Similarly, a range of populations has been studied, from classroom-sized groups to thousands of players, providing both quality one-shot and longitudinal studies. These approaches make good models for new researchers in this area. Research methods in these studies seem to be primarily questionnaire-based, however, lacking in more neuropsychological and hard science data, which represent a significant opportunity for future research.

Sociology Research on MMORPGs

Sociology-based studies on MMORPGs have focused on an investigation into social relationships and behaviors in virtual environments. This work has been both theoretical and empirical in nature. Much of the debate in this research centers on comparison studies of how virtual relationships and behaviors compare to face-to-face social encounters (Hussain & Griffiths, 2008; O'Brian & Levy, 2008). A 3-year longitudinal study employing over 60 terabytes of data from the most popular MMORPGs and researchers from four different universities found that online gaming communities are so massive that they can be used to mirror traditional communities (Srivastava et al., 2009). This is to say that research models used in traditional sociological studies can be applied to MMORPG communities. The full impact of this major study on sociological research into MMORPGs has not yet been seen; potentially this could help promote an increase in the number of MMORPG-based studies, as sociological research models are directly applicable to massive virtual worlds. This field promises to be interesting to watch in the years to come.

ESL Research on MMORPGs

Finally, research based in ESL and applied linguistics have in part, as with education studies, provided anecdotal models for using MMORPGs in the classroom (Weininger & Shield, 2003) as well as listed their benefits to language learners (Bryant, 2008; Svennson, 2003). In my own research (Anderson, 2007) I have found significant linguistic evidence of high levels of interaction and solidarity in MMORPG players. Additionally, levels of interaction have been found to be higher for MMORPGs than for traditional CMC (Anderson, 2008). For the most part, however, research making use of linguistic methodologies and data is lacking, despite numerous linguistics studies based on traditional CMC.

CURRENT TRENDS IN MMORPG RESEARCH

Research into MMORPGs over the last decade has both strengthened and expanded their use in support of learning as noted in the updated benefits section earlier in this chapter. This original chapter noted a problem with the limited number of studies done on the medium citing it's newness at the time of original publication (2010). Since that time a large number research has been published with Sourmelis, Ioannou and Zaphris' literature review (2017) focusing on ($n = 49$) studies between 2010-2016 and the ($n = 29$) more recent studies noted in to this revised chapter. One constant that remains however is the lack of centralized research into the medium. As noted in this and repeated by Sourmelis, Ioannou and Zaphris (2017) MMORPG learning based research is spread across multiple academic fields each with their own methodologies goals, making it difficult to synthesize and generalize. Still, publication platforms for such research has increased with the release of a number of specialized edited volumes and academic serials such as *The International Journal of Virtual and Personal Learning Environments*.

Examining specific directions of recent research the largest growth was seen in ESL and applied linguistics research with a number of articles focusing on the use of MMORPGs to support second language learning noting the medium alleviated communication anxiety, promoted transferable language skills, and engaged learners (Adris & Yamat, 2015; Bytheway; Yang & Quadir, 2018; Yasar, 2018; Zhang et al., 2018). Research into second language learning specifically has grown so much that quite recently Yunjin Kim (2018) did a meta-synthesis which examined ($n = 30$) studies published from 2008-2018. Four major categories that focused on outcomes of second language learning and MMORPGs were noted: Communication, collaboration, interaction, and motivation. Here it was found that a majority of the published work on MMORPGs and second language learning reported the positive effects of the medium regardless of age, gender, game experience or level of game playing, language skills or knowledge. Finally Kim (2018) suggests a needed further analysis of the effects of game performance, game playing experience, and gaming behaviors, on language learning production to strengthen findings and better understand how specifically about the medium is beneficial.

Another academic field that has seen growth in the last decade is psychology. Perhaps the biggest name in MMORPG research since its first inception, Nick Yee (2014) published a research-based popular book, *The Proteus Paradox*, looking into psychological landscapes of MMORPGs. Here he covers everything from negatives such as racism and sexual harassment, to complex matters such as romantic relationships and avatar identification psychology. Ultimately he notes the pedagogical benefits and limits of the medium and challenges players and game makers to make and perpetuate more virtual worlds open to creativity and critical thinking. Building on the initial trends noted above research into avatar identification continues. Sibilla and Mancini (2018) interestingly found that many players view their avatars as an idealized version of themselves both physically and/or psychologically and tend to see the virtual world as an extension of the offline world. Conversely, another set of players create avatars that are quite different from themselves and tend to view the MMORPG world as completely separate from the offline world and are enthusiastic about it, recognizing its revolutionary potential. Further research to empirically validate these finding may better help to understand the underpinnings of skill transfer between game and real life worlds.

Generalized education research into MMORPGs continues through the popularity of MMUVEs and *Minecraft* in particular has eclipsed it within the realm of serious game and virtual world research. Anderson (2014) found empirical evidence supporting the medium for social constructivist and connectivist based learning. Malliarakis el al. (2017) also used an empirical model to show the comparative educational gains against a control group. As noted earlier in the chapter Snelson et al. (2017) and Barr (2017) have done interpretive research into benefits of the medium for post graduate level skills. And while limited, sociological research continues into the use of MMORPGs with the aforementioned research examining the benefits of leadership skills (Thumlert et al., 2018) and developing and maintaining friendship (Martončik & Lokša 2017; Ramierz, 2018; Zhang & Kaufman 2017), as well as examining social interactions confirming that the MMORPG world does not substitute for but supplements real life and expand its possibilities (Sergeyeva et al. 2018).

FUTURE RESEARCH DIRECTIONS

As the body of MMORPG research continues to grow, the focus needs to shift from isolated reports and anecdotal classroom models to strong theoretical models, and more specifically toward providing a greater body of empirical research to support these models. The study of the use of MMORPGs occurs across multiple academic disciplines and the standards and traditions of research in those disciplines strongly influence the studies done (Bernard et al., 2004). Thus, to date, a large amount of empirical research on the subject of MMORPGs comes from psychology. Researchers such as Yee (2005, 2006, 2014), Anderson (2014), Martončik and Lokša (2017), Malliarakis et al. (2017), and Steinkuehler (2004, 2005; Steinkuehler & Duncan, 2008) have led the use of empirical techniques to operationalize and measure many of the theoretical models advanced by MMORPG theorists. More empirical studies of the quality of these two researchers' studies are needed to help provide support for the use and study of MMORPGs in educational contexts. Additionally, as research on MMORPGs remains scattered across multiple disciplines and journals, the study of MMORPGs would benefit from a consolidated research platform for publication.

This chapter has attempted to present the many complex reasons why currently available MMORPGs can easily be adapted to instruction and aid in learning. While the popular MMUVE *Minecraft* has a dedicated version for K-12 education the official refocusing of popular MMORPGs for educational purposes has not yet occurred. As noted earlier, a reexamination of the medium for educational purposes with a comparative model for the inclusion of other more recent genres of online games is needed. As MMORPG research continues to build and develop it must keep in line with current trends in the field of gaming instead of focusing solely on traditional computer based MMORPGs.

CONCLUSION

This chapter has attempted to create an overview of the dynamics and importance of the continuing use of MMORPGs as an instructional medium. This was achieved by creating, supporting and then reexamining a definition of the medium and then developing and expanding a conceptual framework for the use of MMORPGs in support of learning. When possible, this was done with direct empirical and theoretical evidence from studies to date. The proposed definition argues that MMORPGs are a melding of standard video games (with an emphasis on CRPGs) and CMC-based forms of social interaction. MMORPGs also offer players a wide range of game-based interaction and goal types that exceed elements found in any single type of video game. In support of learning and a conceptual model, it was argued that MMORPGs have much to offer potential learners and instructors in aiding cognition, motivation, blending of external resources, and socio-psychological skills and issues. MMORPGs have also been shown to support naturalistic learning and problem-solving skills while providing entertainment and motivation for users to continue learning. Furthermore, as MMORPGs are highly social in nature and encourage both collaborative and competitive play, they promote good communication and leadership skills and require well-thought-out coordinated strategies in order for players to be successful. Ultimately, MMORPGs have the potential to serve as an excellent medium for educational purposes as seen in the many studies both theoretical and empirical covered in this enhanced chapter. The number of instructors implementing MMORPGs into their classrooms is ever-increasing, as is the variety of MMORPGs available to instructors and learners. Much as is the case with all educational technology, effectively applying MMORPGs to pedagogical design requires that teachers understand the complex workings and interactions within the games and adjust to trends in the medium adapting those which benefit creativity and learning skills.

Continued research tells us that MMORPGs excel in tapping into player interests and providing a wide variety of interaction and skill types. In the last decade, a large and increasing number of studies have provided a growing body of empirical support for claims made concerning the benefits of the medium for learning. MMORPGs also appear to be beneficial in aiding online social presence and motivation issues frequently reported in distance education instruction. Finally, psychological research suggests that in addition to cognitive and social skills, MMORPGS can also help in a therapeutic manner with emotional skills. MMORPGs appear to have the potential to be a useful tool in education, compounded by the growing popularity of the medium in both classroom and home settings. What is currently needed the most is more quality empirical research to test the many theoretical claims made by current MMORPG studies.

REFERENCES

Adris, N., & Yamat, H. (2015). Massively Multiplayer Online Role-Playing Games (MMORPG) as Virtual Grounds for Second Language Learning: Players' Perception. *Proceedings of the International Seminar on Language Teaching ISeLT.*

Akcaoglu, M. (2013). Using an MMORPG in a language classroom: Stories versus tutors as source of motivation. In Y. Baek & N. Whitton (Eds.), *Cases on digita l game - based learning: Methods, models and strategies*. IGN Publishing. doi:10.4018/978-1-4666-2848-9.ch002

Anderson, B. (2008). *Operationalizing online interaction in distance education: A register comparison of IRC and MMORPG corpora*. Retrieved on October 22, 2008 from http://pine.ucc.nau.edu/boa/mmoircinteraction/

Anderson, B. (2010). *MMORPGs in support of learning: Current trends and future uses*. Academic Press.

Anderson, B. (2014). Massive Multiplayer Online Role Playing Games and Interaction: A Measurable Model of Interaction for Online Learning. *International Journal of Virtual and Personal Learning Environments*, *5*(2), 28–39. doi:10.4018/ijvple.2014040103

Appleton, R. (2016, October 26). The MMORPG genre is dead, and we killed it. *The Fresno Bee*. Accessed on January 9, 2019 from: https://www.fresnobee.com/entertainment/ent-columns-blogs/video-games/article98016107.html

Barr, M. (2017). Video games can develop graduate skills in higher education students: A randomised trial. *Computers & Education*, *113*, 86–97. doi:10.1016/j.compedu.2017.05.016

Bartle, R. (2013). *The Decline of MMOs*. Accessed on January 9th 2019 from: https://mud.co.uk/richard/The%20Decline%20of%20MMOs.pdf

Barton, M. (2007). *The history of computer role playing games: Parts I, II and III*. Retrieved from http://www.gamasutra.com/features/20070223b/barton_01.shtml

Baylor, A. L. (2002). Agent-based learning environments for investigating teaching and learning. *Journal of Educational Computing Research*, *26*(3), 249–270. doi:10.2190/PH2K-6P09-K8EC-KRDK

Baylor, A. L. (2003). *Evidence That Multiple Agents Facilitate Greater Learning*. Paper presented at the AI-ED, Sydney, Australia.

Baylor, A. L., & Kim, Y. (2006). A social-cognitive framework for pedagogical agents as learning companions. *Educational Technology Research and Development*, *54*(6), 569–596. doi:10.100711423-006-0637-3

Bernard, R. M., Abrami, P. C., Lou, Y., Borokhovski, E., Wade, A., Wozney, L., ... Huang, B. (2004). How does distance education compare with classroom instruction? A meta-analysis of the empirical literature. *Review of Educational Research*, *74*(3), 379–439. doi:10.3102/00346543074003379

Bonk, C., & Dennen, V. (2005). *Massive multiplayer online gaming: A research framework for military training and education* (Technical Report No. 2005-1). Washington, DC: U.S. Department of Defense (DUSD/R): Advanced Distributed Learning (ADL) Initiative. Retrieved from http://mypage.iu.edu/cjbonk/GameReport_Bonk_final.pdf

Bryant, T. (2008). Using *World of Warcraft* and other MMORPGs to foster a targeted, social, and cooperative approach toward language learning. *Academic Commons, 12*(4), 23–35.

Castronova, E., Bell, M., Cornell, R., Cummings, J., Falk, M., Ross, T., ... Field, A. (2009). Synthetic worlds as experimental instruments. In M. Wolf & B. Perron (Eds.), *The video game theory reader 2*. New York: Routledge.

Chen, C., Sun, C., & Hsieh, J. (2008). Player guild dynamics and evolution in massively multiplayer online games. *Cyberpsychology & Behavior, 11*(3), 293–301. doi:10.1089/cpb.2007.0066 PMID:18537499

Chen, Z. H., Chen, H. H. J., & Dai, W. J. (2018). Using narrative-based contextual games to enhance language learning: A case study. *Journal of Educational Technology & Society, 21*(3), 186–198.

Childress, M., & Braswell, R. (2006). Using massively multiplayer online role-playing games for online learning. *Distance Education, 27*(2), 187–196. doi:10.1080/01587910600789522

Conole, G. (2008). New schemas for mapping pedagogies and technologies. *Ariadine, 56*.

de Freitas, S., & Griffiths, M. (2007). Online gaming as an educational tool in learning and training. *British Journal of Educational Technology, 38*(3), 535–537. doi:10.1111/j.1467-8535.2007.00720.x

Di Filippo, L. (2017). MMORPG as Locally Realized Worlds of Action. In M. Boni (Ed.), *World Building. Transmedia, Fans, Industries*. Amsterdam, The Netherlands: Amsterdam University Press. doi:10.2307/j.ctt1zkjz0m.16

Ducheneaut, N., Yee, N., Nickell, E., & Moore, R. (2006). Building an MMO with mass appeal: A look at gameplay in *World of Warcraft*. *Games and Culture, 1*(4), 281–317. doi:10.1177/1555412006292613

Eatough, V., Davies, M. N. O., Griffiths, M. D., & Chappell, D. (2006). *Everquest*—It's just a computer game right? An interpretative phenomenological analysis of online gaming addiction. *International Journal of Mental Health and Addiction*, 4205–4216.

Ebner, M., & Holzinger, A. (2007). Successful implementation of user-centered game based learning in higher education: An example from civil engineering. *Computers & Education, 49*(3), 873–890. doi:10.1016/j.compedu.2005.11.026

Foote, R. (2018, February 4). *Who rules entertainment industry? Video games vs. film & music*. Accessed on January 14th, 2019 from: http://www.kfvs12.com/story/31140647/who-rules-the-entertainment-industry/

Fredrick, T. (2018, January 17). *Who rules entertainment industry? Video games vs. film & music*. Accessed on January 15th, 2019 from: https://www.insidermonkey.com/blog/12-highest-grossing-video-games-of-all-time-518819/?singlepage=1

Gadgets 360. (2018). *World of Warcraft Subscription Numbers Reportedly Revealed.* Accessed on January 9th 2019 from: https://gadgets.ndtv.com/games/news/world-of-warcraft-wow-subscription-numbers-battle-of-azeroth-1932930

Griffith, E. (2018, November 8). Major Video Games Make More Money Than Blockbuster Movies. *The Entrepreneur.* Accessed on January 14th, 2019 from: https://www.entrepreneur.com/article/323001

Griffiths, M., Davies, N., & Chappell, D. (2004). Online computer gaming: A comparison of adolescent and adult gamers. *Journal of Adolescence, 27*(1), 87–96. doi:10.1016/j.adolescence.2003.10.007 PMID:15013262

Griffiths, M., & King, R. (2015). Are Mini-games Within RuneScape Gambling or Gaming? *Gaming Law Review and Economics, 19*(9), 640–643. doi:10.1089/glre.2015.1995

Griffiths, M., van Rooij, T., Kardefelt-Winther, D., Starcevic, V., Kiraly, O., Pallesen, S., ... Demetrovics, Z. (2015). Working towards an international consensus on criteria for assessing internet gaming disorder: A critical commentary on Petry et al (2014). *Addiction (Abingdon, England), 111*(1), 167–17. doi:10.1111/add.13057 PMID:26669530

Gunawardena, L., & McIsaac, M. (2003). Theory of distance education. In D. H. Jonassen (Ed.), *Handbook of research for educational communications and technology.* New York: Simon and Schuster Macmillan.

Heimer, R. (2018, June 5). *How many play League of Legends.* Accessed on January 10, 2019 from: https://www.unrankedsmurfs.com/blog/players-2017

Hill, M. (2005). *The RPG evolution.* Retrieved from http://iml.jou.ufl.edu/projects/Spring05/Hill/

Hussain, Z., & Griffiths, M. D. (2008). Gender swapping and socializing in cyberspace: An exploratory study. *Cyberpsychology & Behavior, 11*(1), 47–53. doi:10.1089/cpb.2007.0020 PMID:18275312

Instructional Technology Council. (2008). *2007 Distance Education survey Results.* Accessed on Sept. 9 2008.from: http://4.79.18.250/file.php?file=/1/ITCAnnualSurveyMarch2008.pdf

Jakobsson, M., & Taylor, T. (2003). The *Sopranos* meets *EverQuest*: Social networking in massively multiplayer online games. *Melbourne International Digital Arts and Culture Conference (Melbourne-DAC).* Retrieved from http://hypertext.rmit.edu.au/dac/papers/Jakobsson.pdf

Kardefelt-Winther, D. (2015). Making the case for hypothesis-driven theory testing in the study of Internet Gaming Disorder. *Addictive Behaviors*, 64. PMID:26455330

Kim, J. (2008). *"Narrative" or "tabletop" RPGs.* Retrieved from http://www.darkshire.net/~jhkim/rpg/whatis/tabletop.html

Kim, Y. (2018). Analysis of research trends focusing on outcomes in language learning using MMORPGs. *Multimedia-Assisted Language Learning, 21*(4), 111–142.

Lester, J. C., Converse, S. A., Kahler, S. E., Barlow, S. T., Stone, B. A., & Bhoga, R. S. (1997). The persona effect: Affective impact of animated pedagogical agents. *Proceedings of 1997 Conference on Human Factors in Computing Systems*. Retrieved from http://www.acm.org/sigchi/chi97/proceedings/paper/jl.htm

Lo, S., Wang, C., & Fang, W. (2005). Physical Interpersonal Relationships and Social Anxiety among Online Game Players. *Cyberpsychology & Behavior*, *8*(1), 15–20. doi:10.1089/cpb.2005.8.15 PMID:15738689

Malliarakis, C., Satratzemi, M., & Xinogalos, S. (2017). CMX: The Effects of an educational MMORPG on learning and teaching computer programming. *IEEE Transactions on Learning Technologies*, *10*(2), 219–235. doi:10.1109/TLT.2016.2556666

Manocha, U. (2017). *MMORPGs and Their Effect on Players*. Accessed on January 22 from: http://scholarworks.sjsu.edu/art108

Martončik, M., & Lokša, J. (2017). Do World of Warcraft (MMORPG) Players Experience Less Loneliness and Social Anxiety in Online World (Virtual Environment) Than in Real World (Offline)? *Computers in Human Behavior*, *56*, 127–134. doi:10.1016/j.chb.2015.11.035

MMOG chart.com. (n.d.). Retrieved from http://MMOG chart.com

MMORPG.com. (n.d.). Retrieved from http:// mmorpg.com / gamelist.cfm

Moreno, R., Mayer, R. E., Spires, H. A., & Lester, J. C. (2001). The case for social agency in computer-based teaching: Do students learn more deeply when they interact with animated pedagogical agents? *Cognition and Instruction*, *19*(2), 177–213. doi:10.1207/S1532690XCI1902_02

Morgan, C., & Cotten, S. R. (2003). The relationship between Internet activities and depressive symptoms in a sample of college freshmen. *Cyberpsychology & Behavior*, *6*(2), 133–143. doi:10.1089/109493103321640329 PMID:12804025

Murphy, B. (2017, December 9). *Gaming's future is and has always been massively multiplayer*. Accessed on January 12, 2019 from: https://venturebeat.com/2017/12/09/gamings-future-is-and-has-always-been-massively-multiplayer/

Nebel, S., Schneider, S., & Rey, G. D. (2016). Mining Learning and Crafting Scientific Experiments: A Literature Review on the Use of Minecraft in Education and Research. *Journal of Educational Technology & Society*, *19*(2), 355–366.

Neverax. (2009). *Saga of Ryzom*. [Computer game]. Winch Gate Property Limited.

O'Brian, M., & Levy, R. (2008). Exploration through virtual reality: Encounters with the target culture. *Canadian Modern Language Review*, *64*(4), 663–687. doi:10.3138/cmlr.64.4.663

O'Neil, H. F., Wainess, R., & Baker, E. L. (2005). Classification of learning outcomes: Evidence from the computer games literature. *Curriculum Journal*, *16*(4), 455–474. doi:10.1080/09585170500384529

Paik, P. C. H. (2017). Study of player attitudes regarding MMORPG avatar customization in the transformation stage. *Journal of Korea Game Society*, *17*(3), 7–20. doi:10.7583/JKGS.2017.17.3.71

Pan, C., & Sullivan, M. (2008). *Game-based learning: Guidelines, challenges, recommendations*. Presented at AETC Convention 2008, Orlando, FL.

Peris, R., Gimeno, M. A., Ibáñez, I., Ortel, G., Peris, R., Pinazo, D., & Sanchiz, M. (2002). Online chat rooms: Virtual spaces of interaction for socially oriented people. *Cyberpsychology & Behavior*, *5*(1), 43–51. doi:10.1089/109493102753685872 PMID:11990974

Pivec, M. (2007). Play and learn: Potentials of game-based learning. *British Journal of Educational Technology*, *38*(3), 387–393. doi:10.1111/j.1467-8535.2007.00722.x

Pu, B. (2018, November 28). What are loot boxes? FTC will investigate $30B video game industry. *NBC News*. Accessed on January 17, 2019 from: https://www.nbcnews.com/tech/tech-news/loot-boxes-gambling-video-games-ftc-look-it-n941256

Ramierz, F. (2018). From Good Associated to True Frineds: An Exploration of Friendship Practices in Massively Multiplayer Online Games. In K. Lakkaraju (Ed.), *Social Interactions in Virtual Worlds: An Interdisciplinary Perspective*. New York: Cambridge University Press. doi:10.1017/9781316422823.004

Rehak, B. (2003). Playing at being: Psychoanalysis and the avatar. In M. Wolf & B. Perron (Eds.), *The video game theory reader*. London: Routledge.

Riegle, R., & Matejka, W. (2006). Dying to learn: Instructional design and MMORPGs. *21st Annual Conference on Distance Teaching and Learning*. Retrieved from http://people.coe.ilstu.edu/rpriegle/mmorpg/index.htm

Rilstone, A. (1994). Role playing games: An overview. *Inter*Action, 1*. Retrieved from http://www.rpg.net/oracle/essays/rpgoverview.html

Rovai, A. P. (2007). Facilitating online discussions effectively. *The Internet and Higher Education*, *10*(1), 77–88. doi:10.1016/j.iheduc.2006.10.001

Royce, B. (2017). *Monetization expert: MMOs are dying because of clueless design, not insufficient demand.* Accessed on January 9th 2019 from: https://massivelyop.com/2017/07/11/monetization-expert-mmos-are-dying-because-of-clueless-design-not-insufficient-demand/

Schrader, P., & McCreery, M. (2007). The acquisition of skill and expertise in massively multiplayer online games. *Educational Technology Research and Development*, *56*(5), 557–574.

Schroeder, R. (Ed.). (2002). *The social life of avatars: Presence and interaction in shared virtual environments*. London: Springer-Verlag. doi:10.1007/978-1-4471-0277-9

Sergeyeva, O., Tsareva, A., Zinoveva, N., & Kononova, O. (2018). *Social Skills Amongst MMORPG-Gamers: Empirical Study*. Accessed on January 28, 2019 from: https://www.shs-conferences.org/articles/shsconf/pdf/2018/11/shsconf_cildiah2018_01008.pdf

Shaw, E., Johnson, W. L., & Ganeshan, R. (1999). *Pedagogical agents on the Web*. Retrieved from http://www.isi.edu/isd/ADE/papers/agents99/agents99.htm

Sibilla, F., & Mancini, T. (2018). I am (not) my avatar: A review of the user-avatar relationships in Massively Multiplayer Online Worlds. *Cyberpsychology (Brno)*, *12*(3), 4. doi:10.5817/CP2018-3-4

Sigil. (2009). *Vanguard Saga of Heroes* [Computer game]. Sony Online Entertainment.

Smith, J. (2008). Facebook to blame for "friendship addiction." *Therapy Today*, *19*(9), 10–11.

Smith, S. (2017, Fall). Stepping Out Of The Classroom Into Virtuality: Using MMORPGS To Teach History. *Teaching History: A Journal of Methods*, 73-80.

Smyth, P. (2007). Beyond self-selection in video game play: An experimental examination of the consequences of massively multiplayer online role-playing game play. *Cyberpsychology & Behavior*, *10*(7), 32–39. PMID:17927543

Snelson, C., Wertz, C. I., Onstott, K., & Bader, J. (2017). Using World of Warcraft to Teach Research Methods in Online Doctoral Education: A Student-Instructor Duoethnography. *Qualitative Report*, *22*(5), 1439–1456.

Snodgrass, J. G., Dengah, H. J. F. II, Lacy, M. G., Bagwell, A., Van Oostenburg, M., & Lende, D. (2017). Online gaming involvement and its positive and negative consequences: A cognitive anthropological "cultural consensus" approach to psychiatric measurement and assessment. *Computers in Human Behavior*, *66*, 291–302. doi:10.1016/j.chb.2016.09.025

Sonstroem, E. (2006). Do you really want a revolution? Cybertheory meets real-life pedagogical practice in Franken MOO and the conventional literature classroom. *College Literature*, *33*(3), 148–170. doi:10.1353/lit.2006.0044

Sourmelis, T., Ioannou, A., & Zaphiris, P. (2017). Massively Multiplayer Online Role Playing Games (MMORPGs) and the 21st century skills: A comprehensive research review from 2010 to 2016. *Computers in Human Behavior*, *67*, 41–48. doi:10.1016/j.chb.2016.10.020

Srivastava, J., Williams, D., Contractor, N., & Poole, S. (2009). *The Virtual World Exploratorium Project*. American Association for the Advancement of Science (AAAS) Conference, Chicago, IL.

Stargame, A. (2018, September 24). *The past and future of MMORPGs*. Accessed on January 9, 2019 from: https://medium.com/@alexstargame/the-past-and-future-of-mmorpgs-c23bfed473f

Steinkuehler, C. (2004) Learning in massively multiplayer online games. In Y. Kafai, W. Sandoval, N. Enyedy, A. Nixon, & F. Herrera (Eds.), *Proceedings of the sixth ICLS*. Mahwah, NJ: Erlbaum.

Steinkuehler, C. (2005). *Cognition and learning in massively multiplayer online games: A critical approach* (Unpublished dissertation). University of Wisconsin, Madison, WI.

Steinkuehler, C., & Duncan, S. (2008). Scientific habits of mind in virtual worlds. *Journal of Science Education and Technology*, *17*(6), 530–543. doi:10.100710956-008-9120-8

Svensson, P. (2003). Virtual worlds as arenas for language learning. *Language learning online: Towards best practice*, *10*(1), 123–142.

The Longman Dictionary of Contemporary English Online. (n.d.). Retrieved from http://www.ldoceonline.com/

Thumlert, K., de Castell, S., & Jenson, J. (2018). *'Training Grounds' to Sociotechnical Actors: Do MMORPG's Presage/Prestage the Futures of Leadership and Work?* Paper presented at DIGRA 2018, Turin, Italy.

Turkle, S. (1995). *Life on the screen: Identity in the age of the Internet*. New York: Simon & Schuster.

Van Eck, I. E. (Ed.), *Gaming and cognition: Theories and practice. from the learning sciences*. Hershey, PA: Information Science. doi:10.4018/978-1-61520-717-6

Van Eck, R. (2006). Building intelligent learning games. In D. Gibson, C. Aldrich, & M. Prensky (Eds.), *Games and simulations in online learning: Research & development frameworks*. Hershey, PA: Idea Group. doi:10.4018/978-1-59904-304-3.ch014

Wagner, M. (2008). *Massively multiplayer online role-playing games as constructivist learning environments in K-12 education: A Delphi study* (Doctoral thesis). Retrieved from http://edtechlife.com/?page_id=2008

Wauters, R. (2008, October 29). *World of Warcraft* to surpass 11 million subscribers. *New York Times*.

Waxman, C., Lin, M., & Michko, G. (2003). *A meta-analysis of the effectiveness of teaching and learning with technology on student outcomes*. Naperville: Learning Point Associates.

Wei, J. (2006). *The role of everyday users in MMORPGs*. Retrieved on August 28, 2007, from Driftreality: http://www.driftreality.com/london/mmorpgs.users.pdf

Weininger, M., & Shield, L. (2003). Promoting oral production in a written channel: An investigation of learner language MOO. *Computer Assisted Language Learning*, *16*(4), 329–349. doi:10.1076/call.16.4.329.23414

Wilson, D. (1992, November). Computer games: Academic obstacle or free-speech? *The Chronicle of Higher Education*, 18.

World of Warcraft. (2018). *Story*. Access on January 22nd from: https://worldofwarcraft.com/en-us/story

WoW Web Stats. (n.d.). Retrieved February 20, 2009, from: http://wowwebstats.com/

Yang, H., Wu, C., & Wang, K. (2007). An empirical analysis of online game service satisfaction and loyality. *Expert Systems with Applications*, *36*(2), 1816–1825. doi:10.1016/j.eswa.2007.12.005

Yang, J. C., & Quadir, B. (2018). Effects of Prior Knowledge on Learning Performance and Anxiety in an English Learning Online Role-Playing Game. *Journal of Educational Technology & Society*, *21*(3), 174–185.

Yasar, S. (2018). The Role Of Massively Multiplayer Online Role - Playing Games In Extramural Second Language Learning: A Literature Review. *Journal of Educational Technology and Online learning, 1*, 3.

Yee, N. (2005). The psychology of MMORPGs: Emotional investment, motivations, relationships, and problematic usage. In R. Schroeder & A. Axelsson (Eds.), *Social life of avatars II*. London: Springer-Verlag.

Yee, N. (2006). The demographics, motivations and derived experiences of users of massively-multiuser online graphical environments. *Presence (Cambridge, Mass.)*, *15*(3), 309–329. doi:10.1162/pres.15.3.309

Yee, N. (2014). *The Proteus paradox: How online games and virtual worlds change us — and how they don't*. New Haven, CT: Yale University Press.

Zeibart, A. (2018). *WoW Archivist: The Gates of Ahn'Qiraj*. Access on January 22nd from: https://www.engadget.com/2011/04/19/wow-archivist-the-gates-of-ahnqiraj/

Zhang, F., & Kaufman, D. (2017). Massively Multiplayer Online Role-Playing Games (MMORPGs) and Socio-Emotional Wellbeing. *Computers in Human Behavior*, *73*, 451–458. doi:10.1016/j.chb.2017.04.008

Zhang, Y. (2017). Language Learning Enhanced by Massive Multiple Online Role-Playing Games (Mmorpgs) and the Underlying Behavioral and Neural Mechanisms. *Frontiers in Human Neuroscience*, *11*(2), 1–7. PMID:28303097

ADDITIONAL READING

Bartle, R. (2003). *Designing virtual worlds*. New Riders Games.

Cameron, B., & Dwyer, F. (2005). The effect of online gaming, cognition and feedback type in facilitating delayed achievement of different learning objectives. *Journal of Interactive Learning Research*, *16*(3), 243–358.

Childress, M., & Braswell, R. (2006). Using massively multiplayer online role-playing games for online learning. *Distance Education*, *27*(2), 187–196. doi:10.1080/01587910600789522

Jakobsson, M., & Taylor, T. (2003). *The* Sopranos *meets* EverQuest*: Social networking in massively multiplayer online games*. Presented at the Melbourne International Digital Arts and Culture Conference. Retrieved from http://hypertext.rmit.edu.au/dac/papers/Jakobsson.pdf

Kim, Y. (2018). Analysis of research trends focusing on outcomes in language learning using MMORPGs. *Multimedia-Assisted Language Learning*, *21*(4), 111–142.

Murphy, B. (2017, December 9). Gaming's future is and has always been massively multiplayer. Accessed on January 12, 2019 from: https://venturebeat.com/2017/12/09/gamings-future-is-and-has-always-been-massively-multiplayer/

Schrader, P., & McCreery, M. (2007). The acquisition of skill and expertise in massively multiplayer online games. *Educational Technology Research and Development*, *56*(5), 557–574.

Schroeder, R. (Ed.). (2002). *The social life of avatars: Presence and interaction in shared virtual environments*. London: Springer-Verlag. doi:10.1007/978-1-4471-0277-9

Snodgrass, J. G., Dengah, H. J. F. II, Lacy, M. G., Bagwell, A., Van Oostenburg, M., & Lende, D. (2017). Online gaming involvement and its positive and negative consequences: A cognitive anthropological "cultural consensus" approach to psychiatric measurement and assessment. *Computers in Human Behavior*, *66*, 291–302. doi:10.1016/j.chb.2016.09.025

Sourmelis, T., Ioannou, A., & Zaphiris, P. (2017). Massively Multiplayer Online Role Playing Games (MMORPGs) and the 21st century skills: A comprehensive research review from 2010 to 2016. *Computers in Human Behavior*, *67*, 41–48. doi:10.1016/j.chb.2016.10.020

Svensson, P. (2003). Virtual worlds as arenas for language learning. *Language Learning Online: Towards Best Practice*, *10*(1), 123–142.

Taylor, T. L. (2006). *Play between worlds: Exploring online game culture*. The MIT Press. doi:10.7551/mitpress/5418.001.0001

Yee, N. (2006). The demographics, motivations and derived experiences of users of massively-multiuser online graphical environments. *Presence (Cambridge, Mass.)*, *15*(3), 309–329. doi:10.1162/pres.15.3.309

Yee, N. (2014). *The Proteus paradox: How online games and virtual worlds change us — and how they don't*. New Haven, CT: Yale University Press.

KEY TERMS AND DEFINITIONS

Applied Linguistics: Research into language with relevance to real-world issues and often a focus on second language learning.

CRPG: Computer role playing game. A video game genre in which players controls the actions and choices of character(s) in a well-defined fictional world.

MMORPG: Massive multiplayer online role playing game. An online video role playing game where thousands of users can play together on a single server.

NPC: Non-player character. A computer-controlled avatar in an MMORPG or CRPG often responsible for directing players on quests, selling and buying their items, and/or explaining game mechanics.

PnPRPG: Pen and paper role playing game. A game such as *Dungeons and Dragons* in which players assume the roles of characters in a fictional setting and act out the roles within a partially improvised narrative.

PVE: Player vs. environment. A mode of MMORPGs in which players work collaboratively to defeat computer-controlled AI opponents.

PVP: Player vs. player. A mode of MMORPGs in which players compete against each other often in violent clashes.

Sandbox: A style of MMORPG in which quests and stronger narratives are lacking and free exploration of the virtual world is encouraged.

Serious Game Studies: The study of the educational benefits of games designed for purposes other than entertainment.

ENDNOTE

1 On a side note and quite interestingly, in serious gaming research there is a decided gap in empirical studies which examine the role of self-learning and games. This is one aspect in which further research is needed and that the field of serious game study as a whole would benefit from.

Section 4

Applications in Development:

New Frontiers in Education and Training

Chapter 11

Augmented Reality-Based Training Systems for Teaching Health and Safety Procedures in Construction

Inma García-Pereira
Universitat de València, Spain

Cristina Portalés
https://orcid.org/0000-0002-4520-2250
Universitat de València, Spain

Sergio Casas
https://orcid.org/0000-0002-0396-4628
Universitat de València, Spain

María Vidal-González
Universitat de València, Spain

Jesús Gimeno
Universitat de València, Spain

ABSTRACT

Traditional teaching methods are not always efficient, especially in areas where the concepts to teach relate to physical work that must be done outside the classroom. This is the case of the construction sector, where the teaching of safety procedures is crucial to reduce the number of accidents, but traditional methods fail to highlight the importance of these procedures. The use of computer simulation through new technologies such as augmented reality (AR) can engage more students in order to better understand the concepts. In addition, they can visualize virtual elements superimposed on the real world to simulate the real situations they will later face in construction. This chapter deals with the simulation, by means of AR technology, of teaching procedures in the construction sector. It presents ARFAT, an application for mobile devices that makes use of AR to teach health and safety procedures about three elements: formwork, scaffolds, and falsework.

DOI: 10.4018/978-1-5225-7987-8.ch011

INTRODUCTION

The use of Augmented Reality (AR) for educational purposes can provide a great added value to the contents that are intended to be taught. For instance, when the target audience is not necessarily familiar with new technologies, AR can be a great ally since the interaction in this paradigm occurs in a simple and intuitive way, as it provides the ability to enhance/augment reality by means of a seamless interaction between virtual and real objects. In this regard, knowledge can be acquired in a more entertaining way, almost like in a game, helping users learn the contents easily, something that is very important in the construction sector where many workers lack a formal education.

Other interaction paradigms based on computer simulations, such as Virtual Reality (VR), can also provide interesting features in the education field, but AR has the ability to provide spatial cues by means of the distribution of computer generated elements that can be used to explain concepts in the real environment, without having to extract/teleport the user to a different simulated world (as occurs in VR). In this sense, AR technology allows visualizing virtual objects in a real environment when they are not really there. For example, a worker could visualize a virtual scaffolding blended with the image of a real facade, in real time and in situ, enhancing the sensation that the scaffolding really belongs to the real environment. It is even possible to interact with it and to move around in order to see it from different perspectives.

With a computer simulation, placing users in spaces where they are not currently located is increasingly easy. Although AR focuses on augmenting a real environment with specific virtual objects designed to enhance existing elements or particular situations, AR can be also a good tool to simulate completely hypothetical situations. This avoids having to move the user to real spaces when it is not possible (because they have not yet been built, because they are far away, because it would not be profitable, because the necessary material is not yet available, because some learning or training is recommended before going to the real space, etc.). This would be somehow similar to a VR application. However, in AR users will always be in contact with their current location, enhancing the sensation that what they are experiencing is believable.

On the other hand, in the construction industry it is essential to have a sufficient level of key competences, safety standards, and specific procedures to ensure both the safety of workers and the correct and efficient construction of buildings. To acquire this knowledge, the traditional use of books can be complemented with practical exercises in which AR can be used. In this way, users can consolidate and practice the knowledge learned by practicing in simulated environments. In this sense, AR technology can play an important role as practicing from a simulated and even a remote place (e.g. at home or at the classroom), is easier and safer than in a construction site. Indeed, the AR technology provides a simple and economical way to represent a construction environment, including its peculiar characteristics. Thus, a student or worker can make use of a tablet (provided with an AR application) to simulate that he or she is in a building site. The AR application would reproduce the necessary steps to safely provide the user with the necessary devices in the building site (fences, signs, guides, harnesses...). In the same way, situations such as changes in the weather or in the conditions of the ground can be simulated so that the student or worker understands better the different challenging and/or dangerous situations that can occur in the real life.

In this chapter, the authors will focus on how AR can help in designing training systems for qualified and non-qualified workers from the construction industry. These kind of systems will prospectively improve their basic competences, their knowledge of safety and of the assembly of certain elements of work, keys to successfully follow up their training and hence their professional career. Specifically, this work will show the mobile application ARFAT (The Augmented Reality Formwork Assembly Training), a European project that aims to elevate workers' health and safety level. As it is explained throughout the chapter, this application provides the two levels of augmentation described earlier: a pure AR-based paradigm where the virtual objects are meaningfully registered and aligned with respect to real objects and another mode where AR is used to show a simulated virtual scene which is, however, not designed to enhance a particular real object. The first mode is designed to be used in a construction site, whereas the second mode is designed to be used at home or at the classroom.

To that end, this chapter is organized as follows. In a first section, a review on the state of the art of different AR applications for the construction sector is presented and discussed through different examples, with a special mention of AR educational tools. In the next section, the ARFAT application is presented as a case study for safety training and education through AR applications in the construction sector. Finally, the discussion and conclusion sections present the advantages of this application according to the environment and the current moment in which it is framed and possible future research directions are included.

BACKGROUND

Augmented Reality Technology

AR is a well-known emerging technology by which virtual data (images, sound, haptic stimuli, etc.) can be added to the user's perception of the real world. This is achieved by simultaneously combining real and virtual objects which are registered in a 3D space, making AR an interactive technology in real-time (Azuma, 1997). Although nowadays AR has gained a lot of interest from many stakeholders, the truth is that AR is not really a new technology. In fact, the term "Augmented Reality" was first coined more than 25 years ago by (Caudell & Mizell, 1992) in order to describe a Head Mounted Display (HMD) used by electricians during the reparation and maintenance of aircrafts. This display showed virtual information on top of images of the real environment. Since then, the AR technology has evolved both in terms of hardware and conceptual definition. Today, it is no longer linked to a particular display technology and goes beyond the visualization of virtual elements over images of the real world. In fact, the current definition of AR is now much broader, including additional elements other than just blending virtual and real information. This is aligned with the work done by Azuma (1997), in which he defined Augmented Reality as the technology that simultaneously: 1) combines real and virtual objects which 2) are registered in the 3D space and 3) are interactive in real-time. This means that the synthetic information is not just placed on top of the real objects, as in some of the early works working with HMDs. They have to be registered in 3D, so that the integration of virtual and real objects is spatially consistent from the user's perspective. Additionally, this might apply to other computer generated information that is not based on visual stimuli, such as spatial sound.

Other authors have reported the advantages of AR in comparison to other technologies. According to Billinghurst & Kato (2002), AR provides simultaneously a number of advantages that other technologies cannot offer at the same time:

- **The Ability to Enhance/Augment Reality**: By using this technology, physical entities that are present in the real environment can be enhanced with computer generated synthetic data, such as images, sounds, 3D virtual models, haptic stimuli, etc. that are not present in the real scene. This feature is the one that provides the name to the AR technology, and it is the reason why it has a special potential for the construction sector. It is a technology that allows users to obtain further information than what is initially apparent, and thus it can be used to include warnings on elements, show hidden elements, give indications on how to proceed, etc.
- **Seamless Interaction Between Virtual and Real Objects:** The seam of an interface was defined by Ishii, Kobayashi, & Arita (1994). A seam of an interface is a functional, temporal, spatial or cognitive element that forces the user to change the way in which he/she interacts with the interface. The AR technology brings the opportunity to perform the interaction in a natural seamless way, since users can perceive and interact with synthetic elements as if they belong to the real environment, without excluding or hiding the real objects, unlike other technologies such as Virtual Reality, in which the real world is purposely hidden from the user.
- **Smooth Transition Between the Real and the Virtual Environments:** This ability is a very important feature for many tasks related to the construction sector (e.g. supervision), since it enables a simple and natural way to monitor real elements and conditions, which is substantially different from performing those tasks through a model or a depiction of the real element with a static display on a computer. According to Milgram and Kishino (1994), interfaces can be categorized or placed on a continuum depending on the amount of synthetic information generated and rendered by a computer, which is referred to as the reality-virtuality continuum or the Milgram's continuum. At one of the edges of the continuum is placed the real environment (0% virtual); at the other edge, the purely virtual one (VR, 100% virtual); between these two edges there is a wide variety of interfaces in which both environments are blended. This includes the AR or the Augmented Virtuality (AV) technologies, depending on the predominance of real (AR) or virtual (AV) objects in the scene. The amount of virtual content can be varied and will depend on the particular need the application is targeted at.
- **It Supports a Tangible Interface:** In AR applications, there is a very intimate relationship between virtual objects and the physical world, as both have to be blended, taking into account the spatial relationship between them in real time. Physical objects can be augmented through virtual ones, and they may even overlap dynamically. Additionally, these objects can be accessible to all users, which is known as *public use*, or may be individualized for each user (*private use*), so that particular interactions can be defined for different users providing customized experiences. Similarly, physical/tangible objects can be used to manipulate virtual elements in an intuitive manner in such a way that users can feel they are actually touching the virtual elements. The advantage of this characteristic is that users do not require any prior knowledge about a particular software application, since the interfaces appear natural to them, as they are in the real world. This could also be very important for tasks related to the construction sector, because users may need to learn to use different protocols and even different software elements to carry out their work. With AR, it is possible to simplify this by making use of tangible interfaces as natural interaction metaphors that are quickly identifiable and very easy to use.
- **The Presence of Spatial Cues for Face-To-Face and Remote Collaboration:** The AR technology allows that the computer-generated elements of the application be spatially distributed according to the physical environment. Thus, the specific location in which they appear will provide

information and can be very important in certain applications. This can also be of interest for the construction sector, for instance for the *in situ* inspection of industrial processes and machines or the *in situ* training.

Most AR applications deal with visual stimuli (3D objects, images, videos, text, etc.) by merging virtual objects with images of the real world, which are computationally generated in real-time. Other applications expand the concept of augmenting the reality by introducing other kind of stimuli, including haptic, acoustic, tactile or even olfactive information (Casas, Portalés, García-Pereira, & Fernández, 2017). Usually, the image of the real world comes from a camera feed, which is then visualized on a screen merged with the computer-generated virtual information. Visual displays include both mobile devices and other kind of setups, such as AR mirrors (Portalés, Gimeno, Casas, Olanda, & Giner, 2016). However, in recent years the use of smart mobile devices has been increasing, and this increase has impacted the deployment of AR applications, which are referred to as mobile AR. This type of AR application can be of great utility in the construction sector, since desktop-based solutions are impractical for most construction sites.

Mobile AR provides many potential benefits since it can be used in a wide variety of scenarios ranging from medical treatment and rehabilitation (Kilgus et al., 2015; Son-Lik Tang, Chee-Keong Kwoh, Ming-Yeong Teo, Ng, & Keck-Voon Ling, 1998) to learning and training (Dunleavy & Dede, 2014; Wu, Lee, Chang, & Liang, 2013), engineering and construction (Boyer, 2018; Gimeno, Morillo, Casas, & Fernández, 2011), and entertainment and cultural heritage (Galatis, Gavalas, Kasapakis, Pantziou, & Zaroliagis, 2016; Díaz, Boj, & Portalés, 2016; Martínez, Casas, Vidal-González, Vera, & García-Pereira, 2018). Additionally, research has been conducted on how computer simulations by means of augmented reality can be used to help students feel immersed in certain situations (Squire & Klopfer, 2007). However, this popularity does not directly imply that all AR applications can be successfully applied in real environments. In particular, in the construction sector, there are special environmental conditions (electromagnetic noise, dust, changing light conditions, etc.) that make it challenging to build robust AR applications. An example of the use of AR in a hostile environment is presented in work by Alam, Katsikas, Beltramello and Hadjiefthymiades (2017), where AR and VR are used to help improving the supervision and maintenance in the Large Hadron Collider (LHC) at CERN, Geneva.

Augmented Reality for Teaching and Training Purposes

AR has proven in multiple studies to be a great technology in the learning and training area (Yuen, Yaoyuneyong, & Johnson, 2011; Nincarean, Alia, Halim, & Rahman, 2013). Its natural usage and easy interaction with the digital environment makes it a highly usable tool for a wide range of users, from preschool kids (Tomi & Rambli, 2013) to the elderly (Kurz et al., 2014). Additionally, thanks to AR, teaching can reach certain user profiles that have serious difficulties for learning, including as people with disabilities. For example, Sevilla, Vera, Herrera and Fernández (2018) presented a project that uses spatial augmented reality and virtual reality technologies to help persons with autism spectrum disorder to develop areas in which they usually have problems.

Moreover, when in a certain population there is a deficiency in the learning of particular concepts that affect public safety, it is important to act quickly. For instance, AR can help correct certain attitudes rooted in a population, providing recommendations and awareness of different problems. In this regard, Vera, Gimeno, Casas, García-Pereira and Portalés (2018) presented a serious game designed to improve driving safety awareness and learning for both adults and children of Kingdom of Saudi Arabia because this country is one of the leaders in mortality rates due to road traffic accidents.

Another benefit of AR is that it helps to locate the user in certain dangerous situations that cannot be easily reproduced under normal circumstances. Being prepared to act in catastrophe situations can help save lives, and Mobile Augmented Reality (MAR) can provide a learner with a simulated disaster experience. In a study by Yamashita, Taki and Soga (2012), AR is used to help users learning about earthquake disasters, for example, quickly identify dangerous and safe points during an earthquake.

The AR technologies that can be used in education are diverse and offer different possibilities (Kesim & Ozarslan, 2012). The choice of the type of device will depend both on the final purpose and the available economic resources. In educational environments, one of the most common devices is the Handheld Displays, along with desktop AR, because of their reduced cost. The increase of the capabilities and features of smartphones and tablets, ubiquitous Internet access, combined with an affordable price, mean that MAR can be used more and more widely for teaching and training purposes (Chatzopoulos, Bermejo, Huang & Hui, 2017). In this sense, diverse research works that use MAR in this area can be found. For instance, in Turkan, Radkowski, Karabulut-Ilgu, Behzadan & Chen (2017), an application for teaching structural analysis by MAR is designed. This matter is a critical part of the curriculum in almost all civil, architectural and construction engineering programs, but the majority of students do not appear to have a sound understanding of fundamental concepts. This study concludes, after the user evaluation, that AR has potential to contribute to students' learning because of its interactivity and 3D visualization features. A similar conclusion is reached in a study describing the use of MAR to implement an assistant teaching system (Pan et al., 2017).

Augmented Reality in the Construction Sector

One of the purposes of the existing AR applications available for the construction sector in the academic literature is to inspect buildings. It is well known that there is a gap between the predicted and the measured energy performance of buildings once they are constructed (de Wilde, 2014). In this regard, AR can guide the inspectors during the inspection process and/or help them to better document the inspection process (Portalés, Casas, Gimeno, Fernández, & Poza, 2018). For instance, the work described in Webster, Feiner, MacIntyre, Massie and Krueger (1996), shows the potential of X-ray AR vision for architectural construction, inspection, and renovation. Another AR system is presented in Feiner, MacIntyre, Höllerer and Webster (1997) for urban environments, where users are allowed to make annotations in real time. In work by Schoenfelder and Schmalstieg (2008), an AR application was presented that enabled comparing planned buildings with the ones actually built.

More recently, in a study by Golparvar-Fard and Ham (2013) a method based on an energy performance AR environment was presented to visualise and analyze the deviations between buildings' actual and simulated energy performances. Other scholars investigated the issues and needs of current defect management practices in the construction industry, also giving a conceptual system framework for construction defect management that integrated ontology and AR with building information modelling (Park, Lee, Kwon, & Wang, 2013). A mobile defect management AR application was presented in work by Kwon, Park and Lim (2014), enabling workers and managers to automatically detect dimension errors and omissions in situ. Finally, studies show that an AR application can be used to help inspectors better document the inspection process of energy efficient pre-fab modular buildings (García-Pereira,

Gimeno, Portalés, Vidal-González, & Morillo, 2018; Portalés et al., 2018). All these examples show that AR is one of most interesting and useful technologies that can be applied to the inspection of buildings.

Augmented Reality in the Construction Sector for Teaching and Training Purposes

On the other hand, regarding AR educational tools in the construction sector, not many works can be found. The most interesting example (Le et al., 2015) proposes a framework using mainly mobile-based VR for construction safety education that provides the construction workers with virtual tools to improve knowledge about safety procedures and regulations on the construction sites. AR is also frequently used in the early stages of a construction project for the design and presentation of the final version of the construction site, in order to prepare or adjust details that could be more difficult to perceive in a 2D image (Zollmann et al., 2014). The typical applications of AR-based construction safety management consist of safety planning, safety training and education, and safety inspection (Park & Kim, 2013), but there are not too many examples.

There are studies focused on identifying what areas of the construction industry could be benefited by the use of AR (Shin & Dunston, 2008) or how it might be exploited to detect damages in buildings (Dong, Feng, & Kamat, 2013; Kamat & El-Tawil, 2007), to name some few examples. There are also investigations that use technologies different from AR for education and training in safety procedures (Pedro, Le, & Park, 2015; Teizer, Cheng, & Fang, 2013). However, very few of them focus on the use of AR for learning in the construction sector (Behzadan & Kamat, 2013). In a study by Li, Yi, Chi, Wang and Chan (2018), the authors perform a review that confirms the shortage of works relative to AR-based training systems for teaching health and safety procedures in construction. This is the goal of ARFAT, the application for mobile devices that is presented here. It is a novel tool that can provide great benefits in the teaching of safety procedures in construction.

CASE STUDY: ARFAT

The Augmented Reality Formwork Assembly Training (ARFAT) is an application for mobile devices developed thanks to the ERASMUS+ Programme: Cooperation for Innovation and the Exchange of Good Practices (Project Code: 2016-1-PL01-KA202-026102). As a result of the project, a training system is being created, consisting of a paper manual, an application for mobile devices, and a set of supporting media files. This chapter focuses on the AR application ARFAT, the development of which has just finished (Arfat | augmented reality formwork assembly training.).

Motivation, Objectives, and Target Audience

The European Directive 2001/45/EC requires appropriate measures be taken to improve safety and health at work. In particular, work at heights (i.e. formworks, scaffolding works) is reported as one of the most dangerous among types of construction work. In fact, falls from height are the most common causes of serious accidents, often fatal, throughout the European Union. One of the main reasons is that current training methods are insufficient. Research suggests that workers are not interested in classic trainings and do not pay much attention when they receive this type of training. The use of mobile devices (smartphones, tablets), computer simulation, modern AR technology and supporting media files can make the training procedure much more interesting and, even, unforgettable (Lin, Son, & Rojas, 2011).

One way to do this is to structure the system in training modules sequenced in a very easy way, supported by AR simulations, in order to train students in those necessary key competences to better understand more complex procedures. In addition, depending on the location of the users, it is interesting to offer different ways of visualizing the virtual information and performing the exercises. For example, if a student is at home or in the classroom, 3D models must appear in the real world at a proper scale and alignment, so that they fit on the user's table, for example. On the other hand, if a worker is in a building site, it may be more interesting to represent elements such as scaffolding or signs in real-size, to see how they should fit into the construction being carried out.

All these elements have been taken into account when developing ARFAT, an application aimed at construction engineers, construction workers, stakeholders and associations in the construction sector, Small and Medium Enterprises (SMEs) and companies (construction sector), Vocational Education and Training (VET) providers, and technical universities. As can be seen, the profile of the users is quite broad, so their ability in the use of new technologies can be very varied. Based on their experience, the authors firmly believe that AR simulations can be a great ally for the interaction to be simple and intuitive, facilitating, in this way, the learning process.

Thereby, the main goal of this European project is to develop innovative solutions, adapted to sectoral needs, modern formworks, and scaffolding works training in order to improve safety and health in the construction sector. Specifically, ARFAT focuses on three recurrent elements used in construction: formwork, scaffolds and falsework. As explained in the paper manual of the project:

These three elements are very relevant for the management of construction projects, since they are temporary works equipment for the support and assembly of structural building parts until these structures have reached a sufficient load bearing capacity as well as for the creation of workplaces. This construction equipment is relevant to the work progress, to the construction project´s economy as well as to the safety of work processes and adherence to the time schedule. They are important for design and safety of workplaces from which, for example, assembly works can be carried out and accompanies a building in the whole life cycle, in the phase of construction, during the operation in the case of possible repair or modernization works as well as in case of demolition.

Training and learning in the correct use of formworks, falsework and scaffolds is very important because they are complex engineering systems, which require special care and the use of experts and specialists in their design and use on construction sites. This is the main purpose of the application described below.

Description of the System

The application is structured around twelve procedures, described in Table 1. The majority of the procedures are exercises designed to be solved using AR technology, although some of them consist of simply visualizing a multimedia resource. When the application is accessed, and after passing the start screen (shown in Figure 1), the ARFAT tool shows the selection menu of the twelve procedures, depicted in Figure 2. When the user resolves an exercise, it appears in this menu with a star that indicates that it has been passed successfully, as can be seen in procedure 7 of Figure 2. At the top of this screen, the user can choose between two different display modes, as explained below. In addition, from the procedures window, some additional settings can be accessed. These settings allow the users to select between four different languages (English, German, Polish and Spanish) and to see an explanatory legend of the different icons that appear in the application.

As can be seen in Table 1, the dynamics of the exercises vary from one procedure to another so that users do not get bored. For example, some exercises consist of selecting elements in the right order,

Figure 1. Start screen of the ARFAT mobile device application

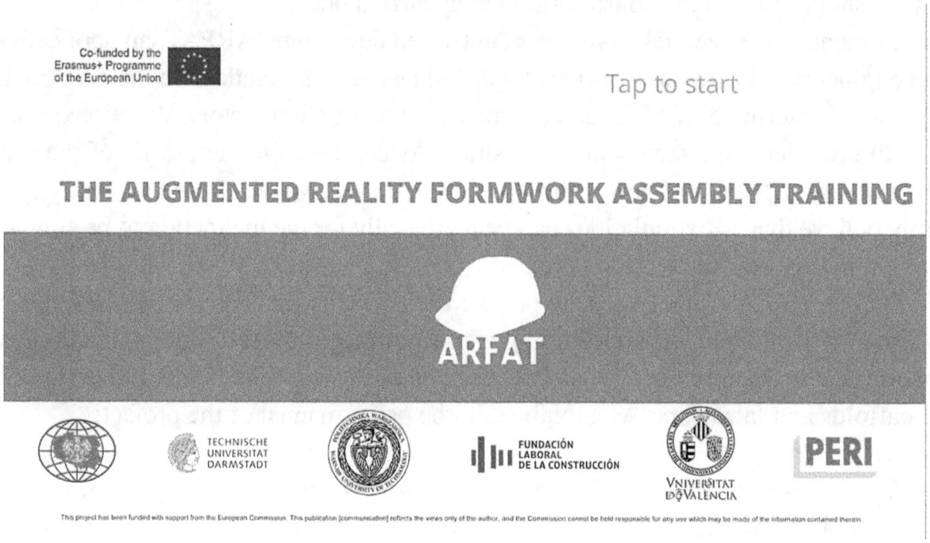

Figure 2. Part of the procedure selection menu of the ARFAT application, with the 1:20 display mode selected and procedure 7 solved successfully

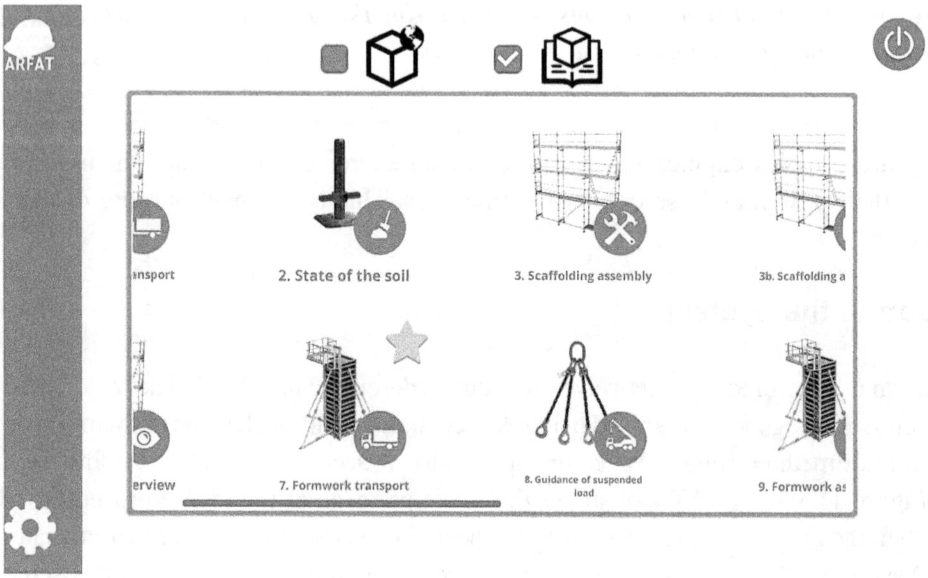

Table 1. Description of the ARFAT procedures

No	Title	Description of the AR procedure	Additional Characteristics
1	Scaffolding transport	Select each one of the elements and drag it towards one of the modular pallets or grid boxes, as appropriate.	
2	State of the soil	Please touch the place where the mistake was made during scaffolding. Then, press each tool icon to see how it should be done correctly.	Explanation of errors in text format.
3	Scaffolding assembly	Drag and drop each element in the correct place and correct order to assemble the scaffolding.	
3b	Scaffolding assembly		Explanatory video.
4	Scaffolding usage	• Identify the missing items of the modular facade scaffolding. • Finish identification. • Drag each element from the menu to its place. • You failed detecting the shortcomings. Press each play icon to see the possible consequences.	Explanation of errors through AR simulations.
5	Scaffolding usage		Explanatory video.
6	Scaffolding disassembly	Select each element in the correct order according to the disassembly procedure.	Disassembly of each element through an AR simulation.
7	Formwork transport	• Select each element and drag it towards the modular pallet, the grid box or the table lift, as appropriate. • Drag each lifting equipment (slings) from the menu to this place. Press each sling icon to see the placement of the selected transport equipment and the formwork material movement.	Material movement through a VR animation.
8	Guidance of suspended load	Place the suspended load over the highlighted area. Press the different hand signals to move the mobile crane.	Small window in the lower right corner of the screen to always see the worker head-on.
9	Formwork assembly	Drag and drop each element in the correct place and correct order to assemble the formwork.	
10	Formwork usage		Explanatory video.
11	Formwork disassembly	Select each element in the correct order according to the disassembly procedure.	Disassembly of each element through an AR simulation.

others in placing elements in their correct place, and others in stopping errors or giving instructions in the appropriate way. In addition, some exercises incorporate elements of randomness so that each time users do it, they face different situations. Figure 3 shows procedure 1 in different stages of realization and from different points of view. Some procedures include animations that explain the way in which certain tasks must be performed or that simulate what would happen if certain elements were not well placed. Some of these animations are made in VR, although most have been developed with AR simulations. Figure 4 shows how in procedure 4, the option is given to visualize small AR simulations that show what would happen in reality if the errors that the user had made during the exercise were real. On the other hand, Figure 5 shows procedure 7, which explains, through a VR animation, how the material should be transported.

Figure 3. Procedure 1 from different points of view and in different stages: in the beginning (A) and finished (B)

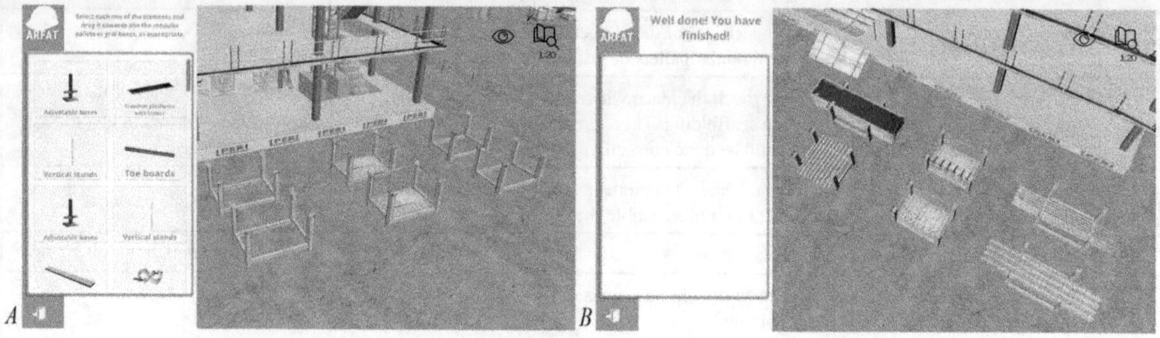

Figure 4. The user has failed in the detection of two missing items of the modular facade scaffolding in procedure 4. By clicking on the play icons (A) he or she can see an AR simulation of the consequences of the error (B).

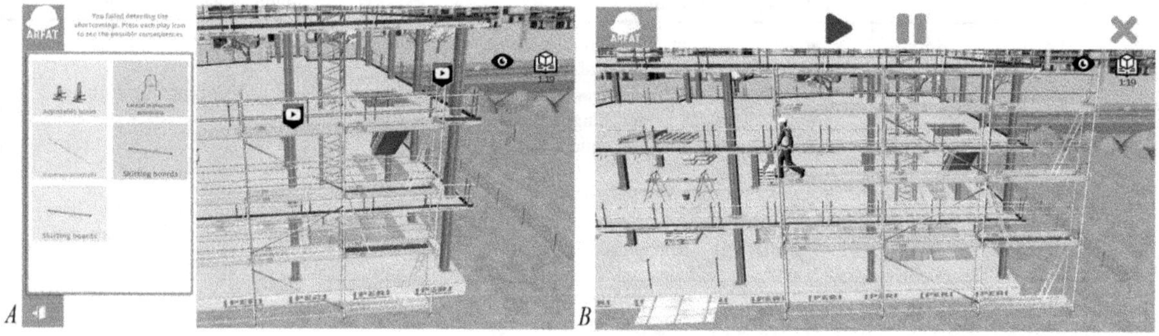

Figure 5. The user has finished procedure 7 and, by clicking on each sling icon (A), he or she can see a VR animation about how the material should be transported (B).

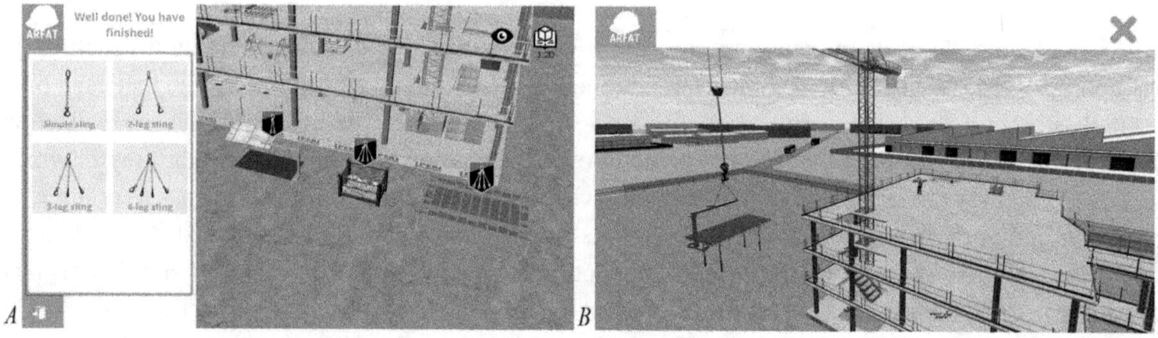

Before interacting with a virtual element of the AR application, it is necessary that the application detects and tracks an AR marker that is related to a given object, so the virtual object is loaded and both the virtual and real objects are properly aligned. An example of this is depicted in Figure 6. Once the user begins to perform the exercise, he or she can physically move the mobile device to navigate through the virtual environment that has appeared superimposed in the real world. In this way, users will be able to approach or move away from the elements of the scene or surround a building just by moving their mobile device. This is because the application performs a kind of extended tracking of the mobile device in relation to the AR marker which can work even if the marker is not always in the point of view of the camera. Therefore, the user can lose sight of the AR marker, and the virtual elements will not disappear from the real world, as it usually happens in traditional AR. This feature makes the immersion of users greater, and, therefore, they focus more on the exercises they are doing and internalize the lessons better. As Figure 7 shows, the same element can be seen from different angles and distances. Users achieve this by simply moving their mobile devices.

Each procedure has two display modes: 1:20 scale and 1:1 scale (real scale). In Figure 2, at the top of the application screen, the two icons that allow the selection of one mode or another can be seen. In the 1:20 mode, the elements necessary to solve the exercises (scaffolding, formwork...) are located in a virtual construction site environment with a scale reduced to the size of the AR marker. Therefore, this mode of visualization is designed to be used in a classroom or any other place away from real construction. On the other hand, the 1:1 mode only shows the elements that are necessary to perform each procedure, without any additional decorative elements. In this way, the user can use the AR application in a real construction visualizing the elements of scaffolding and formwork in real size superimposed

Figure 6. User pointing with the tablet's camera to the AR marker

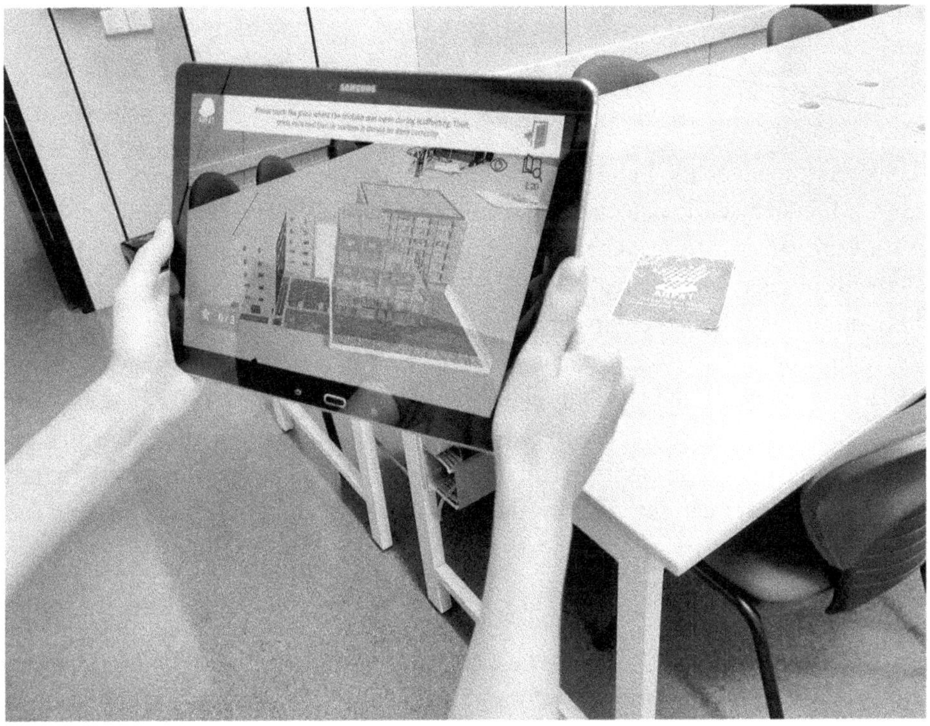

Figure 7. Screenshots of procedures 9 (A and B) and 11 (C, D, E and F) from different points of view and in different display modes: 1:20 (A, B, D, E and F) and 1:1 (C).

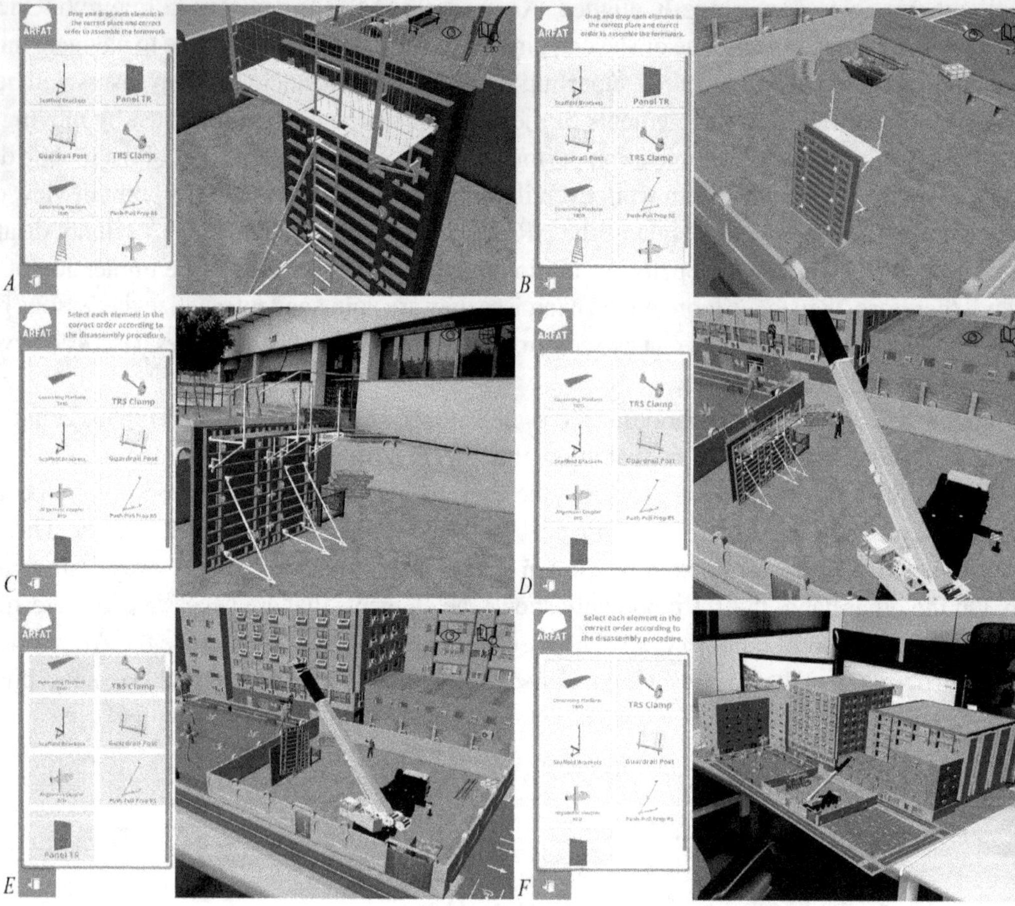

on the real construction elements. Figure 8 shows procedure 7 in the two modes of visualization, and Figure 9 shows a life-size scaffold located in a real environment. These two modes of visualization make ARFAT a very versatile tool, since it can be used both in a real construction environment to see the virtual elements aligned with the real objects of the construction site or in a classroom to explain to students the lessons using a virtual environment.

In addition to this, once each exercise is being performed in one of the two modes, the display scale can be varied. In the 1:20 mode, the elements can be viewed from a scale 1:100 to a scale of 1:2, whereas in the 1:1 mode, the scale can vary between 9:1 and 1:9. Thanks to this option, the size of the virtual elements can be adapted to the real environment in which the application is being used. In the upper right corner of the screen, the user can see the current scale of the elements, as can be seen in figures 3-9.

Implementation

The AR-based training system ARFAT has been developed with the Unity 3D video game engine. This tool is a flexible and powerful platform used to create interactive applications and games in both 2D and

Figure 8. Procedure 7 in 1:20 display mode (A) and in 1:1 display mode (B)

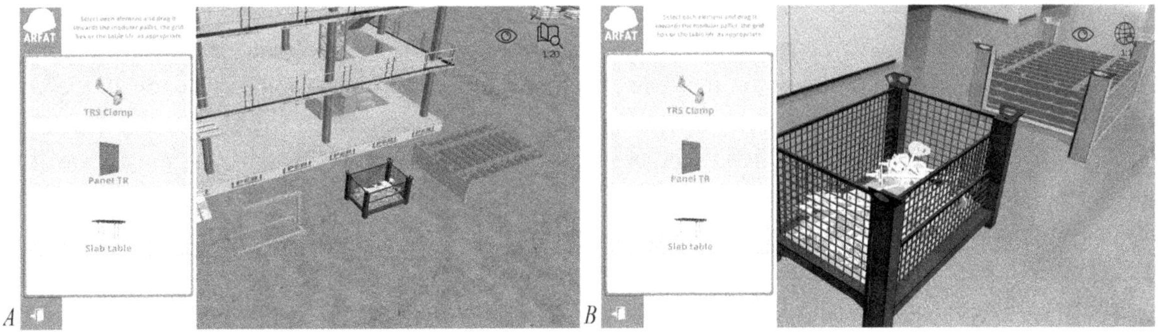

Figure 9. Real-life scaffolding on a real environment during the realization of procedure 4 in 1:1 display mode

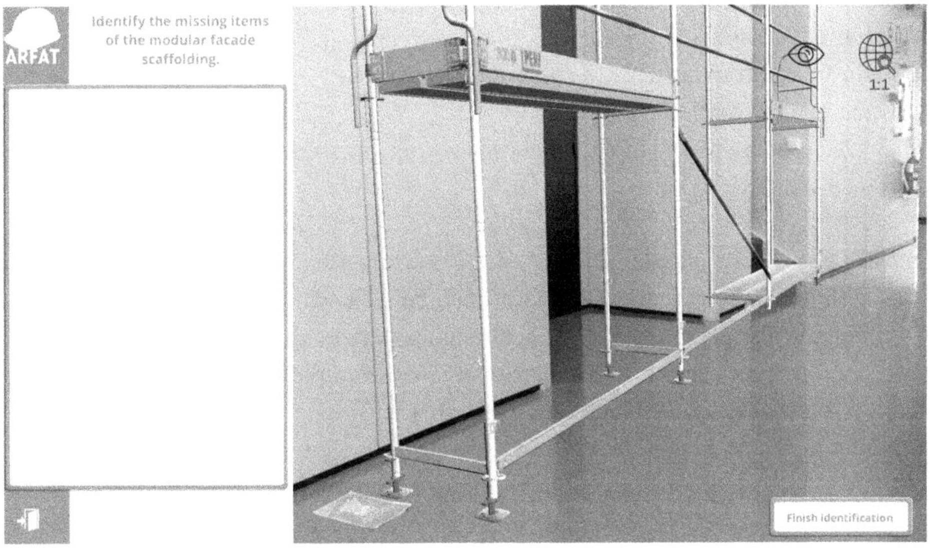

3D. One of the main characteristics of Unity is that it allows to efficiently export the developments to a large number of different platforms. In this way, and thanks to this feature, ARFAT works on mobile devices with both Android and iOS operating systems.

For the integration of AR in the system, Vuforia has been used. Vuforia is a software development kit (SDK) for mobile devices that enables the creation of AR applications. The different procedures have been developed using the Extended Tracking feature from Vuforia SDK. This feature allows users to keep interacting with the digital augmented information even when the camera is not pointing at the AR marker or tracking has been lost. Therefore, user experience is enhanced as users are able to visualize virtual objects with proper scale and perspective, keeping them properly aligned with the real world with respect to the position defined by the initial AR marker setup. Moreover, the system, through the use of Vuforia SDK, allows users to access some of the features of state-of-the-art AR Frameworks ARKit and ARCore in supported devices.

DISCUSSION AND FUTURE RESEARCH DIRECTIONS

As mentioned throughout this chapter, AR technology has the ability to motivate students in learning. This makes it easier for them to retain the concepts that teachers are trying to teach them. In the construction sector, this feature is especially crucial because of the importance of learning health and safety procedures. Memorizing the correct way to assemble, use, disassemble and transport the formworks, falsework, and scaffolds is vital for the safety of the workers, as their lives are at risk. Thanks to the use of AR simulations, learning these procedures can be much more enjoyable so that users pay more attention and better internalize the concepts.

The development of the ARFAT application and its use in the construction sector can mean a qualitative leap in the way teaching is performed in this sector. This mobile application provides many advantages over traditional teaching methods thanks to the use of AR and the incorporation of useful features, such as:

- Different modes of interaction with the elements to solve each exercise
- Incorporation of randomness in several exercises
- Reproduction of AR and VR simulations
- Possibility of modifying the scale of the virtual elements
- Two different display modes
- Flexibility (once the application establishes tracking, it is not necessary for the user to continuously focus on the AR marker.)

Because of the positive results that the use of AR is providing in the construction sector as can be seen in the research and developments that have been carried out so far, it is easy to foresee that this technology will be increasingly used to teach health and safety procedures in this sector. Different lines of research are open to improve the user experience. For example, more and more developments are focused on the so-called AR markerless technology, that is: instead of using an AR marker, a cloud of points from the environment is generated to perform the tracking (Abhishek et al., 2018; Lee, Chau, Chau & Ng, 2017). On the other hand, the improvement of technology is causing tablets and smartphones to be increasingly replaced by AR glasses or AR helmets, which can lead to greater user immersion (Huang et al., 2018; Kumar, Krishna, Pagadala & Kumar, 2018). Another line of remarkable research is the use of collaborative systems, in which no longer does a single user engage with the application, but the tool allows the user to share the real or virtual space with more users who can help him or her in learning (Casas, Portalés, García-Pereira & Gimeno, 2019; Martín-Gutiérrez, Fabiani, Benesova, Meneses & Mora, 2015).

Despite the advantages of using virtual technologies in education (e.g. increasing students' motivation, providing more interaction than conventional learning methods, allowing a constructivist approach of learning), how best to integrate these technologies in a stable way in an educational environment has not yet been clearly defined (Martín-Gutiérrez, Mora, Añorbe-Díaz & González-Marrero, 2017). In this regard, it is important to continue researching how to overcome current barriers, such as the resistance of traditional learning environments to integrate educational innovations, the opposition of some teachers to adopting new technologies, and the costs involved in their implementation and maintenance. However, the quick evolution of MAR makes this incorporation more feasible and affordable than ever before for educational institutions and students.

The AR application presented in this chapter as a case study has been developed as part of a European project that has already finished. However, we have opened diverse future research directions in order to ensure the sustainability of the project and the exploitation of its results. For instance, the way to structure learning content in ARFAT, based on procedures, would be easily extrapolated to other sectors of education, beyond that of construction. Therefore, an interesting line of research would be the development of a general framework that allows creating, in a simple and methodical way, educational AR applications for mobile devices based on the resolution of procedures. On the other hand, the ARFAT application would be easily exportable to other types of devices, such as HMDs, which would allow a greater immersion of the user during the resolution of the procedures.

CONCLUSION

The large number of accidents that occur in the construction sector due to the incorrect assembly of formwork, scaffolds and falsework, suggests the need to use new teaching methods in this sector that provide safer environments to accomplish these tasks. In this chapter, the authors argue that the AR technology stands out as a good candidate to deal with such innovative teaching methods, as it provides an in-situ high interactive environment avoiding the risks associated to the real work in such tasks. In order to deal with the current methods associated with this technology, this chapter includes a review of the state of the art of the use of AR-based tools in the construction sector, paying special attention to its use for teaching and training purposes. Although the many benefits that this technology can bring to the field, it is remarkable the lack of examples that can be found in the literature, making evident the need to advance in the research, design and development of new methods and tools making use of AR.

After the review of the different works and developments available in the academic literature pointing out the current needs for the field in this regards, this chapter presents a dedicated approach and computational solution consisting of an application for mobile devices that uses the AR technology to teach health and safety procedures in the construction sector, both in-situ and in a classroom environment. This solution was developed as part of the ARFAT project, funded under the European Commission Erasmus+ Programme. The multiple advantages and novelties provided by this application, which are addressed and discussed in the scope of this chapter, make the authors optimistic to continue working in this research direction. Most remarkable are the advantages over traditional methods that the tool here presented brings, thanks to the AR technology, such as: the different modes of interaction with the elements to solve each exercise, the incorporation of randomness in several exercises, and the reproduction of AR and VR simulations.

ACKNOWLEDGMENT

The ARFAT project (2016-1-PL01-KA202-026102) is supported by the ERASMUS+ Programme: Cooperation for Innovation and the Exchange of Good Practices and the Spanish Ministry of Science, Innovation and Universities (program: “University teacher formation”).

REFERENCES

Abhishek, M. T., Aswin, P. S., Akhil, N. C., Souban, A., Muhammedali, S. K., & Vial, A. (2018, December). Virtual Lab Using Markerless Augmented Reality. In *2018 IEEE International Conference on Teaching, Assessment, and Learning for Engineering (TALE)* (pp. 1150-1153). IEEE. 10.1109/TALE.2018.8615245

Alam, M. F., Katsikas, S., Beltramello, O., & Hadjiefthymiades, S. (2017). Augmented and virtual reality based monitoring and safety system: A prototype IoT platform. *Journal of Network and Computer Applications*, *89*, 109–119. doi:10.1016/j.jnca.2017.03.022

Arfat. (n.d.). Retrieved from http://www.arfat.il.pw.edu.pl/

Azuma, R. T. (1997). A survey of augmented reality. *Presence (Cambridge, Mass.)*, *6*(4), 355–385. doi:10.1162/pres.1997.6.4.355

Behzadan, A. H., & Kamat, V. R. (2013). Enabling discovery-based learning in construction using telepresent augmented reality. *Automation in Construction*, *33*, 3–10. doi:10.1016/j.autcon.2012.09.003

Billinghurst, M., & Kato, H. (2002). Collaborative augmented reality. *Communications of the ACM*, *45*(7), 64–70. doi:10.1145/514236.514265

Boyer, S. A. (2018). *SCADA supervisory control and data acquisition*. The Instrumentation, Systems and Automation Society.

Casas, S., Portalés, C., García-Pereira, I., & Fernández, M. (2017). On a first evaluation of ROMOT—A RObotic 3D MOvie Theatre—For driving safety awareness. *Multimodal Technologies and Interaction*, *1*(2), 6. doi:10.3390/mti1020006

Casas, S., Portalés, C., García-Pereira, I., & Gimeno, J. (2019). Mixing Different Realities in a Single Shared Space: Analysis of Mixed-Platform Collaborative Shared Spaces. In *Harnessing the Internet of Everything (IoE) for Accelerated Innovation Opportunities* (pp. 175–192). IGI Global. doi:10.4018/978-1-5225-7332-6.ch008

Caudell, T. P., & Mizell, D. W. (1992). Augmented reality: An application of heads-up display technology to manual manufacturing processes. *Proceedings of the Twenty-Fifth Hawaii International Conference on System Sciences*, *2*, 659-669. 10.1109/HICSS.1992.183317

Chatzopoulos, D., Bermejo, C., Huang, Z., & Hui, P. (2017). Mobile augmented reality survey: From where we are to where we go. *IEEE Access: Practical Innovations, Open Solutions*, *5*, 6917–6950. doi:10.1109/ACCESS.2017.2698164

de Wilde, P. (2014). The gap between predicted and measured energy performance of buildings: A framework for investigation. *Automation in Construction*, *41*, 40–49. doi:10.1016/j.autcon.2014.02.009

Díaz, D., Boj, C., & Portalés, C. (2016). HybridPLAY: A new technology to foster outdoors physical activity, verbal communication and teamwork. *Sensors (Basel), 16*(4), 586. doi:10.339016040586 PMID:27120601

Dong, S., Feng, C., & Kamat, V. R. (2013). Sensitivity analysis of augmented reality-assisted building damage reconnaissance using virtual prototyping. *Automation in Construction, 33*, 24–36. doi:10.1016/j.autcon.2012.09.005

Dunleavy, M., & Dede, C. (2014). Augmented reality teaching and learning. In J. Spector, M. Merrill, J. Elen, & M. Bishop (Eds.), *Handbook of research on educational communications and technology* (pp. 735–745). New York, NY: Springer. doi:10.1007/978-1-4614-3185-5_59

Feiner, S., MacIntyre, B., Höllerer, T., & Webster, A. (1997). A touring machine: Prototyping 3D mobile augmented reality systems for exploring the urban environment. *Personal Technologies, 1*(4), 208–217. doi:10.1007/BF01682023

Galatis, P., Gavalas, D., Kasapakis, V., Pantziou, G., & Zaroliagis, C. (2016). Mobile augmented reality guides in cultural heritage. *Proceedings of the 8th EAI International Conference on Mobile Computing, Applications and Services*, 11-19. 10.4108/eai.30-11-2016.2266954

García-Pereira, I., Gimeno, J., Portalés, C., Vidal-González, M., & Morillo, P. (2018). *On the design of a mixed-reality annotations tool for the inspection of pre-fab buildings*. Paper presented at the Spanish Computer Graphics Conference (CEIG), Madrid, Spain. doi:10.2312/ceig.20181157

Gimeno, J., Morillo, P., Casas, S., & Fernández, M. (2011). An augmented reality (AR) CAD system at construction sites. In Y. C. N. Andrew (Ed.), *Augmented reality* (pp. 15–32). Rijeka: IntechOpen. doi:10.5772/26801

Golparvar-Fard, M., & Ham, Y. (2013). Automated diagnostics and visualization of potential energy performance problems in existing buildings using energy performance augmented reality models. *Journal of Computing in Civil Engineering, 28*(1), 17–29. doi:10.1061/(ASCE)CP.1943-5487.0000311

Huang, C. Y., Thomas, J. B., Alismail, A., Cohen, A., Almutairi, W., Daher, N. S., ... Tan, L. D. (2018). The use of augmented reality glasses in central line simulation:"see one, simulate many, do one competently, and teach everyone. *Advances in Medical Education and Practice, 9*, 357–363. doi:10.2147/AMEP.S160704 PMID:29785148

Ishii, H., Kobayashi, M., & Arita, K. (1994). Iterative design of seamless collaboration media. *Communications of the ACM, 37*(8), 83–97. doi:10.1145/179606.179687

Kamat, V. R., & El-Tawil, S. (2007). Evaluation of augmented reality for rapid assessment of earthquake-induced building damage. *Journal of Computing in Civil Engineering, 21*(5), 303–310. doi:10.1061/(ASCE)0887-3801(2007)21:5(303)

Kesim, M., & Ozarslan, Y. (2012). Augmented reality in education: Current technologies and the potential for education. *Procedia: Social and Behavioral Sciences, 47*, 297–302. doi:10.1016/j.sbspro.2012.06.654

Kilgus, T., Heim, E., Haase, S., Prüfer, S., Müller, M., Seitel, A., ... Schlemmer, H.-P. (2015). Mobile markerless augmented reality and its application in forensic medicine. *International Journal of Computer Assisted Radiology and Surgery, 10*(5), 573–586. doi:10.100711548-014-1106-9 PMID:25149272

Kumar, N. M., Krishna, P. R., Pagadala, P. K., & Kumar, N. S. (2018, August). Use of Smart Glasses in Education-A Study. In *2018 2nd International Conference on I-SMAC (IoT in Social, Mobile, Analytics and Cloud)(I-SMAC)* (pp. 56-59). IEEE.

Kurz, D., Fedosov, A., Diewald, S., Güttier, J., Geilhof, B., & Heuberger, M. (2014). [Poster] towards mobile augmented reality for the elderly. *2014 IEEE International Symposium on Mixed and Augmented Reality (ISMAR)*, 275-276. 10.1109/ISMAR.2014.6948447

Kwon, O., Park, C., & Lim, C. (2014). A defect management system for reinforced concrete work utilizing BIM, image-matching and augmented reality. *Automation in Construction, 46*, 74–81. doi:10.1016/j.autcon.2014.05.005

Le, Q. T., Pedro, A., Lim, C. R., Park, H. T., Park, C. S., & Kim, H. K. (2015). A framework for using mobile based virtual reality and augmented reality for experiential construction safety education. *International Journal of Engineering Education, 31*(3), 713–725.

Lee, L. K., Chau, C. H., Chau, C. H., & Ng, C. T. (2017, June). Using Augmented Reality to Teach Kindergarten Students English Vocabulary. In *2017 International Symposium on Educational Technology (ISET)* (pp. 53-57). IEEE. 10.1109/ISET.2017.20

Li, X., Yi, W., Chi, H., Wang, X., & Chan, A. P. C. (2018). A critical review of virtual and augmented reality (VR/AR) applications in construction safety. *Automation in Construction, 86*, 150–162. doi:10.1016/j.autcon.2017.11.003

Lin, K., Son, J. W., & Rojas, E. M. (2011). A pilot study of a 3D game environment for construction safety education. *Journal of Information Technology in Construction, 16*(5), 69–84.

Martín-Gutiérrez, J., Fabiani, P., Benesova, W., Meneses, M. D., & Mora, C. E. (2015). Augmented reality to promote collaborative and autonomous learning in higher education. *Computers in Human Behavior, 51*, 752–761. doi:10.1016/j.chb.2014.11.093

Martín-Gutiérrez, J., Mora, C. E., Añorbe-Díaz, B., & González-Marrero, A. (2017). Virtual technologies trends in education. *EURASIA Journal of Mathematics Science and Technology Education, 13*(2), 469–486.

Martínez, B., Casas, S., Vidal-González, M., Vera, L., & García-Pereira, I. (2018). TinajAR: An edutainment augmented reality mirror for the dissemination and reinterpretation of cultural heritage. *Multimodal Technologies and Interaction*, 2(2), 33. doi:10.3390/mti2020033

Milgram, P., & Kishino, F. (1994). A taxonomy of mixed reality visual displays. *IEICE Transactions on Information and Systems, 77*, 1321–1329.

Nincarean, D., Alia, M. B., Halim, N. D. A., & Rahman, M. H. A. (2013). Mobile augmented reality: The potential for education. *Procedia: Social and Behavioral Sciences*, *103*, 657–664. doi:10.1016/j.sbspro.2013.10.385

Pan, X., Sun, X., Wang, H., Gao, S., Wang, N., & Lin, Z. (2017, November). Application of an assistant teaching system based on mobile augmented reality (AR) for course design of mechanical manufacturing process. In *2017 IEEE 9th International Conference on Engineering Education (ICEED)* (pp. 192-196). IEEE.

Park, C., & Kim, H. (2013). A framework for construction safety management and visualization system. *Automation in Construction*, *33*, 95–103. doi:10.1016/j.autcon.2012.09.012

Park, C., Lee, D., Kwon, O., & Wang, X. (2013). A framework for proactive construction defect management using BIM, augmented reality and ontology-based data collection template. *Automation in Construction*, *33*, 61–71. doi:10.1016/j.autcon.2012.09.010

Pedro, A., Le, Q. T., & Park, C. S. (2015). Framework for integrating safety into construction methods education through interactive virtual reality. *Journal of Professional Issues in Engineering Education and Practice*, *142*(2), 04015011. doi:10.1061/(ASCE)EI.1943-5541.0000261

Portalés, C., Casas, S., Gimeno, J., Fernández, M., & Poza, M. (2018). From the paper to the tablet: On the design of an AR-based tool for the inspection of pre-fab buildings. preliminary results of the SIRAE project. *Sensors (Basel)*, *18*(4), 1262. doi:10.339018041262 PMID:29671799

Portalés, C., Gimeno, J., Casas, S., Olanda, R., & Giner, F. (2016). Interacting with augmented reality mirrors. In J. Rodrigues, P. Cardoso, J. Monteiro, & M. Figueiredo (Eds.), *Handbook of research on human-computer interfaces, developments, and applications* (pp. 216–244). Hershey, PA: IGI Global. doi:10.4018/978-1-5225-0435-1.ch009

Schoenfelder, R., & Schmalstieg, D. (2008). *Augmented reality for industrial building acceptance*. Paper presented at the 2008 IEEE Virtual Reality Conference, Reno, NV. 10.1109/VR.2008.4480755

Sevilla, J., Vera, L., Herrera, G., & Fernández, M. (2018). *FORHHSS-TEA, support to the individual work system for people with autism spectrum disorder using virtual and augmented reality*. Paper presented at the Spanish Computer Graphics Conference (CEIG), Madrid, Spain. doi:10.2312/ceig.20181155

Shin, D. H., & Dunston, P. S. (2008). Identification of application areas for augmented reality in industrial construction based on technology suitability. *Automation in Construction*, *17*(7), 882–894. doi:10.1016/j.autcon.2008.02.012

Squire, K., & Klopfer, E. (2007). Augmented reality simulations on handheld computers. *Journal of the Learning Sciences*, *16*(3), 371–413. doi:10.1080/10508400701413435

Tang, Kwoh, Teo, & Ling. (1998). Augmented reality systems for medical applications. *IEEE Engineering in Medicine and Biology Magazine*, *17*(3), 49–58. doi:10.1109/51.677169 PMID:9604701

Teizer, J., Cheng, T., & Fang, Y. (2013). Location tracking and data visualization technology to advance construction ironworkers' education and training in safety and productivity. *Automation in Construction*, *35*, 53–68. doi:10.1016/j.autcon.2013.03.004

Tomi, A. B., & Rambli, D. R. A. (2013). An interactive mobile augmented reality magical playbook: Learning number with the thirsty crow. *Procedia Computer Science*, *25*, 123–130. doi:10.1016/j.procs.2013.11.015

Turkan, Y., Radkowski, R., Karabulut-Ilgu, A., Behzadan, A. H., & Chen, A. (2017). Mobile augmented reality for teaching structural analysis. *Advanced Engineering Informatics*, *34*, 90–100. doi:10.1016/j.aei.2017.09.005

Vera, L., Gimeno, J., Casas, S., García-Pereira, I., & Portalés, C. (2018). *A hybrid virtual-augmented serious game to improve driving safety awareness*. Paper presented at the Advances in Computer Entertainment Technology, London, UK. doi:10.1007/978-3-319-76270-8_21

Webster, A., Feiner, S., MacIntyre, B., Massie, W., & Krueger, T. (1996). Augmented reality in architectural construction, inspection and renovation. *ASCE Third Congress on Computing in Civil Engineering*, 913-919.

Wu, H., Lee, S. W., Chang, H., & Liang, J. (2013). Current status, opportunities and challenges of augmented reality in education. *Computers & Education*, *62*, 41–49. doi:10.1016/j.compedu.2012.10.024

Yamashita, N., Taki, H., & Soga, M. (2012). A learning support environment for earthquake disaster with a simulation of furniture falling by mobile AR. *2012 International Conference on Information Technology Based Higher Education and Training (ITHET)*, 1-5. 10.1109/ITHET.2012.6246053

Yuen, S. C., Yaoyuneyong, G., & Johnson, E. (2011). Augmented reality: An overview and five directions for AR in education. *Journal of Educational Technology Development and Exchange*, *4*(1), 11. doi:10.18785/jetde.0401.10

Zollmann, S., Hoppe, C., Kluckner, S., Poglitsch, C., Bischof, H., & Reitmayr, G. (2014). Augmented reality for construction site monitoring and documentation. *Proceedings of the IEEE*, *102*(2), 137–154. doi:10.1109/JPROC.2013.2294314

KEY TERMS AND DEFINITIONS

AR Marker: Any object that can be placed in a scene to provide a fixed point of reference of position and/or scale. It allows the device that is generating the AR content to calculate the position and orientation of its camera.

Augmented Reality: The technology that simultaneously combines real and virtual objects that are interactive in real-time and are registered in a three-dimensional space.

Interaction: A kind of action that occurs as two or more objects have an effect upon one another.

Mobile AR: A special form of AR in which mobile devices are used to visualize real and virtual content. The view of the real word is typically obtained by means of the mobile device's camera.

Point Cloud: Set of vertices that represents the surface of objects and helps the AR applications to recognize the patterns to locate the augmented content relative to it.

Serious Game: Game oriented learning and training through entertainment.

Tracking: Continuous location of the user viewpoint acquiring his or her position and orientation in the real world.

Chapter 12
CSI4FS®: A Markerless Augmented Reality Game – A Novel Approach to Crime Scene Investigation Training

Ian Levstein
Marshall University, USA

Lenora Jean Justice
Morehead State University, USA

ABSTRACT

This chapter describes the development of a game-based markerless augmented reality smartphone application (CSI4FS®) that complements traditional crime scene investigation training. The intent is to make a strong case for the use of augmented reality in a forensic science training environment. It includes a brief outline of the issue followed by a history of augmented reality in education and training, simulation use in high-risk professions generally and in education specifically, and augmented reality use in crime scene investigation. Both marker-based and markerless technologies are discussed, followed by a description of the augmented reality application and some of the challenges involved in the creation of that application. Overall, the purpose of this chapter is to introduce a potential solution that will help college students learn crime scene investigation techniques more effectively than with the more traditional training methods.

INTRODUCTION

The body just lay there – still and lifeless! There was blood everywhere… but blood spatter never looked like this! It was her third day on the job and there had not been accurate preparation for this. Nothing she learned so far was really useful… because the real crime scene bore almost no resemblance to the training scenarios chosen by her instructor. Every crime scene she had encountered in training was staged within the walls of the same three rooms.

DOI: 10.4018/978-1-5225-7987-8.ch012

On television, crime scene investigation (CSI) is often portrayed as glamorous and even mysterious to some extent. Television investigators seem to have all manner of equipment and resources at their disposal and recreating the crime scene in a laboratory environment or testing all the collected samples happens within a few minutes or hours. The popularity of such television shows as CSI (aired October, 2000) and NCIS (aired September, 2003) have created what is known as the CSI Effect: the belief that forensic science is more than it really is. The CSI Effect causes problems in the judicial system because juries often have a higher expectation of forensic science than actually exists – which hinders the prosecution, while those same juries simultaneously hold an unrealistic expectation of forensic science's reliability – which hinders the defense (Schweitzer & Saks, 2007; Weaver, Salamonson, Koch, & Porter, 2012).

While the CSI Effect has been a problem for the legal system, it has certainly been good business for forensic science graduate programs across the U.S. In 2004, the Forensic Science Education Program Accreditation Commission (FEPAC) was formed. In 2005 there was only one FEPAC-accredited master's degree program in the U.S., but by 2017 there were 19 accredited graduate programs at the master's level and 26 accredited undergraduate programs (FEPAC, 2017). There is a drawback to this also, though. Students entering forensic science programs expect to use the high-tech equipment that has lured them into this profession having first seen it on television. Where crime scene investigation education and training is concerned, the reality often does not meet their expectations and the staged sets are rarely a reflection of what they encounter in the field.

This chapter will describe the traditional crime scene investigation training practice at a mid-Atlantic academic institution, describe the use of augmented reality in education and training generally and in crime scene investigation specifically, compare and contrast the two main types of augmented reality applications, discuss the use of game-based augmented reality for training, and then discuss the development of a markerless game-based augmented reality smartphone application for crime scene investigation training.

BACKGROUND

In higher education, crime scene investigation training has traditionally taken place within a full-immersion simulation – a house or other facility where staged sets are created by the instructor for that specific purpose. The biggest drawback to this traditional method, however, is that the sets *are* staged. The trainer creates the specifics; the trainer creates the reality – and scenarios are limited because tight course scheduling means that the instructor can only cover the basics of investigation. The settings are largely static and rarely represent what is truly encountered by investigators. Further, after each training session, the staged sets must then be recreated and reset for the next group – both of which are time-consuming tasks. The question most often *not* asked is whether this method of training actually helps the student to learn.

To process a crime scene thoroughly, six steps must be taken sequentially in order to preserve evidence suitable for analysis and later probative purposes in court (adapted from Gardner and Bevel, 2009):

1. **Assessing**: Although this is the first step of an investigation, it is continuous and ongoing. First, a perimeter is established to bring the crime scene under control. Often, a second perimeter is established within the first one so that police and other emergency responders who have a purpose at the scene do not arbitrarily enter or damage the scene further. Factors such as the size of the crime

scene, lighting, and environmental conditions are all taken into consideration. Assessment then involves determining the full scope of the crime scene, ensuring crime scene integrity, ensuring that any search warrants are correct and signed, developing an appropriate team approach, determining an appropriate search technique, and ensuring the safety of the crime scene investigation team.

2. **Observing**: At this step, the crime scene investigator looks for persons and objects in plain sight. The investigator carefully examines the scene and observes details and content that may be altered by subsequent crime scene processing (such as the order of bedding on top of a victim) or altered by time (such as ice cubes in a glass). The investigator will often locate a vantage point near the perimeter and, simply, stop and look – and then document via notes or audio recording, everything that is seen.
3. **Documenting**: This involves the creation of photographs, video recordings, and sketches that show the full and complete context of the crime scene as found by the investigative team. It also includes notes prepared by the investigator during the initial scene observation. Order and purpose are most important, and nothing is done out of sequence. Photographs are often taken in groups of three: an overall photo that captures the condition of the scene before any alteration can occur, a photo that establishes evidence to show its context within the scene, and a close-up photo to show detail that may not be otherwise evident. The investigator will often use a marker containing a ruler to frame evidence-establishing and close-up photographs. Sketches, similar to floor plans, are often drawn to map the crime scene and show the relationship of objects in a room with objects in other rooms.
4. **Searching**: Searching the crime scene is an intrusive process and is done only after the scene context is documented. Searching ensures that all evidence and details are noted, and critical observation plays an important role throughout this step. Objects may be found beneath, behind, or inside other objects, or in positions where easy observation is not possible. Crime scene searches are conducted in multiple iterations to ensure that all evidence is located and nothing is missed.
5. **Collecting**: Collecting evidence is an intrusive process. Evidence must be collected without destroying or damaging that evidence since improperly collected evidence can prevent or cause problems with its subsequent analysis. Collection must be done with the forensic analyst in mind and evidence must be secured in the most appropriate method possible. The only exception that allows collection to be done prior to documentation is if the evidence is fragile and is prone to significant alteration as crime scene processing unfolds – such as in the case of a shoe mark in dirt as a storm is imminent, or a small fiber on the floor at the crime scene. When fragile evidence is collected, documentation must take place immediately following the collection. The onus is on the investigator to know what kinds of evidence are possible at any given crime scene.
6. **Analyzing**: Finally, analysis of the crime scene completes the process. Such on-scene analysis includes examining bullet trajectories or defining the origin of a blood spatter pattern. It can also include processing surfaces with various chemicals for fingerprints. On-scene analysis is always intrusive and is done only after all other evidence items are documented and collected. During analysis, the investigator could encounter new evidence and must then be prepared to backtrack and reprocess the scene to ensure that the new evidence is fully documented.

With these six steps in mind, students are often asked to look around the scene, pick out evidence, and attempt to exploit it for its probative value. Two questions are asked: 1) What hints and clues are there? and 2) How does this help us solve the crime? These questions form the basis for the class instruction.

A game-based augmented reality application has several advantages to this more traditional method of crime scene investigation training: 1) it creates a dynamic environment and frees both the trainer and the student from the confines of a house or other facility where staged sets are used; 2) it is available on demand; 3) evidence can be identified, gathered, and tagged without disturbing the original crime scene; 4) the crime scene can be reset multiple times within a few seconds; and 5) it appeals to college students who are already comfortable with the use of smartphone applications.

Within a 21st Century context, traditional crime scene investigation training is somewhat archaic. It is time consuming for the trainer and ultimately unsatisfactory for the graduate once in the field. Small changes can and should be made to bring CSI into a modern context. Currently, tape measures are used to determine the distance between, for example, the body of a victim and blood spatter on a wall. The distance and angle can suggest possible positions for where people and objects were during the crime – but two people are required, one at each end. An electronic laser device that measures both distance and angle is just as accurate and can be used without the need for a second person.

While this traditional method of training has been reliably tested over the years, today's students may actually prefer a different training method. Today's students – those born after 1988, who grew up in a digital, media-saturated world, and who are nicknamed digital natives – increasingly prefer a digital approach to their studies (Palfrey & Gasser, 2013). Anderson and Jiang (2018) indicate that smartphone ownership is now at 95% among teens. Potnis and Allard (2018) note that as many as 76% of students have used their smartphone to specifically access academic information and digital natives have expectations that correspond to quick and convenient access to information. Further, Ma, Steger, Doolittle and Stewart (2018) note that smartphones have both permeated the academic environment and can facilitate collaboration through engagement. To that end, a markerless game-based augmented reality application is one potential solution for teaching crime scene investigation skills to students who prefer a digital learning environment.

AUGMENTED REALITY IN EDUCATION AND TRAINING

Augmented reality is generally described as a digital experience in which computer-generated, location-specific content is used to enhance the real world (Yuen, Yaoyuneyong, & Johnson, 2011). Augmented reality seamlessly integrates digital information with a user's environment in real time (Bacca, Baldiris, Fabregat, Graf, & Kinshuk, 2014; Bower, Howe, McCredie, Robinson, & Grover, 2014; Zak, 2014).

Augmented reality differs from virtual reality in that virtual reality gives the user a sense of presence – that is, of actually being in that environment rather than simply observing that environment (Ausburn and Ausburn, 2010) and that virtual reality presence refers to the illusion of non-mediation. Non-mediation is the sense that the user has actually been somewhere. The person is not merely an observer in the virtual reality activity, but an active, immersed participant (Rothbaum, Hodges, Smith, Lee, & Price, 2000). Where virtual reality creates a full-immersion simulation to mimic true reality, augmented reality uses overlays to enhance reality – so augmented reality lies midway between the real environment and the virtual environment; it bridges the gap between them in a seamless way (Lee, 2012). Augmented reality is less complex than virtual reality and can introduce digital information such as audio, video, graphics, and satellite-based global positioning system (GPS) data into a real environment. Where virtual reality has focused on sophisticated head-mounted displays linked to a computer, augmented reality has focused almost exclusively on mobile broadband devices (Wasko, 2013) and the most common form of augmented reality is through the integration of GPS data and graphics as an application for a smartphone.

A Brief History Leading to a Paradigm Shift

In 1901, author L. Frank Baum, perhaps best known for his book *The Wonderful Wizard of Oz*, described the use of an augmented reality device. In his book, *The Master Key*, Baum described a display device that overlays data onto real life. In the book, a boy accidentally touches the Master Key of Electricity and encounters a creature who gives him a gift. Baum writes:

Therefore, that you may judge all your fellow-creatures truly, and know upon whom to depend, I give you the Character Marker. It consists of this pair of spectacles. While you wear them every one you meet will be marked upon the forehead with a letter indicating his or her character. The good will bear the letter 'G,' the evil the letter 'E.' The wise will be marked with a 'W' and the foolish with an 'F.' The kind will show a 'K' upon their foreheads and the cruel a letter 'C.' Thus you may determine by a single look the true natures of all those you encounter. (p. 94)

The character marker pair of spectacles nicely foreshadows some of the features used in modern day augmented reality devices. It is unlikely that Baum could have predicted the wealth of augmented reality devices we know today or the many ways in which augmented reality would impact our lives, but markers are still used today as part of an augmented reality display. While its entertainment value is certainly well known, the use of augmented reality in simulations and trainings is slowly coming into its own as a teaching tool, but it still has not been widely adopted despite being used for training and education as far back as the late 1920s. In 1929, Edward Link introduced the Link Trainer – a flight simulator to aid and enhance pilot training.

Simulation entered medical student training in the 1930s with the introduction of the simulated patient (Gaba, 2004). Decades later, driven by the development of high-end graphics for computer gaming, the realism needed to catapult the potential of augmented reality in medical student education was realized (Macedonia, 2002; Rosen, 2008). In the 1990s, high-fidelity patient models were introduced to medical student training. They offered realistic joints, skin tension, muscles, and in some of the more sophisticated models, a functioning heart and lung system (Gordon, Wilkerson, Shaffer, & Armstrong, 2001; Rodgers, Securro, & Pauley, 2009).

In addition to medical and military combat training, such simulations have now entered the fields of air traffic control (Glover & Lygeros, 2004), hazardous waste management (West, Slatin, Sanborn, & Volicer, 2009), and firefighting (Dugdale, Pavard, Pallamin, el-Jed, & Maugan, 2004), and they continue to be used in helicopter, airplane, naval, and submarine training (Macedonia, 2002; Rosen, 2008). Simulation training technology provides a valuable hands-on learning experience without risk of damage to equipment, and without risk of harm to students, instructors, clients, and observers. Prior to 2007, and due to the cost of developing high quality models, augmented reality was largely limited to the domains of medicine, firefighting, the military, and other high-risk professions, but its popularity was about to explode. A paradigm shift was imminent; in 2007, Apple introduced the iPhone.

In 2007, a convergence of technology laid the groundwork for the explosive growth of augmented reality: broadband Internet access was widely available, many companies were building cellular networks using site towers across the U.S., digital natives were going off to college and, perhaps most importantly,

Apple introduced the iPhone. The iPhone was the first mobile device that supported an operating system (iOS), a touch screen, a camera, an MP3 player, a calculator, a virtual keyboard, Wi-Fi capability for broadband Internet access, and a GPS locator for navigation (Carmigniani et al., 2011; Yuen et al., 2011). It was also a phone! One of the most significant features of the iPhone was the user's ability to download applications that extended and enhanced the iPhone's capabilities – so an already useful device became not only more powerful, but also more personal.

In 2008, the first Android smartphone based on the Linux operating system was released by T-Mobile Communications. By 2015, the iPhone would hold over 43% of the smartphone market, with the top three Android manufacturers (Samsung, LG, and Motorola) holding 27%, 9% and 4% of the market share respectively (Heisler, 2015). Coupled with the increasing availability of applications, there was an explosive growth of smartphones which heralded the first popular use of augmented reality in higher education, although the use of augmented reality in the K-12 classroom would not become practical until 2010, when Apple released the iPad (Green, Lea, & McNair, 2014).

Early Use of Augmented Reality in Education

In higher education, augmented reality was quickly introduced into a variety of courses:, mathematics, engineering, geometry, medicine, e-learning systems, e-commerce, architecture, science education, and interior design (Billinghurst & Henrysson, 2009; Cho, Lee, Lee, & Yang, 2007; von Jan, Noll, Behrends, & Albrecht, 2012; Kaufmann, Schmalstieg, & Wagner, 2000; Liarokapis, 2006; Liarokapis et al., 2004; Noh, Sunar, & Pan, 2009; Phan & Choo, 2010; Shelton & Hedley, 2002; Zhu, Owen, Li, & Lee, 2004). Yuen et al. (2011) note that augmented reality has the potential to both engage and motivate students. Indeed, considerable education resources are now being directed at mobile augmented reality systems for use in education (Bower et al., 2014).

One of the best known early uses of augmented reality in education was a game called Mad City Mystery®. The game's purpose was to help students develop scientific argumentation skills by solving a puzzle. In the game-based scenario students could take on the role of a doctor with information about the medical history of the characters, an environmental expert with information about local toxins, or a government official with similar information. Students had to work collaboratively in groups of three, and to solve the puzzle they were required to read texts, understand and discuss their meaning, and formulate ideas based on those readings. They had to speculate based on what they read while looking for new information to aid their understanding (Squire & Jan, 2007).

In 2008, a group at Harvard University created HARP – the Handheld Augmented Reality Project. They designed a game called Alien Contact! to teach math skills to middle and high school students. Their goal was to study a designed learning environment using augmented reality and a wireless handheld device with GPS. As students moved around, a map on the device displayed objects and virtual people superimposed on their location. The game required students to work in teams of four (roleplaying as a chemist, cryptologist, computer hacker, or FBI agent) to solve math puzzles and determine the alien's true intent. Similar to Mad City Mystery®, the students must work collaboratively to solve the scenario (O'Shea, Mitchell, Johnston, & Dede, 2009).

2010 and Onward

Apple introduced the iPad in 2010 and schools quickly realized its tremendous potential due to its low cost relative to a laptop computer, ease of use, and its storehouse of existing applications. Within a few months, educational applications became available for a wide range of school subjects including science, mathematics, geography, chemistry, history, computer science, sociology, engineering, and ethics (Crellin, Adda, & Duke-Williams, 2010; Estapa & Nadonly, 2015; Kaufmann et al., 2000; Lee, 2012; Merchant, Goetz, Cifuentes, Keeney-Kennicutt, & Davis, 2014; Warburton, 2009). Many schools began to adopt 1:1 programs where each student in a class had an iPad for his or her own use. This made education personal for students and gave them both a hands-on approach and more control over their own education (Foote, 2012). The 1:1 programs, however, were not without problems; inventory control including loss or damaged units was a constant issue (Hoffman, 2013).

The use of smartphone applications in such areas as medical training was also being tested. In their study of medical students' use of augmented reality with a smartphone, Albrecht, Folta-Schoofs, Behrends, and von Jan (2013) found that when tested against the use of text books only, the augmented reality component caused a significant improvement in diagnosis and prognosis performance. The ability to visualize a wound on a patient was more valuable than a static photo of the same wound printed in a text book.

Constructivist theory is almost always evident in an augmented reality environment since students are free to explore and learn either on their own or with minimal guidance from the teacher. The students can create and ponder their own spaces (Wasko, 2013). In the past few years, educators have started to see new possibilities in the classroom as a result of the 2016 frenzy surrounding Pokémon GO®. Hoping to capitalize on the game's popularity, teachers discovered new possibilities in social studies, local geography, local history, math, mapping, literacy, and physical education (Doran & Davis, 2016). One of the most valuable aspects of augmented reality is the ability to scale objects. Whether a microscopic molecule, a tree, a planet, or the vastness of space, augmented reality can easily display the objects on a handheld device. This allows students to better understand, through direct manipulation, the relationships and properties that exist. Perhaps most importantly of all, augmented reality helps to create an authentic learning environment (Classroom Learning with augmented reality, 2010). Students can explore course material in such areas as astronomy and geography where real-world first-hand experience is neither feasible nor possible.

Vendors also have now started to showcase the viability of augmented reality and are projecting its possible uses in the classroom. Location-based content is available that can help teach about a local environment. Wikitude, a mobile augmented reality technology provider, allows both sights and events to be seen as a layer above a smartphone's display; SekaiCamera allows users to leave notes using text or audio in locations around the world – both valuable sites in a geography or environmental classroom. AdSugar Media has an application that demonstrates the application of physics by using augmented reality models displayed and triggered across multiple mobile smartphones (Bower et al., 2014).

One of the most interesting uses of augmented reality in education, although still in discovery, is augmented reality books. Introduced in 2011, a 42-page book titled *The Future is Wild: The Living Book* demonstrates the potential of augmented reality to encourage reading. Two augmented reality books, one that teaches about the different layers of the Earth's structure and another that animates wildlife while teaching about nature, were published in the last few years (Yuen et al., 2011). Another such augmented reality book provides three-dimensional (3D) characters that appear once readers wear special glasses, similar to the character marker glasses envisioned by Baum in 1901. Although their results were ultimately inconclusive, Cheng and Tsai (2016) studied the interaction of parents and children while reading an augmented reality picture book. What is perhaps most remarkable, is that a study of this sort was undertaken at all.

AUGMENTED REALITY ENTERS LAW ENFORCEMENT

Use in High-Risk Profession Training

In high-risk professions, live training has the potential to cause great harm to oneself or others and so computer-based simulations driven by augmented reality have become the de facto method for student and professional training in medicine and surgery (Ahmed & Dann, 2015; Khan, Aydin, Khan, Dasgupta, & Ahmed, 2015), and in other difficult or dangerous situations. In 1929, Edwin Link introduced a flight simulator, the Link Trainer. Since then, simulation technology has enabled both student and professional pilots to gain experience without endangering life and limb in as close to a real-world situation as possible (Page, 2000). The US Army Air Corps purchased six Link Trainers in 1934 as a result of the deaths of twelve pilots over a 78-day period because the pilots were not familiar with Instrumental Flight Rules. By 1955, the Federal Aviation Administration required commercial pilots to recertify on a simulator to maintain their license (Rosen, 2008). During the early 1960s, the NASA's Gemini program used a combination of both analog and digital simulators, but by the launch of Apollo 7 in 1968, digital simulators were used exclusively for astronaut training. One direct consequence of the Link Trainer was the sophisticated simulation technologies that became available driven by the military's need for high-resolution graphics (Macedonia, 2002).

Use by Law Enforcement

Of the many high-risk, high-danger professions taking advantage of simulation training, law enforcement is notably missing from the list. While the FBI uses simulation for rapid-response and hostage situation training, non-Federal law enforcement has been slow to embrace computer-based augmented reality simulation training for cadets and active duty officers with the possible exception of firearms training and high-speed chase techniques (Forsythe, 2004).

In courtrooms, however, computer-animated crime scene reconstruction is replacing the more traditional photographs and verbal descriptions (Agarwal, Gupta, Gupta, & Gupta, 2011; Gee, Escamilla-Ambrosio, Webb, Mayol-Cuevas, & Calway, 2010; Lee & Pagliaro, 2013). Simulation technology plays an important role by allowing the court members to not just view the crime scene but to experience what happened at a crime scene (Schofield, 2009; Xu, 2012). Computer vision, 3D graphics, motion tracking, natural language visualization, and forensic computing are all changing the landscape of the courtroom. While the level of interactivity and the level of detail are dependent on the crime, their relevance, authenticity, and fairness must still be verified before being used as evidence (Ma, Zheng, & Lallie, 2010).

Although not specific to CSI, a descriptive study of twenty-six forensic science students found that students enhanced their critical thinking through simulation environments (Baker, 2009). Further, 100% of the students reported improved knowledge of forensic evidence collection, and 88% improved their understanding of the investigative process. Baker (2009) noted that role-playing, active learning, and critical thinking were mutually reinforcing in a simulation environment.

While Wethal (2010) notes that CSI is largely a hands-on applied discipline relying on experience and competence, in their study on virtual reality simulation, Grantcharov et al. (2004) determined that confidence, knowledge, and critical decision skills improved significantly for students who train using simulation technology.

Use in Crime Scene Investigation Training

While classroom instruction aids CSI training, Baker (2009) suggests that an augmented reality simulation can be used to achieve a superior field experience. Augmented reality technology can provide the novice crime scene investigator with the opportunity to apply theory and think critically. Further, the best simulations involve learner participation using all of the senses: auditory, visual, and psychomotor (Baker, 2009). An augmented reality simulation can provide hands-on learning that is engaging for the student while teaching creativity, collaboration, and critical thinking skills (Johnson, Adams & Cummins, 2012).

Simulations have been used successfully in medicine, air traffic control, pilot training, law enforcement, firefighting, and other professions (Dugdale et al., 2004; Gaba, 2004; Glover & Lygeros, 2004; Gordon et al., 2001; Page, 2000; Rosen, 2008; Schofield, 2009; Xu, 2012). Wayne et al. (2008) found simulation training to be significantly superior to traditional education because it offered heightened sensory response to a situation. An augmented reality application is one potential solution for providing an enhanced real-world CSI experience for forensic science training that complements the traditional method of CSI training.

MARKER-BASED VS. MARKERLESS AUGMENTED REALITY

There are two main types of augmented reality technology: marker-based and markerless. A marker is simply an image that provides the platform upon which an augmented reality object can be superimposed. With markerless technology, a GPS tracking system coupled with image recognition is used to display the augmented reality information (Lee, 2012). Markerless is the more complex technology of the two.

Both marker-based and markerless technologies require computer software to create the augmented reality images. The two most common software packages used to create such images are Unity® and Vuforia®. While both are free for non-commercial use, Vuforia® requires registration. Creation and manipulation of objects within these two software packages also necessitates knowledge of the C# programming language.

The simplest form of augmented reality for a mobile device uses a marker-based technology. Using marker-based technology, an augmented reality object can be superimposed on the marker. As the marker moves, the augmented reality image moves; as the marker turns, the augmented reality image turns. The augmented reality image, however, can never be removed from the marker; the augmented reality image is always dependent on the existence of the marker. Without the marker, the augmented reality image cannot exist.

Creating a marker-based augmented reality object is a process involving several steps: creating a marker, creating the augmented reality object, and finally bringing all the components together so that they work seamlessly. An effective marker is highly textured with high contrast, no repeating elements, no single focus area, and a good distribution of content. The camera that displays the augmented reality object must be able to see the marker from any angle and at a reasonable distance in order to properly render the augmented reality object.

Once the marker is created, it can then be imported into Unity® as a plane with dimensions visible only on the x and y axes, and while a printed marker has a definite thickness to it (z axis), it is negligible with respect to the camera. Activating a webcam from within Unity® forces focus on the marker and superimposes the object onto or above the plane of the marker. It is also possible to superimpose a dynamic object – an animated object – onto a marker. Unity® does not natively support animated augmented reality objects so a workaround is required. Using Photoshop, it is possible to import an animated GIF, deconstruct the GIF into its component frames or layers, and then create a PSD file that contains an image of the GIF's animation sequence from beginning to end. The PSD file can then be imported into Unity®, which splices the image into its component frames and recompiles the animated sequence. The webcam is then able to project the animated object above the plane of the marker.

Marker-based augmented reality is restrictive because the augmented reality object depends on the existence of the marker. It follows, therefore, that the only viable method for a truly mobile product is through the use of a markerless application. In contrast to marker-based technology, markerless augmented reality technology uses data from a satellite-based GPS or other location-based information to superimpose an augmented reality image on a real environment. Markerless technology allows an application to be used anywhere without the restrictions placed on it by marker-based technology (Bacca et al., 2014).

GAME-BASED AUGMENTED REALITY IN EDUCATION AND TRAINING

As technology advances, there has been an increased desire to enhance learning with emergent technologies to provide students with enriched learning environments (Bacca et al., Radu, 2014). The common approaches to teaching with augmented reality include situated learning, inquiry-based learning, collaborative learning, and game-based learning (Saltan & Arslan, 2017). This section focuses on game-based learning with augmented reality in education and training situations.

Simply described, game-based learning uses a game platform as a learning environment. In this way, game content and game play enhance knowledge and skills while game activities are challenging and involve problem-solving (Qian & Clark, 2016). Many find this type of learning satisfying as they feel a sense of accomplishment when completing tasks and a sense of control over their learning and performance (Qian & Clark, 2016; Crandall et al., 2015). Research has shown that students find game-based learning more engaging than either traditional teaching or by the use of other technology-enhanced teaching methods (Connolly, Boyle, MacArthur, Hainey, & Boyle, 2012; Crandall et al., 2015; Huizenga, Admiraal, Akkerman, & Dam, 2009; Li & Tsai, 2013). However, several factors determine the success of game-based learning. For example, Qian & Clark (2016) suggest that the academic topic, learner preferences, and even participant age can influence learning from games. Conversely, they suggest that some games can fail to engage students if they are narrowly focused on academic content, target lower level literacy, provide drill and practice methods, and stress memorization of facts. Games that provide meaningful learning will combine established learning theories like social constructivism and flow theory with game design elements such as immediate feedback, adaptive challenge, clear goals, variable rewards, and low-stakes failure (Qian & Clark, 2016).

When it is not possible to find a good educational game to fit a class, many educators turn to what is known as gamification. This strategy uses elements of games, such as points, badges, tasks/goals, and levels, in an educational context (Bidarra & Rusman, 2017). Ideally, incorporating the mechanics of gaming into educational activities makes learning more effective and, potentially, more gratifying. To increase engagement and motivation, educators will often add in other gaming elements such as digital narratives, immersive technologies, mobile technologies, and augmented reality.

Augmented reality was first combined with video games in 2000 with ARQuake® v1.2.0, which was developed by Bruce Thomas (Das, Zhu, McLaughlin, Bilgrami, & Milanaik, 2017). A decade later, augmented reality games expanded to mobile technology and several famous augmented reality games, including Zombies, Run! ® v6.1.0 and DJ Rivals® v2.0.2, became popular worldwide. However, this popularity pales in comparison to the release of Pokémon GO®, which was downloaded more than 500 million times and had more than 20 million active users on a daily basis (Das et al., 2017).

Augmented reality games immerse the player in a virtual narrative in which s/he must play a given role that allows her/him to gain authentic knowledge and/or skills that apply to the real world as well as to the game world (Bower et al., 2014; Castellanos & Perez, 2017). The skills learned from playing these games can easily translate to real-life applications (Bower et al., 2014; Mumtaz et al., 2017). Additionally, many of these augmented reality games provide social benefits by giving players online interactions where informal conversations and relationships can develop. For example, Das et al. (2017) suggest that children with autism have positive social interactions with peers and family members when playing Pokémon GO®. Bower et al. (2014) suggest that another benefit from playing augmented reality games is enhanced motivation and authentic learning and/or thinking.

Lee (2012) claims that augmented reality gaming is particularly relevant to education and training in both academic and corporate situations. Augmented reality games can easily be adapted to a variety of subjects and circumstances to allow failsafe practice and problem solving using real-world contexts and tools. These games can improve practical skills, spatial ability, and conceptual understanding with authentic simulated experiences that are thought to increase learner motivation while enhancing learning retention and performance (Barsom, Graafland, & Schijven, 2016; Bendicho, Mora, Añorbe-Díaz, & Rivero-Rodríguez, 2017; Bower et al., 2014). Additionally, augmented reality games can provide access to learning that may be too costly or impractical for a school or organization (Bacca et al., 2014; Bower et al., 2014). Situations such as medical, military, police, first responder, disaster, and triage trainings are too high-risk to allow real-life practice, but augmented reality games allow the simulation of critical situations that give these professionals a failsafe environment in which to practice interaction and complex spatial orientation (Barsom et al., 2016; Foronda et al., 2017).

The rapid advancement of augmented reality games has had a tremendous impact on education and training. Their potential for cognitive and skill-based learning in a failsafe environment makes augmented reality games a tremendous tool for learning.

CSI4FS®: A MARKERLESS GAME-BASED APPLICATION FOR CRIME SCENE INVESTIGATION TRAINING IN DEVELOPMENT

The concept of game-based augmented reality as an educational and training tool is not new (for example ARQuake® and Mad City Mystery®), but the technology is now sufficiently sophisticated that everyone with a smartphone has the required infrastructure to support it (Zak, 2014). For the purposes of a mobile application, a marker-based application is simply not sufficient – because it would be useful only if the user had access to the specific marker. To be fully mobile and usable in any location, a markerless application is required. A markerless application allows the game to be used anywhere without any marker-based restrictions.

The application, Crime Scene Investigation for Forensic Science (CSI4FS®), is a game-based markerless augmented reality application that allows the student to walk through a crime scene, receive and tag important information, collect evidence items into custody, interpret the evidence, and maintain the chain of custody – all without disturbing the original crime scene. A crime scene scenario is given at the beginning of play, and the goal of the game is to solve the mystery. This method has several advantages to the more traditional method of crime scene investigation training: 1) the dynamic environment frees both the trainer and the student from the confines of staged sets; 2) it is available on demand; 3) tagging, identifying, and gathering evidence does not affect the original crime scene; 4) the scenarios can be quickly reset; and 5) college students are already comfortable with the use of smartphone applications. One additional benefit is the ability to easily modify the program for professional development by making the scenarios specific to the needs of each training site or different law enforcement agency.

To make this game-based markerless augmented reality application viable, the underlying infrastructure capable of receiving location services, translating the application's programing, and displaying that information on an Android smartphone must exist. All recent smartphones have the equivalent of a built-in GPS locator and although, strictly speaking, GPS refers only to a U.S.-based satellite navigation system, it has generally come to mean any combination of location services. GPS applications that use actual satellite data are available, but for most purposes, location services use a combination of GPS data coupled with Wi-Fi hotspot or cell tower identification which then use the Internet to query an online database. Often, a smartphone will combine all of these methods to give the best position.

For a user's position to be displayed on a map, the phone must first obtain a map. Most modern map data is obtained in real time over the Internet, but maps can also be downloaded offline or provided on a storage device such as a micro-SD card. Google Maps® is one of the most popular and most often used mapping services for smartphones.

Realization of the CSI4FS® application required the use of the Unity® game engine and the C# programming language. Unity® v5.5.4 was used to create the basic application and to create the augmented reality aspect of the application. The C# scripting language was used to modify the various parameters of the application and to tap into the Android's location services subroutine. Cost of development was not an issue. The Unity® game engine is available at no charge and the time to develop the application was donated freely. It is the author's intent to make the application available free of charge to the education community.

For the initial lesson, game-play was not a consideration. Development centered on getting the application to work by superimposing appropriate augmented reality objects against the real-life background captured by the smartphone's camera. Touching an object on the screen brought up information about crime scene investigation. Among the augmented reality objects used, were a camera, knife, USB flash drive, tablet, cell phone, and other articles often found at a crime scene. That first instructional lesson was alpha- and beta-tested in February and March, 2018 and was released to the public in early April, 2018. Subsequent lessons are currently in development. Alpha-testing refers to the initial release of the application to a select, hand-picked group. Alpha-testers work through the application and report any major problems they encounter. Once those problems are addressed and corrected, the application is then released for beta-testing. Beta-testing involves a much larger group of users – most of whom the author doesn't know. Beta-testers provide valuable feedback covering everything from functionality to appearance. They also report minor issues or personal preferences as a means to improve the application when released to the general public. Alpha- and beta-testing provides valuable information that will ultimately improve the application.

Comments from the various alpha- and beta-testers were favorable. Many enjoyed the simple user interface and the rotation of augmented reality objects. They all agreed that the text was clear and that presenting the simulation in the form of a lesson enhanced both the application's appeal and its usefulness. In response to one tester's suggestion, the text color was subsequently lightened to make it more readable. Another tester suggested including information about the landscape design of the application and to make sure users rotated their devices appropriately. The tester also suggested clarification on the process of touching and holding an object else the on-screen information appears and disappears too quickly to follow. These suggestions were incorporated into the beta release.

There were also comments regarding features for future versions of the application. Several testers suggested the use of a menu screen at the beginning of play so that when several lessons have been developed, users can choose which lesson to review. One suggestion was the use of a toolbar at the top of the screen where, once an augmented reality object was viewed, its icon would then reside in the toolbar. This would help to serve as a checkpoint in case the user wanted to go back and review an item after having already seen the simulation – even within the same lesson. One tester suggested spawning the augmented reality objects in various locations so that the user would then have to hunt around for the objects as a means of making the simulation more interactive. One tester suggested that the application incorporate a portrait design so that the phone did not need to rotate. There also needs to be an increased emphasis on the mystery aspect of the game to make it more enjoyable for the end user. Also, introducing drop-down lists that allowed users to select and pursue different paths of inquiry, even if those paths were ultimately incorrect, would better help the students to focus on correct assessments and analysis.

It is important to note that CSI4FS® is still in development. Game elements such as fun, simplicity, multiple levels of play, story, and graphics will be developed and enhanced as the application evolves. While still basic in terms of development, when fully realized, features of the application will include the ability to tag evidence (e.g. blood spatter, DNA, documents, shell casings, shoe prints, and tire treads), check for signs of arson or explosives, document bullet trajectory, and maintain a chain of custody. After downloading and installing the application, game play will include multiple levels of play with increasing ambiguity to help develop the player's technique, a background story to each crime scene, the ability to assign point values to clues, and the ability to reset the scenario. Because this application was intended to complement traditional crime scene investigation training, two sworn law enforcement officers acted as subject matter experts for the application.

CONCLUSION

Although her lessons and classrooms had filled her head with knowledge, she could thank her trendsetting professor for her skills. It was her third day on the job and she handled herself with confidence and poise. She calmly collected samples and identified blood spatter as she had practiced in her CSI4FS® training scenarios. If her professor had not embraced this new technology, she would be as lost as her partner now looked. Too bad... she would have to help her partner get more hands-on practice to build those crime scene investigation skills. Sigh!

The history of augmented reality spans over 115 years and its place in simulation training dates back to the late 1920s. Medical education has been taking advantage of simulations since the 1930s and high-fidelity patient models were introduced in the 1990s. Augmented reality was introduced to higher education classrooms by 2007 and to the K-12 classroom by 2010. There is currently tremendous room for expansion because augmented reality accounts for less than 6% saturation in the K-12 classroom. As the technology improves and gains a wider user base, the costs will inevitably fall, and augmented reality will likely become a more permanent fixture in the K-12 classroom of tomorrow. For crime scene investigation training, using an augmented reality application such as CSI4FS® will complement the traditional training methods which will appeal to a new generation of learners.

The blending of real-world and virtual-world elements create new learning environments. Students find the interactive features of augmented reality engaging and motivating. Educators appreciate the immersive technology as a way for their students to build knowledge and skills that easily translate into real-world scenarios. With the advancement of augmented reality into trainings, crime scene investigation education is being revolutionized. Given the potential advantages of learning with augmented reality, the pervasiveness of mobile technology, and the adaptability of this technology, a markerless game-based augmented reality application such as CSI4FS® may be the answer to preparing students for the real world of crime scene investigation.

REFERENCES

Agarwal, A., Gupta, M., Gupta, S., & Gupta, S. C. (2011). Systematic digital forensic investigation model. *International Journal of Computer Science and Security*, *5*(1), 118–131.

Ahmed, S., & Dann, S. (2015). The virtual future of education and training. *The Bulletin of the Royal College of Surgeons of England*, *97*(10), 431–432. doi:10.1308/rcsbull.2015.431

Albrecht, U., Folta-Schoofs, K., Behrends, M., & von Jan, U. (2013). Effects of mobile augmented reality learning compared to textbook learning on medical students: Randomized controlled pilot study. *Journal of Medical Internet Research*, *15*(8), e182. doi:10.2196/jmir.2497 PMID:23963306

Anderson, M., & Jiang, J. (2018). *Teens, social media & technology 2018*. Washington, DC: Pew Internet & American Life Project. Retrieved from http://publicservicesalliance.org/ wp-content/uploads/2018/06/Teens-Social-Media-Technology-2018-PEW.pdf

Ausburn, L. J., & Ausburn, F. B. (2010, December). Spheres of reality: A conceptualization of desktop virtual environments in career and technical education and an implementation training model. *Proceedings of the National Career and Technical Education Research and Professional Development Conference.* Retrieved from http://citeseerx.ist.psu.edu/viewdoc/download?doi=10.1.1.454.7019&rep=rep1&type=pdf

Bacca, J., Baldiris, S., Fabregat, R., & Graf, S., & Kinshuk. (2014). Augmented reality trends in education: A systematic review of research and applications. *Journal of Educational Technology & Society*, *17*(4), 133–149.

Baker, T. E. (2009). Police Criminalistics: Learning Modalities and Evaluation. *Forensic Examiner*, *18*(3), 52–56.

Barsom, E. Z., Graafland, M., & Schijven, M. P. (2016). Systematic review on the effectiveness of augmented reality applications in medical training. *Surgical Endoscopy*, *30*(10), 4174–4183. doi:10.100700464-016-4800-6 PMID:26905573

Baum, L. F. (1901). *The master key: An electrical fairy tale*. Indianapolis, IN: Bowen-Merrill Company.

Bendicho, P. F., Mora, C. E., Añorbe-Díaz, B., & Rivero-Rodríguez, P. (2017). Effect on Academic Procrastination after Introducing Augmented Reality. *EURASIA Journal of Mathematics, Science & Technology Education*, *13*(2), 319–330.

Bidarra, J., & Rusman, E. (2017). Towards a pedagogical model for science education: bridging educational contexts through a blended learning approach. *Open Learning: The Journal of Open, Distance and E-Learning, 32*(1), 6-20.

Billinghurst, M., & Henrysson, A. (2009). Mobile architectural augmented reality. *Mixed Reality in Architecture, Design and Construction*, 93-104.

Bower, M., Howe, C., McCredie, N., Robinson, A., & Grover, D. (2014). Augmented Reality in education – cases, places and potentials. *Educational Media International*, *51*(1), 1–15. doi:10.1080/09523987.2014.889400

Carmigniani, J., Furht, B., Anisetti, M., Ceravolo, P., Damiani, E., & Ivkovic, M. (2011). Augmented reality technologies, systems and applications. *Multimedia Tools and Applications*, *51*(1), 341–377. doi:10.100711042-010-0660-6

Castellanos & Perez, (2017). New Challenge in Education: Enhancing Student's Knowledge through Augmented Reality. *Augmented Reality*, 273-293.

Cheng, K., & Tsai, C. (2016). The interaction of child-parent shared reading with an augmented reality (AR) picture book and parents' conceptions of AR learning. *British Journal of Educational Technology*, *47*(1), 203–222. doi:10.1111/bjet.12228

Cho, K., Lee, J., Lee, J. S., & Yang, H. S. (2007, September). A realistic e-learning system based on mixed reality. In *13th International Conference on Virtual Systems and Multimedia* (pp. 57-64). Academic Press.

Classroom Learning with augmented reality. (2010). *Trends in EdTech Wiki*. Retrieved from http://aug-reality.pbworks.com/w/page/9469033/Classroom%20Learning%20with%20AR

Connolly, T. M., Boyle, E. A., MacArthur, E., Hainey, T., & Boyle, J. M. (2012). A systematic literature review of empirical evidence on computer games and serious games. *Computers & Education*, *59*(2), 661–686. doi:10.1016/j.compedu.2012.03.004

Crandall, P. G., Engler, R. K. III, Beck, D. E., Killian, S. A., O'Bryan, C. A., Jarvis, N., & Clausen, E. (2015). Development of an augmented reality game to teach abstract concepts in food chemistry. *Journal of Food Science Education*, *14*(1), 18–23. doi:10.1111/1541-4329.12048

Crellin, J., Adda, M., & Duke-Williams, E. (2010). The use of simulation in digital forensics teaching. *11th Annual Conference of the Higher Education Academy, Information and Computer Science Group*. Retrieved from http://eprints.port.ac.uk/1597/1/Crellin1.pdf

Das, P., Zhu, M. O., McLaughlin, L., Bilgrami, Z., & Milanaik, R. L. (2017). Augmented Reality Video Games: New Possibilities and Implications for Children and Adolescents. *Multimodal Technologies and Interaction, 1*(2), 8. doi:10.3390/mti1020008

Doran, L., & Davis, M. R. (2016). As Pokémon craze grows, educators weigh game's value. *Education Week, 35*(37).

Dugdale, J., Pavard, B., Pallamin, N., el-Jed, M., & Maugan, L. (2004). Emergency fire incident training in a virtual world. *Proceedings ISCRAM*, 167-172.

Estapa, A., & Nadonly, L. (2015). The effect of an augmented reality enhanced mathematics lesson on student achievement and motivation. *Journal of STEM Education: Innovations & Research, 16*(3), 40–48.

Foote, C. (2012). The evolution of a 1:1 iPad program. *Internet Schools, 1*(15-18).

Forensic Education Program Accreditation Commission. (2017). *Forensic Education Program Accreditation Commission (FEPAC) accreditation standards.* Author.

Foronda, C. L., Alfes, C. M., Dev, P., Kleinheksel, A. J., Nelson, D. A. Jr, O'Donnell, J. M., & Samosky, J. T. (2017). Virtually Nursing: Emerging Technologies in Nursing Education. *Nurse Educator, 42*(1), 14–17. doi:10.1097/NNE.0000000000000295 PMID:27454054

Forsythe, C. (2004). The future of simulation technology for law enforcement: Diverse experience with realistic simulated humans. *FBI Law Enforcement Bulletin, 73*(1), 19–23.

Gaba, D. M. (2004). The future vision of simulation in health care. *Quality & Safety in Health Care, 13*(Suppl.1), i2–i10. doi:10.1136/qshc.2004.009878 PMID:15465951

Gardner, R. M., & Bevel, T. (2009). *Practical crime scene analysis and reconstruction.* CRC Press. doi:10.1201/9781420065527

Gee, A. P., Escamilla-Ambrosio, P. J., Webb, M., Mayol-Cuevas, W., & Calway, A. (2010). Augmented crime scenes: Virtual annotation of physical environments for forensic investigation. In *Proceedings of the 2nd ACM Workshop on Multimedia in Forensics, Security and Intelligence* (pp. 105-110). ACM. 10.1145/1877972.1877999

Glover, W., & Lygeros, J. (2004). A stochastic hybrid model for air traffic control simulation. *Hybrid Systems: Computation and Control, 2993*, 372–386.

Gordon, J. A., Wilkerson, W. M., Shaffer, D. W., & Armstrong, E. G. (2001). "Practicing" medicine without risk: Students' and educators' responses to high-fidelity patient simulation. *Academic Medicine, 76*(5), 469–472. doi:10.1097/00001888-200105000-00019 PMID:11346525

Grantcharov, T. P., Kristiansen, V. B., Bendix, J., Bardram, L., Rosenberg, J., & Funch-Jensen, P. (2004). Randomized clinical trial of virtual reality simulation for laparoscopic skills training. *British Journal of Surgery, 91*(2), 146–150. doi:10.1002/bjs.4407 PMID:14760660

Green, M., Lea, J. H., & McNair, C. L. (2014). Reality check: Augmented reality for school libraries. *Teacher Librarian, 41*(5), 28–34.

Heisler, Y. (2015, November 9). Samsung keeps bleeding market share to Apple's benefit. *BGR News*. Retrieved from http://bgr.com/2015/11/09/iphone-vs-samsung-apple-marketshare/

Hoffman, A. M. (2013). Students' perceptions of on-task behavior and classroom engagement in a 1:1 iPad school. *English Leadership Quarterly*, *36*(2), 9–18.

Huizenga, J., Admiraal, W., Akkerman, S., & Dam, G. T. (2009). Mobile game-based learning in secondary education: Engagement, motivation and learning in a mobile city game. *Journal of Computer Assisted Learning*, *25*(4), 332–344. doi:10.1111/j.1365-2729.2009.00316.x

Johnson, L., Adams, S., & Cummins, M. (2012). The NMC horizon report: 2012 higher education edition. *The New Media Consortium*. Retrieved from http://bibliotecadigital. org/bitstream/001/563/1/2012-Horizon-Report-HE.pdf

Kaufmann, H., Schmalstieg, D., & Wagner, M. (2000). Construct3D: A virtual reality application for mathematics and geometry education. *Education and Information Technologies*, *5*(4), 263–276. doi:10.1023/A:1012049406877

Khan, R., Aydin, A., Khan, M. S., Dasgupta, P., & Ahmed, K. (2015). Simulation-based training for prostate surgery. *BJU International*, *116*(4), 665–674. doi:10.1111/bju.12721 PMID:24588806

Lee, H. C., & Pagliaro, E. M. (2013). Forensic evidence and CSI. *Journal of Forensic Investigation.*, *1*(2), 5.

Lee, K. (2012). Augmented reality in education and training. *TechTrends*, *56*(2), 13–21. doi:10.100711528-012-0559-3

Li, M. C., & Tsai, C. C. (2013). Game-based learning in science education: A review of relevant research. *Journal of Science Education and Technology*, *22*(6), 877–898. doi:10.100710956-013-9436-x

Liarokapis, F. (2006). An exploration from virtual to augmented reality gaming. *Simulation & Gaming*, *37*(4), 507–533. doi:10.1177/1046878106293684

Liarokapis, F., Mourkoussis, N., White, M., Darcy, J., Sifniotis, M., Petridis, P., ... Lister, P. F. (2004). Web3D and augmented reality to support engineering education. *World Transactions on Engineering and Technology Education*, *3*(1), 11–14.

Ma, M., Zheng, H., & Lallie, H. (2010). Virtual reality and 3D animation in forensic visualization. *Journal of Forensic Sciences*, *55*(5), 1227–1231. doi:10.1111/j.1556-4029.2010.01453.x PMID:20533989

Ma, S., Steger, D. G., Doolittle, P. E., & Stewart, A. C. (2018). Improved Academic performance and student perceptions of learning through use of a cell phone-based personal response system. *Journal of Food Science Education*, *17*(1), 27–32. doi:10.1111/1541-4329.12131

Macedonia, M. (2002). Games, simulation, and the military education dilemma. In *Internet and the University: 2001* (pp. 157–167). Forum. Retrieved from https://net.educause.edu/ir/ library/pdf/ffpiu018.pdf

Merchant, Z., Goetz, E. T., Cifuentes, L., Keeney-Kennicutt, W., & Davis, T. J. (2014). Effectiveness of virtual reality-based instruction on students' learning outcomes in K-12 and higher education: A meta-analysis. *Computers & Education*, *70*, 29–40. doi:10.1016/j.compedu.2013.07.033

Mumtaz, K., Iqbal, M. M., Khalid, S., Rafiq, T., Owais, S. M., & Al Achhab, M. (2017). An E-Assessment Framework for Blended Learning with Augmented Reality to Enhance the Student Learning. *Eurasia Journal of Mathematics. Science & Technology Education, 13*(8), 4419–4436.

Noh, Z., Sunar, M. S., & Pan, Z. (2009, August). A review on augmented reality for virtual heritage system. In *International Conference on Technologies for E-Learning and Digital Entertainment* (pp. 50-61). Springer Berlin Heidelberg. 10.1007/978-3-642-03364-3_7

O'Shea, P., Mitchell, R., Johnston, C., & Dede, C. (2009). Lessons learned about designing augmented realities. *International Journal of Gaming and Computer-Mediated Simulations, 1*(1), 1–15. doi:10.4018/jgcms.2009010101

Page, R. L. (2000). Brief history of flight simulation. *SimTecT 2000 Proceedings*, 11-17.

Palfrey, J. G., & Gasser, U. (2013). *Born digital: Understanding the first generation of digital natives.* Basic Books.

Parametric Technology Corporation. (2016). *Vuforia® Plug-in for Unity® v6.2.10* [Computer Software]. Available from http://www.vuforia.com

Phan, V. T., & Choo, S. Y. (2010). Interior design in augmented reality environment. *International Journal of Computers and Applications, 5*(5).

Potnis, D., & Allard, S. (2018). Training LIS Students as Mobile Technology Consultants for Libraries and Not-for-profit Organizations. *Journal of Education for Library and Information Science, 59*(4), 253–264. doi:10.3138/jelis.59.4.2018-0002

Qian, M., & Clark, K. R. (2016). Game-based Learning and 21st century skills: A review of recent research. *Computers in Human Behavior, 63*, 50–58. doi:10.1016/j.chb.2016.05.023

Radu, I. (2014). Augmented reality in education: A meta-review and cross-media analysis. *Personal and Ubiquitous Computing, 18*(6), 1533–1543. doi:10.100700779-013-0747-y

Rodgers, D. L., Securro, S. Jr, & Pauley, R. D. (2009). The effect of high-fidelity simulation on educational outcomes in an advanced cardiovascular life support course. *Simulation in Healthcare, 4*(4), 200–206. doi:10.1097/SIH.0b013e3181b1b877 PMID:21330792

Rosen, K. R. (2008). The history of medical simulation. *Journal of Critical Care, 23*(2), 157–166. doi:10.1016/j.jcrc.2007.12.004 PMID:18538206

Rothbaum, B. O., Hodges, L., Smith, S., Lee, J. H., & Price, L. (2000). A controlled study of virtual reality exposure therapy for the fear of flying. *Journal of Consulting and Clinical Psychology, 68*(6), 1020–1026. doi:10.1037/0022-006X.68.6.1020 PMID:11142535

Saltan, F., & Arslan, Ö. (2017). The Use of Augmented Reality in Formal Education: A Scoping Review. *Eurasia Journal of Mathematics, Science & Technology Education, 13*(2).

Schofield, D. (2009). Animating evidence: Computer game technology in the courtroom. *Journal of Information Law and Technology*, *1*, 1–21.

Schweitzer, N. J., & Saks, M. J. (2007). The CSI effect: popular fiction about forensic science affects the public's expectations about real forensic science. *Jurimetrics: The Journal of Law, Science, and Technology*, 357-364.

Shelton, B. E., & Hedley, N. R. (2002). Using augmented reality for teaching earth-sun relationships to undergraduate geography students. In *Augmented Reality Toolkit, The First IEEE International Workshop* (pp. 8-pp). IEEE. 10.1109/ART.2002.1106948

Squire, K. D., & Jan, M. (2007). Mad City Mystery®: Developing scientific argumentation skills with a place-based augmented reality game on handheld computers. *Journal of Science Education and Technology*, *16*(1), 5–29. doi:10.100710956-006-9037-z

Unity Technologies. (2017). *Unity® v5.5.4* [Computer Software]. Available from http://www.unity3d.com

von Jan, U., Noll, C., Behrends, M., & Albrecht, U. V. (2012). mARble – Augmented reality in medical education. *Biomedizinische Technik. Biomedical Engineering*, *57*(Suppl. 1), 67–70. doi:10.1515/bmt-2012-4252

Warburton, S. (2009). Second Life in higher education: Assessing the potential for and the barriers to deploying virtual worlds in learning and teaching. *British Journal of Educational Technology*, *40*(3), 414–426. doi:10.1111/j.1467-8535.2009.00952.x

Wasko, C. (2013). What teachers need to know about augmented reality enhanced learning environments. *TechTrends*, *57*(4), 17–21. doi:10.100711528-013-0672-y

Wayne, D. B., Didwania, A., Feinglass, J., Fudala, M. J., Barsuk, J. H., & McGaghie, W. C. (2008). Simulation-based education improves quality of care during cardiac arrest team responses at an academic teaching hospital: A case-control study. *Chest Journal*, *133*(1), 56–61. doi:10.1378/chest.07-0131 PMID:17573509

Weaver, R., Salamonson, Y., Koch, J., & Porter, G. (2012). The CSI effect at university: Forensic science students' television viewing and perceptions of ethical issues. *The Australian Journal of Forensic Sciences*, *44*(4), 381–391. doi:10.1080/00450618.2012.691547

West, C., Slatin, C., Sanborn, W., & Volicer, B. (2009). Computer-based simulation in blended learning curriculum for hazardous waste site worker health and safety training. *International Journal of Information and Communication Technology Education*, *5*(1), 62–73. doi:10.4018/jicte.2009010105 PMID:19430576

Wethal, T. (2010, March). Beyond books & lecture: Students and law enforcement get hands-on experience in the Marshall University crime scene house. *Law Enforcement Technology*, 46–50.

Xu, F. (2012). Crime scene reconstruction based on virtual reality. *Journal of Criminal Law*, *17*(3), 149–160.

Yuen, S., Yaoyuneyong, G., & Johnson, E. (2011). Augmented reality: An overview and five directions for augmented reality in education. *Journal of Educational Technology Development and Exchange*, *4*(1), 119–140. doi:10.18785/jetde.0401.10

Zak, E. (2014). Do you believe in magic? Exploring the conceptualization of augmented reality and its implications for the user in the field of library and information science. *Information Technology and Libraries (Online)*, *33*(4), 23–50.

Zhu, W., Owen, C. B., Li, H., & Lee, J. H. (2004). Personalized in-store e-commerce with the promopad: An augmented reality shopping assistant. *Electronic Journal for E-commerce Tools and Applications*, *1*(3), 1–19.

KEY TERMS AND DEFINITIONS

C#: A computer scripting language.

CSI: Crime scene investigation.

Forensic Science: Any science that can be used in the legal system.

Game-Based Learning: A type of game play that has defined learning outcomes.

Higher Education: Education beyond 12th grade.

Law Enforcement: A system that enforces the laws governing a society.

Marker-Based Technology: A type of augmented reality that uses a real object to display digitally created objects.

Unity: A software program used to create digital environments.

Chapter 13
A Constructivist Desktop Virtual Reality-Based Approach to Learning in a Higher Education Institution

Serpil Meri-Yilan
https://orcid.org/0000-0003-1132-568X
Agri Ibrahim Cecen University, Turkey

ABSTRACT

Virtual reality (VR) technology has recently started shaping learning, especially language learning, with the aim of immersing learners into a VR learning environment. However, because of the high system cost of fully immersive VR, desktop VR has been implemented and preferred in educational settings. Based on a constructivist approach, desktop VR has drawn attention to the need for learner autonomy and an authentic VR learning environment. Therefore, this chapter describes empirical research on desktop VR-based learning using a constructivist approach. The research examined university students' interaction and perceptions of learning in this kind of learning environment. Based on the empirical findings gathered from observations and interviews, this chapter has aimed to discuss not only the issues observed both in previous studies and in this chapter, but also additional issues such as scaffolding, self-paced learning, collaboration, and learner differences in order for learning to occur in a well-designed desktop VR learning environment.

INTRODUCTION

The use of Information and Communication Technology (ICT) has been the target of the researchers and educators for decades to create a more efficient language-learning environment (Blake, 1998). The recent research on ICT has gone beyond regarding 'the computer as a tool or partner' but has focused on regarding 'it as a virtual environment where' (Schwienhorst, 2002, p.196) interaction can happen. The interaction in a virtual learning environment can be between students and teachers; students and

DOI: 10.4018/978-1-5225-7987-8.ch013

students; and students and the learning content, tool or online materials. As language and interaction have a fundamental relationship, especially in second and foreign language learning (Loewen & Sato, 2018), various pedagogical interventions have been embedded in the learning environment to foster the relationship between language and interaction. With the incorporation of ICT into language learning, pedagogical interventions have been provided through synchronous or asynchronous computer-mediated communication (Young, 2018), Massive Open Online Courses (MOOCs) (Lambert & Hassan, 2018), mobile-assisted language learning (Botero, Questier, Cincinnato, He & Zhu, 2018) or virtual worlds (Yeh & Wan, 2019).

The advancement in language learning through the abovementioned pedagogical interventions indicates the diversity of interaction in e-learning settings. Learners are engaged with peers or their teacher in person in face-to-face learning, whereas, in online courses, they interact with others via discussion boards or forums, learning content individually and connecting with each other synchronously or asynchronously. Using mobile phones enables learners to exchange information, for instance, within an application anytime and anywhere, whereas virtual worlds create a learning environment where they can improve their learning alone or collaboratively. Despite all these pedagogical inventions, learner interaction within a virtual learning environment has been largely ignored when discussing language learning through ICT.

The gap in fostering interaction via ICT has drawn attention to Virtual Reality (VR). VR has recently been regarded as an efficient and educational tool (Lee, Wong, & Fung, 2009; Martín-Gutiérrez, Mora, Añorbe-Díaz, & González-Marrero, 2017) to teach courses, from science and engineering education (de Jong, Linn, & Zacharia, 2013) to geography (Virvou & Katsionis, 2008) to language learning (Repetto, 2014). VR is described as 'the use of computer graphics systems in combination with various display and interface devices to provide the effect of immersion in the interactive 3D computer-generated environment' (Pan, Cheok, Yang, Zhu & Shi, 2006, p.20). Its efficiency is related to its availability and mobility on desktops (Madathil, Frady, Hartley, Bertrand & Alfred, 2017), and the promotion of learner interaction (Fernandes, Raja, & Eyre, 2003; Madathil et al., 2017). Interaction is an essential component in language learning (Loewen & Sato, 2018), and VR can address this in conjunction with learner engagement. On the one hand, VR has been widely used for adult education in universities (Ott & Freina, 2015), particularly in research on language processes (Repetto, 2014). On the other hand, research has drawn attention to the drawbacks and limits of language learning in VR with regard to the pedagogical and diversity-related concerns in a language-learning environment (Prensky, 2016).

Therefore, this chapter addresses the research gap in interaction and learning through virtual reality based programs in higher education. It sets out to answer two research questions:

1. How do learners interact with a desktop-VR based learning environment?
2. What do learners think about their learning in a desktop-VR based learning environment?

This chapter describes desktop VR for language learning and discusses a constructivist approach in VR learning before presenting previous studies on learners' experience and perception of learning in desktop VR. Next, it introduces empirical findings from Turkish students' use of VR software and ultimately provides suggestions for improving VR for language learning.

BACKGROUND

Desktop VR-Based Learning

VR is classified into two types: immersive and non-immersive (Mills & Noyes, 1999; Suh & Lee, 2005). In immersive VR, using interactive devices such as a head-mounted display (HMD), glove and helmet is important for users to be 'surrounded by the enclosed virtual learning environments' (Suh & Lee, 2005, p.675). According to Bowman, Kruijff, LaViola and Poupyrev (2001), immersive VR with interactive devices enables users to experience 'movement of the viewpoint from one location to another' (p.98). Witmer and Singer (1998) define this action as presence, 'the subjective experience of being in one place or environment, even when one is physically situated in another' (p.225). In non-immersive, sometimes called desktop, VR (Mujber, Szecsi & Hashmi, 2004), 'the interactive three-dimensional (3-D) computer generated program in a multimedia environment is presented on a conventional personal computer and is usually explored using keyboard, mouse, wand, joystick or touch screen' (Lee et al., 2009, p.832). 'Games, simulations or virtual worlds' (Lee & Wong, 2014, p.2) can be considered desktop VR learning environments. Considering the research of Lee and Wong (2014), this chapter regards non-immersive VR as desktop VR without using interactive devices such as a head-mounted display (HMD), glove and helmet and by assigning the work or learning to each student.

There have been arguments on the level of interaction provided by desktop VR, as it does not encourage users to use interactive devices. Suh and Lee (2005) argue that using desktop VR without interactive devices potentially restricts users to experience what users see and hear from their speakers when users do not wear a HMD, helmet and glove. However, as immersive VR is expensive to implement (Huang, Rauch, & Liaw, 2010; Magyari, 2011) and impractical in some ways (Bowman & McMahan, 2007), website owners, designers and researchers have preferred to implement desktop VR (Suh & Lee, 2005) and evaluate the sufficiency of its immersion (Bowman & McMahan, 2007; Cummings & Bailenson, 2016). Although Mizell, Jones, Slater and Spanlang (2002) find that there is no significant difference between immersive and non-immersive VR, other studies comparing two types of VR demonstrate the advantage of non-immersive VR. Wann and Mon-Williams (1996) state that desktop-VR based learning can be adequate in learning environments when desktop VR allows users to 'navigate, traverse and engage' (p.829). The study by Kahani and Beadle (1997) indicates that WWW-based desktop VR performs better than immersive VR as desktop VR can provide collaboration among users. Despite desktop VR's benefits of being low-cost and higher accessibility, they find that immersive VR is more advantageous than desktop VR in terms of enhancing interaction between the system and user (Kahani and Beadle, 1997). However, Ausburn and Ausburn (2008) claim that desktop VR has recently been updated with new features and developments and has the capacity to give benefits to trainers and learners. Despite desktop VR's inefficiency in offering a 'real' immersion into VR, some argue that desktop VR can provide sufficient interaction leading to immersion (Fernandes et al., 2003; Madathil et al., 2017). Dalgarno, Hedberg and Harper (2002) posit that 'the sense of presence or immersion in a 3D environment occurs as a consequence of the fidelity of representation and the high degree of interaction or user control, rather than being a unique attribute of the environment' (p.150). The fidelity is related to the degree to which the images or objects in a 3D environment play in a realistic way (Dalgarno, Hedberg, and Harper, 2002). The fidelity of representation in desktop VR encourages users to 'improve learning outcomes and student engagement in an active learning environment' (Madathil et al., 2017, p.1) as an educational tool. As understood from the aforesaid research, non-immersive VR is beneficial in providing economically attractive and accessible (Madathil et al., 2017) learning environments.

Constructivist Approach in VR Learning

According to the constructivist approach, learners are active in learning environments and use their previous knowledge to build their new knowledge (Huang et al., 2010). Although the constructivist approach seems related with ICT in educational settings, constructivism dates back to the studies by Jean Piaget, Leon Vygotsky (Solomonidou, 2009), Socrates, Jerome Bruner (Amineh & Asl, 2015) and John Dewey (Huang et al., 2010). Socrates highlighted that constructivism can occur in the conversations between the teacher and learner while questioning constructs the knowledge. Bruner related his discovery learning to constructivism and claimed that students have a role in constructing knowledge by combining their past and present learning experiences (Huang et al., 2010). Dewey (1916 cited in Huang et al., 2010) argued that it is the relationship between a learner and the environment, which leads to a productive interaction. According to him, learners' interests should be taken into account to trigger motivation, which will inspire learners to perceive and understand problems (Dewey, 1916 cited in Huang & Liaw, 2018). Similarly, Piaget stressed that constructivism occurs through the interaction between a learner and learning environment (Solomonidou, 2009).

It is generally accepted that the knowledge construction process can be promoted within an authentic and real learning environment (Alam, 2017; Bhattacharjee, 2015; Brooks & Brooks, 1999; Honebein, 1996; Jonassen, 1994; Lainema & Makkonen, 2003; Wilson & Cole, 1991). The main goal of constructing a realistic environment in a constructivist approach overlaps that of VR. Therefore, a number of researchers have explored and discussed VR and constructivism (i.e. Chen et al., 2004; Chuah, Chen and Teh, 2011; Clarke, Dede, Ketelhut & Nelson, 2006; Dalgarno et al., 2002; Fernandes et al., 2003; Huang & Liaw, 2018; Hu, Zhu, Pan, Li & Ju, 2003; Huang et al., 2010; Lin & Yan, 2015; Madathil et al., 2017; Ozkan, 2017).

Huang et al. (2010) discuss learners' attitudes about VR based on constructivism. When applying the constructivist approach into designing a virtual reality-learning environment, they propose the following learning strategies:

- **'Situated Learning':** VR should facilitate users to feel present in a real-world learning environment. In the artificial learning environment, the interaction between learning objects in VR and users is meant to trigger immersion and presence.
- **'Role Playing':** VR should prepare an interactive learning environment where users can take a role, for example, with 3D characters or avatars.
- **'Cooperative/Collaborative Learning':** VR can be more effective when social scaffolding is provided. Social scaffolding in VR can be created when two or more learners are engaged in learning and helping each other.
- **'Problem-Based Learning':** VR should direct learners to explore problems and construct new knowledge in this process.
- **'Creative Learning':** Problem-solving and reflective learning activities should be integrated into VR to lead to creativity (Huang et al., 2010, pp. 1173-1175).

Huang et al. (2010) evaluate those learning strategies in collaborative VR settings. They draw the attention to five issues of VR design based on a constructivist approach: functionality and usability, the skills of educators, design within mixed reality environments, cost effectiveness, and further exploration of VR devices to study learning, learning performance and attitudes, and to ascertain whether VR meets learning needs.

Huang and Liaw (2018) further explore a desktop VR- based environment within constructivism and find out that 'perceived self-efficacy and perceived interaction are two crucial factors affecting perceived ease of use' and 'perceived usefulness and learning motivation' (p.91). They describe perceived interaction as the 'degree to which a learner is able to interact with other learners or with the learning system', whereas perceived self-efficacy is the 'degree to which a learner has confidence that he/she is able to operate the learning system' (Huang & Liaw, 2018, p.101). They conclude that perceived ease of use, perceived usefulness and motivation affect learner intention to use VR. However, more studies should look at learners' actual performance in VR and the relationship between learner motivation and learning in VR (Hunag & Liaw, 2018) since VR has changed not just gaming but also learning.

Learners' Experience and Perception of Learning in Desktop VR

As fully immersive VR needs expensive equipment, attention has shifted to the study of desktop VR (Ausburn & Ausburn, 2008). Therefore, a number of studies have investigated learning in desktop VR software in terms of science education (i.e. Lee et al., 2009; Lee et al., 2010; Lee & Wong, 2014), language learning (Lin a& Lan, 2015; Ozkan, 2017; Zhai, 2017), gaming (Merchant, Goetz, Cifuentes, Keeney-Kennicutt and Davis, 2014; Sousa et al., 2009) and different learner characteristics (Ausburn, Martens, Washington, Steele & Washburn, 2009; Chuah et al., 2011: Lee & Wong, 2014).

Ausburn et al. (2009) reviewed gender issues in a desktop VR learning environment with a cross-case analysis of two previously published studies in Oklahoma State University. The views of forty-two post-secondary surgical technology students and eighty adults representing the general population showed that there was a difference between females and males in using VR. Females performed well when the familiar environment was simple without any labels and visual identifiers. However, when they encountered an unfamiliar complex learning environment, they had difficulty navigating and feeling confident. That might be because of inexperience in VR learning environments and the additional cognitive load that this format introduced.

Santos et al. (2009) compared user performance in immersive and non-immersive VR. Forty-two participants who had no experience in VR systems except games played a game in both desktop and with the HMD. Data from observation, a perception questionnaire, and interviews gave important results about the similarities and differences between the uses of two types of VR. On the one hand, users seemed to enjoy both of them. On the other hand, user performance was better in desktop VR because they were more familiar with the desktop. Nonetheless, they were more satisfied with the HMD, although some reported feeling sick and disoriented because of the cables. This study shows the need to improve immersive VR and the potential adequacy of non-immersive VR.

Lee et al. (2009) explored the comparison between a desktop virtual reality-based learning environment and a traditional learning environment. The study conducted pre- and post-tests and a questionnaire to measure science education students' perceived learning and satisfaction. Three hundred seventy high school students were divided into two groups: control and treatment groups. The findings demonstrated that the latter who learned with VR software had more positive academic achievement and performance.

Lee et al. (2010) furthered the study and found that the level of perceived learning and satisfaction is dependent on the provision of active learning in a VR learning environment. Based on this study, Lee and Wong (2014) examined the effects of desktop VR-based learning environment on learners' spatial abilities. The study pointed out that desktop VR-based learning positively affects learners with low spatial abilities and facilitates student-centered learning. These studies included the cognitive load theory and showed that learners were not exposed to 'extraneous cognitive load' (Lee and Wong 2014, p.11) as they were engaged and interacting with the learning activities, which helped reduce the cognitive load.

Merchant et al. (2014) examined the overall effect of VR-based teaching in K-12 and higher education. The meta-analysis of studies on games, simulation and virtual worlds indicated that they were effective in enhancing learning goals, with games being the most effective. The studies on simulations revealed the importance of providing feedback appropriate to the type of task performed.

Lin and Lan (2015) looked at the studies on language learning in VR-based environments. It demonstrated that the factors most often considered included 'interactive communication; behaviors, affections and beliefs; and task-based instruction' (Lin & Lan, 2015, p.486). Taken together, the research indicated that VR is a feasible learning tool to learn languages, especially in higher education. Although the study did not focus on the investigation of language learning aspects such as learning styles, it did draw attention to the need for more research on language learning in VR settings.

Ozkan (2017) conducted a study on using immersive VR for language education in higher education. The findings showed that teachers were eager to teach Intensive English Program by applying VR into their classroom. Also, they indicated that VR-based training program was 'visual, motivating, fun, authentic, anxiety-removing, interactive [and] autonomous' (Ozkan, 2017, p.42). However, they agreed that VR could not be used as the core of teaching but as complementary as teachers were not sufficiently enthusiastic and knowledgeable to apply VR into classrooms.

Many recent studies have examined creating and using 360° videos for foreign language learning (Berns, Mota, Ruiz-Rube & Dodero, 2018; Bonner & Reinders, 2018; Godwin-Jones, 2016; Kavanagh, Luxton-Reilly, Wüensche & Plimmer, 2016; Lloyd, Rogerson & Stead, 2017; Pilgrim & Pilgrim, 2016; Repetto, Germagnoli, Triberti & Riva, 2018). Consistent with the study by Ozkan (2017), these studies all agreed that 360° videos in VR-based language learning environments should be incorporated into classroom learning and teaching. Furthermore, Zhai (2017) discussed how VR can foster foreign language learning based on a constructivist approach, with the interaction between users and a VR learning environment constructing genuinely immersive foreign language learning.

Considering the discussion and conclusion from the above-mentioned studies, desktop VR still needs exploring. These studies have mostly looked at the use of VR and users' perception of learning or teaching through VR. However, there is a need to investigate the interaction provided through desktop VR. As the technology-assisted learning is developing, knowledge is being enhanced. Desktop VR has been in use as an easy and simple way to transmit and construct this knowledge. It can be concluded from previous studies that the main aim of VR is to facilitate users' immersion and interaction and to help them to feel present in a real-world learning environment without regard to whether the tools they use are technically considered fully immersive or non-immersive VR.

STUDENT PERCEPTIONS OF LANGUAGE LEARNING WITH VR TOOLS

The focus of the chapter is to provide a significant contribution to the current discussion of desktop VR-based learning as it presents empirical findings on two issues that have been highlighted in the previous studies: interaction within VR and learners' perception of their learning in VR.

Participants

Eleven students aged between 19 and 22 (9 females and 2 males) in the Preparatory Class in the Department of Interpretation and Translation at a University in Turkey participated in this study. Their English level was intermediate according to the proficiency exam they took before their course. During the course, they were improving their English to pass the class. In the meantime, they were eager to learn a second foreign language. They were inexperienced in using VR for any purposes, let alone for educational purposes, with the exception of the male students who said that they played VR games a few times before.

The researcher informed each participant about the research, the research tool, and methodology. They declared their consent and agreed with the assurance of their anonymity. Therefore, each of them were nicknamed with an English name in the analysis and presentation of data.

A VR Tool: ImmerseMe

This research used a new VR-based language learning tool, ImmerseMe, which was established in 2015 (ImmerseMe, 2018) and is still in development. The company provided a one-month trail at the request of the research for the purposes of this study. Currently, learners can use the program in a Chrome desktop application, with the addition of apps, Cardboard and VR headset applications to be released in 2019.

ImmerseMe was implemented in this study because of its following features:

- **Learning Activities:** It has over 500 scenarios and learning activities for beginner, intermediate and advanced learners. Figure 1 shows that different topics such as bakery, bar, café, fish and chip shop, grocer, hotel, museum, restaurant, school and street are included to teach English. Learners can perform learning activities, for example, buying a loaf of bread or buying a pastry under the bakery topic.
- **Language Variety:** There are nine languages such as German, Spanish, French, English, Japanese, Chinese, Italian, Greek and Indonesian to learn.
- **Simulation:** The program simulates daily conversations, such as ordering coffee in London, a baguette in Paris, tapas in Spain or an obento box in Tokyo in the target language (TL).
- **Authenticity:** By providing 360° YouTube-based videos, the program offers an authentic location to learn a language.
- **Self-Paced Learning:** Learners can pace their learning on their own or with a tutor, as shown in Figure 2. In this study, participants chose on their own which activity to start accomplishing.
- **Feedback:** The program uses Google-based sound recognition software, which is aimed at helping learners feel like they are having a conversation with a native speaker in the target language. If the learner replies or speaks correctly in a given situation, the program moves into the next learning activity. Otherwise, the learner is asked to try again.

Figure 1. A screenshot of English activities in ImmerseMe (© 2018, ImmerseMe. Used with permission.)

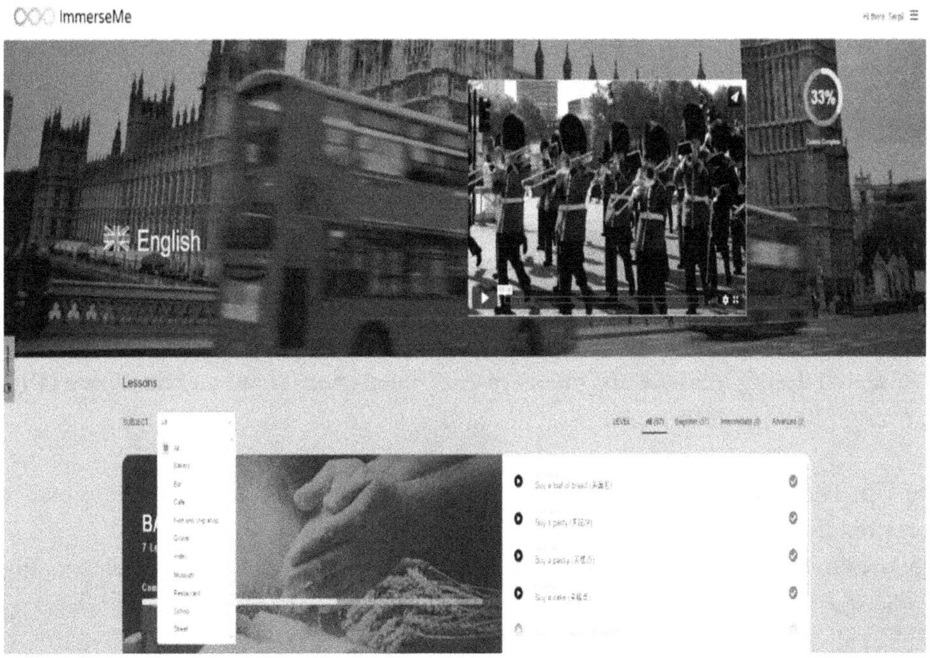

Figure 2. A screenshot of languages with percentages of learning activities accomplished in ImmerseMe (© 2018, ImmerseMe. Used with permission.)

Data Collection Methods and Analysis

Data was gathered from different research instruments (Lin & Lan, 2015) and analyzed based on a qualitative research design. The research combined elements of a descriptive case study (Yin, 1994) to describe data in question, asking 'for instance, what different strategies are used by a reader and how the reader uses them' (Zainal, 2007, p.3), and an interpretive case study (McDonough & McDonough, 1997), 'interpret[ing] the data by developing conceptual categories, supporting or challenging the assumptions made regarding them' (Zainal, 2007, p.3). Direct observation and semi-structured interviewing of 11 students occurred twice, in the first week of April and the first week of May 2018. Participants used the ImmerseMe program in English for their experience and were allowed to select their language of choice for their second experience with the program. Both interactions were followed by individual interviews. Research design followed the model of van Someren, Barnard and Sandberg (1994), Katalin (2000) and Young (2005) as follows:

1. **Setting Up**: The researcher arranged a silent room with a laptop for students to feel comfortable and carry out the activities (van Someren et al., 1994).
2. **Giving Instructions:** The researcher introduced ImmerseMe and told participants that the main aim of the study was not to evaluate their success or failure but to see their learning process (van Someren et al., 1994) and reminded that they would perform the activities as if they were at home. They were also free to choose any learning activity.
3. **Warming-Up:** Each participant performed 'a pre-task orientation' (Gibson, 1997, p.58) to be familiar with the tool and a new e-learning environment (van Someren et al., 1994). Each of them was free to choose the activity and perform it alone.
4. **Behavior of the Researcher:** Based on the work of Imler and Eichelberger (2011), the researcher directly and silently observed the students' activities as it helps when exploring the use of e-learning tools. They were observed for 30 minutes individually (Eveland Jr. & Dunwoody, 2000). In the first twenty minutes, they performed learning activities in English, while afterwards they pursued any other language they preferred.
5. **Follow-Up Interviews**: In order to 'validate' the data from direct observation (Qi, 1998 cited in Charters, 2003, p.73), each participant answered 11 follow-up interview questions. Interviewing was conducted to examine students' perceptions of their learning in VR. This study did not distinguish VR from the VR tool, ImmerseMe while asking their views on their learning. The research drew from the research model of Lee et al. (2010) to create interview questions. Table 1 shows the constructs of VR in the research model of Lee et al. (2010) and interview questions based on the definitions of these constructs.

The data from observations and interviews were analyzed in NVivo; transcripts of students' performance and their responses to interview questions were coded inductively and deductively (Hesse-Biber & Leavy, 2011). Based on the background of the research and research questions, two main codes were deductively created as learner interaction within VR and beliefs about VR. The other main code was inductively created as the comparison between learners' first and second learning experience in VR. Inter-coder reliability of coding data was assured with more than 80 percent agreement between two experts performing coding functions (Miles & Huberman, 1994).

Table 1. Interview questions in the present study based on the constructs of VR designed by Lee et al. (2010)

Constructs of VR (Lee et al., 2010)	Description of the constructs by Lee et al. (2010)	Interview questions in the present study
VR features	• Representational fidelity is the degree of realism of the images and content. • Immediacy of control is the ability to make movements, direct oneself and explore objects.	• Do you think you have learned anything? • Can you describe your learning in VR? • What do you think of your learning in VR?
Usability	• The quality of the technology can be understood within statements in perceived usefulness (i.e. important, relevant, useful or valuable). • The accessibility of the technology can be within statements in perceived ease of use (i.e. convenient, controllable).	• In which ways do you find it useful/not useful or successful/unsuccessful?
Presence	• The psychological thinking of being present in the learning environment.	• Did you feel you were present there while learning in VR?
Motivation	• The psychological factor for learning performance.	• How did you feel while learning in VR?
Cognitive benefits	• Memorization. • Understanding. • Application. • Overall view of learning achievement.	• Do you think you can apply what you have learned or seen here into another learning environment?
Control and active learning	• Students make their own decisions to pace, practise and sequence their learning.	• Do you think you were active and responsible for learning?
Reflective thinking	• Critical thinking of students' own learning.	• Do you think you linked your knowledge with your previous knowledge?
Learning outcomes	• Psychomotor outcomes (i.e. efficiency, accuracy or response magnitude). • Cognitive outcomes (i.e. comprehension, knowledge, application or analysis). • Affective outcomes (i.e. satisfaction, attitude or appreciation).	• What did you learn new? • Were you satisfied with your learning?

Findings

Participants' Interaction With ImmerseMe

Table 2 indicates codes generated based on students' interaction during the observation, including: use of tutorial video in English and in (an)other language(s), sequencing learning activities in order, repetition of words, note-taking of words encountered in learning activities, viewing of 360° videos and expression of motivation, either positive or negative, while performing activities.

It was observed that participants watched the tutorial video more while carrying out the activities in English than other languages. Nine of them preferred to learn French as they stated that they would choose French course in their first year, whereas others preferred Spanish because of their interest. Brenna first tried to do Spanish and accomplished the activities very quickly. When she saw that she succeeded in it, she moved into Chinese; however, she had difficulty in it and just tried a few times. Similarly, Tim did both French and Spanish. Although he could not pass the activities very easily and quickly, he said that he would try even if it would take very long. Six participants followed the sequence of the topics

Table 2. Participants' interaction with ImmerseMe during the first observation

Participants	Tutorial video (English)	Tutorial video (other language(s))	Sequencing	Repetition of words	Note-taking	360° view	Motivation
Heidi	Yes	No	Yes	Yes	Yes	Yes	Yes
Kate	Yes	No	No	No	Yes	Yes	Yes
Gabby	Yes	No	No	Yes	Yes	No	Yes
Sara	Yes	No	Yes	Yes	No	No	Yes
Mia	Yes	Yes	No	Yes	Yes	No	Yes
Scarlet	Yes	No	No	Yes	Yes	No	Yes
Alice	Yes	No	Yes	Yes	Yes	No	Yes
Brenna	Yes	No	No	No	No	Yes	No
Britney	No	No	Yes	No	No	No	No
Harry	Yes	No	Yes	Yes	Yes	Yes	Yes
Tim	Yes	No	Yes	Yes	No	No	Yes

with learning activities in the order provided by ImmerseMe, while others first scrolled and looked over topics and then decided to choose a learning activity.

Table 2 also suggests that there is an indication of the relationship between repetition and note taking of words and motivation. Although they repeated and took notes of words in English, participants did just note taking of the pronunciation of words in other languages when they failed in speaking in this language. During the first observation time, Brenna and Britney did not express their motivational feelings. Apart from them, all of the participants applauded and smiled happily for passing the activity in another language. They also thought and expressed aloud their motivation by saying 'Good!', 'Done. I am perfect, I swear!', and 'I like it.' Tim thought aloud that the tool was wrong, and that he was speaking correctly when the program rejected his responses. Heidi said that she was fed up with its rejection and added 'Please accept my pronunciation.' Less than half of them (i.e. Heidi, Kate, Brenna and Harry) watched the conversation in 360° videos from different angles by dragging the mouse. Additionally, Gabby checked the pronunciation of words in Google translation and Oxford dictionary in the laptop, whereas Scarlet and Alice did this in their mobile dictionary applications.

Table 3 presents participants' interaction with VR features during the second observation.

In this data, tutorial video was excluded as a code because no participants watched the video in the second observation. That might be because they had already watched it in the previous observation, or they were more focused on accomplishing the activities. It was observed that the participants were less sequential in the second observation. Only Gabby, Sara and Britney performed activities in the suggested order. There were similar results between the first and second observations in repetition and note taking of words and motivation. However, Sara took a note of the pronunciation in the second observation, whereas Mia and Harry did not. Likewise, Mia and Sara did not express their feelings but just focused on the activities.

It was observed that the participants talked aloud about their feelings more in the second observation. For example, Kate looked at the school in the French learning activity and said 'The school in French is too long.' She also showed her feelings towards the word she had difficulty in pronouncing by saying

Table 3. Participants' interaction with ImmerseMe during the second observation

Participants	Sequencing	Repetition	Note-taking	360° view	Motivation	English subtitles
Heidi	No	Yes	Yes	Yes	Yes	No
Kate	No	No	Yes	Yes	Yes	Yes
Gabby	Yes	Yes	Yes	No	Yes	No
Sara	Yes	Yes	Yes	Yes	No	Yes
Mia	No	Yes	No	Yes	No	Yes
Scarlet	No	Yes	Yes	Yes	Yes	No
Alice	No	Yes	Yes	Yes	Yes	No
Brenna	No	No	No	Yes	No	No
Britney	Yes	No	No	Yes	No	Yes
Harry	No	Yes	No	Yes	Yes	No
Tim	No	Yes	No	Yes	Yes	Yes

'I will not forget you, the word (brilliant).' Encountering a new word, she said, 'Senior citizen, what does it mean?' After this, she looked up the word in the Oxford dictionary in her mobile phone. Gabby talked about her reason for accomplishing the activities in English by saying 'I have an exam on Friday, so I will do the activities in English'. When she was doing the activities in the grocery topic, she showed her focus by stating 'Definitely, I will buy something.' Sara mentioned the similarities between Turkish and English people when doing the restaurant activities by saying 'It is similar with Turkey. People are looking at the people who are taking videos inside the restaurant.' She was surprised at seeing a museum shop and no dust in the street. Mia complained about a limitation of the tool, saying 'I wish I could get closer to the items, so I can see how much they are.' When doing the activities, she did not just focus on the conversation but environment as well, stating 'It is bright outside.' Britney corrected herself by saying 'I used to say expresso but now espresso.' As in the first observation, participants were observed to use mobile dictionaries and Google. Only Tim tried a different tactic, unsuccessfully trying to use the voice in the mobile dictionary to pronounce and pass the activity. Participants mostly performed French activities because of their plans to study the language. However, Sara chose German because she wished to communicate with her German stepsister. Five participants were observed to click on English subtitles in the activities of another language.

Participants' Perceptions of ImmerseMe

Participants expressed their thoughts about their learning within ImmerseMe during the first and second interview sessions. All of the participants agreed in both the first and second interview sessions that they learned something new, especially pronunciation and vocabulary in both English and other languages. More than half of them thought that ImmerseMe positively improved their learning processes in terms of learning the culture of the TL, other languages such as French, and pronunciation; they reflected positively on interactive communication, conversation with 'real people' in a foreign country with the TL, and on learning easily and enjoyably. That might be because they had already experienced VR while playing games with VR glasses. Perhaps because of their previous immersive gaming experience, Harry and Tim expressed some dissatisfaction, stating that they did not feel like learning in a VR learning environment without VR glasses.

In order to gain a better understanding of their views on learning, each of them was asked to describe their learning within VR in both the first and second interview sessions as indicated in Table 4. Table 4 shows that they did not change their descriptions of learning over time but added more knowledge to it. For example, Kate defined her learning by trying in the first interview, while improving with practice in the second interview. Likewise, in the first interview Gabby regarded her learning as receiving a transmission of knowledge, indicating that ImmerseMe improved her listening and writing. However, in the second interview, she explained that ImmerseMe both taught her and helped her to become active in learning by correcting her 'mislearning' and seeing her mistakes. Mia gave similar descriptions of her learning process as "patient" in both sessions but added learning by communication, interaction with a person, and learning through repetition in the latter interview.

They listed the advantages of ImmerseMe as follows:

- Improving speaking, listening, pronunciation and vocabulary (Heidi, Kate, Gabby, Sara, Mia, Scarlet, Alice, Brenna & Tim) and critical thinking (Kate),
- Providing learning activities in different languages (Kate, Mia & Sara) and English subtitles (Britney),
- Increasing motivation (Kate, Britney) and cultural awareness (Alice)
- Allowing the user to search something in a different website or open a new tab (Gabby)
- Making one repeat the word (Sara & Britney)
- Watching 360° videos (Sara, Mia, Alice & Harry)

Table 4. Participants' description of their learning within ImmerseMe in the first and second interview sessions

Participants	Description in the first interview	Description in the second interview
Heidi	Instead of going abroad like England with a high cost, learning English here where I am staying.	Communication and improvement.
Kate	Learning by trying, even if it is difficult.	Getting improved in each practice.
Gabby	Hearing for listening and understanding for writing.	Correcting my previous learning and seeing my mistakes.
Sara	Effective.	I realized I mispronounced. And I realized lifestyle there.
Mia	Learning patiently. All good things come to those who wait.	Fun but it needs patience. Communication and interaction with a person and repetition
Scarlet	Learning with a meaning.	Improvement.
Alice	Real learning.	Learning with foreign people.
Brenna	Easy learning.	Good but easy learning.
Britney	Learning by talking face-to-face	Improving pronunciation and vocabulary.
Harry	Learning for pronunciation with an additional help resource.	Learning languages with a second online language resource.
Tim	Learning with others in VR.	Learning new vocabulary with British accent like going abroad with 360° videos.

- Correcting one's learning (Gabby).

However, some of them (i.e. Kate, Gabby, Mia and Scarlet) also saw the repetition as a disadvantage of ImmerseMe. That might be because ImmerseMe waited until they could pronounce correctly in order for them to move on to the next activity. As they stated, ImmerseMe sometimes did not recognize what they said and they had to repeat themselves many times to proceed further in the activities. Kate suggested that ImmerseMe could be improved to give useres, for instance, a 10-time trial to pronounce. After that much trial and error, the user could go to the next activity, even if s/he failed. Sara recommended that back and forward buttons could be included visibly. She also thought that ImmerseMe could not recognize her voice because she was sick. Moreover, Tim stated that he failed in some activities because of his soft voice, which ImmerseMe could not recognize correctly. He suggested that it should include American English and the definition of a word after clicking on it. Mia wanted to see a phonetic transcription of the word to speak better. Alice found communication very fast, whereas Tim and Brenna proposed longer conversations. Tim and Harry wished to experience ImmerseMe with VR glasses. Heidi perceived a lack of activities and topics, especially in English.

When asked how they felt while learning with ImmerseMe, students reported that it motivated them to learn better and further their learning, especially in the second interview session. For instance, Gabby talked about feeling curious and motivated to learn in the first interview session, while in the second interview session, she reported speaking hurriedly because she felt like she was speaking face-to-face with a foreigner. Sara described feeling like she was in a competition in the first interview, while in the second, she described herself as interacting and communicating with other people. Britney mentioned that she was motivated to be aware of her pronunciation in the first session, while in the second, she expressed that she could see her progress and even forgot about the exam she was preparing for.

In both interview sessions, all of the participants stated that they felt present while performing activities in ImmerseMe, especially with the help of 360° videos and the incorporation of native speakers of the TL. However, Tim and Harry noted again that they would have felt more immersed with VR glasses. In the same vein, all of them thought that they could apply what they had learned or seen in ImmerseMe into another learning environment, particularly in terms of pronunciation and vocabulary. Moreover, all of them agreed that they were active and responsible for their learning while learning in VR as ImmerseMe made them realize their mispronunciation, correct themselves, and make progress in their learning. Kate saw her learning as 'self-learning'. Sara gave similar responses indicating active learning by noting in the first interview that she was correcting herself, whereas stating in the second interview that she was very careful while speaking. Brenna said 'I was like there. I was like living my little life, buying bread and making friends.'

Furthermore, the participants continued to report linking their new knowledge with their previous knowledge. Gabby expressed this notion with the saying: 'many a mickle makes a muckle.' Sara considered her previous knowledge 'latent learning' in the second interview session, whereas she had focused on correcting herself in the first interview session. In the first interview session, Kate talked about pronunciation and showing links between English and French, while in the second session, she indicated that she had gained the ability to take notes and that she could get excited while learning. Finally, in the second interview session, all participants continued to express satisfaction with learning within ImmerseMe.

However, the comparison between the first and second interview sessions gave further data about the participants' views on VR learning. Their thoughts changed over time in that they focused on the improvement in pronunciation and vocabulary learning in the first interview session, while in the second interview session, they discussed their improvement in learning not only in English but also other languages. When asked to compare their first and second experiences with ImmerseMe, nearly all participants indicated that they realized more over time what the videos contained, including what the environment looked like and how people behaved. For instance, Kate and Mia showed surprise that museums in London had a shopping area, whereas 'it does not have here, we sell in market.' Kate said. Mia added that 'no photo or no touch is stressed in our museums but not here.' Sara indicated her realizations in the café activity by saying 'there is a warm welcome as it happens in Turkey, but it is more expensive.'

DISCUSSION

A number of studies (i.e. Ausburn et al., 2009; Chuah et al., 2011; Lee et al., 2009; Lee et al., 2010; Lin & Lan, 2015; Merchant et al., 2014; Ozkan, 2017; Santos et al., 2009, Zhai, 2017) have looked at desktop VR-based learning, focusing on gender issues, comparisons between immersive and non-immersive VR, VR's effectiveness, emotional aspects of VR learning, and language learning with VR, especially in high school education. However, there is still a need to further research on the issue of desktop VR-based language learning (Lin & Lan, 2015). The empirical findings presented in this chapter aimed to examine learners' interaction and perceptions of desktop VR-based learning based on a constructivist approach, drawing from the research model of Lee et al. (2010) to discuss the constructs of VR including VR features, usability, presence, motivation, cognitive benefits, control and active learning, reflective thinking and learning outcomes.

VR features include representational fidelity and immediacy of control (Lee et al, 2010). Confirming the study by Lee et al. (2010), this chapter's findings suggest that desktop VR-based learning tools can provide realistic images and videos for learners, even if the tool is non-immersive. Although users might be unable to make movements, even simple movements, for instance, to get closer to images and objects in the 360° videos, learners can watch 360° videos from different angles by dragging with the mouse (i.e. immediacy of control).

In terms of usability, language learning tools can aid in improving language learning skills, especially listening and speaking, vocabulary and pronunciation, and note-taking by increasing motivation and cultural awareness through an immersive experience. In order to create a constructivist-learning environment, the tools should also consider a non-restricted learning environment where users can go to another website independently if they need to or where they can sequence their learning on their own. Although this is consistent with the study by Huang and Liaw (2018), this study also suggests the interrelationship between perceived self-efficacy and perceived interaction, and perceived ease of use and perceived usefulness. Perceived ease of use and perceived usefulness affect perceived self-efficacy and perceived interaction to that extent that a user-friendly environment increases learning motivation and interaction with the tools, as shown in the present study.

Similar to other studies (Bowman & McMahan, 2007; Cummings & Bailenson, 2016; Dalgarno et al., 2002), this study highlights that the feeling of presence and immersion in a learning environment is more important than a VR tool's status as a full immersion or non-immersion experience. Students' comparison of cultures and environments between in Turkey and other countries featured in the activities illustrate students' immersion and presence in desktop VR. However, it is true that learners who have previously experienced a fully immersive VR environment might not feel as satisfied with the immersion experience offered by desktop VR as those who have not.

Consistent with the study by Lee et al. (2010), this study suggests that there is an interrelationship among motivation, learning outcomes, and cognitive benefits. In this chapter, learners who repeated and took note of words they wanted to improve and learn had more 'dialogic interaction' (Lantolf & Aljaafreh, 1995, p.620) using self-talk as an affective strategy (White, 1995). In the same vein, VR features including presence, usability, control, and active and reflective learning affected their motivation, which increased over time. This argues that the more learners experience VR, the more they further their learning and increase their motivation. However, the lack in guidance or appropriate feedback might cause them to feel discouraged at accomplishing the activities and continuing within VR, as indicated in Chuah et al. (2011), as well.

Cognitive benefits of VR can be memorization, understanding, and application. Corroborating the studies by Antonietti, Rasi, Imperio and Sacco (2000) and Lee et al. (2010), this study indicates that learners can gain these benefits through their use of VR. The current study shows that note taking promotes memorization, whereas evaluation of learning shows understanding. Students' plans to use what they learned in other future learning environments indicate application.

Control and active learning contributes to learning outcomes (Lee et al., 2010) and motivation as indicated in this study. The feeling of presence facilitates control and active learning. By this, learners feel more careful in accomplishing the task, which, in a desktop VR-based language learning tool, means speaking with a native person in a foreign country like belonging to this country. Above all, some of learners regard this as self-learning. This chapter also discusses that the more they use VR, the more they feel responsible for language learning.

Reflective thinking directly contributes to learning outcomes (Lee et al., 2010) as seen in this chapter. Although students showed this kind of thinking directly in the study by Lee et al. (2010) saying that 'I read, understand and reflect…' (Lee et al., 2010, p.1436), reflective thinking was exhibited in this study with through participants' self-talk, their talk about the usefulness of VR features, their ability to understand and apply what they have learned, and their ability to evaluate their learning.

Possible learning outcomes include psychomotor, cognitive, and affective outcomes (Lee et al., 2010). This study did not measure psychomotor outcomes but included the thoughts of students to show that learners can gain cognitive and affective outcomes by repetition of words and correcting their mistakes. It suggests that the more they use VR, the more cognitive outcomes appear. Learning pronunciation and vocabulary in English is a cognitive outcome in the first observation, whereas learning this in other languages is a cognitive outcome in the second observation. Affective outcomes, suggested by participants' motivation and satisfaction with the program, remained steady through both parts of the study.

This chapter also draws attention to other issues in desktop VR such as scaffolding which is a crucial factor in the effectiveness of a desktop VR-based learning tool (Meri-Yilan, 2017). A study by Chuah et al. (2010) argued that the design of VR must include sufficient scaffolding or guidance to be effective. E-feedback, feedback in e-learning environments (Tuzi, 2004) can play a role in the kind of scaffolding needed to promote learning in VR learning environments. In the program studied here, feedback was provided in terms of allowing participants to progress to another activity. Users were allowed to progress to another activity when it was accomplished or warned: 'Great attempt, please try again.' (ImmerseMe, 2018). In this case, the scaffolding or guidance provided seemed not to be enough. Students needed more scaffolding to move forward or back to activities or acquire more information about the aims of the activities. Otherwise, their motivation could decrease.

This study shows that self-paced learning can occur in desktop VR when users, rather than teachers, can determine the curriculum according to their competences and abilities (Kumar, Packer & Koller, 2010). In this way, self-paced learning can promote learner autonomy (Rhode, 2009). However, in order to enhance self-paced learning, a desktop VR-based learning environment should not only be designed with enough scaffolding and guidance, but also with flexibility in the environment. For instance, in this study, learners tended to open a new tab or use their mobile phone, find an online learning resource such as a dictionary website or application with which they were familiar, and search the pronunciation or meaning of a word on their own. Therefore, the environment should be flexible enough to include these tools within the program.

FUTURE RESEARCH DIRECTIONS AND LIMITATIONS OF THE STUDY

As VR is evolving, research on VR needs furthering (Ezawa & Danely, 2016) in order to see its potential usefulness in education (Huang & Liaw, 2018), especially in language learning. The empirical findings of this chapter confirmed Lee et al. (2010)'s research model of VR but included other issues to consider. Overall, the chapter suggests further studies to design and evaluate a desktop VR-based learning environment with the following concepts:

- The constructs of VR based on Lee et al. (2010)'s research model, which includes VR features (i.e. representational fidelity and immediacy of control), usability, presence, motivation, cognitive benefits, control and active learning, reflective thinking and learning outcomes;
- Scaffolding, which provides enough support and guidance so that users can navigate and develop their learning on their own;
- Self-paced learning, which leads to learner autonomy;
- Opportunities for collaboration, which facilitates the feeling of presence and immersion into the learning environment; and
- Strategies that take learner differences into account

Additionally, further studies might examine VR over a longer period and incorporate pre- and post-tests to compare learning before and after the VR experience. As the present study used a small sample size of eleven students, further studies should include more participants and consider gender balance. Finally, comparative studies that examine immersive versus non-immersive VR language learning environments, including new technologies such as augmented reality technology, would be beneficial to the field.

CONCLUSION

This chapter presented empirical research on desktop VR-based language learning, investigating learners' interaction and perceptions of learning within a desktop VR learning environment. Even if it has been argued that desktop VR does not provide a full immersion, this study showed that learners were observed to feel more present and immersed into the VR environment when they were more familiar with VR. However, the feeling of immersion or presence is dependent on some issues implemented in a desktop VR program, software or tool. The issues in Lee et al. (2010)'s research model were confirmed within this chapter in that VR features, usability, presence, motivation, cognitive benefits, control and active learning, reflective thinking and learning outcomes should be taken into account. Learning can be promoted with real-like images and 360° videos. Interaction can be facilitated with a user-friendly desktop VR environment. Scaffolding, self-paced learning, collaboration and learner differences should be regarded as issues to consider in the design of a desktop VR tool. Scaffolding can be provided with e-feedback to play a role in tutoring or guiding learners. Self-paced learning is related to learner autonomy. The more learners are free and flexible in the desktop VR learning environment, the more they can pace their learning journey. Moreover, they may need to collaborate with peers or natives, especially in a desktop VR-language learning environment. If the tool can consider learner differences, it will be effective for more learners. Therefore, the designers of an authentic desktop VR-based learning program or tool should take these factors into account to enhance learning.

ACKNOWLEDGMENT

This research was supported by ImmerseMe.

REFERENCES

Alam, M. M. (2017). Constructivism and the classroom curriculum. *The International Journal of Indian Psychology*, *5*(1), 20–29. doi:10.25215/0501.103

Amineh, R. J., & Asl, H. D. (2015). Review of constructivism and social constructivism. *Journal of Social Sciences, Literature and Languages*, *1*(1), 9-16. Retrieved from https://pdfs.semanticscholar.org/3890/3f4a7255496f75124d639e14e9b810c17370.pdf

Antonietti, A., Rasi, C., Imperio, E., & Sacco, M. (2000). The representation of virtual reality in education. *Education and Information Technologies*, *5*(4), 317–327. doi:10.1023/A:1012057608694

Ausburn, L. J., & Ausburn, F. B. (2008). New Desktop Virtual Reality Technology in Technical Education. *Journal of Educational Technology*, *4*(4), 48–61. Retrieved from https://files.eric.ed.gov/fulltext/EJ1097807.pdf

Ausburn, L. J., Martens, J., Washington, A., Steele, D., & Washburn, E. (2009). A cross-case analysis of gender issues in desktop virtual reality learning environments. *Journal of STEM Teacher Education*, *46*(3), 6. Retrieved from https://ir.library.illinoisstate.edu/cgi/viewcontent.cgi?article=1103&context=jste

Berns, A., Mota, J. M., Ruiz-Rube, I., & Dodero, J. M. (2018, October). Exploring the potential of a 360° video application for foreign language learning. In *Proceedings of the Sixth International Conference on Technological Ecosystems for Enhancing Multiculturality* (pp. 776-780). ACM. 10.1145/3284179.3284309

Bhattacharjee, J. (2015). Constructivist approach to learning–an effective approach of teaching learning. *International Research Journal of Interdisciplinary & Multidisciplinary Studies*, *1*(4), 23-28. Retrieved from http://oaji.net/articles/2015/1707-1438677336.pdf

Blake, R. (1998). The role of technology in second language learning. In H. Byrnes (Ed.), *Learning foreign and second languages: Perspectives in research and scholarship* (pp. 209–237). New York: Modern Language Association.

Bonner, E., & Reinders, H. (2018). Augmented and Virtual Reality in The Language Classroom: Practical Ideas. *Teaching English with Technology, 18*(3), 33–53.

Botero, G. G., Questier, F., Cincinnato, S., He, T., & Zhu, C. (2018). Acceptance and usage of mobile assisted language learning by higher education students. *Journal of Computing in Higher Education, 30*(3), 426–451. doi:10.100712528-018-9177-1

Bowman, D. A., Kruijff, E., LaViola, J. J. Jr, & Poupyrev, I. (2001). An Introduction to 3-D User Interface Design. *Presence Teleoperators VR, 10*(1), 96–108. doi:10.1162/105474601750182342

Bowman, D. A., & McMahan, R. P. (2007). Virtual Reality: How Much Immersion Is Enough? *Computer, 40*(7), 36–43. doi:10.1109/MC.2007.257

Bronack, S., Sanders, R., Cheney, A., Riedl, R., Tashner, J., & Matzen, N. (2008). Presence pedagogy: Teaching and learning in a 3D virtual immersive world. *International Journal on Teaching and Learning in Higher Education, 20*(1), 59–69.

Brooks, J. G., & Brooks, M. G. (1999). *In search of understanding: The case for constructivist classrooms.* ASCD.

Charters, E. (2003). The use of think-aloud methods in qualitative research an introduction to think-aloud methods. *Brock Education Journal, 12*(2). Retrieved from https://brock.scholarsportal.info/journals/brocked/home/article/view/38

Chen, C. J., Toh, S. C., & Fauzy, W. M. (2004). The theoretical framework for designing desktop virtual reality-based learning environments. *Journal of Interactive Learning Research, 15*(2), 147–167. Retrieved from https://www.learntechlib.org/primary/p/12841/

Chuah, K.-M., Chen, C.-J., & Teh, C.-S. (2011). Designing a desktop Virtual Reality-based learning environment with emotional consideration. *Research & Practice in Technology Enhanced Learning, 6*(1), 25–42. Retrieved from http://ezproxy.lib.swin.edu.au/login?url=http://search.ebscohost.com/login.aspx?direct=true&db=ehh&AN=85289244&site=ehost-live&scope=site

Clarke, J., Dede, C., Ketelhut, D. J., & Nelson, B. (2006). A design-based research strategy to promote scalability for educational innovations. *Educational Technology, 46*(3), 27–36. Retrieved from https://www.jstor.org/stable/44429300

Cummings, J. J., & Bailenson, J. N. (2016). How immersive is enough? A meta-analysis of the effect of immersive technology on user presence. *Media Psychology, 19*(2), 272–309. doi:10.1080/15213269.2015.1015740

Dalgarno, B., Hedberg, J., & Harper, B. (2002). The contribution of 3D environments to conceptual understanding. In O. J. McKerrow (Eds.), *Winds of Change in the Sea of Learning: Proceedings of the 19th Annual Conference of the Australasian Society for Computers in Learning in Tertiary Education* (vol. 1, pp. 149-158). Auckland, New Zealand: UNITEC, Institute of Technology.

de Jong, T., Linn, M. C., & Zacharia, Z. C. (2013). Physical and Virtual Laboratories in Science and Engineering Education. *Science*, *340*(6130), 305–308. doi:10.1126cience.1230579 PMID:23599479

Eveland, W. P. Jr, & Dunwoody, S. (2000). Examining Information Processing on the World Wide Web Using Think Aloud Protocols. *Media Psychology*, *2*(3), 219–244. doi:10.1207/S1532785XMEP0203_2

Ezawa, K., & Danely, C. (2016). Virtual & Augmented Reality. In *Investment Themes in 2016*. Citigroup Inc. Retrieved from https://ir.citi.com/UEfBZ0oas9qLzjz9EjXThOLsmRLtDgNWGwJItg1klVI-GIVm8iFTGvkYnWQPFZ41DjNzOSXl9kuQ%3D

Felder, R., & Silverman, L. (1988). Learning and teaching styles in engineering education. *Engineering Education*, *78*(7), 674-681. Retrieved from http://www4.ncsu.edu/unity/lockers/users/f/felder/public/Papers/LS-1988.pdf

Fernandes, K. J., Raja, V. H., & Eyre, J. (2003). Immersive learning system for manufacturing industries. *Computers in Industry*, *51*(1), 31–40. doi:10.1016/S0166-3615(03)00027-7

Gibson, B. (1997). Talking the test: Using verbal report data in looking at the processing of cloze tasks. *Edinburgh Working Papers in Applied Linguistics*, *8*, 54–62. Retrieved from https://files.eric.ed.gov/fulltext/ED409713.pdf

Godwin-Jones, R. (2016). Emerging Technologies Augmented Reality and Language Learning: From annotated vocabulary to place-based mobile games. *Language Learning & Technology*, *20*(3), 9–19.

Hesse-Biber, S. N., & Leavy, P. (2011). *The practice of qualitative research* (2nd ed.). London: SAGE.

Honebein, P. C. (1996). Seven goals for the design of constructivist learning environments. *Constructivist learning environments: Case Studies in Instructional Design*, 11-24.

Hu, W., Zhu, J., Pan, Z., Li, Y., & Ju, C. (2003). Learning by doing: A Case for Constructivist 3D Virtual Learning Environment. *Eurographics*. Retrieved from http://diglib.eg.org/EG/DL/Conf/EG2003/edu/edu2.pdf

Huang, H. M., & Liaw, S. S. (2018). An analysis of learners' intentions toward virtual reality learning based on constructivist and technology acceptance approaches. *International Review of Research in Open and Distance Learning*, *19*(1), 91–115. doi:10.19173/irrodl.v19i1.2503

Huang, H. M., Rauch, U., & Liaw, S. S. (2010). Investigating learners' attitudes toward virtual reality learning environments: Based on a constructivist approach. *Computers & Education*, *55*(3), 1171–1182. doi:10.1016/j.compedu.2010.05.014

Imler, B., & Eichelberger, M. (2011). Using screen capture to study user research behavior. *Library Hi Tech*, *29*(3), 446–454. doi:10.1108/07378831111174413

ImmerseMe. (2017). *LinkedIn: ImmerseMe*. Retrieved from https://www.linkedin.com/company/immerseme-ltd

ImmerseMe. (2018). *ImmerseMe: VR-based language learning*. Retrieved from https://immerseme.co/#home

Jonassen, D. H. (1994). Thinking Technology: Toward a Constructivist Design Model. *Educational Technology, 34*(4), 34–37. Retrieved from https://www.learntechlib.org/p/171050/

Kahani, M., & Beadle, P. (1997, February). Comparing Immersive and Non-Immersive Virtual Reality User Interfaces for Management of Telecommunication Networks. *IEEE International Conference on Telecommunication (ICT97).*

Katalin, E. (2000). "Please, keep talking": The 'think-aloud' method. *Novelty, 7*(3), 48–59. Retrieved from http://deal.elte.hu/pages/novelty/htm2/vol73/elekes.htm

Kavanagh, S., Luxton-Reilly, A., Wüensche, B., & Plimmer, B. (2016, November). Creating 360 educational video: A case study. In *Proceedings of the 28th Australian Conference on Computer-Human Interaction* (pp. 34-39). ACM. 10.1145/3010915.3011001

Kumar, M. P., Packer, B., & Koller, D. (2010). Self-paced learning for latent variable models. In *Proceedings of Advances in Neural Information Processing Systems Conference* (pp. 1189-1197). Vancouver, Canada: Academic Press. Retrieved from http://papers.nips.cc/paper/3923-self-paced-learning-for-latent-variable-models

Lainema, T., & Makkonen, P. (2003). Applying constructivist approach to educational business games: Case REALGAME. *Simulation & Gaming, 34*(1), 131–149. doi:10.1177/1046878102250601

Lambert, L. A., & Hassan, H. (2018). MOOCs and international capacity building in a UN framework: Potential and challenges. In W. L. Filho, M. Mifsud, & P. Pace (Eds.), *Handbook of lifelong learning for sustainable development* (pp. 155–164). Cham: Springer. doi:10.1007/978-3-319-63534-7_11

Lantolf, J. P., & Aljaafreh, A. (1995). Second language learning in the zone of proximal development: A revolutionary experience. *International Journal of Educational Research, 23*(7), 619-632.

Lee, E. A., Wong, K. W., & Fung, C. C. (2009). Learning Effectiveness in a Desktop Virtual Reality-Based Learning Environment. *Proceedings of the 17th International Conference on Computers in Educations*, 832–839.

Lee, E. A., Wong, K. W., & Fung, C. C. (2010). How does desktop virtual reality enhance learning outcomes? A structural equation modeling approach. *Computers & Education*. doi:10.1016/j.compedu.2010.06.006

Lee, E. A. L., & Wong, K. W. (2014). Learning with desktop virtual reality: Low spatial ability learners are more positively affected. *Computers & Education, 79*, 49–58. doi:10.1016/j.compedu.2014.07.010

Lepadatu, I. (2012). Use self-talking for learning progress. *Procedia: Social and Behavioral Sciences, 33*, 283–287. doi:10.1016/j.sbspro.2012.01.128

Lin, T., & Lan, Y.-J. (2015). Language learning in Virtual Reality environments: Past, present, and future. *Journal of Educational Technology & Society, 18*(4), 486–497.

Lloyd, A., Rogerson, S., & Stead, G. (2017). Imagining the potential for using virtual reality technologies in language learning. In M. Carrier, R. M. Damerow, & K. M. Bailey (Eds.), *Digital language learning and teaching: Research, theory, and practice* (pp. 222–234). London: Routledge. doi:10.4324/9781315523293-19

Loewen, S., & Sato, M. (2018). Interaction and instructed second language acquisition. *Language Teaching, 51*(3), 285–329. doi:10.1017/S0261444818000125

Madathil, K. C., Frady, K., Hartley, R., Bertrand, J., Alfred, M., & Gramopadhye, A. (2017). An empirical study investigating the effectiveness of integrating virtual reality-based case studies into an online asynchronous learning environment. *Computers in Education Journal, 8*(3), 1–10.

Magyari, D. P. (2011). *Head Mounted Display Device. U.S. Patent No. 9,250,444.* Washington, DC: U.S. Patent and Trademark Office. Retrieved from https://patentimages.storage.googleapis.com/e3/be/a6/61e1e1178149d2/US9250444.pdf

Martín-Gutiérrez, J., Mora, C. E., Añorbe-Díaz, B., & González-Marrero, A. (2017). Virtual technologies trends in education. *Eurasia Journal of Mathematics. Science and Technology Education, 13*(2), 469–486. doi:10.12973/eurasia.2017.00626a

McDonough, J., & McDonough, S. (1997). *Research Methods for English Language Teachers.* London: Arnold.

Merchant, Z., Goetz, E. T., Cifuentes, L., Keeney-Kennicutt, W., & Davis, T. J. (2014). Effectiveness of virtual reality-based instruction on students' learning outcomes in K-12 and higher education: A meta-analysis. *Computers & Education, 70*, 29–40. doi:10.1016/j.compedu.2013.07.033

Meri-Yilan, S. (2017). *'Take your time' to 'find yourself!' An exploration of scaffolded autonomous e-learning environments amongst international students in a UK university* (Unpublished Doctoral dissertation). University of Southampton, Southampton, UK.

Miles, M., & Huberman, M. (1994). *Qualitative Data Analysis.* London: Sage.

Mills, S., & Noyes, J. (1999). Virtual reality: An overview of user-related design issues. Revised Paper for Special Issue on 'Virtual reality: User Issues' in Interacting with Computers, May 1998. *Interacting with Computers, 11*(4), 375–386. doi:10.1016/S0953-5438(98)00057-5

Mizell, D. W., Jones, S. P., Slater, M., & Spanlang, B. (2002). Comparing immersive virtual reality with other display modes for visualizing complex 3D geometry. *Boeing and University College.* Retrieved from https://pdfs.semanticscholar.org/cbea/003ce3c84f7dd9da0cfca10e7fdc1666b65a.pdf

Mujber, T. S., Szecsi, T., & Hashmi, M. S. (2004). Virtual reality applications in manufacturing process simulation. *Journal of Materials Processing Technology, 155*, 1834–1838. doi:10.1016/j.jmatprotec.2004.04.401

Ott, M., & Freina, L. (2015). A literature review on immersive virtual reality in education: State of the art and perspectives. In *The International Scientific Conference eLearning and Software for Education* (pp. 133–141). Editura Universităţii Naţionale de Apărare "Carol I". Retrieved from http://www.loweurope.eu/articleDetail?articleID=fcbe1578-8df8-4284-96b6-c82f91e34f3d

Ozkan, B. (2017). The Reflections of English as a Foreign Language Teachers' on the Use of Virtual Reality in Classroom Practice (International Black Sea University Case). *Journal of Education in Black Sea Region, 2*(2), 34–43. doi:10.31578/jebs.v2i2.40

Pan, Z., Cheok, A. D., Yang, H., Zhu, J., & Shi, J. (2006). Virtual reality and mixed reality for virtual learning environments. *Computers and Graphics (Pergamon)*, *30*(1), 20–28. doi:10.1016/j.cag.2005.10.004

Pilgrim, J. M., & Pilgrim, J. (2016). The Use of Virtual Reality Tools in the Reading-Language Arts Classroom. *Texas Journal of Literacy Education*, *4*(2), 90–97.

Prensky, M. (2016). Virtual Reality in the Language Learning Classroom. *On the Horizon*, *9*(5), 1–6. doi:10.1108/10748120110424816

Repetto, C. (2014). The use of virtual reality for language investigation and learning. *Frontiers in Psychology*, *5*. doi:10.3389/fpsyg.2014.01280 PMID:25414691

Repetto, C., Germagnoli, S., Triberti, S., & Riva, G. (2018). Learning into the wild: A protocol for the use of 360° videos for language learning. In P. Cipresso, S. Serino, Y. Ostrovsky, & J. T. Baker (Eds.), *Pervasive Computing Paradigms for Mental Health: 7th International Conference, MindCare 2018, Boston, MA, USA, January 9-10, 2018, Proceedings* (Vol. 253, p. 56). Springer. 10.1007/978-3-030-01093-5_8

Rhode, J. (2009). Interaction equivalency in self-paced online learning environments: An exploration of learner preferences. *The International Review of Research in Open and Distributed Learning*, *10*(1). doi:10.19173/irrodl.v10i1.603

Santos, B. S., Dias, P., Pimentel, A., Baggerman, J. W., Ferreira, C., Silva, S., & Madeira, J. (2009). Head-mounted display versus desktop for 3D navigation in virtual reality: A user study. *Multimedia Tools and Applications*, *41*(1), 161–181. doi:10.100711042-008-0223-2

Schwienhorst, K. (2002). Why virtual, why environments? Implementing virtual reality concepts in computer-assisted language learning. *Simulation & Gaming*, *33*(2), 196–209. doi:10.1177/1046878102332008

Sims, E. M. (2007). Reusable, lifelike virtual humans for mentoring and role-playing. *Computers & Education*, *49*(1), 75–92. doi:10.1016/j.compedu.2005.06.006

Solomonidou, C. (2009). Constructivist design and evaluation of interactive educational software: a research-based approach and examples. *Open Education - The Journal for Open and Distance Education and Educational Technology*, *5*(1), 6-24. Retrieved from https://ejournals.epublishing.ekt.gr/index.php/openjournal/article/viewFile/9693/9857.pdf

Suh, K.-S., & Lee, Y. E. (2005). The Effects of Virtual Reality on Consumer Learning : An Empirical Investigation. *Management Information Systems Quarterly*, *29*(4), 673–697. doi:10.2307/25148705

Tuzi, F. (2004). The impact of e-feedback on the revisions of L2 writers in an academic writing course. *Computers and Composition*, *21*(2), 217–235. doi:10.1016/j.compcom.2004.02.003

van Someren, M. W., Barnard, Y. F., & Sandberg, J. A. C. (1994). *The think aloud method: A practical guide to modelling cognitive processes*. London: Academic Press. doi:10.1016/0306-4573(95)90031-4

Virvou, M., & Katsionis, G. (2008). On the usability and likeability of virtual reality games for education: The case of VR-ENGAGE. *Computers & Education*, *50*(1), 154–178. doi:10.1016/j.compedu.2006.04.004

Vygotsky, L. S. (1980). *Mind in society: The development of higher psychological processes*. Harvard University Press.

Wann, J., & Mon-Williams, M. (1996). What does virtual reality NEED?: Human factors issues in the design of three-dimensional computer environments. *International Journal of Human-Computer Studies*, *44*(6), 829–847. doi:10.1006/ijhc.1996.0035

White, C. (1995). Autonomy and strategy use in distance foreign language learning: Research findings. *System*, *23*(2), 207–221. doi:10.1016/0346-251X(95)00009-9

Wilson, B., & Cole, P. (1991). A review of cognitive teaching models. *Educational Technology Research and Development*, *39*(4), 47–64. doi:10.1007/BF02296571

Witmer, B., & Singer, M. (1998). Measuring Presence in Virtual Environments: A Presence Questionnaire. *Presence (Cambridge, Mass.)*, *7*(3), 225–240. doi:10.1162/105474698565686

Woo, Y., & Reeves, T. C. (2007). Meaningful interaction in web-based learning: A social constructivist interpretation. *The Internet and Higher Education*, *10*(1), 15–25. doi:10.1016/j.iheduc.2006.10.005

Yeh, E., & Wan, G. (2019). The Use of Virtual Worlds in Foreign Language Teaching and Learning. In M. Khosrow-Pour (Ed.), Computer-Assisted Language Learning: Concepts, Methodologies, Tools, and Applications (pp. 1949-1972). IGI Global.

Yin, R. (1994). *Case Study Research: Design and Methods* (2nd ed.). Beverly Hills, CA: Sage Publishing.

Young, E. H. (2018). *Promoting Second Language Learning Through Oral Asynchronous Computer-Mediated Communication* (Unpublished PhD thesis). Brigham Young University. Retrieved from https://scholarsarchive.byu.edu/etd/7051

Young, K. A. (2005). Direct from the source: The value of 'think-aloud' data in understanding learning. *Journal of Educational Enquiry*, *6*(1), 19–33. Retrieved from https://opus.lib.uts.edu.au/bitstream/10453/6348/1/2005002113.pdf

Youngblut, C. (1998). *Education uses of virtual reality technology (No. IDA Document Report no. D2128)*. Alexandria, VA: Institute for Defense Analyses. Retrieved from http://papers.cumincad.org/data/works/att/94ea.content.pdf

Zainal, Z. (2007). Case study as a research method. *Jurnal Kemanusiaan*, (9), 1-6. Retrieved from http://psyking.net/htmlobj-3837/case_study_as_a_research_method.pdf

Zhai, N. (2017). The Application of Virtual Reality Technology in Building Immersive Foreign Language Teaching Environment. *DEStech Transactions on Engineering and Technology Research*.

ADDITIONAL READING

Abdelaziz, M. A., Alaa El Din, M., & Senousy, M. B. (2014). Challenges and Issues in Building Virtual Reality-Based e-Learning System. *International Journal of e-Education, e-Business, e-Management Learning*, *4*(4), 320. Retrieved from https://pdfs.semanticscholar.org/1c77/1c3b1d08e6cd68776d9f7e5ab4ac4d7b7598.pdf

Biocca, F., & Levy, M. R. (Eds.). (2013). *Communication in the age of virtual reality*. Hove, UK: Routledge.

Burdea, G. C., & Coiffet, P. (2003). *Virtual reality technology* (2nd ed.). New Jersey: Wiley-Interscience. doi:10.1162/105474603322955950

Burkle, M. & Kinshuk (2009). Learning in virtual worlds: The challenges and opportunities. *International Conference on CyberWorlds, IEEE Conference Publications* (pp. 320-327). Doi: 10.1109/CW.2009.56

Furht, B. (Ed.). (2008). *Encyclopedia of multimedia*. Boston, MA: Springer Science & Business Media; doi:10.1007/978-0-387-78414-4

Moore, A. A., & McAvoy, S. (2007). Teaching through experiencing. In S. Cawood, M. Fiala, & D. H. Steinberg (Eds.), *Augmented reality: A practical guide* (pp. 205–218). Raleigh, NC: Pragmatic Bookshelf.

Schuemie, M. J., Van Der Straaten, P., Krijn, M., & Van Der Mast, C. A. (2001). Research on presence in virtual reality: A survey. *Cyberpsychology & Behavior*, *4*(2), 183–201. doi:10.1089/109493101300117884 PMID:11710246

Schwienhorst, K. (1998). The 'third place'–virtual reality applications for second language learning. *ReCALL*, *10*(1), 118–126. doi:10.1017/S095834400000433X

Shih, Y. C., & Yang, M. T. (2008). A collaborative virtual environment for situated language learning using VEC3D. *Journal of Educational Technology & Society*, *11*(1), 56–68.

KEY TERMS AND DEFINITIONS

Authentic Virtual Reality (VR) Learning Environment: An environment that enables learners to interact and be immersed into learning in VR by the help of the computer interfaces.

Collaboration: One learner learns and works with one or more than one person.

Constructs of Virtual Reality: The components that structure VR.

Desktop Virtual Reality: Programs, software, or tools that simulate a real or real-like environment provided with 360° videos that can be watched on computers or laptops.

ImmerseMe: A VR tool that teaches different languages with 360° scenarios created in the target language country and characterized by native people.

Interaction: The communication process that can happen between people or a person and a tool, program, or software.

Learner Differences: This term shows that learners have differences in learning in terms of learning styles, perceptions, experiences, motivation, and attitudes.

Scaffolding: The process in which users are assisted to follow their learning paths on their own but with the help of the guidance in a VR learning environment. For instance, e-feedback in a learning activity in a VR-based learning program shows the right answer and may tell whether they have made a mistake or not.

Self-Paced Learning: In this term, learners can pace their learning; for example, they decide how much time to spend on an activity.

Compilation of References

Abdullah, F. S., & Hosseini, K. (2012). Discursive enactment of power in Iranian high school EFL classrooms. *GEMA Online Journal of Language Studies*, *12*(2), 375–392.

Abhishek, M. T., Aswin, P. S., Akhil, N. C., Souban, A., Muhammedali, S. K., & Vial, A. (2018, December). Virtual Lab Using Markerless Augmented Reality. In *2018 IEEE International Conference on Teaching, Assessment, and Learning for Engineering (TALE)* (pp. 1150-1153). IEEE. 10.1109/TALE.2018.8615245

Adkins, D., & Guerreiro, M. (2018). Learning styles: Considerations for technology enhanced item design. *British Journal of Educational Technology*, *49*(3), 574–583. doi:10.1111/bjet.12556

Adris, N., & Yamat, H. (2015). Massively Multiplayer Online Role-Playing Games (MMORPG) as Virtual Grounds for Second Language Learning: Players' Perception. *Proceedings of the International Seminar on Language Teaching ISeLT.*

Affouf, M., & Walsh, T. P. (2007). An assessment of web-based homework in the teaching of college algebra. *The International Journal for Technology in Mathematics Education*, *14*(4), 163–167.

Agarwal, A., Gupta, M., Gupta, S., & Gupta, S. C. (2011). Systematic digital forensic investigation model. *International Journal of Computer Science and Security*, *5*(1), 118–131.

Ahmed, S., & Dann, S. (2015). The virtual future of education and training. *The Bulletin of the Royal College of Surgeons of England*, *97*(10), 431–432. doi:10.1308/rcsbull.2015.431

Akcaoglu, M. (2013). Using an MMORPG in a language classroom: Stories versus tutors as source of motivation. In Y. Baek & N. Whitton (Eds.), *Cases on digita l game - based learning: Methods, models and strategies*. IGN Publishing. doi:10.4018/978-1-4666-2848-9.ch002

Alain, M. (2014). *MOOCs: New research questions and method?* Retrieved from https://prezi.com/owhcvtpwsu5q/moocs-new-research-questions-and-method/

Alam, M. F., Katsikas, S., Beltramello, O., & Hadjiefthymiades, S. (2017). Augmented and virtual reality based monitoring and safety system: A prototype IoT platform. *Journal of Network and Computer Applications*, *89*, 109–119. doi:10.1016/j.jnca.2017.03.022

Alam, M. M. (2017). Constructivism and the classroom curriculum. *The International Journal of Indian Psychology*, *5*(1), 20–29. doi:10.25215/0501.103

Albrecht, U., Folta-Schoofs, K., Behrends, M., & von Jan, U. (2013). Effects of mobile augmented reality learning compared to textbook learning on medical students: Randomized controlled pilot study. *Journal of Medical Internet Research*, *15*(8), e182. doi:10.2196/jmir.2497 PMID:23963306

Alexander, B., Becker, S. A., Cummins, M., & Giesinger, C. H. (2017). Digital literacy in higher education, part II: An NMC horizon project strategic brief.: Vol. 3. Austin, TX: The New Media Consortium.

Allcoat, D., & von Mühlenen, A. (2018). Learning in virtual reality: Effects on performance, emotion and engagement. *Research in Learning Technology*, 26.

American Historical Association. (n.d.). *Statement of Excellence in Classroom Teaching of History.* Retrieved May 26, 2010 from http://www.historians.org/teaching/policy/ExcellentTeaching.htm

Amineh, R. J., & Asl, H. D. (2015). Review of constructivism and social constructivism. *Journal of Social Sciences, Literature and Languages*, *1*(1), 9-16. Retrieved from https://pdfs.semanticscholar.org/3890/3f4a7255496f75124d639e14e9b810c17370.pdf

An, D., & Carr, M. (2017). Learning styles theory fails to explain learning and achievement: Recommendations for alternative approaches. *Personality and Individual Differences*, *116*, 410–416. doi:10.1016/j.paid.2017.04.050

Anderson, B. (2008). *Operationalizing online interaction in distance education: A register comparison of IRC and MMORPG corpora*. Retrieved on October 22, 2008 from http://pine.ucc.nau.edu/boa/mmoircinteraction/

Anderson, B. (2010). *MMORPGs in support of learning: Current trends and future uses*. Academic Press.

Anderson, M. & Jackson, D. (2000). Computer systems for distributed and distance learning. *Journal of Computer Assisted Learning, 16*(1), 213-228.

Anderson, B. (2014). Massive Multiplayer Online Role Playing Games and Interaction: A Measurable Model of Interaction for Online Learning. *International Journal of Virtual and Personal Learning Environments*, *5*(2), 28–39. doi:10.4018/ijvple.2014040103

Anderson, C., & Hounsell, D. (2007). Knowledge practices: 'doing the subject' in undergraduate courses. *Curriculum Journal*, *18*(4), 463–478. doi:10.1080/09585170701687910

Anderson, M., & Jiang, J. (2018). *Teens, social media & technology 2018*. Washington, DC: Pew Internet & American Life Project. Retrieved from http://publicservicesalliance.org/ wp-content/uploads/2018/06/Teens-Social-Media-Technology-2018-PEW.pdf

Anderson, R. C. (1982). Allocation of attention during reading. In A. Flammer & W. Kintsch (Eds.), *Discourse processing* (pp. 292–305). New York: North Holland Publishing Company. doi:10.1016/S0166-4115(08)62699-0

Anderson, R. D. (2002). Reforming science teaching: What research says about inquiry. *Journal of Science Teacher Education, 13*(1), 1–12. doi:10.1023/A:1015171124982

Anderson, T., Rourke, L., Garrison, R., & Archer, W. (2001). Assessing teacher presence in a computer conferencing context. *Journal of Asynchronous Learning Networks, 5*(2), 17.

Anstine, J., & Skidmore, M. (2005). A small sample study of traditional and online courses with sample selection adjustment. *Journal of Economic Education, 36*(1), 107–127.

Antonietti, A., Rasi, C., Imperio, E., & Sacco, M. (2000). The representation of virtual reality in education. *Education and Information Technologies, 5*(4), 317–327. doi:10.1023/A:1012057608694

Appleton, R. (2016, October 26). The MMORPG genre is dead, and we killed it. *The Fresno Bee*. Accessed on January 9, 2019 from: https://www.fresnobee.com/entertainment/ent-columns-blogs/video-games/article98016107.html

Arbaugh, J., Cleveland-Innes, M., Diaz, S., Garrison, D., Ice, P, & Richardson, J. (2008). Developing a community of inquiry instrument: Testing a measure of the Community of Inquiry framework using a multi-institutional sample. *The Internet and Higher Education, 11*(3-4), 133-136. doi:10.1016/j.iheduc.2008.06.003

Arbaugh, J.B., Bangert, A., & Cleveland-Innes, M. (2010). Subject matter effects and the Community of Inquiry (CoI) framework: An exploratory study. *The Internet and Higher Education, 13*(1-2), 37-44. doi:10.1016/j.iheduc.2009.10.006

Arbaugh, J. B. (2005). How much does “subject matter” matter? A study of disciplinary effects in on-line mba courses. *Academy of Management Learning & Education, 4*(1), 57–73. doi:10.5465/amle.2005.16132549

Arbaugh, J. B., Godfrey, M. R., Johnson, M., Pollack, B. L., Niendorf, B., & Wresch, W. (2009). Research in online and blended learning in the business disciplines: Key findings and possible future directions. *Internet and Higher Education, 12*(1), 71–87. doi:10.1016/j.iheduc.2009.06.006

Arfat. (n.d.). Retrieved from http://www.arfat.il.pw.edu.pl/

Ausburn, L. J., & Ausburn, F. B. (2010, December). Spheres of reality: A conceptualization of desktop virtual environments in career and technical education and an implementation training model. *Proceedings of the National Career and Technical Education Research and Professional Development Conference.* Retrieved from http://citeseerx.ist.psu.edu/viewdoc/download?doi=10.1.1.454.7019&rep=rep1&type=pdf

Ausburn, L. J., & Ausburn, F. B. (2008). New Desktop Virtual Reality Technology in Technical Education. *Journal of Educational Technology, 4*(4), 48–61. Retrieved from https://files.eric.ed.gov/fulltext/EJ1097807.pdf

Ausburn, L. J., Martens, J., Washington, A., Steele, D., & Washburn, E. (2009). A cross-case analysis of gender issues in desktop virtual reality learning environments. *Journal of STEM Teacher Education*, *46*(3), 6. Retrieved from https://ir.library.illinoisstate.edu/cgi/viewcontent.cgi?article=1103&context=jste

AVALON Learning NING. (2012). Retrieved June 6, 2012, from http://avalon-project.ning.com/

Azuma, R. T. (1997). A survey of augmented reality. *Presence (Cambridge, Mass.)*, *6*(4), 355–385. doi:10.1162/pres.1997.6.4.355

Bacca, J., Baldiris, S., Fabregat, R., & Graf, S., & Kinshuk. (2014). Augmented reality trends in education: A systematic review of research and applications. *Journal of Educational Technology & Society*, *17*(4), 133–149.

Baddeley, A. D. (1997). *Human memory: Theory and practice* (Rev ed.). Hove, UK: Psychology Press.

Baker, T. E. (2009). Police Criminalistics: Learning Modalities and Evaluation. *Forensic Examiner*, *18*(3), 52–56.

Bandura, A. (2002). Social cognitive theory in cultural context. *Applied Psychology*, *51*(2), 269–290. doi:10.1111/1464-0597.00092

Barabasi, A. (2003). *Linked: How everything is connected to everything else and what it means*. New York, NY: Penguin Books.

Barab, S., Thomas, M., Dodge, T., Carteaux, R., & Tuzun, H. (2005). Making learning fun: Quest Atlantis, a game without guns. *Educational Technology Research and Development*, *53*(1), 86–107. doi:10.1007/BF02504859

Barkand, J & Kush, J. (2009). GEARS: A 3D virtual learning environment and virtual social and educational world used in online secondary schools. *Electronic Journal of e-Learning, 7*(3), 215 – 224.

Baron, N. S. (2017). Reading in a digital age. *Phi Delta Kappan*, *99*(2), 15–20. doi:10.1177/0031721717734184

Barr, M. (2017). Video games can develop graduate skills in higher education students: A randomised trial. *Computers & Education*, *113*, 86–97. doi:10.1016/j.compedu.2017.05.016

Barsom, E. Z., Graafland, M., & Schijven, M. P. (2016). Systematic review on the effectiveness of augmented reality applications in medical training. *Surgical Endoscopy*, *30*(10), 4174–4183. doi:10.100700464-016-4800-6 PMID:26905573

Bartle, R. (2013). *The Decline of MMOs*. Accessed on January 9th 2019 from: https://mud.co.uk/richard/The%20Decline%20of%20MMOs.pdf

Barton, M. (2007). *The history of computer role playing games: Parts I, II and III*. Retrieved from http://www.gamasutra.com/features/20070223b/barton_01.shtml

Barzilai, S. (2017). "Half-reliable": A qualitative analysis of epistemic thinking in and about a digital game. *Contemporary Educational Psychology*, *51*, 51–66. doi:10.1016/j.cedpsych.2017.06.004

Bates, T. (2014). *Comparing xMOOCs and cMOOCs: Philosophy and practice*. Retrieved from https://www.tonybates.ca/2014/10/13/comparing-xmoocs-and-cmoocs-philosophy-and-practice/

Baum, L. F. (1901). *The master key: An electrical fairy tale*. Indianapolis, IN: Bowen-Merrill Company.

Bawden, D. (2001). Information and digital literacies: A review of concepts. *The Journal of Documentation*, *57*(2), 218–259. doi:10.1108/EUM0000000007083

Bawden, D. (2008). Origins and concepts of digital literacy. In C. Lankshear & M. Knobel (Eds.), *Digital literacies: Concepts, policies & practices* (pp. 17–32). New York: Peter Lang Publishing.

Baylor, A. L. (2003). *Evidence That Multiple Agents Facilitate Greater Learning*. Paper presented at the AI-ED, Sydney, Australia.

Baylor, A. L. (2002). Agent-based learning environments for investigating teaching and learning. *Journal of Educational Computing Research*, *26*(3), 249–270. doi:10.2190/PH2K-6P09-K8EC-KRDK

Baylor, A. L., & Kim, Y. (2006). A social-cognitive framework for pedagogical agents as learning companions. *Educational Technology Research and Development*, *54*(6), 569–596. doi:10.100711423-006-0637-3

Beaufort, A. (2004). Developmental Gains of a History Major: A Case for Building a Theory of Disciplinary Writing Expertise. *Research in the Teaching of English*, *39*(2), 136–185.

Behzadan, A. H., & Kamat, V. R. (2013). Enabling discovery-based learning in construction using telepresent augmented reality. *Automation in Construction*, *33*, 3–10. doi:10.1016/j.autcon.2012.09.003

Bellés-Fortuño, B. (2006*). Discourse markers within the university lecture genre: A contrastive study between Spanish and North-American lectures* (Unpublished doctoral dissertation). Universitat Jaume I, Spain.

Bendicho, P. F., Mora, C. E., Añorbe-Díaz, B., & Rivero-Rodríguez, P. (2017). Effect on Academic Procrastination after Introducing Augmented Reality. *EURASIA Journal of Mathematics, Science & Technology Education*, *13*(2), 319–330.

Bernard, R. M., Abrami, P. C., Lou, Y., Borokhovski, E., Wade, A., Wozney, L., ... Huang, B. (2004). How does distance education compare to classroom instruction? A meta-analysis of the empirical literature. *Review of Educational Research*, *74*(3), 379–439. doi:10.3102/00346543074003379

Berns, A., Mota, J. M., Ruiz-Rube, I., & Dodero, J. M. (2018, October). Exploring the potential of a 360° video application for foreign language learning. In *Proceedings of the Sixth International Conference on Technological Ecosystems for Enhancing Multiculturality* (pp. 776-780). ACM. 10.1145/3284179.3284309

Bernstein, B. (1971). *Class, codes and control* (Vol. 1). London: Routledge and Kegan Paul. doi:10.4324/9780203014035

Bhattacharjee, J. (2015). Constructivist approach to learning–an effective approach of teaching learning. *International Research Journal of Interdisciplinary & Multidisciplinary Studies, 1*(4), 23-28. Retrieved from http://oaji.net/articles/2015/1707-1438677336.pdf

Bidarra, J., & Rusman, E. (2017). Towards a pedagogical model for science education: bridging educational contexts through a blended learning approach. *Open Learning: The Journal of Open, Distance and E-Learning, 32*(1), 6-20.

Billinghurst, M., & Henrysson, A. (2009). Mobile architectural augmented reality. *Mixed Reality in Architecture, Design and Construction*, 93-104.

Billinghurst, M., & Kato, H. (2002). Collaborative augmented reality. *Communications of the ACM, 45*(7), 64–70. doi:10.1145/514236.514265

Blackman, S. (2005). Serious Games...and Less! *Computer Graphics, 39*(1), 12–16. doi:10.1145/1057792.1057802

Blake, R. (1998). The role of technology in second language learning. In H. Byrnes (Ed.), *Learning foreign and second languages: Perspectives in research and scholarship* (pp. 209–237). New York: Modern Language Association.

Blasing, M. T. (2010). Second language in Second Life: Exploring interaction, identity and pedagogical practice in a virtual world. *SEEJ, 54*(1), 96–117.

Blin, F., Nocchi, S., & Fowley, C. (2013). Mondes virtuels et apprentissage des langues: Vers un cadre théorique émergent. *Recherches et Applications, 54*, 94–107.

Boellstorff, T. (2015). Three real features for virtual worlds. *Journal of Virtual Worlds Research, 8*(2), 1–5. doi:10.4101/jvwr.v8i2.7167

Bogost, I. (2007). *Persuasive games: the expressive power of videogames*. Cambridge, MA: MIT Press.

Bonk, C. J., Lee, M. M., & Sheu, F.-R. (2014). *Research on self-directed informal learners in open educational environments and massively open online courses*. Presented at AECT, Anaheim, CA. Retrieved from http://trainingshare.worldisopen.com/pdfs/Self-Directed_Lrng_MOOCs_Open_Ed_AECT_Bonk_et_al_Friday_paper_session--Title-Change.pdf

Bonk, C., & Dennen, V. (2005). *Massive multiplayer online gaming: A research framework for military training and education* (Technical Report No. 2005-1). Washington, DC: U.S. Department of Defense (DUSD/R): Advanced Distributed Learning (ADL) Initiative. Retrieved from http://mypage.iu.edu/cjbonk/GameReport_Bonk_final.pdf

Bonner, E., & Reinders, H. (2018). Augmented and Virtual Reality in The Language Classroom: Practical Ideas. *Teaching English with Technology, 18*(3), 33–53.

Botero, G. G., Questier, F., Cincinnato, S., He, T., & Zhu, C. (2018). Acceptance and usage of mobile assisted language learning by higher education students. *Journal of Computing in Higher Education, 30*(3), 426–451. doi:10.100712528-018-9177-1

Bouchard, P. (2009). Pedagogy without a teacher: What are the limits? *International Journal of Self-Directed Learning*, *6*(2), 13–22. Retrieved from http://www.sdlglobal.com

Boucouvalas, M. (2009). Revisiting the concept of Self in self-directed learning:Towards a more robust construct for research and practice in a global context. *International Journal of Self-Directed Learning*, *6*(1), 1–9. Retrieved from http://www.sdlglobal.com

Bower, M., Howe, C., McCredie, N., Robinson, A., & Grover, D. (2014). Augmented Reality in education – cases, places and potentials. *Educational Media International*, *51*(1), 1–15. doi:10.1080/09523987.2014.889400

Bowers, K. W., Ragas, M. W., & Neely, J. C. (2009). Assessing the value of virtual worlds for post-secondary instructors: A survey of innovators, early adopters and the early majority in SL. *International Journal of Humanities and Social Science*, *3*(1), 40–50.

Bowman, D. A., Kruijff, E., LaViola, J. J. J. Jr, & Poupyrev, I. (2001). An Introduction to 3-D User Interface Design. *Presence Teleoperators VR*, *10*(1), 96–108. doi:10.1162/105474601750182342

Bowman, D. A., & McMahan, R. P. (2007). Virtual Reality: How Much Immersion Is Enough? *Computer*, *40*(7), 36–43. doi:10.1109/MC.2007.257

Boyd, D., & Crawford, K. (2012). Critical questions for Big Data. *Information Communication and Society*, *15*(5), 662–679. doi:10.1080/1369118X.2012.678878

Boyer, S. A. (2018). *SCADA supervisory control and data acquisition*. The Instrumentation, Systems and Automation Society.

Boyle, C., & Rivers, N. A. (2016). A version of access. *Technical Communication Quarterly*, *25*(1), 29–47. doi:10.1080/10572252.2016.1113702

Brislin, R. (1981). *Cross-cultural encounters: Face-to-face interactions*. New York, NY: Pergamon Press.

Britt, M. A., & Aglinskas, C. (2002). Improving Students' Ability to Identify and Use Source Information. *Cognition and Instruction*, *20*(4), 485–522. doi:10.1207/S1532690XCI2004_2

Bronack, S., Sanders, R., Cheney, A., Riedl, R., Tashner, J., & Matzen, N. (2008). Presence pedagogy: Teaching and learning in a 3D immersive world. *International Journal on Teaching and Learning in Higher Education*, *20*(1), 59–69.

Bronack, S., Sanders, R., Cheney, A., Riedl, R., Tashner, J., & Matzen, N. (2008). Presence pedagogy: Teaching and learning in a 3D virtual immersive world. *International Journal on Teaching and Learning in Higher Education*, *20*(1), 59–69.

Brooks, J. G., & Brooks, M. G. (1999). *In search of understanding: The case for constructivist classrooms*. ASCD.

Brown, A. (1992). Design experiments: Theoretical and methodological challenges in creating complex interventions in classroom settings. *Journal of the Learning Sciences*, *2*(2), 141–178. doi:10.120715327809jls0202_2

Bruner, J. (1990). *Acts of meaning*. Cambridge, MA: Harvard University Press.

Bryant, T. (2008). Using *World of Warcraft* and other MMORPGs to foster a targeted, social, and cooperative approach toward language learning. *Academic Commons*, *12*(4), 23–35.

Burgess, M. L., Slate, J. R., Rojas-LeBouef, A., & LaPrairie, K. (2010). Teaching and learning in Second Life: Using the Community of Inquiry (CoI) model to support online instruction with graduate students in instructional technology. *The Internet and Higher Education, 13*(1-2), 84-88. doi:10.1016/j.iheduc.2009.12.003

Campbell, C., & Jane, B. (2012). Motivating children to learn: The role of technology education. *International Journal of Technology and Design Education*, *22*(1), 1–11. doi:10.100710798-010-9134-4

Carmigniani, J., Furht, B., Anisetti, M., Ceravolo, P., Damiani, E., & Ivkovic, M. (2011). Augmented reality technologies, systems and applications. *Multimedia Tools and Applications*, *51*(1), 341–377. doi:10.100711042-010-0660-6

Carvin, A. (2000). More than just access: Fitting literacy and content into the digital divide equation. *EDUCAUSE Review*, *35*(6), 38–47. Retrieved from http://www.educause.edu/ero

Casas, S., Portalés, C., García-Pereira, I., & Fernández, M. (2017). On a first evaluation of ROMOT—A RObotic 3D MOvie Theatre—For driving safety awareness. *Multimodal Technologies and Interaction*, *1*(2), 6. doi:10.3390/mti1020006

Casas, S., Portalés, C., García-Pereira, I., & Gimeno, J. (2019). Mixing Different Realities in a Single Shared Space: Analysis of Mixed-Platform Collaborative Shared Spaces. In *Harnessing the Internet of Everything (IoE) for Accelerated Innovation Opportunities* (pp. 175–192). IGI Global. doi:10.4018/978-1-5225-7332-6.ch008

Castellanos & Perez, (2017). New Challenge in Education: Enhancing Student's Knowledge through Augmented Reality. *Augmented Reality*, 273-293.

Castronova, E., Bell, M., Cornell, R., Cummings, J., Falk, M., Ross, T., ... Field, A. (2009). Synthetic worlds as experimental instruments. In M. Wolf & B. Perron (Eds.), *The video game theory reader 2*. New York: Routledge.

Caudell, T. P., & Mizell, D. W. (1992). Augmented reality: An application of heads-up display technology to manual manufacturing processes. *Proceedings of the Twenty-Fifth Hawaii International Conference on System Sciences, 2,* 659-669. 10.1109/HICSS.1992.183317

Center for Universal Design (CUD). (2008). *North Carolina State University*. Retrieved from https://projects.ncsu.edu/design/cud/index.htm

Centre for Excellence in Universal Design (CEUD). (2014). *How to make accessible documents*. Retrieved from http://universaldesign.ie/Products-Services/Customer-Communications-Toolkit-for-the-Public-Service-A-Universal-Design-Approach/Digital-and-Web-Based-Communication-Systems-and-Services/How-to-make-accessible-documents/

Chapman, J., & Rich, P. (2017, January). Identifying motivational styles in educational gamification. *Proceedings of the 50th Hawaii International Conference on System Sciences*. 10.24251/HICSS.2017.157

Charters, E. (2003). The use of think-aloud methods in qualitative research an introduction to think-aloud methods. *Brock Education Journal, 12*(2). Retrieved from https://brock.scholarsportal.info/journals/brocked/home/article/view/38

Chatzopoulos, D., Bermejo, C., Huang, Z., & Hui, P. (2017). Mobile augmented reality survey: From where we are to where we go. *IEEE Access: Practical Innovations, Open Solutions, 5*, 6917–6950. doi:10.1109/ACCESS.2017.2698164

Chavis, D. M., Lee, K. S., & Acosta, J. D. (2008). *The Sense of Community (SCI) Revised: The Reliability and Validity of the SCI-2*. Paper presented at the 2nd International Community Psychology Conference, Lisboa, Portugal.

Chen, C. J., Toh, S. C., & Fauzy, W. M. (2004). The theoretical framework for designing desktop virtual reality-based learning environments. *Journal of Interactive Learning Research, 15*(2), 147–167. Retrieved from https://www.learntechlib.org/primary/p/12841/

Chen, C., Sun, C., & Hsieh, J. (2008). Player guild dynamics and evolution in massively multiplayer online games. *Cyberpsychology & Behavior, 11*(3), 293–301. doi:10.1089/cpb.2007.0066 PMID:18537499

Cheney, A., Sanders, R., Matzen, N., & Tashner, J. (2009). Instructional design and pedagogical issues with Web 2.0 tools. In T. Kidd & I. Chen (Eds.), *Wired for Learning: An Educator's Guide to Web 2.0*. Charlotte, NC: Information Age Publishing.

Cheng, K., & Tsai, C. (2016). The interaction of child-parent shared reading with an augmented reality (AR) picture book and parents' conceptions of AR learning. *British Journal of Educational Technology, 47*(1), 203–222. doi:10.1111/bjet.12228

Chen, J. A., Metcalf, S. J., & Tutwiler, M. S. (2014). Motivation and beliefs about the nature of scientific knowledge within an immersive virtual ecosystems environment. *Contemporary Educational Psychology, 39*(2), 112–123. doi:10.1016/j.cedpsych.2014.02.004

Chen, J. A., Tutwiler, M. S., Metcalf, S. J., Kamarainen, A., Grotzer, T., & Dede, C. (2016). A multi-user virtual environment to support students' self-efficacy and interest in science: A latent growth model analysis. *Learning and Instruction, 41*, 11–22. doi:10.1016/j.learninstruc.2015.09.007

Chen, J. C. (2018). The interplay of tasks, strategies and negotiations in Second Life. *Computer Assisted Language Learning, 31*(8), 960–986. doi:10.1080/09588221.2018.1466810

Chen, Z. H., Chen, H. H. J., & Dai, W. J. (2018). Using narrative-based contextual games to enhance language learning: A case study. *Journal of Educational Technology & Society*, *21*(3), 186–198.

Chickering, A. & Ehrmann, S.C. (1996, October). Implementing the seven principles: Technology as lever. *Association of Adult Higher Education Journal,* 3-6.

Childress, M., & Braswell, R. (2006). Using massively multiplayer online role-playing games for online learning. *Distance Education*, *27*(2), 187–196. doi:10.1080/01587910600789522

Cho, K., Lee, J., Lee, J. S., & Yang, H. S. (2007, September). A realistic e-learning system based on mixed reality. In *13th International Conference on Virtual Systems and Multimedia* (pp. 57-64). Academic Press.

Chuah, K.-M., Chen, C.-J., & Teh, C.-S. (2011). Designing a desktop Virtual Reality-based learning environment with emotional consideration. *Research & Practice in Technology Enhanced Learning*, *6*(1), 25–42. Retrieved from http://ezproxy.lib.swin.edu.au/login?url=http://search.ebscohost.com/login.aspx?direct=true&db=ehh&AN=85289244&site=ehost-live&scope=site

Clarke, J., Dede, C., Ketelhut, D. J., & Nelson, B. (2006). A Design-based Research Strategy to Promote Scalability for Educational Innovations. *Educational Technology, 46*(3), 27-36.

Clarke, J., Dede, C., Ketelhut, D. J., & Nelson, B. (2006). A design-based research strategy to promote scalability for educational innovations. *Educational Technology*, *46*(3), 27–36. Retrieved from https://www.jstor.org/stable/44429300

Clark, R. E. (1983). Reconsidering research on learning from media. *Review of Educational Research*, *53*(4), 445–459. doi:10.3102/00346543053004445

Classroom Learning with augmented reality. (2010). *Trends in EdTech Wiki*. Retrieved from http://aug-reality.pbworks.com/w/page/9469033/Classroom%20Learning%20with%20AR

Clyde, J., & Wilkinson, G. (2009, Fall). *The Digital Mode of History*. Paper presented at Seventy Years On: New Perspectives on the Second World War, Lake Louise, AB. Retrieved from http://www.ucalgary.ca/newperspectives/

Clyde, J., & Thomas, C. (2008). Building and Information Literacy First Person Shooter. *RSR. Reference Services Review*, *36*(4), 366–380. doi:10.1108/00907320810920342

Coates, J. (2004). *Women, men and language: A sociolinguistic account of gender difference in language* (3rd ed.). Harlow: Pearson Education Limited.

Cobb, P., Confre, J., diSessa, A., Lehrer, R., & Schauble, L. (2003). Design experiments in education research. *Educational Researcher*, *32*(1), 9–13. doi:10.3102/0013189X032001009

Coffield, F., Moseley, D., Hall, E., & Ecclestone, K. (2004). *Learning styles and pedagogy in post-16 learning: A systematic and critical review.* Retrieved from Learning and Skills Research Centre: www.LSRC.ac.uk

Cohen, J. (1988). *Statistical power analysis for the behavioral sciences* (2nd ed.). Lawrence Erlbaum.

CollegeConfidential. (2019). *I found the following post about the college and wondering if it is true that they are bankrupt and have a super high crime rate?* Retrieved March 1, 2019, from: https://talk.collegeconfidential.com/suny-general/2107067-suny-plattsburgh-in-new-york.html

Collins, A. (1992). Toward a design science of education. In E. Scanlon & T. O'Shea (Eds.), *New directions in educational technology* (pp. 15–22). New York, NY: Springer. doi:10.1007/978-3-642-77750-9_2

Conference College Composition and Communication (CCCC). (2011). *A Policy on Disability in CCCC*. Retrieved from http://cccc.ncte.org/cccc/resources/positions/disabilitypolicy

Conference on College Composition and Communication (CCCC). (2013). *A position statement of principles and example effective practices for online writing instruction (OWI)*. Retrieved from http://cccc.ncte.org/cccc/resources/positions/owiprinciples

Connolly, T. M., Boyle, E. A., MacArthur, E., Hainey, T., & Boyle, J. M. (2012). A systematic literature review of empirical evidence on computer games and serious games. *Computers & Education, 59*(2), 661–686. doi:10.1016/j.compedu.2012.03.004

Conole, G. (2008). New schemas for mapping pedagogies and technologies. *Ariadine, 56*.

Cooper, S. (2015). Massively Multiplayer Research: Gamifying and (Citizen) Science. In S. P. Walz & S. Deterding (Eds.), The Gameful World: Approaches, Issues, Applications (pp. 487–500). Academic Press.

Cooper, Treuille, Barbero, Leaver-Fay, Tuite, Khatib, … Players. (2010). The challenge of designing scientific discovery games. Proceedings of Foundations of Digital Games.

Costin, H., & Hamilton, D. (2009). Quality in business education as measured by accreditation and ranking systems. *International Journal of Management Education*, *3*(3/4), 249–269.

Crandall, P. G., Engler, R. K. III, Beck, D. E., Killian, S. A., O'Bryan, C. A., Jarvis, N., & Clausen, E. (2015). Development of an augmented reality game to teach abstract concepts in food chemistry. *Journal of Food Science Education*, *14*(1), 18–23. doi:10.1111/1541-4329.12048

Crawford, M. (1995). *Talking difference: On gender and language*. London: Sage.

Crellin, J., Adda, M., & Duke-Williams, E. (2010). The use of simulation in digital forensics teaching. *11th Annual Conference of the Higher Education Academy, Information and Computer Science Group*. Retrieved from http://eprints.port.ac.uk/1597/1/Crellin1.pdf

Cronbach, L. J. (1957). The two disciplines of scientific psychology. *The American Psychologist*, *12*(11), 671–684. doi:10.1037/h0043943

Cummings, J. J., & Bailenson, J. N. (2016). How immersive is enough? A meta-analysis of the effect of immersive technology on user presence. *Media Psychology*, *19*(2), 272–309. doi:10.1080/15213269.2015.1015740

Cybinski, P., & Selvanathan, S. (2005). Learning experience and learning effectiveness in undergraduate statistics: Modeling performance in traditional and flexible learning environments. *Decision Sciences Journal of Innovative Education*, *3*(2), 251–271. doi:10.1111/j.1540-4609.2005.00069.x

Czepielewski, S. (2012). The virtual world of Second Life in foreign language learning. In: S. Czepielewski (Ed.), *Learning a language in virtual worlds: A review of innovation and ICT in language teaching methodology, International conference, Warsaw, 17th November 2011* (pp. 15-24). Warsaw: Warsaw Academy of Computer Science, Management and Administration.

Dalgarno, B., Hedberg, J., & Harper, B. (2002). The contribution of 3D environments to conceptual understanding. In O. J. McKerrow (Eds.), *Winds of Change in the Sea of Learning: Proceedings of the 19th Annual Conference of the Australasian Society for Computers in Learning in Tertiary Education* (vol. 1, pp. 149-158). Auckland, New Zealand: UNITEC, Institute of Technology.

Dalgarno, B., & Lee, M. J. W. (2010). What are the learning affordances of 3-D virtual environments? *British Journal of Educational Technology*, *41*(1), 10–32. doi:10.1111/j.1467-8535.2009.01038.x

Das, P., Zhu, M. O., McLaughlin, L., Bilgrami, Z., & Milanaik, R. L. (2017). Augmented Reality Video Games: New Possibilities and Implications for Children and Adolescents. *Multimodal Technologies and Interaction*, *1*(2), 8. doi:10.3390/mti1020008

de Freitas, S., & Griffiths, M. (2007). Online gaming as an educational tool in learning and training. *British Journal of Educational Technology*, *38*(3), 535–537. doi:10.1111/j.1467-8535.2007.00720.x

de Jong, T., Linn, M. C., & Zacharia, Z. C. (2013). Physical and Virtual Laboratories in Science and Engineering Education. *Science*, *340*(6130), 305–308. doi:10.1126cience.1230579 PMID:23599479

De Laat, M. (2006). *Networked learning* (Doctoral thesis). Retrieved from https://eprints.soton.ac.uk/20358/1/Maarten_De_Laat_Networked_Learning_2006.pdf

de Wilde, P. (2014). The gap between predicted and measured energy performance of buildings: A framework for investigation. *Automation in Construction*, *41*, 40–49. doi:10.1016/j.autcon.2014.02.009

Delfanti, A. (2010). Users and peers: From citizen science to P2P science. *Journal of Clinical Outcomes Management*, *9*(1).

DelGaudio, J. J. (2002). Creating Simulations for Use in Teaching Lower Division U.S. History. *History Computer Review*, *18*(1), 37–52.

Design-Based Research Collective (DBRC). (2003). Design-based research: An emerging paradigm for educational inquiry. *Educational Researcher*, *32*(1), 5–8. doi:10.3102/0013189X032001005

Deterding, D., Dixon, D., Khaled, R., & Nacke, L. (2011). From game design elements to gamefulness: defining "gamification". *MindTrek '11 Proceedings of the 15th International Academic MindTrek Conference: Envisioning Future Media Environments*, 9-15. 10.1145/2181037.2181040

Deutschmann, M., & Panichi, L. (2009a). Instructional design, teacher practice and learner autonomy. In J. Molka-Danielsen & M. Deutschmann (Eds.), Learning and teaching in the virtual world of SL (pp. 27-44). Trondheim: Tapir Academic Press.

Deutschmann, M., Steinvall, A., & Lagerström, A. (2011). Gender-bending in virtual space: Using voice-morphing in Second Life to raise sociolinguistic gender awareness. In S. Czepielewski (Ed.), *Learning a language in virtual worlds: A review of innovation and ICT in language teaching methodology, International conference, Warsaw, 17th November 2011* (pp. 54-61). Warsaw: Warsaw Academy of Computer Science, Management and Administration.

Deutschmann, M., & Panichi, L. (2009b). Talking into empty space? Signalling involvement in a virtual language classroom in SL. *Language Awareness*, *18*(3-4), 310–328. doi:10.1080/09658410903197306

Deutschmann, M., Panichi, L., & Molka-Danielsen, J. (2009). Designing oral participation in SL – A comparative study of two language proficiency courses. *ReCALL*, *21*(2), 206–226. doi:10.1017/S0958344009000196

Di Filippo, L. (2017). MMORPG as Locally Realized Worlds of Action. In M. Boni (Ed.), *World Building. Transmedia, Fans, Industries*. Amsterdam, The Netherlands: Amsterdam University Press. doi:10.2307/j.ctt1zkjz0m.16

Díaz, D., Boj, C., & Portalés, C. (2016). HybridPLAY: A new technology to foster outdoors physical activity, verbal communication and teamwork. *Sensors (Basel)*, *16*(4), 586. doi:10.339016040586 PMID:27120601

Dickey, M. D. (2003). Teaching in 3D: Pedagogical affordances and constraints of 3D virtual environments for synchronous distance learning. *Distance Education*, *24*(1), 105–121. doi:10.1080/01587910303047

Dickey, M. D. (2005). Engaging by Design: How Engagement Strategies in Popular Computer and Video Games Can Inform Instructional Design. *ETR&D*, *53*(2), 67–83. doi:10.1007/BF02504866

Dickey, M. D. (2011). The pragmatics of virtual worlds for K-12 educators: Investigating the affordances and constraints of ActiveWorlds and SecondLife with K-12 in-service teachers. *Educational Technology Research and Development*, *59*(1), 1–20. doi:10.100711423-010-9163-4

Dietze, S., Siemens, D., Tabi, D., & Drachsler, H. (2016). Edotorial: Datasets for learning analytics. *Journal of Learning Analytics*. Retrieved from https://learning-analytics.info/journals/index.php/JLA/article/view/5071

diSessa, A. A. (2000). *Changing minds: Computer, learning, and literacy*. Cambridge, MA: MIT Press. doi:10.7551/mitpress/1786.001.0001

Dong, S., Feng, C., & Kamat, V. R. (2013). Sensitivity analysis of augmented reality-assisted building damage reconnaissance using virtual prototyping. *Automation in Construction*, *33*, 24–36. doi:10.1016/j.autcon.2012.09.005

Doran, L., & Davis, M. R. (2016). As Pokémon craze grows, educators weigh game's value. *Education Week*, *35*(37).

Downes, S. (2010, December 5). The role of the educator. *Huffington Post*. Retrieved from http://huff.to/g7Orh9

Downes, S. (2013). *The quality of massive open online courses*. Retrieved from http://mooc.efquel.org/week-2-the-quality-of-massive-open-online-courses-by-stephen-downes/

Downes, S. (2013, December 4). Learning and performance support systems. *Half an Hour Blogspot*. Retrieved from http://halfanhour.blogspot.com.es/2013/12/learning-and-performance-support-systems.html

Downes, S. (2014). *The MOOC of one*. Retrieved from https://www.slideshare.net/Downes/2014-03-10-valencia

Downes, S. (2018). *Approaching E-Learning 3.0*. Retrieved from https://halfanhour.blogspot.com/2018/09/approaching-e-learning-30.html

Drachsler, H., & Greller, W. (2016). Privacy and analytics: it's a DELICATE issue a checklist for trusted learning analytics. In *Proceedings of the Sixth International Conference on Learning Analytics & Knowledge (LAK '16)*. ACM. 10.1145/2883851.2883893

Dron, J., & Anderson, T. (2007). *Collectives, networks, and groups in social software for e learning*. Paper presented at World Conference on E-Learning in Corporate, Government, Healthcare, and Higher Education (ELEARN), Quebec City, Quebec, Canada.

Drucker, P. F. (1993). *Post-capitalist society*. New York, NY: HarperBusiness.

Ducheneaut, N., Yee, N., Nickell, E., & Moore, R. (2006). Building an MMO with mass appeal: A look at gameplay in *World of Warcraft*. *Games and Culture*, *1*(4), 281–317. doi:10.1177/1555412006292613

Dugdale, J., Pavard, B., Pallamin, N., el-Jed, M., & Maugan, L. (2004). Emergency fire incident training in a virtual world. *Proceedings ISCRAM*, 167-172.

Dunleavy, M., & Dede, C. (2014). Augmented reality teaching and learning. In J. Spector, M. Merrill, J. Elen, & M. Bishop (Eds.), *Handbook of research on educational communications and technology* (pp. 735–745). New York, NY: Springer. doi:10.1007/978-1-4614-3185-5_59

Dunn, R. (1990). Understanding the Dunn and Dunn learning styles model and the need for individual diagnosis and prescription. *Journal of Reading, Writing, and Learning Disabilities International*, *6*(3), 223–247. doi:10.1080/0748763900060303

Duval, E. (2011). Attention please! Learning analytics for visualization and recommendation. *Proceedings of 1st International Conference on Learning Analytics and Knowledge*. 10.1145/2090116.2090118

Eatough, V., Davies, M. N. O., Griffiths, M. D., & Chappell, D. (2006). *Everquest*—It's just a computer game right? An interpretative phenomenological analysis of online gaming addiction. *International Journal of Mental Health and Addiction*, 4205–4216.

Ebner, M., & Holzinger, A. (2007). Successful implementation of user-centered game based learning in higher education: An example from civil engineering. *Computers & Education*, *49*(3), 873–890. doi:10.1016/j.compedu.2005.11.026

Eschenbrenner, B., Nah, F., & Siau, K. (2008). 3-D virtual environments in education: Applications, benefits, issues, and opportunities. *Journal of Database Management*, *19*(4), 91–110. doi:10.4018/jdm.2008100106

Estapa, A., & Nadonly, L. (2015). The effect of an augmented reality enhanced mathematics lesson on student achievement and motivation. *Journal of STEM Education: Innovations & Research*, *16*(3), 40–48.

Eurocall/Calico Virtual World SIG NING. (2012). Retrieved June 13, 2012, from http://virtualworldssig.ning.com/

Eurocall/Calico Virtual World SIG NING. (2012). Retrieved June 6, 2012, from http://virtualworldssig.ning.com/

Euroversity, N. I. N. G. (2012). Retrieved June 13, 2012, from http://euroversity.ning.com

Evans, S. R., Wang, R., Yeh, T.-M., Anderson, J., Haija, R., McBratbey-Owen, P. M., ... Zhang, J. (2007). Evaluation of distance learning in an introduction to biostatistics class: A case study. *Statistics Education Research Journal*, *6*(2), 59–77.

Eveland, W. P. Jr, & Dunwoody, S. (2000). Examining Information Processing on the World Wide Web Using Think Aloud Protocols. *Media Psychology*, *2*(3), 219–244. doi:10.1207/S1532785XMEP0203_2

Ezawa, K., & Danely, C. (2016). Virtual & Augmented Reality. In *Investment Themes in 2016*. Citigroup Inc. Retrieved from https://ir.citi.com/UEfBZ0oas9qLzjz9EjXThOLsmRLtDgNWGwJItg1klVIGIVm8iFTGvkYnWQPFZ41DjNzOSXl9kuQ%3D

Fairclough, N. (2001). *Language and power* (2nd ed.). Harlow: Pearson Education Limited.

Feiner, S., MacIntyre, B., Höllerer, T., & Webster, A. (1997). A touring machine: Prototyping 3D mobile augmented reality systems for exploring the urban environment. *Personal Technologies*, *1*(4), 208–217. doi:10.1007/BF01682023

Felder, R., & Silverman, L. (1988). Learning and teaching styles in engineering education. *Engineering Education*, *78*(7), 674-681. Retrieved from http://www4.ncsu.edu/unity/lockers/users/f/felder/public/Papers/LS-1988.pdf

Felder, R., & Soloman, B. (1994). *Index of learning styles* [Questionnaire]. Unpublished instrument. Retrieved from: http://www4.ncsu.edu/unity/lockers/users/f/felder/public/ILSpage.html

Felder, R., & Spurlin, J. (2005). Applications, Reliability, and Validity of the Index of Learning Styles. *International Journal of Engineering Education*, *21*(1), 103–112. Retrieved from http://www.ijee.ie/

Fernandes, K. J., Raja, V. H., & Eyre, J. (2003). Immersive learning system for manufacturing industries. *Computers in Industry*, *51*(1), 31–40. doi:10.1016/S0166-3615(03)00027-7

Field, A. (2009). *Discovering statistics using SPSS* (3rd ed.). Thousand Oaks, CA: SAGE.

Fisher, G., & Eden, S. (2005). Beyond Binary Choices: Integrating Individual and Social Creativity. *International Journal of Human-Computer Studies*, *63*(4), 482–512. doi:10.1016/j.ijhcs.2005.04.014

Fishman, B., Dede, C., & Means, B. (2015). Teaching and technology: New tools for new times. In D. Gitomer & C. Bell (Eds.), *Handbook of Research on Teaching* (5th ed.). Washington, DC: American Educational Research Association.

Foley, A., & Ferri, B. A. (2012). Technology for people, not disabilities: ensuring access and inclusion. *Journal of Research in Special Educational Needs, 12*(4), 192-200. Retrieved from https://onlinelibrary-wiley-com.librarylink.uncc.edu/doi/pdf/10.1111/j.1471-3802

Foote, C. (2012). The evolution of a 1:1 iPad program. *Internet Schools, 1*(15-18).

Foote, R. (2018, February 4). *Who rules entertainment industry? Video games vs. film & music*. Accessed on January 14th, 2019 from: http://www.kfvs12.com/story/31140647/who-rules-the-entertainment-industry/

Forensic Education Program Accreditation Commission. (2017). *Forensic Education Program Accreditation Commission (FEPAC) accreditation standards.* Author.

Foronda, C. L., Alfes, C. M., Dev, P., Kleinheksel, A. J., Nelson, D. A. Jr, O'Donnell, J. M., & Samosky, J. T. (2017). Virtually Nursing: Emerging Technologies in Nursing Education. *Nurse Educator, 42*(1), 14–17. doi:10.1097/NNE.0000000000000295 PMID:27454054

Forsythe, C. (2004). The future of simulation technology for law enforcement: Diverse experience with realistic simulated humans. *FBI Law Enforcement Bulletin, 73*(1), 19–23.

Fortuño, B. B. (2006). *Discourse markers within the university lecture center: A contrastive study between Spanish and North-American Lectures* (Doctoral Dissertation). Universitat Jaume I.

Fournier, H., & Kop, R. (2010). *Researching the design and development of a Personal Learning Environment.* Paper presented at the PLE Conference, Barcelona, Spain. Retrieved from http://bit.ly/c5ehX4

Fournier, H., & Kop, R. (2015). MOOC learning experience design: Issues and challenges. MOOCs and Open Education. *International Journal on E-Learning, 14*(3), 289-304.

Fournier, H., Kop, R., & Durand, G. (2014). Challenges to Research in MOOCs. *Journal of Online Learning and Teaching / MERLOT, 10*(1). Retrieved from http://jolt.merlot.org/vol10no1/fournier_0314.pdf

Fournier, H., Kop, R., & Sitlia, H. (2011). The Value of Learning Analytics to Networked Learning on a Personal Learning Environment. *1st International Conference on Learning analytics and Knowledge*, Banff, Canada. 10.1145/2090116.2090131

Fredrick, T. (2018, January 17). *Who rules entertainment industry? Video games vs. film & music*. Accessed on January 15th, 2019 from: https://www.insidermonkey.com/blog/12-highest-grossing-video-games-of-all-time-518819/?singlepage=1

Freiermuth, M. (2001). Native speakers or non-native speakers: Who has the floor? Online and face-to-face interaction in culturally mixed small groups. *Computer Assisted Language Learning, 14*(2), 169–199. doi:10.1076/call.14.2.169.5780

Frensch, P. A., & Miner, C. S. (1994). Effects of presentation rate and of individual differences in short-term memory capacity on an indirect measure of serial learning. *Memory & Cognition*, *22*(1), 95–110. doi:10.3758/BF03202765 PMID:8035689

Friesen, N. (2010). Education and the social Web: Connective learning and the commercial imperative. *First Monday*, *15*(12). doi:10.5210/fm.v15i12.3149

Gaba, D. M. (2004). The future vision of simulation in health care. *Quality & Safety in Health Care*, *13*(Suppl.1), i2–i10. doi:10.1136/qshc.2004.009878 PMID:15465951

Gadgets 360. (2018). *World of Warcraft Subscription Numbers Reportedly Revealed*. Accessed on January 9th 2019 from: https://gadgets.ndtv.com/games/news/world-of-warcraft-wow-subscription-numbers-battle-of-azeroth-1932930

Galatis, P., Gavalas, D., Kasapakis, V., Pantziou, G., & Zaroliagis, C. (2016). Mobile augmented reality guides in cultural heritage. *Proceedings of the 8th EAI International Conference on Mobile Computing, Applications and Services*, 11-19. 10.4108/eai.30-11-2016.2266954

Gamage, V., Tretiakov, A., & Crump, B. (2011). Teacher perceptions of learning affordances of multi-user virtual environments. *Computers & Education*, *57*(4), 2406–2413. doi:10.1016/j.compedu.2011.06.015

García-Pereira, I., Gimeno, J., Portalés, C., Vidal-González, M., & Morillo, P. (2018). *On the design of a mixed-reality annotations tool for the inspection of pre-fab buildings*. Paper presented at the Spanish Computer Graphics Conference (CEIG), Madrid, Spain. doi:10.2312/ceig.20181157

Gardner, M. R., & Elliott, J. B. (2014). The Immersive Education Laboratory: Understanding affordances, structuring experiences, and creating constructivist, collaborative processes, in mixed-reality smart environments. *EAI Endorsed Transactions on Future Intelligent Educational Environments*, *1*(1), e6. doi:10.4108/fiee.1.1.e6

Gardner, R. M., & Bevel, T. (2009). *Practical crime scene analysis and reconstruction*. CRC Press. doi:10.1201/9781420065527

Garrison, D., Anderson, T., & Archer, W. (1999). Critical inquiry in a text-based environment: Computer conferencing in higher education. *The Internet and Higher Education*, *2*(2-3), 87–105. doi:10.1016/S1096-7516(00)00016-6

Gass, S. (1999). Discussion: Incidental vocabulary learning. *Studies in Second Language Acquisition*, *21*(2), 319–333. doi:10.1017/S0272263199002090

Gee, J. P. (2005). Good video games and good learning. *Phi Kappa Phi Forum*, *85*(2), 33–37.

Gee, A. P., Escamilla-Ambrosio, P. J., Webb, M., Mayol-Cuevas, W., & Calway, A. (2010). Augmented crime scenes: Virtual annotation of physical environments for forensic investigation. In *Proceedings of the 2nd ACM Workshop on Multimedia in Forensics, Security and Intelligence* (pp. 105-110). ACM. 10.1145/1877972.1877999

Gee, J. P. (2003). *What video games have to teach us about learning and literacy*. New York, NY: Palgrave Macmillan. doi:10.1145/950566.950595

Gee, J. P. (2010). *New Digital Media and Learning as an Emerging Area and "Worked Examples" as One Way Forward*. Cambridge, MA: The MIT Press.

Ghanbarzadeh, R., & Ghapanchi, A. H. (2018). Investigating various application areas of three-dimensional virtual worlds for higher education. *British Journal of Educational Technology*, *49*(3), 370–384. doi:10.1111/bjet.12538

Gibson, B. (1997). Talking the test: Using verbal report data in looking at the processing of cloze tasks. *Edinburgh Working Papers in Applied Linguistics*, *8*, 54–62. Retrieved from https://files.eric.ed.gov/fulltext/ED409713.pdf

Gilster, P. (1997). *Digital literacy*. New York: Wiley Computer Pub.

Gimeno, J., Morillo, P., Casas, S., & Fernández, M. (2011). An augmented reality (AR) CAD system at construction sites. In Y. C. N. Andrew (Ed.), *Augmented reality* (pp. 15–32). Rijeka: IntechOpen. doi:10.5772/26801

Ginns, P., & Ellis, R. (2007). Quality in blended learning: Exploring the relations between on-line and face-to-face teaching and learning. *The Internet and Higher Education*, *10*(1), 53–64. doi:10.1016/j.iheduc.2006.10.003

Global Society of Online Literacy Educators (GSOLE). (2016). *Mission statement*. GSOLE.

Glover, W., & Lygeros, J. (2004). A stochastic hybrid model for air traffic control simulation. *Hybrid Systems: Computation and Control*, *2993*, 372–386.

Godwin-Jones, R. (2016). Emerging Technologies Augmented Reality and Language Learning: From annotated vocabulary to place-based mobile games. *Language Learning & Technology*, *20*(3), 9–19.

Goldstein, E. B. (2008). *Cognitive Psychology: Connecting mind, research, and everyday experience*. Thompson-Wadsworth.

Golparvar-Fard, M., & Ham, Y. (2013). Automated diagnostics and visualization of potential energy performance problems in existing buildings using energy performance augmented reality models. *Journal of Computing in Civil Engineering*, *28*(1), 17–29. doi:10.1061/(ASCE)CP.1943-5487.0000311

Good, B. M., & Su, A. I. (2011). Games with a scientific purpose. *Genome Biology*, *12*(12), 135. doi:10.1186/gb-2011-12-12-135 PMID:22204700

Good, J., Howland, K., & Thackray, L. (2008). Problem-based learning spanning real and virtual words: A case study in SL. *Research in Learning Technology*, *16*(3), 163–172. doi:10.3402/rlt.v16i3.10895

Gordon, J. A., Wilkerson, W. M., Shaffer, D. W., & Armstrong, E. G. (2001). "Practicing" medicine without risk: Students' and educators' responses to high-fidelity patient simulation. *Academic Medicine*, *76*(5), 469–472. doi:10.1097/00001888-200105000-00019 PMID:11346525

Graham, C. R. (2006). Blended learning systems: Definition, current trends, future directions. In C. J. Bonk & C. R. Graham (Eds.), The handbook of blended learning: Global perspectives, local designs (pp. 3-21). San Francisco, CA: Pfeiffer Publishing.

Grandzol, J.R. (2004). Teaching mba statistics online: A pedagogically sound process approach. *Journal of Education for Business, 79*(4), 237-246.

Grantcharov, T. P., Kristiansen, V. B., Bendix, J., Bardram, L., Rosenberg, J., & Funch-Jensen, P. (2004). Randomized clinical trial of virtual reality simulation for laparoscopic skills training. *British Journal of Surgery, 91*(2), 146–150. doi:10.1002/bjs.4407 PMID:14760660

Green, M., Lea, J. H., & McNair, C. L. (2014). Reality check: Augmented reality for school libraries. *Teacher Librarian, 41*(5), 28–34.

Gregory, S., Lee, M. J. W., Dalgarno, B., & Tynan, B. (Eds.). (2016). *Learning in virtual worlds: Research and applications (Issues in distance education)*. Edmonton: AU Press. doi:10.15215/aupress/9781771991339.01

Griffith, E. (2018, November 8). Major Video Games Make More Money Than Blockbuster Movies. *The Entrepreneur*. Accessed on January 14th, 2019 from: https://www.entrepreneur.com/article/323001

Griffiths, M., Davies, N., & Chappell, D. (2004). Online computer gaming: A comparison of adolescent and adult gamers. *Journal of Adolescence, 27*(1), 87–96. doi:10.1016/j.adolescence.2003.10.007 PMID:15013262

Griffiths, M., & King, R. (2015). Are Mini-games Within RuneScape Gambling or Gaming? *Gaming Law Review and Economics, 19*(9), 640–643. doi:10.1089/glre.2015.1995

Griffiths, M., van Rooij, T., Kardefelt-Winther, D., Starcevic, V., Kiraly, O., Pallesen, S., ... Demetrovics, Z. (2015). Working towards an international consensus on criteria for assessing internet gaming disorder: A critical commentary on Petry et al (2014). *Addiction (Abingdon, England), 111*(1), 167–17. doi:10.1111/add.13057 PMID:26669530

Grotzer, T. A., Kamarainen, A., Tutwiler, M. S., Metcalf, S., & Dede, C. (2013). Learning to reason about ecosystems dynamics over time: The challenges of an event-based causal focus. *Bioscience, 63*(4), 288–296. doi:10.1525/bio.2013.63.4.9

Grow, G. (1991). Teaching learners to be self-directed. *Adult Education Quarterly, 41*(3), 125–149. doi:10.1177/0001848191041003001

Gunawardena, L., & McIsaac, M. (2003). Theory of distance education. In D. H. Jonassen (Ed.), *Handbook of research for educational communications and technology*. New York: Simon and Schuster Macmillan.

Guth, S., & Helm, F. (2010). *Telecollaboration 2.0*. Bern: Peter Lang. doi:10.3726/978-3-0351-0013-6

Hamari, J., Koivisto, J., & Sarsa, H. (2014). Does Gamification Work? – A Literature Review of Empirical Studies on Gamification. *Proceedings of the 47th Hawaii International Conference on System Sciences*. 10.1109/HICSS.2014.377

Hammick, J. K., & Lee, M. J. (2014). Do shy people feel less communication apprehension online? The effects of virtual reality on the relationship between personality characteristics and communication outcomes. *Computers in Human Behavior, 33*, 302–310. doi:10.1016/j.chb.2013.01.046

Hancock, A. B., & Rubin, B. A. (2015). Influence of communication partner's gender on language. *Journal of Language and Social Psychology, 34*(1), 46–64. doi:10.1177/0261927X14533197

Hanus, M. D., & Fox, J. (2015). Assessing the effects of gamification in the classroom: A longitudinal study on intrinsic motivation, social comparison, satisfaction, effort, and academic performance. *Computers & Education, 80*, 152–161. doi:10.1016/j.compedu.2014.08.019

Hargittai, E. (2005). Survey Measures of Web-Oriented Digital Literacy. *Social Science Computer Review, 23*(3), 371–379. doi:10.1177/0894439305275911

Hargittai, E., & Hsieh, Y. P. (2012). Succinct Measures of Web-Use Skills. *Social Science Computer Review, 30*(1), 95–107. doi:10.1177/0894439310397146

Hartley, J. (1998). *Learning and Studying. A research perspective*. London: Routledge. doi:10.4324/9780203270189

Hartmann, T., & Klimmt, C. (2006). Gender and computer games: Exploring females' dislikes. *Journal of Computer-Mediated Communication, 11*(4), 2. doi:10.1111/j.1083-6101.2006.00301.x

Hayden, K. A. (2003). *Lived experience of students searching for information* (Unpublished doctoral dissertation). University of Calgary, Alberta, Canada.

Hayden, K. A., Rutherford, S., & Pival, P. (2006). *WISPR (Workshop on the Information Search Process for Research)*. Alberta: University of Calgary Libraries and Cultural Resources. Accessed on May 26, 2010 at http://webapps3.tlc.ucalgary.ca:9080/wispr/app

Hayden, K. A., Rutherford, S., & Pival, P. (2006). WISPR (Workshop on the Information Search Process for Research) in the Library. *Journal of Library Administration, 45*(3), 427–443.

Heimer, R. (2018, June 5). *How many play League of Legends*. Accessed on January 10, 2019 from: https://www.unrankedsmurfs.com/blog/players-2017

Heisler, Y. (2015, November 9). Samsung keeps bleeding market share to Apple's benefit. *BGR News*. Retrieved from http://bgr.com/2015/11/09/iphone-vs-samsung-apple-marketshare/

Helling, T. S., Dumire, R. D., & Augustosky, K. (2009). Incentives for scholarly activity at university and independent general surgery residencies: Current practices. *American Journal of Surgery, 197*(3), 360–364. doi:10.1016/j.amjsurg.2008.11.004 PMID:19245915

Herring, S. C. (2010). Who's got the floor in computer-mediated conversation? Edelsky's gender patterns revisited. *Language@Internet, 7*, article 8. Retrieved April 9, 2013, from http://www.languageatinternet.org/articles/2010/2857

Hesse-Biber, S. N., & Leavy, P. (2011). *The practice of qualitative research* (2nd ed.). London: SAGE.

Hewett, B. L. (2015). *Reading to learn and writing to teach: Literacy strategies for online writing instruction*. Bedford, MA: St. Martin's.

HewettB. L.DePewK. E. (Eds.). (2015). Foundational practices of online writing instruction. Retrieved from https://wac.colostate.edu/books/perspectives/owi/

Hew, K. F., & Cheung, W. S. (2010). Use of three-dimensional (3-D) immersive virtual worlds in K-12 and higher education settings: A review of the research. *British Journal of Educational Technology*, *41*(1), 33–55. doi:10.1111/j.1467-8535.2008.00900.x

Hidi, S., & Renninger, K. A. (2006). The four-phase model of interest development. *Educational Psychologist*, *41*(2), 111–127. doi:10.120715326985ep4102_4

Hill, M. (2005). *The RPG evolution*. Retrieved from http://iml.jou.ufl.edu/projects/Spring05/Hill/

Hirschman, L. (1994). Female-male differences in conversational interaction. *Language in Society*, *23*(3), 427–442. doi:10.1017/S0047404500018054

Hitt, A. (2018). Foregrounding accessibility through (inclusive) universal design in professional communication curricula. *Business and Professional Communication Quarterly*, *81*(1), 52–65. doi:10.1177/2329490617739884

Hobbs, R., & Coiro, J. (2019). Design features of a professional development program in digital literacy. *Journal of Adolescent & Adult Literacy*, *62*(4), 401–409. doi:10.1002/jaal.907

Hoffman, A. M. (2013). Students' perceptions of on-task behavior and classroom engagement in a 1:1 iPad school. *English Leadership Quarterly*, *36*(2), 9–18.

Holmes, J. (2006). *Gendered talk at work: Constructing gender identity through workplace discourse*. Malden, MA: Blackwell. doi:10.1002/9780470754863

Holmes, J., & Schnurr, S. (2006). 'Doing femininity' at work: More than just relational practice. *Journal of Sociolinguistics*, *10*(1), 31–51. doi:10.1111/j.1360-6441.2006.00316.x

Honebein, P. C. (1996). Seven goals for the design of constructivist learning environments. *Constructivist learning environments: Case Studies in Instructional Design*, 11-24.

Honebein, P. C. (1996). Seven goals for the design of constructivist learning environments. In B. Wilson (Ed.), *Constructivist learning environments: Case studies in instructional design*. Englewood Cliffs, NJ: Educational Technology Publications.

Hosford, C. C., & Siders, W. A. (2010). Felder-Soloman's index of learning styles: Internal consistency, temporal stability, and factor structure. *Teaching and Learning in Medicine*, *22*(4), 298–303. doi:10.1080/10401334.2010.512832 PMID:20936578

Hoy, B. (2018). Teaching History with Custom-Built Board Games. *Simulation & Gaming*, *49*(2), 115–133. doi:10.1177/1046878118763624

Hu, L., Du, Z., Tong, Q., & Liu, Y. (2013). Context-aware recommendation of learning resources using rules engine. *IEEE 13th International Conference on Advanced Learning Technologies*. Retrieved from https://ieeexplore.ieee.org/stamp/stamp.jsp?tp=&arnumber=6601899

Hu, W., Zhu, J., Pan, Z., Li, Y., & Ju, C. (2003). Learning by doing: A Case for Constructivist 3D Virtual Learning Environment. *Eurographics*. Retrieved from http://diglib.eg.org/EG/DL/Conf/EG2003/edu/edu2.pdf

Huang, C. Y., Thomas, J. B., Alismail, A., Cohen, A., Almutairi, W., Daher, N. S., ... Tan, L. D. (2018). The use of augmented reality glasses in central line simulation:"see one, simulate many, do one competently, and teach everyone. *Advances in Medical Education and Practice*, *9*, 357–363. doi:10.2147/AMEP.S160704 PMID:29785148

Huang, H. M., & Liaw, S. S. (2018). An analysis of learners' intentions toward virtual reality learning based on constructivist and technology acceptance approaches. *International Review of Research in Open and Distance Learning*, *19*(1), 91–115. doi:10.19173/irrodl.v19i1.2503

Huang, H. M., Rauch, U., & Liaw, S. S. (2010). Investigating learners' attitudes toward virtual reality learning environments: Based on a constructivist approach. *Computers & Education*, *55*(3), 1171–1182. doi:10.1016/j.compedu.2010.05.014

Huizenga, J., Admiraal, W., Akkerman, S., & Dam, G. T. (2009). Mobile game-based learning in secondary education: Engagement, motivation and learning in a mobile city game. *Journal of Computer Assisted Learning*, *25*(4), 332–344. doi:10.1111/j.1365-2729.2009.00316.x

Hulstijn, J. (1989). Implicit and incidental second language learning: Experiments in the processing of natural and partly artificial input. In H. W. Dechert (Ed.), Interlingual processes (pp. 47-73). Tubigen: Narr.

Hurter, S. R. (2003). Elusive or Illuminating: Using the Web to Explore the Salem Witchcraft Trials. *OAH Magazine of History*, *17*(4), 60–61. doi:10.1093/maghis/17.4.60

Hussain, Z., & Griffiths, M. D. (2008). Gender swapping and socializing in cyberspace: An exploratory study. *Cyberpsychology & Behavior*, *11*(1), 47–53. doi:10.1089/cpb.2007.0020 PMID:18275312

Hutchings, M., Hadfield, M., Howarth, G., & Lewarne, S. (2007). Meeting the challenges of active learning in web-based case studies for sustainable development. *Innovations in Education and Teaching International*, *4*(33), 331–343. doi:10.1080/14703290701486779

IDEO. (2009). *Human centered design toolkit* (2nd ed.). Retrieved from http://www.ideo.com/work/item/human-centered-design-toolkit/

Imler, B., & Eichelberger, M. (2011). Using screen capture to study user research behavior. *Library Hi Tech*, *29*(3), 446–454. doi:10.1108/07378831111174413

ImmerseMe. (2017). *LinkedIn: ImmerseMe*. Retrieved from https://www.linkedin.com/company/immerseme-ltd

ImmerseMe. (2018). *ImmerseMe: VR-based language learning*. Retrieved from https://immerseme.co/#home

Inman, C., Wright, V. H., & Hartman, J. A. (2010). Use of SL in K-12 and higher education: A review of research. *Journal of Interactive Online Learning*, *9*(1), 44–63.

Instructional Technology Council. (2008). *2007 Distance Education survey Results*. Accessed on Sept. 9 2008.from: http://4.79.18.250/file.php?file=/1/ITCAnnualSurveyMarch2008.pdf

Ishii, H., Kobayashi, M., & Arita, K. (1994). Iterative design of seamless collaboration media. *Communications of the ACM*, *37*(8), 83–97. doi:10.1145/179606.179687

Itti, L. (2007). *Visual Salience*. Scholarpedia. doi:10.4249cholarpedia.3327

Jakobsson, M., & Taylor, T. (2003). The *Sopranos* meets *EverQuest*: Social networking in massively multiplayer online games. *Melbourne International Digital Arts and Culture Conference (Melbourne-DAC)*. Retrieved from http://hypertext.rmit.edu.au/dac/papers/Jakobsson.pdf

Jarmon, L., Traphagan, T., Mayrath, M., & Trivedi, A. (2009). Virtual world teaching, experiential learning, and assessment: An interdisciplinary communication course in SL. *Computer Education*, *53*(1), 169–182. doi:10.1016/j.compedu.2009.01.010

Jauregi, K., & Canto, S. (2012). Enhancing meaningful oral interaction in Second Life. *Procedia: Social and Behavioral Sciences*, *34*, 111–115. doi:10.1016/j.sbspro.2012.02.023

JISC. (2008). *Effective practice with e-Portfolios, supporting 21st century learning*. Bristol, UK: JISC Innovation Group.

Jochems, W., Merriënboer, J. J. G. v., & Koper, R. (Eds.). (2004). *Integrated e-learning: Implications for pedagogy, technology & organization*. New York: RoutledgeFalmer. doi:10.4324/9780203416365

Johnson, L., Adams, S., & Cummins, M. (2012). The NMC horizon report: 2012 higher education edition. *The New Media Consortium*. Retrieved from http://bibliotecadigital. org/bitstream/001/563/1/2012-Horizon-Report-HE.pdf

Joint, N. (2003). Information literacy evaluation: Moving towards virtual learning environments. The Electronic Library, 21(4), 322.

Joksimovic, S., Gaševic, D., Kovanovic, V., Riecke, B. E., & Hatala, M. (2015). Social presence in online discussions as a process predictor of academic performance. *Journal of Computer Assisted Learning*, *31*(6), 638–654. doi:10.1111/jcal.12107

Jonassen, D. H. (1997). *INSYS 527: Designing constructivist learning environments*. Retrieved July 20, 2011, from http://www.coe.missouri.edu/~jonassen/INSYS527.html

Jonassen, D. H. (1994). Thinking Technology: Toward a Constructivist Design Model. *Educational Technology*, *34*(4), 34–37. Retrieved from https://www.learntechlib.org/p/171050/

Joy, E. H., & Garcia, F. E. (2000). Measuring learning effectiveness: A new look at no-significant-difference findings. *Journal of Asynchronous Learning Networks*, *4*(1), 33–39.

Kafai, Y. B. (2010). The World of Whyville: Living, Playing, and Learning in a Tween Virtual World. *Games and Culture*, *5*(1), 3–22. doi:10.1177/1555412009351264

Kahani, M., & Beadle, P. (1997, February). Comparing Immersive and Non-Immersive Virtual Reality User Interfaces for Management of Telecommunication Networks. *IEEE International Conference on Telecommunication (ICT97).*

Kamarainen, A., Metcalf, S., Grotzer, T., & Dede, C. J. (2015). Exploring ecosystems from the inside: How immersion in a multi-user virtual environment supports epistemologically grounded practices in ecosystem science instruction. *Journal of Science Education and Technology*, *24*(2), 148–167. doi:10.100710956-014-9531-7

Kamat, V. R., & El-Tawil, S. (2007). Evaluation of augmented reality for rapid assessment of earthquake-induced building damage. *Journal of Computing in Civil Engineering*, *21*(5), 303–310. doi:10.1061/(ASCE)0887-3801(2007)21:5(303)

Kardefelt-Winther, D. (2015). Making the case for hypothesis-driven theory testing in the study of Internet Gaming Disorder. *Addictive Behaviors*, 64. PMID:26455330

Karpova, E., Correia, A.-P., & Baran, E. (2009). Learn to use and use to learn: Technology in virtual collaboration experience. *Internet and Higher Education*, *12*(1), 45–52. doi:10.1016/j.iheduc.2008.10.006

Karras, R. W. (1994). Writing Essays That Make Historical Arguments. *OAH Magazine of History*, *8*(4), 54–57. doi:10.1093/maghis/8.4.54

Katalin, E. (2000). “Please, keep talking”: The ‘think-aloud’ method. *Novelty*, *7*(3), 48–59. Retrieved from http://deal.elte.hu/pages/novelty/htm2/vol73/elekes.htm

Kaufmann, H., Schmalstieg, D., & Wagner, M. (2000). Construct3D: A virtual reality application for mathematics and geometry education. *Education and Information Technologies*, *5*(4), 263–276. doi:10.1023/A:1012049406877

Kavanagh, S., Luxton-Reilly, A., Wüensche, B., & Plimmer, B. (2016, November). Creating 360 educational video: A case study. In *Proceedings of the 28th Australian Conference on Computer-Human Interaction* (pp. 34-39). ACM. 10.1145/3010915.3011001

Kee, K., Graham, S., Dunae, P., Lutz, J., Large, A., Blondeau, M., & Clare, M. (2009). Towards a Theory of Good History Through Gaming. *The Canadian Historical Review*, *90*(2), 303–326. doi:10.3138/chr.90.2.303

Ke, F. (2016). Designing and integrating purposeful learning in game play: A systematic review. *Educational Technology Research and Development*, *64*(2), 219–244. doi:10.100711423-015-9418-1

Keil, J., Edler, D., Dickmann, F., & Kuchinke, L. (2019). Meaningfulness of landmark pictograms reduces visual salience and recognition performance. *Applied Ergonomics*, *75*, 214–220. doi:10.1016/j.apergo.2018.10.008 PMID:30509529

Kelly, S. W. (2012). Incidental learning. In N. M. Seel (Ed.), *Encyclopedia of the sciences of learning* (pp. 1517–1518). Boston, MA: Springer US. doi:10.1007/978-1-4419-1428-6_366

Kesim, M., & Ozarslan, Y. (2012). Augmented reality in education: Current technologies and the potential for education. *Procedia: Social and Behavioral Sciences*, *47*, 297–302. doi:10.1016/j.sbspro.2012.06.654

Khan, R., Aydin, A., Khan, M. S., Dasgupta, P., & Ahmed, K. (2015). Simulation-based training for prostate surgery. *BJU International*, *116*(4), 665–674. doi:10.1111/bju.12721 PMID:24588806

Kilgus, T., Heim, E., Haase, S., Prüfer, S., Müller, M., Seitel, A., ... Schlemmer, H.-P. (2015). Mobile markerless augmented reality and its application in forensic medicine. *International Journal of Computer Assisted Radiology and Surgery*, *10*(5), 573–586. doi:10.100711548-014-1106-9 PMID:25149272

Kim, J. (2008). *"Narrative" or "tabletop" RPGs*. Retrieved from http://www.darkshire.net/~jhkim/rpg/whatis/tabletop.html

Kim, B. (2015). Designing Gamification in the Right Way. *Library Technology Reports*, *51*, 29–35.

Kim, B., Gupta, D., & Clyde, J. (2016). Gamefulness in designing digital game-based learning through a role playing game. In M. A. Tekeuchi, P. Preciado, & J. V. Koc (Eds.), *Ideas 2016: Designing for Innovation Selected Proceedings* (pp. 41–55). Calgary, Canada: University of Calgary.

Kim, S. H., Lee, J., & Thomas, M. K. (2012). Between purpose and method: A review of educational research on 3D virtual worlds. *Journal of Virtual Worlds Research*, *5*(1), 1–18. doi:10.4101/jvwr.v5i1.2151

Kim, Y. (2018). Analysis of research trends focusing on outcomes in language learning using MMORPGs. *Multimedia-Assisted Language Learning*, *21*(4), 111–142.

Kirschner, P. A. (2017). Stop propagating the learning styles myth. *Computers & Education*, *106*, 166–171. doi:10.1016/j.compedu.2016.12.006

Koivisto, J., & Hamari, J. (2014). Demographic differences in perceived benefits from gamification. *Computers in Human Behavior*, *35*, 179–188. doi:10.1016/j.chb.2014.03.007

Kolb, D. (1984). *Experiential learning: Experience as the source of learning and development*. Englewood Cliffs, NJ: Prentice Hall.

Kolb, D. A. (1984). *Experiential learning*. Englewood Cliffs, NJ: Prentice-Hall.

Kollock, P., Blumstein, P., & Schwartz, P. (1985). Sex and power in interaction: Conversational privileges and duties. *American Sociological Review*, *50*(1), 34–46. doi:10.2307/2095338

Kondratova, I., Molyneaux, H., O'Donnell, S., & Al-Digeil, M. (2015). *Quick Dive Environmental Scan for the LPSS Visioning Exercise*. Internal report.

Kop, R. (2010). The design and development of a personal learning environment: Researching the learning experience. *Proceedings of the European Distance and E-learning Network Annual Conference 2010*. Retrieved from https://nrc-publications.canada.ca/eng/view/accepted/?id=0728bc9b-1907-49c1-90bd-0f7ea87a0cad

Kop, R., & Carroll, F. (2011). Cloud computing and creativity: Learning on a massive open online course. *EURODL*, 1–11. Retrieved from http://www.eurodl.org/?p=special&sp=articles&article=457

Kop, R., & Fournier, H. (2013). *Developing a framework for research on personal learning environments*. ELearning Papers n.º 35. Retrieved from http://openeducationeuropa.eu/fr/node/131234

Kop, R. (2011). The challenges to connectivist learning on open online networks: Learning experiences during a massive open online course. *International Review of Research in Open and Distance Learning*, *12*(3), 19. doi:10.19173/irrodl.v12i3.882

Kop, R., & Bouchard, P. (2011). The role of adult educators in the age of social media. In M. Thomas (Ed.), *Digital education*. London: Palgrave MacMillan. doi:10.1057/9780230118003_4

Kop, R., & Fournier, H. (2010). New dimensions to self-directed learning in an open networked learning environment. *International Journal of Self-Directed Learning*, *7*(2).

Koski, J. (2017). Reflections of history: Representations of the Second World War in *Valkyria Chronicles*. *Rethinking History*, *21*(3), 396–414. doi:10.1080/13642529.2016.1256625

Koutropoulos, A., Gallagher, M. S., Abajian, S. C., de Waard, I., Hogue, R. J., Keskin, N. O., & Rodriguez, C. O. (2012). Emotive vocabulary in MOOCs: Context & participant retention. *European Journal of Open, Distance and E-Learning, 2012*(1). Retrieved from http://www.eurodl.org/materials/contrib/2012/Koutropoulos_et_al.pdf

Kumar, M. P., Packer, B., & Koller, D. (2010). Self-paced learning for latent variable models. In *Proceedings of Advances in Neural Information Processing Systems Conference* (pp. 1189-1197). Vancouver, Canada: Academic Press. Retrieved from http://papers.nips.cc/paper/3923-self-paced-learning-for-latent-variable-models

Kumar, N. M., Krishna, P. R., Pagadala, P. K., & Kumar, N. S. (2018, August). Use of Smart Glasses in Education-A Study. In *2018 2nd International Conference on I-SMAC (IoT in Social, Mobile, Analytics and Cloud)(I-SMAC)* (pp. 56-59). IEEE.

Kurz, D., Fedosov, A., Diewald, S., Güttier, J., Geilhof, B., & Heuberger, M. (2014). [Poster] towards mobile augmented reality for the elderly. *2014 IEEE International Symposium on Mixed and Augmented Reality (ISMAR)*, 275-276. 10.1109/ISMAR.2014.6948447

Kwon, O., Park, C., & Lim, C. (2014). A defect management system for reinforced concrete work utilizing BIM, image-matching and augmented reality. *Automation in Construction*, *46*, 74–81. doi:10.1016/j.autcon.2014.05.005

LACE. (n.d.). Retrieved from http://www.laceproject.eu/lace/

Ladegaard, H. (2011). 'Doing power' at work: Responding to male and female management styles in a global business corporation. *Journal of Pragmatics*, *43*(1), 4–19. doi:10.1016/j.pragma.2010.09.006

Lainema, T., & Makkonen, P. (2003). Applying constructivist approach to educational business games: Case REALGAME. *Simulation & Gaming*, *34*(1), 131–149. doi:10.1177/1046878102250601

Lambert, L. A., & Hassan, H. (2018). MOOCs and international capacity building in a UN framework: Potential and challenges. In W. L. Filho, M. Mifsud, & P. Pace (Eds.), *Handbook of lifelong learning for sustainable development* (pp. 155–164). Cham: Springer. doi:10.1007/978-3-319-63534-7_11

Lantolf, J. P., & Aljaafreh, A. (1995). Second language learning in the zone of proximal development: A revolutionary experience. *International Journal of Educational Research*, *23*(7), 619-632.

Latour, B. (1999). *Pandora's hope: Essays on the reality of science studies*. Cambridge, MA: Harvard University Press.

Latour, B., & Woolgar, S. (1986). *Laboratory life: The construction of scientific facts* (2nd ed.). Princeton, NJ: Princeton University Press.

Laurillard, D. (1993). *Rethinking university teaching: A framework for the effective use of educational technolgy*. London: Routledge.

Laurillard, D. (2007). Modelling benefits-oriented costs for technology enhanced learning. *Higher Education*, *54*(1), 21–39. doi:10.100710734-006-9044-2

Lear, J., Ansorge, C., & Steckleberg, A. (2010). Interactivity/community process model for the online education environment. *Journal of Online Teaching and Learning*, *6*(1).

Lee, E. A. L., & Wong, K. W. (2014). Learning with desktop virtual reality: Low spatial ability learners are more positively affected. *Computers & Education*, *79*, 49–58. doi:10.1016/j.compedu.2014.07.010

Lee, E. A., Wong, K. W., & Fung, C. C. (2009). Learning Effectiveness in a Desktop Virtual Reality-Based Learning Environment. *Proceedings of the 17th International Conference on Computers in Educations*, 832–839.

Lee, E. A., Wong, K. W., & Fung, C. C. (2010). How does desktop virtual reality enhance learning outcomes? A structural equation modeling approach. *Computers & Education*. doi:10.1016/j.compedu.2010.06.006

Lee, H. C., & Pagliaro, E. M. (2013). Forensic evidence and CSI. *Journal of Forensic Investigation.*, *1*(2), 5.

Lee, K. (2012). Augmented reality in education and training. *TechTrends*, *56*(2), 13–21. doi:10.100711528-012-0559-3

Lee, L. K., Chau, C. H., Chau, C. H., & Ng, C. T. (2017, June). Using Augmented Reality to Teach Kindergarten Students English Vocabulary. In *2017 International Symposium on Educational Technology (ISET)* (pp. 53-57). IEEE. 10.1109/ISET.2017.20

Lenhart, A., Kahne, J., Middaugh, E., Macgill, A. R., Evans, C., & Vitak, J. (2008). *Teens, Video Games, and Civics: Teens' Gaming Experiences Are Diverse and Include Significant Social Interaction and Civic Engagement*. Pew Internet & American Life Project.

Lepadatu, I. (2012). Use self-talking for learning progress. *Procedia: Social and Behavioral Sciences, 33*, 283–287. doi:10.1016/j.sbspro.2012.01.128

Le, Q. T., Pedro, A., Lim, C. R., Park, H. T., Park, C. S., & Kim, H. K. (2015). A framework for using mobile based virtual reality and augmented reality for experiential construction safety education. *International Journal of Engineering Education, 31*(3), 713–725.

Lester, J. C., Converse, S. A., Kahler, S. E., Barlow, S. T., Stone, B. A., & Bhoga, R. S. (1997). The persona effect: Affective impact of animated pedagogical agents. *Proceedings of 1997 Conference on Human Factors in Computing Systems*. Retrieved from http://www.acm.org/sigchi/chi97/proceedings/paper/jl.htm

Levin, H. (2018). *Privatizing education: Can the school marketplace deliver freedom of choice, efficiency, equity, and social cohesion?* London, UK: Taylor & Francis. doi:10.4324/9780429498015

Liarokapis, F. (2006). An exploration from virtual to augmented reality gaming. *Simulation & Gaming, 37*(4), 507–533. doi:10.1177/1046878106293684

Liarokapis, F., Mourkoussis, N., White, M., Darcy, J., Sifniotis, M., Petridis, P., ... Lister, P. F. (2004). Web3D and augmented reality to support engineering education. *World Transactions on Engineering and Technology Education, 3*(1), 11–14.

Ligorio, M. B., & Van der Meijden, H. (2008). Teacher guidelines for cross-national virtual communities in primary education. *Journal of Computer Assisted Learning, 24*(1), 11–25. doi:10.1111/j.1365-2729.2007.00240.x

Li, M. C., & Tsai, C. C. (2013). Game-based learning in science education: A review of relevant research. *Journal of Science Education and Technology, 22*(6), 877–898. doi:10.100710956-013-9436-x

Lim, C. P., Nonis, D., & Hedberg, J. (2006). Gaming in a 3D multiuser virtual environment: Engaging students in science lessons. *British Journal of Educational Technology, 37*(2), 211–231. doi:10.1111/j.1467-8535.2006.00531.x

Lin, K., Son, J. W., & Rojas, E. M. (2011). A pilot study of a 3D game environment for construction safety education. *Journal of Information Technology in Construction, 16*(5), 69–84.

Lin, T.-J., Wang, S.-Y., Grant, S., Chein, C.-L., & Lan, Y.-J. (2014). Task-based teaching approach of Chinese as a foreign language in Second Life through teachers' perspectives. *Procedia Technology, 13*, 16–22. doi:10.1016/j.protcy.2014.02.004

Lin, T., & Lan, Y.-J. (2015). Language learning in Virtual Reality environments: Past, present, and future. *Journal of Educational Technology & Society, 18*(4), 486–497.

Lin, Y., Dowell, N., Godfrey, A., Choi, H., & Brooks, C. (2019). Modeling gender dynamics in intra and interpersonal interactions during online collaborative learning. *LAK19. Proceedings of the 9th International Conference on Learning Analytics & Knowledge*, 431-435. 10.1145/3303772.3303837

Liu, X., Magjuka, R. J., Bonk, C. J., & Lee, S. (2007). Does sense of community matter? An examination of participants' perceptions of building learning communities in online courses. *The Quarterly Review of Distance Education*, *8*(1), 9–24.

Li, X., Yi, W., Chi, H., Wang, X., & Chan, A. P. C. (2018). A critical review of virtual and augmented reality (VR/AR) applications in construction safety. *Automation in Construction*, *86*, 150–162. doi:10.1016/j.autcon.2017.11.003

Lloyd, A., Rogerson, S., & Stead, G. (2017). Imagining the potential for using virtual reality technologies in language learning. In M. Carrier, R. M. Damerow, & K. M. Bailey (Eds.), *Digital language learning and teaching: Research, theory, and practice* (pp. 222–234). London: Routledge. doi:10.4324/9781315523293-19

Loewen, S., & Sato, M. (2018). Interaction and instructed second language acquisition. *Language Teaching*, *51*(3), 285–329. doi:10.1017/S0261444818000125

Longo, D. (2012). Learning a Second Language in a learning community "Second Life": Critical issues and possible developments. *Conference proceedings international conference ICT for language learning 5th conference edition*. Florence: Pixel.

Lo, S., Wang, C., & Fang, W. (2005). Physical Interpersonal Relationships and Social Anxiety among Online Game Players. *Cyberpsychology & Behavior*, *8*(1), 15–20. doi:10.1089/cpb.2005.8.15 PMID:15738689

Lund, H. H., Klitbo, T., & Jessen, C. (2005). Playware technology for physically activating play. *Artificial Life and Robotics Journal*, *9*(4), 165–174. doi:10.100710015-005-0350-z

Lynch, M., & Woolgar, S. (1990). Introduction: Sociological orientations to representational practice in science. In M. Lynch & S. Woolgar (Eds.), *Representation in scientific practice*. Cambridge, MA: MIT Press.

Macedonia, M. (2002). Games, simulation, and the military education dilemma. In *Internet and the University: 2001* (pp. 157–167). Forum. Retrieved from https://net.educause.edu/ir/ library/pdf/ffpiu018.pdf

Mackness, J., Waite, M., Roberts, G., & Lovegrove, E. (2013). Learning in a small, task-oriented, connectivist MOOC: Pedagogical issues and implications for higher education. *The International Review of Research in Open and Distributed Learning*, *14*(4). doi:10.19173/irrodl.v14i4.1548

Maclellan, E. (2005). Conceptual learning: The priority for higher education. *British Journal of Educational Studies*, *53*(2), 129–147. doi:10.1111/j.1467-8527.2005.00287.x

Madathil, K. C., Frady, K., Hartley, R., Bertrand, J., Alfred, M., & Gramopadhye, A. (2017). An empirical study investigating the effectiveness of integrating virtual reality-based case studies into an online asynchronous learning environment. *Computers in Education Journal*, *8*(3), 1–10.

Mager, A. (2014). Defining Algorithmic Ideology: Using Ideology Critique to Scrutinize Corporate Search Engines. *TripleC*, *12*(1), 28–39. doi:10.31269/triplec.v12i1.439

Maggioni, L., VanSledright, B., & Alexander, P. A. (2009). Walking on the Borders: A Measure of Epistemic Cognition in History. *Journal of Experimental Education*, *77*(3), 187–213. doi:10.3200/JEXE.77.3.187-214

Magnussen, R. (2007). Games as a platform for situated science practice. In Worlds in play: International perspectives on digital games research (pp. 301–311). New York, NY: Peter Lang.

Magnussen, R. (2008). *Representational inquiry in science learning games* (Unpublished doctoral dissertation). Aarhus University, Copenhagen, Denmark.

Magnussen, R. (2009). Representational inquiry competences in science games. In S. G. A. Rodrigues (Ed.), *Multiple literacy and science education: ICTs in formal and informal learning environments* (pp. 360–370). Hershey, PA: IGI Global. doi:10.4018/978-1-61520-690-2.ch017

Magnussen, R., & Elming, A. L. (2017) Student re-design of deprived neighborhoods in Minecraft: Game-assisted community-driven urban development. In *12th International Conference on Computer Supported Collaborative Learning, CSCL 2017*. Drexel University and The University of Pennsylvania.

Magnussen, R., Hansen, S. D., Planke, T., & Sherson, J. F. (2014). Games as a Platform for Student Participation in Authentic Scientific Research. *The Electronic Journal of E-learning*, *12*(3), 258–269.

Magyari, D. P. (2011). *Head Mounted Display Device. U.S. Patent No. 9,250,444*. Washington, DC: U.S. Patent and Trademark Office. Retrieved from https://patentimages.storage.googleapis.com/e3/be/a6/61e1e1178149d2/US9250444.pdf

Malliarakis, C., Satratzemi, M., & Xinogalos, S. (2017). CMX: The Effects of an educational MMORPG on learning and teaching computer programming. *IEEE Transactions on Learning Technologies*, *10*(2), 219–235. doi:10.1109/TLT.2016.2556666

Ma, M., Zheng, H., & Lallie, H. (2010). Virtual reality and 3D animation in forensic visualization. *Journal of Forensic Sciences*, *55*(5), 1227–1231. doi:10.1111/j.1556-4029.2010.01453.x PMID:20533989

Manocha, U. (2017). *MMORPGs and Their Effect on Players*. Accessed on January 22 from: http://scholarworks.sjsu.edu/art108

Marsick, V. J., & Volpe, M. (1999). The nature and need for informal learning. *Advances in Developing Human Resources*, *1*(3), 1–9. doi:10.1177/152342239900100302

Marsick, V. J., & Watkins, K. E. (1990). *Informal and incidental learning in the workplace*. London: Routledge.

Martínez, B., Casas, S., Vidal-González, M., Vera, L., & García-Pereira, I. (2018). TinajAR: An edutainment augmented reality mirror for the dissemination and reinterpretation of cultural heritage. *Multimodal Technologies and Interaction*, *2*(2), 33. doi:10.3390/mti2020033

Martín-Gutiérrez, J., Fabiani, P., Benesova, W., Meneses, M. D., & Mora, C. E. (2015). Augmented reality to promote collaborative and autonomous learning in higher education. *Computers in Human Behavior, 51*, 752–761. doi:10.1016/j.chb.2014.11.093

Martín-Gutiérrez, J., Mora, C. E., Añorbe-Díaz, B., & González-Marrero, A. (2017). Virtual technologies trends in education. *EURASIA Journal of Mathematics Science and Technology Education, 13*(2), 469–486.

Martín-Gutiérrez, J., Mora, C. E., Añorbe-Díaz, B., & González-Marrero, A. (2017). Virtual technologies trends in education. *Eurasia Journal of Mathematics. Science and Technology Education, 13*(2), 469–486. doi:10.12973/eurasia.2017.00626a

Martončik, M., & Lokša, J. (2017). Do World of Warcraft (MMORPG) Players Experience Less Loneliness and Social Anxiety in Online World (Virtual Environment) Than in Real World (Offline)? *Computers in Human Behavior, 56*, 127–134. doi:10.1016/j.chb.2015.11.035

Ma, S., Steger, D. G., Doolittle, P. E., & Stewart, A. C. (2018). Improved Academic performance and student perceptions of learning through use of a cell phone-based personal response system. *Journal of Food Science Education, 17*(1), 27–32. doi:10.1111/1541-4329.12131

Matei, S. (2015). Games as a Genre of Historical Discourse. The Past on Fast Forward. *Proceedings of DiGRA 2015: Diversity of play: Games – Culture – Identity.*

Maxwell, A. (2010). Assessment Strategies for a History Exam, or, Why Short-Answer Questions are Better than In-Class Essays. *The History Teacher, 43*(2), 233–245.

Mayrath, M. C., Traphagan, T., Heikes, E. J., & Trivedi, A. (2009). Instructional design best practices for SL: A case study from a college-level English course. *Interactive Learning Environments, 19*(2), 125–142. doi:10.1080/10494820802602568

McCabe, M. (2007). Assessment, blending and creativity: The abc of technology in mathematics teaching. *The International Journal for Technology in Mathematics Education, 14*(1), 54–59.

McClymer, J. F., & Moynihan, K. J. (1977). The Essay Assignment: A Teaching Device. *The History Teacher, 10*(3), 359–371. doi:10.2307/491847

McDonough, J., & McDonough, S. (1997). *Research Methods for English Language Teachers*. London: Arnold.

McGinn, M. K., & Roth, W. M. (1999). Preparing students for competent scientific practice: Implications of recent research in science and technology studies. *Educational Researcher, 28*(3), 14–24. doi:10.3102/0013189X028003014

McKerlich, R., & Anderson, T. (2007). Community of inquiry and learning in immersive environments. *Journal of Asynchronous Learning Networks, 11*(4), 35–53.

McKerlich, R., Riis, M., Anderson, T., & Eastman, B. (2011). Student perceptions of teaching presence, social presence, and cognitive presence in a virtual world. *Journal of Online Teaching and Learning, 7*(3).

McLaren, C. H. (2004). A comparison of student persistence and performance in online and classroom business statistics experiences. *Decision Sciences Journal of Innovative Education*, *2*(1), 1–10. doi:10.1111/j.0011-7315.2004.00015.x

Melchor-Couto, S. (2017). Foreign language anxiety levels in Second Life oral interaction. *ReCALL*, *29*(1), 99–119. doi:10.1017/S0958344016000185

Melchor-Couto, S. (2018). Virtual World Anonymity and Foreign Language Oral Interaction. *ReCALL*, *30*(02), 232–249. doi:10.1017/S0958344017000398

Merchant, Z., Goetz, E. T., Cifuentes, L., Keeney-Kennicutt, W., & Davis, T. J. (2014). Effectiveness of virtual reality-based instruction on students' learning outcomes in K-12 and higher education: A meta-analysis. *Computers & Education*, *70*, 29–40. doi:10.1016/j.compedu.2013.07.033

Meri-Yilan, S. (2017). *'Take your time' to 'find yourself!' An exploration of scaffolded autonomous e-learning environments amongst international students in a UK university* (Unpublished Doctoral dissertation). University of Southampton, Southampton, UK.

Metcalf, S. J., Tutwiler, M. S., Kamarainen, A. M., Grotzer, T. A., & Dede, C. J. (2013). Multi-user virtual environments to promote middle school ecosystem science learning and attitudes about science. American Educational Research Association (AERA) Conference, San Francisco, CA.

Metcalf, S. J., Kamarainen, A. M., Torres, E., Grotzer, T. A., & Dede, C. (2018). EcoMUVE: A Case Study on the Affordances of MUVEs in Ecosystem Science Education. In Y. Qian (Ed.), *Integrating Multi-User Virtual Environments in Modern Classrooms* (pp. 1–25). Hershey, PA: IGI Global. doi:10.4018/978-1-5225-3719-9.ch001

Metcalf, S. J., Kamarainen, A., Tutwiler, M. S., Grotzer, T. A., & Dede, C. J. (2013). Teacher perceptions of the practicality and effectiveness of immersive ecological simulations as classroom curricula. *International Journal of Virtual and Personal Learning Environments*, *4*(3), 66–77. doi:10.4018/jvple.2013070105

Mezirow, J. (2000). *Learning as transformation: Critical perspectives on a theory in progress*. New York: Jossey-Bass.

Miles, M., & Huberman, M. (1994). *Qualitative Data Analysis*. London: Sage.

Milgram, P., & Kishino, F. (1994). A taxonomy of mixed reality visual displays. *IEICE Transactions on Information and Systems*, *77*, 1321–1329.

Miller, T., & Bell, L. (2002). Consenting to what? Issues of access, gate-keeping and 'informed' consent. In M. Mauthner, M. Birch, J. Jessop, & T. Miller (Eds.), Ethics in qualitative research (pp. 53-69). London, UK: Seven Oakes. doi:10.4135/9781849209090.n3

Miller, R. E. (2015). On digital reading. *Pedagogy*, *16*(1), 153–164. doi:10.1215/15314200-3158717

Mills, J. D. (2004). Student's attitudes toward statistics: Implication for the future. *College Student Journal*, *38*(3), 349–360.

Mills, S., & Noyes, J. (1999). Virtual reality: An overview of user-related design issues. Revised Paper for Special Issue on 'Virtual reality: User Issues' in Interacting with Computers, May 1998. *Interacting with Computers, 11*(4), 375–386. doi:10.1016/S0953-5438(98)00057-5

Miyazaki, H., Takeuchi, M., & Nakajima, E. (2009). *Demon's Souls* [video game]. Atlus & Sony Computer Entertainment.

Mizell, D. W., Jones, S. P., Slater, M., & Spanlang, B. (2002). Comparing immersive virtual reality with other display modes for visualizing complex 3D geometry. *Boeing and University College*. Retrieved from https://pdfs.semanticscholar.org/cbea/003ce3c84f7dd9da0cfca10e7fdc1666b65a.pdf

MMOG chart.com. (n.d.). Retrieved from http://MMOG chart.com

MMORPG.com. (n.d.). Retrieved from http:// mmorpg.com / gamelist.cfm

Mojang. (2009). *Minecraft* [video game]. Sweden.

Molka-Danielsen, J., Panichi, L., & Deutschmann, M. (2010). Reward models for active language learning in 3D virtual worlds. In Y. Peng, G, Kou, F. I. S. Ko, Y. Zeng, & K. D. Kwack (Eds.), *Information sciences and interaction sciences: The 3rd international conference on information sciences and interaction sciences* (pp. 97-109). Chengdu.

Monahan, G. W. (2002). Acting Out Nazi Germany: A Role-Play Simulation for the History Classroom. *Teaching History, 27*(2), 74–85.

Moon, S., Birchall, D., Williams, S., & Vrasidas, C. (2005). Developing design principles for an e-learning programme for sme managers to support accelerated learning at the workplace. *Journal of Workplace Learning, 17*(5/6), 370–384. doi:10.1108/13665620510606788

Moore, J. L., & Bass, R. (Eds.). (2017). *Understanding writing transfer: Implications for transformative student learning in higher education*. Sterling, VA: Stylus Publishing.

Moreno, R., Mayer, R. E., Spires, H. A., & Lester, J. C. (2001). The case for social agency in computer-based teaching: Do students learn more deeply when they interact with animated pedagogical agents? *Cognition and Instruction, 19*(2), 177–213. doi:10.1207/S1532690XCI1902_02

Morgan, C., & Cotten, S. R. (2003). The relationship between Internet activities and depressive symptoms in a sample of college freshmen. *Cyberpsychology & Behavior, 6*(2), 133–143. doi:10.1089/109493103321640329 PMID:12804025

Moser, S., & Zumbach, J. (2018). Exploring the development and impact of learning styles: An empirical investigation based on explicit and implicit measures. *Computers & Education, 125*, 146–157. doi:10.1016/j.compedu.2018.05.003

Mossberger, K., Tolbert, C. J., & Stansbury, M. (2003). *Virtual inequality: Beyond the digital divide*. Washington, DC: Georgetown University Press.

Mujber, T. S., Szecsi, T., & Hashmi, M. S. (2004). Virtual reality applications in manufacturing process simulation. *Journal of Materials Processing Technology, 155*, 1834–1838. doi:10.1016/j.jmatprotec.2004.04.401

Mumtaz, K., Iqbal, M. M., Khalid, S., Rafiq, T., Owais, S. M., & Al Achhab, M. (2017). An E-Assessment Framework for Blended Learning with Augmented Reality to Enhance the Student Learning. *Eurasia Journal of Mathematics. Science & Technology Education, 13*(8), 4419–4436.

Munslow, A. (2003). *The New History*. Toronto: Pearson Longman.

Munslow, A. (2007). *Narrative and History*. New York: Palgrave MacMillan.

Murphy, B. (2017, December 9). *Gaming's future is and has always been massively multiplayer*. Accessed on January 12, 2019 from: https://venturebeat.com/2017/12/09/gamings-future-is-and-has-always-been-massively-multiplayer/

Muzzy Lane. (2010). *Making History: The Calm and the Storm & Making History II: The War of the World*. Making History Series. Accessed on May 26, 2010 http://making-history.com

Naidu, S. (2002). Designing and evaluating instruction for e-learning. In P. L. Rogers (Ed.), *Designing instruction for technology-enhanced learning* (pp. 134–159). London: Idea Group. doi:10.4018/978-1-930708-28-0.ch008

National Disability Authority (NDA). (2014). *The 7 principles*. Retrieved from http://universaldesign.ie/What-is-Universal-Design/The-7-Principles/

National Research Council. (2012). *A framework for K-12 science education: Practices, cross-cutting concepts, and core ideas*. Washington, DC: The National Academies Press.

Nebel, S., Schneider, S., & Rey, G. D. (2016). Mining Learning and Crafting Scientific Experiments: A Literature Review on the Use of Minecraft in Education and Research. *Journal of Educational Technology & Society, 19*(2), 355–366.

Nelson, B. C., & Ketelhut, D. J. (2007). Scientific inquiry in educational multi-user virtual environments. *Educational Psychology Review, 19*(3), 265–283. doi:10.100710648-007-9048-1

Neverax. (2009). *Saga of Ryzom*. [Computer game]. Winch Gate Property Limited.

New Media Consortium and EDUCAUSE Learning Initiative. (2007). *The horizon report: 2007 edition*. Retrieved from http://www.nmc.org/publications/2007-horizon-report

NGSS Lead States. (2013). *Next Generation Science Standards: For States, By States*. Achieve, Inc.

Nguyen, D. (2018). The university in a world of digital technologies: Tensions and challenges. *Australasian Marketing Journal, 26*(2), 79-82.

Niche. (2019). *Terrible*. Retrieved January 19, 2019, from: https://www.niche.com/colleges/suny-plattsburgh/reviews/?rating=Terrible

Nicholson, S. (2015). A recipe for meaningful gamification. In *Gamification in education and business* (pp. 1–20). Cham: Springer.

Nielsen, J., Bærendsen, N. K., & Jessen, C. (2009). Music-making and musical comprehension with robotic building blocks. *Proceedings of the 4th International Conference on E-Learning and Games: Learning by Playing. Game-based Education System Design and Development*, 399-409.

Nincarean, D., Alia, M. B., Halim, N. D. A., & Rahman, M. H. A. (2013). Mobile augmented reality: The potential for education. *Procedia: Social and Behavioral Sciences*, *103*, 657–664. doi:10.1016/j.sbspro.2013.10.385

Noh, Z., Sunar, M. S., & Pan, Z. (2009, August). A review on augmented reality for virtual heritage system. In *International Conference on Technologies for E-Learning and Digital Entertainment* (pp. 50-61). Springer Berlin Heidelberg. 10.1007/978-3-642-03364-3_7

Nonaka, I., Toyama, R., & Konno, N. (2001). Seci, ba, and leadership: A unified model of dynamic knowledge creation. In I. Nonaka & D. Teece (Eds.), *Managing industrial knowledge creation, transfer and utilization*. Thousand Oaks, CA: Sage. doi:10.4135/9781446217573.n2

Norman, D. (2013). The design of everyday things (Revised & Expanded Ed.). New York: Basic Books.

O'Barr, W. M., & Atkins, B. K. (1980). "Women's Language" or "Powerless Language"? In S. McConell-Ginet, R. Borker, & N. Furman (Eds.), *Women and language in literature and society* (pp. 93–110). New York: Praeger.

O'Brian, M., & Levy, R. (2008). Exploration through virtual reality: Encounters with the target culture. *Canadian Modern Language Review*, *64*(4), 663–687. doi:10.3138/cmlr.64.4.663

O'Neil, H. F., Wainess, R., & Baker, E. L. (2005). Classification of learning outcomes: Evidence from the computer games literature. *Curriculum Journal*, *16*(4), 455–474. doi:10.1080/09585170500384529

O'Shea, P., Mitchell, R., Johnston, C., & Dede, C. (2009). Lessons learned about designing augmented realities. *International Journal of Gaming and Computer-Mediated Simulations*, *1*(1), 1–15. doi:10.4018/jgcms.2009010101

OECD. (2000). *Knowledge management in the learning society*. Paris, France: OECD Publications.

Oliver, M., & Carr, D. (2009). Learning in virtual worlds: Using communities of practice to explain how people learn from play. *British Journal of Educational Technology*, *40*(3), 414–426. doi:10.1111/j.1467-8535.2009.00948.x

Omale, N., Hung, W. C., Luetkehans, L., & Cooke-Plagwitz, J. (2009). Learning in 3-D multiuser virtual environments: Exploring the use of unique 3-D attributes for online problem-based learning. *British Journal of Educational Technology*, *40*(3), 480–495. doi:10.1111/j.1467-8535.2009.00941.x

Online Learning Consortium (OLC). (2016). *Report: One in four students enrolled in online courses*. Retrieved from https://onlinelearningconsortium.org/news_item/report-one-four-

Online Writing Instruction Community (OWI Community). (2015). *Our Mission.* Retrieved from http://www.owicommunity.org/

Organization Homepage. (n.d.). Retrieved from https://www.glosole.org/

Oswal, S. K. (2013). Exploring accessibility as a potential area of research for technical communication: A modest proposal. *Communication Design Quarterly Review*, *1*(4), 50–60. doi:10.1145/2524248.2524261

Oswal, S. K., & Meloncon, L. (2014). Paying attention to accessibility when designing online courses in technical and professional communication. *Journal of Business and Technical Communication*, *28*(3), 271–300. doi:10.1177/1050651914524780

Ott, M., & Freina, L. (2015). A literature review on immersive virtual reality in education: State of the art and perspectives. In *The International Scientific Conference eLearning and Software for Education* (pp. 133–141). Editura Universităţii Naţionale de Apărare "Carol I". Retrieved from http://www.loweurope.eu/articleDetail?articleID=fcbe1578-8df8-4284-96b6-c82f91e34f3d

Otto, S. K., & Pusack, J. P. (2009). Computer-assisted language learning authoring issues. *Modern Language Journal*, *93*(1), 784–801. doi:10.1111/j.1540-4781.2009.00973.x

Ozkan, B. (2017). The Reflections of English as a Foreign Language Teachers' on the Use of Virtual Reality in Classroom Practice (International Black Sea University Case). *Journal of Education in Black Sea Region*, *2*(2), 34–43. doi:10.31578/jebs.v2i2.40

Pace, D. (2004). Decoding the Reading of History: An Example of the Process. *New Directions for Teaching and Learning*, *2004*(98), 13–21. doi:10.1002/tl.143

Paek, S., Hoffman, D. L., & Saravanos, A. (2017). Spatial contiguity and incidental learning in multimedia environments. *British Journal of Educational Technology*, *48*(6), 1390–1401. doi:10.1111/bjet.12488

Page, R. L. (2000). Brief history of flight simulation. *SimTecT 2000 Proceedings*, 11-17.

Paik, P. C. H. (2017). Study of player attitudes regarding MMORPG avatar customization in the transformation stage. *Journal of Korea Game Society*, *17*(3), 7–20. doi:10.7583/JKGS.2017.17.3.71

Palfrey, J. G., & Gasser, U. (2013). *Born digital: Understanding the first generation of digital natives.* Basic Books.

Pan, C., & Sullivan, M. (2008). *Game-based learning: Guidelines, challenges, recommendations.* Presented at AETC Convention 2008, Orlando, FL.

Pan, X., Sun, X., Wang, H., Gao, S., Wang, N., & Lin, Z. (2017, November). Application of an assistant teaching system based on mobile augmented reality (AR) for course design of mechanical manufacturing process. In *2017 IEEE 9th International Conference on Engineering Education (ICEED)* (pp. 192-196). IEEE.

Panichi, L. (2012). Virtual Worlds: An opportunity for thinking about learning. In: S. Czepielewski (Ed.), *Learning a language in virtual worlds: A review of innovation and ICT in language teaching methodology, International conference, Warsaw, 17th November 2011* (pp. 25-32). Warsaw: Warsaw Academy of Computer Science, Management and Administration.

Panichi, L. J. (2015). *Participation in language learning in virtual worlds: An exploratory case-study of a business English course* (Unpublished PhD thesis). University of Hull. Retrieved from https://hydra.hull.ac.uk/resources/hull:11583

Panichi, L., & Deutschmann, M. (2012). Language learning in virtual worlds: Research issues and methods. In M. Dooly & R. O'Dowd (Eds.), *Researching online foreign language interaction and exchange: Theories, methods and challenges* (pp. 207–234). Bern: Peter Lang.

Pan, Z., Cheok, A. D., Yang, H., Zhu, J., & Shi, J. (2006). Virtual reality and mixed reality for virtual learning environments. *Computers and Graphics (Pergamon)*, *30*(1), 20–28. doi:10.1016/j.cag.2005.10.004

Parametric Technology Corporation. (2016). *Vuforia® Plug-in for Unity® v6.2.10* [Computer Software]. Available from http://www.vuforia.com

Park, C., & Kim, H. (2013). A framework for construction safety management and visualization system. *Automation in Construction*, *33*, 95–103. doi:10.1016/j.autcon.2012.09.012

Park, C., Lee, D., Kwon, O., & Wang, X. (2013). A framework for proactive construction defect management using BIM, augmented reality and ontology-based data collection template. *Automation in Construction*, *33*, 61–71. doi:10.1016/j.autcon.2012.09.010

Pashler, H., McDaniel, M., Rohrer, D., & Bjork, R. (2008). Learning styles: Concepts and evidence. *Psychological Science in the Public Interest*, *9*(3), 105–119. doi:10.1111/j.1539-6053.2009.01038.x PMID:26162104

Pedro, A., Le, Q. T., & Park, C. S. (2015). Framework for integrating safety into construction methods education through interactive virtual reality. *Journal of Professional Issues in Engineering Education and Practice*, *142*(2), 04015011. doi:10.1061/(ASCE)EI.1943-5541.0000261

Peris, R., Gimeno, M. A., Ibáñez, I., Ortel, G., Peris, R., Pinazo, D., & Sanchiz, M. (2002). Online chat rooms: Virtual spaces of interaction for socially oriented people. *Cyberpsychology & Behavior*, *5*(1), 43–51. doi:10.1089/109493102753685872 PMID:11990974

Peterson, E. R., Rayner, S. G., & Armstrong, S. J. (2009). Researching the psychology of cognitive style and learning style: Is there really a future? *Learning and Individual Differences*, *19*(4), 518–523. doi:10.1016/j.lindif.2009.06.003

Pettit, J., & Street, K. (2007). *Heaven & Hell on Earth: The Massacre of The "Black" Donnellys.* Great Unsolved Mysteries in Canadian History. Accessed on May 26, 2010. http://www.canadianmysteries.ca/sites/donnellys/home/indexen.html

Phan, V. T., & Choo, S. Y. (2010). Interior design in augmented reality environment. *International Journal of Computers and Applications*, *5*(5).

Phillips, A., Smith, G., Cook, M., & Short, T. (2016). Feminism and procedural content generation: Toward a collaborative politics of computational creativity. *Digital Creativity*, *27*(1), 82–97. doi:10.1080/14626268.2016.1147469

Phillips, J. (2002). The Dinosaurs Didn't See It Coming, But Historians Had Better: Computer-Aided Activities in the History Classroom. *History Computer Review*, *18*(1), 27–36.

Pilgrim, J. M., & Pilgrim, J. (2016). The Use of Virtual Reality Tools in the Reading-Language Arts Classroom. *Texas Journal of Literacy Education*, *4*(2), 90–97.

Pivec, M. (2007). Play and learn: Potentials of game-based learning. *British Journal of Educational Technology*, *38*(3), 387–393. doi:10.1111/j.1467-8535.2007.00722.x

Ponton, M. (2005). The relationship between self-efficacy and autonomous learning: The development of new instrumentation. *International Journal of Self-Directed Learning*, *5*(2), 50–58. Retrieved from http://www.sdlglobal.com

Popovich, C. J., & Neel, R. E. (2005). Characteristics of distance education programs at accredited business schools. *American Journal of Distance Education*, *19*(1), 229–240. doi:10.120715389286ajde1904_4

Portalés, C., Casas, S., Gimeno, J., Fernández, M., & Poza, M. (2018). From the paper to the tablet: On the design of an AR-based tool for the inspection of pre-fab buildings. preliminary results of the SIRAE project. *Sensors (Basel)*, *18*(4), 1262. doi:10.339018041262 PMID:29671799

Portalés, C., Gimeno, J., Casas, S., Olanda, R., & Giner, F. (2016). Interacting with augmented reality mirrors. In J. Rodrigues, P. Cardoso, J. Monteiro, & M. Figueiredo (Eds.), *Handbook of research on human-computer interfaces, developments, and applications* (pp. 216–244). Hershey, PA: IGI Global. doi:10.4018/978-1-5225-0435-1.ch009

Potnis, D., & Allard, S. (2018). Training LIS Students as Mobile Technology Consultants for Libraries and Not-for-profit Organizations. *Journal of Education for Library and Information Science*, *59*(4), 253–264. doi:10.3138/jelis.59.4.2018-0002

Prensky, M. (2003). Computer Games and Learning – digital game-based learning. In Handbook of Computer Game Studies (pp. 97-122). Cambridge, MA: MIT Press.

Prensky, M. (2016). Virtual Reality in the Language Learning Classroom. *On the Horizon*, *9*(5), 1–6. doi:10.1108/10748120110424816

Prinsloo, P., & Slade, S. (2017). Ethics and Learning Analytics: Charting the (Un)Charted, Handbook of Learning Analytics. Academic Press. doi:10.18608/hla17.004

Pu, B. (2018, November 28). What are loot boxes? FTC will investigate $30B video game industry. *NBC News*. Accessed on January 17, 2019 from: https://www.nbcnews.com/tech/tech-news/loot-boxes-gambling-video-games-ftc-look-it-n941256

Qian, M., & Clark, K. R. (2016). Game-based Learning and 21st century skills: A review of recent research. *Computers in Human Behavior, 63*, 50–58. doi:10.1016/j.chb.2016.05.023

Radu, I. (2014). Augmented reality in education: A meta-review and cross-media analysis. *Personal and Ubiquitous Computing, 18*(6), 1533–1543. doi:10.100700779-013-0747-y

Ramierz, F. (2018). From Good Associated to True Frineds: An Exploration of Friendship Practices in Massively Multiplayer Online Games. In K. Lakkaraju (Ed.), *Social Interactions in Virtual Worlds: An Interdisciplinary Perspective*. New York: Cambridge University Press. doi:10.1017/9781316422823.004

Ratemyprofessors. (2019). *If possible don't attend*. Retrieved March 3, 2019, from: http://www.ratemyprofessors.com/campusRatings.jsp?sid=968

Ravipati, S. (2017). *Outsmarting the Machine: Redesigning Education to Make Students, Teachers Relevant in the Algorithm Age, Transforming Education Through Technology*. Centre in discussion with Lee Rainie from PEW's Research Centre.

Rehak, B. (2003). Playing at being: Psychoanalysis and the avatar. In M. Wolf & B. Perron (Eds.), *The video game theory reader*. London: Routledge.

Reinders, H., & Wattana, S. (2015). Affect and willingness to communicate in digital game-based learning. *ReCALL, 27*(1), 38–57. doi:10.1017/S0958344014000226

Repetto, C. (2014). The use of virtual reality for language investigation and learning. *Frontiers in Psychology, 5*. doi:10.3389/fpsyg.2014.01280 PMID:25414691

Repetto, C., Germagnoli, S., Triberti, S., & Riva, G. (2018). Learning into the wild: A protocol for the use of 360° videos for language learning. In P. Cipresso, S. Serino, Y. Ostrovsky, & J. T. Baker (Eds.), *Pervasive Computing Paradigms for Mental Health: 7th International Conference, MindCare 2018, Boston, MA, USA, January 9-10, 2018, Proceedings* (Vol. 253, p. 56). Springer. 10.1007/978-3-030-01093-5_8

Reynolds, R. E. (1992). Selective attention and prose learning: Theoretical and empirical research. *Educational Psychology Review, 4*(4), 345–391. doi:10.1007/BF01332144

Reynolds, R., Sheperd, C., Kreek, C., Lapan, R., & Goetz, E. (1990). Differences in the use of selective attention by more successful and less successful tenth-grade readers. *Journal of Educational Psychology, 82*(4), 749–759. doi:10.1037/0022-0663.82.4.749

Rhode, J. (2009). Interaction equivalency in self-paced online learning environments: An exploration of learner preferences. *The International Review of Research in Open and Distributed Learning, 10*(1). doi:10.19173/irrodl.v10i1.603

Rideout, V. J., Foehr, U. G., & Roberts, D. F. (2010). *Generation M²: Media in the Lives of 8-to 18-Year-Olds*. Henry J. Kaiser Family Foundation.

Riegle, R., & Matejka, W. (2006). Dying to learn: Instructional design and MMORPGs. *21st Annual Conference on Distance Teaching and Learning*. Retrieved from http://people.coe.ilstu.edu/rpriegle/mmorpg/index.htm

Rilstone, A. (1994). Role playing games: An overview. *Inter*Action, 1*. Retrieved from http://www.rpg.net/oracle/essays/rpgoverview.html

Rodgers, C. R., & Raider-Roth, M. B. (2006). Presence in teaching. *Teachers and Teaching, 12*(3), 265–287. doi:10.1080/13450600500467548

Rodgers, D. L., Securro, S. Jr, & Pauley, R. D. (2009). The effect of high-fidelity simulation on educational outcomes in an advanced cardiovascular life support course. *Simulation in Healthcare, 4*(4), 200–206. doi:10.1097/SIH.0b013e3181b1b877 PMID:21330792

Rohrer, D., & Pashler, H. (2012). Learning styles: Where's the evidence? *Medical Education, 46*(7), 634–635. doi:10.1111/j.1365-2923.2012.04273.x PMID:22691144

Ropovik, I. (2015). A cautionary note on testing latent variable models. *Frontiers in Psychology, 6*, 1715. doi:10.3389/fpsyg.2015.01715 PMID:26594192

Rosen, K. R. (2008). The history of medical simulation. *Journal of Critical Care, 23*(2), 157–166. doi:10.1016/j.jcrc.2007.12.004 PMID:18538206

Rothbaum, B. O., Hodges, L., Smith, S., Lee, J. H., & Price, L. (2000). A controlled study of virtual reality exposure therapy for the fear of flying. *Journal of Consulting and Clinical Psychology, 68*(6), 1020–1026. doi:10.1037/0022-006X.68.6.1020 PMID:11142535

Rovai, A. P. (2007). Facilitating online discussions effectively. *The Internet and Higher Education, 10*(1), 77–88. doi:10.1016/j.iheduc.2006.10.001

Rovai, A. P., Wighting, M. J., Baker, J. D., & Grooms, L. D. (2009). Development of an instrument to measure perceived cognitive, affective, and psychomotor learning in traditional and virtual classroom higher education settings. *Internet and Higher Education, 12*(1), 7–13. doi:10.1016/j.iheduc.2008.10.002

Royce, B. (2017). *Monetization expert: MMOs are dying because of clueless design, not insufficient demand.* Accessed on January 9th 2019 from: https://massivelyop.com/2017/07/11/monetization-expert-mmos-are-dying-because-of-clueless-design-not-insufficient-demand/

Royle, K. (2009). Computer games and realising their learning potential: Crossing Borders, Blurring Boundaries and Taking Actition. *Game Based Learning Video Games, Social Media & Learning*. Retrieved May 26, 2010 http://www.gamebasedlearning.org.uk/content/view/67/

Royle, K., & Clarke. (2003). *Making the case for computer games as a learning environment*. University of Wolverhampton. Retrieved May 26, 2010 http://citeseerx.ist.psu.edu/viewdoc/download?doi=10.1.1.110.2561&rep=rep1&type=pdf

Rughinis, R., & Matei, S. (2015). Play to Remember: The Rhetoric of Time in Memorial Video Games. In Human-Computer Interaction, Part II (pp. 628-639). Springer International Publishing.

Russell, T. L. (2002). *The no significant difference phenomenon as reported in 355 research reports, summaries and papers: A comparative research annotated bibliography on technology for distance education*. North Carolina State University: Office of Instructional Telecommunications. Retrieved from http://www.nosignificantdifference.org/

Russell, W. B. III, & Pellegrino, A. (2008). Constructing Meaning from Historical Content: A Research Study. *Journal of Social Studies Research*, *32*(2), 3–15.

Russo, T., & Benson, S. (2005). Learning with invisible others: Perceptions of online presence and their relationship to cognitive and affective learning. *Journal of Educational Technology & Society*, *8*(1), 54–62.

Ryan, R. M., & Deci, E. L. (2000). Self-determination theory and the facilitation of intrinsic motivation, social development, and well-being. *The American Psychologist*, *55*(1), 68–78. doi:10.1037/0003-066X.55.1.68 PMID:11392867

Sadera, W. A., Robertson, J., Song, L., & Midon, M. N. (2009). The role of community in online learning success. *MERLOT Journal of Online Teaching and Learning, 5*(2), 277-284. Retrieved September 15, 2011 from http://jolt.merlot.org/vol5no2/sadera_0609.pdf

Sadler, R. (2012). *Virtual worlds for language learning: From theory to practice*. Bern: Peter Lang.

Saltan, F., & Arslan, Ö. (2017). The Use of Augmented Reality in Formal Education: A Scoping Review. *Eurasia Journal of Mathematics, Science & Technology Education, 13*(2).

Salvador, F., De Holan, P. M., & Piller, F. (2009). Cracking the code of mass customization. *MIT Sloan Management Review*, *50*(3). Retrieved from http://www.ie.edu/microsites/comunicacion/Sem%2018%20mayo%202009/Salvador,%20De%20Holan%20&%20Piller.pdf

Sanders, R.L. & Melton, S. (2010). The AETZone experience: A qualitative analysis of the use of presence pedagogy in a 3D immersive learning environment. *MERLOT Journal of Online Learning and Teaching, 6*(1).

Santos, B. S., Dias, P., Pimentel, A., Baggerman, J. W., Ferreira, C., Silva, S., & Madeira, J. (2009). Head-mounted display versus desktop for 3D navigation in virtual reality: A user study. *Multimedia Tools and Applications*, *41*(1), 161–181. doi:10.100711042-008-0223-2

Sawyer, R. K. (2006). Educating for innovation. *Thinking Skills and Creativity*, *1*(1), 41–48. doi:10.1016/j.tsc.2005.08.001

Scheelf, E. (2008). Gender and academic discourse: Global restrictions and local possibilities. *Language in Society*, *38*(4), 515–538.

Scheffel, M., Drachsler, H., Stoyanov, S., & Specht, M. (2014). Quality indicators for learning analytics. *Journal of Educational Technology & Society*, *17*(4), 117–132.

Scherer Bassani, P. B. (2011). Interpersonal exchanges in discussion forums: A study of learning communities in distance learning settings. *Computers & Education*, *56*(4), 931–938. doi:10.1016/j.compedu.2010.11.009

Schoefegger, K., Seitlinger, P., & Ley, T. (2010). Towards a User Model for Personalized Recommendations in Work-Integrated Learning: A Report on an Experimental Study with a Collaborative Tagging System. *Procedia Computer Science*, *1*(2), 2829–2838. doi:10.1016/j.procs.2010.08.008

Schoenfelder, R., & Schmalstieg, D. (2008). *Augmented reality for industrial building acceptance.* Paper presented at the 2008 IEEE Virtual Reality Conference, Reno, NV. 10.1109/VR.2008.4480755

Schofield, D. (2009). Animating evidence: Computer game technology in the courtroom. *Journal of Information Law and Technology*, *1*, 1–21.

Schrader, P., & McCreery, M. (2007). The acquisition of skill and expertise in massively multiplayer online games. *Educational Technology Research and Development*, *56*(5), 557–574.

Schreurs, B., de Laat, M., Teplovs, C., & Voogd, S. (2014). Social learning analytics applied in MOOC-environment. eLearning Papers. *OpenEducationEuropa, 36*, 45-48. Retrieved from http://openeducationeuropa.eu/en/download/file/fid/33697

Schroeder, R. (Ed.). (2002). *The social life of avatars: Presence and interaction in shared virtual environments*. London: Springer-Verlag. doi:10.1007/978-1-4471-0277-9

Schugurensky, D. (2000). *The forms of informal learning: Towards a conceptualization of the field* (Working paper 19-2000). Retrieved from: http://www.oise.utoronto.ca/depts/sese/csew/nall/res/19formsofinformal.htm

Schunk, D. H. (2004). *Learning theories: An educational perspective.* Upper Saddle River, NJ: Pearson Prentice Hall.

Schweitzer, N. J., & Saks, M. J. (2007). The CSI effect: popular fiction about forensic science affects the public's expectations about real forensic science. *Jurimetrics: The Journal of Law, Science, and Technology*, 357-364.

Schwienhorst, K. (2002). Why virtual, why environments? Implementing virtual reality concepts in computer-assisted language learning. *Simulation & Gaming*, *33*(2), 196–209. doi:10.1177/1046878102332008

Selverian, M., & Hwang, H. (2003). In search of presence: A systematic evaluation of evolving VLEs. *Presence (Cambridge, Mass.)*, *12*(5), 512–522. doi:10.1162/105474603322761306

Senge, P. M., Kleiner, A., Roberts, C., Ross, R., & Smith, B. (1999). *The fifth discipline fieldbook: Strategies and tools for building a learning organization.* New York: Doubleday.

Sergeyeva, O., Tsareva, A., Zinoveva, N., & Kononova, O. (2018). *Social Skills Amongst MMORPG-Gamers: Empirical Study*. Accessed on January 28, 2019 from: https://www.shs-conferences.org/articles/shsconf/pdf/2018/11/shsconf_cildiah2018_01008.pdf

Sevilla, J., Vera, L., Herrera, G., & Fernández, M. (2018). *FORHHSS-TEA, support to the individual work system for people with autism spectrum disorder using virtual and augmented reality*. Paper presented at the Spanish Computer Graphics Conference (CEIG), Madrid, Spain. doi:10.2312/ceig.20181155

Shaffer, D. W., & Gee, J. P. (2005). *Before every child is left behind: How epistemic games can solve the coming crisis in education* (Tech. Rep. No. 2005-7). Madison, WI: University of Wisconsin-Madison, Center for Education Research.

Shaffer, D. W. (2006). Epistemic frames for epistemic games. *Computers & Education*, *46*(3), 223–234. doi:10.1016/j.compedu.2005.11.003

Shaffer, D. W. (2007). *How computer games help children learn*. New York, NY: Palgrave Macmillan.

Shaw, E., Johnson, W. L., & Ganeshan, R. (1999). *Pedagogical agents on the Web*. Retrieved from http://www.isi.edu/isd/ADE/papers/agents99/agents99.htm

Shea, P., & Bidjerano, T. (2010). Learning presence: Towards a theory of self-efficacy, self-regulation, and the development of a communities of inquiry in online and hybrid learning environments. *Computers & Education, 55*(4), 1721-1731. Elsevier Ltd. doi: . doi:10.1016/j.compedu.2010.07.017

Shelton, B. E., & Hedley, N. R. (2002). Using augmented reality for teaching earth-sun relationships to undergraduate geography students. In *Augmented Reality Toolkit, The First IEEE International Workshop* (pp. 8-pp). IEEE. 10.1109/ART.2002.1106948

Shen, K., & Khalifa, M. (2008). Exploring multidimensional conceptualization of social presence in the context of online communities. *International Journal of Human-Computer Interaction*, *24*(7), 722–748. doi:10.1080/10447310802335789

Shin, D. H., & Dunston, P. S. (2008). Identification of application areas for augmented reality in industrial construction based on technology suitability. *Automation in Construction*, *17*(7), 882–894. doi:10.1016/j.autcon.2008.02.012

Sibilla, F., & Mancini, T. (2018). I am (not) my avatar: A review of the user-avatar relationships in Massively Multiplayer Online Worlds. *Cyberpsychology (Brno)*, *12*(3), 4. doi:10.5817/CP2018-3-4

Siemens, G. (2008). *Learning and knowing in networks: Changing roles for educators and designers*. Paper presented at the University of Georgia IT Forum, Athens, GA. Retrieved from http://bit.ly/170fVM

Sigil. (2009). *Vanguard Saga of Heroes* [Computer game]. Sony Online Entertainment.

Sims, E. M. (2007). Reusable, lifelike virtual humans for mentoring and role-playing. *Computers & Education*, *49*(1), 75–92. doi:10.1016/j.compedu.2005.06.006

Sitzmann, T., Kraiger, K., Stewart, D., & Wisher, R. (2006). The comparative effectiveness of web-based and classroom instruction: A meta-analysis. *Personnel Psychology*, *59*(1), 623–664. doi:10.1111/j.1744-6570.2006.00049.x

SLED list – SL Educators. (n.d.). Retrieved June 6, 2012, from https://lists.secondlife.com/cgi-bin/mailman/listinfo/educators

Smith, S. (2017, Fall). Stepping Out Of The Classroom Into Virtuality: Using MMORPGS To Teach History. *Teaching History: A Journal of Methods,* 73-80.

Smith, G. G., Heindel, A. J., & Torres-Ayala, A. T. (2008). E-learning commodity or community: Disciplinary differences between online courses. *The Internet and Higher Education*, *11*(1), 152–159. doi:10.1016/j.iheduc.2008.06.008

Smith, J. (2008). Facebook to blame for "friendship addiction." *Therapy Today*, *19*(9), 10–11.

Smyth, P. (2007). Beyond self-selection in video game play: An experimental examination of the consequences of massively multiplayer online role-playing game play. *Cyberpsychology & Behavior*, *10*(7), 32–39. PMID:17927543

Snelson, C., Wertz, C. I., Onstott, K., & Bader, J. (2017). Using World of Warcraft to Teach Research Methods in Online Doctoral Education: A Student-Instructor Duoethnography. *Qualitative Report*, *22*(5), 1439–1456.

Snodgrass, J. G., Dengah, H. J. F. II, Lacy, M. G., Bagwell, A., Van Oostenburg, M., & Lende, D. (2017). Online gaming involvement and its positive and negative consequences: A cognitive anthropological "cultural consensus" approach to psychiatric measurement and assessment. *Computers in Human Behavior*, *66*, 291–302. doi:10.1016/j.chb.2016.09.025

Søby, M. (2003). *Digital competence: From ICT skills to digital "bildung" (ITU Report June 10, 2003)*. Oslo: University of Oslo.

Solomonidou, C. (2009). Constructivist design and evaluation of interactive educational software: a research-based approach and examples. *Open Education - The Journal for Open and Distance Education and Educational Technology*, *5*(1), 6-24. Retrieved from https://ejournals.epublishing.ekt.gr/index.php/openjournal/article/viewFile/9693/9857.pdf

Sonstroem, E. (2006). Do you really want a revolution? Cybertheory meets real-life pedagogical practice in Franken MOO and the conventional literature classroom. *College Literature*, *33*(3), 148–170. doi:10.1353/lit.2006.0044

Sourmelis, T., Ioannou, A., & Zaphiris, P. (2017). Massively Multiplayer Online Role Playing Games (MMORPGs) and the 21st century skills: A comprehensive research review from 2010 to 2016. *Computers in Human Behavior*, *67*, 41–48. doi:10.1016/j.chb.2016.10.020

Spice, B. (2014). Press release. Google sponsors Carnegie Mellon Research to improve effectiveness of online education. Paying attention to how people learn promises to enhance MOOCs. *Carnegie Mellon News*. Retrieved from http://bit.ly/1l6NsON

Spring, D. (2015). Gaming history: Computer and video games as historical scholarship. *Rethinking History*, *19*(20), 207–221. doi:10.1080/13642529.2014.973714

Squire, K. (2005). *Game-Based Learning An X-Learn Perspective Paper*. MASIE Centre: ELearning Consortium.

Squire, K. D. (2004). Changing the Game: What Happens When Video Games Enter the Classroom? *Innovate*. Retrieved May 26, 2010 http://www.innovateonline.info/index.php?view=article&id=82

Squire, K., & Klopfer, E. (2007). Augmented reality simulations on handheld computers. *Journal of the Learning Sciences*, *16*(3), 371–413. doi:10.1080/10508400701413435

Squire, K. D., & Jan, M. (2007). Mad City Mystery®: Developing scientific argumentation skills with a place-based augmented reality game on handheld computers. *Journal of Science Education and Technology*, *16*(1), 5–29. doi:10.100710956-006-9037-z

Squire, K., & Barab, S. (2004). Replaying history: engaging urban underserved students in learning world history through computer simulations games. *International Conference on Learning Science. Proceedings of the 6th international conference on Learning sciences*, 505-512.

Squire, K., Giovanetto, L., Devane, B., & Durga, S. (2005). From Users to Designers: Building a Self-Organizing Game-Based Learning Environment. *TechTrends*, *49*(5), 34–74. doi:10.1007/BF02763688

Srivastava, J., Williams, D., Contractor, N., & Poole, S. (2009). *The Virtual World Exploratorium Project*. American Association for the Advancement of Science (AAAS) Conference, Chicago, IL.

Stadler, M. A. (1997). Distinguishing implicit and explicit learning. *Psychonomic Bulletin & Review*, *4*(1), 56–62. doi:10.3758/BF03210774

Stargame, A. (2018, September 24). *The past and future of MMORPGs*. Accessed on January 9, 2019 from: https://medium.com/@alexstargame/the-past-and-future-of-mmorpgs-c23bfed473f

Steinkuehler, C. (2005). *Cognition and learning in massively multiplayer online games: A critical approach* (Unpublished dissertation). University of Wisconsin, Madison, WI.

Steinkuehler, C. (2004) Learning in massively multiplayer online games. In Y. Kafai, W. Sandoval, N. Enyedy, A. Nixon, & F. Herrera (Eds.), *Proceedings of the sixth ICLS*. Mahwah, NJ: Erlbaum.

Steinkuehler, C., & Duncan, S. (2008). Scientific habits of mind in virtual worlds. *Journal of Science Education and Technology*, *17*(6), 530–543. doi:10.100710956-008-9120-8

Sternberg, R. J., Grigorenko, E. L., & Zhang, L. (2008). Styles of learning and thinking matter in instruction and assessment. *Perspectives on Psychological Science*, *486*(6), 486–506. doi:10.1111/j.1745-6924.2008.00095.x PMID:26158974

Steyaert, J. (2002). Inequality and the digital divide: Myths and realities. In S. Hick & J. McNutt (Eds.), *Advocacy, activism, and the Internet* (pp. 199–211). Chicago, IL: Lyceum.

Still, B., & Crane, K. (2017). *The fundamentals of user-centered design: A practical approach*. New York: Taylor & Francis Group. doi:10.4324/9781315200927

Strang, K. D. (2016c). Do the critical success factors from learning analytics predict student outcomes? *Journal of Educational Technology Systems*, *44*(3), 273-299. Retrieved from http://ets.sagepub.com/content/0047239515615844/0047239515615853/0047239515615273.abstract

Strang, K. D. (2014). Cognitive learning strategy as a partial effect on major field test in business results. *Journal of Education for Business*, *89*(3), 142–148. doi:10.1080/08832323.2013.781988

Strang, K. D. (2015a). *Handbook of Research Design in Business and Management*. New York: Palgrave Macmillan. doi:10.1057/9781137484956

Strang, K. D. (2015b). Effectiveness of instructor-led collaborative learning in the classroom. *Journal of Applied Research in Higher Education*, *7*(2), 1–16. doi:10.1108/JARHE-07-2012-0018

Strang, K. D. (2016a). Testing young business students for technology acceptance and learning performance. *International Journal of Learning Technology*, *11*(3), 238-265. doi:10.1504/IJLT.2016.079036

Strang, K. D. (2016b). How student behavior and reflective learning impact grade in online business courses. *Journal of Applied Research in Higher Education*, *8*(3), 390–410. doi:10.1108/JARHE-06-2015-0048

Strang, K. D. (2016d). Can online student performance be forecasted by learning analytics? *International Journal of Technology Enhanced Learning*, *8*(1), 26–47. doi:10.1504/IJTEL.2016.075950

Strang, K. D. (2017a). Predicting student satisfaction and outcomes in online courses using learning activity indicators. *International Journal of Web-Based Learning and Teaching Technologies*, *12*(1), 32–50. doi:10.4018/IJWLTT.2017010103

Strang, K. D. (2017b). Beyond engagement analytics: Which online mixed-data factors predict student learning outcomes? *Journal of Education and Information Technologies*, *22*(3), 917–937. doi:10.100710639-016-9464-2

Strang, K. D., & Shimer, M. (2017). Compressed school week cultural bias against English Second Language student performance on standardized exams. *Global Journal of Human-Social Sciences-G:Linguistics & Education*, *17*(5), 37–48. doi:10.17406/GJHSS

Strang, K. D., & Vajjhala, N. R. (2017). Student resistance to a mandatory learning management system in online supply chain courses. *Journal of Organizational and End User Computing*, *29*(3), 49–67. doi:10.4018/JOEUC.2017070103

Stričević, I. (2018). Literacies in the Digital Age New Teaching Paradigms and Solutions for Academic Libraries. In *Proceedings of the 5th International Symposium on Emerging Trends and Technologies in Libraries and Information Services (ETTLIS)*. Bettis University.

Studentsreview. (2019). *OMG!! worst school ever and only went beacause*. Retrieved January 18, 2019, from: https://www.studentsreview.com/NY/SUNYPL_comments.html?type=negative&page=2

Suh, K.-S., & Lee, Y. E. (2005). The Effects of Virtual Reality on Consumer Learning : An Empirical Investigation. *Management Information Systems Quarterly*, *29*(4), 673–697. doi:10.2307/25148705

Sullivan, F. R., Kapur, M., Madden, S., & Shipe, S. (2015). Exploring the Role of 'Gendered' Discourse Styles in Online Science Discussions. *International Journal of Science Education*, *37*(3), 484–504. do i:10.1080/09500693.2014.994113

Sunderland, J. (2004). Classroom interaction, gender, and foreign language learning. In B. Norton & K. Toohey (Eds.), Critical pedagogies and language learning (pp. 222-241). Cambridge. doi:10.1017/CBO9781139524834.012

Sunderland, J. (1998). Girls being quiet: A problem for foreign language classrooms? *Language Teaching Research*, *2*(1), 48–62. doi:10.1177/136216889800200104

Sunderland, J. (2000). New understandings of gender and language classroom research: Texts, teacher talk and student talk. *Language Teaching Research*, *4*(2), 149–173. doi:10.1177/136216880000400204

Svensson, P. (2003). Virtual worlds as arenas for language learning. *Language learning online: Towards best practice, 10*(1), 123–142.

Swan, K. P., Richardson, J. C., Ice, P., Garrison, D R., Cleveland-innes, M., & Arbaugh, J. B. (2008). Validating a measurement tool of presence in online communities of inquiry. *E-Mentor, 2*(24), 1-12. Retrieved from http://www.e-mentor.edu.pl/e_index.php?numer=24&all=1

Swan, K. (2003). Learning effectiveness: What the research tells us. In J. Bourne & J. C. Moore (Eds.), *Elements of quality online education: Practice and direction* (Vol. 3, pp. 13–45). Needham, MA: Sloan Consortium.

Tallent-Runnels, M. K., Thomas, J. A., Lan, W. Y., Cooper, S., Ahern, T. C., Shaw, S. M., & Liu, X. (2006). Teaching courses online: A review of the research. *Review of Educational Research*, *76*(1), 93–135. doi:10.3102/00346543076001093

Tang, Kwoh, Teo, & Ling. (1998). Augmented reality systems for medical applications. *IEEE Engineering in Medicine and Biology Magazine*, *17*(3), 49–58. doi:10.1109/51.677169 PMID:9604701

Teach Access. (2019). *About us*. Retrieved from http://teachaccess.org/about/

Teizer, J., Cheng, T., & Fang, Y. (2013). Location tracking and data visualization technology to advance construction ironworkers' education and training in safety and productivity. *Automation in Construction*, *35*, 53–68. doi:10.1016/j.autcon.2013.03.004

ten Have, P. (1991). Talk and institution: A reconsideration of the 'asymmetry' of doctor-patient interaction. In D. Boden & D. H. Zimmerman (Eds.), *Talk and social Structure: Studies in ethnomethodology and conversation analysis* (pp. 138–163). Cambridge, UK: Polity Press.

Tey, J., (1968). *The Daughter of Time*. Scarborough, Canada: Bellhaven House ltd.

The Longman Dictionary of Contemporary English Online. (n.d.). Retrieved from http://www.ldoceonline.com/

Thomas, W., Boechler, P., deJong, E., Stroulia, E., & Delaney, M. (2012). Incidental Learning and Salience in Virtual Worlds. In T. Bastiaens, & G. Marks (Eds.), *Proceedings of World Conference on E-Learning in Corporate, Government, Healthcare, and Higher Education 2012* (pp. 1686-1690). Chesapeake, VA: AACE.

Thumlert, K., de Castell, S., & Jenson, J. (2018). *'Training Grounds' to Sociotechnical Actors: Do MMORPG's Presage/Prestage the Futures of Leadership and Work?* Paper presented at DIGRA 2018, Turin, Italy.

Tobin, K. (2001). To Think On Paper: Using Writing Assignments in the World of History Survey. *The History Teacher*, *34*(4), 497–508. doi:10.2307/3054202

Tomi, A. B., & Rambli, D. R. A. (2013). An interactive mobile augmented reality magical playbook: Learning number with the thirsty crow. *Procedia Computer Science*, *25*, 123–130. doi:10.1016/j.procs.2013.11.015

Tough, A. M. (1979). Choosing to learn. Toronto: The Ontario Institute for Studies in Education (OISE).

Toyoda, E., & Harrison, R. (2002). Categorization of text chat communication between learners and native speakers of Japanese. *Language Learning & Technology*, *6*(1), 82–99.

Tsai, P.-J., Hwang, G.-J., Tseng, J. C. R., & Hwang, G.-H. (2008). Computer-assisted approach to conducting cooperative learning process. *International Journal of Distance Education Technologies*, *6*(1), 49–66. doi:10.4018/jdet.2008010104

Tsui, L. (1999). Courses and Instruction Affecting Critical Thinking. *Research in Higher Education*, *40*(2), 185–200. doi:10.1023/A:1018734630124

Tuckman, B. W. (1999). *Conducting Educational Research* (2nd ed.). Belmont, CA: Wadsworth Group.

Turkan, Y., Radkowski, R., Karabulut-Ilgu, A., Behzadan, A. H., & Chen, A. (2017). Mobile augmented reality for teaching structural analysis. *Advanced Engineering Informatics*, *34*, 90–100. doi:10.1016/j.aei.2017.09.005

Turkle, S. (1995). *Life on the screen: Identity in the age of the Internet*. New York: Simon & Schuster.

Tuzi, F. (2004). The impact of e-feedback on the revisions of L2 writers in an academic writing course. *Computers and Composition*, *21*(2), 217–235. doi:10.1016/j.compcom.2004.02.003

Unigo. (2019). *What is your overall opinion of this school?* Retrieved March 2, 2019, from: https://www.unigo.com/colleges/suny-college-at-plattsburgh

Unity Technologies. (2017). *Unity® v5.5.4* [Computer Software]. Available from http://www.unity3d.com

University of North Carolina at Charlotte. (2019, Spring). *LBST 2301: The rhetoric of digital design* [Course Syllabus]. Author.

Valve Corporation. (2007). *Source SDK*. Bellevue, WA: Valve Corporation.

van Deursen, A. J. A. M., & van Dijk, J. A. G. M. (2009). Using the internet: Skill related problems in users' online behavior. *Interacting with Computers*, *21*(5–6), 393–402. doi:10.1016/j.intcom.2009.06.005

van Deursen, A. J. A. M., & van Dijk, J. A. G. M. (2010). Measuring internet skills. *International Journal of Human-Computer Interaction*, *26*(10), 891–916. doi:10.1080/10447318.2010.496338

van Deursen, A. J. A. M., & van Dijk, J. A. G. M. (2016). Modeling traditional literacy, internet skills and internet usage: An empirical study. *Interacting with Computers*, *28*(1), 13–26. doi:10.1093/iwc/iwu027 van Dijk, J. A. G. M. (2005). *The deepening divide: Inequality in the information society*. Thousand Oaks, CA: Sage Pub.

van Dijk, J. A. G. M., & van Deursen, A. J. A. M. (2014). *Digital skills: Unlocking the information society*. New York, NY: Palgrave Macmillan; doi:10.1057/9781137437037

Van Eck, I. E. (Ed.), *Gaming and cognition: Theories and practice. from the learning sciences*. Hershey, PA: Information Science. doi:10.4018/978-1-61520-717-6

Van Eck, R. (2006). Building intelligent learning games. In D. Gibson, C. Aldrich, & M. Prensky (Eds.), *Games and simulations in online learning: Research & development frameworks*. Hershey, PA: Idea Group. doi:10.4018/978-1-59904-304-3.ch014

van Someren, M. W., Barnard, Y. F., & Sandberg, J. A. C. (1994). *The think aloud method: A practical guide to modelling cognitive processes*. London: Academic Press. doi:10.1016/0306-4573(95)90031-4

Van Wel, L., & Royakkers, L. (2004). Ethical issues in web data mining. *Ethics and Information Technology*, *6*(2), 129–140. doi:10.1023/B:ETIN.0000047476.05912.3d

Van Zwanenberg, N., Wilkinson, L. J., & Anderson, A. (2000). Felder and Silverman's Index of Learning Styles and Honey and Mumford's Learning Styles Questionnaire: How do they compare and do they predict academic performance? *Educational Psychology*, *20*(3), 365–380. doi:10.1080/713663743

Vaughan, N. D. (2010). A hybrid community of inquiry approach: Linking student engagement and course redesign. *The Internet and Higher Education, 13*(1-2), 60-65. Elsevier Inc. doi: . doi:10.1016/j.iheduc.2009.10.007

Vera, L., Gimeno, J., Casas, S., García-Pereira, I., & Portalés, C. (2018). *A hybrid virtual-augmented serious game to improve driving safety awareness*. Paper presented at the Advances in Computer Entertainment Technology, London, UK. doi:10.1007/978-3-319-76270-8_21

Verbert, K., Manouselis, N., Ochoa, X., Wolpers, M., Drachsler, H., Bosnic, I., & Duval, E. (2012). Context-aware recommender systems for learning: A survey and future challenges. *IEEE Transactions on Learning Technologies, 5*(4), 318-335. Retrieved from https://ieeexplore.ieee.org/stamp/stamp.jsp?tp=&arnumber=6189308

Virvou, M., & Katsionis, G. (2008). On the usability and likeability of virtual reality games for education: The case of VR-ENGAGE. *Computers & Education*, *50*(1), 154–178. doi:10.1016/j.compedu.2006.04.004

Voelker, D. J. (2008). Assessing Student Understanding in Introductory Courses: A Sample Strategy. *The History Teacher*, *41*(4), 506–518.

Voinescu, A., & David, D. (2019). The effect of learning in a virtual environment on explicit and implicit memory by applying a process dissociation procedure. *International Journal of Human-Computer Interaction*, *35*(1), 27–37. doi:10.1080/10447318.2018.1424102 von Jan, U., Noll, C., Behrends, M., & Albrecht, U. V. (2012). mARble – Augmented reality in medical education. *Biomedizinische Technik. Biomedical Engineering*, *57*(Suppl. 1), 67–70. doi:10.1515/bmt-2012-4252

Vrasidas, C., & Zembylas, M. (2004). Online professional development: Lessons from the field. *Education + Training*, *46*(6/7), 326–334. doi:10.1108/00400910410555231

Vygotsky, L. S. (1978). *Mind in society: The development of higher psychological process*. Cambridge, MA: Harvard University Press.

Vygotsky, L. S. (1980). *Mind in society: The development of higher psychological processes*. Harvard University Press.

Wagner, M. (2008). *Massively multiplayer online role-playing games as constructivist learning environments in K-12 education: A Delphi study* (Doctoral thesis). Retrieved from http://edtechlife.com/?page_id=2008

Walters, P., & Kop, R. (2009). Heidegger, digital technology and post-modern education: From Being-in-cyberspace to meeting on MySpace. *Bulletin of Science, Technology & Society*, *29*(4), 278–286. doi:10.1177/0270467609336305

Wang, A. (2017). *Learning English in a Multi-User Virtual Environment : Exploring Factors Affecting Participation (PhD dissertation)*. Sundsvall: Mid Sweden University. Retrieved from http://urn.kb.se/resolve?urn=urn:nbn:se:miun:diva-30795

Wang, A. (2017). Using Second Life in an English Course: How does the technology affect participation? *International Journal of Computer-Assisted Language Learning and Teaching*, *7*(1), 66–85. doi:10.4018/IJCALLT.2017010105

Wang, C. X., Song, H., Stone, D. E., & Yan, Q. (2009). Integrating SL into an EFL program in China: Research collaboration across the continents. *TechTrends*, *53*(6), 14–19. doi:10.100711528-009-0337-z

Wang, C. X., Song, H., Xia, F., & Yan, Q. (2009). Integrating SL into an EFL program: Students' perspectives. *Journal of Educational Technology Development and Exchange*, *2*(1), 1–16. doi:10.18785/jetde.0201.01

Wann, J., & Mon-Williams, M. (1996). What does virtual reality NEED?: Human factors issues in the design of three-dimensional computer environments. *International Journal of Human-Computer Studies*, *44*(6), 829–847. doi:10.1006/ijhc.1996.0035

Warburton, S. (2009). Second Life in higher education: Assessing the potential for and the barriers to deploying virtual worlds in learning and teaching. *British Journal of Educational Technology*, *40*(3), 414–426. doi:10.1111/j.1467-8535.2009.00952.x

Warschauer, M. (1997). Computer-mediated collaborative learning: Theory and practice. *Modern Language Journal*, *81*(4), 470–481. doi:10.1111/j.1540-4781.1997.tb05514.x

Warschauer, M., & Liaw, M. L. (2010). *Emerging technologies in adult literacy and language education*. Washington, DC: National Institute for Literacy. doi:10.1037/e529982011-001

Wasko, C. (2013). What teachers need to know about augmented reality enhanced learning environments. *TechTrends*, *57*(4), 17–21. doi:10.100711528-013-0672-y

Wauters, R. (2008, October 29). *World of Warcraft* to surpass 11 million subscribers. *New York Times*.

Waxman, C., Lin, M., & Michko, G. (2003). *A meta-analysis of the effectiveness of teaching and learning with technology on student outcomes*. Naperville: Learning Point Associates.

Wayne, D. B., Didwania, A., Feinglass, J., Fudala, M. J., Barsuk, J. H., & McGaghie, W. C. (2008). Simulation-based education improves quality of care during cardiac arrest team responses at an academic teaching hospital: A case-control study. *Chest Journal*, *133*(1), 56–61. doi:10.1378/chest.07-0131 PMID:17573509

Weaver, R., Salamonson, Y., Koch, J., & Porter, G. (2012). The CSI effect at university: Forensic science students' television viewing and perceptions of ethical issues. *The Australian Journal of Forensic Sciences*, *44*(4), 381–391. doi:10.1080/00450618.2012.691547

Webster, A., Feiner, S., MacIntyre, B., Massie, W., & Krueger, T. (1996). Augmented reality in architectural construction, inspection and renovation. *ASCE Third Congress on Computing in Civil Engineering*, 913-919.

Wehner, A. K., Gump, A. W., & Downey, S. (2011). The effects of Second Life on the motivation of undergraduate students learning a foreign language. *Computer Assisted Language Learning*, *24*(3), 277–289. doi:10.1080/09588221.2010.551757

Wei, J. (2006). *The role of everyday users in MMORPGs*. Retrieved on August 28, 2007, from Driftreality: http://www.driftreality.com/london/mmorpgs.users.pdf

Weininger, M., & Shield, L. (2003). Promoting oral production in a written channel: An investigation of learner language MOO. *Computer Assisted Language Learning*, *16*(4), 329–349. doi:10.1076/call.16.4.329.23414

Weller, M. (2007). *Virtual learning environments*. New York, NY: Routledge.

Weller, M. A. (2011). Pedagogy of abundance. *Revista Española de Pedagogía*, *249*, 223–236.

West, C., & Zimmerman, D. H. (1983). Small insults: A study of interruptions in conversations between unacquainted persons. In B. Thorne, & N. Henley (Eds.), Language, Gender, and Society (pp. 102-117). Rowley: Newbury House.

West, C., Slatin, C., Sanborn, W., & Volicer, B. (2009). Computer-based simulation in blended learning curriculum for hazardous waste site worker health and safety training. *International Journal of Information and Communication Technology Education*, *5*(1), 62–73. doi:10.4018/jicte.2009010105 PMID:19430576

Wethal, T. (2010, March). Beyond books & lecture: Students and law enforcement get hands-on experience in the Marshall University crime scene house. *Law Enforcement Technology*, 46–50.

Whately, D., & Harris, N. (2010). *Hero Engine.* Simutronics Corporation. Author spoke Harris at Game Developers Conference, San Francisco, CA. Website accessed May 26, 2010 http://www.heroengine.com/home

Whelchel, A. (2007). Using Civilization Simulation Video Games in the World History Classroom. *World History Connected*, *4*(2), 1–14.

White, C. (1995). Autonomy and strategy use in distance foreign language learning: Research findings. *System*, *23*(2), 207–221. doi:10.1016/0346-251X(95)00009-9

Wigham, C. R. (2012). *The interplay between non-verbal and verbal interaction in synthetic worlds which supports verbal participation and production in a foreign language* (Unpublished PhD thesis). Université Blaise Pascal - Clermont-Ferrand II. Retrieved from https://halshs.archives-ouvertes.fr/tel-01077857/document

Wigham, C. R., & Chanier, T. (2013). A study of verbal and nonverbal communication in Second Life – the ARCHI21 experience. *ReCALL*, *25*(1), 63–84. doi:10.1017/S0958344012000250

Wigham, C. R., Panichi, L., Nocchi, S., & Sadler, R. (2018). Interactions for language learning in and around virtual worlds. *ReCALL*, *30*(2), 153–160. doi:10.1017/S0958344018000022

Wilson, B., & Cole, P. (1991). A review of cognitive teaching models. *Educational Technology Research and Development*, *39*(4), 47–64. doi:10.1007/BF02296571

Wilson, B., & Ryder, M. (1996). Dynamic learning communities: An alternative to designed instructional systems. *Proceeding of Selected Research and Development Presentations at the 1996 National Convention of the Association for Educational Communications and Technology.*

Wilson, D. (1992, November). Computer games: Academic obstacle or free-speech? *The Chronicle of Higher Education*, 18.

Witmer, B., & Singer, M. (1998). Measuring Presence in Virtual Environments: A Presence Questionnaire. *Presence (Cambridge, Mass.)*, *7*(3), 225–240. doi:10.1162/105474698565686

Woken, M. D., & Swales, J. (1989). Expertise and authority in native-non-native conversations: The need for a variable account. In S. Gass, C. Madden, D. Preston, & L. Selinker (Eds.), *Variation in second language acquisition: Discourse and pragmatics* (pp. 211–227). Clevedon, UK: Multilingual Matters.

Wolf, M. (2018). *Dear reader, come home: The reading brain in a digital world.* New York: HarperCollins.

Woo, Y., & Reeves, T. C. (2007). Meaningful interaction in web-based learning: A social constructivist interpretation. *The Internet and Higher Education*, *10*(1), 15–25. doi:10.1016/j.iheduc.2006.10.005

World of Warcraft. (2018). *Story.* Access on January 22nd from: https://worldofwarcraft.com/en-us/story

WoW Web Stats. (n.d.). Retrieved February 20, 2009, from: http://wowwebstats.com/

Wu, H., Lee, S. W., Chang, H., & Liang, J. (2013). Current status, opportunities and challenges of augmented reality in education. *Computers & Education*, *62*, 41–49. doi:10.1016/j.compedu.2012.10.024

Xu, F. (2012). Crime scene reconstruction based on virtual reality. *Journal of Criminal Law*, *17*(3), 149–160.

Yamashita, N., Taki, H., & Soga, M. (2012). A learning support environment for earthquake disaster with a simulation of furniture falling by mobile AR. *2012 International Conference on Information Technology Based Higher Education and Training (ITHET)*, 1-5. 10.1109/ITHET.2012.6246053

Yang, H., Wu, C., & Wang, K. (2007). An empirical analysis of online game service satisfaction and loyality. *Expert Systems with Applications*, *36*(2), 1816–1825. doi:10.1016/j.eswa.2007.12.005

Yang, J. C., & Quadir, B. (2018). Effects of Prior Knowledge on Learning Performance and Anxiety in an English Learning Online Role-Playing Game. *Journal of Educational Technology & Society*, *21*(3), 174–185.

Yasar, S. (2018). The Role Of Massively Multiplayer Online Role - Playing Games In Extramural Second Language Learning: A Literature Review. *Journal of Educational Technology and Online learning, 1*, 3.

Yee, N. (2005). The psychology of MMORPGs: Emotional investment, motivations, relationships, and problematic usage. In R. Schroeder & A. Axelsson (Eds.), *Social life of avatars II*. London: Springer-Verlag.

Yee, N. (2006). The demographics, motivations and derived experiences of users of massively-multiuser online graphical environments. *Presence (Cambridge, Mass.)*, *15*(3), 309–329. doi:10.1162/pres.15.3.309

Yee, N. (2014). *The Proteus paradox: How online games and virtual worlds change us — and how they don't*. New Haven, CT: Yale University Press.

Yeh, E., & Wan, G. (2019). The Use of Virtual Worlds in Foreign Language Teaching and Learning. In M. Khosrow-Pour (Ed.), Computer-Assisted Language Learning: Concepts, Methodologies, Tools, and Applications (pp. 1949-1972). IGI Global.

Yeo, A., & Alibali, M. W. (2018). Does visual salience of action affect gesture production? *Journal of Experimental Psychology. Learning, Memory, and Cognition*, *44*(5), 826–832. doi:10.1037/xlm0000458 PMID:29648868

Yin, R. (1994). *Case Study Research: Design and Methods* (2nd ed.). Beverly Hills, CA: Sage Publishing.

Young, E. H. (2018). *Promoting Second Language Learning Through Oral Asynchronous Computer-Mediated Communication* (Unpublished PhD thesis). Brigham Young University. Retrieved from https://scholarsarchive.byu.edu/etd/7051

Youngblut, C. (1998). *Education uses of virtual reality technology (No. IDA Document Report no. D2128)*. Alexandria, VA: Institute for Defense Analyses. Retrieved from http://papers.cumincad.org/data/works/att/94ea.content.pdf

Young, K. A. (2005). Direct from the source: The value of 'think-aloud' data in understanding learning. *Journal of Educational Enquiry*, *6*(1), 19–33. Retrieved from https://opus.lib.uts.edu.au/bitstream/10453/6348/1/2005002113.pdf

Yuen, S. C., Yaoyuneyong, G., & Johnson, E. (2011). Augmented reality: An overview and five directions for AR in education. *Journal of Educational Technology Development and Exchange*, *4*(1), 11. doi:10.18785/jetde.0401.10

Zainal, Z. (2007). Case study as a research method. *Jurnal Kemanusiaan*, (9), 1-6. Retrieved from http://psyking.net/htmlobj-3837/case_study_as_a_research_method.pdf

Zak, E. (2014). Do you believe in magic? Exploring the conceptualization of augmented reality and its implications for the user in the field of library and information science. *Information Technology and Libraries (Online)*, *33*(4), 23–50.

Zeibart, A. (2018). *WoW Archivist: The Gates of Ahn'Qiraj*. Access on January 22nd from: https://www.engadget.com/2011/04/19/wow-archivist-the-gates-of-ahnqiraj/

Zhai, N. (2017). The Application of Virtual Reality Technology in Building Immersive Foreign Language Teaching Environment. *DEStech Transactions on Engineering and Technology Research*.

Zhang, F., & Kaufman, D. (2017). Massively Multiplayer Online Role-Playing Games (MMORPGs) and Socio-Emotional Wellbeing. *Computers in Human Behavior*, *73*, 451–458. doi:10.1016/j.chb.2017.04.008

Zhang, Y. (2017). Language Learning Enhanced by Massive Multiple Online Role-Playing Games (Mmorpgs) and the Underlying Behavioral and Neural Mechanisms. *Frontiers in Human Neuroscience*, *11*(2), 1–7. PMID:28303097

Zheng, D., & Newgarden, K. (2012). Rethinking language learning: Virtual worlds as a catalyst for change. *International Journal of Learning and Media*, *3*(2), 13–36. doi:10.1162/ijlm_a_00067

Zhu, D., Luo, Y., Dai, L., Shao, X., Zhou, Q., Itti, L., & Lu, J. (2018). Salient object detection via a local and global method based on deep residual network. *Journal of Visual Communication and Image Representation*, *54*, 1–9. doi:10.1016/j.jvcir.2018.03.017

Zhu, W., Owen, C. B., Li, H., & Lee, J. H. (2004). Personalized in-store e-commerce with the promopad: An augmented reality shopping assistant. *Electronic Journal for E-commerce Tools and Applications*, *1*(3), 1–19.

Zollmann, S., Hoppe, C., Kluckner, S., Poglitsch, C., Bischof, H., & Reitmayr, G. (2014). Augmented reality for construction site monitoring and documentation. *Proceedings of the IEEE*, *102*(2), 137–154. doi:10.1109/JPROC.2013.2294314

Zuengler, J. (1989). Performance variation in NS-NNS interactions: Ethnolinguistic difference or discourse domain? In S. Gass, C. Madden, D. Preston, & L. Selinker (Eds.), *Variation in second language acquisition: Discourse and pragmatics* (pp. 218–235). Clevedon, UK: Multilingual Matters.

Zywno, M. S. (2003). *A contribution to the validation of score meaning for Felder-Soloman's Index of Learning Styles.* Paper presented at 2003 Annual Conference, Nashville, TN. Retrieved from http://asee.org

About the Contributors

Bodi Anderson received his Master's in TESOL/Applied Linguistics in 2002 and doctorate in Curriculum and Instruction with a focus on Educational Technology from Northern Arizona University in 2012. He has been teaching for twenty years with seventeen at the post-primary level. He is currently an associate professor of Educational Technology at Indian River State College in Florida where he is deeply involved in the school's institute for academic excellence in addition to his B.S. education program teaching, and has previously taught at multiple universities in the US and Japan. His primary research interests include cultural contexts in online learning and virtual world and game-based learning.

Patricia Boechler is a Professor in the Department of Educational Psychology. Dr. Boechler's educational background is in psychology and cognitive science with a research focus on cognition, learning and technology. She has training and experience in the areas of cognitive theory and testing, learning theory, computational modeling as well as experience in investigating navigation and learning with educational technologies such as multimedia, web-based learning and virtual environments. For the past sixteen years, Dr. Boechler's research has been interdisciplinary, incorporating aspects of psychology, technology and education. Dr. Boechler is interested in understanding how various technologies (websites, on-line communication applications, video games, virtual reality applications) can be optimized for educational purposes. She is currently the Director of the Technology and Learning Sciences lab in Educational Psychology.

Leslie Bolt is Associate Professor of Research in the Department of Leadership and Educational Studies in the Reich College of Education at Appalachian State University specializing in mixed methods educational research methodology and evaluation research. Prior to this, he was the Director of Institutional Effectiveness and Director of Institutional Research at Blue Ridge Community College in Virginia. He also was a tenured faculty member and administrator in various roles at at James Madison University for 30 years. His Ph.D. is in Research and Evaluation from the University of Virginia with post-doctoral work in Advanced Statistical Analysis of large data sets at Stanford University.

Sergio Casas-Yrurzum has a master's degree in Computer Engineering and also a bachelor's degree in Telecommunications Engineering - Telematics Specialty. He received the Spanish National Award on University Studies in 2008. He received his Ph.D. in Computational Mathematics at the University of Valencia in 2014. He works as a senior researcher in the Robotics Institute (IRTIC) of the University of Valencia, where he is also a part-time professor at the School of Engineering (ETSE). His expertise is in the simulation field with special focus on Virtual Reality, Augmented Reality and motion cueing.

Jason A. Chen is the Gerdelman Family Term Distinguished Associate Professor of Education at the College of William & Mary's School of Education. The questions that drive his research have to do with the variety of ways that innovative technologies can be used as a tool for motivation and engagement. Rather than assuming that technology is inherently motivating for students (it's not!), Jason is interested in understanding the types of technologies that can be used to support students' developing interests in science, and their confidence in being able to succeed in STEM fields. Recently, with the help of a National Science Foundation grant, Jason has begun to explore the affordances of using mixed-reality virtual environments in combination with intensive training to teach university faculty how to disrupt pernicious implicit biases that impede efforts to diversify our STEM classrooms and fields of study. Jason earned his Ph.D. from Emory University in 2010, and then accepted a postdoctoral research fellowship at Harvard University from 2010-2012. In 2012, he earned the Early Career Award from the American Psychological Association in Educational Psychology. Jason is, at heart, a teacher, having taught high school chemistry and physics in Seattle, WA and Atlanta, GA.

Amelia Cheney is Professor in and Program Director for the Educational Media/Instructional Technology program in the Department of Leadership and Educational Studies at Appalachian State University, where she has taught in 3D immersive environments since 2006. Prior to joining the faculty, Dr. Cheney had more than thirteen years experience in K-12 education, including serving as a high school teacher and a Chief Technology Officer for two school districts. She is a Past-President and current Board member of the North Carolina Technology in Education Society (NCTIES). Dr. Cheney also serves as Executive Director of the Consortium for Research in Immersive and Online Learning Environments (CRIOLE). Her current research is focused on constructivist teaching and learning in immersive environments, particularly issues of community, presence, and the building of relationships.

Jerremie Clyde is an Associate Librarian at the University of Calgary. Currently he is head of the Military Museums Library & Archive, a branch of the University of Calgary's Library system and Canada's largest military history library. In addition to his teaching, reference, collections, and administrative duties he engages in game-based learning research with multiple collaborators. His work has included integrating gameful design into graduate-level teacher education, building digital game-based learning environments to teach emotional intelligence to peace officers, and most recently using Minecraft and scaffolded social media engagement to teach students about WWI propaganda and modern media literacy. When not engaging directly in academic pursuits he operates a sustainable mixed farm North of Calgary.

Chris Dede is the Timothy E. Wirth Professor in Learning Technologies at Harvard's Graduate School of Education (HGSE). His fields of scholarship include emerging technologies, policy, and leadership. From 2001-2004, he was Chair of the HGSE department of Teaching and Learning. In 2007, he was honored by Harvard University as an outstanding teacher, and in 2011 he was named a Fellow of the American Educational Research Association. From 2014-2015, he was a Visiting Expert at NSF, Directorate of Education and Human Resources. Chris has served as a member of the National Academy of Sciences Committee on Foundations of Educational and Psychological Assessment, a member of the U.S. Department of Education's Expert Panel on Technology, and a member of the 2010 National Educational Technology Plan Technical Working Group. In 2013, he co-convened a NSF workshop on new technology-based models of postsecondary learning; and in 2015 he led two NSF workshops on data-intensive research in the sciences, engineering, and education. Chris also was an International

Steering Committee member for the Second International Technology in Education Study, and he has participated in technology-based learning initiatives for various Global South countries. He leads the adult capacity building strand of the Reaching Every Reader initiative at Harvard and MIT. His edited books include: Scaling Up Success: Lessons Learned from Technology-based Educational Improvement; Digital Teaching Platforms: Customizing Classroom Learning for Each Student; Teacher Learning in the Digital Age: Online Professional Development in STEM Education; Virtual, Augmented, and Mixed Realities in Education; and Learning Engineering for Online Education: Theoretical Contexts and Design-Based Examples.

Mats Deutschmann is professor of English at Örebro University, Sweden. He has been working with online language learning since the early 2000s, and is one of the pioneers in Virtual World language pedagogy, a field which he has published widely in. More recently, his research also includes language stereotyping and developing methods for raising awareness of these issues.

Helene Fournier is a Research Officer with the National Research Council Canada's Digital Technologies Research Centre. Dr. Fournier joined the NRC in 2002 and holds a Ph.D. in Educational Psychology from McGill University. Her research area is educational technology and she has participated in several research projects focused on the application and evaluation of advanced technologies in the training sector, in distance education, and more recently in learner-centered research and development of Personal Learning Environments. She has contributed to the advancement of research in the field of distance education, online learning, adult learning, and more recently to educational learning analytics in the context of Massive Open Online Courses. She has published widely in peer reviewed journals and at international conferences.

Kim Frumin studies online teacher professional learning and research-practice partnerships at the Harvard Graduate School of Education.

Inma García-Pereira was born in Valencia, Spain in 1985. She received a M.S. degree in Audiovisual Communication (2008) and a M.S. degree in Computer Engineering (2016), both from the University of Valencia, Spain. She received the FPU grant (2016-present) by the Spanish Ministry of Science, Innovation and Universities to complete her Ph.D. at the Institute of Robotics and Information and Communication Technologies (IRTIC) of the University of Valencia, Spain. She currently works as a Junior Researcher in the IRTIC at the University of Valencia, where she is also a part-time professor at the School of Engineering (ETSE). She belongs to the ARTEC group, dedicated to 3D interactive graphics, virtual reality, augmented reality and civil simulation. Currently, she is developing her doctorate in the field of indoor real-time locating systems and its application to augmented reality. Her research interests include augmented and virtual reality, RTLS, collaborative shared environments, multimedia applications and multimodal interaction systems.

Jesús Gimeno Sancho received a Master's degree (2008) and Ph.D. in Computer Science from the University of Valencia (2016), with a dissertation titled "Contributions to the Authoring of Augmented Reality Contents for Education, Industry and Construction Sectors". Currently he is a researcher at the IRTIC Institute and part-time professor at the University of Valencia. His research interests include augmented reality, virtual reality, motion capture, real time simulation, advanced user interfaces and mobile computing. He has served also as visiting scientist at the Augmented Reality Group at Bauhaus Universitat (Weimar, Germany, 2008) and at VRAC Center at Iowa State University (Ames IO, USA, 2010).

Tina Grotzer, a senior researcher at Project Zero and faculty member at the Harvard Graduate School of Education, is a cognitive scientist who studies learning in formal and informal contexts. She teaches courses in cognition, pedagogy, instructional design, learning, and school design. She is a recipient of a Career Award from the National Science Foundation (NSF) and a Presidential Early Career Award for Scientists and Engineers (PECASE) from the U.S. Government. In addition to many articles, her published works include the book, Learning Causality in a Complex World, and the Causal Patterns in Science Curriculum series.

Lenora Jean (Jeannie) Justice graduated with an Ed.D. in curriculum and instruction from the University of Florida. She has taught at the high school, GED/adult high school, undergraduate, and graduate levels for over 20 years. She currently teaches educational technology courses and advises both masters and doctoral students at Morehead State University in Morehead, Kentucky.

Amy Kamarainen is a senior research manager at the Harvard Graduate School of Education where she manages research related to the EcoLearn projects. Amy is an ecosystem scientist who holds a B.S. in Zoology from Michigan State University and a Ph.D. from the University of Wisconsin – Madison. Her Ph.D. work focused on studying the movement and fate of pollutants in aquatic ecosystems using environmental sensors, historical data, and models. She applies her understanding of ecosystems science and research to the design and evaluation of technologies that support science learning inside and outside of the classroom.

Ian Levstein holds an Ed.D. in Educational Technology Leadership from Morehead State University. He taught high school and GED/adult education for 16 years including 2½ years at a Federal prison. He is currently the Computer Operations Manager at Marshall University's Forensic Science Center in Huntington, West Virginia.

Rikke Magnussen is an associate professor at Department of Communication, Aalborg University. Her main research interest is how digital learning design can open new types of collaborative science practice and innovation processes to support community driven science in and outside formal education. She currently leads the research and development project Community Drive.

Cat Mahaffey is a Senior Lecturer in the University Writing Program at the University of North Carolina at Charlotte. She is a Quality Matters (QM) Certified Master Reviewer, serves on the executive board of the Global Society of Online Literacy Educators (GSOLE), and is an active member of the Online Writing Instruction (OWI) Standing Group of the Conference on College Composition and Communication (CCCC). Her research interests include OWI, digital literacy, and digital design. In addition, she is currently a Ph.D. student in the Technical Communication and Rhetoric program at Texas Tech University.

Terry McClannon is Associate Professor in the Educational Media/Instructional Technology program and Department Chair in the Department of Leadership and Educational Studies in the Reich

College of Education at Appalachian State University. Dr. McClannon has taught a variety of academic courses in the areas of Instructional Technology, higher Education, and school administration during his tenure at Appalachian. He has expertise in the development of Online and hybrid courses utilizing both synchronous and asynchronous technologies. Dr. McClannon has unique experiences in the utilization of immersive learning environments and other innovative technologies to engage students and build a greater sense of presence in online courses.

Serpil Meri-Yilan received her MA and Ph.D. in Applied Linguistics for Language Teaching from University of Southampton in 2011 and 2017, respectively, and BA in English Language Teaching from Ataturk University in 2009. She has served as a language advisor and coach; editor, reviewer and proof reader of academic papers; translator and private tutor. She is currently a lecturer in the Department of Interpretation and Translation in Foreign Language School at Ibrahim Cecen University of Agri. She writes and presents about the topics of computer-assisted language learning, foreign language learning and teaching, virtual reality, e-learning, scaffolding, digital storytelling, learner autonomy and motivation.

Shari J. Metcalf is a Senior Researcher at the Harvard Graduate School of Education, where her research centers on the design and evaluation of computer–based tools for learning through scaffolded environments in which students can engage in authentic, project-based, constructivist activities. For the past 11 years she has served as Project Director for the EcoLearn research group, whose research projects include EcoMUVE, EcoMOBILE, EcoXPT and EcoMOD – curricula that use virtual and augmented reality to provide highly immersive and engaging learning experiences in ecosystem science for elementary and middle school students. Her focus is on how to support students doing science – strategies for visualizing complex processes, conducting virtual experiments, and collaboratively representing and testing hypotheses. Shari works with teachers and students in classrooms to determine the effectiveness of new software and curricula, using design-based research methods to study learning and teaching in the field.

Heather Molyneaux is an Analyst at the National Research Council Canada and current member of the Cybersecurity team. She has over a decade of experience in Human Computer Interaction (HCI). Her interests include visual analysis of communication technologies, participatory design and user studies in education and healthcare technologies, and HCI related aspects of AI, augmented reality and Cybersecurity.

Cristina Portalés Ricart is MSc. in Geodesy and Cartography from the Universidad Politécnica de Valencia and MSc. in Surveying and Geoinformation from Technische Universität Wien (2003). Research fellow at the Mixed Reality Laboratory of the University of Nottingham (2005) and at the Interaction and Entertainment Research Centre of the Nanyang University of Singapore (2006), both in the area of computer vision. In 2008 she received the Ph.D. degree from the UPV. From 2011-2012 she worked at AIDO (Industrial Association of Optics, Colour and Imaging), where she was primarily involved in technical management of the FP7 funded project SYDDARTA. In 2012 she received the Juan de la Cierva post-doctoral grant by the Spanish Ministry to join IRTIC (Research Institute of Robotics and Information and Communication Technologies), where she continued researching in accurate 3D reconstruction. Her current research interests are focused on geometric calibration, image processing, 3D reconstruction, multispectral imaging, augmented reality and human-computer-interaction.

Robert Sanders has served as the Associate Dean of the Cratis D. Williams School of Graduate Studies at Appalachian State University since January 2014. From 2003-2011, he served on the faculty at Appalachian State University as a Professor of Library Science. Before moving to the Graduate School, Sanders also served as the Chair of the Department of Leadership and Educational Studies in the Reich College of Education at ASU from 2011-2014. Sanders has worked professionally as a teacher, media specialist, school administrator, and as an instructional technology consultant. He also served as the Director of Distance Education for the Southwest Ohio Regional Distance Learning Network and later as the President of para instructional designs, an e-Learning design company based in Cincinnati, OH. He is the past president of both the Ohio Distance Learning Association and the League of Worlds, an international virtual world collaborative. He is the author, coauthor, and editor of books and articles on collaboration, community formation, and constructivist pedagogy in immersive learning environments. His current research is focused on the symbiotic relationship of Action Learning pedagogy and 3D virtual worlds.

Anders Steinvall, Ph.D., is a Senior Lecturer in English Linguistics at the Department of Language Studies, Umeå University, Sweden. He is an experienced teacher of English language courses and linguistics courses. He has taught campus courses as well as online language courses and has worked with computer assisted language learning (CALL) tools for more than 20 years. He has participated in pedagogical projects involving the use of ICT in higher education covering many different fields: online assessment; use of peer-based intervention and key-stroke logging as tools for developing students' translations; use of wikis to help students contextualize vocabulary learning; use of ICT support in order to calibrate peer review procedures; use of Second Life for awareness raising activities relating to sociolinguistic phenomena, to mention a few. A firm believer in socio-cultural and social-constructivist views of learning, Steinvall uses ICT as a support tool for students, but also as tool for stimulating discussions and debriefings so that students reach new heights of learning.

Kenneth Strang has more than 270 mostly-sole-authored scholarly publications. He is a professor who teaches and supervises undergraduate, graduate and doctoral students across five disciplines: business administration, management information systems, marketing/consumer behavior, supply chain management and economics/statistics. Ken has a doctorate in project management (operations research), an MBA (strategic management), a BSBA (marketing), an AAS (IT) all with summa cum laude/honors. Plus he is an internationally licensed Project Management Professional (PMI, USA), a Certified Research Professional (IIPMR, USA), a Certified Network Administrator (Novell, USA), a Certified Supply Chain Specialist/Procurement Professional (IIPMR, USA) and a Fellow Life Management Institute with distinction (LOMA, USA). Dr. Strang has lifetime grants over $7 million, and he has won several honors including a Behavior Energy Climate Change Fellowship from the American Council for an Energy-Efficient Economy, the Emerald Literati award and Duke of Edinburgh community service medal, along with several presidential citations.

Wayne Thomas received his M.Ed from the department of Educational Psychology in Technology in Education from the University of Alberta in 2013. During his time with the Technology and Learning Science lab in Educational Psychology, much of his research focused on the topics of virtual environments and learning within educational contexts. In 2014 he returned to teaching, integrating some of his findings into the field. Wayne currently works for the Government of Alberta in the Ministry of Education with internal and external stakeholders in the field of education. He maintains a keen interest in multimedia and educational technologies that can be leveraged to enhance student learning experiences.

Trisha Vickrey is a researcher in Jeff Mower's laboratory in the Department of Agronomy and Horticulture at University of Nebraska-Lincoln. She is currently investigating flower color pathways in plants. She is also a lecturer in the Department of Chemistry. Trisha received a M.Ed. in education policy and management from the Harvard Graduate School of Education, a Ph.D. in chemistry from the University of Virginia, and a B.S. in chemistry from the University of Mississippi.

María Vidal-González was born in Castellón, Spain in 1992. She has a degree in Multimedia Engineering and a master's degree in Artificial Intelligence, Pattern Recognition and Digital Imaging. She's been working as a Junior Researcher in the Institute of Robotics and Information and Communication Technologies (IRTIC) at the University of Valencia since 2014. She is part of the ARTEC group, dedicated to 3D interactive graphics, virtual reality, augmented reality and civil simulation.

Ashlyn C. Walden is a Senior Lecturer in the University Writing Programs at the University of North Carolina at Charlotte. In addition to teaching First Year Writing, she also serves at the Associate Editor of RE: Composing, A Writing Studies Journal, a homegrown text used in UNCC's FYW course. Research interests primarily include: fostering inquiry-based research in the writing classroom, digital composition and design, and Universal Design practices. To extend these interests, Ashlyn maintains active professional development affiliations with the Global Society of Online Literacy Educators (GSOLE), and is the current associate editor of one of the organization's publications, Research in Online Literacy Education (ROLE).

Airong Wang is a Senior Lecturer at Xi'an Jiaotong-Liverpool University, China. She obtained her Ph.D. degree in English from Mid-Sweden University, Sweden. Her research centers on language learning and teaching in virtual environments, especially English classes in 3D virtual worlds, using mobile phones or using VR. During the past few years, she has published in reputable journals, including SCI-indexed journals.

Glenn Wilkinson is a Senior Instructor in the Department of History at the University of Calgary and Fellow of the Royal Historical Society. His teaching and research interests include media history, film and history, British and European cultural history, and military history. He is currently working on a study of post-1945 British war films examining the cultural and social significance of World War II to post-war Britain in the 15 years after the end of the war. His four teenaged children spend an inordinate amount of time playing digital games, in particular Minecraft and Bioshock.

Index

P

R

S

T

U

V

www.ingramcontent.com/pod-product-compliance
Lightning Source LLC
LaVergne TN
LVHW062134300926
849161LV00010B/2525
* 9 7 8 1 5 2 2 5 7 9 8 7 8 *